Grandpa
Hyppy

To Emma Tom + Alice
Tim '05

MAJOR-GENERAL SIR EDMUND LEACH. K.C.B.
Colonel of the Regiment, 1904-1921.

Frontispiece.

THE QUEEN'S OWN ROYAL WEST KENT REGIMENT - 1914-1919

BY

C. T. ATKINSON

Late Captain, Oxford University O.T.C.

LONDON

SIMPKIN, MARSHALL, HAMILTON, KENT & Co., Ltd

MCMXXIV

Printed and bound by Antony Rowe Ltd, Eastbourne

To the
Undying Memory of our Fallen Comrades
this History of
The Queen's Own Royal West Kent Regiment
in the Great War
is Dedicated.

   . . . " *These Men resigned to hope*
Their unknown chances of happiness.
And in the face of Death
They were minded to resist and suffer,
Rather than to fly and save their lives.
They fled from dishonour.
But on the Battle Field their feet stood fast,
And in an instant, at the height of their fortune,
They passed away from the scene
Not of their fear,
But of their Glory."

FOREWORD.

HAVING been appointed to the Colonelcy of the Regiment as successor to our beloved Colonel of 17 years, Major-General Sir Edmund Leach, K.C.B.; whose resignation through ill-health two years ago we all so much regretted, and whose death, just as this History is about to be published, we so deeply deplore; it devolves upon me to write its Foreword.

In doing so, my uppermost feeling is one of immense pride in the glorious service recorded in this History of our Regiment throughout the Great War.

It is the record of Twenty-two Battalions, and one Depôt. Of these, Eleven Battalions served abroad on active service, in which 6,866 of all ranks " gave all that they had," and some 21,000 became casualties, while the Honours gained complete a record of which any Regiment might be justly proud.

To us of the Regiment, however, it is the way in which the service was rendered, that gives us our feeling of pride.

When I arrived in France early in 1915, I had the extreme pleasure of hearing on all sides, of the high reputation our Regiment had won by their tenacity in holding trenches at whatever cost.

There is the story, which will be remembered as long as the Regiment exists, of the old private soldier at Neuve Chappelle in 1914, told by Major Molony in his History of the First Battalion in the Great War. I make no apology for repeating it here, because it gives a living example of that spirit which is the treasure of the Regiment.

FOREWORD.

The Germans had over-run the trenches on the left of the Battalion, and that flank was left in the air.

Major Molony writes:—" None could have blamed them if, attacked in flank and rear, they had, as a unit, withdrawn from a position which, had not The Queen's Own proved the contrary, would have been accepted by all as impossible. They were told to stay and, desperate and nearly officerless, stay they did. One young soldier, almost a boy, observing men of other units trickling to the rear, began to look over his shoulder. In another instant he might have been gone, but an old Private seized hold of him none too tenderly, shouting ' None of that, my lad! We don't do that in The Queen's Own.' "

Here, in the " We," lies the secret of it all. Pride of Regiment, the pride which means " We can do nothing that does not become a soldier," and which is, in the highest degree, *esprit-de-corps*. It was this pride, that lived and had its being in every Battalion of the Regiment, which enabled it, in the unprecedented difficulties of the Great War, to present the resolute front that is told of in this History.

Such a spirit comes from more than discipline, is above even the highest sense of duty, and is beyond the power of any system, however good, to produce. It comes, I feel perfectly certain, from that Comradeship, nay, that Friendship which gives the mutual and invincible confidence which has so long existed, and, I cannot doubt, will continue to exist between our officers, warrant officers, non-commissioned officers and men.

FOREWORD.

With this superb spirit the Regiment will always act up to its motto, " Quo fas et gloria ducunt," and will ever be worthy, as it has proved itself in this Great War, of the Grand Word we wear so proudly beneath the White Horse of Kent upon our caps—

" INVICTA."

E. A. H. ALDERSON,
LIEUTENANT-GENERAL,
Colonel The Queen's Own Royal West Kent Regiment.

February, 1924

PREFACE.

THE special difficulties of writing the history of a regiment of British infantry of the Line in the war of 1914-1918 can only be really appreciated by those who have ventured on the attempt. The place of the regiment in the British Army is important and peculiar; regimental traditions and sentiment, all that is covered by the phrase " esprit de corps," have played a part of incalculable importance in the history of the British Army, which is much the same as saying " the history of the British Empire "; their influence over the fortunes of the war of 1914-1918 was by no means the least of the many factors which affected its course, what they contributed towards making possible that miracle of improvisation, the " New Armies " of Great Britain, must most certainly not be overlooked. It is only natural that regiments should desire to have the history of their achievements and experiences in this great struggle put together.

Unfortunately, it is undeniable that for purposes of narration the regiment is not a convenient unit. It is not a tactical unit as the Division and the battalion are; it is only for certain purposes an administrative unit; it is not an exact unit of measurement as it is in foreign armies, for a British regiment may have had as many as forty battalions or as few as six, and these great variations in size involve corresponding variations in experiences between one regiment and another. It did not necessarily follow that because a regiment put a score of battalions into the field between 1914-1918 it was therefore represented on many fronts, or that because it had but few battalions its experiences were confined to one or two quarters. As a rule the different

PREFACE.

battalions of a regiment all served in different Divisions, except in the Territorials or in the Divisions composed of " local " Service battalions it was unusual for any two battalions of the same regiment to have gone through the same actions, much more to have fought side by side.

Normally each battalion means to the would-be regimental historian a separate set of incidents, often involving a good deal of detail of what other units were doing at its side, but as a rule each battalion's story is quite disconnected from the stories of the other battalions of the regiment. There is thus a great lack of unity and coherence about the experiences of a regiment, and the larger the number of its battalions the more varied and distinguished its achievements, the more marked the difficulty of combining them into one narrative. The battalion makes a better subject for a narrative, it is small enough to be treated in real detail, space can be found in a battalion history for the many minor incidents that bring back the conditions and the circumstances that distinguished different phases of the war, to bring out the characteristics of the many individuals who made up and influenced the battalion. That a battalion history needs to be written by someone who served in it goes without saying; it should be intimate and individual.

That an ideal regimental history would consist of a collection of separate accounts of all the different battalions, each written by someone with inside knowledge, may be admitted, but not perhaps without some qualification. So spacious a method of treatment is bound to be expensive; it must also involve a good deal of overlapping. Even though the different battalions may have all taken part in different stages of such major operations as the Somme or Third Ypres there would bound to be repetitions. Even in a battalion history some account of strategical situations and tactical conditions is needed to explain the why and wherefore of

PREFACE.

what the battalion was called on to attempt, the reasons for its success or failure, the importance of the individual episode in which it shared. The attempt to combine in one narrative the stories of the different battalions at any rate reduces considerably this overlapping, and without trying to provide anything like a comprehensive story of the war ought to give a better impression of what a very distinguished regiment of the Line contributed towards the final victory of Great Britain and her Allies than the piece-meal method of treatment can produce.

This volume, therefore, represents an attempt to put on record the part played in the war by all the battalions of The Queen's Own, whether they served overseas or were occupied with the maintenance of those actively employed. Between them these battalions served in all but one of the major theatres of war, took part in nearly fifty operations officially reckoned as "battles" in France and Flanders alone, and in nearly a dozen elsewhere, besides innumerable minor actions, had over twenty-one thousand casualties, including nearly seven thousand killed, received hundreds of distinctions and honours and earned many more. Necessarily, therefore, their record has had to be severely compressed in order to keep it within anything like moderate dimensions, details that might have given life and individuality to the accounts of the different battalions have had perforce to be omitted, and extensive periods have had to be cursorily summed up. The main aim of the volume has been to produce as accurate a record of the achievements and experiences of The Queen's Own as the often imperfect evidence will allow and to bring this within the compass of a volume which could be produced at a price within the means of all members of the Regiment.

It will be noticed that in the text honours and decorations have not been mentioned after the names of officers and men and that initials have only been

PREFACE.

inserted where needed to distinguish between individuals of the same name. This has been done in order to economize space, a matter of some importance, while to secure accuracy in the matter of decorations would have entailed an expenditure of time and labour quite disproportionate to its importance. Economy of space again is the justification and apology for the use of the abbreviation " R.W.K.," by which a really substantial saving has been effected. The general remarks on the situations and the references to the doings of other units have been as far as possible severely kept down, the aim being merely to mention those things which nearly affected the fortunes of The Queen's Own.

In the matter of maps and plans the main object has been to provide all the diagrams needed to elucidate the actions and movements described in the text. These diagrams are in most instances copied or adapted from plans in the War Diaries of the different battalions or of the Brigades and Divisions in which they served. A few have been taken from "Invicta" or the *Queen's Own Gazette*. It has been decided to have a large number of rather rough diagrams rather than the smaller number of more elaborate and detailed maps which was the other alternative, partly from considerations of price, partly because in trench warfare in particular the narrative must otherwise have been considerably enlarged.

For one who has not the honour of being a member of the great Regiment whose story he is trying to tell, who has not even had the privilege of having served with any of its battalions at any time, the task of writing its history presents special difficulties. Not to know the personal equation is a grave disadvantage, it leaves the compiler dependent on written records which he has probably often misinterpreted where he has not had the great advantage of being assisted and corrected by those more fortunately situated. At the same time, for writing a regimental history inside knowledge is perhaps rather less essential than for writing the story

PREFACE.

of a battalion; no one could have much inside knowledge of more than a minority of the battalions of a regiment, and one who is equally a stranger to them all at least approaches all from the same standpoint.

In the compilation of this account the chief source of evidence is naturally that contained in the official War Diaries which every unit is required by Field Service Regulations to keep. When it has been admitted that the War Diaries are often inadequate, that as a foundation for a narrative history they lack much of what is most wanted, the compiler must still express a real debt of gratitude to those who kept them, often under very difficult conditions and without much idea of the purpose for which this onerous duty was imposed upon them. Naturally War Diaries vary in value; some are good as a rule, others are good more occasionally, of others it may be said that had they fallen into the hands of the Germans during the war they would have afforded singularly little satisfaction or profit to their captors' Intelligence Section—to that extent they also may perhaps be reckoned good.

As a rule the defect of the War Diary lies in its reticence. It was not indeed a battalion of The Queen's Own which could find no more to say about the battle of the Aisne than : " Sept. 14th.—Battle of the Aisne; hard fighting, heavy casualties, rain at night "; but one battalion—which shall remain unspecified—omitted to record the departure of a C.O. who had commanded it in the field for over a year. All with one accord fail to provide copies of the recommendations submitted on behalf of officers and men who had distinguished themselves, and those who do mention the award of honours or decorations usually omit to mention the service for which the reward was conferred, or the occasion on which the incident occurred. Occasionally reference is made in the text of a Diary to a special report on some action, no copy of which is attached to the Diary. It is touching, however, to notice the confidence which

PREFACE.

those who have not kept or read Battalion Diaries place in them as repositories of information. Often officers who have been asked to supply information to fill gaps in the story have written back cheerfully: " That was the day when Pte. X did such good work with his Lewis gun, but no doubt there will be full details about him in the Battalion Diary." Still, though they have left a most tantalising amount unsaid, the battalion Diaries have provided the information which forms the backbone of this account, though, of course, efforts have been made to check and supplement their information from other sources.

To follow the fortunes of a battalion a good many sources other than its own Diaries have to be laid under contribution. In the first place Diaries of the Brigade and Division in which it served are indispensable, and in some cases those of the other battalions of the brigade have also been consulted. For access to all these Diaries the compiler's thanks are in the first place due to Brig.-Gen. J. E. Edmonds, Director of the Military Branch of the Historical Section of the Committee of Imperial Defence, and to the Staff of that Section, more particularly to Mr. E. A. Dixon. Every facility has been placed in his way and the help that the Section has given has been unfailing and invaluable.

After the War Diaries comes the *Q.O.G.* It was no small achievement to keep the paper going throughout the war, and its Editors, Colonel Brock in particular, are to be heartily congratulated on a notable feat, which it is believed no other regimental paper equalled. It has been of the utmost value and has greatly lightened the task of the compiler of this account. The earlier numbers are naturally the more valuable, they are allowed to mention many things with a degree of preciseness and definiteness, which was prohibited later on when the heavy hand of the Censorship had descended on regimental journals. Even then it continued to give casualty lists, information as to appointments, promo-

PREFACE.

tions, honours and awards, which has been of great value in the compilation of this account. To have, for example, lists of D.S.O.'s, M.C.'s and D.C.M.'s given in the *Q.O.G.*, often with the statement of the services for which these decorations were awarded, has saved hours that must otherwise have been devoted to the laborious task of chasing them through the *London Gazette*, though it must be admitted that in a good many cases the information given has lacked the identifications of time and place needed before the episode could be utilised in the narrative. Many of these deeds, therefore, have had to be omitted, and some, it is to be feared, may, despite all precautions, be incorrectly identified.

Beyond the War Diaries, the *Q.O.G.* and the *London Gazette*, the main sources utilised have been the official dispatches, notably those of Sir Douglas Haig, General Montgomery's "Fourth Army in the Hundred Days," which helps to elucidate the story of the 6th and 7th Battalions, with two histories of Divisions, the Fifth and the Eighteenth, in which battalions of The Queen's Own served and, naturally, the two battalion histories which have been published for the 1st and 8th Battalions. Colonel Wenyon and Major H. S. Brown have produced an admirable account of the 8th Battalion, which has been of the greatest assistance. "Invicta," Major Molony's history of the 1st Battalion, unfortunately only appeared after this account had been written, and it has only been possible to utilize it to make some corrections and minor additions. Reference is made in the text to the few other works utilized, to one or two articles like General Wauchope's accounts of the Qalat Shergat operations, but for the majority of "war books"—other than histories of different units—the compiler must confess to a profound distrust which has caused him to leave them severely alone.

But to all the information contained in these different sources the compiler has been fortunate enough to

PREFACE.

be able to add a great deal which has been provided by surviving officers and men. A certain amount was collected by Captain Palmer, the first secretary of the Regimental History Committee, before the book was begun, a great deal more has been supplied by those who have been kind enough to read over, criticise and amplify the chapters dealing with the events with which they themselves were familiar. To get into touch with the different battalions in this way has been of the greatest help. Where the official sources have often been jejune and unilluminating the information thus obtained has been specially welcome. It has frequently helped the compiler to avoid pitfalls into which he would otherwise have blundered; it has brought into relief things that did not deserve to be overlooked. Those who have helped in this way have been many, so numerous that it would hardly be possible to mention them all and invidious to make a selection of names from among them. The compiler would therefore like to thank all these helpers collectively, many of them for welcome encouragement as well as for help; he must, however, be allowed to thank Colonel Charles Bonham-Carter for all he has done to help him. Colonel Bonham-Carter has taken on himself the laborious duty of preparing and checking the appendices, he has been indefatigable in getting hold of the right people to supply information, he has been a kind as well as a helpful critic; if this volume in any way fulfils its object of providing an accurate record of the doings of The Queen's Own in the greatest of all its wars it is very largely due to Colonel Bonham-Carter's keenness, energy and encouragement. That it falls far short of doing full justice to a truly remarkable record the compiler is painfully conscious. C. T. A.

[For permission to reproduce plans and photographs and help in doing so the Regimental History Committee is much indebted to the Author of "Invicta," and to its Publishers (Messrs. James Nisbet & Co.), to the Authors of "The History of the 8th Battalion," and to its Publishers (Messrs. Hazell, Watson, & Viney), and to the Editor of the *Queen's Own Gazette*.]

CONTENTS.

CHAPTER I

MOBILIZATION—MONS—THE RETREAT

The Queen's Own on August 4th, 1914. Mobilization. 1st Battalion crosses to France. Advance to Mons. In action on Mons—Condé Canal. The German attack. The Brandenburg Grenadiers meet The Queen's Own. Beginning of the retreat. Le Cateau. Retreat from Le Cateau. Action of Crépy en Valois. End of Retreat   1—28

CHAPTER II

THE MARNE AND AISNE

Situation on September 6th. The British advance. Forcing the Petit Morin and Marne. Von Kluck's retreat. Advance to the Aisne. The passage of the Aisne. In trenches at Missy. Beginnings of trench-warfare   29—42

CHAPTER III

LA BASSEE AND NEUVE CHAPELLE

The move to Flanders. The advance against La Bassée. Held up at Vermelles. Under the Third Division. Stopping a gap. Withdrawal to Neuve Chapelle. The new position. German attacks renewed. The attack of October 27th. Neuve Chapelle lost. The counter-attack of October 28th. The stand at the cross-roads. Relieved. In line opposite Messines. Move to Ypres. The first experience of "the Salient"   43—63

CHAPTER IV

EXPANSION

The 2nd Battalion in India. The 3rd Battalion. Guard-finding and draft providing. Second Line Territorial battalions formed. 1/4th and 1/5th

CONTENTS.

Battalions to India. Raising "Service" battalions. The start of the 6th. The 7th Battalion formed. The 8th and 9th Battalions. The Volunteers ... 64—77

CHAPTER V

THE FIRST WINTER—HILL SIXTY—SECOND YPRES

Trench Warfare, 1914—1915. Wastage. In the Wulverghem Line. Moved to the Salient. Redressing the balance. Hill Sixty. The Assault. Consolidating the position. Resisting counter-attacks. Back into action. The gas attack. The counter-attack of April 23rd. Holding on. Hill 60 lost: the effort to recover it ... 78—97

CHAPTER VI

MESOPOTAMIA IN 1915

2nd Battalion ordered to Mesopotamia. At Qurna. The move to Ahwaz. The operations in Arabistan. Amara. Move to the Euphrates. Nasiriya ... 98—111

CHAPTER VII

TRENCH WARFARE, 1915

The "New Armies" in France. The 6th Battalion at Ploegsteert. The 7th Battalion's move to France. 1st Battalion in Flanders: its move to the Somme. The 7th Battalion's first experience of active service ... 112—123

CHAPTER VIII

LOOS

The 8th Battalion in training. Its move overseas. The attack at Loos. The Twenty-Fourth Division's task. The 8th Battalion's "baptism of fire": its losses. The 6th Battalion brought South. Gun Trench. The attack of October 8th. The capture of Gun Trench. Trench warfare ... 124—138

CONTENTS.

PAGES

CHAPTER IX

THE TERRITORIALS IN 1915—SUVLA —NEW BATTALIONS

1/4th and 1/5th Battalions in India. Formation of the " Kent Battalion," renamed 2/4th. Move of 2/4th to Gallipoli. At Suvla. Move to Egypt. 3rd Battalion. Draft for 2nd Battalion sent to 7th R.D.F. Formation of 10th, 11th and 12th Battalions. 9th and 12th Battalions converted into Training Reserve Battalions 139—152

CHAPTER X

FROM LOOS TO THE SOMME

Lull on the Western Front. 1st Battalion at Arras. 6th Battalion at Givenchy. The fighting for the Hohenzollern Craters. 7th and 8th Battalions during first half of 1916. 10th and 11th Battalions in France 153—165

CHAPTER XI

MESOPOTAMIA IN 1916

B and D Companies, 2nd Battalion, on the Tigris. Defence and capitulation of Kut al Amara. Sufferings of the prisoners. Headquarter wing of 2nd Battalion at Nasiriya. Butaniya. 2/4th Battalion in Egypt. The advance across Sinai 169—179

CHAPTER XII

THE SOMME

Preparations. 7th Battalion on July 1st. 6th Battalion at Ovillers la Boisselle. 7th Battalion at Trones Wood. The defence of Trones Wood. 1st Battalion at High Wood. The attack on Switch Trench. 1st Battalion at Longueval. 8th Battalion at Guillemont. The defence of Delville Wood. 6th Battalion back in the line. The fighting for Ration Trench 180—203

xvii

CONTENTS.

PAGES

CHAPTER XIII
THE SOMME—(*continued*)

September on the Somme. 1st Battalion again in action. Falfemont Farm and Leuze Wood. The Tank attack of September 15th. The 10th and 11th Battalions at Flers. The 7th Battalion at Thiepval. The fight for the Schwaben Redoubt. The attack of October 7th: the 10th and 11th Battalions at Le Sars, the 6th at Guedecourt. The 7th's last fight on the Somme: Desire Trench. The 7th's losses on the Somme   204—224

CHAPTER XIV
FROM THE SOMME TO ARRAS

The close of the Somme. 1st Battalion at Givenchy: the raid of February 10th. 6th Battalion at Blangy: the Arras front. 7th Battalion on the Ancre: the attack of February 14th. 8th Battalion in the Loos salient. At Lens. 10th and 11th Battalions in Flanders: raids and bombardments   225—241

CHAPTER XV
ARRAS

The Spring offensive. 1st Battalion on the Vimy Ridge. 6th Battalion at Observation Ridge: Monchy le Preux. Advance by 8th Battalion. Offensive continued: 1st Battalion on April 23rd. Attack of May 3rd: 6th Battalion at Gun Trench: 7th Battalion at Cherisy: 1st Battalion at Oppy. End of the offensive: 6th Battalion: 1st Battalion   242—260

CHAPTER XVI
MESSINES

The Flanders offensive—The 8th Battalion in the Spring of 1917—The battle of Messines: the 10th and 11th Battalions in action: the 8th Battalion consolidate. The 11th Battalion's attack on Optic Trench. The 7th Battalion move to Flanders. The 1st and 6th Battalions on the Arras front.

CONTENTS.

Preparing for the new offensive. The 3/4th Battalion selected for service in France 261—274

CHAPTER XVII
THIRD YPRES

The beginning of the new offensive: the 10th and 11th Battalions attack astride the Canal. Hollebeke taken. Consolidating under difficulties. Unfavourable weather as a cause of delay. The 7th Battalion at Stirling Castle. The 8th Battalion at Inverness Copse: the German counterattack of September 8th and its repulse. The attack resumed: the 11th Battalion on September 20th. Tower Hamlets taken. The 10th Battalion in action. The 11th's honours 275—290

CHAPTER XVIII
THIRD YPRES—(*continued*)

The 1st Battalion's return to the Salient. The German attack of October 3rd repulsed. October 4th: a successful advance. The 7th Battalion in action again. The attack on Poelcapelle: mud the chief obstacle. The 3/4th Battalion in the Salient. The 1st Battalion's second attack (October 26th). A disastrous day 291—303

CHAPTER XIX
INFANTRY HILL

The 6th Battalion in the Monchy sector. The tactical situation. The loss of Long Trench. Long Trench retaken. The attack on Hook Trench: the Germans driven back. The raid on Strap and Buckle Trenches 304—315

CHAPTER XX
CAMBRAI

The Tank attack. The Hindenburg Line broken. The 6th take Lateau Wood. Major Alderman's death. Holding on under difficulties: an unsatisfactory situation. The counter-attack of November

CONTENTS.

PAGES

30th: the stand at Battalion Headquarters: the front line companies overwhelmed. The Germans checked. The 6th nearly wiped out: the task of reconstruction   316—325

CHAPTER XXI

PALESTINE AND MESOPOTAMIA IN 1917.

The Eastern theatres in 1917. The 2/4th move up to the front. The first attack on Gaza: the demonstration along the coast. The second attack: the capture of Samson Ridge. The checkmate on the Gaza front. The fresh attack. Beersheba taken. The fighting for Hill 1250. The advance up the Hebron Road. Jerusalem taken. The storming of Tel Aziziye Ridge. The 5th Battalion on active service: its arrival at Baghdad. The 2nd Battalion transferred to the Tigris   326—339

CHAPTER XXII

ITALY

Caporetto and its consequences. The Forty-First Division moved to Italy. The march across Lombardy. In line on the Piave. The Fifth Division in Italy. The recall to France   340—345

CHAPTER XXIII

THE LAST WINTER

The "man-power" problem. The 6th Battalion at Fleurbaix: raids and counter-raids. The 7th at Houthulst Forest: its move to the Oise. The reduction of brigades to three battalions: its grave disadvantages. The 8th at Hargicourt: its move to Vadencourt. The 3/4th broken up   346—355

CHAPTER XXIV

THE GERMAN ATTACK

The German attack of March 21st. The 7th Battalion overwhelmed: the defence of Durham

CONTENTS.

Post. The retreat of the Eighteenth Division: rear-guard actions. The remnant of the 7th moved round to Amiens and amalgamated with the 12th Entrenchment Battalion. The attack on the 8th Battalion: the Germans held up at Vadencourt. The Twenty-Fourth Division forced back. Across the Somme. The stand at Fonches Cross-roads. Back to the Amiens Defence Line. The German advance stayed. The 8th's achievement   356—369

CHAPTER XXV

THE GERMAN ATTACK—(*continued*)

The disbanding of the 11th Battalion: its record. The 10th thrown into the fight. The stand at Vaulx—Vraucourt: the battalion overwhelmed. The 6th Battalion brought down from Flanders. The stand on the Ancre. Aveluy Wood. The Germans held up. The reconstituted 7th in action again. The defence of Amiens. The fighting round Hangard. Villers-Bretonneux. A successful counter-stroke. What the 7th went through   370—386

CHAPTER XXVI

THE CHANNEL PORTS IN DANGER AND THE LAST SUMMER

The return of the 1st Battalion. The German offensive on the Lys. The Fifth Division at Nieppe Forest. The advance stopped. The counter-stroke at Plate Becque: a fine achievement. The 6th on the Albert front: the attack at Bouzincourt. The 7th reconstructed. The 8th back at Lens. The 10th in Flanders again   387—400

CHAPTER XXVII

TURNING THE TABLES

August 8th, 1918: the turn of the tide. The work of the Third Corps. The 7th's attack. The 6th at Morlancourt: Sergeant Harris' V.C. The battle-front shifted. The Third Army strike at

CONTENTS.

Bapaume. The 1st Battalion at Irles and the advance of the Fourth Army from the Ancre: the 6th and 7th in action. Trones Wood again. The capture of Saillisel. The Germans driven back to the Hindenburg Line ... 401—420

CHAPTER XXVIII

PREPARING FOR THE DECISIVE BLOW

The 8th Battalion at Lens: the defence of Dean's Post. Another V.C. Preparing to break the Hindenburg Line. The 6th and 7th at Epehy: a stubborn resistance. The 1st at Gouzeaucourt. The battle spreads to Flanders: the 10th's advance on Menin ... 421—434

CHAPTER XXIX

THROUGH THE HINDENBURG LINE

The attack on the Cambrai—St. Quentin front. The 6th reach the Canal. The advance past Cambrai: The 8th join in: Awoignt and Haussy. The 1st Battalion on the Selle. The 7th at Le Cateau: the attacks of October 23rd and 26th. The First Army on the move: the 6th Battalion's advance from Lens to St. Amand. Colonel Dawson wounded again. The 10th in the advance to the Scheldt ... 435—449

CHAPTER XXX

THE LAST BATTLE

The Germans defence weakening. The last big attack. The 8th at Bavai. The 1st near Maubeuge. The 7th in Mormal Forest. The 10th's last fight. The Armistice ... 450—456

CHAPTER XXXI

EASTERN THEATRES IN 1918

The 2/4th's last actions. The "Indianization" of the Army in Palestine. The 2/4th broken up. A quiet time for the 2nd and 5th Battalions. The

CONTENTS.

advance on Tekrit. The passage of the Fattah Gorge. The 5th in action. Qalat Shergat : a fine attack. The Turkish surrender. The 5th at Mosul 457—469

CHAPTER XXXII
DEMOBILIZATION

After the Armistice. The Army of Occupation. Colonel Dawson's death. The 1st reduced to cadre and brought home. Its reconstruction. The return of the 2nd Battalion. The 3rd disembodied. The 1/4th gets a chance in Afghanistan : its return. The 5th in garrison in Mesopotamia : it comes home. The end of the 7th and 8th Battalions : their records. The 6th and 10th on the Rhine : their disbandment and their achievements. The War Memorial : its unveiling. The laying up of the Colours 470—484

APPENDICES.

I The Depôt and the Comforts and Prisoners of War Funds 485—499

II The Roll of Honour 501—584

III Honours, Rewards and Decorations 585—614

IV Mentions in Dispatches 615—622

V Units of The Queen's Own and their Commanding Officers 623—629

LIST OF MAPS AND SKETCH PLANS.[1]

			PAGE
Map	A	THE WESTERN FRONT	At end of book
,,	B	MESOPOTAMIA	468
Sketch	1	AREA ROUND MONS	8
,,	2	POSITION ON MONS—CONDÉ CANAL	14
,,	3	THE BRITISH RIGHT AT LE CATEAU	22
,,	4	CREPY EN VALOIS	28
,,	5	THE ADVANCE ACROSS THE MARNE AND OURCQ	36
,,	6	MISSY SUR AISNE	40
,,	7	AREA W. AND N.W. OF LA BASSEE	50
,,	8	NEUVE CHAPELLE	58
,,	9	HILL 60	96
,,	10	NASIRIYA	108
,,	11	HULLUCH AND BOIS HUGO	132
,,	12	GUN TRENCH	138
,,	13	SUVLA	144
,,	14	HOHENZOLLERN CRATERS	160
,,	15	KUT EL AMARA	170
,,	16	BUTANIYA	176
,,	17	MONTAUBAN	184
,,	18	THE OVILLERS FRONT	186
,,	19	THE ATTACK OF JULY 3RD, 1916	188
,,	20	TRONES WOOD	192

[1] The majority of these sketch-plans are taken from or based on maps in the official War Diaries, one or two have been supplied or amended by officers who were present at the actions illustrated. Nos. 2 and 15 are taken from the *Q.O.G.*, No. 8 has been adapted from the map in *Invicta*.

LIST OF MAPS AND SKETCH PLANS.

			PAGE
Sketch	21	HIGH WOOD	196
,,	22	DELVILLE WOOD AND FALFEMONT FARM	200
,,	22A	TRENCHES NEAR POZIERES	202
,,	23	N.E. PORTION OF THE SOMME BATTLEFIELD	220
,,	24	SCHWABEN REDOUBT	216
,,	25	POSITIONS BETWEEN THIEPVAL AND MIRAUMONT	234
,,	26	THE GIVENCHY RAID	230
,,	27	THE VIMY RIDGE	244
,,	28	OBSERVATION RIDGE—APRIL 9TH, 1917	248
,,	29	POSITIONS N.E. OF MONCHY	254
,,	30	CHERISY	258
,,	31	MESSINES	268
,,	32	THE ATTACK OF JULY 31ST, 1917	280
,,	33	TOWER HAMLETS RIDGE	290
,,	34	THE MENIN ROAD	302
,,	35	POELCAPELLE	298
,,	36	INFANTRY HILL	314
,,	37	CAMBRAI	324
,,	38	GAZA AND BEERSHEBA	334
,,	39	MOY	360
,,	40	THE RETREAT OF THE 7TH R.W.K.	362
,,	41	VADENCOURT	366
,,	42	OPERATIONS OF 8TH R.W.K., MARCH, 1918	370
,,	43	VAULX-VRAUCOURT	374

LIST OF MAPS AND SKETCH PLANS.

			PAGE
Sketch	44	OPERATIONS OF 6TH R.W.K. ON THE ANCRE	378
,,	45	VILLERS-BRETONNEUX	384
,,	46	PLATE BECQUE	392
,,	47	BOUZINCOURT	396
,,	48	AREA BETWEEN THE ANCRE AND THE SOMME	418
,,	49	ATTACK OF 7TH R.W.K., AUGUST 8TH, 1918	408
,,	50	AREA N.W. OF BAPAUME	412
,,	51	EPEHY—PEIZIERES	436
,,	52	THE LENS AREA	424
,,	53	GOUZEAUCOURT	432
,,	54	AREA E. OF CAMBRAI	440
,,	55	THE SELLE	442
,,	56	HECQ	454
,,	57	THE ADVANCE FROM LENS	446
,,	58	THE ADVANCE ACROSS THE SCHELDT	456
,,	59	COUNTRY N.E. OF JERUSALEM	458
,,	60	QALAT SHERGAT	466

ERRATA.

PAGE	
182	Under " July 1st, 1916, 7th Battalion," should occur cf. Sketch 17.
201	The reference should be to Sketch 22a.
204	,, ,, ,, ,, ,, 22.
208	,, ,, ,, ,, ,, 23.
212	,, ,, ,, ,, ,, 24.
217	,, ,, ,, ,, ,, 23.
221	,, ,, ,, ,, ,, 25.
282	Under " 7th Battalion " insert cf. Sketch 34.
284	Under " September 8th " insert cf. Sketch 34.

LIST OF PHOTOGRAPHS.

MAJOR-GENERAL SIR EDMUND LEACH, K.C.B.	*Frontispiece*
	To Face Page
BRIG.-GENERAL A. MARTYN and BRIG.-GENERAL S. H. PEDLEY	4
MAJOR M. P. BUCKLE	54
COLONEL C. N. WATNEY and COLONEL F. A. FRAZER	68
COLONEL P. M. ROBINSON and LIEUT.-COL. H. D. BUCHANAN-DUNLOP	120
LIEUT.-COL. E. F. VENABLES and COLONEL E. VANSITTART	136
COLONEL R. J. WOULFE-FLANAGAN and COLONEL A. T. F. SIMPSON	178
LIEUT.-COL. J. T. TWISLETON-WYKEHAM-FIENNES and LIEUT.-COL. J. C. PARKER	198
LIEUT.-COL. A. F. TOWNSHEND	208
COLONEL A. WOOD MARTYN and LIEUT. COL A. C. CORFE	262
LIEUT.-COL. L. H. HICKSON and LIEUT.-COL. B. JOHNSTONE	296
CAPTAIN (A/LIEUT.-COL.) W. J. ALDERMAN	318
BT.-MAJOR (T/LIEUT.-COL.) N. I. WHITTY and LIEUT.-COL. H. J. WENYON	368
SERGT. T. J. HARRIS	406
LIEUT. D. J. DEAN	422
LIEUT. C. H. SEWELL	500
BT.-MAJOR (T/LIEUT.-COL.) W. R. A. DAWSON	470
THE UNVEILING OF THE CENOTAPH	480

CHAPTER I.

PRECAUTIONARY PERIOD.

THE twelve years which followed the South African War of 1899-1902 saw the British Army but infrequently engaged in even minor operations of war. It was nevertheless a momentous time, of strenuous training, of digesting and utilizing the experiences of South Africa, of organization and preparation if not of actual fighting. It was moreover pre-eminently a period of "rumours of war." More than once the war-clouds seemed on the verge of bursting but passed away without doing so until some believed they never would break: indeed, after the Agadir crisis had left peace unbroken there was some excuse for those who did not at once appreciate the seriousness to the British Empire of the situation created by the murder of the Austrian heir-apparent at Serajevo. But as the troubled month of July 1914 neared its eventful close it became increasingly apparent that this time the long imminent danger was not to be averted—that the British Empire must inevitably be involved in the developments of the Balkan crisis. With the progress of the diplomatic and political crisis a regimental history may be excused from dealing, but for The Queen's Own the turning point came with the issue on July 27th of the orders to adopt the measures prescribed for the "precautionary period" preceding actual mobilization.

Of the five battalions of the Regiment existing in July 1914 the 1st (Lieut.-Col. A. Martyn) was at Dublin, being assigned to the 13th Brigade of the Fifth Division,[1] the 2nd (Lieut.-Col. S. H. Pedley) was on

---

[1] This was commanded by Brigadier-General G. J. Cuthbert, and included also the 2nd K.O.S.B.'s, 2nd Duke of Wellington's and 2nd K.O.Y.L.I. The Fifth Division (Major-Gen. Sir C. Fergusson) was on mobilization allotted to the Second Corps.

PRECAUTIONARY PERIOD.

1914

the Indian establishment and was in the Third Indian (Lahore) Division, having its headquarters and four companies at the hill station of Dalhousie and its other four companies at Multan, its normal station. The 3rd, the Special Reserve unit, of which Sir A. Griffith-Boscawen was Lieut.-Col., had been embodied for its annual training on the 27th and was at Shorncliffe; the two Territorial battalions, the 4th (Lieut.-Col. C. N. Watney) and 5th (Lieut.-Col. F. A. Frazer), were also under arms for, with the rest of the Home Counties Division, they were marching across Hampshire to spend the greater part of their fortnight's training on Salisbury Plain.

1st Battalion

On receipt of the "precautionary period" orders all officers and men of the 1st Battalion were recalled from leave and in common with the rest of the Army steps were taken to anticipate a certain amount of the work of mobilization, orders for which were regarded as inevitable. But the necessity of finding large detachments for duties in Dublin, mainly guarding bridges and other points on the railway, put a serious strain on the battalion, and when the expected orders to mobilize finally arrived on the afternoon of August 5th these guard duties greatly hindered the progress of mobilization. As far as possible they were assigned to men unfit for service overseas who numbered nearly 200, though of these only four were really medically "unfit," the remainder being so classified for being under 19 or not having completed their recruit's course. But even so officers and N.C.O.'s had to be found for these duties when wanted for mobilization purposes.

Those actually serving with the battalion and ready to proceed overseas came to 22 officers and nearly 450 men, the balance of the war establishment having to be found from the Army Reserve. If in 1899 the response of the Reservists to the summons to the colours had been excellent, in 1914 it was even better. Within a few hours of the posting of the notices Maidstone

MOBILIZATION.

was inundated with Reservists. But Major P. M. Robinson, the Officer Commanding the Depôt, and his staff were equal to the emergency, although, as the 3rd Battalion was already embodied, the number of officers at the Depôt was accordingly reduced. However, willing helpers were plentiful, notably Major Couch; he had just finished his term as Quarter-Master at the Depôt on August 1st, but within four days he was back at his old post and busier than ever before.

August, 1914
1st Battalion

Such was the celerity with which the Reservists answered the call and were equipped and dispatched to Dublin that on the afternoon of the second day of mobilization no less than 320 had reached the battalion, followed by 270 more next day. With them came five Special Reserve Officers, Lieuts. Anderson, Sewell, Snelgrove, Whitehouse and Holloway. Lieut. Anstruther of the 2nd Battalion, who was home on leave, and Captain Snow, of the Reserve of Officers, also joined, bringing the battalion up to war-strength. Against these increases, however, must be set the departure for Maidstone on August 7th of Captain Snow and Lieuts. Anstruther and Snelgrove, with 15 N.C.O.'s, they having been detailed to form the nucleus of the new 6th (Service) Battalion, for whose formation orders had just been issued, while five days later Captain Lynch White, and 2nd-Lieut. Dawson were ordered to the Depôt on the reduction of the War Establishment to 25 officers.[1]

1.—The officers who proceeded overseas with the battalion were: Lieut.-Col. A. Martyn (C.O.); Major P. M. Buckle, D.S.O. (2nd in command); Lieut. G. B. Legard (Adjutant); Lieut. H. G. Rogers (Quartermaster); Lieut. D. J. Johnson (Machine Gun Officer); Lieut. W. Newton (Transport Officer). "A" Company: Captains G. D. Lister (commanding) and C. F. H. Keenlyside, Lieuts. P. F. Wilberforce Bell and C. K. Anderson, 2nd-Lieuts. S. K. Gore and A. A. E. Chitty. "B" Company: Major C. G. Pack Beresford (commanding), Captain W. C. O. Phillips, Lieuts. F. Fisher and D. C. C. Sewell, 2nd-Lieut. M. F. Broadwood. "C" Company: Major P. Hastings (commanding), Lieuts. W. V. Palmer, C. A. M. Holloway, W. K. Ames and J. H. Whitehouse. "D" Company: Captains R. M. G. Tulloch (commanding) and H. D. Buchanan-Dunlop, Lieuts. H. B. H. White and N. P. J. K. McClelland; R.S.M., H. S. Doe.

MOBILIZATION.

August, 1914
3rd Battalion

Meanwhile the normal routine of the 3rd Battalion's training had been abruptly interrupted. It had gone into camp on July 27th with 16 officers and just over 500 other ranks, and was carrying on as usual despite the atmosphere of tension and uncertainty. Its first real intimation of the serious things afoot came with an order on August 1st to find an armed guard with ball ammunition for the Naval seaplane station at Westgate-on-sea. Then in the small hours of August 3rd the Adjutant, Captain Waring, was aroused by a telegram ordering the battalion to move at once to its " peace station." The camp was promptly struck, a special train secured, and by 9 a.m. the battalion was back at Maidstone only to find that it should have been sent to Fort Darland at Chatham. To that spot, destined to become only too familiar to The Queen's Own if they found it disused, unfrequented and approached only by a land way overgrown with weeds, the battalion proceeded forthwith. In the course of the next few days it was required to find detachments to proceed to Sheerness to guard prisoners of war, German waiters and merchant sailors for the most part, to Gravesend for Customs duties, and to Faversham to guard powder works. On August 9th it moved to its " war station " at Chattenden, where it relieved a Territorial battalion of The Queen's. Here it took over guard duties at several important points, notably the big magazines at Chattenden and Lodge Hill, with Kingsnorth seaplane station and Upnor, where the ammunition from the big magazines was loaded on to the warships. The surplus Reservists from the Depôt had joined the battalion, but even so the guard duties were so heavy that the men got very few " nights in bed " and were kept busy by day also.

1st Battalion

At Dublin mobilization proceeded rapidly and with great smoothness, apart from the guard-finding duties, and had been completed some days before the time for embarkation arrived; indeed, but for delays over pro-

Photo by]   [*G. C. Beresford, Brompton Road, S.W.*

BRIG.-GENERAL S. H. PEDLEY, C.B.
Commanded 2nd Battalion in 1914-1915 and 1916.

BRIG.-GENERAL A. MARTYN, C.B., C.M.G.
Commanded 1st Battalion, 1914.

TRANSPORT TO FRANCE.

curing harness for the heavy-draught horses, all was ready by August 8th. It was on August 13th that the battalion embarked on the s.s. "Gloucestershire," amid scenes of much enthusiasm. This was an 8,000-ton vessel, but as she had Brigade Headquarters with the 2nd K.O.S.B.'s and the 2nd Duke of Wellington's also on board, the strain on the accommodation was enough to make the voyage uncomfortable. Fortunately the sea was calm and neither "U" boats nor the German High Seas Fleet made the least attempt to interfere with the passage of the "B.E.F." to France. Havre was reached without incident about 11 a.m. on August 15th, and after another three hours the "Gloucestershire" went alongside the quay and disembarkation began. After unloading the transport the battalion spent an uncomfortable night in sheds on the quay, moving early next morning to a rest camp five miles out. This was thronged by the people of Havre, who displayed the greatest interest and enthusiasm and made strenuous efforts to induce the men to part with cap-badges and other souvenirs. But the stay at this rest camp was not long, and soon after midnight the battalion started for the railway station, where it entrained by 5 o'clock. "After leaving Havre," wrote one officer in his diary, "the whole journey was a sort of triumphal progress. At every station there were crowds of people with cigarettes, little flags, sweets and flowers for the men. Great cheering, hand-shaking, kissing of hands. Many shouted 'Guillaume' (meaning the German Emperor) and then pretended to cut their throats. In the towns the windows were full of people for half-a-mile on each side of the railway waving flags and handkerchiefs, and shouting 'Hip, Hip, Hurrah, Vive l'Angleterre.'"

A 16-hour journey by Rouen and Amiens brought the battalion to Landrecies early on August 18th; detrainment was soon over and the battalion marched away to Maroilles, four miles distant, where it and the

August, 1914
1st Battalion

August 16th, 1914

August 17th, 1914

MONS.

August, 1914
1st Battalion
Duke's were to billet. Here three days were spent, mainly in route-marching and musketry, while the British force completed its concentration. Of what was happening the troops knew little, except that the Germans were advancing in great force through Belgium, that the gallant resistance of Liège had been already overcome, that the British had been assigned a position on the left of General Lanrezac's Fifth French Army and that heavy fighting had already begun in Alsace and Lorraine. But of the strength of the Germans in Belgium no exact knowledge had as yet reached even the French Headquarters, and when, on the evening of August 20th, the orders for the advance of the British were issued, regimental officers and men were expecting to be launched in a counter-stroke at the German right.

Aug. 21st 1914
These orders prescribed for the Second Corps an advance to an area West of Maubeuge, the billets assigned to the Fifth Division being Houdain — Gommegnies—Hargnies. This involved for the 13th Brigade a trying march of 17 miles in hot weather, which tried the Reservists sorely, for most of them were in bad training and therefore unequal to the weight they had to carry. Still the R.W.K. had under thirty men who failed to reach their billets at Houdain along with

Aug. 22nd, 1914
the battalion. Next day's march was worse; during most of it the route lay over the cobble stones of the roads through the mining villages which stretch South and West of Mons. On this day the battalion found the advanced guard of its brigade and led the Division from Houdain, across the Franco-Belgian frontier at Athis, through Dour, to Bossu. Here the vanguard was diverted from Hornu, its original destination, to St. Ghislain. On reaching that place, a large village of

See Sketch 1
6,000 inhabitants, it was ordered to take up and entrench a position along the Mons-Condé Canal, from St. Ghislain on the left to Mariette, where touch was established with the Third Division, who continued the

MONS.

outpost line past Mons. D Company (Captain Tulloch) was on the right, holding the railway bridge just North of St. Ghislain, C (Major Hastings) on the left, the K.O.S.B.'s continuing the line to the Westward and connecting up with the 14th Brigade. Aug. 22nd, 1914
1st Battalion

Reports had been received from the Divisional Cyclists that they had already established touch with the enemy and, fired by the prospect of a speedy encounter, all ranks fell busily to work, entrenching, barricading roads and bridges, loop-holing houses and garden-walls and clearing the foreground. The position was fair, the Southern canal bank being 10 feet above the general level commanded the low ground to the North, though C Company had to take post just North of the canal[1] as houses and other buildings would have masked its fire had it remained on the Southern bank, and even so the field of fire was somewhat broken by trees and bushes. These, however, served to conceal the British positions from the enemy. The line assigned to the battalion was long over 2,000 yards, and included a railway bridge, a road bridge and a foot bridge. But its length was a less unsatisfactory feature than the absence of any good artillery position just South of the canal, which made it very difficult to give the infantry along the canal adequate artillery support.

The afternoon passed uneventfully, though C and D were hard at work till late into the evening, and remained in the trenches with the M.G. Section[2] when the rest of the battalion went into billets at Hornu. Directly it was light next morning the work of entrenching was resumed, and before long the battalion was so well dug in that it was congratulated on the excellence of its trenches by the R.E. themselves. About 8 o'clock things began to get lively. The Divisional squadron, one of the 19th Hussars, and the Cyclists passed through the outposts and pushed Northwards Aug. 23rd, 1914

---
[1] Part of D also was north of the Canal.
[2] The M.G. Section of the Duke's also was with C Company.

7

MONS.

Aug. 23rd, 1914
1st Battalion

through Tertre to feel for the enemy. A Company (Captain G. D. Lister) followed them, having been warned about 5.30 a.m. to cross the canal and take position South of Tertre in readiness to cover the mounted troops should they be driven back. Captain Lister moved to within about 400 yards of Tertre and disposed his platoons to cover the exits from that village. No. 1 (2nd-Lieut. Gore) was on the left on the main road to St. Ghislain, Nos. 2 and 3 (Lieuts. Bell and Anderson) were echeloned back to the right, No. 4 (2nd-Lieut. Chitty) was retained in reserve behind No. 2, who occupied a small farm just East of the road. No. 1's field of fire was about 250 yards, Nos. 2 and 3 with nearly twice as much, being much better off. But the line of retreat to the main position was made difficult by numerous wire fences and deep ditches, and though Captain Lister detailed men to cut the wire, there was scanty time for such work, for before long[1] several cyclists came full tilt down the road from Tertre and announced that the enemy were close at hand. Five minutes later infantry began debouching in numbers from Tertre, and A Company had the satisfaction of opening a highly effective fire. It could be seen that the enemy were losing heavily and very soon his infantry halted and opened a brisk fire in return.

See Sketch 2

By a fortunate chance an officer of the 12th (Brandenburg) Grenadier Regiment of the Third (Brandenburg) Corps, by which the battalion was being attacked, has left a full and vivid account of this action. Captain Walter Bloem, a reserve officer of the Brandenburg

---

[1] There are most irreconcilable differences between the times given in the War Diaries and other authorities, but apparently the attack of the German Ninth Corps on the Third Division in the Nimy-Obourg salient N. and N.E. of Mons, which began about 9 a.m., preceded that of the Third Corps on the Canal line further West; The Queen's Own, therefore, though the first battalion in the Fifth Division to become engaged can hardly claim to have been the first battalion in the British Army to have come into conflict with the Germans, cf. *Military Operations*, 1914, I., pp. 67 ff.

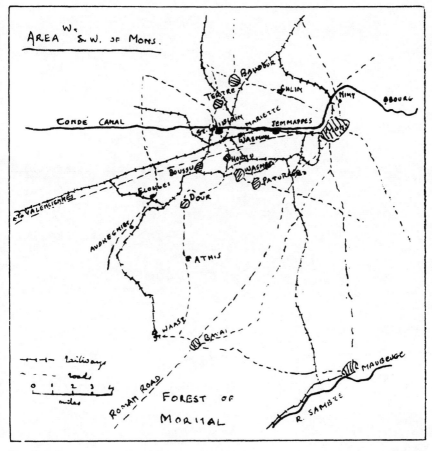

MONS.

Aug. 23rd, 1914
1st Battalion

Grenadiers, was a well-known novelist; his "Vormarsch" is certainly among the best written German war-books and his narrative is a handsome tribute to British markmanship and tactics.[1] As Captain Bloem tells the story the 12th Grenadiers had halted in Baudour, a village about a mile N.E. of Tertre, after a twelve-mile march, and were having a meal when suddenly cavalry scouts galloped in to report contact with the English in Tertre and that the canal line was held in strength.[2] At once the 3rd (Fusilier) Battalion pushed forward to clear Tertre, the 1st (Bloem's) was ordered to advance on its right through the woods N. and N.W. of the village, the 2nd being for the time held in reserve. A Company had thus to sustain the direct attack of a whole battalion, while another threatened its left. At first the German attack from Tertre made little headway against the accurate and well-controlled fire of A Company, but to maintain his advanced position for any length of time was clearly beyond Captain Lister's power; however, he had just received a request to cover the retirement of the cavalry, and he therefore decided to hang on, although a field battery had come into action South of Baudour and the infantry attacking astride the Tertre-Hornu road had increased so much in numbers that half the reserve platoon had to be sent up to reinforce Lieut. Gore. But A Company fired steadily, and the German accounts testify amply to its effectiveness. The commander of the Fusilier battalion had to reinforce his leading company with two others[3] and even then it was not till the 1st Battalion worked its way round Tertre and deployed beyond the Fusiliers that A began to yield

---

[1] *The Queen's Own Gazette* of March, 1918 contains a translation of an abbreviation of Captain Bloem's story, which was translated in full in the *Journal of the Royal United Service Institution* for November, 1919.

[2] A troop of cavalry had been fired on by D Company about 9.30 a.m., but at long range and without much effect.

[3] *cf.* "*Mons*"—the monograph issued by the German General Staff.

MONS

Aug. 23rd, 1914
1st Battalion

ground. There was nothing to be seen of the cavalry for whose sake Captain Lister was hanging on, and as his orders were to withdraw "if things were getting too hot," he decided shortly before noon to start retiring. He brought up the rest of his reserve platoon to No. 2's position, where they lined a deep dyke, and, covered by their fire, Lieut. Gore's party got well away. But the German infantry were now pressing closer, and though A Company fired with increasing effect and unshaken steadiness the retirement involved more casualties than the earlier part of the fight. Lieut. Anderson had been killed before the retirement began, Captain Lister himself was badly wounded and had to be left behind, refusing to let losses be risked in trying to get him away, 2nd-Lieut. Chitty was also hit but was got back safely. Altogether nearly half the company were hit, and of these two-thirds were killed or missing, for the German pressure was too strong to allow of getting the more severely wounded away.[1] Indeed, the last platoon had Germans within 100 yards of it in front and pressing on both its flanks before it got away. But the company had done well; it had, as the *Official History* (p. 71) says, "made a magnificent fight and inflicted far heavier losses than it had received"; certainly it had left its mark on the Brandenburg Grenadiers, whose Fusilier Battalion alone had lost its commander, a company commander, several other officers and many men.

Once the survivors of A had re-crossed the canal the companies in the main position began to get good targets, though at considerable ranges. B (Major Pack Beresford) had by now been brought up and four guns of the 120th Battery, R.F.A., had been placed on the canal bank. However, the Germans brought no less than six field batteries in action S.E. of Tertre, and this

---

[1] Pte. Donovan, of C, who went forward to assist Lieut. Wilberforce Bell in bringing in one of the wounded of A, was afterwards awarded the D.C.M. for his gallantry, the first of the many won by The Queen's Own in the war.

MONS.

overwhelming superiority silenced these guns and forced them to evacuate their advanced position, though another section of the 120th, more fortunately placed on a pit heap rather further East, remained in action till evening, lending the battalion invaluable support. The German guns then turned on to the infantry position but found it extremely hard to locate, so well had the positions been chosen and concealed, and although the volume of fire they developed did much damage to houses and garden-walls the battalion's defence was quite unshaken and its casualties were light. A dummy trench at the end of the railway bridge proved most successful in attracting the bulk of the enemy's attention and the care which had been devoted to concealing the real trenches was amply repaid.

Meanwhile the 2nd Battalion of the 12th Grenadiers had reinforced its comrades and advanced East of Tertre against D, the Fusiliers in the centre opposing B and C, while the 1st Battalion apparently attacked the K.O.S.B.'s right as well as the left of C. Captain Bloem may not have actually encountered The Queen's Own, but part of his battalion did, and his experience of British musketry may be taken as typical of the whole German attack along the canal line. Working forward by rushes, at first 100 yards or more, gradually shortening to 50 or 30, the Brandenburg Grenadiers felt themselves opposing an invisible enemy whose bullets swept unceasingly over the level water-meadows, inflicting heavier casualties with each rush till the whole meadow was spread with little grey dots and the impetus of the attack completely broken. At one point Bloem and his men got forward almost unchecked for 300 yards, getting within 120 yards of the canal. But as they rose to their feet for a final charge which should carry the position, a devastating fire mowed them down. "The enemy," he writes, "appeared to have been waiting for this moment ... they had lured us, cunningly, as close as possible so as to destroy us the more certainly and

Aug. 23rd, 1914
1st Battalion

Aug. 23rd, 1914
1st Battalion

thoroughly." The few survivors of the first wave of the attack found themselves pinned to the ground within a short distance of the British position, unable to move, with their ammunition exhausted—to little purpose, for the few British casualties were chiefly due to shell fire—and conscious that they could not offer effective resistance to the counter-attack they were instantly expecting. Not till darkness came to conceal their movements could Bloem and his men creep back to where the shattered Grenadiers were trying to rally just South of Tertre, exhausted, dejected, suffering from " the crushing knowledge of defeat . . . . a severe defeat . . . . and that inflicted by the English, the English at whom we laughed."

Bloem's account, moreover, is fully confirmed by the more matter of fact version in the Staff monograph. This admits quite frankly the complete failure of the Grenadiers, their heavy losses, their inability to produce any real impression on the defence. According to it a supreme effort at an advance was attempted about 6.30 p.m., but was completely frustrated by the burst of rapid fire that greeted it.

Certainly, when evening came, the battalion could feel satisfied with the results of the day's fighting. Well sheltered in good trenches and well screened from the enemy's observation the three companies along the canal bank had suffered only trifling losses, although from 1 p.m. two German field batteries had fairly plastered their line with shrapnel from about 2,500 yards range. D, indeed, had had but one man killed and two wounded[1] and were inclined to complain that the Germans had not come near enough to please them, their advance having come to a standstill about noon fully 500 yards away, and up to 1 p.m. Captain Tulloch had not had occasion to put his reserve platoon into line or to replenish his ammunition. Further West, B

---

[1] Captain Buchanan-Dunlop was wounded in the head but continued at duty till August 28th, when he was forced to go to hospital.

MONS.

and C had been more vigorously attacked and had had better opportunities; "they made a nice target. . . . if you were a third-class shot you were bound to hit something," one private in B reported. But here also the attack had been stopped before it had got to anything like close quarters, and the ineffectiveness of the German rifle fire made a great impression on the troops, who would have been ashamed to do such poor shooting at such comparatively short ranges.

Aug. 23rd, 1914
1st Battalion

Nowhere, indeed, on the Fifth Division's front had the German experiences been very encouraging; they had driven in the advanced detachments but had then been absolutely held and had suffered very severely. But against the Third Division they had achieved rather more, though here, too, their losses had been extremely heavy. They had managed to cross the canal and the 9th Brigade had fallen back from the line Mariette-Nimy to a second position South of Mons, running East from Frameries, while the 8th Brigade had had to evacuate its advanced position in the salient East of Mons. At the point of junction between the Third and the Fifth Divisions the Germans were actually South of the line held by the Fifth, and were thus in a position to outflank the battalion, whose right from about 4 p.m. could see the Germans crossing the bridges in numbers, though quite out of range. Actually the 8th Grenadiers seem to have begun pushing Westward towards Hornu and Wasmuel, for about 4.30 p.m. D Company came under fire from their right rear and a little later some Germans appeared further in rear, but were promptly beaten off by the cooks and transport men and other details who snatched up their rifles and opened fire. Another party attacked the section of the 120th Battery on the slag heap, to the right flank of D, and captured one of the guns, but there their success ended and D, though exposed, maintained its position without difficulty.

MONS.

Aug. 23rd, 1914
1st Battalion

However, the Fifth Division's right flank was clearly insecure and, moreover, the strategical situation of the British force had become highly dangerous. Not only had the French offensive in Lorraine been checked, but equal unsuccess had attended their Third and Fourth Armies which had sought to counter the German move through Belgium by advancing into Belgian Luxembourg. The enforced retreat of these Armies towards the Meuse had left the French Fifth Army on the Sambre and the British on its flank exposed to the converging attacks of three German Armies, the Third from the East, the Second from the North-East, and the First from the North. Indeed the German attack on Lanrezac had already developed on the 22nd, and von Bulow's men[1] were actually pushing the French back over the Sambre as the British moved forward to Mons. Indeed the British position at Mons was already compromised before it was taken up, and it was only maintained on the 23rd in response to an urgent request from General Lanrezac for help against the right wing of the Germans who were pressing him back. Sir John French, warned by his air reports of the presence of large German forces on his front, could not promise this, but he had agreed to hold his ground for 24 hours, with the result that the British found themselves confronted by von Kluck's whole Army, no less than three Corps of which had been engaged against the Second Corps. Moreover, information had come in that strong German columns were moving on Condé beyond the British left, and as the day's fighting had seen the French Fifth Army driven still further back, Sir John French had no alternative to being enveloped and overpowered but a prompt retreat. Accordingly during the night orders were issued for a retirement to a line running East and West through Bavai.

Before this, however, the Fifth Division had begun

[1] The Second German Army.

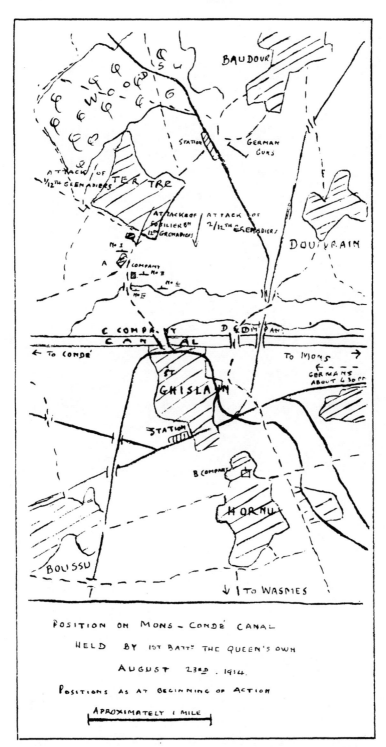

MONS.

withdrawing from the canal to a line from East of Wasmes through Dour and Hainin, level with the new line of the Third. Orders reached Colonel Martyn about 9.30 p.m. to withdraw his battalion at midnight, destroying all bridges as soon as his men were across. With the Germans so close to the battalion's front, and already on its right flank at Wasmuel, the operation presented difficulties, but Colonel Martyn arranged to maintain the most advanced positions to the last, companies retiring by alternate sections, and then withdrawing the last detachment man by man. While the movement was in progress the Germans made two attacks; both were beaten off with ease and were probably little more than patrols trying to find out if the British were still holding their positions. Soon after midnight all troops were reported back across the canal, whereupon the bridges were blown up. Actually one section under Sergt. Fittal was left on the wrong side, never having received orders to retire, and there it remained undisturbed by the enemy till about 4 a.m. Then the Germans approached and summoned it to surrender, whereupon the little party opened fire, drove back the detachment which had approached them, and, falling back to the bridge which had been only partially destroyed, successfully negotiated the passage of its ruins with the loss of only four wounded and rejoined just as the battalion was giving them up for lost.

After quitting the canal the battalion re-assembled South of St. Ghislain and then fell back towards Wasmes, two miles back, passing through the Duke's, who were now in the front line of the Brigade on some steep and wooded ground just outside the town. On reaching Wasmes, about 6 a.m., the battalion remained halted for some time in the square, which was getting the brunt of the heavy shelling which the town was receiving. However, by taking cover close up to the houses serious casualties were averted.

*Aug. 23rd, 1914
1st Battalion*

Aug. 24th, 1914

See Sketch 1

15

MONS.

Aug. 24th, 1914
1st Battalion

Meanwhile the Germans were across the canal in force and soon began pressing forward against the Fifth Division, besides endeavouring to exploit their previous evening's success in penetrating between the two Divisions of the Second Corps by out-flanking the right of the Fifth. However, two battalions of the 15th Brigade had been brought across to a position between Wasmes and Paturages and successfully held up the out-flanking movement. But in that intricate and complicated tangle of houses, slag-heaps, winding roads and railway lines it was impossible to keep touch all along the line, and there were gaps through which the enemy could get forward. Thus the Duke's were before long hard pressed and under a nasty enfilade fire from some guns which had been run up by hand to within 600 yards. A and B Companies were, therefore, sent to their help under Major Pack Beresford, and though their field of fire was indifferent they gave the Duke's splendid support, as that battalion's Diary acknowledges. The Germans at first pressed on in close formation as though expecting to find the place evacuated and were severely punished. However, B suffered severely: Major Pack Beresford was shot down in leading his men forward, Captain Philipps and Lieut. Broadwood were also killed and Lieut. Sewell badly wounded.[1]

Soon after these companies had gone off, C was detailed to take up a position near the railway station and then D prolonged the line to the left. By this time the Duke's and the other troops in the firing line were hard pressed, no less than six German battalions were engaged with them (*Official History*, p. 99), and against such odds they could no longer hold on. Accordingly, about 11.30 a.m., they were ordered to retire and Major Hastings was ordered to use C and D as a rearguard to cover their retirement. For some time after the

[1] He subsequently died of wounds.

MONS.

Duke's and A and B had passed through their line,[1] C and D held their ground. Heavy shelling was going on but mostly passed harmlessly over the heads of the battalion for the Germans were apparently searching for the British guns further back, and the German rifle fire was most ineffective, the Yorkshire Light Infantry on the left and the guns assisting to keep their infantry at a respectful distance. But the German efforts against the front of the Fifth Division were not very determined, they were relying rather on the turning movement of their Fourth Corps against Elouges and Audregnies and the wider sweep of their Second Corps still further West to envelop the British left and drive the whole force in on Maubeuge. That effort was, however, frustrated, largely by the gallant stand of the 1st Norfolks and 1st Cheshires, aided by " L," R.H.A. and the 119th Battery, between Elouges and Audregnies, and when at last C and D fell back they had a hot and exhausting but unmolested retirement to the Bavai line. At one moment C laid an ambush for any Germans who might be pressing forward and thought they had trapped an over-enterprising section, but some men of another battalion showed up inopportunely and alarmed the Germans, who retired hastily, robbing C of its chance. Eventually the Divisional squadron took over all rear-guard duties and C made its way to rejoin the battalion, the rest of which had already arrived in bivouac at St. Waast lez Bavai.

Aug. 24th, 1914
1st Battalion

All ranks were fairly exhausted that evening from fatigue and want of sleep and food; they had had nothing to eat since the previous day's breakfast and had been fighting and marching for 36 hours almost continuously. But an even more exhausting march was in store for the battalion next day. By 3.20 a.m. it had

Aug. 25th, 1914

[1] It would seem that part, at any rate, of the Duke's never received this order and remained in position for over an hour longer, but it is not clear whether A and B were with them or recevied the order, and fell back earlier. But, in any case, the retirement from Wasmes was not pressed.

THE RETREAT FROM MONS.

Aug. 25th, 1914
1st Battalion

paraded ready to move off with the Division along the long straight road which skirts the Western edge of the Forest of Mormal. Once the sun was up the day proved stiflingly hot; what breeze there was came from the East and was screened off the long column by the great forest, and the men stumbled along without water or food other than was produced by the villagers along the road. The very straightness of the apparently unending road seemed to add to the length of the march. To be retreating after having had so much the best of the first encounter with the enemy was perplexing and disturbing: it was obvious something had gone wrong elsewhere or why were the British retiring before an enemy they had defeated, and why were they abandoning to the tender mercies of the Germans the friendly inhabitants whose cordial welcome they had so recently enjoyed. In the course of the day a report was received of Uhlans threatening the column on the West, on which the battalion was detailed to guard the transport, but no Uhlans appeared to give it the satisfaction of another encounter. But the men stood the strain well and stuck grimly to their task; there was no straggling, march discipline was excellent. Still it was a very weary battalion which, about 5 p.m., found itself bivouacking just West of the great road on rolling ground about two miles S.W. of Le Cateau. To add to its trials the rain, which had been threatening all the afternoon, came down in torrents just as the bivouac was reached. No supplies were forthcoming, the emergency rations had been eaten, and what with fatigue, rain, mud and hunger the battalion spent an unpleasant night with the prospect of more rear-guard work in the morning. Orders had been received that the 13th Brigade would take up a rear-guard position at daybreak and hold it till 11 a.m. to let the rest of the Division get well away. Accordingly, at 4 a.m. the Brigade stood to arms and took up its position. The battalion was detailed to dig trenches 800 yards behind the front

Aug. 26th
See Sketch 3

LE CATEAU.

line trenches held by the Yorkshire L.I. on the right and the K.O.S.B.'s on the left, the intention being that these should be held to cover the retirement of the front line. However, soon after 7 a.m. the news came round that the orders were changed, there would be no retreat, the Second Corps were going to give battle. *(Aug. 25th, 1914 1st Battalion)*

The dispositions of the Brigade, made with a view to covering a withdrawal, were not altogether suitable to the requirements of a pitched battle. But there was no time for alterations, for firing broke out almost immediately on the extreme right, East of Le Cateau, and shortly afterwards German guns started shelling the position. It was lucky that the ground gave the battalion some cover, for it's tools had been left behind at St. Ghislain and the men had only their entrenching implements to dig with. Fortunately the soil was favourable, and with everybody working hard quite fair cover had been obtained before the bombardment became heavy.

Thus The Queen's Own spent the early stages of the battle lying inactive in second-line trenches, fairly well sheltered from the enemy's fire but unable to see much of what was happening, except to it's right front, still less to inflict any damage on the enemy. As the morning wore on the firing grew heavier and a tremendous number of shells passed over the battalion; these, however, were obviously searching for a battery of 60-pounders some way in rear of the infantry, and casualties were few. From time to time, also, the battalion came in for spells of machine-gun fire but these, too, were evidently aimed at some other target, and did little damage. In the lulls of the firing it was possible to see something of what was happening to the right front, where the bulk of the Divisional Artillery was posted in close support of the infantry in the front line. It was easy to see that these guns, which were under a heavy converging fire, were having a very bad time, though the gunners stuck to their work magnificently *(Aug. 26th, 1914 1st Battalion)*

19

LE CATEAU.

Aug. 26th, 1914
1st Battalion

and maintained a steady fire in return. The right of the British front line rested on a spur just West of and above Le Cateau, which lies in the hollow of the Selle valley. The Germans were pushing forward up the valley, making good use of the dead ground; they were also attacking in front and had, moreover, established themselves on the high ground North and N.E. of Le Cateau, so the situation on the British right was from the start never very satisfactory. From the battalion's right trenches more than one gallant attempt to reinforce the firing line was witnessed, but it was not itself called upon to advance so had nothing to do but to lie still and wait. Soon after mid-day it became obvious to the watchers that the British right could hardly hope to maintain its position much longer. "After what seemed hours to me," writes one officer in his diary, "we saw the limbers galloping forward to try to get the guns back. One battery[1] galloped past our trenches within a few yards. The Captain was leading and shouting 'Come on, boys,' at the top of his voice. Another lot went forward to the battery on our right and another past the left of our trenches. After a bit they came back, but it was a sad sight; very few returned, and they had great difficulty in moving the horses. I saw one gun from our right front coming back at a slow walk, dragged by four horses. The two gunners were flogging for their lives, and shells were bursting all over them. Of the lot that passed close to us[1] I think two guns came back and were going out at a good pace. . . . To our right front I could see a dismal wreck of guns and limbers where the battery had been."[2]

What had happened was, that about 1.30 p.m. Sir Charles Ferguson had been compelled to report to General Smith-Dorrien that on the right of the Fifth Division a retirement was inevitable, upon which the Corps had issued orders at 1.50 that the Fifth Division

[1] Probably the 122nd Battery.
[2] Probably the 52nd Battery.

LE CATEAU.

should begin withdrawing when necessary and that the Third and Fourth[1] should conform. The attempt to save the guns was accordingly made somewhere between 2 and 2.30 p.m., and almost directly afterwards the Germans swarmed up out of the Selle valley and overwhelmed the troops on the extreme right of the British line. These were the 2nd Suffolks and some detachments of the 2nd Manchesters and 2nd Argyll and Sutherlands, who had reinforced them during the morning. Pressing on West across the Roman road, the Germans fell upon the Yorkshire Light Infantry in flank; while the rest of the Manchesters and of the Argyll and Sutherlands to the right rear of the advanced trenches were forced to fall back past the right of the R.W.K. The battalion's turn had come, and it looked as though it must soon be closely engaged.

Aug. 26th, 1914
1st Battalion

However, for some reason or another the German infantry displayed little eagerness to push forward along the spur East of the Roman road, while immediately West of it they were delayed for nearly an hour by the stubborn resistance of the Yorkshire Light Infantry. Further to the left the attack had not been favoured by dead ground as it had been on the right, and had hardly got across the Cambrai road when the retirement began, so that here the Germans were in no position to pursue closely. Thus the battalion, contrary to its expectations, was never pressed, although for a time its right was quite uncovered; it had a few targets at long range on which it opened fire, apparently with good effect, but no advance in force came, and in the end the battalion retired practically unmolested. The retirement took place in two stages, the first to just near Reumont, where the battalion halted and took up a new covering position. This move was carried out by short rushes and under heavy shelling and rifle and machine-

[1] This Division had come under General Smith-Dorrien's command when the decision to stand and fight was taken.

LE CATEAU.

Aug. 26th, 1914
1st Battalion
gun fire, but with the greatest steadiness and very few casualties.[1] Here the battalion remained for about an hour while troops were retiring down and East of the Roman road. The situation seemed made for the German cavalry, but none appeared. Their guns maintained a heavy fire but without much result, and at last, between 4.30 and 5 p.m. Colonel Martyn, being satisfied that all formed bodies of the Fifth Division were already to the rear of his battalion, and that his task had been accomplished, gave orders to retire.

Passing wide of Reumont, the battalion regained the main road mid-way between that village and Maurois; companies closed into fours and moved off down the road. It was utterly congested with transport of every kind, with ambulances full of wounded and with men of every unit in the Division, all streaming on towards St. Quentin. Rain was falling steadily, and as darkness came on the confusion naturally increased. To retain march formation while pushing on through this crowd was extremely difficult and the battalion's progress was of the slowest. But there was no loss of formation or cohesion. Exhausted as they were the men trudged steadily on in good order, till about 10 p.m. Estrees, a village 7 miles beyond Reumont was reached, where orders to halt and bivouac were received. Fortunately some tea and bread was forthcoming and officers and men sank down upon the mud to rest. It was the briefest of rests. By 1 a.m. the battalion was again under arms, though the mass of transport on the road delayed its moving off till after 3 a.m.

Aug. 27th, 1914

This day's march took the battalion through St. Quentin, beyond which it halted about 9 a.m. for a couple of hours, to Ollezy, S.E. of Ham, which it reached about 3 p.m., being put into billets for something more like a rest. A certain amount of reorganization of the Brigade had been effected: men who had

---

[1] Captain Tulloch was wounded in the head and Lieuts. Ames and Whitehouse were hit but continued at duty.

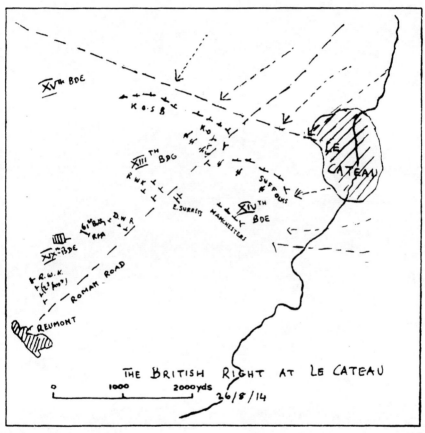

THE RETREAT FROM MONS.

become detached during the night march had been col- _{Aug. 28th,} lected and sorted out to their units. "It was astonish- _{1st Battalion} ing," wrote one of the Fifth Division's Brigadiers, "how the men responded . . . those who had become detached seemed to have one idea only, and that was to find their proper unit as soon as possible." The Queen's Own, however, had not only left the field in good order, but, where some other units had become temporarily dissolved, had kept together in a way which spoke volumes for the discipline and spirit of all ranks.

Another early start and another trying day awaited the battalion on the 28th, which brought it through Noyon to a bivouac at La Pommeraye. "This march of about 16 miles," writes one officer, "was—perhaps owing to the extreme fatigue we had gone through— one of the worst we had experienced. It rained nearly all day, but was close and hot, and we were wet through. The road was blocked with transport, and the men were taking advantage of any chance of a lift or the loan for a short distance of the mounted troops' horses, and hanging on to the stirrups to get some assistance. . . . It was nothing like such a fast march as we had had, but just seemed the finishing touch to human endurance."

By this time the British force had placed itself out of the immediate reach of its enemies, partly owing to its extraordinary endurance and powers of marching, but partly to von Kluck's misconception of the situation and the consequent misdirection of his marches after Le Cateau. What would have happened had he pressed on in direct pursuit of Smith-Dorrien on August 27th must remain problematical. If the British were exhausted, the Germans were no whit less weary and had lost extremely heavily both at Mons and Le Cateau, but the S.W. direction which von Kluck gave to his march on the 27th took him away from the British and prevented him from doing anything to improve the advantage which his numerical superiority and his preponderance in artillery had procured him on August 26th.

23

THE RETREAT FROM MONS.

Aug. 29th, 1914
1st Battalion

Sir John French could therefore give his weary troops a welcome day of rest on the line they had reached on the evening of the 28th, which ran from South of La Fère (First Corps) to the area Noyon-Carlepont, where Smith-Dorrien's wing had halted. This rest allowed of further sorting-out and re-organization; it was possible to take more accurate stock of losses and to make the necessary re-distribution of officers and N.C.O.'s to companies and platoons. During the morning the Fifth Division heard much firing to the Northward, where German cavalry were pressing back the covering screen of British cavalry along the Ham-Noyon road, but the R.W.K., though easily the strongest unit in their Brigade and almost the strongest in the Division, were not called upon to turn out in support of the cavalry, and could enjoy and profit by the halt to the utmost. But by 7 p.m. they were on the move again, having been ordered to proceed to billets at Carlepont, four miles away. The move proved a most wearisome performance, the column was nearly four miles long, the road was hopelessly congested, and after getting on by a hundred yards at a time punctuated by long halts, the troops finally bivouacked along the roadside in column of route. Early next morning the march was resumed, and for another grilling day the battalion toiled through hilly country, arriving in the afternoon at Jaulzy, just South of the Aisne, where the 13th Brigade billeted. From Jaulzy the retreat was continued next day to Crépy en Valois, 20 miles away; the heat was again great, and to push on over rather indifferent roads up the steep hills which fringe the Aisne valley was fatiguing work. But with every day's march the men who had managed to stick it out were getting into better training, and as supplies were now being regularly issued none of the marches after August 29th were quite as bad as the earlier stages of the retreat.

Aug. 30th, 1914

Aug. 31st, 1914

See Sketch 4

At Crépy en Valois the battalion had to find outposts covering the town to the North and N.E., from the

THE RETREAT FROM MONS.

Crépy-Fresnoy la Rivière road on the right to the Séry valley on the left. This line was about one-and-a-half miles long and was continued on the right by the Duke's. There were rumours that German cavalry were near at hand, but the outposts passed an unmolested night, though C Company, on the left, heard sounds as if the Germans were entering a village opposite them. To the left of the Division's line there was something of a gap before the right of the Fourth Division was reached South of the Forest of Compiègne, the only troops in this space being the 1st Cavalry Brigade, at Néry.

But if the night had been quiet the morning of September 1st saw active contact between British and Germans renewed all along the line. On the previous day von Kluck had again changed direction and was now bearing down to the S.E., on what he believed to be the open flank of the French Fifth Army. This Army had delayed its retreat to give battle to von Bülow on August 29th, near Guise, and had had none the worst of the encounter. Von Kluck's move was part of the new enveloping movement which the German Headquarters had evolved to outflank the French on the West simultaneously with an attack in force on the Lorraine front; this last was to pierce the French line above Nancy and the net result was to eclipse Sedan. But German Headquarters in framing this scheme, and von Kluck in carrying out his part in it, both appeared to be calculating that the British forces were a negligible quantity; it was, therefore, no slight surprise to them to be sharply received wherever they encountered the British by a force which was evidently quite ready to give a good account of itself. Certainly the German cavalry and Jäger, who ran up against The Queen's Own, had no reason to regard the Fifth Division as something to be ignored.

The original orders for the Fifth Division for September 1st would have started it on the march soon after 6 a.m., but the start was delayed on receiving news that

Sept. 1st
1914
1st Battalion

CREPY EN VALOIS.

Sept. 1st, 1914
1st Battalion

the Third Corps[1] was engaged and the outposts of the 13th Brigade had an unexpectedly long wait in their positions. Soon after daybreak German infantry[2] began feeling their way forward in small number towards the British outposts, but they were promptly fired upon and driven back. However, they continued to come on until it became evident that a real attack was developing. By 8 a.m. a brisk action was in progress, especially on the left, where C Company brought up its support platoons for a flanking movement, which proved fairly effective as a counter-stroke. The Duke's were also engaged, though against them the attack was less vigorous, the brunt of the action falling on The Queen's Own, which was effectively supported by two batteries of the 27th Brigade, R.F.A. a little North of Crépy. These guns found good targets in infantry and dismounted cavalry advancing down the Bethancourt-Crépy road, and the battalion's fire also proved very effective. By 9.30 a.m. the Germans were attacking in some force, and though easily held, as long as the battalion maintained its ground, they were near enough to make things awkward for A and D in the centre when, about 10 a.m., orders for a withdrawal were issued. However, these two companies were well supported by the K.O.S.B.'s and the artillery, and got safely away. C, on the left, having to retire over very exposed ground, was also in trouble, but the Bedfords helped it to extricate itself safely, and the men behaved with exemplary steadiness under heavy fire. Unluckily, shortly before the retirement began C had had the misfortune to lose Major Hastings, who was badly wounded in the thigh, but refused assistance when his men tried to get him away. With him Lieut. Ames had also to be left behind, he had been hit in the stomach earlier on and was also in a desperate condition. Both these officers subse-

---

[1] The Fourth Division and 19th Brigade had been so organized as from August 31st.
[2] These seem to have been the five Jäger battalions attached to Von der Marwitz's Cavalry Corps (*Official History*, p. 240).

CREPY EN VALOIS.

quently succumbed to their wounds, and thus within ten days of the opening of the campaign all the four company commanders had been put out of action. Sept. 1st, 1914 1st Battalion

B Company meanwhile remained in position, never having received orders to retire. The Yorkshire Light Infantry, who had come up on the Duke's right, had some effective shooting at Germans getting out of motor lorries, while B had the satisfaction of putting out of action a machine-gun mounted in a lorry. Finally about noon the Duke's and the Yorkshire Light Infantry received orders to retire, and with them B fell back. At Sablières the rearguard passed through the 14th Brigade, but there was no pursuit, any disposition on the part of the German cavalry to press having been severely discouraged by the fate of a couple of squadrons which caught a salvo of lyddite from the howitzers and were pretty well annihilated.

Thus the Fifth Division drew off unmolested and in a happy frame of mind, as one diary notes, over its most successful little rearguard action. The brunt of it had fallen on The Queen's Own, but even its casualties, apart from the loss of Major Hastings and Lieut. Ames, were light.[1]

That evening found the battalion in billets at Silly le Long, near Nanteuil, whence the next day's march, only 11 miles, brought it to Cuisy, just North of the Marne. From this point the direction of the marches was altered; after crossing the Marne the troops turned away to their left, moving more or less S.E. up the valley, covered by cavalry North of the river and quite unmolested by the enemy. The night of September 3rd/4th the R.W.K. spent in comfortable billets at Coulommiers, a village S.W. of La Ferté sous Jouarre, enjoying their first really good rest for ten days, a rest which was pro- Sept. 2nd, 1914 Sept. 3rd-4th, 1914

---

[1] The battalion's total loss up to its arrival on the Aisne (September 12th), was 30 killed, 43 wounded and missing, 110 missing, 82 wounded; of these August 23rd and 24th accounted about 140, details for La Cateau and Crépy have not been preserved. Several of the " missing " rejoined during the halt on the Aisne.

THE RETREAT FROM MONS.

Sept. 5th, 1914
1st Battalion

longed till after dark on the 4th. Then the 13th Brigade, acting as rearguard to the Division, moved off South shortly before midnight for what was to prove the last stage of the great retreat from Mons. This night-march took it through the Forest of Creçy, and contrasted pleasantly with the hot and exhausting daytime marches of the last fortnight. About 9 a.m. on the 5th the battalion reached bivouac at Tournan and had the double satisfaction of being joined by its "first reinforcement"[1] and of receiving the welcome news that the retreat was over, that the next day's march would be an advance to meet the enemy. This information was a positive tonic. Continual retirement to which there seemed no end was inevitably depressing and showed that the hoped-for improvement in the situation had not yet taken place. The change in the orders indicated that the tide had turned.

[1] These amounted to Lieut. Vicat and 84 men, and with them came Lieut. Palmer, who had been detached on railway duty on August 21st and had been prevented from rejoining earlier by a badly sprained ankle. The party had left Dublin a week after the battalion, and had barely reached Havre when the German advance made it necessary to shift the British base to St. Nazaire. On this the detachment left Havre by rail on August 30th for the new Advanced Base at Le Mans and after two days there entrained again on the night of September 2nd/3rd, reached Coulommiers early on the 4th and arrived at Tournan just before the battalion came in. Its arrival brought the battalion up to 17 officers and over 800 men.

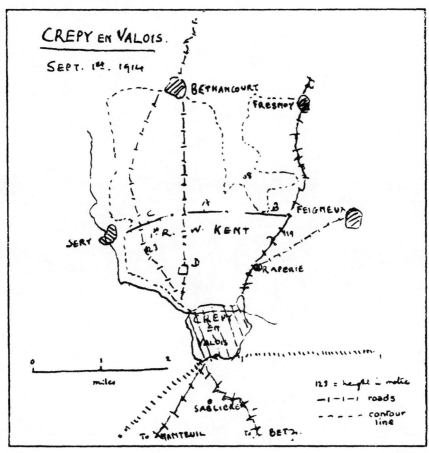

CHAPTER II

THE MARNE.

When, on the evening of September 5th, the welcome orders for the advance reached the British Army the actual situation was that the bulk of the German First Army was South of the Grand Morin with its right midway between Coulommiers and Lagny and its left N.E. of Montceaux. Opposite its left and left centre was the Fifth French Army, now under General Franchet d'Esperey. The British Army, in position from Rozoy on the right to North of Brie Comte Robert on the left, was about 8 miles away from von Kluck's right, while more than 12 miles lay between it and Franchet d'Esperey, this gap being in some measure filled by a French cavalry corps. Some way behind von Kluck's right rear, and North of the Marne near Meaux, was his flank guard, one corps and a cavalry division; this, in the course of the day, became engaged with Manoury's new Sixth French Army, now advancing N.E. from Paris. Directly the news of this advance reached von Kluck it was recognised as a serious menace to his flank and communications, and he suspended his advance, brought his right and right-centre corps, II and IV, back over the Grand Morin to meet this new enemy, and directed von der Marwitz's IInd Cavalry Corps to move S.W. on Lumigny and Rozoy to cover their flank.[1] Thus just as the British started to advance a gap was opening in the German line opposite them, and it was their advance into this gap until they were behind the left flank of von Kluck's new line on the Lower Ourcq, which constitutes the British contribution to the great battle of the Marne. Their continued advance would have

Sept. 5th, 1914
1st Battalion

See Sketch 5

---

[1] These orders were issued about 10 p.m., September 5th.

THE MARNE.

Sept. 5th, 1914
1st Battalion

rendered his position untenable, and, therefore, just when it was going decidedly in his favour, von Kluck had to break off his struggle with Manoury. Once again over-rating the damage inflicted on the British in the first encounters, von Kluck had so much under-estimated the force necessary to hold them up that they were able to play a decisive part in the battle without ever having to engage much more than the advanced guards of their columns.

Sept. 6th, 1914

The orders for September 6th issued to the Second Corps on the previous evening gave it as its objective the line La Houssaye-Villeneuve le Comte, the Fifth Division being on the left and advancing on Villeneuve. For this day's march the 13th Brigade was detailed as advanced guard and The Queen's Own, much the strongest battalion in the Brigade, had the satisfaction of finding the vanguard. Parading before 4 a.m., A and B Companies started off at the head of the column and, passing through the 14th Brigade, who had been on outpost, pushed steadily N.E. through the Forest of Crécy. Everyone was in high spirits and anxious for an encounter with the enemy; they were not, however, to have this satisfaction as, although the Divisional cavalry and cyclists encountered a few Uhlans, no opposition was met with before Villeneuve was reached about 8 am. Here an outpost line was taken up by A and B with C and D in support. Sounds of firing could be heard away to the S.E., and about 1 p.m. orders were received to continue the advance, but this time in an Easterly direction, Dammartin being now the objective assigned. The K.O.Y.L.I. had now taken over the vanguard duty, and the march to Dammartin was accomplished without incident, though the mounted troops accounted for several German cavalry patrols. Shortly before reaching Dammartin the Brigade was halted and ordered to bivouac, but almost immediately the order was cancelled and the march resumed to Courtry, which was reached about 8 p.m. The day's advance, 17 miles,

THE MARNE.

had brought the Second Corps to the Grand Morin, on the Northern bank of which it established its outposts after a little fighting. On its right the First Corps had met more serious opposition from the main body of von der Marwitz's Cavalry Corps; this had retired early in the afternoon, but the First Corps had been so much delayed that it was behind the Second and did not reach the Grand Morin. On September 7th, therefore, the Second Corps did not advance far, having to wait till the First got up level, and for the battalion the day proved uneventful. The 13th Brigade did not start its march till the morning was well advanced, and then moved to Boissy le Chatel without encountering the enemy, though signs of his recent presence were plentiful enough. "Every village had been turned inside out by the Germans," writes an officer, "and bottles were as thick as peas." Meanwhile the First Corps had reached the Grand Morin, and the Germans had retired behind the Petit Morin almost without offering any opposition. _{Sept. 6th, 1914 1st Battalion} _{Sept. 7th, 1914}

The next day, however, was to see more fighting. The continued pressure of the French Sixth Army had forced von Kluck to transfer his two remaining corps, the IIIrd and IXth, to the Ourcq and thus left von Bülow to maintain his ground against Franchet d'Esperey without their assistance. The IInd German Cavalry Corps began drawing off Westward across the front of the British and left only a rearguard, including four Jäger battalions, about La Ferté sous Jouarre, on which the British Third Corps was advancing. Thus on the Ist German Cavalry Corps devolved the main task of holding up the British on the Petit Morin, and the day's fighting took the shape of several sharp actions for the crossings of that stream, the First Corps attempting the passage at Bellot and Sablonnieres, the Second at Orly and St. Cyr, further West. The Petit Morin, running through a deep and heavily wooded ravine, afforded ideal rearguard positions, but the British were not to be _{Sept. 8th, 1914}

THE MARNE.

Sept. 8th, 1914
1st Battalion

denied and the passages were all forced after sharp fighting, a good many casualties being inflicted on the enemy and nearly 300 prisoners, with several machine-guns, taken by the Second Corps alone.

The Fifth Division's share in this action was the forcing of the passage at St. Cyr and St. Ouen, held by the 5th German Cavalry Division and attached Jäger. The 13th Brigade once again found the advanced guard for the Division and had as its vanguard A and B Companies, 1st R.W.K. Starting about 4 a.m. the vanguard soon found the 3rd Cavalry Brigade held up under a brisk artillery fire on the Petit Morin at St. Cyr. The advanced guard was at once deployed, and advanced to support the cavalry, the K.O.Y.L.I. on the right and the R.W.K. on the left of the Doué-Mauroy road. But the enemy's artillery, which had been skilfully placed, gave considerable trouble and could not be located or silenced. Meanwhile the 14th Brigade, moving to the right of the 13th, pushed down to the river and, crossing higher up at St. Ouen, co-operated effectively also with the troops of the Third Division further to the right. By 1 p.m. the enemy were beginning to withdraw and the firing line of the 13th Brigade was approaching the river, which was crossed in the end with little difficulty. St. Cyr was carried and the 13th and 14th Brigades, pushing on unopposed by Champtortel, reached Noisement, three miles North of the river, at dusk. It had been a hard day for the battalion, which had been on the move since before daybreak, but partly owing to the thickness of the woods which had concealed both sides from each other, it had got off practically without casualties. The day had, however, had most important results. Of the 1st Cavalry Corps, the Guard Division had been thrust back N.E. and no longer interposed between the British and the Marne, the other division, the 5th, had been even more sharply handled and had retired some miles behind the Marne, so that

THE MARNE.

von Kluck found it necessary to detail General von Kraewel's infantry brigade of the IXth Corps to support his cavalry, while a whole division of the IIIrd Corps, which was just about to be thrown in against Manoury, had to wheel about and march back towards the Marne.

Sept. 8th, 1914 1st Battalion

However, these reinforcements came too late to prevent the British crossing the Marne. On their left the Third Corps was held up at La Ferté sous Jouarre, where the bridges had been destroyed, and did not get across until the afternoon, but the Second Corps had the advanced guards of both its divisions on the right bank before 8 a.m., and the First Corps on the right advanced even more rapidly. But in the course of the morning the Second Corps met with considerable opposition, especially in front of the Fifth Division S.E. of Montreuil aux Lions. Here once again guns concealed in thick woods defied all efforts to locate them, and as von Kraewel's brigade had been thrown into the fight at this point the 14th Brigade, which was acting as advanced guard, found its progress checked. There was some confused fighting in the thick woods around Pisseloup and Le Limon; it was difficult to keep direction in such a blind country and the enemy's positions were well-chosen and hard to locate accurately, while enfilade fire from Chamoust, on the left front of the attack, proved very effective. The 13th Brigade had, therefore, to be called upon. It had stood to arms about 4 a.m., had crossed the Marne at Mery and halted. It was ordered to push two battalions forward on the left of the 14th Brigade to make for Montreuil and, if possible, dislodge the troublesome concealed battery. The R.W.K. were told off for the task and, followed by the K.O.Y.L.I., they pushed forward about 3 p.m. up the valley road towards Courcelles. As they advanced they met with a good many wounded of the 14th Brigade, making their way to the rear and reporting that the D.C.L.I. on the left of the 14th Brigade had been

Sept. 9th, 1914

THE MARNE.

Sept. 9th, 1914
1st Battalion

heavily counter-attacked. However, no enemy were encountered, and soon after 5 p.m. the leading companies, B and C, had established themselves on high ground about Moitiébard, and Major Buckle reported that he was pushing out two platoons of D to his right, in which direction the enemy were said to be. No contact with the Germans, however, followed and the battalion dug itself in, having received orders to push on to Montreuil early in the morning. It would seem from the accounts given by the 14th Brigade that the advance of these two battalions had proved effective even though they had not fired a shot. On their approach the German counter-attack against the D.C.L.I. had been suspended while von Kraewel hastened to disengage directly it became dark and fell back to Gandelu, 6 miles North of Montreuil. Von Kluck's Army was in full retreat, its left, imperilled by the British advance, going first and being covered by vigorous action on the part of the right wing.

Sept. 10th, 1914

In the pursuit of September 10th, marked by more than one sharp rearguard action and by the capture of over 1,000 German prisoners, The Queen's Own had no very active part. The chief fighting and the substantial captures of prisoners occurred on the lines of march of the First Corps and Third Division, and though the Fifth captured many stragglers it met with nothing like serious opposition. The battalion had started off for Montreuil in the small hours and by good leading succeeded, despite the woods and darkness, in arriving there about 5 o'clock. But the only Germans in Montreuil were dead or wounded, and the inhabitants reported that the enemy had cleared out an hour before.

After a couple of hours' halt, which allowed breakfasts to be eaten in the main street in pouring rain, the battalion was off again before 8 o'clock, pushing on through Gandelu to Chézy. The road was strewn with the débris of an army in retreat, ammunition carts, some full, some empty, broken down waggons, dead and

THE AISNE.

wounded horses, packs and equipment of every kind. Despite the rain the men's spirits were high, all this encouraging evidence of the hurried nature of the German retreat showed those who had endured the long tramp from Mons to Tournan that indeed the tables were turned and that they were getting their own back. At Chézy, which was reached about 6 p.m., the battalion bivouacked and was joined by a draft of 185 men,[1] which raised it practically up to strength again. Sept. 10th, 1914
1st Battalion

September 11th brought a hard march in pouring rain, but no fighting. The battalion, leading the Division again, marched at 5 a.m., and after covering 15 miles arrived at Hartennes at 3 p.m., wet through. However, it was able to get some excellent billets and a good night's rest. The British were now within a short distance of the Aisne, which would form a serious obstacle to a further advance should the Germans elect to stand and fight. It was all important, therefore, to discover their intentions, whether the bridges had been destroyed and whether the passage of the river would be opposed. The 13th Brigade, still keeping its place at the head of the column, started off before 6 a.m. on September 12th, close in rear of the cavalry. This was another day of heavy rain, but of recovered touch with the enemy, for after passing through Chacrise and Serches and reaching the hills overlooking the Aisne at Ciry, the battalion came up with the 3rd Cavalry Brigade, who had been held up by the enemy's guns and could not get on. The battalion deployed into battle formation and advanced into Ciry, while the battalion scouts under Lieut. Moulton-Barrett pushed forward to the river to reconnoitre Missy Bridge and discover if it was held. The patrol did not manage actually to reach the bridge, but, on getting within 150 yards, drew a heavy fire which provided all the information required,

Sept. 11th, 1914

See Sketch 6

Sept. 12th, 1914

---

[1] With this draft were Lieuts. Moulton-Barrett (from the Regular establishment of the 3rd Battalion) and Furber (3rd R.W.K.), and 2nd-Lieut. Russell (newly commissioned from the R.M.C.).

THE AISNE.

Sept. 12th, 1914
1st Battalion

though, thanks to the bad shooting of the Germans, Lieut. Moulton-Barrett and his men got back with only one casualty. Shortly afterwards the battalion received orders to fall back to Serches as no billets were available. This meant a five-miles' tramp back in the rain for very tired men, but good billets at the end of it.

But if the Second Corps had not secured the bridges over the Aisne the Third Corps on its left had been more fortunate, and its leading troops had not only managed to begin crossing the half-destroyed bridge at Venizel, two miles below Missy, before midnight, but the 11th Brigade had pushed rapidly forward across the low-lying fields near the river bank and seized the higher ground about Bucy le Long before daybreak on

Sept. 13th, 1914

the 13th. This prompt and daring stroke had therefore effected a considerable alteration in the tactical situation on the British left when the Fifth Division again advanced to the Aisne on the morning of September 13th. With the Fourth Division already well across it was possible for the Engineers to throw another bridge across the bend of the river between Venizel and Missy without being prevented by the enemy. This was at Moulin des Roches, a mile above Venizel, to which spot the 14th Brigade was diverted. Meanwhile The Queen's Own had renewed their efforts to secure a passage at Missy for the 13th Brigade.

Starting about 4 a.m., the battalion pushed forward to Sermoise, where B and C Companies deployed astride the road leading down to Missy Bridge. Directly B began to advance towards the river it came under a very heavy fire from the far bank, both from rifles and machine-guns. This inflicted a good many casualties, and unfortunately among those killed was Captain Fisher, who had gone ahead to reconnoitre the line of advance. The battalion thus lost one of its most capable junior officers, a man of real character and great promise. But well supported by the artillery on the heights

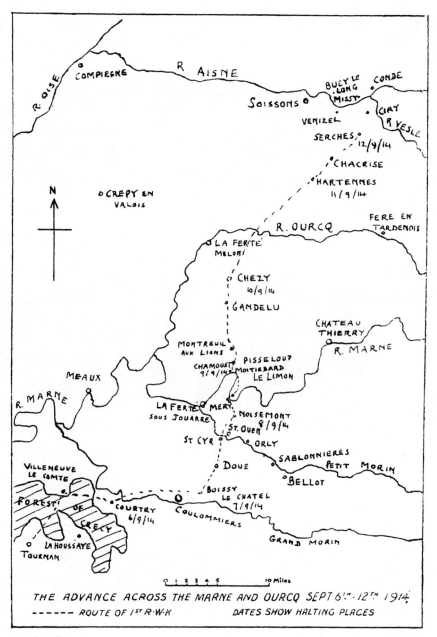

THE ADVANCE ACROSS THE MARNE AND OURCQ SEPT 6TH - 12TH 1914.
------ ROUTE OF 1ST R.W.K.   DATES SHOW HALTING PLACES

THE AISNE.

behind, B pressed on nevertheless, and Nos. 6 and 8 Platoons established themselves on the river bank not far from the bridge and opened a heavy fire against the enemy on the far side. The bridge, a three-span iron-girder structure, had had its northernmost span blown up, and the passage was held by the Germans in some force, while their guns replied vigorously to the British bombardment. The advanced detachment was accordingly ordered back to the Northern edge of Gobinne Wood, as there was little to be gained by clinging to its rather exposed position, where it to some extent masked the fire of its own guns. In doing this B was so unfortunate as to lose Lieut. Vicat, another valuable and popular officer, and shortly afterwards the whole company was withdrawn to the railway embankment East of Sermoise, where it entrenched, C meanwhile maintaining its position and keeping up a steady fire. For some time the artillery duel continued, while the 14th Brigade began crossing the river at Moulin des Roches and advancing across the low ground towards the village of St. Marguerite to support the Fourth Division, who had been counter-attacked but were making some progress. Either because of this threat to their flank, or because of the effects of the artillery bombardment, the defenders of Missy Bridge thought it expedient to fall back, and when, about 3 p.m., C Company pushed forward again they found the bridge-head unoccupied. Just before this 2nd-Lieut. Holloway had worked his way down to the river-bank, located a German machine-gun and managed to get one of the British guns on to it, effectually silencing it.

On Lieut. Holloway's report that the bridge-head had been evacuated the rest of the battalion advanced to the bridge. Luckily a small boat had been discovered which would take five men, and in this, using sticks instead of the missing oars, Lieut. Holloway, Sergt. Hodge, and three men crossed the river. One

THE AISNE.

Sept. 13th, 1914
1st Battalion

of the men took the boat back and in five minutes' time a second boat-load was across. The party thereupon pushed forward into the wood, encountered and rushed a German picquet and gained the far edge. More men were constantly coming over, and by 6.30 forty were on the edge of the wood ready to advance. Just then a strong German patrol appeared advancing down the road. It was getting dark, but against the light of a burning village in the rear they were clearly visible and gave a good target, and a few minutes' firing soon sent them to the right-about. After that the passage went on without further interruption, though twice during the evening the Germans made attacks which the covering party beat off with ease. The 59th Field Co. R.E. fitted up a raft to supplement the means of ferrying, and before long C and A Companies were across and entrenching in the wood, while the rest of the battalion was gradually transferred to the right bank as the night wore on.

Meanwhile the 14th Brigade, co-operating with the Fourth Division, had advanced against the Southern end of the Chivres spur, the dominating tactical feature in this part of the line. Neither the Fourth Division attacking from the West nor the 14th Brigade attacking from the South could effect much, but the 14th reached and passed St. Marguerite and established itself between that village and a point just West of Missy, ready to renew the advance next morning. The 15th Brigade, which had followed the 14th across at Moulin des Roches, was directed to push forward and prolong the line of the 14th by attacking Missy. But for the R.W.K. and for the K.O.S.B.'s, who had followed them across and taken post in the woods to their right, an active part in the attack was not possible. Their position was commanded from the slopes of the Condé spur, some 900 yards away, and to have advanced without more artillery support than was available would have been useless. As it was, the two battalions were under

Sept. 14th, 1914

THE AISNE.

a heavy fire throughout the day and were not very fortunate in getting targets at which to fire back. They could only hold on and improve their positions. <small>Sept. 14th, 1914 1st Battalion</small>

The attack on the Chivres position at first went well, and some of the East Surreys and Bedfords made their way some distance up the spur. But in the woods direction was hard to keep; there was confusion and congestion in the firing-line, and finally the attackers withdrew to a new line, slightly in advance of their starting points. As the village of Missy was included in this, the battalion was able to push forward during the night and take up a new position along the road from the bridge to Missy. Three companies were in the firing-line, A and B, East of the road and facing E, D on their left just South of Missy, flung back to face North, while C was held in reserve on the West of the road. The position had many defects; it was difficult to dig deep trenches as about three feet down water was reached, the Germans on the Chivres-Condé spur overlooked the low ground between Missy and the river and their snipers, well concealed in the woods on the hillside and along the river bank above the bridge, proved very troublesome, though at 900 yards, the distance to the foot of the ridge, they did not make very good practice. But the worst feature was that whereas the German guns could play upon the British trenches with much effect, they were themselves mostly out of the reach of the British artillery, which could not be brought across the river in the Missy area and had to put up with positions on the hills some way back from the left bank. The Fifth Division, therefore, would not get from its artillery the support needed to push forward, and only by pushing forward could it find positions from which its artillery could support it adequately. <small>September, 1914</small>

This was perhaps the main reason for the comparative inactivity to which the Fifth Division and Third Corps, the left wing of the British Army, found themselves

THE AISNE.

September, 1914
1st Battalion

committed from September 15th onwards. Below Condé the artillery position favoured the Germans so much that to have renewed the attack which had been checked at the Chivres spur would have had little prospect of success. The Germans on their part made no effort to drive back into the river the troops who had established themselves on the right bank, but contented themselves with keeping them under an intermittent shell-fire. This varied greatly in intensity and effect; sometimes it amounted to a regular bombardment, as on September 20th, when Missy received a severe dose and was very much damaged, some days passed without a single casualty from shell-fire, but on the other hand a single shell would inflict several. Thus on September 19th D Company lost three splendid N.C.O.'s in Sergts. Fitzgerald, Barden and Warnett, all killed by the same shell. Another day the machine-gun section had its wagon blown to pieces, three horses killed, and Lieut. Johnston, the machine-gun officer, put out of action by concussion. On the whole, however, the snipers were responsible for more casualties, especially at first. After that the men were pretty well dug in, communication trenches had been dug and screens of branches planted in the road so much interfered with the view of the snipers that men could move about outside the trenches in day-time without at once attracting bullets. Fortunately, also, if the wetness of the ground made life in the trenches very uncomfortable it greatly diminished the effects of the high explosive shells, whose bursts often did no more than cover those near at hand with mud and water. But the fortnight which the battalion spent in these trenches at Missy was a costly period, judged by the standards of later days of that "trench warfare" to which the British Army was getting its first introduction. The total casualties on the Aisne came to two officers killed (Captain Fisher and Lieut. Vicat) with 31 other ranks, two officers wounded

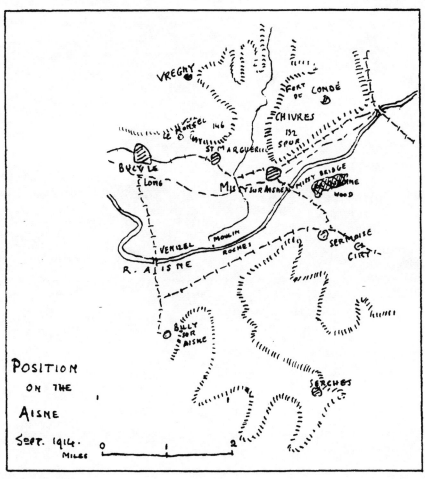

THE AISNE.

(Lieuts. Wilberforce-Bell and Johnston), with 96 men.[1] On the other hand the sick-rate was unexpectedly low, considering the frequent rains, the wet state of the trenches and the lack of all those appliances like gumboots, which were later on to make life in trenches more endurable. At first especially, the men were never dry and had to sleep in wet clothes without a chance of changing them or getting a wash. Nevertheless, only one officer (Captain Bonsor) and under 40 men had to be sent to hospital for sickness. These losses were more than balanced by the arrival on the 23rd of 176 men under 2nd-Lieuts. Pownall[2] and Harding.[2] This draft included a few recovered wounded and stragglers, and on the 18th Captain Tulloch, who had been wounded at Le Cateau, rejoined, while Captains Grant,[3] Beeman[4] and Bonsor,[4] and 2nd-Lieuts. Tinné,[2] Williams[2] and Kerr[2] arrived a couple of days earlier. At the end of September, therefore, the battalion was practically up to strength.

September, 1914 1st Battalion

During this period communication with the left bank, where the battalion transport remained at Sermoise, was maintained by a pontoon bridge established by the R.E. just below Missy Bridge, but less in view of the enemy. Across this rations and ammunition had to be brought up and wounded evacuated, entailing much work on the Quarter Master and his staff. But the transport which had had a dozen casualties from a couple of shells on the 13th was lucky in escaping very lightly from its nightly journeys down to the river, and never failed to carry out its tasks.

At length, on October 1st, came the welcome tidings that relief was at hand, and that evening the 2nd Lancashire Fusiliers, of the Fourth Division, turned up to

Oct. 1st, 1914

---
[1] These include the losses suffered on September 12th-14th in the passage of the river.
[2] From the R.M.C.
[3] Of the 2nd Battalion.
[4] Of the 3rd Battalion.

THE AISNE.

Oct. 2nd, 1914
1st Battalion

take over the position. The first of the many " reliefs " the battalion was to carry out was completed without incident in the small hours of October 2nd, and, thanks to a fog, the battalion was well out of range of shell-fire before daylight. After so many days cramped up in trenches with little chance of exercise marching was painful; many men found their feet and legs so swollen that they had difficulty in keeping up. Reaching Couvrelles by 8.30 a.m. the battalion had hardly had time for more than a wash and a change of clothes before the prospects of the week's rest with which it had been indulging itself were dispelled by orders to be off again. That evening it started on the move which was to take it to even heavier fighting than it had yet experienced.

CHAPTER III

THE MOVE TO FLANDERS.

From the moment when the German stand on the heights North of the Aisne had checked the advance of their French and British pursuers the main interest of the campaign had shifted away from the stalemate along the Chemin des Dames to the open Western flank of both armies. It was there only that a decision could be reached and the last half of September had seen a succession of efforts at outflanking, as first the French and then the Germans hurried corps after corps to the one quarter where the fighting had not yet stabilized itself into trench warfare. It was probably partly because the units holding the stabilized front were being called on to extend to their flanks and to take over more of the line, so as to make the troops relieved available at other points, that there had been no German counter-attack on the none too strong British left and that the R.W.K. had not had to resist any serious attack in the Missy position. They were now to be denied the relief they had so well earned because the British were to quit the Aisne and be transferred back to their original position on the French left. Administrative reasons alone made this expedient, as the supply services of the British were necessarily much complicated and impeded when their line of communications ran across those of the French armies. Moreover, the very special interest which the British had in saving from the Germans what was left of Belgium and in keeping them back from the Channel ports rendered their transfer to Flanders particularly appropriate.

This transfer was accordingly begun by extending the line of the Fourth Division to the right as far as Missy and by relieving the Third by units of the Sixth.[1]

September, 1914
1st Battalion

October, 1914

[1] This had reached the Aisne on September 17th, just too late for the battle, and had been placed in Army reserve.

THE MOVE TO FLANDERS.

October, 1914
1st Battalion

By the morning of October 3rd the Second Corps was able to report itself as concentrated in the appointed area. This for the Fifth Division meant the country round Nampteuil, Maast, Droizy, Launoy and Long Pont, the 13th Brigade having the first two assigned to it. The battalion, which had left Couvrelles at 7 p.m, on October 2nd, reached Maast at 9.15 p.m., and billeted in an enormous cave, crowded and none too comfortable quarters, though the rest after the trenches was most welcome. From Maast it started off again next evening for Hartennes, and eventually on October 7th found itself at the railway station of Pont St. Maxence. The marches had been made at night in order to conceal the move from the inquisitive eyes in the German aeroplanes, and for the same reason the men had had to keep well under cover by day. Night marches, however, proved fruitful in checks and stoppages and were an exhausting experience, men often falling asleep as they marched, and dropping down the moment they halted.

October 8th

At Pont St. Maxence the battalion entrained late on October 7th in two trains, the first of which reached Abbeville early next morning, the second not till the afternoon. Directly the second trainload had detrained the battalion started off on a cold and tiring march to Gueschart, whence it proceeded next night, partly by marching and partly in motor-omnibuses, to Vaulbon. Its first experience of this method of transporting troops was not too favourable. The motors did not turn up till many hours late, then missed their way and went miles too far, and eventually landed their passengers at Vaulbon later and more fatigued than if they had marched all the way.

October 9th

At Vaulbon the battalion found itself in the concentration area of the Second Corps, which had now assembled in readiness to advance N.E. to the Aire—La Bassée canal just West of Bethune, from which it might strike most effectively at the flank of the Ger-

LA BASSÉE.

mans, who were closely engaged near Vermelles, N.W. of Lens, with the left corps of the French line, the 21me. The British cavalry were pushing N. and N.E. ahead of the Second Corps towards the Forest of Nieppe, in touch with French cavalry on their right, who were falling back over the Lys before superior forces of Germans advancing from the N.E. Meanwhile the Third Corps, having in its turn left the Aisne, was detraining round St. Omer.

<small>October, 1914
1st Battalion</small>

On October 11th the forward move began. The 13th Brigade, now commanded by Brigadier-General W. B. Hickie, who had replaced General Cuthbert (invalided) on October 2nd, was for the first day's march in Corps reserve and followed uneventfully in the wake of the Fifth Division to Vaudricourt, where it billeted. The orders for October 12th were for an advance N.E. of Bethune to the line Festubert—Fosse, with the Third Division on the left, the Fifth on the right, and the 13th Brigade again in Corps reserve. But the day was not far advanced when news came in that the Germans had driven the French out of Vermelles and that General Maudhui (G.O.C. 21me Corps) wanted British assistance for the counter-attack he proposed to make. The 13th Brigade, which had reached Beuvry about 10 a.m., was therefore diverted to the right and given as its objective a line from N.W. of Vermelles through Burbure to Pont Fixe on the canal, the battalion being on the right and therefore next the French. By 3 p.m. the Brigade had reached the position of deployment and the attack began. Directly the British moved forward, however, they came under a very heavy enfilade fire from the direction of Vermelles: they pushed on for some distance, but the fire was too hot and soon brought the attack to a standstill. The right flank was completely " in the air," for the expected French counter-attack had never been launched, and without more support on the right the British could not get on; indeed, as the ridge which the leading line had reached

<small>Oct. 12th, 1914
See Sketch 7</small>

LA BASSÉE.

Oct. 12th, 1914
1st Battalion

was nicely ranged by the German machine-guns, the battalion withdrew a little and dug in along a road running N.E. from Noyelles lez Vermelles, with some advanced trenches 200 yards further East, and this line was maintained, though after dark the Germans attempted a counter-attack, which was successfully repulsed.[1] The Duke's, on the battalion's left, and the K.O.S.B.'s, who were beyond them reaching to the canal, had been unable to get any further forward and had also to dig in as best they could. North of the canal also the Fifth Division had become engaged all along its line, which reached from Pont Fixe to Rue des Chavattes, whence the Third Division continued it Northward.

Oct. 13th, 1914

For the next day the 13th Brigade's orders were to co-operate as before with the French counter-attack on Vermelles. This was to be preceded by an artillery bombardment, and while that was going on the infantry were to retain their positions. Actually this proved to be all that the R.W.K. were called on to do all day; it was another unsatisfactory day. On the right, the French made no progress against Vermelles, and until they got up level with its right the 13th Brigade could not move. On the left a German counter-attack drove the right battalion of the 15th Brigade back to Pont Fixe, and in consequence the K.O.S.B.'s, who had advanced a little, were checked. By 3 p.m. the 13th Brigade reported that it was heavily engaged along its whole front in a fire fight, and not until after dark did the Germans abandon their efforts to push back the British line. After dark indeed A Company and the machine-guns, now under Lieut. Palmer, made a small advance to a rather better position. During the day General Hickie had been compelled to go sick, so Colonel Martyn became acting Brigadier and Major Buckle took his place in command of the battalion.

---

[1] The battalion's casualties on this day came to just under 50.

LA BASSÉE.

October 14th proved equally uneventful for the battalion. Not until the late afternoon was the expected French attack launched, and though the battalion did what it could to help it with covering fire, it soon had to stop shooting when the French advance masked its fire. At 7 p.m., however, French troops relieved the battalion, which withdrew into billets near Beuvry.

Oct. 14th, 1914
1st Battalion

Three days of comparative quiet followed for the battalion, which was at first held in reserve to the 14th Brigade, and then lent to the Third Division, along with the K.O.Y.L.I., to act as its Divisional reserve. Not until the 18th was it called upon to return to the firing line. By that time the Third Division had made substantial progress, had pushed the Germans back well East of the La Bassée-Estaires road, and had established itself on the Aubers Ridge. On the previous evening the Lincolnshires of the 9th Brigade had stormed Herlies and the 7th Brigade on their right had got within half-a-mile of Illies. Some of its battalions, however, were in need of relief, and early on the 18th the R.W.K. left some very indifferent billets in Neuve Chapelle to relieve the 3rd Worcesters opposite Illies. In this position the battalion was E. of La Hue and had the 2nd South Lancashires on its right and the 1st Wiltshires on the left. But the German position was very strong, and in the last day or two their resistance had appreciably stiffened, as reinforcements had arrived from less active parts of the front: indeed the Intelligence had located the whole German VII. Corps, in addition to cavalry and Jägers, in front of General Smith-Dorrien's troops. Moreover, the Third Division was now so far ahead of the French cavalry on its left that that flank was liable to be enfiladed, and though the Fifth Division had gained ground East of Givenchy, and its left had advanced down the Estaires-La Bassée road level with the right of the Third, there could be no converging movement on La Bassée till the French, South of the canal, could get well beyond the line

Oct. 15th-17th, 1914

Oct. 18th-19th, 1914

47

LA BASSÉE.

Oct. 18th-19th, 1914

reached by the 13th Brigade. The line which the British had reached on October 17th was indeed to be the high-water mark of their advance. Four years were to pass before they got beyond it, and throughout the 18th and 19th of October the battalion could do no more than maintain and improve its position as the troops on its flank were completely held up. The battalion's patrols were active but found the enemy in strength and on the alert, and 2nd-Lieut Kerr was wounded while engaged in this work. Snipers, too, were busy on both sides, and it was clear that if the Germans were to be pushed further back reinforcements must be put in. Thus, though more than one German counter-attack was beaten off, the most determined being one delivered early on the 19th, the line had not

Oct. 20th, 1914

been advanced when, early on the 20th, the Worcesters arrived to take over, and the battalion withdrew to the Bois de Biez for a promised two days' rest.

Promises of rest, however, were beginning to be regarded as certain indications of a hard time coming. Shortly after mid-day an urgent message arrived for the battalion to support the South Lancashires, who were being heavily attacked. By 3 o'clock, therefore, the battalion was moving back to the trenches, but on reaching a farm half-a-mile North of Lorgies, it was halted and placed in reserve as the attack had already been checked, mainly by very effective fire from our artillery. Here, therefore, it spent the night, but

Oct. 21st, 1914

early next morning the South Lancashires were again attacked in force, and this time the Germans succeeded in breaking through them near Le Transloy, and thrust them back, inflicting heavy casualties on them. The Worcesters' flank was thus exposed, and their right company was forced back, though those further to the left held on some time longer before being compelled to retire on La Hue Farm. On the right the D.C.L.I., though themselves heavily attacked in front, threw back their line to cover their left, and maintained their

LA BASSÉE.

position very stubbornly. But there was a dangerous gap in the line and the battalion had to fill it if the Germans were to be stopped. Two companies were at once put in, one on the right, to gain touch with the D.C.L.I., the other on the left, toward La Bouchaine, to help the Worcesters to counter-attack. Thanks largely to the fire which the 41st Battery, R.F.A., maintained on the gap, the counter-attack was most successful. The Germans had advanced nearly a quarter-of-a-mile, but for the most part did not stand their ground, retiring rapidly as C Company advanced, and though all the advanced trenches of the 7th Brigade were not re-occupied, a line was taken up connecting the 14th Brigade with the Wiltshires, who had held on unshaken on the left of the 7th Brigade. Thus the immediate danger was averted and a renewed German advance early that evening was beaten off. But the loss of Le Transloy made it necessary to draw back the line held by the 7th Brigade. In the course of the night, therefore, a new line was taken up, the battalion being behind the Lorgies-La Hue road.[1] Just before moving back it had beaten off another German attack, but during the 22nd it was not seriously troubled either by infantry or artillery. The German snipers were busy, but they gave some targets for our snipers, and more than one German patrol came in for heavy punishment.

Oct. 21st, 1914
1st Battalion

Oct. 22nd, 1914

Still, October 22nd proved a bad day for the Second Corps. The village of Violaines, S.W. of the position held by the battalion, had been rushed by the Germans early in the morning, counter-attacks had failed to recover it, and this left the centre of the British line in a most unsatisfactory position. On the left of the Third Division also the expulsion of the French cavalry from Fromelles had accentuated the already very pronounced salient about Herlies. General Smith-Dorrien had no

[1] The two other companies had come up after dark and rejoined those which had been employed in restoring the line.

NEUVE CHAPELLE.

Oct. 23rd, 1914
1st Battalion

See Sketch 8

option, therefore, but to withdraw to a new line, already reconnoitred and to some extent prepared, running North from the canal in front of Givenchy, bending round N.E. along the Rue du Bois and passing East of Neuve Chapelle. To this line a retreat was accordingly accomplished on the night of October 22nd/23rd. Strong parties were left in the trenches to be evacuated until the new line was taken up, and under their cover the withdrawal was not only safely completed, but was concealed from the Germans, who gave the abandoned trenches a good shelling before they discovered there was no one in them.

In the new line the battalion was assigned a position which was to become famous in the annals of the Regiment. Just South of Neuve Chapelle the Rue du Bois running W.S.W. to E.N.E. joins the main road from La Bassée, which runs about S.S.E. to N.N.W. towards Estaires. From the road junction (afterwards known as " Port Arthur ") a road goes off about N.E., practically continuing the Rue du Bois to Neuve Chapelle. The main road marked the right of the battalion's line, which extended about 400 yards to the left, the front line being 250 yards East of the Port Arthur-Neuve Chapelle road, West of which Battalion Headquarters and the reserve company's trenches were placed. To the front, turnip fields and ploughed land stretched for about 400 yards to the hamlet of Ligny le Petit, while to the left front and more opposite Neuve Chapelle itself was the Bois de Biez, in those days affording plenty of cover to attacking forces, so that its nearness to the British line was a serious disadvantage. Trenches of sorts had been begun, but they needed all available labour to improve them. Fortunately the delay of the Germans in advancing gave time for the work. It was 2.30 p.m. before their leading scouts reached the houses in front, and soon after that the troops in the front trenches were pretty briskly engaged, finding targets in the Germans who were

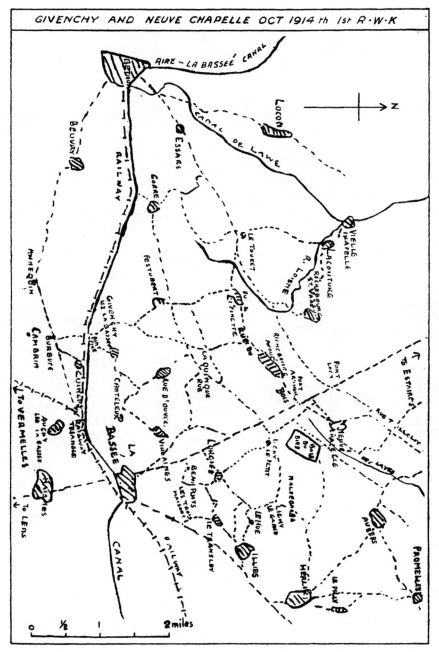

NEUVE CHAPELLE.

attempting to establish themselves in the houses, and being heavily fired on in return, though as yet there was little shelling. Of that plenty was to come.[1]

During the night of the 23rd/24th B Company heard what sounded like digging going on close to their front, a heavy fire was therefore opened, and the noise soon ceased. At daybreak a good many German corpses along the line of an intended advanced trench testified to the effectiveness of B's shooting, and during the morning the enemy attempted no advance. But early in the afternoon his guns opened fire, not only field guns, but large howitzers, 6 inches in calibre and more, whose shells, descending at a steep angle, wrecked completely anything they struck. Luckily the soil was soft, which diminished considerably the effect of the bursts, but fire trenches and dug-outs such as the battalion had been able to make proof against shrapnel could not compete with these "Black Marias," and when these guns got the range of the British line, as they did on the 26th, the trenches were blown to pieces and many casualties sustained. Luckily more than one alternative position was available and, by shifting men about, casualties were to some extent kept down. But the ordeal to which the men were subjected was a severe one, alike for those in the firing-line and for those, equally exposed, in support or reserve. It was now that Major Buckle's wonderful example of calm and courage had a most remarkable effect in steadying and encouraging the men. As Major Molony has written (*Invicta*, p. 287) " the great personal influence of this officer over the whole battalion was one of the greatest factors which helped to bring it through these days of trial and crisis." But the worst of it was that the

Oct. 24th - 26th 1914
1st Battalion

---

[1] Up to this time the battalion had not suffered many casualties since leaving the Aisne. Except for the 50 incurred on October 13th, it had got off lightly. The only officer casualties had been 2nd-Lieut. Kerr, wounded on patrol on October 18th, and Captain Grant, hit in the leg by a sniper on the 22nd, while Lieuts. Furber and McClelland had been invalided, as was Lieut. Newton also, on October 25th.

NEUVE CHAPELLE.

**Oct. 24th - 26th, 1914
1st Battalion**

damage done to the trenches by these heavy shells very much diminished the protection they afforded against shrapnel, and gave opportunities to the German snipers and machine-gunners. To repair trenches or to dig out men buried under the débris meant exposure to a stream of bullets. But volunteers for these perilous tasks were never wanting, and their gallantry was rewarded more than once by men being dug out alive.

For the first two days in this new position the Germans made no determined effort against the battalion, though they shelled it steadily and managed, during the nights, to dig new trenches within about 150 yards of its front line. Their main efforts were directed further North, against Neuve Chapelle itself, though one or two weak attacks on the battalion were beaten off on both days, while under cover of darkness renewed efforts were made to push up close and dig in. It was before the days of Very lights, and if sounds of digging were heard all that could be done was to open fire in the direction of the noise; this, however, was done with good effect. On the morning of October 25th, for example, a length of newly-turned earth was seen some way in front of B.'s trench. No movement could be detected, and L/Cpl. Wright[1] therefore volunteered to go out over the top to see what actually was there. Rapid fire was opened to cover him and enabled him to get out and back and report that there was no one in the trench save some dead Germans. That evening Sergt. Bishop

Oct. 26th, 1914

took out a party after dark and filled in the trench. On the 26th shelling opened about 7 o'clock and continued with increased vehemence all day, reaching an intensity not yet experienced.[2] Both to the right and left of the

---

[1] He was subsequently awarded the D.C.M.
[2] On the 26th the battalion had D, B and A Companies in the firing-line, in that order from right to left, A having one platoon to the left of the lane to Ligny le Petit. Each company had two platoons in support and C Company was in reserve.

NEUVE CHAPELLE.

Oct. 26th, 1914
1st Battalion

battalion the German infantry attacked, but not until late in the day did it get the satisfaction of having good targets to shoot at. When the attack came it was directed mainly against D Company on the right, who had been getting the worst of the bombardment and had lost Captain Tulloch, badly concussed by a shell bursting close to him. But D, unshaken by the shelling, shot steadily and straight at the advancing enemy, met with the bayonet the few Germans who reached the parapet, and maintained its line triumphantly. That night D Company, which had had over 50 casualties, including Captain Beeman and 2nd-Lieut. Harding,[1] was relieved by C and went back to a new reserve position rather further in rear.

The front-line companies were not the only ones to be busy that day. Early in the afternoon a renewed attack broke through the left of the 7th Brigade, North of Neuve Chapelle. The Germans poured into the village seeking to roll up the Wiltshires from the left. That battalion put up a splendid fight; its reserves checked the German advance beyond the village and counter-attacking cleared the Southern half of the village before two platoons of C Company could arrive from the reserve trenches of the R.W.K. Returning to their trenches these platoons were promptly summoned to the right flank, which was reported to have been left uncovered by the retirement of the next battalion. No. 9 Platoon was sent off, but arrived just in time to join the reserves of the K.O.Y.L.I. in a counter-attack, which regained the small section of that regiment's trenches which the Germans had managed to rush, all those of the enemy who had penetrated into the gap being satisfactorily disposed of and a dozen

---

[1] These officers seem to have been killed by a direct hit when on their way back to the front line from Battalion Headquarters, as they were never seen alive again after leaving. On this day the battalion also lost Captain Keenlyside, who was mortally wounded; while 2nd-Lieut. Whitehouse went sick and 2nd-Lieut. Pownall was wounded.

NEUVE CHAPELLE.

Oct. 27th, 1914
1st Battalion

prisoners taken from the 158th Regiment of the VIIth Corps.

With daylight on October 27th the men in the front line trenches of the R.W.K. were not a little encouraged by the number of German dead and wounded to be seen lying out in front of the line. Several efforts were made, notably by Corpl. Verrall, to take out water to the wounded, but as the Germans fired on the men engaged in this task it had to be abandoned. About the same time a German patrol, trying to work down a dry ditch leading into the battalion's line, was met and repulsed by Major Buckle and Corpl. Verrall, the Major himself accounting for six Germans with his revolver. However, the day was to bring the hard-pressed 7th Brigade and its neighbours of the 14th along the Rue du Bois no relief, but an accentuation of trouble. All efforts to recover the Northern part of Neuve Chapelle proved fruitless, while in the course of the morning the Wiltshires were once more outflanked through a retirement beyond their left. This time the German effort to roll them up was more successful, and early in the afternoon the left of the R.W.K.'s front trenches came under fire from their flank and rear, while some of the Wiltshires were pressed back upon Battalion Headquarters and the reserve trenches. Major Buckle at once ordered D Company (now in reserve) to turn out to their assistance. All turned now on the possibility of stopping the Germans by holding the lane from Ligny le Petit, on which the left of the front trenches rested. As D pushed up to the lane the supports of A lined it nearer to the front trenches and, seeing help coming, many of the Wiltshires turned and joined the line. But in organizing the stand Major Buckle was killed and about the same time Captain Legard also fell mortally wounded, the battalion thus losing two of its finest officers at a most critical moment. Their inspiration and example were not lost. D, though only 80 strong,

Major M. P. BUCKLE, D.S.O.

Commanded 1st Battalion, October, 1914.
Killed in action, 27th October, 1914.

NEUVE CHAPELLE.

pushed forward to the lane, and, together with the sup- Oct. 27th, 1914
ports of A,[1] opened such a heavy fire that the Germans, 1st Battalion
instead of pressing on straight, either worked off to their right or halted and opened fire in reply, bunching into masses which, at 250 yards range, presented excellent targets. C.S.M. Penny did splendid work, behaving with the utmost coolness, walking along smoking a cigarette and directing the fire of his men calmly and collectedly, and the determination with which this improvised line was held kept the Germans at bay, despite their superiority in numbers, till about 5 p.m. the 9th Bhopals, of the lately arrived Lahore Division, came up from Pont Logy. This battalion, pushing forward till it joined up with the left of the flung-back R.W.K. line, swept the Germans back across the Port Arthur-Neuve Chapelle road. On its left other Indian units continued the line to and beyond Pont Logy, a continuous front being thus formed in a rough semi-circle West of Neuve Chapelle. Meanwhile the front line companies had stuck to their position quite unshaken by the bombardment or the danger to their flank and taking every chance of inflicting punishment on the enemy.[2]

But the position was far from satisfactory, and the Oct. 28th, 1914
Third Division accordingly determined to counter-attack Neuve Chapelle with all the troops available. In this attack, timed for 11.15 on October 28th, the battalion was to open covering fire to assist the 9th Bhopals, who were to attack to the South of the village,

---

[1] Apparently the left platoon of A had also to be brought back to cover the flank at the point marked L on the map opposite p. 58 of *Invicta*.

[2] On this day the battalion had 2nd-Lieuts. Holloway and Williams wounded as well as losing Major Buckle and Captain Legard. As Captain Tulloch's injuries had involved his being sent to hospital, the command devolved on Captain Battersby, who arrived that very evening. The day was also notable for the gallantry of Pte. G. H. Johnson, who left his trench in full daylight, made his way to a field gun which had been left in No Man's Land and removed first the sights, and then, after a second journey, the breech-block also, though within 200 yards of the enemy. He received the D.C.M.

55

NEUVE CHAPELLE.

Oct. 28th, 1914
1st Battalion

while the 47th Sikhs and two companies of the Sappers and Miners attacked the village itself. The assault was preceded by a bombardment, to which the German guns replied in great volume, the trenches of the battalion coming in for an extremely heavy shelling. However, the attack was at first successful, and the 47th Sikhs and the Sappers and Miners who made a magnificent charge, got well into Neuve Chapelle. But the Bhopals, coming under a heavy shrapnel fire, were soon brought to a stop without reaching the trenches they were attacking or getting into touch with the 47th. The Sikhs, therefore, finding themselves unsupported were unable to withstand the vigorous German counter-attacks, and about 1 o'clock they were driven out of the village and fell back fighting on Pont Logy. Before this a strong attack had developed against the 14th Brigade and against B and C Companies, R.W.K. in the front trenches. Supported by heavy shelling and machine-gun fire the Germans advanced by rushes, only to be brought to a standstill about 100 yards away; beyond that point they failed to advance, having apparently suffered too heavily, though they continued to send up more lines from the rear. Some effective combined shooting by a small party of C Company put one troublesome machine-gun out of action, and despite casualties B and C maintained their line intact. But while they were fully occupied in keeping this attack at bay the Germans advanced in force against the Bhopals, just as that regiment was beginning to retire to the trenches from which its attack had started. The Bhopals had fought well while they had their own British officers to lead them, but with almost all these out of action they gave way and recoiled in disorder across the La Bassée-Estaires road and behind the front trenches of The Queen's Own. On this A and D Companies were hastily pushed forward to stem the German advance, but there was great confusion, and A and D

NEUVE CHAPELLE.

were not strong enough to stem the rush.[1] Much re- Oct. 28th, 1914
duced by the fighting of the previous days they had no 1st Battalion
time to take up a position before the Bhopals with the
Germans at their heels were right upon them. Lieut.
Gore was killed making a stand on the La Bassée road,
as was C.S.M. Penny also, and in the end most of A and
D were carried away in the Bhopals' retreat. They had
lost all their officers, Captain Battersby had been
killed, Lieut. Palmer had been wounded and disabled
in fetching D from the reserve trenches, and
there was no one to take command. About 300 or
400 Germans pressed on after the Bhopals, reaching
the trench where Battalion Headquarters had been
established; the situation was most critical, it looked as
if the companies in the firing-line could not possibly
retain their position and as if there was nothing to stop
the Germans. However, nothing could have surpassed
the steadiness with which B and C stuck to their fire-
trenches, even with the enemy right in their rear and
with shots coming into them from behind. They were
heavily attacked in front but they never wavered, and
kept the Germans back. C.S.M. Crossley was conspicuous by his coolness and the skill with which he
handled his men, and the steadiness and tenacity of the
defence was a wonderful proof of their discipline
and of the spirit with which The Queen's Own
were inspired.

This determined stand was of vital importance; had
these companies gone back they would have uncovered
the flank of the 14th Brigade and the whole line along
the Rue du Bois might have been rolled right up with
far-reaching consequences. However, the Germans do
not seem to have pushed their advance beyond the La

---

[1] According to one account there was some uncertainty and mis-
understanding as to the orders. It is said that the Bhopals had been
ordered to retire, as the Germans, by recovering the village, were in
a position to outflank them. But at the Battalion Headquarters of
The Queen's Own nothing was known of this, and there was no idea
whatever of retiring.

NEUVE CHAPELLE.

Oct. 28th, 1914
1st Battalion

Bassée road. This may have been because they were under fire from the dismounted men of the 2nd Cavalry Brigade, who had been hurried down from Messines and had just taken over the trenches near Pont Logy; it is possible also that they were deterred by the tenacity of B and C and feared to be caught in a trap if they pressed on. This can only be surmised, but it may well have seemed as if B and C must have known that ample reserves were at hand or they would never have held on in so precarious a position. Anyhow the Germans did not press on and meanwhile all available reserves had been ordered up when the failure of the attempt to recover Neuve Chapelle became known. These reserves consisted of fragments of several battalions, more than one reduced to the strength of a company, all exhausted with a fortnight's almost continuous fighting, but their arrival sufficed. A line was hastily patched up connecting the right of the cavalry with the still intact front trenches of The Queen's Own, and thus at last the danger was averted. By dusk, too, the attack on B and C had died down and Lieut. Moulton-Barrett, the senior officer in the firing-line, was able to send out patrols to find out what had happened in the rear of the trenches. Shortly afterwards he, too, was wounded and had to hand over the command to Lieut. H. B. H. White, who, with 2nd-Lieut. Russell, alone remained effective. Lieut. White promptly got in touch with Brigade Headquarters, and with its concurrence he decided to throw back his left flank, evacuating the trenches which B had held so tenaciously all day and placing that Company almost at right angles to the old line. B, therefore, despite its arduous day, had to turn to and dig for the greater part of the night. During the night the remnants of A and D, under 100 strong, who had been rallied by C.S.M.'s Mockford and Duffield, were brought up and were set on to assist in the entrenching. By morning the new trenches had been dug to such purpose that the battalion

Oct. 29th, 1914

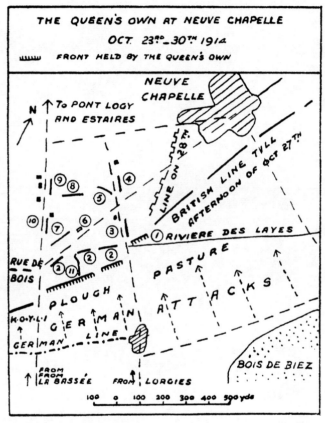

Face Page 58.   SKETCH 8.

1.—One platoon A Company till p.m., 27th.
2.—Original support line.
3.—A Company's supports and platoon from 1 on p.m., 27th.
4.—D Company from reserve on p.m., 27th.
5.—Second position of D Company, p.m., 27th.
6.—Battalion Headquarters.
7.—C Company in reserve on 25th, two platoons C in support on 27th.
8.—D Company in reserve on 27th.
9.—D Company on 28th. Lieut. Gore killed here.
10.—A Company on 28th. C.S.M. Penny killed here.
11.—Left of B Company when refused after 28th.

NEUVE CHAPELLE.

was warmly complimented by the Brigade Staff, and the position had been made fairly secure. C Company was still in the old firing-line, with B flung back to the left along the new line, A and D being in support behind B. The total strength of the battalion in trenches was now between 300 and 400, but with only two company officers. Its losses had been crippling,[1] but what it had achieved is difficult to appraise without exaggeration. There was hardly a moment in all that terrible month when the Germans were nearer to breaking through the British line than at the Neuve Chapelle cross-roads on October 28th. That they failed to improve their opportunity may be in large measure put down to the tenacity with which The Queen's Own had clung to a position which to all seeming was indefensible.

Oct. 29th, 1914
1st Battalion

After the heavy fighting of October 27th-28th a day of mere intermittent shelling and machine-gun fire, such as the 29th proved, was one almost of repose, and with evening came the welcome news that the battalion would be relieved by the Meerut Division. It was no mere rumour. Shortly after midnight the 1st Seaforths appeared and the weary remnants of the R.W.K. marched off by Le Touret, where they found the transport awaiting them, to billets at Merville, and thence next day the Cæstre area, where the Fifth Division was collecting for badly needed rest and re-organization.

Oct. 30th, 1914

Oct. 31st, 1914

But the battalion's hopes were once more to be disappointed. Heavy fighting as the Second Corps had had round La Bassée, the last days of October had seen even more desperate struggles in the Ypres salient and on the Messines Ridge, and the loss of Messines and Wytschaete and the straits to which the First Corps was reduced denied to the exhausted units of the Fifth

---

[1] The total casualties at Neuve Chapelle have never been accurately ascertained, under the circumstances it could hardly be expected that they should have been, but of the fifteen officers, seven were killed and six wounded, and the losses in " other ranks " were estimated as about 450.

MESSINES.

Nov. 1st, 1914
1st Battalion

Division their hardly-earned repose. The afternoon of November 1st found the battalion on the march North to support the cavalry, who were forming a new line West of the Messines Ridge to link up the left of the Third Corps with the French. Colonel Martyn had rejoined that day, and the total numbers present with the battalion were 560 other ranks, but still there were only two company officers. However, before the battalion actually went into trenches again, seven officers[1] had arrived with 76 other ranks, so that there were enough officers to go round the companies. Captain Buchanan-Dunlop, who had recovered from wounds received at Mons, rejoined on November 2nd and took over command next day from Colonel Martyn, who had now been definitely appointed to command the 13th Brigade. The battalion had owed much in peace and in war to Colonel Martyn and the reputation it had earned was due in no small measure to his outstanding ability as a trainer of troops and to his coolness and resourcefulness as a commander in the field.

For the first ten days of November the battalion remained facing the Messines Ridge, being either in billets at Neuve Eglise or in support trenches. Though not actually employed in the front line it came in for much shelling and had several casualties, while at the same time the Brigade lost General Martyn, who was wounded on November 7th. Two days later Lieut. White went sick and was invalided. Lieut. Rogers, the Quarter-Master, who had accomplished wonders in the way of getting the rations up to the men despite all kinds of difficulties and dangers, was still at his post, but of the combatant officers who had come out with the battalion and served continuously with it Lieut. White was the last survivor. The chief incident of these days was a special visit paid by Sir Horace Smith-Dorrien to the battalion on the

---

[1] These were mostly Special Reserve officers of other regiments, but included Lieut. J. E. G. Brown, of the 2nd Battalion.

YPRES.

8th for the special purpose of congratulating and thanking it for what it had done. He explained the necessity for keeping out of the papers particulars of the gallant deeds and achievements of individual regiments, showed why our men had to go on performing great things without those at home ever learning what their own regiment was doing, and added that when the time came for these things to be known " in no records will be published better deeds than those of this battalion." "I am perfectly certain," he said, "that there is not another battalion that has made such a name for itself as the Royal West Kent." He spoke with special appreciation of the way in which Lieuts. White and Russell had handled the battalion after all the other officers had fallen, and said that he had brought their names before the notice of the Commander-in-Chief.[1]

<small>Nov. 1st-12th 1914
1st Battalion</small>

Between La Bassée and the Messines Ridge the struggle had by this time quieted down into what was soon to be classed as "normal trench warfare," no major operation being attempted by either side; in front of Ypres, however, there had been no relaxation of the severe pressure on the First Corps. The Germans had not yet abandoned hopes of a break through, and after the defeat, on November 11th, of the Prussian Guard's special effort against the thinly-held British line, it became necessary to draw on the Second Corps for another couple of battalions. Thus on November 13th the R.W.K. found themselves on the road to Ypres along with the K.O.Y.L.I. It was growing dark when they first sighted the town whose name will always be associated with the great stand of the "Old Army." It was as usual being heavily shelled, but the battalion, moving in companies at ten minutes' intervals, negotiated the passage without casualties, and, turning off to the right, reached Lord Cavan's headquarters, a mile-and-a-half East of Zillebeke. Here it received orders to take over

<small>Nov. 13th, 1914</small>

---

[1] Both these officers received the D.S.O.

YPRES.

Nov. 13th–19th, 1914
1st Battalion

some trenches held by the London Scottish and to come under the orders of the 7th Brigade. It had been raining all day, the roads were deep in mud and pitted with shell-holes, though the " Salient " as a whole was anything but the abomination of desolation which the battalion was to find it in the autumn of 1917. The relief was accomplished by midnight, and within an hour the indefatigable Quarter Master had arrived with rations and hot tea.

The battalion was now on the right of the First Corps, in the woods to the N.E. of Klein Zillebeke, an area it was to know only too well in the spring of 1915. The line was in places within thirty yards of the enemy's trenches, but this very proximity had the compensation that the Germans could not shell our trenches without grave danger of hitting their own men, while the débris of fallen trees and broken branches, to which the shelling had reduced the woods, formed an impenetrable abatis which took away all fear of the enemy rushing the position. But it was a great place for snipers, and the Germans were extremely active, though they were to a great extent subdued by the gallantry and skill of Pte. Turnbull of B Company, who went out in front of the trenches time after time to hunt down the enemy's marksmen. He always used a German rifle and supplied himself with ammunition from his victims and others whom he found dead. Every time he came back he brought trophies with him, and he succeeded in accounting for many Germans before he was finally wounded in the foot.[1]

2nd-Lieut. Walker was another who distinguished himself greatly here; he made several daring reconnaissances, locating enemy's working parties and indicating the positions to the artillery; thus on one occasion the enemy, when bolting from a house 300 yards away on which he had ranged the guns, gave good targets to the infantry and were well punished. Usually, however,

---

[1] He was subsequently awarded a very well-deserved D.C.M.

YPRES.

Nov. 13th-19th, 1914
1st Battalion

the Germans did not expose themselves much, confining themselves chiefly to sniping and machine-gun fire and to shelling the support trenches and the tracks along which rations and supplies came up and by which wounded were removed. The task of the transport was most arduous; it had to come up at night from 7 miles away over roads full of shell-holes, bringing the " cookers " and water-carts as far as the reserve trenches, from which the Quarter-Master Sergeants had the rations and water taken up to the front line along rides in the woods which were swept by the enemy's snipers and machine-guns. But the work was done with great regularity and efficiency.

The outstanding incident of this period was the attack delivered on November 17th by the German IIIrd Corps. This came mainly against the troops some way to the left of the battalion, but the Guards on its right were also heavily attacked, and C Company were able to get in most effective enfilade fire, inflicting heavy loss on the enemy, who pressed forward with much determination in close formation but were repulsed all along the line. It was the closing phase in the great struggle for Ypres; after this failure the Germans did not renew the attempt which had cost them so much, though in defeating it the " Old Army " had been worn down till but a scanty remnant survived of the men who had faced von Kluck at Mons. Two days later the battalion was relieved and withdrew to Dranoutre, where it was met by Major Robinson, who had come out from the 6th Battalion to take over command. Its week in the Salient had cost it over 50 casualties, while two officers[1] were invalided. But the German effort to reach the Channel had been stemmed and a less exhausting, if still strenuous and costly, period lay before the battalion in the immediate future.

[1] Captain Corrie, Scottish Rifles (attached), and 2nd-Lieut. Littleboy.

CHAPTER IV.

INDIA, 1914.

Aug.-Dec., 1914
2nd Battalion

While the 1st Battalion had been marching and fighting, gaining new honours and reputation for The Queen's Own, the other battalions had been going through very varied experiences. The 2nd Battalion had found itself assigned to the rôle of " Internal Security Troops," and had therefore remained in India when the Lahore Division mobilized for service in France. Some of its officers were taken for Staff employment, Major Joslin for example was given a post on the lines of communication of the Indian Expeditionary Force in France, while those who were at home on leave, like Lieuts. Anstruther, Wilberforce Bell and Brown, were retained for duty either with the 1st Battalion or with the new " Service " battalions. Their places were filled by the promotion from other regiments of 2nd-Lieuts. Elton, Howe, Madgett and Piggott, and of Colour-Sergt. Harrison of the battalion, but though some changes of station followed on the mobilization of those Divisions of the Indian Army detailed for active service the battalion had to carry on its daily round with little change. Two companies, C and G[1] were sent to Karachi to relieve the 1st Lancashire Fusiliers, being replaced at Multan by E and F from Dalhousie, and before the end of the year Headquarters moved to Nasirabad, while two companies were sent to Hyderabad (Scinde) and small detachments posted at various other places, but not till the middle of January did it at last receive the welcome orders to mobilize for active service.

3rd Battalion

To the 3rd Battalion the mobilization scheme assigned the double duty of manning an important section of the

[1] The battalion was still organised in eight companies.

THE SPECIAL RESERVE.

Aug.-Dec., 1914
3rd Battalion

Thames defences and of keeping the battalions on active service up to strength. After spending nearly six weeks at Chattenden, a time of many rumours and alarms, with chases after non-existent spies who were supposed to be cutting telegraph wires and similar excursions, it had returned on September 18th from Fort Darland, where Headquarters were stationed with several outlying detachments; two companies under Captain P. A. Wilson were united with similar parties from the 3rd Queen's and 5th and 6th Middlesex to form a special " training battalion," and several smaller parties had to be found to act as guards and garrisons. To combine the double function of holding defences and training drafts was very difficult, especially at first when the battalion was short of Regular N.C.O.'s and those from the Reserve were a little rusty and had not got back their old habits of command. Moreover, the battalion had so many places to guard—in November, 1914, Tilbury Fort, Thames Haven, Kynoch's Town and several other points were added to its list—that it was extremely scattered, and the administrative work and supervision were made extraordinarily difficult. The demands for guards and sentry duties were heavy, but plenty of men were available, though naturally the numbers present fluctuated considerably as draft after draft was sent off.[1] To those serving on the Special Reserve engagement were soon added the surplus Reservists and the " details " left behind by the 1st Battalion, the recruits and young soldiers. Then, as the wave of recruiting brought men in hundreds to the Depôt, they were passed on to the 3rd Battalion as quickly as they could be clothed and equipped. Many of them were anything but new recruits; any number of old soldiers who had finished their time with the Reserve came flocking back to the colours. These included many experienced N.C.O.'s whose usefulness in dealing with the great influx of raw recruits can hardly

[1] The first draft was sent off on August 26th.

THE SPECIAL RESERVE.

Aug.-Dec., 1914
3rd Battalion

be over-estimated. Many of these old soldiers were drafted off to the newly-formed Service battalions, thereby providing a real link between the older battalions and the new additions, a channel whereby regimental traditions could be handed on, so that the newcomers might feel themselves really part of the Regiment in spirit. Early in 1915 there were over 150 old N.C.O.'s serving at the Depôt or with the 3rd Battalion or one or other of the Service battalions, while many others had already gone overseas in drafts. Before that time, too, another element had begun to replenish the 3rd Battalion, the recovered sick and wounded from the 1st. By the beginning of December 130 of these were already with the 3rd Battalion, which had settled down to its work of preparing the drafts for which there was so constant a demand. The wastage of the Mons retreat and of the desperate fighting of October and November was far in excess of anything that had been estimated, but the 3rd Battalion proved equal to the demands upon it.

With officers it was the same. The 3rd had been under establishment in August, though less so than many Special Reserve units, and of its subalterns four, Lieuts. Anderson, Sewell, and Whitehouse, and 2nd Lieut. Holloway, had accompanied the 1st Battalion to France, indeed, with the many calls on the battalion to find officers for different employments there was a time in August, 1914, when Colonel Boscawen, the C.O., and Lieut. Wingfield-Stratford, who was acting as both Adjutant and Quarter-Master, as Captain Waring was away at Maidstone helping at the Depôt, were the only officers at Headquarters and had actually to share the duties of Orderly Officer. Owing to the formation of the Service battalions the 3rd lost the advantage of having with it the Regular officers from the Depôt, who according to "pre-war" plan were to have become 3rd Battalion officers on mobilization. However, there was an immediate influx of its old members, among

THE SPECIAL RESERVE.

them Captains Mills, B. W. Parker, Tuff and Battersby. With them came any number of new faces, newly commissioned Regulars from the R.M.C., some eight of whom had been gazetted to the Regiment before the end of October, undergraduates from Oxford and Cambridge and representatives of almost every well-known public school, most of them with O.T.C. experience, with Rugby and Marlborough contributing specially large quotas, as Colonel Boscawen had established a special connection with those schools. Then, as the seriousness of the crisis became increasingly apparent, there set in from the Colonies and India, from the United States and the Argentine and every country under the sun, a stream of men who had thrown up their jobs and come home to serve, men of experience and capacity, rather maturer than the schoolboys and undergraduates of the O.T.C., some of the finest officer-material imaginable. These the 3rd received, trained[1] and passed to the front in due course. Colonel Boscawen was indefatigable in his efforts to get the right type of officer and the Regiment was to benefit greatly by the pains he took on this most important question. Aug.-Dec., 1914
3rd Battalion

The work of the Special Reserve battalions between 1914-1918 affords little material for description. They saw no active service as battalions, they had an unending round of duties, increasing and unchanging, monotonous perhaps, but absolutely essential. They were not in the limelight, but none the less their work was invaluable and indispensable.

The Territorial battalions of the Regiment were, as already mentioned, under arms when war broke out. Their annual training had begun at Longmoor, near Aldershot, on July 26th, four days later they started for Salisbury Plain, and had just reached its Eastern 4th and 5th Battalions

---

[1] A special training camp was formed just outside Fort Darland for the training of young officers from the brigades holding the Thames and Medway Defences.

THE TERRITORIALS.

<small>4th and 5th Battalions Aug.-Dec., 1914</small>

edge on August 3rd when they were recalled to their Headquarters to prepare to mobilize. Mobilization orders arrived on the 5th; twenty-four hours later the Kent Brigade was at its war stations at Dover. A few days were spent here in entrenching positions, finding examining posts on the roads, patrolling and other activities, and then the battalions moved back to Canterbury, where it was expected that they would be put through the six months additional training which was supposed to be needed to fit the Territorials for active service. But within a very few days the critical nature of the situation had swept away most pre-conceived ideas as to what was to be done in war time, and the Territorials, who had been enlisted and organized as a Home Defence force and been repeatedly assured by responsible persons that nothing more was expected of them, were being asked to volunteer for foreign service. If the immediate response was not quite unanimous it was not to be wondered at, but all the officers of both the 4th and 5th Battalions volunteered and so did the greater proportion of the men. However, many of the men were too young for service abroad and others were found medically unfit, so it was at first proposed to form one foreign service battalion out of the 4th and 5th to be under Colonel Watney, of the 4th, and to unite the remainder as a home service battalion under Colonel Frazer of the 5th. This arrangement was, however, never carried through, as after a short time so many more men volunteered for foreign service and so many recruits were joining that it became clear that each battalion could provide two units, one for foreign service, one for home. By this time (middle of September) the Kent Brigade had moved to Sandwich and the adjacent villages, and there the foreign service units remained till their departure overseas, the home service, or " Reserve " battalions as they were styled, being formed at Sevenoaks and Bromley respectively under

Photo by] [J. Weston and Son, Folkestone.

COLONEL F. A. FRAZER, D.S.O., T.D.
Commanded 1/5 Battalion, 1914-1918.

Photo by] [Elliott and Fry, Ltd., Baker Street, W.

COLONEL C. N. WATNEY, C.I.E., T.D.
Commanded 1/4 Battalion until April, 1919.

Face Page 68.

THE TERRITORIALS.

Colonel Simpson,[1] an old commanding officer of the 4th Battalion, and Colonel E. Bassett Willis, second-in-command of the 5th. These two battalions started with about 200-300 men each but quickly filled up with recruits. By the middle of November, when they moved to the neighbourhood of Ascot, both were fairly well up to strength, though it well illustrates the unprepared state in which the country had found itself that the New Year arrived before the "Home Counties Reserve Division," to which these battalions belonged, received serviceable rifles. *4th and 5th Battalions Aug.-Dec., 1914*

The foreign service which the 4th and 5th Battalions had been asked to undertake proved not to be the service at the actual "front" for which they had thought that they were volunteering, but garrison duty in India, where Territorials were wanted to set free the majority of the Regular units to reinforce the Army in France. This employment appeared to many of the 4th and 5th to be but a poor form of service, but it was of vital importance since it rendered possible the successive arrival in France of the Eighth, Twenty-Seventh and Twenty-Eighth Divisions, all urgently needed, nor could the Twenty-Ninth Division have been sent to the Dardanelles without the move to India of the Home Counties and Wessex Territorials.

The two battalions actually sailed from Southampton on October 29th. Their voyage to India was a protracted business, taking over five weeks, long waits at Port Said, Suez and finally Aden spinning it out considerably. Both battalions, however, reached Bombay early in December, and the end of the year found the 4th stationed at Jubbulpore and the 5th at Jhansi where it relieved D Company of the 2nd Battalion.

Meanwhile there had been added to the Regiment not one "Service" battalion only, but four. The forma- *Service Battalions*

---

[1] Col. Simpson was appointed to command the new unit on September 19th, and six days later the nucleus of the battalion arrived at Sevenoaks from Sandwich and was sent into billets.

EXPANSION.

Service Battalions

tion of all these additional battalions and the creation not of one but of many "New Armies" is the most prodigious feat of military organization that history records. It easily eclipses Napoleon's wonderful efforts to recreate for the campaign of 1813 the Grand Army which had perished in Russia and the gallant attempt of the Third Republic to replace the armies lost at Sedan and Metz; it surpasses the achievements of the American Civil War in extent and still more because there both combatants started on an equality of unpreparedness. When the raising of "the First Hundred Thousand," familiarly called "K 1," was originally ordered its formation seemed to many of those responsible for raising and training it a sufficiently formidable task. When on "K 1" there followed "K 2" and "K 3" and "K 4," till the numbers of the New Army Divisions soared into the Thirties and Forties, the problems of officering, equipping, arming, disciplining and training these great hosts seemed absolutely insuperable. In the end nearly two years elapsed before these new forces were to exercise any marked influence on the fortunes of the war; the intervening period saw many dangerous moments, when it looked as if the New Armies would after all come too late, as if, long before the great effort of raising and preparing these extemporised forces could be completed, the enemy must overwhelm the old originals of the Regular Army and the Special Reservists and Territorials who were helping them to hold up the German attacks while an unready Empire armed. But the knowledge that these great forces were being got ready helped to sustain the overmatched British Expeditionary Force of 1914 and the Spring of 1915, and from the first the officers and men of the old battalions listened with eager interest for news of the new off-shoots from the common stem, just as to these new members of each regiment one of the inspiring motives was to prove themselves worthy of the

EXPANSION.

Regiment and of the men who were carrying on at the front till they should come.

Of all the Service battalions of The Queen's Own the 6th was perhaps the most closely connected with the 1st Battalion, as it may fairly claim to have started life at Dublin when Captain Snow and Lieut. Anstruther and fifteen N.C.O.'s were detailed to provide its nucleus. It received a further link with the 1st Battalion in Captain Lynch White and 2nd Lieut. Dawson, who were left behind on the reduction of the War Establishment. But if the infant 6th Battalion saw the light at Dublin its closest associations are with Colchester and Purfleet. It was to Colchester that the original nucleus with the earliest accretions proceeded and where it increased to something like a battalion. At Purfleet, to which it moved at the end of August, recruits continued to come in until the battalion was completed up to establishment. It was allotted to the 37th Brigade of the Twelfth (Eastern) Division of the "First New Army," the other units of the brigade being the 6th Queen's, 6th Buffs and 7th East Surreys. Major Robinson, the C.O. at the Depôt, was its first commanding officer, Captain Wingfield Stratford its first adjutant, and with the aid of the nucleus of Regular officers and men left behind,[1] of the old soldiers who rejoined and of retired officers who, like Major F. H. Hotham, Captain H. C. W. Beeching, and 2nd-Lieut. E. Hudson,[2] came back to serve, the 6th's progress towards efficiency was remarkable. For subalterns it had splendid material. To Lord Kitchener's appeal for 2,000 young officers for the "First New Army" there had been an enormous response, applications for subalterns' commissions had fairly inundated the War Office and the five training camps for young officers in which the selected candi-

Aug.-Dec., 1914 6th Battalion

---

[1] Captain J. C. Parker, who joined from the Depôt and took command of B Company, was another of the Regulars who helped to make the new battalion.

[2] Promoted to Captain in October, 1914.

EXPANSION.

Aug.-Dec., 1914
6th Battalion

dates were given a month's preliminary instruction contained without any exaggeration the very pick of the Universities and Public Schools. The keenness and energy of all ranks was unbounded and everybody faced with real cheerfulness the discomforts involved in life under canvas at Purfleet in late autumn. As long as fine weather lasted things were not too bad, but November proved wet, and, as the ground on which the battalion was encamped was below the level of the Thames the camp soon became a sea of mud, while the nights were damp and foggy. The men had only a thin blue uniform, not as warm as the khaki issue which was not served out till a good deal later, and the overcrowding of the tents added to their discomfort, so the move into huts at Sandling Junction, early in December, was very welcome. These huts, however, were far from finished, some of them only leaked, the majority made no pretence of keeping out the rain, and the mud surpassed that of Purfleet; so another move, this time to billets in Hythe, proved necessary and popular. The end of the year found the 6th R.W.K. already a well-established battalion, considering themselves quite old soldiers when compared with the junior units of the Regiment, well advanced with their programme of training, considering the time available, and the shortage of arms and equipment from which all the New Armies were suffering. The battalion had had several changes among its senior officers. Colonel Robinson had left it in November to take command of the 1st Battalion and was succeeded by Colonel G. E. Even, formerly of the Indian Army. Major Hotham had died suddenly at the end of October and was succeeded as second-in-command by another old officer of the Regiment, Major E. F. Venables, who joined at Sandling in December, while Captain Lynch White had departed to France, as had also Captain Waterfield, of the 45th Sikhs, who had been attached to the battalion for some months and had proved an

EXPANSION.

<small>Aug.-Dec., 1914
6th Battalion</small>

admirable trainer of recruits. Captain Snow also left to take up a Staff appointment.

<small>7th Battalion</small>

The formation of the 7th Battalion, part of the Eighteenth Division of the " Second New Army,"[1] had been begun at Purfleet early in September. A small nucleus of officers was provided from the 6th Battalion, including Lieuts. Anstruther, who became Adjutant, and Snelgrove, while Captain G. St. C. Stevenson joined as second-in-command with the rank of Major, Colonel A. W. Prior, formerly of the North Staffords, being appointed to the command, while the battalion was fortunate in obtaining the services of many old N.C.O.'s formerly in the Regiment. Like the 6th, it drew for its subalterns mainly on the Universities and Public Schools and had a very fine set of young officers, the majority of whom had received a month's instruction before joining, even if they had not already learnt the elements of their work in the O.T.C. Thus the battalion started under good auspices and made rapid progress. It was at Purfleet till the beginning of October, then moved to a camp at Belhus Park, returning to huts at Purfleet before the end of the year.

<small>Sept.-Dec., 1914
8th Battalion</small>

The raising of yet a third Service battalion was ordered early in September. Its start was somewhat unpropitious. On the 12th the overcrowded Depôt disgorged some 800 men, who found themselves suddenly planted down in camp at Shoreham without a single officer to form the 8th R.W.K., a unit of the 72nd Brigade of the Twenty-Fourth Division, which, like the 37th and 55th Brigades, included battalions of The Queen's (8th), Buffs (8th) and East Surreys (9th). There were tents but no blankets or equipment of any kind, rations but nothing to cook them with or eat them off, and as the rain was coming down in sheets the first night was a severe trial of the temper and willingness of the men. But with the arrival two days later

---

[1] The battalion was assigned to the 55th Brigade, which included also the 7th Queen's, 7th Buffs, and 8th East Surreys.

EXPANSION.

<small>Sept.-Dec., 1914
8th Battalion</small> of a C.O. in Colonel E. Vansittart, formerly of the 7th Gurkhas, the 8th soon got going, though its progress was naturally even more retarded than that of its predecessors by delays in getting adequate arms, clothing and equipment. Like them, the 8th was fortunate in securing several old officers and over 30 old N.C.O.'s of the Regiment; Major Brock-Hollinshead became second-in-command, and others who joined it were Major O. J. Daniell, Major E. V. O. Hewett, who, however, soon left to command a Service battalion of the South Wales Borderers, Captain A. H. Pullman and Lieut. C. de C. Middleton, who became Adjutant.

<small>Oct.-Dec., 1914
9th Battalion</small> But the addition to the Regiment of three Service battalions and the two Reserve or " Second line " Territorial battalions did not exhaust the recruit-producing capacities of the regimental district. Before the end of October the 3rd Battalion, even after providing drafts amounting to over 400, was positively overflowing with men. The majority of Special Reserve battalions being in this state the War Office issued orders for the formation of yet another " New Army " by the simple process of drafting the necessary numbers from the Special Reserve. Thus on October 24th a 9th R.W.K. came into being, with yet another old officer of The Queen's Own as its C.O., Major Daniell being transferred from the 8th and promoted to Lieut.-Colonel. Major and Hon. Lieut.-Colonel T. T. Burt joined him as second-in-command, while the apparently inexhaustible supply of ex-N.C.O.'s of the Regiment provided a good nucleus of sergeants. By the middle of December the 9th was already above establishment in " other ranks," had Majors and Captains enough to provide company commanders and seconds-in-command, and had received such a flood of 2nd-Lieutenants that rumour declared that a complete company was to be formed from them. Even more than its predecessors the 9th was handicapped by the shortage of arms and equipment, its only rifles for

THE VOLUNTEERS.

some time were 200 of the variety known as " D.P."[1] and its training naturally suffered severely. Chatham was the scene of the battalion's formation, and its early life was spent in billets in the town.

Thus by the end of 1914 The Queen's Own had no less than eleven battalions of one category or another, all doing or preparing to do their part in the greatest struggle in which the Regiment had ever engaged. But behind the eleven battalions there was forming a body which was ultimately to be definitely connected by name with the Regiment and in whose ranks not a few who ultimately joined its ranks perceived their first introduction to military discipline and training. The actual organisation of the Volunteers did not obtain official recognition until the spring of 1915, though before that various unofficial associations had been formed in many places in which men who were unable to join up for full-time service or who were ineligible by reason of age or health were obtaining some degree of military training. It was in April 1915 that the War Office decided not only to authorize but in some degree to organize and correlate these rather spasmodic and irregular formations, and the definite beginning of the Volunteer movement proper in West Kent dates from the appointment of Colonel C. E. Warde, M.P., as inspecting officer. This was followed by the holding of meetings at various places to explain the nature and scope of the organization; efforts were made to raise funds by voluntary subscription for the necessary expenditure, and Deputy Lieutenants were invited to form local committees for their respective districts. A most successful mass meeting for this purpose was held at Maidstone on August 4th 1915, the first anniversary of the declaration of war, and in a short time no less than 12,000 men had given in their names for enrolment in the county, many of whom before long passed

1914-1915 Volunteer Battalions

[1] " Drill purposes only."

THE VOLUNTEERS.

1914-1918 Volunteer Battalions

on into the Royal Defence Corps, some of them even into the Regulars.

With the introduction of the Military Service Act the position of the Volunteers was somewhat altered. A certain number of their members were taken into the Regulars by conscription, their places being mostly taken by " exempted " men, especially when later on the tribunals established under the Act received authority to order such men to join the Volunteers. Thus the strength of the force was fairly well maintained, and by the end of 1916 no less than twelve battalions had been, or were being, formed in Kent, four, the 3rd, 5th, 6th and 8th, being allotted to Mid-Kent—having their headquarters respectively at Cranbrook, Maidstone, Chatham, and Ashford, and five to West Kent, the so-called " Metropolitan area." These were the 7th at Beckenham, the 9th at Bexley Heath, the 10th at Penge, the 11th at Eltham, and the 12th at Sevenoaks. At the end of 1917, however, a drastic reorganisation took place, the Mid-Kent and West Kent groups were amalgamated and re-formed as four Volunteer Battalions of the Royal West Kent Regiment, Colonel Warde, hitherto in command of the Mid-Kent group, taking command of the amalgamated groups. As re-organised the 3rd and 4th Battalions became the 1st V.B., with Tonbridge as headquarters and Colonel Rowlandson, late King's Own Royal Lancasters, in command: the 2nd V.B. was formed from the 5th and 6th Battalions, with Maidstone as headquarters, under Colonel Borton, late Somerset L.I.: the 3rd V.B. was made up of the 7th and 10th, and was commanded by Major Sir Philip Dawson, Penge being its headquarters, while the 9th and 11th went to make up the 4th V.B. at Dartford under Major C. H. Gray. The Ashford battalion had been transferred to the Buffs, and the 12th had never been completely formed. The strength of these four battalions came to 3,000 all told.

THE VOLUNTEERS.

1914-1918 Volunteer Battalions

In the course of 1918 a good deal was done to improve the equipment and efficiency of the Volunteers, who were somewhat extensively employed, the West Kent battalions working hard and efficiently at constructing defences for London, and receiving Regulars' pay, allowances and rations when so employed. The names of the officers now appeared in the Army List, and the force was by this time a factor of real importance in the schemes for the defence of the country. The high level of efficiency which it attained was most creditable to the zeal and energy of all ranks, and though the Volunteers were never called upon to meet the test of having to defend their homes, the work they did, such as preparing defences, guarding vulnerable points, and manning searchlights, was of great value; indeed a composite company from the Kentish Volunteer battalions spent July-August, 1918, on coast defence work at Lydd, attached to the Kent Cyclists. Much of this work must have fallen to other formations but for the existence of the Volunteers, and had that been the case it would have seriously interfered with their training and draft-finding, while thanks to the Volunteers many men were rendered available for service overseas who must otherwise have been retained in England.

CHAPTER V

THE FIRST WINTER.

November, 1914-
March, 1915
1st Battalion

For the British Army the four months which elapsed between the end of the German offensive against Ypres and the opening of the British offensive of 1915 at Neuve Chapelle were a period of unremitting toil, in which it was contending almost more against the forces of Nature than against the Germans. There were intermittent outbursts of activity, each side in turn attempted local attacks, there was heavy fighting round Givenchy in December and again at the end of January, but the main problem was that of holding on to the trenches in conditions of almost indescribable difficulty and discomfort, especially in the wetter parts of the line, where the men had to stand knee or even thigh deep in icy cold water, endeavouring to prevent parapets from dissolving altogether into liquid slime. In the other winters of the war there may have been heavier shelling, the enemy may not have been handicapped as they undoubtedly were in 1914-1915 from the fact that their consumption of munitions had outrun even their preparations, there was certainly more trouble overhead from aeroplanes as well as underneath from mines, and in 1914-1915 there was at least no gas, but in the other winters it was known what a winter of trench-warfare meant, there had been time to devise means for rendering it more tolerable and to accumulate in advance supplies of all the varied trench stores that ingenuity could devise. Moreover, the relieving, refitting and resting of trench garrisons had by then been reduced to a system. Billets, baths, theatrical entertainments, a roster of leave, had been carefully organized. If wood was wanted for rivetting parapets, for making communication trenches passable, it was usually forthcoming in profusion. There were hardships to be endured in the

THE FIRST WINTER.

other winters, at no time could the life in trenches be anything but one of slightly mitigated discomfort. Much was attempted even in 1914-1915 to render the conditions more endurable, but the methods of mitigating the discomfort had not progressed beyond the experimental stage. Moreover, in 1914-1915 the troops had to endure the discomforts far more frequently and for longer periods than they were called upon to do under normal circumstances in the later years. There were no months in reserve for a whole Division, for the simple reason that there were not enough Divisions in France.

November, 1914-March, 1915 1st Battalion

Thus on coming out of the Ypres salient the 1st R.W.K. had a bare week's rest, during which time Major Robinson—as already mentioned—joined and took over command, Captain Dunlop becoming Adjutant, while a big reinforcement arrived with which were Major Bonham-Carter and Lieut. MacNeece. Then on November 27th the battalion went back into trenches again, and from that day to the day before the attack on Hill 60 it was either in the front line, in support trenches, or in immediate reserve, except for about ten days at the end of December, a week at the end of January, ten days in the middle of February, two short periods of four or five days in March, and a week in April. At times the battalion was in trenches for as much as nine days on end, and further it proved necessary to hold the trenches in greater strength than need have been done had more artillery ammunition been available. It was said that the French held their trenches with their guns, the British had to hold them with men, and certainly the strain on the troops that first winter was very great. But it was wonderful how well they stood it. The almost unfailing cheerfulness of the men was really amazing, if it had not been so thoroughly in keeping with the British soldier's habit of taking everything as it came as part of the day's work, something to

THE FIRST WINTER.

November, 1914-March, 1915 1st Battalion

"grouse" about and to treat as a joke. The sick-rate was extraordinarily low considering the conditions, though "trench-feet" and similar ailments caused a large number of admissions to hospital until issues of whale-oil and gum-boots and other measures somewhat reduced the wastage from this cause. But the wastage was heavy: thus of seven officers who joined early in November only one, 2nd-Lieut. Walker, was still with the battalion at the end of February. In all about 50 company officers joined the battalion between the beginning of November 1914 and the end of April 1915: of these, sixteen were killed or died of wounds in that period, a dozen were wounded, as many invalided, and the average duration of their service with the battalion was under forty days. During this same period the casualties among "other ranks" amounted to 109 killed and 224 wounded, apart from sickness and the

November, 1914-April, 1915

heavy losses at Hill 60 and on April 23rd, while the drafts received came to over 1,100.[1] This rate of wastage in trench warfare was far heavier than was to be experienced in subsequent years when defences had been greatly improved, notably by the provision in many parts of the line of dug-outs, which could withstand anything except a really heavy shell, and more especially by the introduction of the "shrapnel-helmet," which did so much to reduce casualties. Through the winter of 1914-1915 casualties through head-wounds were sadly frequent and many valuable lives were lost in this way. Thus on one day in February the battalion lost a promising young officer in 2nd.-Lieut. Pownall and a splendid N.C.O. in Sergt. Verrall, who, coming out as a private, had worked his way up very quickly, distinguishing himself greatly at Neuve Chapelle in October, and whose cheerfulness, calmness and resource had proved a great asset.

[1] On January 1st it was noted that there were still present with the battalion 3 officers and 210 men who had come out with it in August, though these numbers included several who had rejoined after a short absence.

THE FIRST WINTER.

During the early part of these winter months the battalion was opposite the Messines-Wytschaete ridge, which portion of the line the Second Corps had taken over towards the end of November. The Fifth Division was on the right of this line, holding a frontage of about two miles running N. and somewhat W. from the Douve. This was divided into two portions, known as the Neuve-Eglise and Wulverghem sectors, which were originally held by two brigades, with the third in reserve. Later on the 14th Brigade took over the Neuve-Eglise sector permanently, finding its own reliefs, while the 13th and 15th took turn and turn about in the Wulverghem line, withdrawing to St. Jans Cappel or some other village West of the Kemmel and Scherpenberg hills for its turns of rest. It was not a good line, for it represented the final positions attained by the French efforts to recover the Messines ridge and was therefore the result of accident rather than choice. For the most part it ran along a lower ridge opposite the main one from which it was overlooked. It was imperative, therefore, to construct communication trenches between the front line and the supports, and as the weather was extremely wet and keeping the trenches in repair was more than enough occupation by itself, the troops were never without employment. Mud was the outstanding feature of this part of the line. The continued rain reduced the country to a bog, communication trenches rarely existed and, if they did, were invariably impassable,[1] so that reliefs and ration parties had to go up to the front line across the open, and this often meant casualties from machine-gun fire. When not in the firing-line battalions were fully employed on the support trenches or in preparing a second line some distance in rear. Active operations were impossible, quite apart from weather conditions, owing to the

November, 1914-March, 1915
1st Battalion

---

[1] It was not till July, 1915, when the battalion was in the St. Eloi sector that it ever found a communication trench which could be used for the purpose.

THE FIRST WINTER.

<small>November, 1914-March, 1915 1st Battalion</small>

shortage of the ammunition supply, though the gunners made the best use of the scanty daily allowance of shells. Snipers, too, were continually on the alert for targets, while good work was done at night by patrols, Lieut. Brown in particular distinguishing himself by careful reconnaissance and good reports. But, as a whole, December, January, and the early part of February were devoid of outstanding incidents, though the constant hard work put in gradually produced a distinct effect on the trenches, which before long were really quite formidable and even not uncomfortable.[1]

<small>February, 1915</small>

But with the middle of February came a change. The 13th Brigade was resting at Bailleul in Army Reserve and the battalion had just been inspected by the new Brigadier, General Wanless O'Gowan, when on the 19th it received orders to proceed at once to Vlamertinghe, just West of Ypres, and to relieve the 83rd Brigade of the Twenty-Eighth Division in trenches S.E. of Ypres. This portion of the Allied line was just to the right of the trenches held by the battalion from November 13th-19th: the French had taken it over at the end of the battle of Ypres, but had handed it back to the newly-arrived Twenty-Eighth Division of the Fifth Corps at the end of January. This Division, which was composed of battalions drawn from India and other distant stations, had been going through a very bad time. Coming straight from the Tropics to the damp and cold and mud of Flanders, its men had suffered frightfully from sickness and had been succumbing to trench-feet and other complaints at an alarming rate. Moreover, they had opposed to them an active and aggressive Bavarian division, who had given them no opportunity to settle down to the new conditions and methods of warfare. It soon became evident that it

<small>[1] Casualties in the Wulverghem area amounted to one officer (Capt. Mills) and 28 men killed and 49 men wounded; those from invaliding had been higher, and several officers had left to join the Flying Corps or take up Staff appointments, among the latter being Major Bonham-Carter.</small>

THE YPRES SALIENT.

was imperative to relieve the exhausted infantry of the Twenty-Eighth Division, and in the last ten days of February three seasoned brigades from the Second Corps, among them the 13th, were sent up to take the place for the time of the brigades properly belonging to that Division.

February, 1915
1st Battalion

Thus it was that on the evening of February 20th the 1st R.W.K. found themselves taking over the left section of the 83rd Brigade's line. This was to the S.E. of Zillebeke on the Northern side of the railway line from Ypres to Comines, which here ran through a deep cutting. The line extended for some distance to the left past the hamlet of Zwarteleen, which formed a salient. The trenches were in a bad state and required a great deal of work, while the enemy in this quarter had attained a decided supremacy and were very much on the aggressive. Their trench-mortars in particular were to the fore, and at its first tour of duty in the new trenches the battalion came in for a very bad time. On February 22nd part of B Company in the Zwarteleen salient was very heavily bombed by a heavy trench mortar which blew down large portions of the parapet. The Germans then turned machine-guns on to the gaps, making it necessary to thin out the garrison and eventually the survivors were forced for the time to evacuate what remained of their trench after Lieuts. Brown and Burbury had been killed and many other casualties suffered. For over two hours the bombing continued, but the battalion endured the ordeal steadily and hung grimly on. The Germans did not attempt to assault, and when with nightfall the damaged trench was re-occupied, the bombing ceased. All hands then turned on to repair the damages and restore the position, and when the Duke's arrived to relieve the battalion the line was intact. But the day had cost The Queen's Own over forty casualties, 2nd-Lieut. Frost having also been killed and Captain Molony wounded. Lieut. Brown in particular was a

THE YPRES SALIENT.

March-April, 1915
1st Battalion

great loss to the battalion; he had shown himself an excellent officer and had been specially selected by Colonel Robinson for the responsible and dangerous post of Battalion Bombing Officer.

Throughout March the battalion continued in this quarter, relieving and being relieved by the Duke's every second day, except for two periods of rest spent at Ouderdom (March 11th-14th) and Vlamertinghe (March 28th-31st). Sometimes it held the Zwarteleen sector, sometimes that to the right, just North of the Ypres-Comines Canal. This sector contained a trench known as the International Trench, because the Germans held the Southern portion and the British its continuation Northward, a situation which may well have given rise to the legend of the loophole through which British and Germans took it in turns to fire. With the enemy at such close quarters and in an aggressive mood the situation was at times decidedly lively, but the 13th Brigade was not slow in redressing the balance, which on its arrival it had found heavily weighted against the British. Though greatly handicapped by the shortage of artillery ammunition, which prevented our guns, restricted to a maximum of three rounds a day, from replying effectively to the German shelling, The Queen's Own and the other battalions not only improved the trenches out of all recognition, but gradually wrested the ascendancy from the Germans, reduced their snipers to relative inactivity and put matters on a much more satisfactory footing all round. General Bulfin, the commander of the Twenty-Eighth Division, had told General Wanless O'Gowan when the 13th Brigade arrived in his command that he had never seen battalions with more go or spirit or that gave him more complete confidence. When, at the beginning of April, the Twenty-Eighth Division[1] moved to the left to relieve the French in the Broodseinde and Zonnebeke

[1] It had been reconstituted by the return of its original brigades from the Second Corps.

THE YPRES SALIENT.

area, General Bulfin's report showed that his confidence had not been misplaced. "Their energetic and indefatigable work," he wrote, "greatly improved and strengthened the line: their steadiness under trying circumstances gave a sense of security throughout the Division, and their boldness in small enterprises diminished to a great extent the aggressive attitude of the enemy." The G.O.C. Fifth Corps, Sir Herbert Plumer, was not less emphatic in his praise. "The work they have done," was his verdict, "has been equal in value to the winning of many an engagement."

April, 1915
1st Battalion

The 1st Battalion could therefore look on their six weeks under the Twenty-Eighth Division with some satisfaction. Deeds of gallantry had not been few in number: conspicuous among them was the action of Sergt. Dennington and Pte. Bunsell, who, when a portion of a trench had been blown in by shell-fire, went to the help of a man who had been buried in the débris. Working lying on their stomachs within 30 yards of the enemy, they dug and cleared for over an hour, and were at length rewarded by rescuing the man.[1] It had been a difficult and trying time of constant hard work and endurance, in a way a severer test of a battalion's quality than a big fight in the open. It had cost the battalion heavily. Four officers and 65 men had been killed, three officers and 134 men wounded. Among those killed was C.S.M. File, who had come out with the battalion as Machine-Gun Sergeant, had been wounded on September 1st, and actually placed on a hospital ship under orders for home, but managed to get off the ship and rejoined the battalion. Wounded again in December, he had refused to go to hospital and had carried on, setting a splendid example of courage and devotion to duty.

The return of the 13th and 15th Brigades to the command of their own Divisional General did not mean a

---

[1] They were subsequently awarded the D.C.M.

HILL SIXTY.

April, 1915
1st Battalion

change of area. The Fifth Division merely took over the front which the Twenty-Eighth had been holding, and it fell to General Morland[1] to carry out a scheme which had been planned and prepared by General Bulfin. Opposite the right of the Zwarteleen sector

See Sketch 9

there was a large mound formed by the excavation of the railway cutting through the Zwarteleen-Zandvoorde ridge and dignified with the name of " Hill Sixty." Though in itself nothing more than an inconsiderable hummock this mound was the highest point for some distance round and had no little tactical value as an artillery observation post. To deny its use to the enemy's artillery observing officers would be a distinct gain to the British, and the higher authorities had readily accepted the proposal to capture it. Preparations for an attack had been in progress for some time before the Twenty-Eighth Division handed over to the Fifth. Several mines had been excavated under the German trenches and additional artillery concentrated to give the necessary support.

Among the battalions of the 13th Brigade it was The Queen's Own who had the honour of being selected to assault the hill, and during their stay at Vlamertinghe they had carefully rehearsed their task. All arrangements had been carefully thought out and on the evening of April 16th the battalion took its position in the trenches ready for the assault. The hour selected for the attack was 7 p.m. on April 17th, which involved the battalion

April 17th, 1915

being placed in position under cover of darkness on the previous night and having to lie quiet all day waiting for the hour to come. Aeroplanes patrolled up and down to keep the enemy's aircraft from discovering what was coming, but otherwise the day passed without special signs of activity. The actual storming party, C Company (Captain Moulton-Barrett[2]), lay in the

---

[1] He had succeeded Sir C. Fergusson in November.

[2] He had rejoined on February 3rd, on recovering from his wound received at Neuve Chappelle.

HILL SIXTY.

trenches 39 and 40, immediately opposite the hill, with B (2nd-Lieut. Walker) in close support in dug-outs and support trenches. D (Captain Tuff) was in the communication trench further back ready to replace B directly it took C's place in trenches 39-40. A (Captain Lynch-White) was further back in reserve near Battalion Headquarters. A party of R.E. was attached to each of the eight columns into which the stormers were divided, and a strong working party of the K.O.S.B.'s had been detailed to push forward directly the hill was taken and assist in consolidating it.

April 17th, 1915 1st Battalion

At length the long day of waiting came to its close: at 7 p.m. the mines were fired and simultaneously the seventy guns collected to support the attack opened a tremendous bombardment of the German trenches behind and on either side of the hill, of the woods in rear, and the railway cutting. "There was not much noise," writes one account, "but the whole ground shook as if there was an earthquake and a few minutes later bricks, Germans and all kinds of débris were hurtling through the air in all directions." Then C Company leapt forward out of their trenches and dashed for the hill. In a couple of minutes they had swarmed up the slope and fallen upon the Germans who had survived the explosion. The bulk of the garrison of the hill had been wiped out and only some 50 or 60 stood to meet the assailants, but, dazed and shaken, they offered no organised opposition and were for the most part bayonetted: about 20 were taken, and of those who endeavoured to escape many were bombed or shot down as they fled down the communication trenches in rear of the hill, Sergt. Fisher doing most effective work with his machine-gun. The hill had been taken with but seven casualties among the stormers.

To retain the captured position was bound to be more difficult; once the Germans had recovered from their surprise they were sure to counter-attack in force.

HILL SIXTY.

April 17th, 1915
1st Battalion

B Company had joined C on the hill directly after the assault and with it came the two companies of the K.O.S.B.'s detailed as working parties. Consolidation was at once started, for there was much to be done. The explosion had completely demolished the top of the hill, in places the trenches had altogether disappeared and in their place were great craters 20 yards across. The largest of these were on the left flank, though there was another group at the other end. These craters were quickly put into a state of defence by the R.E.'s and K.O.S.B.'s while a firing-line was taken up along the far edge of the hill, which position Major Joslin, who commanded the assaulting party, considered better than the line of the enemy's trench on the crest. Communication trenches back to our old lines were started, one from each flank, and about an hour after the assault it was reported that these were "nearly through," so vigorously had the working-parties plied pick and shovel.

At first the consolidation was but little impeded by the enemy. The precautions for concealing the intention to attack had been successful and the German failure to counter-attack with any promptitude showed how completely they had been surprised. About half-past eight a counter-attack was reported to be threatening, but at 9 p.m. the report was "no attack yet: two companies and four machine-guns ready for it," and though shortly before midnight the enemy's artillery opened on the new trench the message was "firmly established." But when at last the attack came there

April 18th, 1915

was no mistake about it. Soon after midnight the K.O.S.B.'s were ordered to relieve B and C Companies, but before the relief had been completed the Germans started pushing forward in force over the open and from the railway cutting on our right, and at the same time began to press up the communication trenches and to throw bombs into the craters on the left. Their artillery fire had now become very heavy and the support and

HILL SIXTY.

communication trenches came in for a tremendous shell-ing, but the garrison held on unflinchingly and fired with deadly effect. Three times the Germans swarmed forward like great waves, each time they were beaten back, at the third attempt a few gallant men persevered only to be shot down on our parapet. On the left the Germans had more chances of working up close to the British line, and round the craters there was hand to hand fighting and constant bombing. Casualties were now becoming heavy on the hill, the removal of the wounded was made very difficult by the bombardment of the rear of the hill, and many were hit again as they were carried back to the First Aid post in the railway cutting. The brunt of this attack fell on the K.O.S.B.'s, but the portions of B and C Companies under 2nd-Lieuts. Poland and Walker had remained on the hill and continued to share the defence with the K.O.S.B.'s, notably in the left-hand craters, where 2nd-Lieut. Walker did splendid work. Just as he was handing over command on the hill to Major Sladen of the K.O.S.B.'s, Major Joslin was hit and killed, the fourth of the Regiment's field-officers to fall since the beginning of the war. He had, as already mentioned, come to France with the Indian Corps, but had managed to get away from his post on the lines of communication and joined the battalion at the front in February in time to play a leading part in one of the most brilliant and successful of all its exploits.

When the K.O.S.B.'s relieved the original stormers A and D Companies remained in readiness to support them, and almost at once D was called up to reinforce as the Germans were renewing their attacks more vigorously than ever. Several officers fell, among them Captain Tuff, but there were not wanting N.C.O.'s like Sergt. Markham, who took command on his platoon commander's fall and acted with great coolness and resource, directing his men's fire and maintaining their

HILL SIXTY.

April 18th, 1915
1st Battalion

resistance.[1] About 4.30 a.m. the enemy made a most determined effort and managed to get close up, especially on the left, where the two big craters were desperately contested. A then went up, taking with them a large quantity of ammunition of which the K.O.S.B.'s were running short. 2nd-Lieut. Doe taking up his platoon to the left craters about 5 a.m., found 2nd-Lieuts. Walker and Borland with a few of B Company still there, helping the hard-pressed Borderers to maintain the position. 2nd-Lieut. Walker was hit almost immediately after the reinforcements from A arrived, but 2nd-Lieut. Doe's party carried on the defence, keeping the German bomb-throwers effectively at bay by a well-directed rapid fire until their overheated rifles began to get out of action. Sergt. Young won the D.C.M. for conspicuous gallantry in this fighting; he picked up German grenades, threw them back at the enemy, and set a splendid example. Sergts. Weston, Botting and Rabbit were all conspicuous for their gallantry and good leading, while Pte. Hissey took command of a small party, no N.C.O. being available, and established it in a position on the flank of the line so as to cover a weak spot most effectively. Some relief was given to the defenders at a critical moment by a British aeroplane, which hovered over the German lines and caused most of their batteries to cease fire in order to avoid detection. But the trench on the edge nearest to the German lines proved very hard to maintain and the defenders were gradually pressed back to the crest. However, at 8.5 a.m. Captain Lynch-White's message was "still holding the hill," and when half-an-hour later the Duke's came up and relieved the remnants of A and D and of the Borderers the defence had not been seriously shaken.

On relief A and D withdrew to some dug-outs in the railway embankment near Zillebeke Lake, to which B

[1] He was awarded the D.C.M.

HILL SIXTY.

and C had already retired, and in the evening the whole battalion marched off to huts between Ouderdom and Vlamertinghe. They met with a tremendous reception from the other troops in the rest camp while congratulatory messages from persons in authority, from the Commander-in-Chief downwards, testified to the general recognition of their gallantry. A few days later Sir John French, addressing the battalion along with the K.O.S.B.'s and other battalions which had shared in the later stages of the desperate fighting for the hill, spoke in the warmest terms, declaring that " nothing ever required greater tenacity or courage " than what these troops had had to endure.

April, 1915 1st Battalion

" Hill Sixty " may have been only a minor incident in a war of such extent and intensity, but nevertheless it is a source of most legitimate pride to the regiments represented there. After the long and trying months of winter in the mud and marshes through which the Second Army's line ran, this successful attack seemed to mark a new era. It was followed, it is true, by a struggle which dwarfed " Hill Sixty " altogether, and instead of the advance it had seemed to promise the Second Army was desperately pressed to maintain its ground, was forced to give up most of the " Ypres salient," and even Hill 60 itself. But it was only the use of a weapon they were pledged not to employ that won the Germans these successes, and when hardest pressed the Second Army could brace themselves up to their struggle with the thought that the storming and retention of Hill 60 showed that, barring gas, they were better men than the Germans. " Eye Witness " was not far out when he classed the attack and defence of Hill 60 as " among the finest exploits performed by British troops."

But once more the battalion had to take the field again just as a well deserved rest seemed assured. Hill 60 had cost it dear; in addition to Major Joslin, Captain Tuff and 2nd-Lieut. Walker, it had lost Lieut.

91

"SECOND YPRES."

April 22nd, 1915
1st Battalion

Payton,[1] and 2nd-Lieuts. Poland, Craston and Job, the last of whom had only joined the battalion three days before the fight. Four officers, 2nd-Lieuts. Doe, Westmacott, Liebenrood and Borland, were wounded and the casualties among the rank and file exceeded 300. It was an attenuated battalion, therefore, which moved off to relieve the 15th Brigade in the sector between Hill 60 and the canal on the afternoon of April 22nd. But when the head of the column reached Vlamertinghe it became clear that something had gone very much amiss. Transport of every description was pouring into the village from the Eastward along with a crowd of fugitives, mainly French African troops. The wildest rumours were prevalent, and even at that distance from the battlefield a curious smell could be detected. The road was blocked and the battalion found further progress impossible. It had barely halted before orders came cancelling the relief and diverting the 13th Brigade to a position of readiness in fields just West of Ypres, where it remained all night.

April 23rd, 1915

Early next morning fresh orders were received and the brigade moved off N.E. to a position near Brielen, the R.W.K. coming second in the column and following the K.O.S.B.'s. After a short halt at Brielen the Brigade pushed on and crossed the Ypres-Yser canal North of Ypres. As to the position of the enemy little definite information was available, nor was much known as to the general situation, except that the Germans had broken the French line running N.W. from the St. Julien-Poelcappelle road and had completely outflanked the British left where the Canadian Division, commanded by an old officer of The Queen's Own, Lieut.-Gen. Alderson, was putting up a splendid fight. The object of the counter-attack which the 13th Brigade was now to

---

[1] This officer had been for some years in the 3rd Battalion and was in Government service in the Straits Settlements, but had hurried home at once and had reached the front early in February.

"SECOND YPRES."

deliver was to drive back the Germans, whose advance into the gap between St. Julien and the canal menaced the whole of the British troops in the salient. To stop them was imperative; any further advance would make the position of the Fifth Corps absolutely untenable, and it would be doubtful if the bulk of it could be extricated and drawn back to the Westward of Ypres. The extreme urgency of the situation, therefore, required the immediate launching of the counter-attack, even though there had been no time for proper reconnaissance, and the artillery support available was wholly inadequate. Other troops were to co-operate, French on the left and some of the reserves of the Fifth Corps on the right, and the attack was timed for 3 p.m. It was already 2 p.m. when the battalion received its orders and there were $2\frac{1}{2}$ miles to go to reach the position of deployment near St. Jean.

April 23rd, 1915 1st Battalion

The march was carried out under shell-fire but the position was reached in time and the brigade deployed; the K.O.S.B.'s on the right of the first line with their right on the La Brique-Pilckem road, the R.W.K. on the left with the K.O.Y.L.I. and 9th London[1] in support. By deploying in a hollow the battalion managed to get some shelter, and escaped casualties during its deployment. For the attack it was organized in three lines with one platoon per company in the firing-line, of which Captain Moulton-Barrett was in command. Almost directly it started to advance the French began to crowd in upon its firing-line and even crossed its front. This made it necessary to hold back the supporting lines under cover and only push up a platoon at a time as required. Partly owing to this, partly because the ground over which the battalion was advancing gave a little cover, it managed to push forward without the crippling casualties which the K.O.S.B.'s suffered, but even so it could not get to close quarters with

[1] This battalion had been added to the 13th Brigade at the end of November.

"SECOND YPRES."

April 23rd, 1915
1st Battalion

the enemy, whose exact position it was impossible to ascertain. " None of us had any idea where the Germans were," one officer writes; " to this day I don't know whether they were on top of the hill, in front of us, or at the foot of it." They gave no targets to the firing-line, which eventually came to a standstill after advancing about 800 yards. On that line it dug in, holding on till dark, when a withdrawal was made to a better line 100 yards further back. It may have seemed that the 13th Brigade had accomplished nothing but its advance had closed up the gap between the French and the Canadian Division which had been so grave a danger to the whole British position. One eye-witness described the Brigade's advance with the utmost enthusiasm: " They went up," he wrote, " in broad daylight, in skirmishing order, in face of the most awful shell-fire .... I am thankful for the privilege of having been a witness of their heroism."

April 24th, 1915

On this new line the battalion entrenched; the supports came up on the left and prolonged the firing-line in that direction, but before dawn the 4th Rifle Brigade arrived and allowed the battalion to be withdrawn a couple of miles to a field where the welcome battalion-cookers were met. The losses, Lieuts. Bradley and Daubeny killed, 2nd-Lieuts. Maunder and Cobb wounded, 101 other ranks killed, wounded and missing, had not been heavy considering the severity of the shelling and the tremendous rifle-fire to which the battalion had been exposed,[1] but they amounted to nearly a quarter of those in action. Two days' comparative rest followed, mostly spent along the canal bank in support and marked by the arrival of a big draft of 370 men under Captain Knox, recently released from his Territorial Adjutancy, with 2nd-Lieuts. Littleboy and Gross. The battalion was thus fairly up to strength when, in

April 24th-25th, 1915

[1] One officer wrote that the action was an admirable example of " the little real harm shells and bullets make on a properly extended line ... 25 per cent. casualties are heavy, but it was nothing compared to the amount of ammunition expended."

"SECOND YPRES."

the small hours of April 26th it relieved portions of the 2nd D.C.L.I., 1st York and Lancaster and 9th London in front-line trenches, about a mile and a quarter N.W. of Wieltje and joining on to the French near Turco Farm. These trenches, which were to the right of the line reached on the 23rd, represented the high water mark of an advance by a scratch brigade collected from the reserves of the Fifth Corps; they were shallow and gave little cover, but companies had brought up 50 shovels apiece and so could improve them considerably. This was just as well, as the battalion was subjected to a very heavy shell-fire, against which it found itself fairly well protected, though this could not be said of the gas from which it suffered considerably during the next five days. The only protection available was strips of flannel which were damped and tied on over the mouth and nose but proved a rather inadequate expedient. During these days the battalion did not have to advance, its task being to retain its position and do what it could with covering-fire to assist other troops who attacked on its flanks, but neither the Lahore Division, who made two determined attacks, nor the French on their left, achieved any substantial success, and when the battalion were at last relieved by the Fourth Division on April 30th, the German position was unaltered. But these attacks had at any rate stopped the German advance and removed the principal danger that had threatened the Ypres Salient; if The Queen's Own seemed to have achieved little for all the losses they had suffered[1] they had shared in a negative result of real importance, the Salient was still tenable, even if the advanced positions had to be evacuated.

Even now the battalion was not to get the rest it so much needed. After getting, on May 1st-2nd, its

April 26th - May 5th, 1915
1st Battalion

---

[1] The casualties of April 25th-30th came to one officer (2nd Lieut. Croucher) and three men killed, 26 men missing, two officers (2nd Lieuts. Sharpin and Hilder) and 42 men wounded and gassed.

HILL SIXTY LOST.

<small>May 1st.-5th, 1915
1st Battalion</small> first night's real rest since April 21st, it was turned out two nights running owing to alarms East of the canal, and then on the 5th it had to hurry back to Zillebeke as the Germans were again attacking Hill 60. They had had a try on May 1st, but despite their use of gas they had been beaten off by the Dorsets. This time, however, the wind had greatly favoured the gas, and thanks to it they had overwhelmed the Duke's and retaken the hill. On reaching the headquarters of the 15th Brigade, therefore, the battalion were ordered to counter-attack. As on April 17th, it was associated with the K.O.S.B.'s, who were to attack on its right, advancing against Hill 60 itself, while the battalion made for the trenches North of the Hill. A Company was to lead, with D in support, B and C being in reserve. However, the enemy's fire was extremely heavy, the night was dark, the ground unknown and very difficult, owing to wire, old trenches and shell-holes, and the net result was that most of the battalion lost direction, and the advance was unsuccessful. Eventually 2nd-Lieut. Littleboy and about a platoon got into Trench 40, now once again the British front line, but the Hill was not re-taken. Sergt. Robinson, the Signalling Sergeant, almost the only man in the battalion who had been over the ground in daylight and knew it, did splendid work in going round and ascertaining the position of the companies, for which he later on received the D.C.M. Pte. Cork also, one of the stretcher-bearers, obtained the same reward for going out under heavy fire in broad daylight to the help of a wounded man whom it seemed impossible to reach; he not only took him food and water but crawled back 300 yards with the man on his back and safely brought him in to shelter. Eventually as it was clear that there was no chance of a successful attack the battalion was withdrawn just before daylight to support trenches at Larch Wood. C Company was left on the right of the Bedfordshires to protect that battalion's flank should the

<small>May 6th, 1915</small>

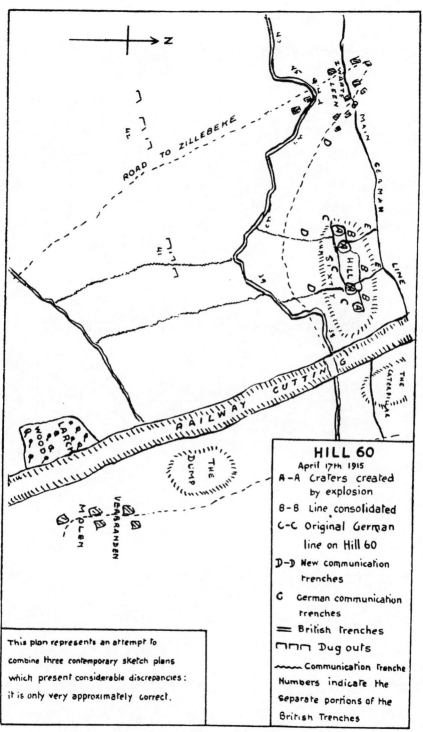

HILL SIXTY LOST.

enemy try to advance from the Zwarteleen salient which they had captured along with Hill 60. No such attempt, however, was made and eventually the battalion was reunited in reserve at Ypres on May 8th. Its casualties during the last four days had been over 100, including 2nd-Lieut. Wild wounded, making its total losses since the beginning of the attack on Hill 60 nineteen officers and nearly 600 men. But the unsuccessful counter-attack on Hill 60 was to be the last severe fight for the battalion for many months to come. No blame can be attached to it for the failure, which merely emphasized the lesson that if a counter-attack is to succeed it should be launched either before the enemy have had time to consolidate and get ready for it or after very careful preparation. Still, it was an unsatisfactory ending to three weeks in which the battalion had earned great distinction and had shown that if but few of the men who had stood in its ranks at Mons on August 23rd were still with it, they had transmitted to the recruits who had replaced them their fighting spirit and powers of endurance, and that The Queen's Own's traditions were safe in the keeping of the successors of the " Old Originals." May 8th. 1915

CHAPTER VI

MESOPOTAMIA, 1915.

January, 1915
2nd Battalion

The long deferred orders to mobilize which reached the 2nd R.W.K. on January 19th, found it scattered over several stations, "apparently all stranded high and dry in India," as one writer put it. Its destination was Mesopotamia; there, as has so often happened, an expedition begun with a limited object was developing into something much larger. The original "I.E.F.,[1] D," consisting of the Sixth Indian (Poona) Division under Lieut.-Gen. Sir Arthur Barrett, had been sent out to secure the pipe-line by which oil was brought down to Abadan Island from the oil-fields to the N.E., and also to prevent any possibility of the Persian Gulf ports being utilized as the base of efforts to foment trouble in India or on the N.W. frontier. Its earlier operations had resulted, by the first week of December, in the occupation of Basra and Qurna, but it soon became apparent that one Division would hardly secure the positions gained against a Turkish counter-attack, and reinforcements from India and Egypt were requisitioned, the 2nd R.W.K. being detailed as the British battalion of the 12th Indian Infantry Brigade, commanded by Major-Gen. K. S. Davison, which was placed under orders for Mesopotamia in January.

Thus on January 28th Headquarters and three companies,[2] with Colonel Pedley in command, left Nasirabad for Bombay, where they arrived two days later, sailing the same day (January 30th) on the s.s.

---
[1] *i.e.*, Indian Expeditionary Force.
[2] The double company system had just been adopted.

MESOPOTAMIA, 1915.

"Elephanta."[1]   At Karachi No. II. Company (late C and G Companies), under Captain Nelson, was picked up, and on February 6th the "Elephanta" reached Basra, where the battalion was transhipped to a river steamer and a couple of lighters for a crowded but fortunately brief voyage up-stream to Qurna, the junction of the Tigris with the old stream of the Euphrates. Here it went into camp on the left bank of the Tigris. The position was none too comfortable, the ground was low-lying, the river was rising steadily, and as it was also raining persistently the troops had to spend almost as much time on digging dams and banks to keep out the water as on defences against the Turks, who were doing all they could to flood the British positions by sending out raiding parties to cut the "bunds" along the river banks some way higher up. This led to some nocturnal encounters with these raiders, who gave considerable trouble, while the Turkish positions, some $2\frac{1}{2}$ miles to the Northward, were occasionally shelled by the British guns; it was one of these bombardments that led to the issue of a Brigade order : "Works and fortifications are not to be used as grand-stands for viewing the effects of artillery fire upon the enemy." There was some sniping at night, but the battalion's main employment was digging in a water-logged country, and eventually

February, 1915 2nd Battalion

---

[1] The battalion embarked 908 strong, being the normal war establishment of a British battalion in India plus 10 per cent. first reinforcements; any men surplus to this establishment or medically unfit were left as a depôt at Nasirabad under Captain Case Morris. The officers who embarked with the battalion were: Lt.-Col. S. H. Pedley (commanding), Major R. J. Woulfe-Flanagan (second-in-command), Captain A. E. Hardy (Adjutant), Lieut. C. H. Battye (Machine Gun Officer), Lieut. J. B. B. Ford (Signalling Officer), Lieut. J. K. Kay (Transport Officer); Lieut. F. Grey (Quartermaster), R.S.M. P. Walker, R.Q.M.S. A. L. Bellion. No. 1 Company: Captains H. D. Belgrave and M. W. Graham, Lieuts. V. S. Clarke and A. G. Balbernie. No. II. Company: Captains J. W. Nelson and A. K. Searight, Lieuts. O. G. Barnes and N. B. Howell, 2nd-Lieut. R. Harrison. No. III. Company: Captains C. R. Ingram and O. Y. Hibbert, 2nd-Lieuts. A. Howe and A. H. Piggott. No. IV. Company: Major C. E. Kitson, Captain M. J. Dinwiddy, Lieut. A. S. Bredon, 2nd-Lieuts. A. C. Elton and C. V. Madgett.

MESOPOTAMIA, 1915.

Feb.-April, 1915
2nd Battalion

the floods rose to such an extent that the camp had to be shifted across the river to rather drier ground in Qurna itself.

At the end of February the battalion moved to Basra, where the conditions were much the same. The camp was situated among date palms in low-lying ground cut up in all directions by irrigation channels. The river being tidal and the soil loose, the water was apt at high tide to percolate through the ground and fill up any hollow or low-lying places, so that the unwary often awoke to find themselves awash in what had seemed overnight a desirable spot for a tent or bivouac. One important duty that fell to the battalion's lot during this time was made very arduous by the floods. This was that of escorting convoys to the outposts at Shaiba, about 12 miles West of Basra, a duty which involved a march there and back of nearly 24 miles through mud and water, in which men often went in up to their knees or even thighs. The whole country looked like a vast lake, and the road could only be distinguished by a line of telegraph posts showing above the water and by various abandoned A.T. carts along the line. On several occasions the mules pulling the carts were drowned and the work was so exhausting that men often had to be helped through the last stages of the march by slinging rifles and joining hands. But the stay at Basra was not to be very long. In February a small British column had been sent off up the Karun River to Ahwaz for the protection of the pipe-line, and on March 3rd this force had an unsuccessful encounter with a much stronger Turkish force backed up by a large number of Arabs. A gun was lost, and only through the steadiness of a small detachment of the Dorsets was disaster narrowly averted. The reinforcement with British infantry of the Ahwaz column was clearly imperative, and the very next day Nos. II. and IV. companies, under Captain Nelson and Major Kitson respectively, with

AHWAZ.

April-June, 1915
2nd Battalion

Major Woulfe-Flanagan in command, was shipped off to Ahwaz, arriving two days later.

The position there was not unlike that at Qurna, the British were occupying an entrenched camp on the river bank with the enemy in observation at a respectful distance. The camp was occasionally shelled, and sniping at night sometimes developed into a serious fusillade, but no definite attack was attempted. A week after the departure of the first half battalion Headquarters followed, having a sharp brush with Arabs on the way up at Ohma Tomair, while five days later the remaining companies also came up. But even then the British force on the Karun remained inactive until after the hard-fought action at Shaiba (April 14th).[1] This decisive repulse of the Turkish counter-stroke down the Euphrates on Basra completely altered the situation, and allowed the concentration in the Ahwaz area of the bulk of the newly-organized Twelfth Indian Division, now under General Gorringe. The main object before it was to teach the Beni Taruf Arabs to abstain from molesting the pipe-line and to drive out of Arabistan the Turkish force which was supporting their opposition.

On April 27th two companies of the battalion formed part of a column which reconnoitred the enemy's camp near Ahwaz, only to find it evacuated; on the news of Shaiba the Turks had retired across the Kharka river and were now 20 miles to the Westward. This was the beginning of six weeks of exhausting operations against a most elusive enemy. It was a strenuous time of hard marching under a burning sun, with the thermometer in the tents going as high as 120 deg., on half rations, with a minimum of kit and rest, sometimes varied by getting among quicksands, into which transport animals sank up

[1] On the day of the action at Shaiba the Turks made a demonstration in force at Ahwaz, shelling the camp heavily and showing infantry more freely than they had previously done. They may have intended to invest Ahwaz had their attack on Shaiba succeeded, but with their defeat at Shaiba their activities round Ahwaz slackened off.

May-June, 1915
2nd Battalion

to their girths. Near the banks of the Kharka there was water, but so brackish that it increased rather than assuaged thirst, being moreover "as warm as soup and about the same colour."[1] The Kharka was both rapid and wide, a serious obstacle which was only crossed with considerable difficulty and the exercise of much ingenuity in improvising methods, though the enemy showed no disposition to make a stand and offered little serious opposition. The battalion had a good deal of skirmishing, but was in reserve on May 15th when one of the chief villages of the district, Khafajiyu, was successfully attacked and destroyed; indeed it had rather to endure hardships and privations than to encounter actual enemies. It was during the march to this village that the battalion suffered special hardships. Its brigade had not crossed the Kharka river at Illa, where the bulk of the force had, and the last stage of the march was a terrible time. Men were fainting everywhere, and as there were only about 20 riding mules to take the place of an ambulance only the worst cases could be given a mount, and the majority, when brought to, had to stagger along as best they could. Sometimes those who were riding had to get off and walk to make room for worse cases. The battalion owed a great deal to its bheestis, who did splendid work, going off to the river at every halt and fetching water back over a considerable distance, thanks to which the men succeeded in completing the march. After the capture of Khafajiyu the brigade crossed the river, though not without difficulty; all the transport animals had to be swum across and the men and equipment to be ferried across on improvised pontoons made of light framework of boxwood covered with canvas and paddled with entrenching shovels, which proved quite effective for the purpose. But the operations were highly successful. A sharp lesson was inflicted on the Beni Taruf, the security of the pipe-line was assured,

[1] cf. "The Long Road to Baghdad," E. Candler, i. 244.

MESOPOTAMIA, 1915.

and Persian Arabistan cleared of the enemy. More- June-July, over, General Gorringe was able to co-operate effectu- 2nd Battalion ally with the advance of the Sixth Indian Division up the Tigris on Amara.

This force, the original " I.E.F. D," now under General Townshend, had defeated the Turkish forces near Qurna in the remarkable amphibious encounter in the marshes generally known as " Townshend's Regatta," in which The Queen's Own was only represented by a little party who had been detailed to act as marines on the river flotilla when the battalion moved to Ahwaz. The steamers had hurried on ahead after the action, reaching Amara on June 3rd and receiving its surrender. To this result General Gorringe's operations contributed directly. They had already diverted Turkish reinforcements from the Tigris, and now a portion of his force threatened to intercept the retreat of the Turkish forces and consequently accelerated their withdrawal. His troops had remained in camp for a few days trying to collect supplies which were none too plentiful, the only fuel available being camel dung. For the whole force to move against Amara was out of the question, but a column was organised under Colonel Dunlop, of the 44th Merwaras, who was commanding the 12th Brigade, as Major-Gen. Lean, who had recently replaced General Davison, had gone sick. This included the battalion (less No. IV. Company), the 67th and 90th Punjabis and a field battery, and this force, cutting loose from its communications, pushed for Amara, while the main body of the force under General Gorringe himself returned to Ahwaz. Colonel Dunlop's column got near enough to hear General Townshend's guns, but a fight was denied it, and in the final move from Bisaitin to Amara, a matter of ten days, in the course of which the marshes had to be crossed, the battalion's trials had reached the culminating point. The heat was intense,

MESOPOTAMIA, 1915.

July, 1915
2nd Battalion

the men were heavily laden, rations were short and water brackish. But if the 2nd R.W.K. had no chance of proving its qualities in action, it distinguished itself by the lowness of its sick rate and by the splendid way in which the men had stuck to their work, often fainting from sheer exhaustion and yet managing to march in with the rear guard.

But the battalion was soon to have fighting of quite sufficient severity to satisfy anyone. General Nixon, who had taken over the Mesopotamian command early in April, had received instructions to prepare for the effective occupation of the Basra vilayet (district) which practically meant securing the Tigris up to Kut al Amara and the Euphrates to Nasiriya. With Townshend already at Amara, nearly 100 miles up-stream from Qurna, it was necessary to secure the left flank by capturing Nasiriya before attempting an advance beyond Amara. The Twelfth Division was detailed for this work and the battalion was accordingly withdrawn down-stream to Basra, where, on July 3rd, a draft joined from India. Five days later a start was made, Headquarters and Nos. I. and III. Companies leaving by steamer for Qurna, whence the Euphrates was followed to a point six miles below Nasiriya. Here General Gorringe's leading brigade had been temporarily brought to a standstill, after having overcome the first opposition encountered a dozen miles lower down.

The battalion found the British troops established in trenches among palm-groves on both banks of the river, with the Turks strongly entrenched opposite them. Anything of the nature of a turning movement was precluded, as except for belts of dry ground extending a few hundred yards inland on both banks of the river the country was under water, so direct attack was inevitable. Some sand hills on the right bank of the Euphrates were believed to be the key of the position, and the battalion was detailed to attack them,

NASIRIYA.

but after Captain Graham had carried out a most daring and useful reconnaissance of the position, the orders were cancelled, and when the attempt was made it was entrusted to a battalion of the 30th Brigade, who despite much gallantry failed to secure the position. In this attack the men had to wade through flood-water, and when they had to withdraw many of the wounded were drowned. However, an attack in the early hours of July 14th had established the British advanced line within about 400 yards of the Turkish trenches, but the battalion was not engaged in this, though it took over the front-line trenches on the 17th and held them for two days under a good deal of sniping. On July 20th the remaining companies[1] arrived, having left Basra on the 16th, but being delayed through their steamer taking the ground in the shallow Hammar Lake; the men had had to be disembarked and to help to haul the steamer over the shallows by means of ropes.

July, 1915
2nd Battalion

By July 23rd General Gorringe had completed his preparations. The 30th Brigade was to attack on the right bank, the 12th on the left. The Turkish trenches on this bank ran back rather obliquely from the river along the edge of a grove of date-palms. On the left of their line were a couple of fortified towers, in rear of which the Maiyadiya creek ran roughly parallel to the trench-line. At the right or river end of the Turkish trenches the lines were about 400 yards apart, and at this point the battalion was posted. It was to lead the attack, some of the 90th Punjabis were in support, the rest of the 90th and the 67th Punjabis holding a trench in continuation to the right of the battalion's front line. The battalion's machine-guns, with the rest of those of the Brigade, were in the trenches of the 90th to assist in giving covering-fire.

July 23rd, 1915
See Sketch 10

---

[1] No. IV. had not shared in the move to Amara but had been sent back from Bisaitin to Ahwaz, and had come direct from that station to Basra, rejoining prior to the move up the Euphrates.

MESOPOTAMIA, 1915.

July 24th, 1915
2nd Battalion

No. III. Company was on the left, the directing flank, with No. I. on its right, No. IV. supported No. III., No. II. being behind No. I.

At 5 a.m. on the 24th the bombardment opened. It was a heavy one judged by Mesopotamian standards, and the guns made good practice, but when the time came for the advance the Turks were by no means shaken and put up a stiff resistance. The leading companies went over the top at 5.30 and pushed rapidly forward. As the date-palms concealed the advance of our infantry from the artillery it was arranged that the left flank of the advancing troops should carry a conspicuous yellow flag to mark the progress of the advance. This naturally attracted the attention of the Turkish marksmen, and many times the flag-bearer was shot down, but as often as this happened the flag was promptly picked up and carried forward unflinchingly by a new bearer. On reaching the edge of the date-palms in front of the trenches the leaders came under a very heavy fire, which for the moment checked the attack. But Major Kitson and the supports were close behind, and as they came up the leading companies pushed on with them. " It was the most magnificent sight," wrote an officer of the 90th Punjabis, " to watch those fellows going up under the terrific fusillade from their front . . . in spite of the casualties, just as if they were on a manœuvre parade. As soon as they got up to the trenches they wheeled round to the right, so we had to stop our fire for fear of hitting them. . . . They got in with their bayonets and all we could see from where we were was Mr. Turk running as if the Devil himself were after him." What had happened was that on the right, even after the arrival of the supports, the next rush had come to a standstill 100 yards from the enemy's trenches. However, while the right companies were firing at the Turkish loopholes and keeping down the rifle-fire of

NASIRIYA.

the defence,[1] Nos. III. and IV. on the left had pushed on unchecked. Here there was a little more cover and, led by Major Kitson, they had got in all mixed up together and carried the Turkish trench. Sergt. Wannell, of No. IV., was one of the first into the Turkish trenches, and led a party from point to point, clearing the Turks out with rifle and bayonet, as well as using bombs[2] with great effect. C.S.M. Elliott was also among the first to reach the enemy's lines and led several bayonet charges, while C.S.M. Newbrook[3] was also conspicuous for gallantry and good leading, remaining with his men, though severely wounded, until the end of the day.

July 24th, 1915
2nd Battalion

Directly Nos. III. and IV. got in on the Turkish flank and began to work to the right, Nos. I. and II. sprang up again and swept over the trenches opposite them, a company of the 90th Punjabis following close behind. A good many Turks were bayonetted there and then, many were taken, and the remainder bolted to their left. Then, while the other two companies pushed straight ahead with their left on the river bank, Nos. I. and II. worked steadily forward toward the towers on the Turkish left. The enemy put up a good fight and reinforcements from the 90th and 67th Punjabis came up to find the firing-line of the battalion beginning to run out of ammunition and held up for the time on the edge of a cleared space; Nos. I. and II. at the towers, Nos. III. and IV. near Thorneycroft Corner on the river bank. It was now about 7.15; the enemy were putting up a stubborn resistance, and Colonel Pedley reported that his left was very weak. Half

---

[1] It says a good deal for British markmanship that when the Turkish dead in these trenches were afterwards examined the majority of them proved to have been shot through the face.

[2] This was the first occasion on which the 2nd Battalion had used bombs, the kind employed being the " Hales " grenade.

[3] All these N.C.O.'s received the D.C.M., together with Ptes. Bye and Bridger, decorated for gallantry in succouring wounded, and Pte. Howe, who went to the assistance of a wounded officer who was attacked by six Turks, five of whom he shot or bayonetted.

MESOPOTAMIA, 1915.

July 24th, 1915
2nd Battalion

a battalion of the 67th Punjabis came up on this flank and reinforced, and thus assisted and replenished with ammunition the battalion got forward again. One company of the 90th Punjabis reached the front of the attack to find about twenty of The Queen's Own, under Sergt. Edwards,[1] well ahead of everyone else, and hotly engaged with about 100 Arabs, but with the aid of the 90th the right-hand tower was rushed about 9 o'clock, and half-an-hour later mixed parties of Punjabis and R.W.K. stormed the second tower after a hard tussle. A fresh advance then drove the enemy beyond the Maiyadiya Creek, four guns being captured at this point and another village with more towers cleared in the process. There was another pause for reorganization and then, about mid-day, another advance, with the 67th Punjabis in the lead this time, and the battalion on their left. Opposition was lessening by now and the enemy's final line of defence, at the Sadanawiya Creek, was carried with much less difficulty than their stubbornly defended original position, the battalion assisting the 67th Punjabis with effective covering-fire, while fine work was done by Captain Nunn, R.N., who came up the river in a stern wheel steamer and, despite heavy fire, enfiladed the Turkish trenches effectively with the 3-pounder which it carried. Meanwhile the 30th Brigade had been equally successful; on both banks the Turks had been routed, and by the evening they were in full retreat.

The great strength of the position attacked, the stubborn resistance offered and the very unfavourable conditions in which the action was fought, a shade temperature over 110 deg. and a damp and humid atmosphere calculated to be exhausting even to the lightly clad,[2] make the action of Nasiriya an achievement worthy of the highest praise, and the battalion's

[1] This N.C.O. received the D.C.M. for his gallantry.

[2] " In no other theatre of war," writes one War Diary, " are men put to such a high test of endurance."

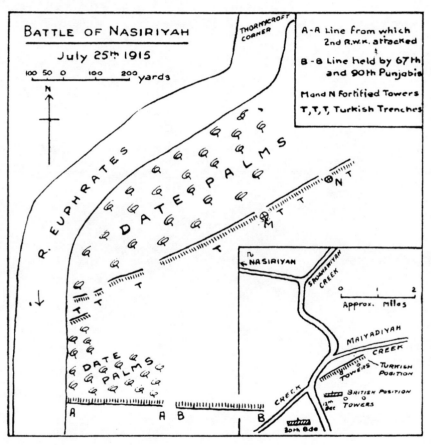

MESOPOTAMIA, 1915.

conduct earned it a well-deserved commendation from General Gorringe. In his despatch describing the Nasiriya operations he wrote that " the gallantry of the Royal West Kent, under Lieut.-Col. Pedley, set an example which was followed without hesitation by the remainder of the brigade. This initial success gave an impetus to the operations, the value of which it is difficult to over-estimate. Too much credit cannot be given for the splendid work they did during that eventful hour." And when addressing the battalion a few weeks later he spoke no less emphatically: " no words of mine," said he, " can adequately express my appreciation and feeling of praise to you for your conduct on July 24th." The D.S.O. was subsequently awarded to Captain Nelson for these operations, Lieut. Balbernie received the M.C., and Colonel Pedley the C.B., while Major Kitson was promoted to Brevet Lieut.-Col.[1]

July-Nov., 1915 2nd Battalion

But the battalion's losses had been heavy; less than 500 of all ranks had actually gone over the top (excluding the machine-gun section, reserve ammunition party and other details), six officers and 150 men were in the casualty list. Three officers had been killed, Captain Graham, a competent and popular officer of over ten years' service, who had been a mainstay of the 2nd Battalion's athletics, Lieut. Howell, another popular leader, and 2nd-Lieut. Elton, who had been promoted into the Regiment shortly after the outbreak of war. Captains Nelson and Ingram were wounded, as well as 2nd-Lieut. Howe. As Captain Searight and Lieut. Barnes had already been invalided, while Major Woulfe-Flanagan and Lieut. Clarke were actually in the Field Ambulance on the river bank just behind the trenches during the action, and were almost immediately afterwards dispatched to India, and Cap-

[1] Captain F. A. Robinson, R.A.M.C., who had been with the battalion since mobilisation also received the M.C. for his gallantry in this action.

tains Belgrave and Hibbert and Lieut. Piggott had received Staff appointments, the battalion was thus left terribly weak in officers and with under 400 rank and file. However, the victory had been decisive enough; all local opposition ceased, the remnants of the Turkish troops—they had lost over 1,000 prisoners and nearly 20 guns, and many hundreds of dead were found in their trenches—decamped to a respectful distance, and Nasiriya was occupied without further fighting, nor was its garrison destined to be troubled by anything more than stray Arab snipers for some months to come.

<small>July-Nov., 1915
2nd Battalion</small>

Directly the town had been occupied the transfer of troops back to the Tigris line for the advance on Kut was begun. In that advance The Queen's Own was represented only by the few men serving as machine gunners on the flotilla which co-operated with General Townshend's force. Some of these distinguished themselves in the battle for Kut, and three, Corpl. Bax and Ptes. Mires and Pannett, earned the D.C.M. for bold and skilful handling of their weapons.[1] But the 12th Brigade was left on the Euphrates and many months were to pass before the battalion saw the last of Nasiriya. Early in August it received a welcome draft of 200 officers and men, volunteers from Territorial battalions in India. These included Lieut. Haslam and 41 men from the 4th R.W.K., and similar detachments from the 5th Battalion under Lieut. Marshall, and from the 5th Buffs and 2/4th and 2/6th Devons. Their arrival brought the battalion's much depleted ranks up to a respectable strength again, and with the improvement in the climate that accompanied the advance of autumn the sick rate declined and a certain number of recovered sick and wounded rejoined. Brig.-Gen. McNab, who had joined the Brigade soon after the fall of Nasiriya, was invalided after about a month and replaced by Brig.-Gen. H. T. Brooking, till then in command at Bushire. Early in November

[1] Pte. Back also received the D.C.M. for gallantry in this action.

MESOPOTAMIA, 1915.

the uneventful course of the battalion's doings was broken by a sudden order for two companies to proceed at once down river to Qurna for employment at Kut al Amara, from which place the Sixth Division had advanced on Baghdad. Nos. II. and IV. Companies accordingly left Nasiriya on November 9th under Major Nelson.[1] There was a general hope that the departure of this detachment was only the prelude to the move of the whole battalion to a more active theatre of operations, twice before it was noted had this happened, but this was not to be, and the end of 1915 found the headquarter wing still at Nasiriya, by which time Major Nelson's detachment was already in its fourth week as part of the closely invested garrison of Kut. A small reinforcement had been received on December 1st consisting of Major Woulfe-Flanagan, Captain Case Morris and 23 men, recovered sick and wounded, but otherwise December had proved quite uneventful.[2]

Nov.-Dec., 1915
2nd Battalion

---

[1] Promoted to that rank on Sept. 1st in a promotion which included no less than eleven Captains and went down as far as Captain Lynch-White.

[2] This chapter was already in page-proof before the publication of Volume I. of the official account of the campaign, written by Brig.-Gen. F. J. Moberly, which gives an excellent account of the operations in Arabistan and at Nasiriya. It has been impossible, therefore, to utilize it in compiling this narrative.

CHAPTER VII

TRENCH WARFARE, 1915.

May, 1915

On a really broad view of the story of the British Army on the Western Front from 1914 to 1918 the most notable features of May 1915 was not the bitter and protracted struggles to keep the Germans out of Ypres, nor the repulse of the Aubers Ridge attack of May 9th, from which so much had been hoped, but the arrival in France of the first instalment of the " New Armies." This marked a real turning point in the story of England's effort. The " Old Army," sustained by the Special Reserve and reinforced by the Territorials, had kept up its end in the face of appalling difficulties and odds; the tide must now begin to flow Eastward.

If at first some had feared that the New Armies would never get a look in, when the " New Army " Divisions did begin to appear they came too late for that immediate reversal of the fortunes of war for which some had fondly hoped. With the situation as thoroughly stabilized as it had become in France in the early summer of 1915 a sudden change was out of the question; it wanted a very big force to achieve even a small success. At the Aisne on September 14th, 1914, the reinforcement of the First Corps by the Sixth Division might have driven back the whole German right, and greatly altered the entire course of the war; in June 1915 such chances were a thing of the past. Still the arrival in quick succession of the Ninth, Fourteenth and Twelfth Divisions was an earnest of a mighty force to be reckoned with seriously by the Germans.

Jan.-June, 1915
6th Battalion

Included in General Wing's Twelfth Division was the senior Service battalion of The Queen's Own. After spending the mid-winter months at Hythe, during which period Colonel Even had left the battalion

TRENCH WARFARE, 1915.

for the War Office and had been succeeded by Major Venables, on which Major Beeching became second-in-command, the 6th R.W.K. had moved to Aldershot at the end of February. Here the remaining portion of its training had been passed, a period of hard work and of many rumours both as to the probable date of the battalion's departure for active service and still more as to its destination. Ultimately it was June 1st before the main body left Aldershot for Folkestone,[1] whence a night passage carried it to Boulogne. It was a good augury for the 6th that the Commandant of the Base Camp should have been a former C.O. of the 1st Battalion, Colonel Maunsell, who had been in command at the Depôt earlier in the war. On June 3rd the battalion entrained again, finding on the train the transport party, machine-gun section and other details under Major Beeching, who had preceded the main body by one day, travelling by Southampton and Havre. A long night journey took it to its detraining station at Wizernes, from which a couple of marches, rather trying to those who were making their first acquaintance with French roads in very sultry weather, brought it well within sound of the guns at Meteren on June 6th. A fortnight in billets followed, then came a week in which the battalion was attached by platoons and companies to the 19th Brigade for instruction in trench-warfare, after which it took over reserve trenches from the Warwickshire Territorials of the Forty-Eighth Division in the famous Ploegsteert Wood. On

Jan.-June, 1915
6th Battalion

[1] The officers who went overseas with the battalion were :—Colonel E. F. Venables, in command; Major H. C. W. Beeching, second-in-command; Captain G. E. Wingfield Stratford, Adjutant; Lieut. L. de B. Barnett, Machine-Gun Officer. A Company: Captains E. Hudson (commanding), and H. G. Margetts, Lieut. G. A. L. Hatton, 2nd-Lieuts. G. Brown, A. B. Francis and W. J. Alderman (Transport Officer). B Company: Captains J. C. Parker (commanding), and C. H. Towse, Lieut. M. L. W. Matthews, 2nd-Lieuts. A. G. Heath, H. C. Harris and J. S. Mann. C Company: Captain A. B. C. Francis (commanding), and W. R. A. Dawson, 2nd-Lieuts. K. Dykes, W. W. Pye and L. C. R. Smith. D Company: Captains R. P. P. Rowe (commanding) and E. T. Williams, 2nd-Lieuts. M. H. Carré, W. B. Hodgson-Smith and J. Langlands, also Captain Logan, R.A.M.C. (attached).

June-Sept., 1915
6th Battalion

the last day of June, the 6th moved up to relieve the 6th Buffs and found itself actually holding part of the British front line, and with the enemy only 150 yards away.

"Plugstreet Wood" in the summer of 1915 was not a particularly active quarter. Shortage of artillery ammunition was necessarily restricting to a minimum the offensive activities of the B.E.F. and the local tactical situation presented no exceptional features. Thus the two-and-a-half months which the 6th spent in this sector, or in the one immediately South of it, were marked by few outstanding incidents. But they were far from being a time of idleness or without value as training. The maintenance and improvement of the trenches involved constant work, vigilant patrolling had to be carried on, in the course of which Captain Dawson distinguished himself by daring and successful reconnaissances, and the battalion found it no easy job to establish an ascendency over the enemy's active and enterprizing snipers. But by the middle of August it was noted that there was a marked diminution in the enemy's rifle-fire, and though his expenditure of trench mortar ammunition had increased no great damage had resulted. On the whole casualties had been low; for July they amounted to 50 all told, 6 men being killed, and one officer, Lieut. Heath, and 43 other ranks wounded; for August they were lower, 5 men killed, two officers, Lieut. Hodgson Smith and 2nd-Lieut. Mann, and 28 men wounded, and as three drafts had joined and the sick-rate had been remarkably low the battalion was well up to strength. A noticeable incident was that which won for the battalion its first D.C.M., the first indeed won by any member of any Service Battalion in the war. This occurred on the morning of July 19th, when Sergt. Cresswell went out from the trenches under very heavy rifle-fire and brought in a wounded officer and a man of the next battalion, who had been hit while patrolling in "No Man's Land" and were lying

TRENCH WARFARE, 1915.

nearly 50 yards out from the line. The usual tour of duty in trenches was six days, following by six out, during which large working parties had constantly to be found. In these periods out of the line several inspections took place. On August 18th the battalion was inspected by Lord Kitchener and commended for its healthy appearance and hard work, while a little later the G.O.C. Second Army, General Sir H. Plumer, expressed himself highly satisfied with what he had seen, and held up to the battalion the glorious example of the 1st Battalion, declaring that he " never wished to have a better battalion under him."

July-Sept., 1915
6th Battalion

September saw the 6th entrusted with its first active enterprise. Between Monmouth House on the right and Essex Farm on the left there was an awkward re-entrant in the line which it was decided to straighten out by constructing a breastwork across the chord of the arc. After dark one evening a strong covering party was pushed out in front and, thus protected, working parties threw up during the hours of darkness a line over 100 yards in length which was connected up with the old line by a communication trench called Sevenoaks Tunnel. The work was carried out without interference from the enemy and was a very satisfactory and useful performance, greatly improving the line. One more tour of duty in these trenches followed, costing the battalion its first officer, Lieut. Bingham Stevens, killed on September 17th, a day of more than usual artillery and trench-mortar activity, and then the 6th moved away from Ploegsteert, passing Southward to the area South-East of Bethune, where, on September 25th, the First Army had delivered its attack on Loos. Its apprenticeship was over,[1] a severe test was before it.

---

[1] The 6th's losses in action up to the end of September came to just 100: 1 officer and 13 other ranks killed, 4 officers and 82 other ranks wounded. It had received drafts amounting to 2 officers and 140 other ranks, and at the end of September it mustered 27 officers and 996 men, of whom 1 officer and 43 men were detached on various employments.

TRENCH WARFARE, 1915.

April-July, 1915
7th Battalion

By this time two more Service battalions had followed the 6th to the front, the 7th and the 8th. The 7th, which had moved from Purfleet to Colchester in April for Brigade training and then to Salisbury Plain for Divisional training, had had experiences not unlike those of the 6th, much hard work compressed into a short space, training not a little delayed by the want of proper weapons and equipment, changes in officers and N.C.O.'s, the most notable being that Major Stevenson, the second-in-command, was not passed for active service. Major Stevenson had done admirable work in building up and training the new unit, and the battalion parted with him with regret. His place was taken by another Regular officer of The Queen's Own, Major J. T. Twisleton-Wykeham-Fiennes, who had till then been detained as a Company Commander at the R.M.C., where Major Stevenson succeeded him, while another link with the pre-war Regiment was provided when Colonel Martyn, who had taken the 1st Battalion out to France, took over command of the 55th Brigade. Various dates had been provisionally fixed for its departure, but it was July before the Eighteenth Division got its orders for France and not till the end of the month did the 7th Battalion set foot in France, landing at Havre on the 27th.[1] It was not destined for any of those parts of the "front" with which the B.E.F. had become familiar, for the Eighteenth Division had been allotted to the newly-formed Third Army which began relieving the French on the right bank of the Somme at the end of July. To Bray, therefore, the 7th

August, 1915

[1] The officers who proceeded overseas with the 7th Battalion were: Colonel A. W. Prior (commanding), Major Fiennes (second-in-command), Captain Anstruther (Adjutant), Lieut. Hackett (Transport Officer), Lieut. Rich (Signal Officer), Lieut. Maloney (Quartermaster), Lieut.-Col. Ryall (D), Captains Phillips (B), Snelgrove (A), Summers (C) (Company Commanders), Captains Webber (D), R. B. Holland (B), Waddington (C) and Latter (A) (Second Captains), Lieuts. Russell, Heaton, Skinner and Warren, 2nd-Lieuts. Dennis, Mackenzie (Machine-Gun Officers), Tindall (Sniping Officer), Emden, J. B. Matthews, Pymm, Johnson, Cross, Proud, Lucas, Lewin, D. S. Freeman, C. S. Stevenson and Longley (Platoon Commanders).

TRENCH WARFARE, 1915.

made its way, and August found the battalion under- Aug., 1915
7th Battalion
going its initiation into trench warfare at Bois Français in the neighbourhood of Carnoy.

It was not the only representative of The Queen's June-July, 1915
1st Battalion
Own in that district, for the 1st Battalion had recently preceded it to the Third Army's area, having reached Corbie by train on July 31st, and had relieved French troops in front of Carnoy on the first anniversary of the declaration of war. Since " Hill 60 " the 1st Battalion had had a quieter time. After a short period of rest it had gone into the trenches again near St. Eloi at the end of May. Here it spent the next two months, tours of duty in the trenches alternating with periods in huts at Dickebusch. The Germans opposite the battalion were fairly lively and there was much trench-mortaring and sniping, varied by occasional bombardments. On June 15th, for example, the British guns developed heavy fire as a diversion in favour of the Third Division's attempt to recover the Bellewarde Ridge near Hooge, while a month later the Germans opened a bombardment which seemed to prelude an attack in force. Actually the German infantry did begin to leave their trenches, but despite the bombardment The Queen's Own were ready for them and promptly opened a rapid fire which sent them packing back to cover and nipped in the bud anything serious that may have been intended. The battalion again was fortunate in missing by a bare half-hour the explosion of a mine under one of the trenches in its sector, an explosion which inflicted 120 casualties on the K.O.Y.L.I., who had just relieved it. As it was the total casualties from May 8th to the end of July came to just over 160,[1] and as several drafts had arrived and a good many officers had joined, the

---

[1] One officer (2nd-Lieut. Richardson) and 30 men killed or died of wounds, 2 officers (Captain Knox and Lieut. Carpenter) and 135 other ranks wounded.

TRENCH WARFARE, 1915.

July, 1915
1st Battalion

battalion was well up to strength[1] when the Fifth Division was transferred to the newly-formed Tenth Corps, under its old Divisional Commander, General Morland, in the Third Army. Before leaving Flanders for the Somme it was reviewed by the Army and Corps Commanders under whom it had been serving and was warmly praised for its splendid work. " You are handing over the line," said the Corps Commander (General Sir C. Ferguson), " to those who succeed you in a very different and improved condition from what it was when you took it over. It remains as a very fine record of the good work you have done." Indeed, the battalion could look back with legitimate satisfaction on its work in the Ypres Salient. If " Hill 60 " had been its most brilliant and outstanding exploit, its counter-attack on April 23rd had been in some ways of even greater importance, while to hold to trenches, as it had so often had to do, under severe punishment to which no effective reply could be made had been in reality an almost more searching test of courage, discipline and endurance.

Aug.-Dec.,
1915
1st and 7th
Battalions

The 1st and 7th Battalions were to find the new line which the British had taken over a somewhat peaceful part of the war. In the five months of 1915 which the 1st spent in the Carnoy sector its total battle casualties came to 56, including 3 officers wounded and 11 men killed or died of wounds, a striking contrast even to the " trench-warfare " losses of the winter of 1914-1915. The losses of the 7th similarly amounted to well under 100. This was partly to be accounted for by the strategical situation. Shortage of munitions was still sufficiently pronounced to preclude any major operation on the British side except the attempted break through

---

[1] During this period Colonel Robinson was made a Brevet Lt.-Col. and Captain Moulton-Barrett awarded the M.C. in recognition of the " Hill 60 " operations. Captains Buchanan-Dunlop and Moulton-Barrett were both invalided home in May, Captain Lynch White taking over the duties of Adjutant, but in July Captain Buchanan-Dunlop rejoined and became second-in-command, being in temporary command for a month as Colonel Robinson was away on sick leave.

TRENCH WARFARE, 1915.

of the First Army at Loos in September. Had that Aug.-Dec., 1915 offensive gone really well the Fifth Division was to 1st Battalion have attacked the Pommiers Ridge which faced the Carnoy sector, but this had to remain a paper project, and the Third Army remained inactive. It was this same shortage of ammunition which prevented the practice of "raiding" from being as extensively followed as it was to be in the summer of 1916 and in the following winter, when for a raid by one or two companies almost as much heavy artillery and ammunition was available as had been vouchsafed to three whole Divisions at Neuve Chapelle in March 1915. Only towards the end of 1915 did the Third Army begin to raid, and then only on a small scale.

But the Germans opposite the Third Army were equally unaggressive, and when they did indulge in an occasional "hate" in the shape of a bombardment by heavy artillery or more often by trench mortars, casualties were much reduced by the well-developed state of the trench system. The ground in this district being largely chalk, the work of cutting out trenches and, in fine weather at any rate, of keeping them in repair was much easier than in the mud and swamps of Flanders, while in the construction of dug-outs, communication trenches and various contrivances to make life in trenches rather less uncomfortable, the French had done much, assisted thereto by the somewhat pacific attitude adopted by both sides. When the 1st Battalion took over the Carnoy trenches the thickness of the parapet was not up to its standard, but this was soon remedied and the parapet made bullet-proof, while other improvements were put in hand, fire-steps were rivetted, trenches deepened and drained, the wire in front of the line repaired. As far as ammunition supply permitted the pacific attitude was abandoned. If there was no major offensive and little artillery activity, snipers and trench mortars were usually busy and the acquisition of an elephant gun warranted to penetrate the enemy's

TRENCH WARFARE, 1915.

Aug.-Dec., 1915
1st Battalion

loop-hole plates and of a catapult capable of throwing hand-grenades across No Man's Land were hailed with satisfaction. Patrols went out frequently but the enemy seemed disinclined to venture much into No Man's Land, and our patrols found little to report. A couple of the 1st Battalion's daily Intelligence Reports will give some idea of the daily round:—

> "Enemy's working parties were seen apparently rivetting parapet in their front line trenches at 6 a.m. in front of 60 Trench. Enemy fired two T.M. (trench mortar) bombs just in front of 52 at 7.45 p.m. last night; our howitzers replied. About midnight working parties were noisy in front of 53. Enemy has been very quiet and done little sniping. They had the wind up last night about 9 p.m., firing a good deal and sending up a number of lights. They apparently imagined we had a patrol out. Enemy refrained from replying in any way to our Catapult Battery this morning."
> —(November 4th, 1915.)
>
> "45 T.M. bombs fired this afternoon elicited a response of four rifle grenades, three of which were "duds." It seems to be impossible to upset the equanimity of the Germans opposite us."— (November 27th, 1915.)

In September Colonel Robinson was promoted to command the 112th Brigade, on which Major Buchanan-Dunlop obtained command of the battalion and Captain Newton became Adjutant, and later in the month Major Lynch White received a Staff appointment.

Aug.-Dec., 1915
7th Battalion

The 7th Battalion found the last five months of 1915 comparatively quiet. In the second week of August it went into the Fifth Division's trenches for instruction, A Company having the good fortune to have its own 1st Battalion as its instructors. Individual instruction was first given, officers, N.C.O.'s and men being shown their duties by the corresponding individuals in the instructing unit. In the next stage the new hands went in by platoons and finally by companies, in each case replacing an equivalent unit. This over, the battalion assumed responsibility for a section of the line on August 23rd. The Eighteenth Division's trenches were to the left of those held by the Fifth and faced the Pommiers Ridge between Fricourt and Montauban. Here the advantage of ground lay with the Germans,

Colonel P. M. ROBINSON, C.B., C.M.G.
Commanded 1st Battalion, 1914, 1915.

Lieut.-Colonel H. D. BUCHANAN DUNLOP, C.M.G., D.S.O.
Commanded 1st Battalion, 1915 and 1916.

TRENCH WARFARE, 1915.

whose trenches were higher up the slope, and as the defences required much work, parapets not being bullet-proof, shelters and dug-outs being most inadequate, communication trenches and parados out of repair, the 7th had a busy time. The Germans were fairly active, and on August 23rd they blew a mine under the left of the battalion's line but found the 7th so much on the alert that they were unable to occupy the crater thus formed or to prevent the battalion occupying and consolidating another crater formed four days later by the explosion of a British counter mine. The 7th came out from its first tour very cheerful and confident. It had suffered a dozen casualties but had fully held its own with the enemy, and had accomplished any amount of useful work.

Until the end of the year the 7th continued in the same area, generally holding the same sector, known as E.1., and relieving and being relieved by the 7th Buffs. The sector had the reputation of being " quiet," but when the 7th first went into it the German snipers were so much in the ascendant that their working parties exposed themselves unhesitatingly, expecting their snipers to keep the British rifle-fire completely under. This situation could not be tolerated, and the 7th set to work to put things right. Fortunately before the battalion had left Salisbury Plain a special squad of snipers had been organised by Major Fiennes, and these men, who had been specially trained and equipped, soon proved their value. The squad was commanded by Lieut. C. G. Tindall, and was composed of 24 picked shots of good physique and intelligence, including, it is to be noted, several men who had in civil life been gamekeepers. These snipers worked in pairs, one man observing, the other shooting. Special positions were chosen and carefully protected and concealed. On the left of the sector the ground rose a little and good positions could be found in old trenches from which the German line could be observed and even enfiladed; on

Aug.-Dec., 1915
7th Battalion

the right places were harder to find, and finally they had to be constructed in the parados of the fire-trench. The men went to their posts just before dawn and remained till dusk, keeping a sharp watch on everything that went on in the German lines and combining intelligence duties with their sniping. So well thought out and executed were these measures that the battalion had soon got the Germans in hand; within two days their snipers had had to move their posts, and before long the Germans were so completely dominated that it proved necessary to forbid our men to sit on top of the parapet, a thing they could not have done with impunity when they first went into the line.[1]

In the same way the machine-gun officer, Lieut. McKenzie, and his detachment set about their work with great zeal and skill. Great care was taken in selecting the sites of the machine-gun emplacements and in controlling their fire. Systematic shooting was practised at points where working parties had been observed or suspected and the intelligence furnished by Lieut. Tindall's snipers enabled the machine-gunners to record several successes. More than once when a fog lifted they found themselves presented with good targets, and the battalion soon acquired a reputation throughout the Division.

Before the end of the year the 7th saw several changes in its senior officers. On October 12th Colonel Prior was forced to relinquish command. He had been a most capable and efficient commander and the battalion was not a little indebted to his instruction and example, but his health proved unequal to the strain of active service. Major Fiennes succeeded to the command, and Captain Phillips became

---

[1] At a meeting of the National Rifle Association in 1916 special reference was made to the success with which a battalion of The Queen's Own had got the upper hand of the Germans in sniping by careful and systematic measures and by developing the science of sniping; it was evidently to the 7th's achievements that the reference was being made.

TRENCH WARFARE, 1915.

second-in-command; Colonel Ryall also went home about the same time, Captains R. B. Holland and Waddington taking command of B and C Companies respectively. About the same time the 7th parted regretfully from General Martyn, who was transferred to a brigade in the Twenty-Second Division, which had just been ordered to Salonica.[1]

Thanks largely to the good work of all ranks on the defences and to the efficiency in offensive work of its machine-gunners and snipers the 7th's total losses up to the end of 1915 were, as already stated, under 100 killed and wounded. A mine explosion on December 21st, at the Tambour, a salient in the British line 50 yards from the German trenches, saw several officers and men gassed, but afforded the battalion its first distinctions; Captain Waddington, who, though himself gassed, not only directed the work of rescue but went down a gallery and brought out three men himself, was awarded the M.C., while D.C.M.'s were awarded to Sergt. Levy, Corpl. Hillyard and Pte. Moore, who were all conspicuous in the work. It was at this same danger spot, the Tambour, that the battalion lost its first officer, Captain Summers being killed there on December 29th while in charge of a "mining fatigue," in which work Lieuts. Russell and Innocent were wounded about the same time. But if neither the battalion nor the Eighteenth Division as a whole had been put to any severe test in their first five months of active service they had been sufficiently tried to prove their worth and give good promise of solid achievements to come, and the end of the year found them steady and efficient soldiers.

[1] General Martyn had previously served in the Balkans with the Gendarmerie and was an interpreter in Turkish, which was the reason for his transfer. The climate of Macedonia, however, proved too much for his health, and he was soon invalided. He subsequently recovered enough to be given the command at the Cape, which he held for over a year.

CHAPTER VIII

LOOS.

Jan.-Aug., 1915
8th Battalion

If the 7th R.W.K. reached the end of 1915 without taking part in any major operation, such was not the lot of the third Service Battalion of the Regiment to go overseas. The 8th Battalion's early experiences had closely resembled those of the 6th and 7th. It had to wait longer for its khaki uniforms, for rifles that could be used for other purposes than learning the manual—it was only issued with service rifles in July—for equipment of every variety. Until "K 1" and "K 2" were fully equipped the wants of "K 3" could not be supplied, and its training was naturally not a little impeded thereby. And it would be absurd to pretend that in the matter of trained instructors "K 3" battalions fared as well as the earlier-formed units. The Regular officers and N.C.O.'s left behind by the 1st Battalion or serving at the Depôt were only a handful, and of the ex-officers and men who rejoined those with the more recent experience were naturally posted to the battalions first for service. Similarly very few of the newly-appointed junior officers of "K 3" had any appreciable degree of military training. It is all the more honour, therefore, to Colonel Vansittart and those associated with him in training the 8th R.W.K., and to the officers and men who had to prepare for service in face of such handicaps and discomforts, that when the battalion came to go overseas it was acknowledged to have become a really fine and efficient unit.

What Hythe and Aldershot had represented in the 6th Battalion's progress towards readiness for service, and Purfleet, Colchester and Codford in the case of the 7th, Shoreham-on-Sea, Worthing and Blackdown had been to the 8th. It had moved to Worthing at the end of November and stayed there till the end of

LOOS.

March, when it returned to Shoreham for another couple of months. The concentration in the Aldershot District at the end of June of the Twenty-Fourth Division had been hailed as the preliminary to the transfer to France, and this followed on August 29th after a peculiarly strenuous final preparation.[1] But the Division was not to go through the same gradual initiation into active service conditions as the Twelfth and Eighteenth had gone through. When it landed in France[2] preparations for the coming offensive by the First Army were already well advanced, and, together with another newly-arrived "K 3" Division, the Twenty-Fourth was allotted to General Haking's Eleventh Corps, which was to constitute the reserves for the attack. To criticise this use of raw and inexperienced troops is easy after the event, as it is also to overlook the administrative difficulties in the way of putting these new Divisions into the line at quiet spots and drawing out more seasoned units for employment in the attack. Certainly the conditions under which the 8th R.W.K. was to endure its baptism of fire demanded the highest qualities of skill and leadership, endurance and discipline.

September, 1915
8th Battalion

The task before the Eleventh Corps was to support the advance of the centre which, covered by defensive flanks to be formed facing La Bassée on the left and Lens on the right, was intended to penetrate the Ger-

See Sketch 11

---

[1] The Division was now under Major-Gen. Sir J. Ramsay, the battalion being in the 72nd Brigade (Brigadier-Gen. Mitford).

[2] The officers who proceeded overseas with the 8th Battalion were as follows: Colonel E. Vansittart (commanding), Major L. Brock-Hollinshead (second-in-command), Captain C. de C. Middleton (Adjutant), Lieut. W. K. Tillie (Machine-Gun Officer), Lieut. S. R. Paul (Transport Officer), Lieut. H. Evans (Quartermaster), R.S.M. A. Lee. A Company: Major A. H. Pullman, Lieuts. R. M. Old, H. S. Brown and L. Gibbs, 2nd-Lieut. C. D. N. Lawson. B Company: Captain R. W. Grant, Lieuts. P. T. Smith and N. B. Green, 2nd-Lieuts. O. Jones, E. A. Bigsby and V. G. Don. C Company: Captains A. C. Edwards and C. A. Hutchinson, Lieut. H. L. Lewis, 2nd-Lieuts. D. H. Watts, M. S. Ell and A. N. Harris. D Company: Major J. C. Chillingworth, Captain P. M. Robertson-Ross, 2nd-Lieuts. H. O. Beer, R. F. T. Burrell, G. de L. Hough and D. W. Plant.

LOOS.

September, 1915
8th Battalion

man positions between Haisnes and Loos, push forward to the Deule Canal and cross it near Pont à Vendin. There, if all had gone well, it might hope to effect a junction with General Foch's Army, which, attacking South of Lens, was to work round that town and then swing leftward to meet the British. The first day's fighting saw the German defences penetrated on a wide front from Loos to the Hohenzollern Redoubt, and a defensive flank satisfactorily established on the right by the Forty-Seventh (London) Division.[1] In the centre, however, a check to the right brigade of the First Division had broken up the force of the attack, fragments only of the Division had reached Hulluch, and that important point had not been secured. Indeed, the Lens-La Bassée road had only been crossed by the First Division on its extreme right at Bois Hugo, and though the Fifteenth had taken Loos and pushed on over Hill 70 against the suburbs of Lens, its left flank was hardly secure.

Further to the left rather less success had attended the efforts of the First Corps; the Seventh and Ninth Divisions had begun well and in places had reached the enemy's second line, but it had proved impossible to take full advantage of the opportunity and before evening on September 25th counter-attacks had begun to press both Divisions back.

For September 26th it was proposed to utilize the Twenty-First and Twenty-Fourth Divisions of the Eleventh Corps, the former to take over Bois Hugo from the First Division and to push forward on the right of the Twenty-Fourth, which was to advance between Bois Hugo and Hulluch flanked on the left by a

---

[1] One unit of this was the 20th (Blackheath and Woolwich) Battalion of the London Regiment, which had been formed on the organization of the Territorial Force out of the old 2nd and 3rd Volunteer Battalions of the Royal West Kent; it had been allowed to retain the regimental badge, and was proud to recall its connection with The Queen's Own. This battalion distinguished itself greatly in the attack and earned several distinctions.

LOOS.

renewed attempt by the First Division against Hulluch. But before these two Divisions could reach their assembly positions a brigade of each had been diverted, one of the Twenty-First to Hill 70, which was being furiously counter-attacked, one of the Twenty-Fourth to assist in the defence of the Hohenzollern Redoubt.

Sept. 21st-25th, 1915 8th Battalion

Moreover, all manner of difficulties had contributed to delay their advance to the front. The area behind the battle zone was congested with every kind of traffic, through which the battalions of the Eleventh Corps could only thread their way slowly and with many checks. The 8th R.W.K. had spent the first three weeks of September encamped near Montreuil, devoting most of its time to field-firing and divisional exercises, and had started to march to the battle area on the evening of September 21st. It was four days, or rather nights, on the road, for its moves were carried out during the hours of darkness, and though the marches were not long the congestion of the roads by the voluminous traffic moving in the same direction caused many delays and made progress slow and exhausting.

Early on September 25th the Division moved forward to Vermelles, where it spent a day of rumours and anticipation, listening to the guns and watching wounded and prisoners coming down from the front. After dark the 72nd Brigade advanced in artillery formation past the Lone Tree trenches, which had so long held up the First Division. The move was covered by the scouts of the 8th R.W.K., who carried their work out well, pushing across the Lens-La Bassée road and reaching Hulluch, which they found held by the enemy. On this, orders were issued to the battalion to capture the village, but they were almost immediately cancelled and the battalion finally moved back to some trenches about 1,000 yards West of the Lens-La Bassée road. It had come under some shell-fire while moving up and rather more after reaching its halting-place, but had only a few casualties. But the men went

Sept. 26th, 1915
8th Battalion

into action next morning with but little water or food and very short of sleep.

The ground over which the Twenty-Fourth Division was to attack sloped down gently for some distance to the Lens-La Bassée road, beyond which it rose gradually to a rearward system of wire and trenches running from East of Hulluch to the outskirts of Lens and about 1,000 yards from the Lens-La Bassée road. Bois Hugo, which jutted out Eastward beyond the rest of the British line, was the key to the situation as it flanked the approach to the German trenches. Unfortunately, some time before the hour fixed for the Twenty-Fourth Division to advance, the Germans counter-attacked Bois Hugo, dislodged from this highly important position the brigade of the Twenty-First Division which was holding it, and filled the wood with machine-guns. The Twenty-First pushed reinforcements forward to recover Bois Hugo, but without any success, and the Twenty-Fourth's chances had already been imperilled when at 11 a.m., on the cessation of the bombardment, the 72nd Brigade advanced. It had been exposed since daybreak to a heavy artillery fire but had found enough shelter in old German trenches to escape heavy casualties, and the men went forward promptly and confidently. To the 8th R.W.K. had been assigned the left of the leading line with the 8th Queen's in support and the 9th East Surreys on the right supported by the 8th Buffs. At first all went well. Nothing could have surpassed the steadiness and regularity of the advance. Though under heavy fire from artillery and rifles from the outset, to which, as the advance progressed, was added machine-gun fire from their flanks, the 8th pressed on without wavering, the East Surreys keeping pace with them. At the Lens-La Bassée road, a natural range-mark for the enemy's gunners, they came in for exceptionally heavy and accurate fire, but still they pushed on. There were some Germans in advanced trenches who fell

LOOS.

back as the 72nd Brigade approached the road, suffering heavily from our men's fire, and the battalion swept on over these trenches, finding them full of German dead. On they went steadily and gallantly, up the gentle slope towards the German wire, though men fell fast as the machine-gun and artillery fire from the flanks increased in intensity. Still the 8th did not falter, and at last reached the German wire only to find it practically intact, for the bombardment, possibly because there had been no chance of effective registration, had been quite ineffective.

Sept. 26th, 1915
8th Battalion

The position was desperate. Some gallant but unavailing efforts were made to get through the wire, in which 2nd-Lieut. Don was conspicuous, but all that most of the men could do was to throw themselves on the ground and attempt to return the enemy's fire. For some time they hung on tenaciously, despite heavy losses, but to no avail. The East Surreys had been shot down wholesale from Bois Hugo, on the other wing the First Division had achieved nothing against Hulluch, and without support on the flanks the position was hopeless. Colonel Vansittart was wounded; one by one almost every other remaining officer was shot down; to hang on longer could only involve further useless sacrifices, and at last the remnants of the battalion had to fall back as best they could over the long space between them and the Lens-La Bassée road. It was then Lieut. Tillie, the machine-gun officer, distinguished himself greatly by the courage and resource which he displayed, and himself actually brought out of action the machine-gun which he had handled with skill and effect during the advance. Major Pullman, too, was conspicuous in this work; though wounded, he steadied the men by his influence and example and did much to extricate the survivors of the battalion in good order.[1]

[1] Major Pullman was awarded the D.S.O. and Lieut. Tillie the M.C., and the D.S.O. was subsequently awarded to Colonel Vansittart for his gallant leading, while 2nd-Lieut. Don was mentioned in despatches.

LOOS.

September, 1915
8th Battalion

When the remnants of the 72nd Brigade were relieved and withdrawn to Mollinghen it was evident that the task before the 8th R.W.K. was practically the reconstruction of the battalion. Of the 24 officers and 800 men who had actually gone into action only Lieut. Tillie and 250 men remained effective. [1]Colonel Vansittart,[x] Major Brock-Hollinshead, Major Chillingworth, Captain Middleton,[x] the Adjutant, Captains Edwards and Hutchinson[x] were all missing, along with Lieuts. Don, Old,[x] Smith, Gibbs, Harris, Burrell, Watts, Ell,[x] Bigsby and Plant; Captain Robertson-Ross and Lieuts. Lawson and Beer were known to be dead; Major Pullman, Captain Grant and Lieuts. Green, Lewis and Hough had been brought in wounded. To the survivors there were added those officers[2] and men who had been with the transport, but the battalion was clearly in no condition to go into action again until it had been completely reconstructed. The survivors were indeed to receive warm praise from the Brigadier, to be told that the 8th had " added glory " to the regiment to which it belonged, that it had been " an example in steadiness and determination . . . not only to the New Armies, but to seasoned troops," and to hear from the Corps Commander that even if the attack had failed to take its objective it had forced the enemy to divert large reserves from General Foch's front and thus had materially assisted the French. Certainly whatever the reasons for the failure to improve the First Army's initial success the 8th in its disastrous " baptism of fire " had done all that in it lay to achieve victory and had well upheld the name of The Queen's Own.

6th Battalion

As the remnant of the 8th was withdrawing from the battle area the 6th was nearing it from the North, and on September 30th the Twelfth Division

---

[1] The officers marked x were subsequently reported wounded and prisoners of war, the remainder were killed.

[2] Lieut. Paul and Lieut. and Quartermaster Evans.

GUN TRENCH.

relieved the Guards in the trenches facing those against which the 8th R.W.K. had been shattered. But in the Division's first tour of duty in this sector the 6th did not have to take over the front line, remaining in support first at Vermelles, then at Mazingarbe, and suffering about 50 casualties from the shelling of its billets. But this period was marked by a sad loss to the battalion together with the whole Twelfth Division, that of the man whom the Division could least afford to lose, its commander, General Wing, killed by a shell near Lone Tree. It is not too much to say that not only did the officers, subalterns and seniors alike, feel that they had lost a personal friend as well as an inspiring and trusted commander, but General Wing was known to and loved by the rank and file as well. He was always in the front trenches; no one was ever surprised to find him crawling along some half-dug sap in close proximity to the German line. He had trained the Division well, had been its real maker and organizer, and it was prepared to follow him anywhere with zeal and confidence.

_{Oct. 1915}
_{6th Battalion}

When the 6th did go into trenches on the night of Oct. 5th/6th, it took over a most curious piece of line. After the Seventh Division's initial success had carried it to the outskirts of Cité St. Elie counter-attacks had forced it back to Gun Trench, about half-way between the German front trenches and Cité St. Elie. Not only this, but the Germans had effected a lodgment in Gun Trench itself and were clinging on to about 150 yards in the centre of it. Thus when the 6th Battalion took over Gun Trench from the 2nd Scots Guards they found Germans between the two companies in the front line. Of these A, on the right, stretched from the Vermelles-Hulluch road Northward, having two platoons in a support trench 150 or 200 yards in rear, which, however, came to an end about level with the Southern end of the German lodgment. On the left C continued the front line N.W. along Stone Alley to within 120 yards of some quarries which

See Sketches 11 & 12

131

LOOS.

October 8th 1915
6th Battalion

formed an important tactical feature. D Company was in rear of A in close support, B being some distance further back. It was clear that the Germans must be promptly dislodged from Gun Trench, and after two days orders were received for an attack to be made on October 8th. These had been days of intermittent artillery fire, by which D in particular was considerably troubled, and of much bombing at the Southern end of the German part of Gun Trench, which together cost the battalion about a dozen casualties, including Lieut. G. W. Brown wounded, while one of the machine-guns was destroyed by an aerial torpedo; the battalion, however, had not been inactive and had taken its chances of replying effectively.

This attack was to be preceded by two hours' shelling, but about noon on October 8th the Germans began an extremely heavy bombardment which became intense between 3 and 4 p.m., doing great damage and inflicting many casualties. This was in fact part of a general bombardment of the Allied positions from Loos round to the Hohenzollern, which was followed by violent counter-attacks on Chalk Pit Wood (West of Bois Hugo), on the Hohenzollern, and on the French positions in front of Loos, attacks which were everywhere completely repulsed. But naturally this counter-bombardment interfered seriously with the battalion's preparations for the attack; all signal wires were cut, and it was not certain whether the British artillery fire was mere retaliation or whether it was the bombardment arranged for and the attack was to be made as planned despite the unexpected element of the German bombardment. The plan was that while the two platoons of A Company not in the actual front line, under Captain Margetts, assaulted Gun Trench over the open,[1] bombing parties were simultaneously to work

[1] Gun Trench ran more or less in the shape of a crescent, so that the platoons which carried out the assault advanced in a slightly slanting direction, while the platoons of A Company in the front line were liable to be shot at from the rear by Germans in a short sap which projected from their part of the trench.

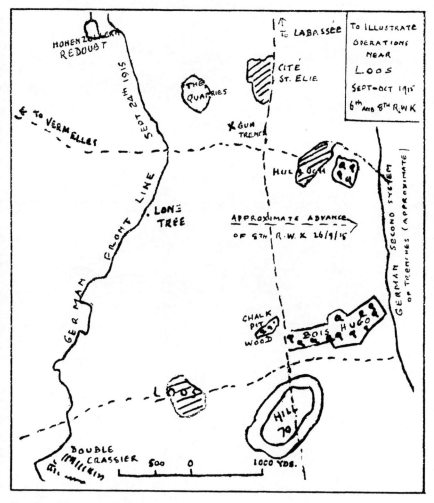

GUN TRENCH.

Oct. 8th, 1915
6th Battalion

inwards from both flanks, and B[1] was detailed to consolidate the position when captured and open up an old communication trench running from the trench held by D Company towards the section held by the enemy.

The German bombardment notwithstanding, there was no thought of cancelling the attack. At 6.16 p.m. the British artillery fire lifted to the German support trench, and Captain Margetts and his men went over the parapet. They at once encountered a very heavy fire, for the bombardment had been very disappointing in its effects, having failed to silence most of the German machine-guns. The Germans were manning their trenches in strength and were also holding a support trench 20 yards in rear of Gun Trench in force; they seemed quite ready for the attack, and had no less than four machine-guns in the short length of trench to be attacked. Captain Margetts fell at once, badly wounded; Lieut. Yates was killed on the parapet of Gun Trench, and casualties were very heavy; only a few men reached the German trench[2] and joined up with the battalion bombers under 2nd-Lieuts. Carré and Friend, who were attacking the Southern end of the trench, while others took shelter in shell-holes just in front of the trench and engaged the defenders with bombs and rifle-fire. Corporal Killick was conspicuous in this work and set a fine example; his own rifle was shattered by a bullet but he picked up another and shot down in succession one after another of the German bombers who were standing up on the parapet and hurling bombs at the shell-holes in which the survivors of the attack were sheltering.

The bombing party meanwhile had at first made considerable headway, indeed they made their way

---

[1] B Company was now under Captain Towse, as Major Parker had just left on promotion to command the 8th Battalion.

[2] Several of these seem to have got into the sap which projected from the German line: this they cleared of Germans and then pushed on to the main trench.

LOOS.

October, 8th 1915
6th Battalion

almost to C Company's block, only to find that fresh Germans seemed continually to be appearing. The truth was that instead of the portion of Gun Trench in German hands being, as it was believed to be, an isolated piece of line, it was joined up with the rest of their line by a trench running into it just beyond C's block, which, owing to the absence of any air photos by which to correct the maps, was quite unknown to the assailants.[1] Hence all the gallant efforts of Lieut. Carré's party were frustrated; he himself was wounded but continued to lead and encourage his men. However, the failure of the main assault allowed the Germans to concentrate their counter-attacks on the Southern end of the trench, while unluckily C Company, being completely out of communication with Battalion Headquarters, had never received news that the attack was to go forward, and so failed to co-operate. Captain Francis, who was on his way up from Battalion Headquarters with orders and instructions, was knocked out by a shell, and it was not known till long afterwards that he had failed to reach the front line. B did what they could by passing up bombs and ammunition, Lieut. Heath being killed when leading his men forward, but in the end the Germans wrested from our bombers the ground they had gained; all that could be done was to re-establish the block and hold on to our original positions. 2nd-Lieut. Carré made his way down to Battalion Headquarters and asked for leave to make another bombing attack, but Colonel Venables would not allow it. 2nd-Lieut. Carré indeed was in no condition for further work; that same day he collapsed and was away from duty for some months.[2]

This unsuccessful effort had cost the battalion over

---

[1] The existence of this trench became known to the platoons of A in the front line under Lieut. Hatton as it was occupied as a fire-trench and was held in strength, the Germans in it firing upon Lieut. Hatton's party who replied vigorously.

[2] Lieut. Carré received the M.C. for this action and the D.C.M. was awarded to Corporal Killick.

GUN TRENCH.

100 casualties in addition to the five officers; 12 men were killed, 39 missing, 53 wounded—the loss falling mainly on A Company. <small>October, 1915 1st Battalion</small> But to have made the effort after the heavy bombardment which the battalion had just endured involved no little courage and determination, and its conduct was highly commended by the Corps Commander, General Haking, who declared that it had shown " fine military qualities." There seems reason, moreover, to believe that its attack on Gun Trench had anticipated and thrown out of gear a projected German effort to extend their holding at this point; certainly the German trenches were packed with men at the time of the attack, and it cost them not a little to retain their hold on Gun Trench.

However, the 6th was to taste of success as well as of failure at Gun Trench. After being relieved by the 7th East Surreys on the evening of October 9th and spending a couple of days in support, it moved further back into Brigade Reserve, but was detailed to find one company to support the 6th Buffs in a renewed attack to be made on October 13th. In this the 7th East Surreys were to tackle Gun Trench, the Buffs on their left attacking a trench running S.E. from the Quarries, which were themselves to be assaulted by the 35th Brigade, the whole being part of a bigger attack comprising Hulluch and the Hohenzollern Redoubt.

The attack by the Buffs, though gallantly made, proved unsuccessful, and D Company, though busily employed in carrying up bombs and water and ammunition, had little actual fighting. C, however, had a much livelier time, and were able to get some of their own back on the Germans for the losses of October 8th. Two platoons went over the top with the East Surreys and assisted them to capture Gun Trench, and then, about 5 p.m., the East Surreys, who were being hard pressed to hold their gains, asked for reinforcements, and the rest of C was sent up under Captain Dawson. <small>October, 13th</small>

135

LOOS.

October 13th 1915 1st Battalion On reaching Gun Trench he took over the left of the captured position with two of his platoons, setting the others to work to dig a communication trench back to the British trench in rear. C Company made the most of its chances; it not only maintained and consolidated the position, despite heavy shelling and machine-gun fire, but cleared and filled in about 50 yards of a German communication trench running back to Cité St. Elie, and in the early morning had the satisfaction of beating off by heavy and accurate rifle-fire a strong and determined counter-attack. 2nd-Lieut. Pye was killed while setting a fine example of coolness and courage to his men, but the Germans were heavily punished and fell back after losing severely. Altogether C's share in the successful defence of Gun Trench was no small one and carried no little credit for the battalion.

October 14th October 14th proved a busy day. C remained in position, while before dawn B was sent up to take over the trenches on its left from the Buffs. There was much to be done to the line, wounded and dead had to be removed or buried, and as the Germans, who were also busy on similar work, exposed themselves somewhat freely snipers and machine-gunners got many chances. That evening the battalion was relieved by the 11th Middlesex and withdrew to Vermelles, moving thence to Verquin on the 19th, where a real rest could be enjoyed. The battalion came out from this first experience of serious fighting with the satisfaction of having acquitted itself well in a really severe trial; it had shown gallantry in attack and steadiness and tenacity in defence. Its total casualties came to 220; three officers and 38 men had been killed; 44 men were missing; 5 officers and 130 men wounded, Lieut. Langlands having been wounded on October 11th and Lieut. L. C. R. Smith in the defence of Gun Trench. But drafts amounting to 130 other ranks had been received on the 11th and 12th and ten young officers joined in the course of the month, so that the battalion was not

Lieut.-Colonel E. F. VENABLES, D.S.O.
Commanded 6th Battalion, 1915.

Colonel E. VANSITTART, D.S.O.
Commanded 8th Battalion, 1914-15.

Face Page 136.

LOOS.

far below strength when, after a week's well-earned rest at Verquin it relieved the 1st Grenadier Guards in trenches W. of the Northern end of the Hohenzollern on October 26th.

Oct.-Nov., 1915
6th Battalion

At this moment the Germans were believed to be preparing to attack, so active reconnaissance was enjoined by the Brigade, but all the patrols sent out by the battalion found the enemy hard at work on his defences, adding to his wire and apparently in a state of nervous tension, expecting to receive rather than to deliver an attack. This tour did actually pass off without any German attack, but the shelling was often very heavy and the persistent rain made it extremely difficult to keep trenches in repair. The line too was in a terrible state: it had been much knocked about in the fighting and was very wet. It was in this period that Captain Towse was killed by shell-fire in the front trenches, and other casualties were numerous. All November the weather continued indifferent, so the turns in the line—all in the Hohenzollern region—which fell to the battalion's lot were extremely arduous and exhausting and resulted in a rapid increase in the sick rate, 33 men went sick after one three days' tour in the front line, and 1 officer and 88 men after another. When it reached Ecquedecques on November 22nd for a rest and refit, the battalion had fallen to barely 750 " present." But its rest was not to be protracted, for early in December the Twelfth Division received orders to move to Bethune and to take over trenches North of Givenchy.

November had been marked for the 6th by the loss of Colonel Venables: he had been wounded in the foot by a shell-splinter on October 8th, but had refused to report sick, and actually remained at duty till November 15th. He had commanded the battalion for ten months, and had been largely responsible for the high level of discipline and efficiency of which it had given proof, and all parted from him with regret. He

Nov.-Dec., 1915
6th Battalion

was succeeded by Major C. S. Owen, of the Royal Welsh Fusiliers, who joined on November 29th and quickly established himself firmly in the confidence and regard of officers and men. About the same time Major Beeching also left the battalion; his departure was much regretted and his part in its history is no small one; he had done fine work in building it up and knitting it together into an united whole, he had been in a very special degree a link between the young battalion and the old Regiment to which it was proud to belong; he had enjoyed the confidence and respect of his brother officers, and in action, notably on October 8th, he had been a tower of strength to less experienced comrades. The 6th owed him no small debt for his example and his influence.

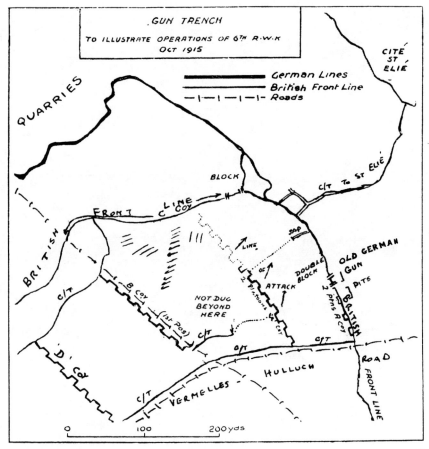

CHAPTER IX.

THE TERRITORIALS IN 1915.

The Regular and the three senior Service battalions were not the only portions of The Queen's Own to see active service in 1915. The opportunity of representing the Regiment in action came to a Territorial battalion also. This was not, however, one of the two " pre-war " Territorial battalions which spent the year with their Headquarters at Jubbulpore and Jhansi respectively, busily employed in preparing themselves for the expected but always deferred orders for " the front," and in going through the various experiences that fall to British battalions in India. Both 4th and 5th R.W.K., 1/4th and 1/5th as they were now styled, had plenty to occupy them, but little to deserve special mention, except the adoption of the four-company organization. Both lost a certain number of men from sickness, and the 1/5th, in addition to losing Lieut. Burr from this cause, suffered a severe loss when Captain Cooper was murdered by two sepoys who ran amok at Jhansi in June and killed three British officers and an N.C.O. Both battalions, as has been mentioned, found drafts to reinforce the 2nd in Mesopotamia and suffered various changes of personnel through officers obtaining staff appointments and through N.C.O.'s and men obtaining commissions, but for both 1915 came to an end without a change of station. ₁₉₁₅ _{1/4th & 1/5th} _{Battalions}

The Territorial unit of The Queen's Own which did see active service in 1915 had come into existence under somewhat remarkable circumstances. While several of the Territorial Divisions had proceeded overseas as complete formations, others had been not a little handicapped and disorganized by the dis- ₁₉₁₅ _{2/4th Batt.}

THE TERRITORIALS IN 1915.

1915
2/4th Batt.

patch of selected individual battalions or R.E. companies to France. The Welsh Division had suffered severely in this way, and when, in the spring of 1915, it was decided to bring it forward for overseas service a whole infantry brigade was needed to supplement what were left of its original units. It was to the Home Counties Reserve Division, then quartered in the Thames and Medway Defence area, that recourse was had. Each of its three brigades, Kent, Middlesex and Surrey, was called on to provide a battalion, which the Kent Brigade formed by taking a company from each of its four battalions. Captain E. W. Dillon commanded the company which the 2/4th contributed to the new unit, with Captain Dowling as his second-in-command, and from the 2/5th came Captains Palmer and Savage. To this composite unit, known in its early days as "the Kent Battalion," the 2/4th R.W.K. in addition supplied a battalion headquarters and a machine-gun section, with a C.O. in Colonel A. T. F. Simpson, and an Adjutant in Captain Johnson. On April 25th the Kent Battalion joined the Welsh Division at Cambridge, moving to Bedford in May, while recruiting was vigorously carried on by the 2/4th and 2/5th R.W.K. to replace the men contributed to the new battalion. Then came a change in the nomenclature of the Kent Battalion. For administrative reasons it was desirable to allot it definitely to one of the two County regiments, and as the 4th R.W.K. had provided the C.O. and battalion headquarters it was to The Queen's Own that it was assigned on June 14th, 1915. Thus Colonel Simpson found himself again commanding a 2/4th R.W.K., while his old battalion of the Home Counties Reserve Division, by this time numbered as the Sixty-Seventh, was renumbered 3/4th,[1] and was reconstituted as a unit for foreign service on July 1st, 1915, whereupon all those who had only undertaken or proved fit for home

April-July
1915
2/4 Batt.

---

[1] Colonel J. D. Laurie had succeeded Colonel Simpson in command.

SUVLA.

service were drafted to a Provisional battalion. The reconstitution of the 3/4th as a foreign service unit made it necessary before the end of the year to raise yet another off-shoot of the 4th Battalion, and on October 26th a 4/4th came into existence to act as the feeding unit for those on active service. Major Disney Roebuck was appointed to command this new unit, and at the same time a 3/5th R.W.K. was formed under Major Jenyns to discharge the same function for the 5th Battalion.

<small>1915
3/4th & 4/4th
Battalions</small>

The 2/4th R.W.K., after a couple of months of "intensive training" at Bedford, received its embarkation orders early in July, and along with them came equipment for a tropical climate so that it was clear that France was not its destination. Actually the Fifty-Third, as the Welsh Division was now numbered, the 2/4th R.W.K. being in the 160th Brigade, had been selected to reinforce the Mediterranean Expeditionary Force for the new effort to secure the Dardanelles by landing in Suvla Bay and simultaneously taking the offensive from the "Anzac" position. Its move to the Eastern Mediterranean was uneventful. Leaving Bedford on July 18th[1] it sailed two days later from Devonport on the s.s. "Northland" and reached Alexandria on the 31st, where it landed the Orderly Room Staff required for Base duties along with a "first reinforcement" provided rather paradoxically by cutting down its strength by 25 per cent, a method of robbing Peter to pay Paul that bordered on the farcical. From Alexandria the "Northland" proceeded to Mudros,

<small>July, 1915
2/4th Batt.</small>

---

[1] Officers who went overseas with 2/4th R.W.K.: Lieut.-Col. A. T. F. Simpson, commanding; Major H. Smithers, second-in-command; Captain F. Johnson, Adjutant; 2nd Lieut. Bailey, M.G.O., Lieut. Ruse, Quartermaster. A Company: Captains Jude and Taunton, Lieuts. Dixon and Filmer, 2nd Lieuts. Larking and Morgan. B Company: Captains Greatorex and Lamarque, Lieuts. Keble and Wood, 2nd Lieuts. Willows and Griffin. C Company: Captains Dillon and Dowling, 2nd Lieuts. H. J. Wilson, L. E. Wilson, Woollett and Le Fleming. D Company: Captains Palmer and Savage, Lieuts. Stern and Tharp, 2nd Lieuts. J. C. Cobb and R. S. Cobb.

SUVLA.

August 8th
2/4th Batt.

where it arrived on August 8th, the day on which the originally bright prospects of the Suvla landing were finally destroyed by the inertia which seemed to paralyse the whole Ninth Corps, and by the fatal withdrawal from the all-important Anafarta Hills of the two battalions who had obtained a foothold on them. The consequences of this were made only too evident in the next day's fighting, and when, on the evening of August

August 10th

10th, the 2/4th landed at West Beach at Suvla the fate of the whole operation was practically settled. Positions which might have been had for the asking on August 8th were firmly held by the Turks in considerable force; their guns were up, surprise had vanished.

Aug. 13th
See Sketch 13

Not till the third day after landing did the 2/4th reach the firing-line; it had spent the intervening time on the beach, digging in, for even the furthest beach was within range of the Turkish guns, unloading lighters and discharging other beach fatigues. It took no part, therefore, in the unsuccessful effort of the rest of the Division to storm the Turkish positions opposite Sulajik, and did not move forward till the evening of August 13th. It was then to find that instead of being in support, as it had expected, it was in the front trenches, if that name could properly be applied to the shallow little scrapes made with entrenching tools, which did duty for trenches on the 700 yards' front assigned to the battalion. Immediately in front the ground was fairly flat but was dotted with bushes and trees, affording ideal cover for the numerous and active Turkish snipers who made it necessary for the men to set promptly to work to improve their scanty cover. But some uncertainty prevailed as to the way in which the existing line was to be regarded; the higher authorities had apparently not yet abandoned hopes of a substantial advance and were disinclined to have the line dug and wired for permanent defence.

It was a trying experience for a raw battalion, newly landed after a three weeks' voyage and decidedly "soft"

SUVLA.

in consequence. Neither officers or men were accustomed to active service conditions, even to make the most of the rather indifferent rations available, and to add to the battalion's troubles Colonel Simpson was among its earliest casualties; he was wounded while going round the position on the morning of the 15th and had to be evacuated, Major Smithers replacing him in command. Gradually, however, as the battalion settled down to the new conditions, things improved. Steps were taken to deal with the snipers, the trenches were deepened and made more habitable and defensible, especially after the night of August 17/18th, when, with the guidance and assistance of a company of the 2nd South Wales Borderers from the famous Twenty-Ninth Division, an advance of 250 yards was made and a straighter line taken up and consolidated. By September 1st, when the battalion was relieved and taken back to Divisional Reserve at West Beach, not only had a satisfactory front line been constructed, but a fair second line was also in existence. The battalion had suffered somewhat severely from snipers, but though occasionally shelled had lost little from this cause, and the arrival, on August 23rd, of the " first reinforcements " left behind at Alexandria, more than balanced the casualties even when those from sickness, already fairly numerous, were included.

The period spent by the 2/4th R.W.K. at Suvla was one of monotonous hardships. Though shelled from time to time and constantly under rifle-fire, which varied from intermittent heavy fusillades to occasional sniping, it had no opportunity of distinguishing itself either in attack or defence, though its discipline, its cheerfulness and its powers of endurance were severely tested and not found wanting, as is clear from the reports of the authorities as to its work and conduct. Periods in the front-line trenches alternated with periods in reserve near the beach, but even in the reserve areas there was no real shelter, either from the weather or from the enemy's

SUVLA

Aug.-Dec., 1915
2/4th Batt.

shell-fire, which was indeed more troublesome there than to the troops in the front line, who had at least the satisfaction of getting their own back in duels with the Turkish snipers, no longer as predominant as when the battalion first went into the line. In reserve, too, there was as much or more hard work; stores had to be loaded and unloaded, roads made and repaired, trenches and dug-outs kept in condition. Battalions in reserve in France usually found that a period out of the line, whether in huts or billets, did mean some degree of comfort and real rest; the troops in Gallipoli had no baths or laundries, no chances of recreation, no "leave," their rations, if plentiful, were monotonous and hard to cook for lack of fuel and appliances. Casualties in action were few, but the battalion dwindled rapidly from sickness till, when it embarked for Mudros on December 13th, it was down to a dozen officers and little over 200 other ranks. Of the officers who went out in July less than half were present at the end of the year and these included some who had been to hospital but had returned to duty. Four officers only had been wounded, and the casualties in action among the rank and file were under a hundred. Of the four original company commanders Captain Dillon went sick in August, Captain Greatorex in November, Captain Jude in December, and only Captain Palmer remained. Major Smithers was invalided early in October and was succeeded by Major Vaughan, a Regular officer from the Devons, who retained command till after the evacuation. No drafts were received, though a party of young officers from the 3/4th R.W.K. arrived just in time for the famous blizzard of November 15th, which did havoc among the trenches, filled the hospitals with exhausted, frost-bitten and incapacitated men, and stands out in memories of Gallipoli as the summit of hardship and misery.

The Fifty-Third Division was about the first to be withdrawn from the Peninsula when evacuation was

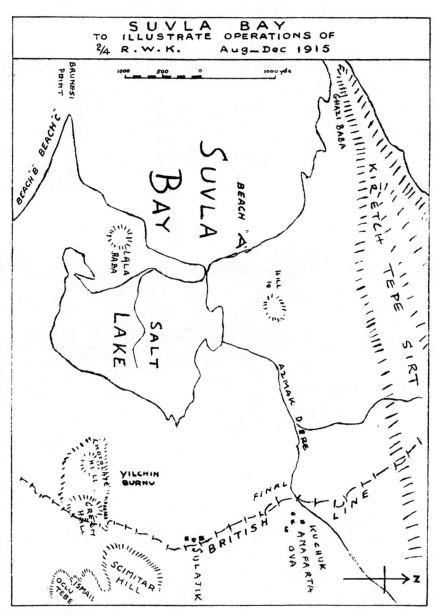

SUVLA.

begun and the remnant of the 2/4th R.W.K., which during the closing days of its stay had been employed on rearward defences round Lala Baba, made but a brief stay at Mudros before embarking for Alexandria. Here the battalion arrived on December 20th, proceeding at once by train to Wardan, near Cairo, where it was to enjoy its first real rest since its arrival in the Eastern Mediterranean. Colonel Vaughan left almost at once to command the 160th Brigade, but the battalion was fortunate in getting back Colonel Simpson, who had just returned from England after recovering from his wounds, and its depleted ranks were replenished by the numerous convalescents whom it found awaiting it in Egypt. Fortunately, if the sick-rate had been very high the number of deaths had been low, and early in 1916 the battalion, rested, refreshed, re-organized and re-equipped, was again an effective unit, though sadly below establishment. Dec., 1915
2/4th Batt.

Of the battalions of The Queen's Own who remained in England throughout 1915 the 3rd carried on with its normal duties of training recruits, finding guards and providing drafts. If its duties remained unchanged this could not be said of its composition. Colonel Sir A. Griffith-Boscawen remained in command[1] and most of the permanent staff continued with the battalion, though in November Captain Waring handed over the Adjutancy to Captain Knox. Major Allfrey left to be second-in-command of the 20th Manchesters and various other officers went off to different employments in England, but the majority of those who left went to one of the battalions on active service, mostly to the 1st and 2nd, for the duty of keeping the Service battalions up to strength was assigned more particularly to the 9th Battalion. This unit, in common with the rest of "K 4," had been converted from an active service into a draft-finding formation early in the year, a change 1915
3rd Battalion

---

[1] He left the battalion in April, 1916, to command a Garrison Battalion of the Hampshire Regiment, being succeeded by Major Barrow.

DRAFTS.

<small>1915
3rd Battalion</small> specially appropriate because "K 4" had originally been formed by splitting up the Special Reserve battalions when they had swollen to unmanageable proportions. But to keep the two Regular battalions up to strength involved a tremendous drain on the 3rd. By the end of the first twelve months of the year it had sent out no less than 2,450 N.C.O.'s and men, the equivalent of two-and-a-half battalions, and this though as yet the 2nd had not begun to make itself felt as a draft consumer. Officers in like manner were trained and sent out with almost greater rapidity, and in the early months not a few were sent to other units which were in even worse straits for trained subalterns than The Queen's Own.

Two drafts from the 3rd Battalion, however, did not find their way to any battalion of the Regiment, being composed of rather older officers and men who, though not up to the strain of active service, were quite fit for garrison duties. One of these went out to Lemnos, the advanced base of the M.E.F., with a Garrison Battalion of the Essex Regiment, the other joined a Garrison Battalion of the Norfolks. Another and much larger draft of 7 officers and over 300 men, despatched in September by the 3rd Battalion to reinforce the 2nd in Mesopotamia, had a remarkable career. Its transport, which also carried similar drafts for the three British battalions of Townshend's Sixth Indian Division, was nearing Suez when it was suddenly diverted to Mudros, and the 1,200 officers and men on board were pitch-forked headlong in the Tenth (Irish) Division, just placed under orders for Salonica and woefully below strength, since but scanty drafts of genuine Irishmen were available. Thus Lieut. Le Cocq and his 300 found themselves forming a substantial proportion of the 7th Royal Dublin Fusiliers, for which battalion they helped to gain not a little credit. Their first fighting was on December 7th-9th 1915 on the Graeco-Bulgarian frontier near Kosturino, when the

DRAFTS AND THE DEPÔT.

Tenth Division made so fine a stand against heavy odds to cover the retreat of the French troops who had pushed up the Vardar in the belated effort to succour the Servians. With the 7th Dublins this detachment did good service again in the fighting on the Struma in the autumn of 1916, and was transferred to Palestine in 1917 in time to share in Allenby's triumph at Gaza and the deliverance of Jerusalem. Some of its officers and a fair number of men ultimately proceeded with the battalion to France in the spring of 1918 and finished the war as members of the 2nd Dublins, into which the 7th had been absorbed. Still it is permissible to wonder whether the campaign in Mesopotamia was not a little adversely affected by the diversion to Salonica of a reinforcement which would have made Townshend's British battalions at Ctesiphon half as strong again. In war trifles sometimes have far-reaching results.

₁₉₁₅ 3rd Battalion

Behind the 3rd Battalion during this period was the Depôt, which continued to receive recruits and pass them on to the various battalions for training as soon as they were equipped, and to carry on all its multifarious other duties. In April 1915 Colonel Maunsell, who had succeeded to the command when Major Robinson had joined the 6th Battalion, received a Staff appointment in France and proceeded overseas; his place was taken by another old officer of The Queen's Own, Colonel Dalison.

1915 The Depôt

Despite the conversion of the 9th Battalion into a draft-finding unit the despatch of the 8th to France did not exhaust the " New Army " battalions which the Regiment was preparing for service. If the Southern and Eastern counties of England did not produce very many of the battalions specially raised by local committees to represent some particular town or occupation, of which the more populous industrial areas of the North and Midlands provided so many, such as the " City battalions " of the King's and the Manchesters or the Yeomen Farmers' Battalion raised in Yorkshire

1915 10th & 11th Battalions

THE LOCAL BATTALIONS.

<small>1915
10th Batt.</small>

for the Sixtieth Rifles, West Kent at any rate raised two such units who were to achieve high distinction.

The earliest of these came into existence in reply to a letter addressed, early in 1915, by the Army Council to Lord Harris, the Vice-Lieut. of the County. This letter requested him to appeal to the local governing bodies in the County for assistance in recruiting a brigade of artillery, the special idea governing the raising of the unit being that as far as possible definite portions should be found by different villages or towns. The County, however, did not feel able to undertake this, but suggested as an alternative that it should raise a battalion of infantry to be commanded by Colonel A. Wood Martyn, the Secretary of the Kent Territorial Association, himself an old officer of The Queen's Own. It was further suggested that as the battalion was to be raised in the Buffs' recruiting area as well as in West Kent it should be known by the title of "Kent County." Actually in the end the bulk of the recruits were raised, not by local authorities as suggested, but by Colonel Wood Martyn, speaking from his own motor car and attended by his own band, the instruments of which belonged to him personally, while the musicians came from Blackpool, none being available in Kent. Moreover, as its commander belonged to The Queen's Own the new unit was allotted to that regiment as its 10th Battalion. Colonel Wood Martyn was well backed up by other old members of the Regiment: Captain C. V. Molony, for example, who had already distinguished himself with the 1st Battalion in the Ypres Salient, joined the new unit on recovering from his wounds, becoming second-in-command with the rank of Major. Penenden Heath Camp, near Maidstone, was the scene of this battalion's earlier days, and if it took some time to reach its establishment, this was only natural, seeing how many recruits the Regimental District had already raised, and that the voluntary system was already on its last legs when the decision to raise the battalion was

THE LOCAL BATTALIONS.

taken. But excellent progress was made in its training and it showed itself inspired by a zealous determination to reach the high standards of efficiency and hard work which the other battalions of The Queen's Own had set up. By the end of 1915 the 10th R.W.K., which had moved into billets at Maidstone on November 1st, had already made great headway.

1915
10th & 11th Battalions

About the same time as the 10th, an 11th Battalion[1] came into existence. The task of raising this unit was entrusted to the Mayor of Lewisham, Mr. R. Jackson, who, backed by a strong local committee, made rapid progress with the undertaking. Lewisham had already contributed a large number of recruits, but within a month from the start 400 men had been collected and more were coming in daily. Major H. L. Searle, from the 8th East Surreys, was transferred to the 11th R.W.K. to command.[2] Major A. J. P. Annesley, of the 9th Battalion, became second-in-command, and a notable acquisition was secured in September when Major A. C. Corfe of the South African Defence Force, who had already done good service under General Botha in German South West Africa, joined and took over A Company. Several old N.C.O.'s joined the new unit, notably Sergt.-Major Goulds and C.S.M. Tranter, a veteran with 18 years' service to his credit, so that even the junior battalion was well supplied with connecting links with the older branches of the Regiment. By the middle of September the battalion was within 200 of its establishment, and on November 12th the 11th R.W.K.

[1] Both the 10th and 11th Battalions belonged to the category of "local" battalions which were not on quite the same footing as other "Service battalions." A "local" battalion was raised by an individual or corporate body who undertook all responsibility for raising, housing, feeding, clothing, equipping and training the unit, appointed officers, and then after a certain number of months produced the battalion for inspection by the War Office, which took it over if the inspection proved satisfactory, and in that case paid the bills for the expenses incurred, which till then had been the risk of the person or body responsible for raising the regiment.

[2] Colonel A. F. Townshend, formerly of the Scottish Rifles, was appointed to the command of the 11th shortly after its move to Aldershot, Colonel Searle being unfit for active service.

THE LOCAL BATTALIONS.

1915
10th & 11th Battalions

was formally "taken over" by the War Office on reaching its full complement. Both the 10th and the 11th had originally been posted to the Thirty-Ninth Division but were subsequently transferred to the Forty-First, the last formed "New Army" Division, the 10th Battalion being in the 123rd Brigade, the 11th in the 122nd. Early in December their Division was concentrated at Aldershot, the 10th moving thither from Maidstone and the 11th from Catford, where it had till then been quartered, and with this these two battalions entered on the last stage of their preparation for war.

1916
12th Batt.

Depôt companies of these two battalions had been left behind at Maidstone and Catford to maintain recruiting, and out of these was formed in February 1916 yet another battalion of the Regiment. This, which was numbered the 12th, was described as a "Local Reserve" battalion. Its original commander was Colonel A. G. Jeffrey of the Wiltshire Regiment, who had with him as company commanders Major Molony, Captains Bowes-Lyon, Bracewell and Hawes, all from the 10th, while the 11th supplied him with a senior Major in Major Annesley and an Adjutant in Captain Stopford-Holland. The battalion was transferred to Northampton at the end of February, where it found itself in a brigade composed of seven similar "Local Reserve" units. Northampton was not a very satisfactory spot as regards facilities for training, but matters improved in May when the battalion moved to Bourley, near Aldershot, shifting later in the summer into barracks in Aldershot itself. Shortly after this the battalion's designation was changed and its connection with the Regiment was officially severed on its becoming the 99th Training Reserve Battalion, the 9th R.W.K. at the same time being converted into the 22nd Training Reserve.

This change was necessitated by the difficulty of adapting the supply of reinforcements to the de-

THE TRAINING RESERVE.

mands of particular regiments. Heavy losses simultaneously suffered by several battalions of one regiment might find its feeding units short of trained recruits, while those of another regiment were overflowing; hence the conversion of " K 4 " and " Local Reserve " battalions into a pool on which all regiments might draw indifferently, regardless of their territorial connections. The plan was doubtless convenient and necessary, but it had obvious drawbacks, and it was a little inconsistent with the insistence of the authorities on the necessity of maintaining a high standard of regimental patriotism and *esprit de corps*. A battalion like the 12th R.W.K., whose officers and N.C.O.'s had nearly all served in that regiment, many of them being old soldiers with long associations with it, lost part of its incentive when the recruits it had trained so carefully and had specially taught to be proud of the chance of doing credit to the old regiment went off to almost any other regiment than The Queen's Own. It did not so much matter that almost from the first recruits had come to the 12th from other counties as well as Kent; it was not difficult to make a Northern or a Midland recruit proud of The Queen's Own, it was disheartening not to have the traditions of The Queen's Own to set before the recruits. About a year later the 99th T.R. became a " graduated battalion "[1] and shortly afterwards found itself becoming a battalion of the Royal Sussex, a regiment and a county with which few of its members had any connection. Indeed, up till that time the " 99th T.R." had cherished its old membership of The Queen's Own, and even the recruits had liked to pretend that they belonged to The Queen's Own, and are believed to have displayed its cap badge when on leave. It was a pity that in allotting it to a definite regiment the authorities should not have taken the trouble to

1916
12th Batt.

---

[1] This meant that it received its recruits at 18½ years of age, kept them six months, was organized into six companies according to age, each company going off overseas together, and that the training could proceed on more systematic lines.

151

THE TERRITORIALS IN 1916.

<small>1916
12th Batt.</small>
inquire who the "99th T.R." had originally been and to have restored it to its old regiment. The officers and N.C.O.'s who had worked so hard at a task rendered difficult by its combination of hurry and monotony would have been gratified and encouraged by such a simple concession.

<small>1916
4th (Reserve)
Battalion</small>
Meanwhile the Territorial battalions still at home had been pursuing the even tenor of their way. In the course of 1916 the 4/4th and 3/5th, the two draft-finding units, were combined into one battalion, known as the 4th (Reserve) Battalion and commanded at first by Lieut.-Col. Disney-Roebuck, to whom Lieut.-Col. McKergown succeeded later on. In June Colonel Simpson, on recovery from illness, took command of the 3/4th, and in September Colonel E. B. Willis resigned command of the 2/5th on transfer to T.F. Reserve. That battalion had just been depleted by finding a draft of nearly 400 N.C.O.'s and men, but it gradually filled up the vacancies. Major Savage was in command of it from September 7th to November 21st, when Lieut.-Col. C. L. Willoughby Wallace was appointed to it as commanding officer.[1]

---

[1] In March, 1916, the Regiment formed yet another unit, a Home Service Garrison Battalion, which did not prove very long-lived, being transferred to the Royal Defence Corps shortly after its formation.

CHAPTER X

FROM LOOS TO THE SOMME.

The lull on the fronts held by the British Armies in France, which had followed the Loos offensive, continued all through the first half of 1916, unbroken by any major operations. This does not mean that there was not much hard fighting, lengthy casualty lists, much activity on the part of Tunnelling Companies, constant local bombardments, that trenches were not lost and won at many points, that raids did not increase in frequency and in scale, that the troops holding the line did not have much to endure and ample opportunities for putting to the proof their discipline, their courage and their skill. But as far as the British Armies were concerned the one serious change was the extension of their line in February 1916. Hitherto in the section of the Allied line from Loos Southward past Arras French troops had interposed between the right of the British First Army and the left flank of the Third. To afford some relief to the French, then very hard pressed at Verdun, this section was taken over, but otherwise nothing of major importance happened. At the same time the local activities of the British, still considerably hampered by the not yet too plentiful supply of ammunition, kept the Germans opposite on the alert and constituted a constant drain on their resources, while as yet the strength of the British Armies in the field was steadily increasing.

_{Oct., 1915-June, 1916}

_{Jan.-June, 1916}

In this long period of strategical inaction the work that fell to the four battalions of The Queen's Own already in France varied greatly. At the beginning of 1916 the sector in which the 1st and 7th were stationed was still conspicuously " quiet," the 6th, who had gone into the line North of Givenchy in the middle of

FROM LOOS TO THE SOMME.

Jan.-Feb., 1916
1st Battalion

December was in a more "lively" quarter, while the 8th found the Ypres Salient, of which they had now had a couple of months' experience, decidedly unrestful. Of the four only the 6th was to see really severe fighting in the first half of 1916, but what it came in for was some of the most desperate of the crater-fighting of the whole winter in which it earned no small credit.

The 1st Battalion had found trenches in chalk country much less comfortable in wet weather than they had been in summer. Conditions went from bad to worse; communication trenches became impassable owing to the depth of sticky mud in which men became embedded and unable to move; water would not drain away, parapets dissolved into adhesive mud. At the New Year there was an important change in the composition of the Fifth Division, four of its original battalions with the 14th Brigade Headquarters were transferred to the Thirty-Second in exchange for the 95th Brigade,[1] two battalions of which, the 14th and 15th R. Warwicks, replaced in the 13th Brigade the K.O.Y.L.I. and Duke's, with whom the R.W.K. had so long co-operated. However, to the battalion's satisfaction it was not parted from the K.O.S.B.'s, with whom it had been so particularly closely associated; indeed, to the end of the war these two battalions continued to serve side by side, and their long and cordial association was fitly commemorated when, after the Armistice the officers of the 1st R.W.K. and of the 2nd K.O.S.B.'s made each other honorary members of each other's messes. Shortly after the New Year the Division was relieved by the Thirtieth Division and withdrew for a month's welcome rest. When the battalion returned to the trenches it was not to the familiar Carnoy sector but to quite new country. The Fifth Division was among those selected to take over the new front, and on February 25th it started on a memorable march to Arras

---

[1] 12th Gloucesters and 14th, 15th and 16th Royal Warwickshires.

FROM LOOS TO THE SOMME.

in the teeth of a raging blizzard from the N.E., over roads congested with traffic and horribly slippery with ice and snow. "The Moscow march" it was called in the Division, but the battalion stood it well, though it was a specially trying time for the regimental transport, which found the frozen roads almost impassable.

March-June, 1916 1st Battalion

By March 4th the relief of the French had been completed and the Fifth Division was holding a sector running Northward from the Scarpe near St. Laurent Blangy to the famous "Labyrinth," just E. of the road from Arras to Lens, the dividing line between the sub-sectors being the road from Arras to Bailleul.[1] This sector, the scene of desperate fighting in the past, had by this time become fairly "quiet," though the enemy had evidently been having things his own way for some time, for his working parties were exposing themselves in a way which argued that they expected an immunity the battalion did not allow them to enjoy.[2] However, though there were occasional heavy bombardments and some mining activity, the four months which the Division spent in this sector were on the whole quiet enough, and the total casualties for the period were little over 60. The most noteworthy incident occurred one unlucky early morning in April when Captain Gross and Lieut. Dobie were caught by a sudden burst of rifle-fire while out in front of the line inspecting the work which had been done during the night by a wiring party. Lieut. Dobie was killed on the spot, Captain Gross very badly wounded. Upon this C.S.M. Crossley, Sergt. Hammond and L/Cpl. Liddamore immediately went to their Captain's assistance, despite the heavy fire which the enemy kept up, and managed to bring him in, but the C.S.M., a valuable N.C.O., who had distinguished himself at Neuve Chapelle, was killed and Captain

---

[1] This was not the Bailleul in the Lys Valley but that S.W. of Douai, less familiar to the British Troops.

[2] The original front line had been evacuated by the French for fear of mining, but the battalion did not find the enemy particularly enterprising.

FROM LOOS TO THE SOMME.

June, 1916
1st Battalion

Gross died of his wounds; the other two men received the D.C.M. for their gallantry. On June 4th again, when the battalion was to relieve the 14th R. Warwicks, the enemy opened a violent bombardment, blew up some mines and attacked. Only about 30 of the battalion were in the trenches, a party on mining fatigue; these luckily escaped without casualties and did great work in helping to beat off what General Stephens, who had succeeded General Kavanagh in command of the Division, described as no mere raid but an evident attempt to secure the high ground in that particular sector. Apart from these episodes the time was uneventful. Officers came and went: in March Captain Waring joined and took over the Adjutant's duties.[1] In April Captain Newton left to become Brigade Major to the 165th Brigade.[2] Drafts appeared fairly frequently and, with good weather and a low sick-rate, the battalion was well over strength when it finally quitted the sector in June and moved South.

Dec., 1915-
June, 1916
6th Battalion

The 6th Battalion, as already mentioned, had moved to the Givenchy district in December, taking over trenches in the area won back from the Germans in the Festubert fighting of May 16th-25th, 1915. It was a wet quarter, the front line had generally to be held by garrisoning " islands " in the less wet parts, and though both artillery and trench mortars were fairly active and the Germans engaged in more than one outburst of violent bombarding the state of the ground rather imposed an unaggressive attitude on both sides. During December and January the battalion had only about 40 casualties in action, though losses through invaliding were higher; however, a big draft which joined on December 24th brought it up to over 900 of all ranks by the end of the year. The first three weeks of February saw the battalion back in Corps Reserve at

---

[1] He relinquished these in June to become second-in-command, being replaced as Acting-Adjutant by Lieut. Healey.

[2] He was killed in October, 1916, when holding this post.

THE HOHENZOLLERN CRATERS.

Gonnehem, during which period the machine-gun detachment was transferred to the Machine-Gun Corps on the formation of the Brigade Machine-Gun Company, Lewis gun sections in each company now taking the place of the Vickers guns. At this time, too, the battalion lost the last of its original company commanders, Captain R. P. P. Rowe, who was invalided home. When the battalion returned to the line after its rest it was to trenches just opposite the Hohenzollern. This sector had been greatly changed since its capture in September by the Ninth Division. Most of the original Redoubt had disappeared, mine craters pitted the ground everywhere; the British held a line not very far in advance of the original West Face of the Redoubt, the German front corresponding roughly to the trench known as the Chord. *Feb.-Mar., 1916 6th Battalion* *See Sketch 14*

The battalion's first two turns in these trenches passed quietly enough, but on March 2nd, while the 6th was out of the line, the 36th Brigade attacked the Chord and took most of it. Counter-attacks followed, and confused but heavy fighting, in the course of which a big crater on the right, known as Triangle Crater, was lost, though elsewhere the Germans were beaten off. Then the 37th Brigade took over from the exhausted 36th, and on March 6th the Buffs essayed the recapture of Triangle Crater, the battalion assisting them with large carrying-parties. Later on, when the Buffs, whose attack had been held up, were being hard pressed to beat off some determined counter-attacks A Company was sent up to reinforce. These detachments, however, escaped with light casualties, less than a dozen all told, and then on the 7th the battalion received orders to relieve the Buffs. By 4.30 p.m. the relief was complete, C Company, under Captain Dawson, was holding the craters, A was in support in Northampton Trench, D and B were further to the right holding Kaiserin Trench as their front line, with their supports in Vigo Street behind. The line was in an appalling state, the trenches were much damaged *March 6th*

THE HOHENZOLLERN CRATERS.

March, 7th, 1916
6th Battalion

and had collapsed in places, the ground was impossibly sticky and slippery and the weather was bitterly cold with wind and snow from the N.E. To have to fight under such conditions and to fight hard was a great tax on the spirit and condition of the battalion. But fighting they had in plenty and of a desperate character.

The enemy was active and aggressive, making repeated bombing attacks on the craters, especially on Nos. I. and II., just short of Triangle Crater. But, despite bombs, rifle-grenades and trench-mortars, C stuck to its posts and beat off every attack. Captain Dawson set a splendid example of courage, resourcefulness and skill, and was the heart and soul of the defence. Though severely wounded he insisted on rejoining his men directly his wound had been dressed, and continued to direct the defence, although wounded a second time, till the German attacks died down somewhere about 3 a.m.[1]

March 8th

At 10 a.m. Captain Matthews brought up D Company to relieve C and to undergo a similar experience. After a fairly quiet day the enemy started attacking again about 6 p.m., coming out of Triangle Crater and directing their attack upon I. and II. But they never effected an entrance, though for over an hour their bombers maintained the attempt, well supported by trench-mortars, machine-guns and artillery. However, the British gunners were on the alert, and the support they gave to the men in the trenches was most effective. Soon after 7 the enemy relaxed his efforts, only to renew them half-an-hour later with redoubled vigour but no better success. The day's casualties were over 80 all told, but fortunately the proportion of killed was exceptionally low.

March 9th

The small hours of the 9th saw a brief renewal of activity, a German attack being successfully nipped in

---

[1] It was for this action that Captain Dawson received the D.S.O., the first of his many distinctions, while Corpl. Everist earned a D.C.M. by creeping forward under heavy fire to ascertain the direction of the attack and so direct the efforts of our bombers.

THE HOHENZOLLERN CRATERS.

the bud. This was followed by intermittent rifle-grenade and trench-mortar fire till dawn. It was now the turn of Captain Williams and B Company to take over the craters. The relief was accomplished under great difficulties: it was colder than ever, the frozen snow made the communication-trenches almost impassable, and after all this fighting the trenches were in an appalling condition, " a mixture of Boche, mud, refuse, dislodged German sand-bags and equipment and unexploded instruments of devilry " was one account of them. B came in for one vigorous attack about 8.30 p.m., Crater A being assaulted while bombers engaged the garrisons of Nos. I. and II. But this effort was no more successful than its predecessors and was soon repulsed. Trench-mortars continued active all night, but the Germans for the time being had shot their bolt, and next morning the battalion was relieved by the Buffs. Its total casualties since taking over the craters had been over 150; 24 men were killed, 3 officers[1] and 132 men wounded, but nevertheless the men came out justifiably elated despite their exhaustion. They had taken a heavy toll of the Germans, had held their own in a kind of warfare in which the German equipment was at the time superior, and had maintained intact the none too defensible position handed over to them.

March 1916 6th Battalion

March 10th

Three days in support followed and then another three in the front line, one company in the craters as before, one in Northampton Trench, two in Kaiserin. This was another period of activity, but of a less pronounced character, the main need being to clear and improve some most dilapidated trenches. The enemy started a bombing attack early on the 14th, but a prompt barrage quenched their activities and one rather feeble effort to rush No. I. Crater was effectively dealt with by Lewis guns, while our snipers were busy and successful, and on one occasion German working parties were detected and promptly dispersed by rapid fire.

March 10th-15th

[1] Captain Dawson, 2nd-Lieuts. Coombs and Wood.

FROM LOOS TO THE SOMME.

March-April 1916
6th Battalion
This tour cost the battalion Lieut. Barker (died of wounds) and 7 men killed, with 2nd Lieut. Ashton and 53 other ranks wounded.

For the next few days the battalion remained in support to the 6th Buffs, having one company up with them each day. On the evening of the 18th the Germans suddenly opened a tremendous bombardment, after which they rushed the craters and managed to secure the front lips of several of them, though the Buffs held on stoutly to the rear lips. Nearly the whole battalion was sent up to support the Buffs; it did good service in helping to recover much of the ground but was lucky in escaping with under 20 casualties, and next morning it went back to Annequin for a week's much-needed rest. It was much below strength now, under 600 for the first time since it had landed.

March 18th

March 19th

On returning to the trenches on March 27th it took over a quieter section of the line, opposite the Quarries, and had little trouble from the enemy though much from the melting snow which flooded the line. Till the end of April it continued in this section or in the Hohenzollern, being then withdrawn to Allouagne for training. April was a fairly active month, but the enemy had replaced their troops in this quarter by a new division, who were reported "jumpy and less aggressive than their predecessors," and there was nothing like the heavy fighting or the long casualty lists of March, 5 men only were killed and 28 wounded, and as several drafts arrived the battalion was over 700 strong when it reached Allouagne, and during the two months it remained out of the line it rose almost up to full strength, even after deducting the numerous "employed" officers and men detached on one account and another. In June Captain Dawson rejoined on recovering from his wounds, while Captain Wingfield-Stratford vacated the Adjutancy on appointment to the Staff of the Twelfth Division, being succeeded by Captain Alderman. Towards the end of June the

April-June, 1916
6th Battalion

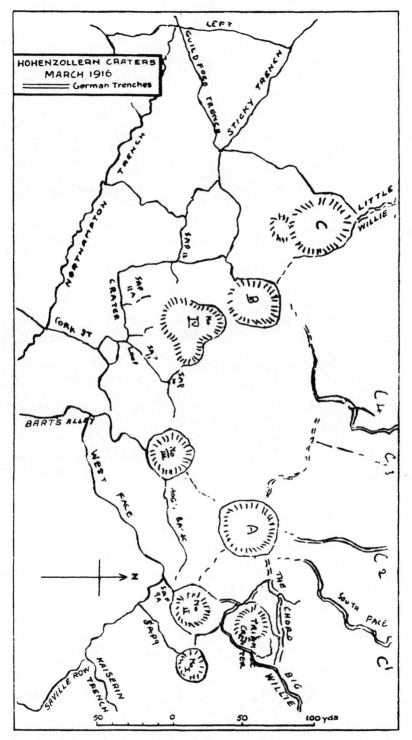

Face Page 160.

SKETCH 14.

FROM LOOS TO THE SOMME.

Twelfth moved South to the Somme area. After so long a spell of rest and training the battalion was not only well up to strength but in the best of condition and readiness for the great battle now so clearly imminent.

Meanwhile the 7th Battalion also had enjoyed nearly a couple of months of respite from the line. After two turns in the trenches in January the battalion went back to Quarrieux and La Houssoye, partly for employment on railway construction, partly to serve as demonstration party to a Divisional School which had just been started with Colonel Fiennes as Commandant and Captain Anstruther among the instructors, Major Phillips taking command during the Colonel's absence. Not till the last half of March did it return to trenches, when its Division took over the extreme right of the Third Army's front. This included a stretch of the actual bank of the Somme N.E. of Suzanne, and involved very novel conditions, as there were posts to be held on the little islands in the marshes through which the river runs. This made the patrolling very complicated. Still, if it was difficult, this patrolling was excellent training for junior officers and men, and some good work was accomplished during April, the whole of which was spent in the line. At the beginning of May the battalion was withdrawn for more training, making a 40 miles' march in four days to the Picquigny district beyond Amiens. Hence in the middle of June it returned to the Carnoy sector and had a couple of spells in the front line before the great offensive began. In the second of these it attempted a raid on the German trenches, but owing to one party of the raiders missing their way the plan miscarried and several casualties were incurred.

<small>Jan.-June, 1916
7th Battalion</small>

<small>March-June, 1916
7th Battalion</small>

After its severe "baptism of fire" at Loos the 8th Battalion had to wait some time before enjoying any real rest. It had barely been brought up to strength by large drafts, including several of its original officers

<small>Oct. 1915-July, 1916
8th Battalion</small>

FROM LOOS TO THE SOMME.

Oct., 1915-July, 1916
8th Battalion

whom it had left behind on going overseas, before it was hurried off into trenches S.E. of Ypres. Major Parker had been transferred from the 6th Battalion to take command on October 6th, and he had Captain Tillie as his Adjutant and Lieut. Evans as his Quarter-Master, while in Captains W. Wood, W. V. Ross, T. P. P. Walker, and C. F. Penton, (one of the old officers of the 8th) he was well off for company commanders. But the battalion had a bad time when it first tasted the pleasures of trench warfare in the sector so familiar to the 1st Battalion earlier in the year. Whether it was the Spoilbank and Bluff sub-sectors on either side of the Canal, or the St. Eloi trenches further to the right, it made little difference; in all alike there was mud and water, dug-outs were non-existent, parapets and parados in the habit of dissolving into a liquid mush, while, if the communication-trenches theoretically provided shelter against shot and shell, they offered those who used them a better chance of being drowned. Fortunately the Germans opposite were in similar plight, though a little better off where, as at St. Eloi, they were higher up the slope and their trenches drained down it towards the British line. They also were too well occupied with keeping the trenches in some sort of repair to spare time for being "offensive," and casualties consequently were not as high as might have been feared from the lack of protection.

From the end of November to the beginning of January the 8th had a welcome and much-needed rest at Bonningues, near St. Omer, during which time it was at last completely re-equipped and brought up to full strength, while Captain Whitty arrived from the 1st

Jan.-June, 1916
8th Battalion

Battalion and became second-in-command. Then followed nearly three months more of the Ypres Salient, this time further to the left, at Hooge and in Sanctuary Wood, a part of the line in which conditions were a little better but the enemy's activity rather greater.

FROM LOOS TO THE SOMME.

One unlucky day, February 19th, when the reserve dug-outs were heavily bombarded, cost the battalion four officers, including Captain Ross and Lieut. W. L. Wigan, a most efficient and popular young Regular who had recently joined the battalion, having served for some time with the 1st Battalion in the previous winter, but on the whole casualties were not very heavy.

Jan.-July, 1916 8th Battalion

In March the battalion was taken back to Berthen, near Bailleul, but instead of getting a rest was almost immediately sent up to the Wulverghem sector, where it remained for three months. Conditions here were decidedly better, but the reputation for quiet which the sector had enjoyed before the Twenty-Fourth Division arrived did not last long. As the weather improved both sides became more active, especially their artillery, while the Germans twice made gas attacks on a large scale. Neither time did the battalion happen to be actually holding the line, but it had large working parties up either in the front trenches or just behind, so that its gas discipline and steadiness were fully tested and stood the trial well. Its most notable experiences were a tremendous bombardment on June 29th, a retaliation for a successful raid by the 8th Queen's, which cost the battalion 40 casualties, and a raid on the night of June 4th/5th by a party under Lieut. Green, who had rejoined after recovering from his Loos wounds. This enterprise, though gallantly carried out, was not successful, the wire being insufficiently cut. A little earlier the battalion had suffered a severe loss in having Captain W. Wood killed on patrol; he was a fine officer who had had 17 years' service in the Regiment before receiving his commission and had done splendid work as a company commander in the 8th.

At the end of June the battalion was withdrawn from the Wulverghem line, but unexpectedly found itself called on for a turn in the Ploegsteert trenches, where it had to wear Australian head-gear in the hope of concealing from the enemy the departure of their previous

FROM LOOS TO THE SOMME.

July, 1916
8th Battalion

opponents. This turn, however, was brief, and by the middle of July the 8th was on the way South, bound for the Somme.

May-Aug.,
1916
10th & 11th
Battalions

Meanwhile two more Service Battalions of The Queen's Own had made their way to France, for early in May the Forty-First Division had gone overseas and had joined the Second Army. At the end of the month, after three weeks of additional training round Moolenacker, near Strazeele, the Division relieved the Ninth in trenches between Armentières and Ploegsteert, so that June found the 10th and 11th R.W.K. receiving their initiation into active service.[1] The Forty-First Division remained in this district nearly three months, a period marked by no very outstanding incidents but nevertheless one of considerable minor activity. There were intermittent bombardments, at times fairly heavy, both battalions tried their hands at raiding the German trenches, though without any marked success, snipers and machine-gunners were busy on both sides, and the casualties of the 10th in the period totalled over 130, including five officers. Among these was Captain

[1] The officers who proceeded overseas with these battalions were as follows :—
10th Battalion : Colonel A. Wood Martyn (commanding), Major W. F. Soames (second-in-command), Captains H. H. Logan (A Co.), E. R. Slaney (Adjutant), G. M. Watney (D Co.), C. H. Wild (B Co.), F. A. Wallis (A Co.), R. L. Pillman, T. J. Guest (Transport Officer), Lieuts. G. F. Drayson, C. H. Wickham, H. I. Jones, G. V. Hinds, A. J. S. Pearson ; 2nd-Lieuts. A. A. Barling, J. A. Tennyson-Smith, F. W. Roberts, F. T. Licence, S. Lawrence, J. K. Ground, G. P. Couch, G. J. Brown, A. Morgan, C. R. Browne, I. T. Grant, G. G. Samuel, F. C. Turnpenny, L. A. H. Gingell, V. Holden, A. W. Edmett, J. R. Coke, Dickinson, 2nd-Lieut. and Quartermaster E. H. Jarrett.
Captain S. H. Beattie joined the battalion on arrival in France and took command of A Company.
11th Battalion : Colonel A. F. Townshend (commanding), Majors A. C. Corfe (second-in-command) and G. A. Heron ; Captains A. J. Jiminez (Adjutant), A. E. Dickinson, S. L. Simmonds, P. Clarke-Richardson, L. V. Stone, R. G. Solbe ; Lieuts. H. W. E. Bainton (Transport Officer), W. E. Roberts (Machine-Gun Officer), C. B. Smith and B. A. Purver ; 2nd-Lieuts. R. G. Rogers, T. G. Platt, A. B. Bateman (Signalling Officer), J. O. Heath (Bombing Officer), G. D. Henderson, P. T. Cooksey, S. Gordon-Smith, C. W. Habrow, C. E. Malpas, S. J. Jones, A. V. D. Morley, F. J. Argent, N. C. Barrs, C. H. Yorke, H. G. R. Prior and H. R. Smith.

FROM LOOS TO THE SOMME.

R. L. Pillman, mortally wounded in leading a raid on July 8th. The 11th got off more lightly with about 20 men killed and three officers and 50 men wounded, the heaviest losses being on June 30th, when the Germans plastered the line with shells in retaliation for an attempted raid by a party under 2nd Lieut. Rogers, which found the wire uncut and had to come back. Both battalions lost rather more from sickness, and as drafts had not been too plentiful both were down to about 800 rank and file, though better off for officers, when they moved South. But if these months were barren of outstanding events they provided a useful apprenticeship in actual warfare for the 10th and 11th Battalions, who profited by this experience, as their record on the Somme was to show when they took their turn in the great offensive.

May-Aug., 1916 10th & 11th, Battalions

CHAPTER XI

KUT AL AMARA.

1916
2nd Battalion

Nov. 1915

Those battalions of The Queen's Own who spent 1916 in the East found it an uneventful year, apart from the tenacious but ill-fated defence of Kut al Amara, in which B and D Companies of the 2nd Battalion shared. These had left Nasiriya on November 9th under the command of Major Nelson, with whom were Captains Dinwiddy and Clarke, 2nd Lieut. Mills, two attached officers, Lieuts. Burns (5th Buffs) and Gregory (4th Devons), C.S.M.'s Crisford and Fletcher, and 322 rank and file. Travelling in native sailing boats they reached Qurna on the 11th, left for Kut two days later on a river steamer, and after a crowded and uncomfortable journey, delayed by running aground several times, reached Kut on the 17th. A week later orders were received to move up to Lajj to reinforce the Sixth Division, which was then actually attacking the Turkish position covering Baghdad.

D Company left that evening by steamer, B marching next morning along with the 14th Hussars. It was a trying march, the guides missed the way, the ground was slippery from heavy rain, and the camels and undersized mules of the transport gave much trouble. However, moving partly by land and partly by steamer the two companies reached Aziziya on the 28th, to find there the Sixth Division, which had won a Pyrrhic victory at Ctesiphon on the 22nd but had then been compelled to retire downstream by the arrival of large Turkish reinforcements. The wing was attached to Sir Charles Melliss's 30th Brigade (2/7th Gurkhas and 24th and 76th Punjabis) in which there was no British battalion.

On November 30th, the Sixth Division resumed its rearward move, the 30th Brigade pushing on ahead

KUT AL AMARA.

because news had been received that the communications had been cut below Kut by Arabs. After covering twenty miles it encamped that night at Shadaif, but before the march could be resumed next morning two British officers of the 7th Cavalry came in with the urgent message from General Townshend that he had been overtaken by the Turks and must fight, so General Melliss must return to his help. At 6.10 a.m., therefore, the 30th Brigade started on its ten-mile march back to Umm al Tubal, arriving about 9 a.m., just as a well-executed counter-stroke had foiled an enveloping movement by the Turks and thrown them back in disorder. The Sixth Division thereupon resumed its retreat with the 30th Brigade as rearguard, fighting a running action with Arab cavalry, who hovered continually on the flanks. General Townshend was determined to profit by the check he had inflicted on his pursuers to get his troops well away from the Turkish main body, and the retreat was continued till Shadie, thirty-six miles from Umm al Tubal, was reached just before midnight, the 30th Brigade having had in addition their march back from Shadaif. The men were utterly exhausted, when they halted they lay down in column and slept as they were, the R.W.K. being lucky in that they were about the only people to get any food, as they happened to find part of their transport. But the forced march had achieved its object, the pursuers had been shaken off: the next day's move brought the retreating troops without molestation to Shumran, only a few miles up-stream of Kut, and on December 3rd the R.W.K. marched into Kut, pitched their camp on the East of the town and promptly set to work on the defences.

The town of Kut stands at the end of a horse-shoe bend in the Tigris, just at the confluence of that river and the Shatt al Hai. The area of the entrenched camp which the Sixth Division established was about two miles in depth and a mile across at the inland end.

Dec., 1915 2nd Battalion

Dec. 1st

Dec. 2nd.

See Sketch 15

KUT AL AMARA.

Dec., 1915 -
Jan., 1916
2nd Battalion

Scarcely any defensive works had as yet been erected; there was only a line of block-houses about 2,000 yards North of the town, and if a successful stand were to be made much more extensive and elaborate defences would be needed. The troops had therefore to set about digging trenches, putting up wire and improving the communications between the front line and positions further to the rear. The 30th Brigade was assigned to the N.W. sector of the defences, being relieved at regular intervals by the 16th Brigade and drawn back to the second line of defence to act as General Reserve.

The fatigues of the march back to Kut were still fresh when the Turks came up and invested the town. On the right bank of the Tigris the garrison had two posts, one at the so-called Woolpress village opposite the town above the junction with the Hai, the other a bridge-head two miles lower down. This last post was still very inadequately consolidated, when, on December 9th the Turks attacked in force and drove in the company of the 67th Punjabis which was holding it. D Company 2nd R.W.K., under Captain Clarke, was sent up from reserve, but it was impossible to recover the bridge-head, and in the end the bridge had to be demolished, an operation gallantly carried out by two young officers and a party of Gurkhas and Sappers and Miners. Still the loss of this connection with the right bank was to be a real disadvantage to the defence.

For the first two months of the siege the Turks pressed extremely hard on the garrison, hoping to capture the town by force before the relieving column, already gathering lower down the river, could come into action. The British units of the garrison had more than their share of the work, for the Indian battalions had lost heavily in British officers, and mainly in consequence— by General Townshend's own admission—they were decidedly shaken and not altogether to be relied on. The wing of the R.W.K. and a company of the 1/4th

KUT AL AMARA.

Hampshires, belonging to the original Kut garrison, formed a composite battalion under Major Nelson, and had a most strenuous and active time. The Turks' advanced trenches were close up, within 50 yards in places, and, despite all the garrison could do to stop them, they gradually worked up nearer till by January 20th they were only 25 yards away. Their snipers were very busy, and at night heavy rifle and machine-gun fire was often maintained. The Turks tried assault after assault, but these were mainly directed against the Fort at the N.E. end of the line, and the only occasion on which the R.W.K.'s section was threatened was on December 25th, when the attempt was met by so heavy and effective a fire that it was nipped in the bud.

When in second line there was much digging to be done, and supports were often required for the front line, so that these periods did not mean any real relief. The R.W.K. were in the front line from December 13th to 18th, from the 22nd to the 26th, from January 1st to 8th, and 15th to 21st. On this last date the river, which had been steadily rising for some days, broke through the bunds along the river bank and flooded both the Turkish advanced trenches and the greater part of the British front line and immediate support trenches. The garrison had to retire across the open to the Middle Line, leaving a strong picquet in the only piece of the support trenches that had been kept out of water. In withdrawing the R.W.K. and Hants had about a dozen casualties from snipers, but they retaliated with good effect on the Turks, who were likewise flooded out of their trenches and compelled to expose themselves. After this a belt of flooded ground intervened between the two sets of trenches, and instead of the Turks being almost within bombing range they were 500 yards away, except for a few advanced posts on some sand-hills in the flooded area. From this time therefore the tactical situation

Dec., 1915, to Jan., 1916 2nd Battalion

KUT AL AMARA.

Jan.-April, 1916
2nd Battalion

and the character of the siege altered. All prospect of an attack in force was at an end and the fighting died down. There was much intermittent shelling and sniping to be endured, but the Turks had abandoned the effort to take Kut by storm and were relying on the slower but surer method of starvation, while concentrating all their forces to keep at bay the troops who were trying to work their way through to Townshend's relief.

It was a dreary and painful time for the garrison. The first reduction in rations had occurred as early as January 20th, when the tea ration was cut down by a half and the battery bullocks were first used for rations. Four days later the troops were put on half-rations of bread and meat, with only $\frac{1}{2}$-oz. of sugar and $\frac{1}{3}$-oz. of tea per diem. On January 29th horse meat was first issued, and after that the quality and quantity of the rations suffered reduction after reduction. The officers' chargers went after General Aylmer's repulse at the Dujailah Redoubt (March 8th), when the last hope of co-operation with the relievers was given up, a fact announced by the sacrifice of the artillery horses. Till then the R.W.K. had been among the troops chosen to lead in any attempt of the besieged to break out; had the sortie proposed for March 8th been attempted 250 R.W.K. and 150 Gurkhas under Major Nelson would have had the honour of being the first to cross to the right bank to secure a bridge-head.

March-April, 1916
2nd Battalion

The last six weeks of the siege were the most trying. The men were getting weaker daily and were hardly capable of getting through the comparatively small amount of work to be done: even the cleaning of trenches had to be performed in short spells with many reliefs. Every possible expedient for eking out the scanty store of food was tried. Nearly everybody was affected by dysentery and the death-rate among the wounded was very high. Meanwhile the relieving column was making effort after effort. But it had the

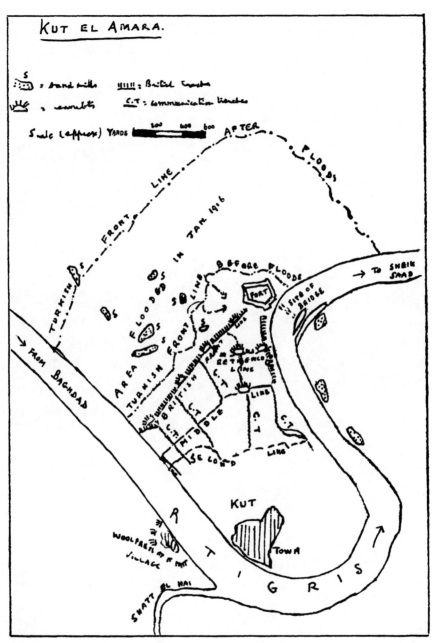

SKETCH 15.

KUT AL AMARA.

Tigris to contend against as well as the stubborn resistance of the Turk playing the defensive game at which he has always shone, and the Tigris was an important factor in the failure to win through. At last on April 29th, after nearly five months, the end came and over 8,000 British and Indian officers and men surrendered to the Turks. Among them were some 300 of The Queen's Own. The detachment's losses had been 22 killed or died of wounds, one died of disease, and 54 wounded.

April, 1916
2nd Battalion

Many of the wounded and a certain number of sick had the good fortune to be among those exchanged against Turkish prisoners in British hands. They thus escaped the fate which overtook the majority of those who remained in Turkish hands and endured the horrors of the long march into captivity in Asia Minor. Weakened by the long and grim struggle against starvation, the prisoners were quite unfit for such exertions, even had their captors been as considerate as the Turks were callous, and their arrangements for feeding them as careful and well organized as they were careless and indifferent. Of the 226 of the 2nd R.W.K. who actually passed into captivity only 69 survived their ordeal: the long march from Kut to Asia Minor accounted for a large number, enfeebled and run down as they all were by the privations and strain of the long-drawn-out siege. Of those who survived the horrors of the march many more perished in the Turkish prison camps from the combined effects of scanty and indifferent food, brutal ill-treatment and overwork, and scandalous neglect of ordinary decencies on the part of their captors.[1] There are few sadder incidents in the history of the British Army than the surrender of Kut and the fate of its defenders, but there

[1] Of the officers Lieut. Gregory alone succumbed to illness; Captain Clarke was one of a party who distinguished themselves by a daring and adventurous escape for which he was awarded the M.C.; they made their way to the coast after many perils and seized a boat in which they managed to make Cyprus.

Jan., 1916
2nd Battalion

are few finer pages than those which tell of this stubborn and tenacious defence; and in this effort of endurance and determination the wing of the 2nd R.W.K. had earned no small credit for the Regiment, which may well be proud of General Melliss's report that the detachment had "upheld the finest traditions of the British Army for grit, cheerfulness and good work throughout the siege."

Meanwhile the headquarter wing of the 2nd Battalion had not been entirely without opportunities of distinction. A certain amount of activity on the part of the troops at Nasiriya was desirable to keep the local Arabs in check. The Turks were leaving no stone unturned to induce them to rise against the British, and information was received which pointed to the probability of a Turkish advance down the Euphrates to renew the effort which had been so completely foiled at Shaiba earlier in the year. Moreover, a move along the Shatt al Hai from Kut was another possibility to be reckoned with, and the 34th Indian Brigade, therefore, which had just arrived from India, was pushed up to reinforce the garrison of Nasiriya, and its arrival allowed a movable column to be organized in which the 2nd R.W.K. were included. On January 7th this force moved out to Butaniya, 12 miles or so North of Nasiriya.

On reaching Butaniya the battalion exchanged with the 5th Queen's from the 12th to the 34th Brigade, of which Brigadier-General Tidswell was in command, parting from its old brigadier, General Brooking, with real regret, a feeling which that officer admittedly shared. Its chance in the field was not slow to come. On January 14th a reconnaissance by the Divisional Commander in the direction of Suwaij was heavily attacked by Arabs directly it started to return to camp. The Queen's, who were experiencing their "baptism of fire," conducted the retirement admirably, but the Arabs were in great force and pressed them hard, so the

BUTANIYA.

R.W.K., with the 114th Mahrattas, had to be pushed out from Butaniya to cover the retirement. This they did with complete success and the Arabs, who had already been heavily punished, broke off the fight and dispersed. The battalion's casualties were trifling, one man being killed and three wounded, but unluckily Colonel Pedley himself was hit in the thigh and, though not dangerously wounded, had to be evacuated to India, on which Major Woulfe-Flanagan took over command. *Jan.-Feb., 1916 2nd Battalion*

For over a month the column continued in camp at Butaniya, the chief occupation of the troops being to find escorts for the convoys to and from Nasiriya. The weather turned extremely cold and to those who had endured the heat of July on the Euphrates it was indeed a change to have blizzards and snow, and such intense cold that cattle died from exposure and that one of the sentries had some kind of fit caused by the cold. Moreover, the distance from Nasiriya made it difficult to supply the troops with anything beyond the merest necessities, and conditions were far from pleasant. By the beginning of February it was fairly evident that the purpose with which the force had been pushed out to Butaniya had been achieved. The tribesmen displayed no disposition to rise, the Intelligence reports showed that there was no Turkish force in the neighbourhood and that no Turkish advance down the Euphrates or along the Shatt al Hai was likely. It was accordingly decided to withdraw to Nasiriya, and on February 5th part of the column returned thither, to be followed two days later by the remainder of the force. *Feb., 1916 2nd Battalion*

Early on February 7th the night outposts which the battalion had been finding were relieved by the 114th Mahrattas and the battalion took post on the camping ground, shortly before the baggage started off at 9.30 escorted by The Queen's. Almost directly hostile Arabs began to appear and some pressed in upon the camp, but were easily held at bay, though the 114th Mahrattas on *Feb. 7th*

BUTANIYA.

Feb. 7th, 1916
2nd Battalion

outpost were more closely pressed. At 10 o'clock the baggage had cleared some sand-hills about two miles from the camp which had been picketed by The Queen's and the cavalry, so the battalion began to fall back, acting as rear-guard to the force. At first the ground was flat and open, and as the enemy could get no cover they did not approach nearer than 1,500 yards and the sand-hills were reached with little trouble. Here a stand was made for over an hour, the enemy working wide round the flanks but not pressing, though one of the outpost companies of the 114th had lost heavily on withdrawing.

In the next stage of the movement, however, in which the battalion was again acting as rear-guard, trouble really began. To the West of the track along which the column was retiring were several villages, the inhabitants of which had been looking on, to all appearances as mere spectators. As the troops passed these Arabs suddenly produced weapons they had been concealing and opened fire, inflicting many casualties. The battalion and a squadron of cavalry were detailed to clear some of these villages and had some sharp fighting while engaged in this work, but kept the Arabs off until another line of sand-hills about two miles further South was reached. Here two Indian battalions, which had come out from Nasiriya, were waiting to take over the rear-guard, and the battalion passed through them and was proceeding to a new position some way further back when the Arabs pressed the new rear-guard so hard that one battalion became extremely unsteady and began to give way. The R.W.K. accordingly had to face about and return to the firing-line, while The Queen's left the baggage and took up a covering position in their place.

The Arabs, who were in great force, came on with much courage and resolution, making skilful use of the cover afforded by the water-courses and nullahs, with which the ground abounded. For a time the situation

BUTANIYA.

was unpleasant: one of the Indian battalions was falling back in disorder, and, as the Brigadier reported, "only the accurate fire of the Mountain Battery (the 30th) and the steady courage of the R.W.K. took off the pressure." But the fighting was quite fierce and the situation critical; on the right it was hand-to-hand, and the Arabs were right in among the men who in some cases were walking away without making any effort either to fight or run. But The Queen's Own rose to the occasion; shooting steadily and coolly, they never let the Arabs close, and did much to relieve the pressure on the right. There were well under 200 rifles in the firing-line that day: out of the 10 officers and 265 other ranks present over 80 men were acting as signallers, machine-gunners or stretcher-bearers, and the remainder fired well over 120 rounds apiece. In the end the Arabs drew off about 4 p.m., discouraged by the rough handling they had received from the R.W.K. and the 114th, and seeing The Queen's appearing in strength on the right rear, and by 6 p.m. Nasiriya was reached. The total casualties came to nearly 400, so that the battalion with only thirty escaped lightly. These included Lieut. Haslam (attached from the 4th Battalion), C.S.M. Newbrook, one of the Nasiriya D.C.M.'s, and 6 men killed, and Lieut. Clough (1/4th R.W.K.) wounded. Captain Hardy received the M.C. for good work in this action and Ptes. Herbert and Vickers the D.C.M. for gallantry in rescuing wounded; indeed the battalion could congratulate itself on having been mainly instrumental in averting what had threatened to prove a very nasty business. The Arabs had shown themselves skilful and enterprising enemies, and it is only the vast scale of the war which reduces the "affair" of Butaniya to insignificance. There have been British campaigns in which it would have ranked as an important engagement and would have obtained far more recognition for the steadiness and gallantry of The Queen's Own.

Feb. 7th, 1916
2nd Battalion

Feb., 1916
2nd Battalion

Two days later the battalion, 10 officers and 294 men, went out with a column under General Tidswell to chastise the Arabs for their treacherous attack of February 7th. Several of the villages mainly concerned were seized and destroyed, towers were blown up and huts burnt. Little opposition was offered, and though the Arabs followed the return to Nasiriya at a respectful distance they never pressed their attacks home; clearly they had learnt their lesson two days earlier. What few casualties occurred—the battalion had two men killed and three wounded—were mainly caused by long-range fire, and the whole operation was most successful. It was the last brush with an enemy which the 2nd was to have for many a long month. All through 1916 and well on into the next year it remained on the Euphrates, occasionally sending out detachments on columns employed in demonstrations or as escorts to Political Officers who made trips on steamers to various points along the river, but no fighting came its way.

1916
2nd Battalion

As the year wore on several drafts arrived to replenish its ranks. On March 30th Captain Wilberforce-Bell arrived with 6 subalterns and 131 men. In June Lieut. Balbernie rejoined with three other officers and 118 men from the Tigris line, the remnant of a detachment which had been attached to the 1st Connaught Rangers of the Lahore Division in the attempts to relieve Kut. These were all who were left out of nearly 500 officers and men who had taken part in the fighting of March, when the Rangers, then in large measure composed of this draft, had distinguished themselves in a sharp action at Abu Roman, capturing a Turkish position on some sand-hills, with 50 prisoners. They were again to the fore at Beit Aiessa on April 17th, when the Rangers, with the rest of the Ferozepore Brigade, held on to captured trenches in the face of massed counter-attacks and inflicted tremendous losses on the enemy. Later on the ranks of the

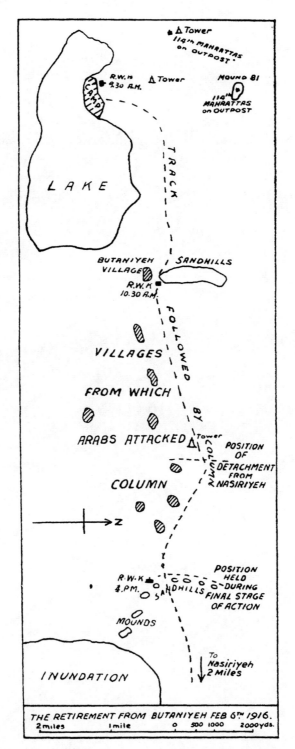

MESOPOTAMIA IN 1916.

party were thinned by a cholera epidemic, and then in May, when the Turks abandoned the Es Sinn position, the survivors helped to advance and occupy it. Though what they had accomplished stands to the credit of another regiment their own had good reason to be proud of them. Another detachment of nearly 80 joined in June, and five officers and 117 men appeared in November. As against this the sick-rate was high, and many officers and men were invalided; and though it proved possible to reorganize the battalion as one of four weak companies in June 1916 it was not until 1917 that its numbers were really brought up to strength. From May 1916 onwards it was in camp at Khamisiya, several miles S.E. of Nasiriya, with the mission of keeping the local Arabs in order, but here too it had an uneventful time under most uncomfortable and trying conditions. An observer who was on the Euphrates that summer[1] has written of embarking sick men of the regiment, of their exhausted, emaciated appearance, their soiled kit, shirts "white with the salt of perspiration, spine-pads and sun-guards half devoured by locusts," of "the pestilential heat," of "the air moist with the exudation of the drying swamp." At Khamisiya there was the additional discomfort of being without fresh water when the Euphrates fell and being consequently reduced to brackish well-water. Certainly the battalion's lot was not one to be envied.

¹⁹¹⁶
^{2nd Battalion}

To the 2/4th Battalion 1916 was a year of much hard work but no opportunities of distinction. The Fifty-Third Division was at first allotted to the "Force in Egypt," which was charged with maintaining order in the Nile Delta and with the operations against the Senussi, as distinct from the "Mediterranean Expeditionary Force," to which was allotted the defence of Egypt and the Canal against Turkish attacks. But by the time the Division had recovered from its losses at

1916
2/4th Batt.

[1] Mr. E. Candler, "The Long Road to Baghdad," I. 282.

EGYPT IN 1916.

1916
2/4th Batt.

Gallipoli and had been re-equipped and re-organized the chief danger from the Senussi was over. Still there was some anxiety lest the trouble should spread, and in February the 160th Brigade was moved to the Fayum oasis to support a Yeomanry brigade which had already been sent there for patrol duties. In this spot the 2/4th spent nearly four months, at first having delightful weather, but as the year advanced so did the temperature, and before the battalion left Fayum for the Suez Canal zone at the end of May it had experienced 120° in the tents for several days on end. The battalion had seen no fighting while at Fayum, but its presence and the demonstration marches undertaken to the chief villages of the district had been effective in suppressing any disposition to revolt. In March Colonel Simpson's health compelled him to relinquish command again and to return to England; he was succeeded by Lieut.-Col. Norton, of the West India Regiment, who retained command till he also was invalided at the end of June; Lieut.-Col. Money, of the Shropshire Yeomanry, then obtained the command, taking over on July 27th. Large drafts, amounting to nearly 500 all told, had brought the battalion practically up to strength.

The move to the Canal zone brought the battalion nearer to the theatre of active operations, though the Southern half of the Canal line was never the scene of fighting. But the battalion was fully employed on keeping in repair a longish line of defence, so long that a continuous trench line could not be maintained and fortified posts were constructed at all the chief features of tactical importance. When the expected Turkish attack finally developed in August, to be decisively repulsed at Romani, the battalion was sent up North to Kantara, but too late for any fighting. Until September 12th it remained at Kantara, training but suffering a good deal from illness. A move to Moascar and two months' more training followed, and

Photo by] [A. Debenham, Cowes.

COLONEL A. T. F. SIMPSON, D.S.O., V.D.
Commanded 2/4 Battalion, 1915 and 1916;
3/4 Battalion in 1916 and 1917.

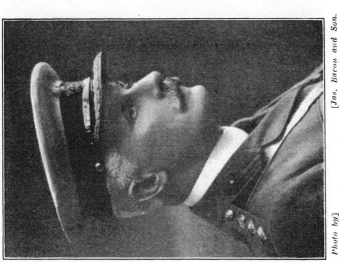

Photo by] [Jas. Bacon and Son.

COLONEL R. J. WOULFE-FLANAGAN, D.S.O.
Commanded 2nd Battalion from 1916.

Face Page 178.

EGYPT IN 1916.

then the battalion returned to Kantara, drew equipment and camels, and on November 27th started off on a four-day march Eastward along the recently-laid wire road. At Khirba a three weeks' halt was made, and then on December 20th the battalion moved up to Railhead, 40 miles further East, in readiness to support the attack on El Arish. However, the Turks did not think El Arish worth a fight and the 2/4th were retained at Railhead for local defence duties. Here the end of the year found it with A Company under Captain Hodgson, detached at Salmanca, and D (Captain Downes) at Mazar. If 1916 had brought it no fighting the year ended with the battalion close up to the front and with every prospect of a more active time near at hand.

1916
2/4th Batt.

CHAPTER XII.

THE SOMME.

July, 1916

As the summer of 1916 drew on it became increasingly evident that the projected British offensive could not be long postponed. The steady increase in the numbers available[1] and the advance in experience and efficiency of the " New Army " Divisions had greatly improved the chances of success. Some relief of the pressure still maintained on Verdun was urgent: moreover, though the second year of the war was nearing its end, the Allies had as yet scored no substantial offensive success in any theatre of importance; despite all their efforts and losses they had merely achieved a negative success by foiling the German efforts to obtain a decision. For months past elaborate preparations had been in progress, involving most careful Staff work as well as tremendous exertions on the part both of the troops at the front and of the munition-workers at home. The accumulation of ammunition and other material, the improvement of communications and water-supplies, the digging of assembly trenches and gun positions, the manifold arrangements for the support and supply of the troops engaged, for the wounded, for the safe housing of ammunition, and for the multifarious other requirements for a modern battle on a great scale—all these were a lengthy and laborious process. The point selected for the attack lay at the junction between the British and the French on the Somme. Here the German positions ran along the Southern and Western slope of the low hills which form the watershed between the middle Somme and the rivers which drain away E. and N. towards Belgium. The French were to attack astride the Somme in an Easterly direction, the British

[1] The rifle strength of the British forces in France rose by nearly 50 per cent. between January 1st, 1916, and June 30th.

THE SOMME.

right from Maricourt to Fricourt was to strike North, while from Fricourt, where the enemy's lines formed a sharply-marked salient, across the Ancre to Serre the centre and left also attacked East.

July, 1916

More formidable defences than the German lines on the Somme have hardly ever existed. The ground had been in German occupation since October 1914, their hold on it had been unshaken by any serious offensive or bombardment: they had had labour and material in abundance and had constructed two systems of defences about two to three miles apart, each consisting of several lines of trenches, lavishly provided with bomb-proof dug-outs, with strong and elaborate wire entanglements many yards in breadth, all the villages and houses in the neighbourhood had been turned into veritable fortresses, the woods had been carefully prepared for defence, and the whole position bristled with well placed and protected machine-guns. Every device known to the military engineer had been utilized to make these lines impregnable; and tremendous as was the volume and intensity of the bombardment which the British opened a week before the assault, even it did not achieve all that had been hoped for: so many machine-guns survived the bombardment that a tremendous toll was taken of the attackers who, too often, reached the German trenches in such diminished numbers that they were unable to withstand the vigorous counter-attacks of the enemy or to retain the ground captured at the first assault. On the British left and centre this was conspicuously the case. Though the German front line was carried at most points the gains could not be maintained, and only on the right, and to a less degree on the right centre between Fricourt and Ovillers, was any ground secured. Fortunately the gains that were secured were so well turned to account that despite the disappointment on the left July 1st 1916 proved the beginning of the turn of the tide.

THE SOMME.

July 1st, 1916   Of the six battalions of The Queen's Own then in France only the 7th was actively engaged on that day. The 1st was still in front of Arras, the 6th, though within the battle area, was held in reserve, the 8th was opposite Messines, and the 10th and 11th were still completing their apprenticeship at Ploegsteert. But 7th Battalion the 7th was fully to sustain the Regiment's reputation. To it, as to its Division as a whole, July 1st was the first great test, and the Eighteenth Division came through the strain splendidly. The frontage allotted for its attack was the ground so familiar to it just S. and W. of Montauban. The Division was the second from the right of the British line, the Thirtieth, who attacked Montauban itself, coming between it and the French. All its three brigades were in line, the 55th being on the right and having the 8th E. Surreys on the right, the 7th Queen's on the left, the 7th Buffs in support, and the 7th R.W.K. in reserve.

July 1st, 1916   At 7.30 a.m. the attack was launched, and though The 7th Battalion Queen's and East Surreys met with determined resistance, they made splendid progress. But before long they were held up, and first the Buffs and then the Battalion had to be thrown into the fight to complete the success. A and C Companies were sent up at 11 o'clock to help the East Surreys capture Train Alley, the back trench of the front system; after securing it they were to push forward against Montauban Alley, an intermediate line parallel with the village itself. Simultaneously D was to advance to and consolidate the Pommiers Line, of which Train Alley formed a part, but its runner was hit and never delivered the orders, and over an hour later the Adjutant discovered D still in the British trenches.

A and C both came in for hard fighting. The German front system had not been completely " mopped up," and A lost nearly all its officers and could not get beyond the Pommiers Line, where Germans were still putting up a stubborn resistance, which, however, was

THE POMMIERS RIDGE.

July 1st, 1616
7th Battalion

before long overcome. Meanwhile C on the right got on better, and Captain Waddington and two platoons had established themselves in Montauban Alley just as, about noon, the Thirtieth Division reached and mastered the village. Here they maintained themselves, consolidating the position with the assistance of the R.E., and gradually other detachments of the battalion worked their way forward. C.S.M. Klein, with the bulk of A Company, pushed up Mine Alley and ultimately joined Captain Waddington; another platoon of A under 2nd/Lieut. File with the other two platoons of C had already reinforced him, and with the assistance of parties of the three other battalions Montauban Alley was made good, despite hostile sniping and machine-gun fire. Splendid work was done by Lieut. Lewin, who laid and repaired telephone wires under heavy fire and successfully maintained communication between Battalion Headquarters and the troops in front; Captain Watkin Williams, R.A.M.C., the Medical Officer attached to the battalion, and his orderly, Sergt. Cook, were also conspicuous; the latter went repeatedly into the open under heavy fire to dress the wounded and bring them into safety. By 2 p.m. the Colonel had brought Battalion Headquarters up to the Pommiers Line, which D was consolidating. He himself pushed up to the front line to find the troops well established, but running short of ammunition. This was replenishing by carrying parties of B and D, but for the rest of that day there was nothing in the nature of a real counter-attack, though the line was for some time rather " in the air," as touch was only obtained with the 53rd Brigade on the left flank quite late in the day. By evening, however, a firm grip on the ridge West of Montauban had been secured.

If the distinction of leading the Division into the enemy's trenches had not fallen to the 7th, it had contributed substantially to confirm the gains achieved by the leading battalions, thereby making

THE SOMME.

<small>July 1st-4th, 1916
7th Battalion</small> the day one of real success for the Eighteenth Division, which had penetrated as far as any other into the hostile lines and had made good all its objectives. It was here that the winning advantage had been secured: the Northward advance of the Eighteenth Division and those on its flanks turned the German positions on the Fricourt-Ovillers front, and this, coupled with the success of the troops who had penetrated the German trenches North of Fricourt and maintained themselves there, forced the Germans back to their second position on the crest of the ridge. They only retired to it, however, after a week's sharp fighting. In this the 7th R.W.K. had only a minor part. It had taken over the new front line of the brigade West of Montauban on the early morning of July 2nd and maintained the position till the evening of the 4th, coming in for a good deal of heavy shelling, but getting some good targets in enemy withdrawing from advanced positions which they could no longer retain. By the time relief came the battalion had suffered 180 casualties, Lieut. Innocent and 36 men being killed, Captain Latter, 2nd Lieuts. Freeman, Heaton, Woodhouse, Phipps and Gregory and 136 men wounded, and one man missing. Considering the importance of the results achieved the 7th could be reckoned fortunate in escaping so lightly. It was to enjoy a week out of the line before it was thrown into an even severer struggle.

<small>July 1st-3rd, 1916
6th Battalion</small> Meanwhile another battalion of The Queen's Own had taken a part in the attack. The Twelfth Division had been in reserve on July 1st, but as the Eighth Division on the left of the Third Corps, to which the Twelfth belonged, had suffered heavily and made but little progress in its attack on Ovillers La Boisselle, the Twelfth relieved it on the night of July 1st/2nd. Thus the 6th R.W.K. found themselves in the front trenches with orders to resume the attack early on July 3rd. The position it had taken over lay just West of the ruins of Ovillers and the task assigned to the 37th Brigade

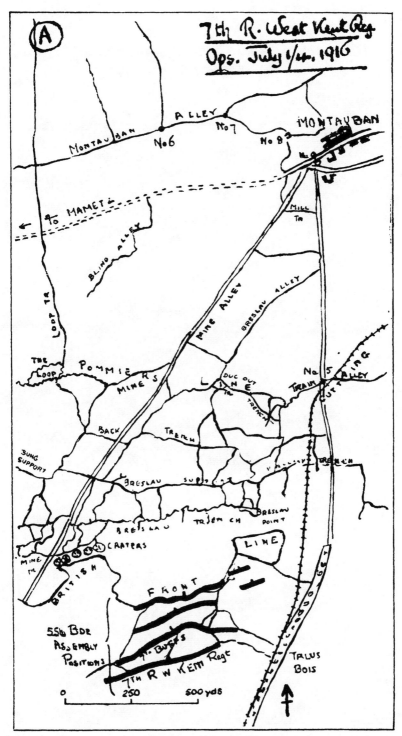

OVILLERS.

was the capture of two small salients in the German front line, which here ran almost due N. and S. To its right the 35th Brigade was also attacking E. and at the same time a larger attack was to be delivered further to the right in a Northerly direction against the line Contalmaison-Mametz Wood, and it was hoped that the two attacks would ultimately unite and cut off the German garrisons still clinging desperately to Ovillers and La Boisselle. But the task before the 37th Brigade was one of no small difficulty. Much of the German wire had escaped destruction by the bombardment, and the two salients to be attacked by The Queen's and the battalion respectively were separated by a stretch of uncut wire 300 yards long, while an even longer belt to the left of the Northernmost salient, the one which the battalion was attacking, put an extension of the attack to that flank out of the question. The Royal Fusiliers, who were opposite this frontage, were told off to give covering fire from rifles and machine-guns, and a smoke barrage had been arranged for the protection of this flank, but the prospect of enfilade fire was a serious menace.

July 3rd,
6th Battalion
See Sketches
18 & 19

The attack was to be delivered by A and C Companies, the former under Captain Barnett on the right, the latter under Captain Hatton on the exposed left flank. Their objective was the German front line, but after capturing it they were to bomb along the trench to both flanks, A having to connect up with the 6th Queen's, C to reach a junction with a communication trench which was to be secured and a double-block erected. Meanwhile B and D under Captains H. C. Harris and Matthews were to pass through A and C and assault the German second line about 300 yards further on. The attack was then to be carried on by the East Surreys, whose objective was a third line of trenches, just North of Ovillers.

It was still dark when at 3.15 a.m. the barrage lifted off the German front line and A and C dashed forward.

THE SOMME.

July 3rd, 1916
6th Battalion

They were met by heavy machine-gun fire, but it failed to stop them, and without a check they were into the German trench and had killed, taken or driven off its defenders, mostly machine-gunners. 2nd Lieut. Coombs led the way with magnificent gallantry: he was the first man of C into the trench, shot down a German who was about to shoot his company commander, and promptly started bombing and clearing the dug-outs. A Company was equally successful, though Captain Barnett was killed after reaching the German trench, and its bombers at once began pushing along to the right with considerable success. Unluckily in the darkness the left platoons of C had gone too far to the left and had come up against uncut wire. Some men managed to win through this and forced their way into the trench, but the majority, including the two platoon commanders, 2nd Lieuts. Montagu and P. V. Roberts, were shot down, and the loss in this way of a specially-selected bombing squad severely handicapped the company's efforts to bomb Northward along the trench and secure the junction with the communication trench. However, the first objective had been secured on a frontage of about 250 yards, and A and C opened a heavy fire on the German second line to cover the advance of the second wave of the attack.

As A and B came charging gallantly forward they were scourged with machine-gun fire from the flanks, and lost so terribly from this that they altogether lacked the weight needed to carry out their task. Moreover, they had been delayed by the congestion in the British trenches, and by the time they reached the German front trench the barrage had already lifted off the second line, which was their objective, and it could be seen that this trench was thickly manned. But, forlorn hope as an attack was, Captain Matthews never hesitated and led the remnants of D Company forward into a perfect hail of bullets, only to be shot down after covering a few yards. His courage found a parallel in the gal-

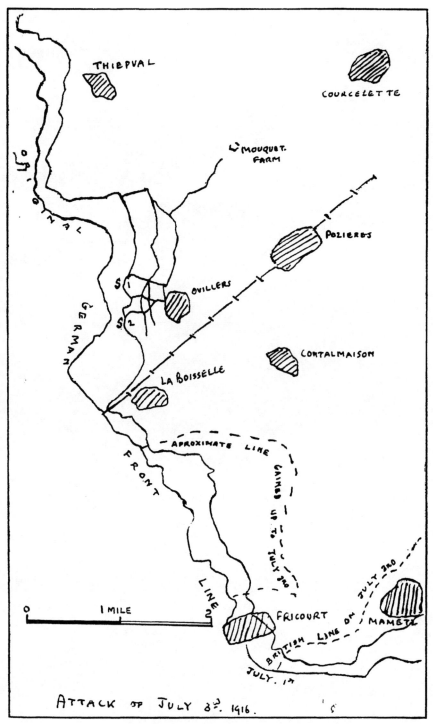

OVILLERS.

lantry with which 2nd Lieut. Latimer, a subaltern recently joined from Rugby, dashed forward ahead of his men, pushed through the wire on the left of the salient and stood up on the German parapet to cheer his men on and point them out the way, till he fell shot through the head.   *July 3rd, 1916 6th Battalion*

After the failure of the supports to reach the German second line the survivors of the attack put up a most gallant fight to retain their gains in the front line. Their position was precarious and isolated. The Queen's, on the right, had come up against uncut wire, in front of which they were mown mercilessly down, only a handful getting through into the German trenches. Thus the 6th were without support on the right and were soon hard pressed on that flank, while on the left a strong point at the junction with the communication trench held up C Company's bombers. They were cut off from reinforcements by the enfilade fire of the machine-guns which swept No Man's Land. Several times the men in the German trench saw parties starting out to dash across the open with ammunition and bags of bombs, but time after time the machine-guns caught them, and it was only by dodging from shell-hole to shell-hole that a very few ever reached their goal. Communication was hard to keep up: a telephone wire was run across but was promptly cut, though a few messages were taken to and fro by runners. Moreover, the bombardment had only too effectually damaged the German front line and it gave but little protection to those trying to consolidate it or to carry on a fire-fight against the Germans manning the second line and the communication trenches.

But bad as was the situation, the 6th put up a splendid fight. 2nd Lieut. Buckle behaved with conspicuous courage and disregard of safety, walking up and down along the German parapet to direct the fire of his men. He was ordered to get down into the trench, but persisted nevertheless until

THE SOMME.

<small>July 3rd, 1916
6th Battalion</small> at last he was hit and killed. Sergt. Knight, of C Company, seeing many of the bomb-carriers shot down in the effort to cross No Man's Land, leapt out of the trench under heavy fire and fetched in two bags of bombs from a fallen carrier, but was himself hit in the head and killed just as he regained the trench. Sergt. Brown and Corpl. Hooker, both of A Company, were also conspicuous by their courage and fine example, and for several hours the 6th stuck tenaciously to their gains, keeping the Germans at bay. Captain Hatton, the senior officer in the captured trenches—for Captain Harris had been killed leading B Company across No Man's Land—had impressed on his men that the Colonel's explicit orders were that the ground taken must be held to the last, and the men responded splendidly. While bombs and ammunition held out they held stubbornly on. But casualties were heavy, the men using the parados of the German trench as their fire position were terribly exposed to the machine-guns, and before long Captain Hatton had only men enough for a couple of bombing squads, one at each end of his line, whom he and his servant managed to keep supplied with bombs by moving up and down the trench to collect bombs off the casualties. When things had reached this pass the end could not be long delayed; Captain Hatton himself was badly wounded about 7 a.m., and a final effort dislodged the few survivors from the trench they had so stoutly defended.

Those few who regained their original trenches spent the rest of the day hanging on there under a heavy shell-fire from the direction of Pozières. But the Germans did not follow them up, they were content to have recovered their own trenches, and that evening the remnants of the 6th were withdrawn to Bouzincourt. The losses had been terrible: 617 officers and men had gone into action, 375 were casualties.

The losses were the more felt because those who had fallen included many of the original members of

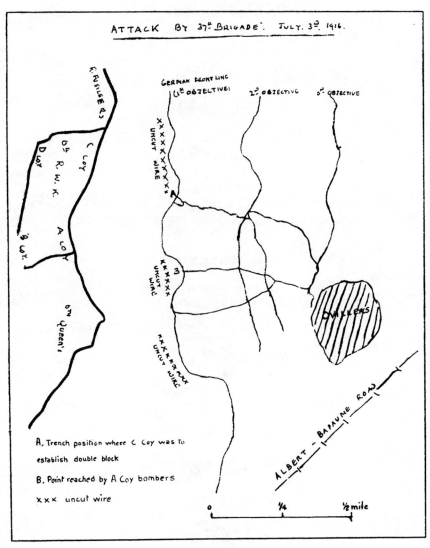

THE SOMME.

the battalion. In addition to the officers already named
Lieuts. J. H. Hughes and B. V. Wood were killed,
2nd Lieut. Coombs also, who had been badly wounded
but managed to crawl back to the British lines, died of
wounds shortly afterwards, while in all ten subalterns
were wounded, making the total loss of officers nineteen. The four company commanders, three of whom
were killed and one, Captain Hatton, wounded and a
prisoner, all belonged to the early days of the 6th, and
among the N.C.O.'s who had fallen were many who
had joined at Purfleet. Loos and the Hohenzollern
Craters had made gaps in the 6th in 1914, and July
3rd went far to wipe it out. Fortunately the practice
had now been established of leaving out from an
attack a proportion of officers, N.C.O.'s and men to
serve as a nucleus on which, in case of need, a battalion
might be built up again, and thanks to this the 6th
had Captain Dawson and a couple of officers and 40
N.C.O.'s and men from each company available, so that
reconstruction could be promptly begun when, on the
9th, the Twelfth Division, which had meanwhile made
substantial progress in the Ovillers neighbourhood, was
relieved and the battalion went back to Vauchelles des
Authoy to rest and re-organize. However, though
reinforced by half-a-dozen officers, including Captain
E. T. Williams, who rejoined on July 20th, its depleted ranks were not adequately replenished. A draft
of 253 arrived on the 22nd, but only 31 belonged to
The Queen's Own, the remainder being promptly transferred to the other units of the Division to which they
properly belonged. The battalion was thus still much
below strength when on July 26th it moved up again
into front trenches between Ovillers and Pozières.
Before this, however, the 1st Battalion had come down
to the battle area and the 7th had been through that
desperate struggle for Trones Wood, which is perhaps
the episode in the whole Somme most closely associated
with the Regiment in the popular mind.

July, 1916
6th Battalion

THE SOMME.

July 13th, 1916
7th Battalion
See Sketch 20

When, on the evening of July 12th, the Eighteenth Division took over the right of the British line considerable progress had been made in clearing the intermediate area between the first and second German systems. East of Montauban Bernafay Wood had been taken and a footing obtained in the Southern end of Trones Wood, and it was this last position which B and C Companies took up that night with D in support on the Eastern edge of Bernafay Wood and A a little further back. As a preliminary to the great attack fixed for the morning of July 14th it was highly desirable that Trones Wood should be completely cleared, and accordingly orders were issued for the battalion to push through the wood from South to North, to the 7th Queen's to attack its Northern end, and to the 7th Buffs to capture a "strong point" at the S.E. corner where Maltzhorn Trench joined the Guillemont Road. It was a difficult task, the lie of the ground and the conditions prevailing in that quarter of the battle-field, where heavy fighting had been in progress for some days, were all against the attackers. The wood had been badly shot about and was a maze of shallow trenches, strong points and shattered trees, while orders were received very late and there was scanty time to prepare for the advance. However, the 7th went forward with dash and determination.

The attack, launched at 7 p.m. on July 13th, after three hours' bombardment, was delivered in the face of a most effective German barrage which inflicted heavy casualties on the support companies as they crossed the open, both Captain Emden of D and Lieut. Skinner, who was in temporary command of A, being hit. However, the battalion made good progress despite stout opposition and many difficulties from the undergrowth and fallen trees which filled the interior of the wood. Heavy and confused fighting such as occurred in Trones Wood is bound to result in disorganization

TRONES WOOD.

and loss of cohesion and direction, and the attack was further impeded by coming up against a couple of "strong points" inside the wood. However, by 7.30 part of B Company, under Captain Holland, reached the Southern branch of the light railway which runs through the wood, only to find that the Germans had somehow got in between them and their starting point and had retaken a "strong point" in the interior of the wood. Captain Holland's party, which had been reinforced by detachments of A and C, under Lieuts. Bartholomew and Hogg, accordingly dug themselves in along the railway and maintained themselves all night, though without any support, practically isolated and constantly attacked, mainly from S. and S.W.

July 13th, 1916 7th Battalion

Meanwhile hardly any news came back from C Company, which had attacked on B's right with orders to change direction to the right on reaching the railway so as to line the Eastern edge of the wood, so Colonel Fiennes therefore sent up the Adjutant, Captain Anstruther, to investigate. Captain Anstruther made his way with some difficulty to the middle of the wood and there found 150 men of A, C and D all mixed up and scattered about; mostly on the Eastern edge, without any unwounded officers and much disorganized. He promptly re-organized these men, posted about 100 with 6 Lewis guns along the Eastern edge, pushed further North with the rest, obtained touch with the very few of The Queen's who had managed to reach the wood in face of the heavy shelling and machine-gun fire, and established three posts about 200 yards from the apex also.[1] Thanks to his energy and initiative the defence of the central portion of the wood was most successfully organized. Corpl. Chapman, whose Lewis gun section had all become casualties, did splendid work in

[1] The precise position reached by the 7th was extremely difficult to ascertain: what makes it seem that the battalion never quite reached the Northern end of the wood, which it was at first believed to have done, was that none of its dead were subsequently found in the Northern portion.

THE SOMME.

July 13th-14th, 1916
7th Battalion

collecting men and showing them how to work the guns, so that he was able to keep his guns in action and contributed greatly to beat off the German attacks. Battalion Headquarters meanwhile had moved up to the S.W. corner and, though attacked, beat off its enemies with rifle and machine-gun fire and bombs. About midnight therefore the situation was that some 250 of the 7th R.W.K. and a few 7th Queen's were established in Trones Wood North of the railway; these were cut off from support by the Germans who had reoccupied the portion South of the railway and were attacking Captain Holland's men from the South, while the Buffs and some East Surreys were still fighting for the "strong point" on the Guillemont Road. The situation was precarious; the Germans were counterattacking vigorously and the party established in the wood was perilously isolated and hard pressed. Still it held its ground and kept the Germans at bay; indeed when in the small hours of July 14th Captain Anstruther was offered two platoons of the 12th Middlesex, who had arrived at Battalion Headquarters, he declined their help, saying that his line was strong enough and that he was beating off all the German attacks. However, as daylight came these attacks increased in force and ammunition began to fail; but eventually, about 6 o'clock, just as a fresh counter-attack was threatening to recover the wood, a dashing counter-attack by the 12th Middlesex and 6th Northamptons, under Colonel F. A. Maxwell, swept Northward through the wood, re-established touch with Captains Anstruther and Holland, and cleared the wood right up to the apex, forcing the surviving Germans out. As the Germans bolted from the wood like driven birds they gave good targets to the riflemen and Lewis gunners along the Eastern edge, who saw their tenacity and endurance well rewarded.

If the story that the 7th had held out, though cut off, for 48 hours must be relegated to the category of war

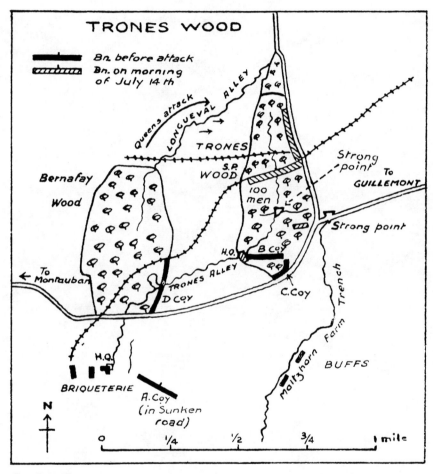

SKETCH 20.

TRONES WOOD.

July, 1916
7th Battalion

correspondents' legends, the battalion's achievement was splendid enough by itself, and the real truth can well stand. General Maxse, the Divisional Commander, wrote warmly and appreciatively of " the brave men of the 7th R.W.K. who, through the night of July 13th/14th, maintained their position in isolated parties in the wood." The capture of Trones Wood had helped appreciably to secure the right flank of the British attack, one of the most successful of the whole Somme offensive. The casualties, nearly 250 all told, were heavy, but not out of proportion to what had been achieved. Lieuts. Skinner and Crosse and 2nd Lieuts. Cathcart, File, Forsyth and Saveall were killed or died of wounds with 28 men, 23 men were missing, 5 other officers and 174 men wounded. This added to the casualties of July 1st-4th had reduced the battalion by half and the rest of the Division being in like case after sharing in the fight for Delville Wood it was transferred before the end of July to the quieter Flanders front.[1]

July 14th had greatly developed the results achieved on the 1st and had established the British firmly on the main ridge, but the frontage on which the German second position had been penetrated was but narrow and some of the fiercest fighting of the whole Somme took place in the effort to extend our gains Eastward past Guillemont and Ginchy, Northward past High Wood and Westward past Pozières to the heights overlooking the Ancre. The German resistance was perhaps never so tenacious as between the middle of July and the end of August; they contested every yard of trench with skill and obstinacy, launched repeated counter-attacks at every point wrested from them, and bombarded with unremitting fury not only the British positions but all the lines of approach.

---

[1] Captain Anstruther received the D.S.O. and Corpl. Chapman the D.C.M., while 12 N.C.O.'s and men were awarded the M.M.

THE SOMME.

July, 1916
1st Battalion

See Sketch 21

The 1st R.W.K. therefore, whose Division came into line between Longueval and Bazentin le Grand on July 19th, came in for heavy and costly fighting. The battalion was in reserve when the Fifth Division made its first attack. This was on July 20th, and had as objective a road running S.E. from the E. corner of High Wood. Partial success only was achieved, and that evening the battalion took over the left of its brigade's front, its left resting on the Southern angle of the wood from which its line followed a track running S.E. It was a hot corner, the situation in High Wood was most obscure and the German artillery most active, while the battalion had to push out many patrols to locate the enemy, and the day's casualties came to 90 in all, though the majority of them were accounted for by a heavy barrage in which one company was caught when moving up. Sergt. Traill distinguished himself greatly by the coolness and skill which he displayed, keeping his platoon together and bringing it through the barrage with very few casualties and then setting a splendid example to his men while they were digging in under heavy fire. Sergt. Davis and L/Cpl. Butler also were conspicuous for the devotion and gallantry with which they went out repeatedly to relay and mend the telephone wires and keep up communication between the front line and Battalion Headquarters. Then, after two strenuous days in the line came another big effort all along the front from Guillemont to Pozières.

In this attack the battalion's special objective was Wood Lane, a trench 400 yards ahead and just beyond the road which the brigade had tried to reach on July 20th. This trench lay over the crest of a gentle slope and could not be seen from our front line. Its capture was essential as a preliminary to the attack on Switch Trench, the main objective of the Division. This, which ran more or less E. and W. through the Northern end of the High Wood, was

July 22nd &
23rd, 1916
1st Battalion

HIGH WOOD.

to be attacked at 1 a.m. on July 23rd, the preliminary attack by the 13th Brigade being timed for 10 p.m. This allowed but little time for bombarding or for accurate location and registration of the object.

July, 22nd-23rd, 1916 1st Battalion

However, the lie of the ground allowed the leading companies, A and B, to advance almost to the crest before the barrage lifted. Thanks largely to this they reached the road almost without a casualty and pushed on towards their objective. But as they topped the crest rifle and machine-gun fire caught them in flank from High Wood and in front from Switch Trench. Many officers and men fell, and though at two points the trench was reached and a lodgement made both parties were unsupported, for the battalion on the right had not got as far forward, and High Wood itself had again proved impregnable. A platoon of C, under Lieut. Peachey, had been detailed to guard the left flank and to capture the strong point believed to exist just inside the Wood, but it was shot down almost to a man and the enfilade machine-gun fire from this strong point proved most effective. Nevertheless both detachments held on with great determination. On the right 30 men of A established themselves in the trench though all their officers had fallen and were only at length dislodged when their supply of bombs ran out. On the left a platoon of B under Lieut. J. J. Scott and Sergt. Franklin occupied about 40 yards of the trench, inflicted many casualties on the Germans and maintained themselves firmly for nearly four hours, though the enemy made several bombing attacks from the left. These were repulsed mainly through the skill and gallantry of Pte. Butlin, who sprang over some German bombs which were just about to explode and, hurling his own bombs at the Germans, drove them back and secured the flank of his party. At another point Sergt. Traill collected a few men, dug in 15 yards from the German trenches, and hung on in this advanced position for several hours, killing several

195

THE SOMME.

July, 1916
1st Battalion

Germans who came out to capture some of the British wounded, and when he finally retired brought back several wounded with him. In the end, however, all these scattered parties had to be withdrawn to the original line. Nearly 400 of those who had started to the attack were casualties, Captain Bennett, Lieuts. Healey and Bartlett, 2nd Lieuts. Cornford, J. A. Fleming, Leatherdale, Cross, Lewinstein, Fox and Gillett were killed, and four other officers wounded. Many who would otherwise have been missing were brought safely in, thanks to the splendid courage and devotion of Corpl. Hatch, the N.C.O. in charge of the stretcher-bearers. He was indefatigable in the work of succour, although he was out for over seven hours, working from shell-hole to shell-hole, carrying men on his back under the heaviest fire, and altogether rescuing nearly 50 wounded before he himself was at last hit. The standard required for the V.C. must indeed have been high when such gallantry only received the D.C.M.[1]

The 1st Battalion's initiation into the Somme had been unfortunate, but no blame could attach to it for failing against a very strong position which was dominated by the all but impregnable High Wood. Officers and men alike had distinguished themselves by numerous acts of devotion and gallantry, and the tenacity with which the advanced parties had clung to their gains had been worthy of the best traditions of The Queen's Own. Indeed, the Divisional commander paid a special visit to congratulate the battalion on its behaviour. At its next attempt it was again confronted with an extremely difficult task. Since the original capture of Longueval and Delville Wood by the Ninth Division on July 14th repeated German counter-attacks had won back much ground, and several divi-

---

[1] Captain Baines, R.A.M.C., who had been serving with the battalion since early in 1915, received the M.C. for his gallantry and devotion to duty in this action.

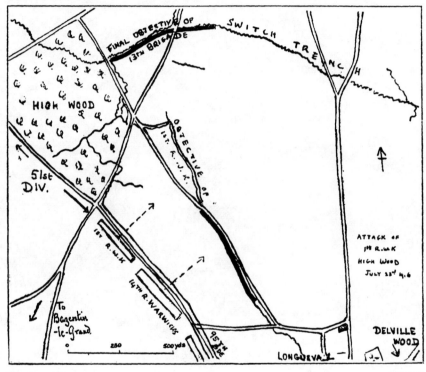

LONGUEVAL.

sions had tried to deprive the Germans of these bones of contention. On the night of July 29th/30th the 13th Brigade went up to relieve the 95th at Longueval, the battalion being in support to the K.O.S.B.'s, who were in Delville Wood itself. It had the greatest difficulty in establishing itself in its proper positions among the ruins of the village; the Germans put down a tremendous barrage, communication between companies and Battalion Headquarters was lost, and merely to reach and hold a support position cost the battalion over 60 casualties. It did not actually take part in the attack, merely having to endure an absolute deluge of 8 inch and 5.9 inch shells while the K.O.S.B.'s succeeded in finally completing the work which the 15th Brigade had begun on July 27th, clearing most of the orchards N.E. of Longueval. _{July, 1916
1st Battalion
See Sketch 22}

After this the Fifth Division was withdrawn to a training area S.E. of Abbeville, where it had three weeks before being called on for yet another effort. When the 1st R.W.K. reached this area it was certainly in need of rest and reinforcements. Its losses had amounted to little short of 600, and included many valuable and experienced officers and N.C.O.'s. It was over a year since the battalion had been engaged in any very heavy fighting and consequently there had been relatively few changes since Hill 60, so that in a way these losses were the more acutely felt. However, about 16 new officers turned up during August with drafts amounting to over 300 men, though a large proportion of these men were recruits with only four months' service, whose training was in so elementary a stage that it was a superhuman task to render them fit to go into action in less than three weeks.

Among the Divisions which took up the struggle after the Fifth withdrew from Delville Wood was the Twenty-Fourth, so that it fell to the lot of the 8th Battalion to push on to the N.E. and E. against the next tactical feature of importance, the ruins which had once _{Aug., 1916
8th Battalion}

197

THE SOMME.

Aug., 1916
8th Battalion

See Sketch 22

August 12th

been Guillemont. The 8th reached the Somme area at the end of July, and went into trenches East of Trones Wood and facing Guillemont on August 11th. Its first trenches were mere apologies for shelter, but the men dug with such vigour that by daybreak they had provided themselves with quite respectable protection, which stood them in good stead next morning when they were subjected to a very severe bombardment. During its first week on the Somme the battalion was mainly occupied in being shelled and in digging; there was no actual hostile attack, but the severity of the shelling may be calculated from the battalion's casualties, which, between August 10th and 18th, came to 6 officers and 146 other ranks, among the killed being 2nd Lieut. S. E. Dove, who had just succeeded Captain Penton, wounded on August 11th, in command of D Company. The chief work put in by the battalion was its construction in two nights of a new trench 800 yards in length and 400 yards further to the front, an operation which it was fortunate to complete without being interrupted by the enemy. The battalion also distinguished itself by good work in bringing in many wounded who were lying out in front of the line, casualties of an attack on Guillemont some days earlier. In this work Captain McLarty, the Medical Officer of the battalion, distinguished himself greatly, labouring incessantly and devotedly and dealing with literally hundreds of cases.

Aug. 19th & 20th

On August 18th the Twenty-Fourth Division attempted the task which had already baffled several others, the capture of Guillemont, and succeeded in establishing a foothold in the ruins of the village and in taking the railway station some distance in the North. The 72nd Brigade was in reserve during the attack, but next night the 8th R.W.K. sent up A Company to take over the post in Guillemont. This consisted of shell-holes rather imperfectly consolidated, and as the Germans were in strength in some quarries only 40 yards

LIEUT.-COLONEL J. C. PARKER.
Commanded 8th Battalion, 1915, 1916, 1917.

LIEUT.-COL. J. T. TWISLETON-WYKEHAM-FIENNES.
Commanded 7th Battalion, 1915, 1916.

DELVILLE WOOD.

off A had a lively time, contending with no little success against bombers and snipers. Moreover they managed to dig a continuous trench facing South and to consolidate two large shell-holes facing East, while on the night of August 20th 2nd Lieut. Roscoe took out a fighting patrol of one platoon which worked its way Eastward and then South into the village, met and disposed of several enemy, and established two new posts to the South which proved useful in preventing the enemy from interfering with the digging of the trench. It was a much improved position which was handed over next night to the 8th Queen's.

August, 1916
8th Battalion

A week out of the line followed, and then came orders to move up to Delville Wood itself.[1] The night of August 30th was perhaps the most trying experience in the battalion's service, a march up in pouring rain, under heavy shell-fire, over tracks which were deep in slippery mud, and this for men burdened with an astonishing load of ammunition, rations and equipment of every kind. The battalion took eleven hours from leaving its assembly trenches to cover one mile and get into position with A Company on the right in Inner Trench and B on its left in Edge Trench, C in support in the wood, D in reserve behind it. "Wood" was already a misnomer, for the constant shelling had reduced the trees to mere stumps amid a tangle of débris.

August 31st

The 8th's first day in Delville Wood coincided with the Germans' last and most formidable attempt to recover the high ground between Guillemont and High Wood. Hardly had a scanty breakfast been finished than the enemy's guns opened a terrific shelling, which they maintained for five hours, inflicting terrible casualties on the troops in the front line, so that two platoons of D had to reinforce. The message from Captain Wenyon of A asking for them was carried down in

[1] As Colonel Parker had gone sick with malaria, Major Whitty was in command of the battalion.

THE SOMME.

Aug. 31st, 1916
8th Battalion

the face of the greatest danger by two wounded men, Ptes. Skerry and Tyrrell, who not only volunteered for the duty but, after managing to deliver the message, actually returned to the front line. At last the German guns lifted, and then, to the satisfaction of the surviving defenders, infantry were seen coming forward and collecting for the assault in a trench about 500 yards away. So admirable was the fire discipline of the British troops that their fire was withheld for nearly another hour till the enemy's advance in force began. Then, indeed, their rifles and machine-guns let him have it and with such good effect that on the right, where the field of fire was good and several guns of the 72nd Company M.G. Corps had escaped the bombardment, A Company stopped the Germans in about 50 yards, inflicting very heavy losses. On the left there was more cover and B was very closely pressed, its commander, 2nd Lieut. Flowers, being among the killed, but it also kept its immediate opponents out. The Germans lost heavily both in the advance and later on when the survivors of the attack tried to get back to cover, but in the evening they made a second attempt. As before they were beaten off both by A and B, but the latter had to throw back its left flank as the Germans had effected a lodgement in the next battalion's frontage at Orchard Trench. This was successfully done by 2nd Lieut. E. G. Brown, who had succeeded to the command of B, and he was ably seconded by C.S.M. Rankin; thanks largely to their efforts the enemy was prevented from

Sept. 1st

improving his advantage and next day a counter-attack threw him out of Orchard Trench. The repulse of this attack was a great feather in the battalion's cap; its steadiness under a heavy bombardment had been equalled by the excellence of its musketry to which the losses inflicted on the Germans testified. The strength in which the Germans had attacked was some testimony to the value they attached

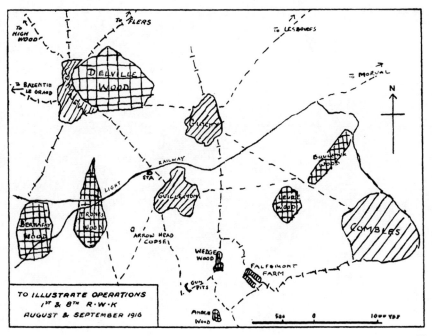

RATION TRENCH.

to the position and to the service rendered by the 8th in repulsing such a determined attack. <small>Sept., 1916 8th Battalion</small>

On the evening of September 2nd the 8th were relieved and went back to Caterpillar Valley between Bernafay and Delville Woods to come in for a gas bombardment lasting five hours; this, however, thanks to good " gas discipline," caused more discomfort than loss. Here the next three days were spent, though it <small>Sept. 3rd-5th</small> was a period of " fatigues " rather than of rest, as large carrying parties had to be found to take rations, water and ammunition up to the front line. One of these errands cost the battalion 2nd Lieut. Roscoe, who had done so well at Guillemont, but on his fall Sergt. Greenaway took charge of the party and carried through the task, though it had to be completed in daylight and under severe fire. By September 5th, when it was relieved and taken back to a village near Abbeville to rest, the 8th R.W.K. had had over 300 casualties, including 13 officers, 3 of whom, with 91 other ranks, had been killed. If it had not taken part in any big forward movement the work the 8th had done in holding and exploiting the advanced positions and in carrying, in digging, and in succouring wounded, had been of no small merit and value.

While the 8th Battalion had been hotly engaged on <small>July-August</small> the right of the British line the 6th had come in for a <small>6th Battalion</small> strenuous fortnight at the opposite end of the battlefront when, on July 27th, it relieved the 7th Worcesters near Ovillers. Here the fighting was of a different character, systematic nibbling away at the German positions rather than large-scale attacks. Hence the 6th experienced much local fighting, attacks on strong points and sections of trenches in which the bomb and the machine-gun were more important than artillery. Since it had been in action progress had been made beyond Ovillers, and on the night of August 3rd/4th a lodgement had been gained in Ration Trench N.E. <small>See Sketch 23</small> of Ovillers. Here the battalion relieved the 6th Buffs

THE SOMME.

August 4th, 1916
6th Battalion
next day and that evening attacked and captured a strong point on the left of its position, at the same time as the 36th Brigade further to the right assaulted and took the greater part of Ration Trench. To maintain and consolidate the ground gained was no easy task; the position was heavily shelled, and in its two days in this bit of line the battalion had nearly 80 casualties, including Captain Alderman and five other officers wounded. But it not only held the ground, beating off one vigorous bombing attack, but actually added to the gains and captured a couple of machine-guns. Sergt. Cooker distinguished himself in this fighting by re-organizing a party of bombers who had been driven back, erecting a new barricade, and then climbing over it to bring in a wounded man under the very noses of the enemy. A short rest followed, in which the battalion received a reinforcement of twelve subalterns, and then on the 10th it returned to the trenches for another effort.

The 35th Brigade were attacking a trench running parallel to Ration Trench and the 37th was co-operating on its left. The objective of the 6th Battalion, which was on the left of the 37th Brigade, was two strong points known as 20 and 81 with the intervening trench.

August 12th
This attack, delivered at 10.30 p.m. on August 12th, found the enemy much on the alert, and A Company on the left could make no headway towards 81; D, however, who got quite close to their objective before German bombers held them up, took a few prisoners and managed to build a block in the trench at the point reached and to maintain it. But the battalion on the right of the 37th Brigade had been unsuccessful and it was useless to press the attack. However, the ground gained commanded the German line just opposite and the 37th Brigade's attack had diverted the Germans' attention from the 35th, who captured their objective on a front of nearly 1,000 yards, inflicting heavy losses

August 13th
on the enemy. Next day the Forty-Eighth Division

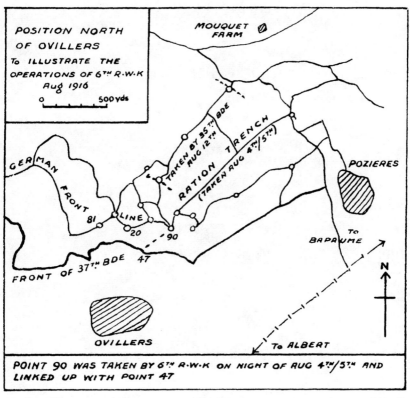

THE SOMME.

relieved the Twelfth and the battalion moved away to the front South of Arras for a month of relative quiet.

Aug.-Sept., 1916
6th Battalion

During this phase of the Somme offensive the progress of the attack had certainly been slower than had been hoped; on no one day between the middle of July and the beginning of September had gains been made approaching those secured on July 14th, but the net results had nevertheless been substantial, and if the British casualties had been heavy the incessant counter-attacks by which the enemy had delayed the advance had been extremely costly and had necessitated the practical abandonment of the attacks on Verdun to provide troops to maintain the struggle on the Somme. If August had seemed to produce little material change in the situation the efforts then made had contributed in no small measure to bring within reach the more tangible results achieved in September.

CHAPTER XIII.

THE SOMME (*Continued*).

Sept., 1916

The third month of the Somme opened with ten days of heavy fighting which saw the final overthrow of the barrier which Guillemont and Ginchy had so long presented to the British advance. In this phase The Queen's Own was represented by the 1st Battalion, though it was not actually against either of those points that it was employed. South and East of Guillemont the chief feature was the ridge on which stood Falfemont Farm with Leuze Wood beyond it. These strongly fortified localities formed part of the same defensive system as Guillemont and their capture was essential to any widening of the area of the attack, more especially if the French were to come up level with the British to attack Combles and the ridges between the Combles valley and the Tortile river.

August 25th
1st Battalion
See Sketch 24

When the Fifth Division returned to the line after its rest it was put in on the extreme British right S.W. and S. of Guillemont and next the French. The 1st R.W.K., who were in the centre of the Divisional front, had to prepare new assembly trenches 400 yards in front of the existing line. This work, of course, could only be undertaken at night, and to cover it patrols had to be thrust out further ahead, which led to a good many brushes with the enemy and not a few casualties, the battalion having over 60 before it was drawn back into reserve on the night of August 29th. But it had carried out its task, an excellent trench had been dug and the preparations carried so far forward

Sept. 3rd

that on September 3rd the Falfemont Farm position could be assaulted. The task was entrusted to the 13th Brigade, who had the K.O.S.B.'s on the right and the 14th R. Warwicks supported by the R.W.K. on the left. At 9 a.m. the K.O.S.B.'s attacked, but though

FALFEMONT FARM.

Sept., 1916
1st Battalion

they went forward magnificently they were unable to capture the Farm, and when at noon the 14th Warwicks and the 95th Brigade on their left delivered the main assault the Warwicks were checked by enfilade fire from the right. However, the 95th Brigade got on well, and in a renewed attack the Warwicks secured some gun pits which B Company assisted them to consolidate. Meanwhile orders were received for the battalion to advance, but they were soon cancelled, not before D Company, which was some way to the left rear of the rest of the battalion, had come under very heavy fire, losing both its officers. Evening, therefore, found the battalion still in support and Falfemont Farm untaken, though Wedge Wood and the trenches N.W. of it had been secured.

Next day, however, the 15th Brigade having relieved the 13th, a renewed attack at last mastered Falfemont Farm, and that afternoon the battalion, which had been left in support to the 15th Brigade, received orders to exploit the success by advancing between the Farm and Wedge Wood. C and D Companies promptly pushed forward towards Leuze Wood, crossing the open with little loss and capturing or otherwise disposing of quite a large number of Germans who were found in shell-holes on the way. About 200 yards short of Leuze Wood a trench was dug which served as the jumping-off ground from which next day the 15th and 95th Brigades advanced successfully through Leuze Wood, though in this advance the battalion was not employed, having been drawn back into support. It was in the front line, however, in front of Leuze Wood on the 10th and 11th, being heavily shelled and having nearly 70 casualties, and then, after a period of rest at Mericourt, returned to the front on the 18th for another week of hard work under shell-fire. Its chief task in this tour was to dig new trenches in front of Morval in preparation for the successful attack of September 25th, in which Morval, Lesbœufs and

Sept. 4th

Sept., 5th

THE SOMME (*Continued*).

Sept., 1916
1st Battalion Combles were captured. But as the 13th Brigade was in Corps Reserve the battalion was not actively engaged, merely providing stretcher and carrying parties for the 95th Brigade. On September 26th the Twentieth Division began relieving the Fifth and the end of the month saw the 1st R.W.K. established once again in billets near Abbeville. Its second turn on the Somme, a period of hard and useful work rather than of any exceptional incidents, had cost it 250 casualties, including 2nd Lieuts. Martin, Hallowes and Pracy and 28 men killed or died of wounds, and ten other officers wounded, making a total casualty list for the Somme of nearly a thousand all told. Lieut.-Col. Buchanan-Dunlop had also had to relinquish command through ill-health on September 12th, on which Major Lynch White was recalled from his Staff appointment to command.

7th, 10th, and
11th Batts. But before the 1st Battalion finally withdrew from the area of active operations two other battalions of The Queen's Own had made their début in offensive warfare, and the 7th was becoming familiar with that second portion of the Somme battlefield with which the Eighteenth Division will always be associated, Thiepval and the ridges above the Ancre. The immediate result of the gains made in the first ten days of September was that a substantial portion of the forward crest of the main ridge was in British hands and with it the advantage, hitherto lacking, of observation over the slopes beyond. It therefore became possible to launch a general attack on a wider front than had been attempted all through August. On the right the Fourteenth Corps was to master the spur which ran N.E. from Ginchy to Morval, in the centre between Delville Wood and High Wood the Fifteenth Corps had the Flers Line as its immediate objective, and on the left between High Wood and the Albert-Bapaume Road the Third Corps was to advance against Martinpuich should the progress of the attack elsewhere warrant it.

THE TANK ATTACK.

In the Fifteenth Corps was now included the Forty- <small>Sept., 1916</small>
First Division, which had reached the battle area at the
beginning of the month and had begun relieving the
Fifty-Fifth in the centre of the Corps front on the
night of September 10th/11th. The 10th was the <small>10th & 11th</small>
first of the Regiment's two battalions in the Forty-First <small>Battalions</small>
Division to come into action. After 24 hours in support positions in Montauban Alley the battalion sent
two companies forward on the evening of September
11th to pass through the 23rd Middlesex, who were
holding the front line North of Delville Wood, and to
construct six strong points 150 yards in advance. This
operation was successfully carried out and the posts
were held next day by B Company, while that evening <small>Sept. 12th</small>
the remaining companies relieved the 23rd Middlesex
in the front line. They were fairly heavily shelled,
especially on the following night, when their brigade <small>Sept.</small>
was being relieved by the 124th Brigade, which was to <small>13th & 14th</small>
be on the right of the Division in the attack with the
122nd on the left and the 123rd in reserve.

The great feature of September 15th was the em- <small>Sept. 15th</small>
ployment of the new weapon whose preparation had <small>1916</small>
been so carefully concealed. If at their first effort the
" tanks " hardly accomplished all that had been hoped
or that was claimed for them at the time, they undoubtedly introduced an element of surprise which produced a great effect upon the German rank and file.
The German Higher Command may have obtained
some idea that this new device would be tried; their
men in the fighting line were certainly unprepared for
the appearance of these extraordinary and formidable if
clumsy and rather uncertain objects. That they were
an encouragement to the British rank and file may also
be accepted as true, if the amount of that encouragement varied considerably with the performances of the
particular tanks with which individual units happened
to co-operate.

THE SOMME (*Continued*).

Sept. 15th
1916
11th Batt.
See Sketch 25

The 11th, the first battalion of The Queen's Own to have experience of co-operation with tanks, was in support trenches N.E. of Delville Wood when the attack opened. It moved forward at " zero " in rear of the 15th Hampshires, the right battalion of the 122nd Brigade, which had as its objectives Switch Trench, Flers Trench and the actual village of Flers. As the 11th started the enemy put down a heavy barrage on the front line and on the assembly positions in rear, causing many casualties which unfortunately included a large proportion of officers, whose loss was sorely felt later. However, the Hampshires made short work of Switch Trench and then, as they swept on towards Flers Trench, the 11th caught them up and went forward together with them. Flers Trench was full of Germans, but very few put up a stiff fight; many surrendered, others bolted towards the village under heavy fire from the machine-guns of the tanks which had by now overtaken the infantry. However, the British barrage was still coming down on Flers so there was a short halt till it should lift. Owing to the heavy casualties among the officers little re-organization could be effected during this pause, and when the lifting of the barrage allowed infantry and tanks to go forward the advance lacked organization and cohesion. Still Flers was cleared after sharp fighting, and some of the battalion pushed on in pursuit of the Germans beyond the village towards its final objective, reaching some trenches known as Box and Cox. In this phase of the attack splendid work was done by C.S.M.'s Hayley and Judge in rallying the men and leading them forward against Flers, where C.S.M. Judge further distinguished himself by capturing 30 prisoners with the aid of a couple of men, while C.S.M. Hayley, whose courage and initiative were conspicuous, was instrumental in capturing a large number of Germans and in organizing the position. Largely by their efforts the advanced line was held

LIEUT.-COL. A. F. TOWNSHEND.
Commanded 11th Battalion, 1916.
Died of wounds, 16th September, 1916.

FLERS.

despite counter-attacks, and meanwhile some of the 124th Brigade established themselves on the East of the village where they also held on.

_{Sept. 15th 1916 11th Batt.}

But in the meantime touch had been to a great extent lost between the advanced troops and those in rear; very little exact information ever reached even Battalion Headquarters, and to the higher authorities further back the situation was most obscure. The Assistant-Adjutant, 2nd Lieut. G. D. Henderson, had gone up to the front just in time to see the battalion pushing into Flers, but except for a message from C.S.M. Judge, " going strong through Flers," no more news came back till about 9.30, when it was reported that the enemy were putting down a heavy barrage upon Flers and the trenches West of it and that men were coming back from the village. Upon this Colonel Townshend went forward to Flers with all the men from Battalion Headquarters, but finding men coming back on both sides of the village he took up a position in Flers Trench and rallied many stragglers. A further retirement to Switch Trench became necessary a little later, and while here Colonel Townshend was mortally wounded by shrapnel. On this the Adjutant, Captain Jiminez, took charge of the party, now some 25 strong, and led it forward again about mid-day and took post in Flers Trench, and this position was retained till after 5 p.m., when orders were received to withdraw to a position S.W. of Delville Wood, where the Brigade was to re-assemble. By this time the Headquarters party had increased to about 40, and on arrival at the rendezvous many other small detachments came in, parties who had spent the day in various positions in and around Flers. Actually it would seem that, despite the shelling and counter-attacks, the village was never lost. There was a good deal of confusion and a good many men seem to have straggled back, but the Germans certainly never recovered the village, for 2nd Lieut. Cooksey and C.S.M. Judge with a party of the 11th

THE SOMME (*Continued*).

Sept. 15th 1916
11th Batt.

remained continuously in occupation of part of the third objective until in the course of the afternoon some of the 124th Brigade relieved them and secured the Hog's Head and Flea Trenches East of the village.

When all remnants had been collected the 11th Battalion was found to have left three officers, Captain Jiminez and 2nd Lieuts. Cooksey and G. D. Henderson, with some 150 men out of a total of 18 officers and 592 other ranks who had gone into action. However, many more stragglers turned up at intervals and the final casualty list was reduced to 13 officers (Lieut.-Col. Townshend, Captain Culley, Lieut. Jones, 2nd Lieuts. G. Smith, Barrs and Mansfield killed, Major Heron, Captain Dickinson, Lieut. Puttock, 2nd Lieuts. H. R. Smith, C. F. Hall, Platt and Cooksey wounded) and 330 other ranks.[1] Colonel Townshend's loss was severely felt; he had been indefatigable in his efforts to bring the battalion up to a high level of efficiency, and it owed not a little to him.

10th Batt.

Meanwhile the 10th, whose brigade had been in reserve, had been much less severely tried. About 10 a.m. orders were received for the 23rd Middlesex to leave the reserve position South of Delville Wood and for the battalion to follow. After a short halt in the original front line the two battalions moved up about 1 p.m. to Switch Trench in face of a heavy barrage, which caused the two companies on the left to swing away to the flank, with the result that they lost touch and became mixed up with the New Zealand Division, who were notably successful to the N.W. of Flers, reaching and crossing the Abbey Road. On reaching Switch Trench the rest of the battalion found plenty of occupation in consolidating and clearing up the position, useful work of an essential character which cost it several casualties from shell-fire if it did not afford much opportunity of earning distinction. It remained in

[1] C.S.M.'s Hayley and Judge received the M.C. for their good work in this attack.

THE SOMME (*Continued*).

position until the night of September 17th/18th, when its Division was withdrawn to the Becordel and Dernancourt area for rest and re-organization. Of this the shattered 11th was in sore need, but the 10th had escaped much more lightly, for its casualties for September 11th-18th only came to 7 officers and 94 other ranks, including Captain H. H. Logan, 2nd Lieuts. Laurence and Stones and 16 men killed, 7 men missing, Colonel Wood-Martyn,[1] Major Beattie and 2nd Lieuts. Edmett and Percival wounded. But despite heavy losses the Forty-First Division and the 10th and 11th R.W.K. had made a good start in active warfare. If its final objective had not been reached, Flers had definitely passed into British keeping, and the advance in this quarter had been carried as far as anywhere.

Sept., 1916
10th & 11th Battalions

The attack of September 15th had not realized the full expectations that had been formed, but its success had at least sufficed to allow of extending the area of active fighting to the West of the Albert-Bapaume road; here since July 1st but little progress had been made against the exceedingly formidable positions on the heights overlooking the Ancre, particularly at Thiepval. If anywhere on the Somme battlefield there were defences which the Germans reckoned impregnable it was the Thiepval section. However, the gains now made in the centre allowed of a converging attack in which the Eighteenth Division had the honour of tackling Thiepval itself while the Eleventh on its right struck at the defences just S.E. and E. of the village.

The 7th Battalion had had an easy time since its hard fighting in July. Its stay on the Flanders front had been uneventful. The trenches it had taken over from the New Zealanders near Bois Grenier were in excellent condition and the Germans opposite proved unaggressive. Casualties, therefore, were few, and thanks to

July-Sept. 1916
7th Battalion

---

[1] During Colonel Wood-Martyn's absence, Major W. F. Soames commanded the battalion with the acting rank of Lieut.-Colonel.

THE SOMME (*Continued*).

July-Sept. 1916
7th Battalion
the arrival of some large drafts—one of 138 joined the battalion just as it left the Somme and another of 102 men from the Suffolk Yeomanry, splendid fighting material, arrived early in September—with twenty new subalterns, the battalion was nearly up to strength again when it returned to the South. It rejoined the Fifth Army before the end of August, but nearly a month elapsed before it went into action again, and in this time it had three weeks of intensive battle-training at Puchevillers, S.E. of Doullens. It cannot be too strongly emphasized that it was by the careful, systematic and definite training which all ranks received in these periods out of the line that units were made capable of returning to the attack after such heavy losses as those of the Eighteenth Division in July, and these periods must not be overlooked even if they must be but briefly passed by.

Sept. 26th
In the actual attack on Thiepval the 55th Brigade was in reserve and the 7th R.W.K. therefore spent the morning of September 26th in a position of readiness. Not till nearly 2 p.m. was it summoned up to Crucifix Corner, the cross roads W. of Aveluy, and placed under the orders of the 54th Brigade who, aided by the 53rd, had taken most of Thiepval but were having great difficulty in completing the reduction of the position in the face of the desperate resistance of a stubborn and confident garrison.
Sept. 27th
By 8.30 next morning, however, the task had been completed without the 7th being employed. The battalion had merely moved up to positions closer to Thiepval, being heavily shelled while doing so and suffering 40 casualties from one single shell.
Sept. 28th
Then on the 28th the indefatigable Eighteenth Division proceeded to attack
See Sketch 26
the extremely strong Schwaben Redoubt some 1,000 yards to the North of Thiepval. In this attack the 54th Brigade was on the left with the 53rd on its right. Here again a stubborn resistance was encountered, and about 11 a.m. D Company had to be put in, partly to

THE SCHWABEN REDOUBT.

assist in consolidating and partly to act as carriers. A little later Battalion Headquarters with C and three platoons of B, all that remained in hand, as several parties had been detached on various errands, moved up to Thiepval Chateau under heavy shell-fire. This party remained in Thiepval all night and moved forward at 3.30 next morning to relieve the troops who had captured the Southern and South-Western portions of the Schwaben Redoubt. Sept. 28th 1916 7th Battalion

Sept. 29th

The relief was a most difficult matter; the situation in the Redoubt was obscure, it was uncertain how much had already been taken, the trenches had been badly damaged, the Germans still held a considerable portion of the Redoubt and several blocks and strong points had to be mastered before any advance could be made. Captain Waddington, going on ahead of his company, C, to reconnoitre the position it was to take over, came upon Germans in possession of a point believed to be in our hands, and was wounded by a bomb, being, indeed, fortunate in escaping capture. In moving up, the company was heavily shelled, which added greatly to the difficulty of the relief, and only No. 9 Platoon was even getting into position when the Germans suddenly delivered an attack in force against its right. No. 9, however, though without any knowledge of the ground or of the enemy's dispositions, and for the moment quite " in the air," put up a stubborn fight and managed to beat the enemy off, inflicting heavy losses upon them. By this time the remaining platoons were reaching the front, and the three available platoons of B, under Captain Holland, were coming up on the left. But the 7th were given little time in which to settle down to their arduous task. The Germans, undeterred by their first repulse, promptly returned to the attack and a savage and determined struggle followed. The Lewis guns did good service, but early in the fight they were all put out of action by German bombs, and the fight resolved itself into a

213

THE SOMME (*Continued*).

Sept. 29th 1916
7th Battalion

regular "soldier's battle," in which all depended on the courage and tenacity of individual N.C.O.'s and men. Most of the officers were hit and the survivors could only exercise control over their immediate neighbourhood. But the men of the 7th were not found wanting. Pte. Tobin, a C Company runner, was conspicuous by his example; he was prominent in repulsing the first German attack and, though badly wounded in the jaw and throat, stuck to his post, encouraging his comrades to keep up their resistance till a second severe wound finally disabled him. He, too, was only one of many. Indeed, when C finally beat the Germans back not a bomb was left nor a round of ammunition, though luckily a little later carrying parties made their way up to the front with fresh supplies.

All through that day extremely hard fighting continued; the German bombing attacks pressed especially heavily against the right, where C Company, after repulsing one attack, was driven back but quickly recovered the ground by a vigorous counter-attack. In the evening an effort was made to master two strong points known respectively as Points 19 and 39; but though the attack was at first successful bombs and grenades ran short and the Germans, who were in great force, at length forced the assailants back. In the intervals between the attacks the position was steadily shelled by the Germans and this and the activity of their snipers made consolidation extremely difficult. However, the work was pushed steadily on, and during the day the various detached parties rejoined so that it proved possible during the night to take over an additional section of the captured trenches on the left, as far as a point known as the Pope's Nose. C Company, moreover, managed in the course of the day to get touch with The Queen's on the right, and thanks to the training the men had received in intensive digging, one of the points on which the Divisional Commander, General Maxse, was most insistent, a fairly good line

THE SCHWABEN REDOUBT.

was established. But the ground was a mass of churned-up earth and half-destroyed trenches, and one of the greatest difficulties was to make certain where the line actually did run.

Sept. 29th 1916 7th Battalion

September 30th opened with a powerful German attack against Point 45 on the right, held by A Company. Once again shortage of rifle-grenades and the superior handiness and range of their egg-bombs enabled the Germans to gain ground; but a counter-attack, ably organized by Sergt. Weller, partly along the trench and partly across the open, recovered most of it and would have done more but that our own guns suddenly opened fire and, firing short, disorganized the advance. However, when the guns lifted, 2nd Lieut. Sutherst headed a fresh attack which drove the Germans right back to the bomb stop from which they had started. For the rest of the day the battalion held on stoutly, and about 2 p.m. a detachment of the Buffs came up for a fresh advance against Points 19 and 39 to co-operate with an assault by the 8th East Surreys against the portion of the Redoubt further to the East. This attack was delivered at 4 p.m., D Company detailing two platoons to help the Buffs. Unluckily the Buffs went too far to the right, Point 19 was left unattacked, and though 2nd Lieuts. Grist and Griffith with their platoons made a most gallant effort to rush it, they were still in No Man's Land short of the objective when the barrage lifted, and were caught by the German artillery and machine-guns and badly cut up.

Sept. 30th

By this time the battalion's numbers were much reduced, C Company was down to 2 officers and 56 men, and the long line it had to hold taxed all its resources and endurance. Nevertheless the ground was held, and on October 1st 2nd Lieut. Sutherst, skilfully using a Stokes mortar to assist his bombers, cleared the Germans out of a double-bombing block on the battalion's right, successfully re-establishing communication with

October 1st

215

THE SOMME (*Continued*).

October 2nd 1916
7th Battalion
the Buffs. On the left and centre also there was desperate fighting. Next day a German attempt on Point 86 was beaten off, but the Germans attacking from Point 16 gained about 60 yards and held it in face of counter-attacks by B Company, which at first regained the ground but were ultimately forced back

Oct. 3rd-5th
by weight of numbers and lack of bombs. The 3rd saw a heavy German attack on the centre beaten off by B, the 4th an advance from Point 16 repulsed by C. On the 5th the battalion co-operated by Lewis gun and rifle-fire in an attempt of the 8th Norfolks to complete the capture of the Schwaben Redoubt, getting good targets in the Germans retiring from before the Norfolks, though in the end little progress was made. That evening the 16th Rifle Brigade (Thirty-Ninth Division) arrived to relieve the battalion, now completely exhausted and terribly reduced by a week of the most strenuous and arduous fighting under difficult conditions of wet and mud. This had cost it heavily. Of all the officers who went into action on the first day only one was still at duty, and he had been wounded three times. Captain R. B. Holland, Lieut. Hackett, 2nd Lieuts. Hudson, Fricker, Ward, Griffith and Roberts had been killed, Captains Waddington and Warren and eight subalterns wounded; of " other ranks " 70 were killed and missing and over 200 wounded. Colonel Fiennes too had gone sick, and in his absence Major Phillips was in command. After such a trial, " the worst days of its life " one of its officers called this time; with all the companies reduced to mere skeletons, it was natural that the battalion was not called on for another serious attack for some weeks, but it had covered itself with credit, had inflicted heavy losses on the enemy, and the positions it had helped to secure were among the most important gains made anywhere on the battle front. Well as the Eighteenth Division had done on July 1st and at Trones Wood, Thiepval

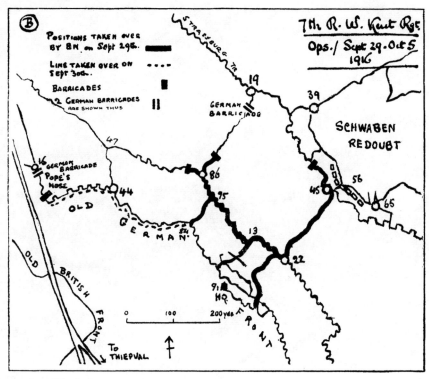

GUEUDECOURT.

and the Schwaben Redoubt were an even bigger achievement.

As the 7th was withdrawing from the front line for its well-deserved rest no less than three battalions of The Queen's Own were preparing for another big attack. After the capture of Combles (September 26th) the French had made substantial progress North of that town towards Sailly-Saillisel, while N.W. of Gueudecourt the Fourth Army had gained ground towards Eaucourt l'Abbaye and Le Sars and was now to attack along its whole front from Les Bœufs to Le Sars. In this not only was the Forty-First Division to participate but the Twelfth was brought down from Wailly (South of Arras) where it had been since the last week in August, having a fairly easy time and escaping with comparatively few casualties. In the last week of September the 6th R.W.K. had been at last brought up to nearly 800 effectives by the arrival of a large draft. On October 1st it took over reserve trenches West of Gueudecourt, which it held till the 4th, when it moved up into support, getting heavily shelled but escaping lightly. On the evening of the 6th it took over the front line on the Northern edge of Gueudecourt ready to attack next day, having the 6th Buffs on the right and the 36th Brigade on the left.

The Forty-First Division were further to the left again, East of Eaucourt l'Abbaye. Since the battle of Flers the 10th R.W.K. had had another turn in the front line from September 28th to October 1st, but it had been comparatively uneventful. The enemy shelled the positions continuously and heavily but did not attempt any counter-attack or succeed in preventing the battalion from pushing forward on the night of September 29th/30th and constructing a fresh line of posts 100 yards further in advance. After three days in the line had cost it just 50 casualties the 10th was relieved and drawn back to Pommiers Redoubt.

Sept.-Oct., 1916
6th, 10th, & 11th Batts.
See Sketch 25

THE SOMME (*Continued*).

Oct., 1916
11th Batt.

The 11th R.W.K. had meanwhile had a much needed chance of reorganization. Major Corfe had succeeded to the command and with Lieut. Puttick as Adjutant had done a great deal to get the battalion into fighting trim despite its heavy losses at Flers. A big draft from the Royal Fusiliers and the arrival of eight officers from the Base had brought it more or less up to strength, but to be called on for another attack so soon after such losses as those of September 15th was a big demand on any unit. In the course of October 3rd and 4th the Forty-First Division relieved the New Zealanders, who had just carried out a highly successful attack on the German trenches of Eaucourt l'Abbaye, capturing a substantial portion of Gird Trench and Gird Support together with a redoubt known as the Circus, between those trenches and Eaucourt. The 124th Brigade went in on the right, the 122nd on the left, so that the 11th R.W.K., who took the left of the brigade frontage, found themselves next the Forty-Seventh Division and with the 15th Hampshires on the right. The objective of the Division was the ridge overlooking Ligny-Thilloy and La Barque, and the battalion before it a part of the Gird Trench system which had so far defied all assaults and was again to prove a formidable obstacle.

Oct. 7th,
1916
11th Batt.

The moment the troops left their trenches (1.45 p.m., October 7th) heavy machine-gun fire enfiladed them from both flanks, and brought the attack to a speedy standstill after 100 yards had been covered. A sunken road leading N.N.E. towards La Barque proved a special hindrance to progress, and as no better success had attended the rest of the Division, all that could be done was to consolidate the line gained. This involved a strenuous night for the survivors of the attack but they received useful assistance from a party of the 12th East Surreys and eventually touch was established with the troops on both flanks, while the great majority of the wounded were safely got away after untiring efforts

LE SARS.

by the stretcher-bearers. Casualties had been heavy, all four company commanders had been hit, Lieuts. Purves and Prior being killed, Captains Stone and Richardson wounded; still, though there were only four officers and less than 100 men[1] left, the line was successfully held till the early hours of the 9th, when the 123rd Brigade replaced the 122nd. Lieut. Henderson was conspicuous for good work in re-organising the end and consolidating the position, and his efforts were fittingly rewarded by the grant of the M.C.[2] The remnants of the 11th were then relieved by the 23rd Middlesex and went back to Switch Trench, where all available reinforcements joined them. Meanwhile the 10th had taken up its position in support to the Middlesex. This battalion once again came off much more lightly than the 11th. It had been in reserve on the 7th, had moved up into the British front line that evening, and had found working parties to help consolidate the advanced position. Nothwithstanding this, and despite being quite heavily shelled while in support, it escaped with one officer killed (Lieut. Grant), two (Captain Wallis and 2nd Lieut. Samuel) wounded, and under 100 casualties in all. It was relieved on the night of October 10th/11th, when the Forty-First Division was replaced by the Thirtieth and bade farewell to the Somme. _{Oct. 7th, 1916 11th Batt.} _{10th Batt.}

The 6th R.W.K., on October 7th, had fared no better than the junior Service battalions. The hostile artillery supporting the front to be attacked had increased considerably in the days preceding the assault and the enemy had in addition organized an extremely powerful machine-gun defence while their trenches were screened from direct artillery observation. The _{6th Battalion}

---

[1] The battalion had taken 16 officers and 465 other ranks into action.

[2] The same honour was deservedly bestowed on Lieut. Bainton, the Transport Officer, who, despite the most adverse conditions, had done splendidly in getting rations and water up to the front trenches and in helping to remove the wounded.

THE SOMME (*Continued*).

Oct. 7th 1916
6th Battalion

battalion had been heavily shelled all the morning and had suffered seriously before it went over the top at 1.45 p.m. in the face of a fierce rifle and machine-gun fire which the British bombardment was unable to subdue. From the first losses were heavy. Neither R.W.K. nor Buffs could get far, though C Company on the left advanced about 150 yards before being held up. It got some shelter from a bank along a road which crossed its front but, being ahead of the troops on its flanks, could do no more than hang on till after nightfall when it got back, bringing in all its wounded.[1] The battalion had to hold on for the rest of the day under a steady barrage, but at midnight The Queen's took over and the remnants of the battalion—companies were down as low as 50 each—took up a position in support, which it held till relieved by the 1st Essex, of the Twenty-Ninth Division, on the evening of the 10th. The casualties were very severe, little short of 300 out of a bare 500 in action. Captain Hall, Lieut. Wilks and 2nd Lieuts. Longuehaye, Stuart and Gray were killed with 23 men, 89 men were missing; Captains Williams and Carré, 2nd Lieuts. Dickinson, Dunt, Hogbin and Paulson and 185 men wounded. The Twelfth Division did make some progress beyond Gueudecourt in the next few days, but the 6th was too shattered to be employed and spent the next week in camp near Montauban, resting and incorporating two large drafts, one of 68 and one of 143, which arrived before the whole Division was drawn out and transferred to its old positions at Wailly.

7th Battalion

The 7th had been the first battalion of The Queen's Own to go into action on the Somme. It was to be the last also to take part in that protracted struggle. Sadly reduced by the long fight for the Schwaben Redoubt, it

---

[1] Pte. F. Brown, one of the battalion stretcher-bearers, distinguished himself in this work, collecting some thirty wounded and getting them into shelters in some old dug-outs, whence they were safely brought in after dark.

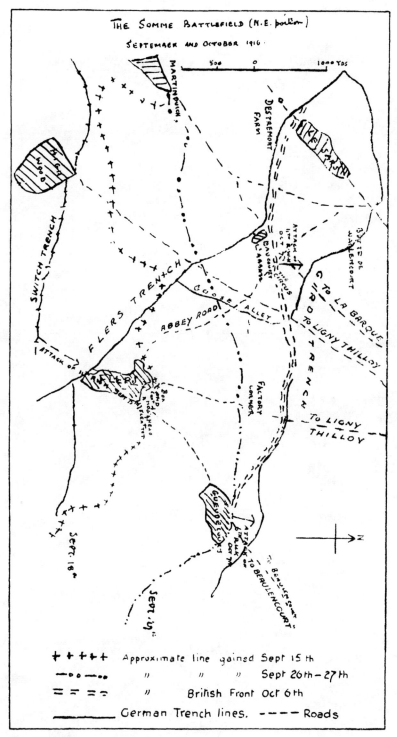

DESIRE TRENCH.

was in reserve on October 17th when the 53rd Brigade, in conjunction with some Canadians further to the right, attacked and took Regina Trench. The 55th Brigade took over the position then captured by the 53rd Brigade and held it till the 29th. The 7th was in the front line from the 26th to 29th, and was notably active in patrolling, 2nd Lieut. Macdonald in particular obtaining most valuable information. After four days' rest at Warloy it came forward again to Albert, had two days in Brigade Reserve, two in the front line, and then moved into reserve trenches, where it remained till the night of November 17th when it took up a battle position in readiness for yet another big attack. *Oct., 1916 / 7th Battalion* *November, 1916*

The plan of this attack was that the 55th Brigade, with the Nineteenth Division on its left and the Fourth Canadian on the right, was to attack the portions of Desire and Grandcourt Trenches between Twenty-Three Road, on the right, and Stump Road. All four battalions were in line, the 7th R.W.K. being in the right centre between the E. Surreys and the Buffs. It had B and D Companies in front, each attacking on a two-platoon front; A was in support, C in reserve. By this time the persistent wet weather which had set in early in October and had contributed so much to the ill-success of the attack of October 7th, had given place to frost and snow. The ground was frozen hard and covered with snow, so that when the attack was launched at 6.10 a.m. the troops showed up clearly against the white ground. However, the attack was pressed with much determination, and the right company, B, got into Desire Trench and established itself there despite much opposition. Its left, however, was " in the air," for D had lost direction and, going off left-handed, soon lost touch with B. Only a few of D ever got back; the company had pushed on over its first objective and had come under very heavy machine-gun fire from a strong point *See Sketch 27* *Nov. 18th*

THE SOMME (*Continued*).

Nov. 18th 1616 7th Battalion
on the left and the survivors had been surrounded by the enemy and killed or taken almost to a man.[1]

A similar fate befell the Buffs and Queen's further to the left. They, too, captured their first objective but, apparently pushing on beyond, were cut off by a German counter-attack which got in behind them, this being the more successful because the Division on their left had been forced back, completely exposing the flank of the 55th Brigade. B Company's position in Desire Trench was, therefore, most precarious, but Major Clare, of the E. Surreys, who was temporarily commanding the battalion,[2] promptly pushed up all available reinforcements, including a Stokes mortar and a bombing party. Thus assisted, B not only maintained its ground, but, inspired by Captain Knight's splendid example, actually extended its gains and cleared Desire Trench as far as Sixteen Street, the point originally fixed as the left of the battalion's objective. Several barricades had to be broken down but the trench was successfully cleared by 2nd Lieut. Dix, who led a bombing party with much courage and determination, while another detachment rushed over the open and got into the trench farther along. Pte. Keleher, who led the bayonet charge with great dash, disposed of a large number of enemy himself, while Corpl. Coleman threw bombs with the greatest skill and accuracy, doing splendid service. Most of the garrison endeavoured to escape by bolting back across the open to Grandcourt Trench but were shot down by the leading platoon of A Company, which 2nd Lieut. Kent[3] brought up opportunely.

[1] The fate of D. was cleared up after the Germans were driven back from this part of the line in February, 1917 (*c.f.* Chap. xiv).

[2] Colonel Fiennes was still away and did not return to the battalion, receiving an appointment at home : a skilful tactician, whose knowledge of his profession inspired respect in officers and men alike, his great ability as a trainer of troops had been no small factor in the 7th's successes.

[3] Captain Knight and 2nd Lieut. Dix were subsequently awarded the M.C., while Corpl. Coleman and Pte. Keleher got D.C.M.'s.

DESIRE TRENCH.

Next morning patrols pushed along Desire Trench as far as Stump Road, the left of the 55th Brigade's objective, and found it evacuated. A welcome supply of food and wine was found in the dug-outs with many other evidences of the haste with which the Germans had departed. It should be added that several British wounded were now recovered who had been most carefully tended and looked after by the Germans, a somewhat unusual occurrence greatly to the credit of the defenders of Desire Trench. During the day the Buffs took over the Western portion of Desire Trench, which allowed the battalion to concentrate its energies on Cross Trench, a communication trench running diagonally across its front. Snipers from this trench had given trouble during the day, but in the evening Captain E. S. Holland and C Company made a most successful advance, reached a strong point at Point 85, three quarters of the way to Grandcourt Trench, and established a block there. Two nights later the 55th Brigade was relieved by the Sixty-First Division and withdrew to an area North of Abbeville.

Nov. 19th
1916
7th Battalion

Nov. 21st

The casualties of the 7th in this last action, by no means its least creditable exploit on the Somme, came to nearly 200; 2nd Lieut. Carter and 22 other ranks were killed, Lieut. Stevenson and 2nd Lieut. Fryer missing with 94 men, mainly of D Company, and 2nd Lieuts. Godley and Taylor wounded with 77 men. With the rest of the Eighteenth Division it could look back on the Somme with special pride. Hardly any other Division had been so frequently or successfully engaged and none had achieved more. It had established a great reputation as a fighting unit and the 7th R.W.K. had proved as efficient and formidable as any battalion in the Division. Indeed, of all the battalions of The Queen's Own engaged in the Somme offensive the 7th had perhaps the finest record; no one would claim for it that it had surpassed the others in devotion and gallantry and endurance, but it had been more often in

THE SOMME (*Continued*).

Nov., 1916
7th Battalion

action and always with success. The new drafts who had replaced the old hands who fell in July had shown themselves inspired by the same zeal and high spirit as their predecessors. Certainly a high spirit and high standard of courage and devotion had been required, for the fighting had been very bitter. The 7th's losses during the period give some clue to the intensity of the fighting and the great part it had played. Its " parapet strength " in the last week of June had been 36 officers and 837 other ranks; it had received drafts amounting to 28 officers and 955 other ranks, yet could only muster 20 officers and 529 men at the end of November.

CHAPTER XIV.

THE THIRD WINTER.

With the capture of Desire Trench the long-drawn out operations on the Somme came to an end. The bad weather which had so seriously hampered their later stages and had prevented the Allies from reaping the full fruits earned in the wearing down process of July and August set in again with increased intensity. Over the greater part of the battle area the condition of the ground absolutely prohibited further attacks and made the maintenance of the advanced position reached and the carrying out of the necessary reliefs quite sufficiently difficult. The strain imposed on the troops in merely holding what had been gained was incredible, it was amazing that men could endure so much; trenches were deep in oozy slime, roads and paths disappeared into morasses, shell-holes pitted the ground in every direction and made movement off the tracks difficult and dangerous; to reach the front line was an achievement, to survive there a struggle against every kind of discomfort, danger and difficulty. But if conditions in the front trenches were indescribable, there was little relief for those in support or immediate reserve. The area in rear of the front line was devoid of shelter, houses and villages were represented by heaps of indistinguishable débris, woods by bare tree-stumps and tangled masses of broken branches.

However, despite the tremendous losses incurred between July and November and the relatively small gains in actual ground the Somme offensive marks a real turning point in the war. The admissions of Ludendorff and Hindenburg, though grudging and reluctant, show clearly how deeply it had affected the Germans, how heavily they had lost, with what difficulty they had maintained their hold and how

THE THIRD WINTER.

Nov., 1916 dark the prospect appeared to them. The bad weather of October had helped them greatly—had the Allies been favoured in 1916 with the splendid autumn weather of 1918 the real results achieved on the Somme would have been unmistakably apparent; but naturally the defence had profited by the handicaps imposed on the assailants by rain and mud, and the delays in the Allied advance had allowed time for the construction of new and formidable lines in rear of the battle-front. Still the prospects of the Allies for 1917 looked bright enough, if only the weather should allow of an early resumption of the offensive on the Somme front and of the extension of the battle-front Northward to take advantage of the precarious position in which the Germans between the Ancre and the Scarpe now found themselves. The Allied advance had turned this portion of the German lines into a sharply marked salient which any further advance across the Upper Ancre would render untenable.

To profit by the exhaustion of the Germans, to leave them no breathing space and to keep them in suspense about the time and locality for the resumption of the attack, the British command had resolved on adopting during the winter months as active an attitude as the weather would allow. All along the line, therefore, from Ypres to the Somme a policy of harassing the enemy by artillery activity, raids, gas attacks, mining and other methods was initiated, so that the battalions of The Queen's Own were likely to be kept busy. When the Somme offensive ended the 1st was in the Bethune area, the 6th in the Wailly sector near Arras, the 7th was just leaving the Ancre heights for Abbeville, the 8th had found its way back to the Hulluch area where it had first seen active service, while the 10th and 11th had been sent up to Flanders and had gone into line S.E. of Ypres before the end of October.

1st Battalion After leaving the Somme the 1st Battalion had moved to the First Army, going into billets at Essars on

THE THIRD WINTER.

October 1st and taking over the support trenches in the centre of its new Divisional front two days later. This frontage extended for over four miles Northward from the La Bassée Canal, being divided into three sectors, Givenchy on the right, Festubert in the centre and Ferme du Bois on the left. Except on the actual Givenchy spur the line ran through low-lying ground, mostly water-logged, and was held not with continuous trenches but with breast-works, and in many places only by isolated posts. From the beginning of October to the end of March the battalion remained in this quarter. The difficulty of moving in this swampy wilderness of ditches and old trenches made great activity in the way of raids and local attacks impossible, and the maintenance of the line involved unending labour. When the battalion first arrived in this district things were very quiet; the enemy were anything but aggressive and seemed nervous and apprehensive of attack; casualties therefore were low, under twenty being suffered in the course of October and November, while those for December would have been little higher had not the enemy suddenly indulged in a heavy bombardment on December 19th which inflicted a dozen casualties. In the course of this Pte. Herbert distinguished himself by going back through the shell-swept zone to ask for artillery support; he was wounded but got back to the telephone and got the guns on to the German trench mortars. When he volunteered for this dangerous errand he was due to start in a day or two for a month's leave. Otherwise the chief incident of the closing months of the year was the return in November of Colonel Buchanan-Dunlop, on which Major Lynch White reverted to second-in-command, while in February Major Waring came out from the Depôt and became Adjutant.

Nov., 1916-March, 1917
1st Battalion
See Sketch 7

But as time wore on the enemy became more active, attempting several small raids, trying to rush saps and giving good targets to snipers and Lewis guns on

THE GIVENCHY RAID.

Feb., 1917
1st Battalion

several occasions. Their chief effort was on February 8th, when a party of about 20 got into one of D Company's saps but were thrust out again after a sharp hand-to-hand fight, leaving several dead behind them. The battalion on its part carried out several minor enterprises and was as active in patrolling as the state of the ground allowed. But its great achievement came in February, when A and B Companies successfully carried

See Sketch 26

out a really big raid against the German lines just N.E. of Givenchy. Its distinctive feature was that it was carried out by daylight and without any preliminary bombardment, though for some days the artillery had been cutting the German wire systematically and the Corps Heavy Artillery had carried out a special programme of counter-battery work designed to ensure that the German gunners should not be at their guns when the raiders went over. In previous tours in the trenches A and B Companies had become specially familiar with their objectives, and just before the attack they had been carefully practised in crossing rough ground, negotiating wire and other obstacles, and had rehearsed their programme over taped-out trenches. No Man's Land was a mass of mine craters and shell-holes, but careful patrolling and reconnaissance by the leaders chosen for the six parties into which the attackers were divided enabled them to guide their men over the broken and intricate ground.

Feb. 10th

The morning of the 10th passed quietly, except for some shooting by 4.5 in. howitzers and some trench mortars, which, if anything, helped to put the enemy off the alert as it was finished two hours and more before 3 p.m., the " zero " hour. The attack was a complete surprise. The wire was well cut and the rapidity with which No Man's Land was crossed on the heels of the barrage enabled the raiders to rush the front line almost without casualties. Such resistance as was offered was speedily quelled. Many Germans were killed, several prisoners taken, and the raiders, pushing

THE GIVENCHY RAID.

on, stormed the German support line 400 yards further on with equal success. Both A Company (Captain Cobb) on the right and B (Captain Scott) on the left reached their objectives. The trenches were cleared, dug-outs discovered and bombed and mine shafts blown up. 2nd Lieut. Jagger, who commanded the left party, was conspicuous for his leadership and his party was specially successful, being much assisted by the skill with which Pte. Thompson, one of the Lewis gunners, covered its advance. 2nd Lieut. Brett and Sergt. Donohu also handled their parties with great skill; the former displayed the greatest coolness in checking his men when he found them getting too near the barrage, and set a splendid example, while Sergt. Donohu guarded the right flank most carefully and was the last man to withdraw. Corpl. Budgeon, one of the " old originals " of 1914, who took over command of another party when Sergt. Lines, its commander, was hit, led his men forward most successfully, penetrated further into the enemy's lines than any other party and inflicted heavy casualties on his opponents. So complete had been the surprise and so effective the counter-battery work that twenty minutes elapsed before any of the enemy's guns opened in reply and then it was only an ineffective effort by a few odd guns. At 3.30 the raiders withdrew; their casualties came to 70, mostly men slightly wounded from following too close on the barrage, or hit later on after the return to the British trenches, for the enemy, who were evidently shaken by their experience, kept on opening heavy shell-fire at intervals. As against that they had taken nearly 30 prisoners from the 264th (Saxon) Infantry Regiment and had inflicted casualties estimated as at least 150 killed, many of the fugitives being caught in our barrage as they fled. A captured officer remarked that he had seen nothing like it on the Eastern Front and had imagined it was the beginning of the spring offen-

THE THIRD WINTER.

Feb.-March, 1917
1st Battalion

sive.[1] Indeed " The Royal West Kents' Givenchy Raid " served as the standard of reference by which the Fifth Division judged similar enterprises in future.

This was the outstanding event of the winter months for the 1st Battalion, though there was an interesting episode in December when two French soldiers turned up on leave from the Somme and asked permission to dig for a box of valuables which they had buried in 1914 near a farm between the support trenches of the Festubert section and what had been the old British front line before May 1915. After some disappointment they succeeded in unearthing the box containing money and valuables worth 15,000 francs and departed in a state of jubilant satisfaction. The battalion remained in the Bethune area till the middle of March, moving thence to Auchel to spend the rest of that month in training for a new offensive. During the battalion's stay in the Bethune area there had been many changes among the officers, company and platoon commanders varied with the exigencies of courses, leave and the return of recovered wounded, though Colonel Buchanan-Dunlop and Majors Lynch White and Waring all continued with the battalion till the new offensive opened in April. In December Lieut. Thorne came out from the 3rd Battalion to take over the Quarter Master's position, and the battalion was very lucky in escaping with few casualties or invalidings among the officers. Fairly substantial drafts were received in November, nearly 250 in all, and another large draft joined in January; but the losses in the Givenchy raid had not been made good when the Fifth Division left the area.[2]

---

[1] Captain Cobb and 2nd Lieuts. Brett and Jagger received the Military Cross for their services in this raid, while D.C.M.'s were awarded to Sergt. Donohu, Corpl. Budgeon and Pte. Thompson.

[2] At this time there were present with the battalion 42 N.C.O.'s and men who had landed with it in August, 1914, and had served consecutively with it ever since, while another 40 " old originals " were still present who had only been away for quite short periods.

THE THIRD WINTER.

Meanwhile the 6th Battalion had spent two very quiet months in its now familiar Wailly sector. This part of the line had never been "active" since the British had taken it over, and though keeping the trenches in repair involved plenty of work the period was barren in incidents of note. Still this gave it plenty of time for assimilating the large drafts, nearly 400 in all, with which its depleted ranks had been filled up. On November 20th Colonel Owen left the battalion to take command of the 36th Brigade—the only C.O. the 6th had in France who did not come from The Queen's Own he had given the battalion of his best and had been a vigorous and effective commander. He was succeeded by Major Dawson, who, though only a substantive Captain, had thus achieved the distinction of rising from junior subaltern to Lieut.-Colonel and battalion commander in little over two years. This appointment gave great satisfaction to all ranks; Dawson had already given ample proof of his capacities and had shown himself fully equal to his new position. Captain Alderman became second-in-command in his place with the rank of Major, and Captain Dove succeeded to the Adjutancy. The New Year found the 6th out of the line at Sombrin, where it remained till the middle of January, when it took over part of the new Divisional front. This was in the actual suburbs of Arras, extending Southwards from the Scarpe on the left to the Arras-St. Quentin Road.

The German trenches here were mostly about 200 yards away, though at Blangy, which was included in this sector, they were much nearer, less than 20 yards off in places; this closeness, however, had advantages, the Germans could not bombard the British front line for fear of hitting their own front trench, and the front line was consequently much safer than the support trenches 150 yards away, which were constantly obliterated. It was a curious bit of the line; it ran right through the ruins of Blangy so that there No Man's

Nov., 1916-March, 1917 6th Battalion

THE ARRAS FRONT.

Nov., 1916-
March, 1917
6th Battalion

Land was a chaotic tangle of bricks, bits of broken roofs and wire, on the left the line ran backwards along the Scarpe and there was an outlying post in the reeds from which the sentries used at intervals to call across to the Australians on the further bank. The trenches here were necessarily shallow and gave the German snipers many chances, and as both sides were active with artillery and trench-mortars it was a more "lively" portion of the front than Wailly. Cold and wet weather at first, followed by hard frost, made life in the trenches very uncomfortable, but the good quarters available for supports and reserves in close proximity to the front made things much more endurable. The remarkable feature about Arras was that though the front line ran through its suburbs and the town was continually under fire, it looked at first sight quite normal, and the population continued to carry on with their daily routine in surprising fashion. Still, many houses which outwardly seemed intact proved on closer inspection to be badly damaged, and by day the town seemed a city of the dead, the only people to be seen in the streets being officers and orderlies on duty. Big cellars abounded, and these had been connected up, and an extensive system of tunnels developed, giving underground communication which proved of enormous value when the great attack was launched.

The battalion was still in this sector when the spring offensive started in April and had, therefore, the advantage of attacking over ground with which it had become thoroughly familiar. It was by this time well up to strength, although of the 43 officers and 1,080 men on its rolls at the end of March 11 officers and over 200 other ranks were not actually with the battalion, being mainly absorbed by the multifarious divisional and brigade employments, courses and schools. It had carried out one raid in March, but the repeated raids which the Twelfth Division had made had put the enemy on the alert; two of the parties pene-

THE THIRD WINTER.

trated successfully into the enemy's trenches to find the front line evacuated and the enemy manning the support line in strength. The main purpose of identification was, therefore, not achieved, though the raiders were withdrawn without many casualties and had reason to believe they had inflicted some loss in the exchange of bombs and rifle-fire with the enemy. March, 1917
6th Battalion

The 7th had enjoyed more than two months of respite after its long spell of fighting and hard work on the heights above the Ancre. After arriving in the Abbeville neighbourhood at the end of November it did not return to the line till the middle of February, though it shifted its billets more than once. Training was energetically carried on and the smartness of the battalion appears to have made a great impression on a large draft which joined in January, one of whom wrote home in some awe of the standard required. " As for guard mounting," he added, " I guess it would beat the Guard changing at Whitehall easily." During this period there were many changes among the officers. Captain Anstruther was in temporary command when the battalion was withdrawn from the line, but early in January Lieut.-Col. E. M. Liddell, of the Duke of Wellington's, was definitely appointed to the command. Captain J. B. B. Ford, who had been invalided home from the 2nd Battalion, came out in December and took over A Company; in January Captains Latter and J. B. Matthews rejoined, while the arrival of a dozen subalterns and a draft of nearly 200 men went some way to repair the losses of the autumn, though the battalion was still much below establishment. Nov., 1916-
Feb., 1917
7th Battalion

When the 7th returned to the front line it found itself holding part of Desire Trench, but somewhat to the left of the line which it had attacked on November 18th. Part of Grandcourt Trench was in British hands, but the continuation of that trench Eastward was still in German keeping, and A Company was accordingly detailed to attack it. The attack, launched See Sketch 25

233

GRANDCOURT TRENCH.

Feb. 14th 1917
7th Battalion

in the early hours of February 14th in two waves, with 2nd Lieuts. Dix and Beckett commanding the leading platoons, at first seemed to go well, and at 7.20 a.m. a report reached Battalion Headquarters that the objective had been taken but that Captain Ford was wounded and 2nd Lieuts. Dix and Beckett killed. Colonel Liddell, therefore, detailed Captain Matthews to take up a platoon of C to reinforce A, and shortly afterwards went up to the front himself to investigate. It then appeared that the whole objective had not been taken; in the darkness direction had been lost, the attackers had got into the left of their objective only and the right platoon had run into uncut wire in front of the strong point which formed the Eastern end of the objective[1] and had been shot down almost to a man. The attack thus resulted in a very limited success and casualties were deplorably heavy; Captain Ford died of his wounds shortly afterward and Captain Matthews was killed in organizing the defence of the portion of the objective taken. He had apparently gone forward to reconnoitre the obstructing strong point as his body was subsequently found quite close to it.

Feb.-April, 1917

This unlucky enterprise was the 7th's chief operation during the winter months. It was resting when, on February 17th, the 53rd and 54th Brigades made a most successful attack on the high ground overlooking Miraumont, and on its next tour in the front line (February 19th-23rd) its patrols, which were extremely enterprising and most successful in collecting useful information, found that the enemy were beginning to retire from the pronounced salient which his positions on the Ancre now presented. This withdrawal was only a preliminary to the general retreat three weeks later out of the larger salient from the Ancre to Arras; but in this beginning of semi-open warfare the 7th had no very active part, though the Eighteenth Division

[1] This was the same "strong point" from which D Company had suffered such heavy losses on November 18th.

THE THIRD WINTER.

shared in the capture of Irles on March 10th, which im- Feb.-April, mediately preceded the main withdrawal. The 7th had 1917 7th Battalion only just had the satisfaction of leaving the desolated area on the heights above the Ancre for the grass and growing crops around Achiet le Grand when, on March 21st, it was withdrawn for another period of training, mostly spent at Wittes, which lasted till nearly the end of April. In February it had had the ill-luck to lose Colonel Liddell, who was wounded: his tenure of command had been brief but long enough to show his great capacities as a leader and commander. He had at once won the heart and confidence of everybody in the battalion. On his being wounded, as Major Phillips was away, Captain Anstruther was again in command until Colonel Hickson joined early in April. He had been serving in East Africa at the outbreak of war, having been seconded to the King's African Rifles, and had been invalided home early in 1916, but had now been passed fit for service again.

The rest which the 8th Battalion enjoyed after its Oct., 1916- exertions on the Somme was not of long duration but March, 1917 8th Battalion it gave time for the re-organization necessary after the recent fighting and losses. Major Whitty was now in command, as after struggling against ill-health all the summer Colonel Parker had been evacuated sick. Lieut. H. S. Brown was Adjutant and Captain Wenyon, 2nd Lieut. E. G. Brown, Lieut. Sir H. W. Hawley and 2nd Lieut. Lock were the company commanders. When the battalion returned to the fighting front it found itself in the First Army, and after one turn in the Berthonval sector, near the Vimy Ridge, was moved up to a quarter with which it was only too familiar. On October 25th it relieved a battalion of the Fortieth Division near Hulluch and had its front See Sketch 11 line just West of that Lens and La Bassée Road the battalion had crossed on September 26th, 1915.

The 8th found its opponents " very much out of hand," using trench mortars with much freedom,

235

THE THIRD WINTER.

Oct., 1916-
March, 1917
8th Battalion

particularly from Posen Crater, a prominent tactical feature on our right where the enemy were only 100 yards away, though No Man's Land widened to nearly 300 yards further to the left. There followed a desperate duel for supremacy in which the 8th plied their opponents with rifle-grenades so assiduously that the enemy soon found they were getting as good as they gave. To their "rum jars" and "pineapples" retaliation in the shape of rifle-grenades was so quickly forthcoming that they gradually desisted from their activities, ceased to start "strafes," and left No Man's Land almost uncontested to the active patrols of the 8th. The battalion spent nearly four months in this sector, six days in the line were usually followed by six in support, another six in the line and then six in reserve. It was a strenuous time, for the line needed constant work, but as the battalion always returned to the same trenches it could carry on a continuous programme and casualties were kept astonishingly low, while though the weather was very cold, trench life was really more endurable in frost than in wet. Just before the end of the year a big draft filled up the gaps left by the Somme fighting, while in January Colonel Parker returned and resumed command.

In February the Division enjoyed a fortnight's rest after which it relieved the Canadians in the line from the Souchez River to just South of Loos. Here the 8th were in the middle of a mass of mining villages, pit-heads and dumps of mine refuse. The 72nd Brigade had the left or Calonne sector, which included a post on the N.W. end of the famous "Double Crassier" of Loos. Here the enemy were in close proximity, within 50 yards, though in the centre their trenches were 600 yards away, being nearer again on the right. The trenches were in an awful state but this was soon remedied by hard work in which the Divisional Pioneers, the 12th Sherwood Foresters, co-operated notably. The chief event of the battalion's stay

See Sketch 52

THE THIRD WINTER.

in this area was a German attack on the Double Crassier post on March 19th, which was beaten off by No. 13 Platoon of D Company under 2nd Lieut. Proctor, largely thanks to L/Cpl. Dent, who bombed back a party which was working round at the base of the mound.[1] Several Germans were killed and the repulse apparently discouraged them, for they did not repeat the attempt and made little effort to dispute No Man's Land, which remained practically the territory of the battalion's patrols. *Feb.-March, 1917 8th Battalion*

The Forty-First Division had moved far afield after quitting the Somme. It had at first enjoyed a few days spent in rest and re-organization, by the 10th R.W.K. at Dernancourt, by the 11th at Ribemont, where it received a draft of 250 men from the 2nd line of the Royal East Kent Mounted Rifles—most magnificent material apart from the welcome addition to its depleted numbers.[2] The Division then moved by rail to Flanders and found itself by the end of October near Reninghelst. The frontage on which the 10th and 11th were now to serve was that S.E. of Ypres, already so familiar to the 1st Battalion. The months which had passed since any of The Queen's Own had held this sector had not seen any change for the better in it. The trenches, which had been left in very bad condition by their last occupants, lay on a slope with the Germans on the crest above them and overlooking the approaches. Even to those who had fought on the Somme this sector was emphatically one to be reckoned notable for its mud, and the task of getting up to the trenches the large quantity of materials required to keep them in repair was as difficult as was that of repairing the trenches when the materials at last reached them. It was astonishing what an appetite for R.E. stores the trenches seemed to possess; the more stuff used in their maintenance the more seemed needed. *Oct., 1916- March, 1917 10th & 11th Battalions*

[1] He received the M.M.
[2] Some officers joined at the same time, among them Major Beadle, who was to have a long spell of service with the battalion.

THE THIRD WINTER.

Oct., 1916-April, 1917 10th & 11th Battalions

The 10th and 11th were to have ample opportunities for becoming accustomed to this area. It was not only the closing months of 1916 which they were to spend there, 1917 was three parts gone before they finally quitted "the Salient." For both battalions the winter and spring of 1916-1917 was an active time. The 11th came in for the larger number of notable incidents in the way of raids and bombardments, but its casualties were nearly twice as high. On the whole, however, the wastage of both battalions was moderate, neither sickness nor battle-casualties being responsible for anything like the numbers of the first winter of the war; while both were kept fairly well up to strength. Several officers who had been wounded on the Somme returned, notably Colonel Wood-Martyn, who rejoined the 10th on January 1st and took over command from Colonel Soames. Captain Jiminez rejoined the 11th in April and resumed duty as Adjutant, relieving Captain Puttick.

10th Batt.

The outstanding feature of this period as far as the 10th were concerned was the splendid "liaison" it established with the artillery covering its sector. This brigade was commanded by Lieut.-Col. Simons, an ex-naval officer, and its gunners were the closest of friends with the 10th. It was arranged that if the enemy seemed restive and inclined to try a raid a code-word should be sent to the guns direct from the front line and not *via* Battalion Headquarters. This arrangement worked splendidly; three times the Germans started to raid the 10th, but each time the barrage came down so instantaneously and effectively that on every occasion the Germans were stopped at their own wire. To this the 10th were largely indebted for the lightness of its casualty list, which only came to five officers and just over 100 men, including two officers, Lieut. Tennyson Smith and 2nd Lieut. Hodges, killed on patrol. Moreover, when the Germans followed up one unsuccessful attempt at a raid by repeating it at the same

RAIDS AND REPULSES.

place and hour, the 10th had the satisfaction of taking two prisoners, the first the Division had captured for months, and of killing all the rest of the party. The battalion's snipers and patrols were busy enough and had the best of several minor encounters, while it behaved with conspicuous steadiness when heavily bombarded at the beginning of May, and the excellence of its work was fully recognised by its Divisional commander, General Lawford. *Oct., 1916- April, 1917 10th Batt.*

The story of the 11th during these months was perhaps marked by rather more outstanding incidents: it was three times subjected to heavy bombardments followed by German raids; and after one fairly satisfactory raid in January, when it was holding the Spoil Bank sector near the Ypres-Comines Canal, was most successful in a second attempt. This was on February 8th when 2nd Lieut. R. S. French took a party over, got well into the German trenches, obtained a valuable identification by capturing 12 prisoners from the 65th Reserve Infantry Regiment of the 208th Division, and inflicted many casualties on the enemy. Though wounded, 2nd Lieut. French accounted for three of the enemy himself and, aided by Sergt. Cozens, whose gallantry and good leading were conspicuous, he brought his party back with a loss of only four killed and a dozen wounded.[1] It was arranged to repeat the raid six hours later, but this time the enemy were decidedly on the alert and the raiders failed to get into the trenches, though they withdrew without casualties. *11th Batt. Feb. 8th, 1917*

The three German attacks which the 11th experienced all occurred within about a month. The first was on March 24th, when the Germans were apparently attempting a much bigger raid which was disorganized by the promptness and efficiency of our artillery retaliation. A small party of raiders came over but was easily beaten off without obtaining any identifications, and the *March 24th 1917*

---

[1] 2nd Lieut. French received the M.C. and Sergt. Cozens the D.C.M.

THE ST. ELOI SECTOR.

March, 1917
11th Batt. way in which Colonel Corfe appreciated and handled the situation was highly commended by the Divisional commander. The battalion's casualties came to some 30, including Lieut. Aylett wounded. The second attempt,

April 7th on April 7th, was apparently in retaliation for a raid by the Forty-Seventh Division. The battalion was then in the St. Eloi sector, not in the Spoil Bank. The bombardment began about 4 p.m. and worked from the centre outwards. Captain T. C. Wright observing this, skilfully moved his men from the danger zone in a way which minimized their casualties although the trenches were much damaged. When the enemy came over, just before 7 p.m., they actually entered the trenches, but were quite unsuccessful in obtaining any prisoners or Lewis guns or other spoil, and were quickly driven out. In retiring to their own lines they were caught in the British barrage and suffered severely, while the 11th were lucky to escape with only 20 casualties. Captain Wright was among the wounded, but his coolness and grasp of the situation well deserved the M.C. he received.

April 20th
1917
11th Batt. The third German attack was the most serious. It came on April 20th when the battalion was again in the St. Eloi trenches, though this time in the right subsector. In the support line at this point there was an important mine-shaft, part of the elaborate mining preparations for the projected big attack by the Second Army, and there was little doubt that this was the main objective of the attack. The bombardment began about 7.30 p.m. and continued till 9 p.m. with great intensity, almost obliterating the front trenches and doing special damage to a crater in front, the whole garrison of which was missing. Captain Frazer, who was in command, rose splendidly to the occasion; he set a fine example of bravery and displayed much tactical skill and resource. He had moved his men to the flanks of the shelled area or sheltered them in the mine-shaft, and directly the barrage lifted he brought them up and

THE ST. ELOI SECTOR.

posted them so adroitly that when the raiders came over they were met with a most effective rifle and Lewis gun fire from the support line, which prevented them getting near the mine-shaft and sent them promptly to the right-about. As they went back they were caught by the British counter-barrage and suffered heavily both from that and from the Lewis guns of the 15th Hampshires, who got into them from the flank, so that the enterprise ended badly for them. The 11th had nearly 30 casualties; 2nd Lieut. Rodney, who had only joined ten days before this, was killed, but the gallantry of the men and the resourcefulness and skill of Captain Frazer, who received the M.C., were warmly praised by the Divisional commander.

April, 1917
11th Batt.

The 11th had certainly added considerably to its reputation by the steadiness and gallantry it had displayed in these actions, and the D.S.O., which was conferred on Colonel Corfe in the June 3rd Honours List was a well-merited recognition both of the battalion's excellent record and of its commander's personal share in bringing it up to its high standard of efficiency and imbuing it with his own fighting spirit and energy. In its first year of active service it had already earned an unusual number of honours and distinctions. The next few months were to make its record in this respect quite remarkable. But before the 10th and 11th were to take part in any major operation other battalions of The Queen's Own had been heavily engaged in the first major offensive of the year, the desperate fighting of April and May 1917 on the Arras front.

CHAPTER XV

ARRAS.

April, 1917

The change in the Allied plan of campaign which had postponed the opening of Sir Douglas Haig's offensive had allowed the Germans to retire " according to plan " on the defences of the Hindenburg Line, more formidable by the middle of April than they would have been a month earlier. But on the greater part of the Third Army's front the Germans had not withdrawn, and the plans originally arranged did not have to be seriously modified to meet the new situation. The 15-mile frontage to be attacked extended from Croisilles, S.E. of Arras, to the Northern end of the Vimy Ridge. Twelve divisions of the Third Army, among them the Twelfth, were detailed for the attack together with the Canadian Corps of General Horne's First Army, which, with the assistance of the 13th Brigade from the Fifth Division, was to tackle the Vimy Ridge. Thus the 1st R.W.K. as well as the 6th took part in the attack, while the 8th—who were on the fringe of it North of the Souchez River—stood ready to join in should the success of the operations lead to an extension of the front.

The defences to be assaulted were fully as formidable as those which had confronted the British forces on the Somme. The defensive belt organized in depth extended in places as far as five miles back and included three separate trench systems. But the British heavy guns and ammunition available exceeded even the preparations for the Somme, and for nearly three weeks before the day fixed for the assault a most systematic bombardment had been carried on, in which the new fuse " 106," which burst the shell the instant it touched the ground, proved most effective in cutting wire. As " zero day " drew nearer the bombardment increased in volume and intensity, while gas was discharged on an

ARRAS.

extensive scale wherever conditions favoured it; by April 9th, when the assault was delivered, the defences had been so effectually battered and the garrisons so shaken and demoralized that the front system was carried over almost the whole line. The advance to the second objective met rather more resistance, but soon after mid-day this, too, was captured. After the attackers passed on beyond the positions which had been within the reach of their preliminary bombardment their fortunes were more chequered, but as a whole the day fully fulfilled the high hopes that had been formed and dealt a really severe blow to the Germans.

In this day of general success two battalions of The Queen's Own had their share of victory. The 13th Brigade's task was to pass through the Second Canadian Division after it had captured its second objective and to carry on the advance to where the Eastern edge of the Vimy Ridge dips steeply to the low ground beyond. The 1st Battalion had moved up into assembly trenches at Neuville St. Vaast on the evening of April 8th, but did not advance till 7.30 a.m., two hours after zero. As it started snow was falling heavily, which added considerably to the difficulty of crossing ground already devastated by the bombardment and pitted with craters and shell holes. The tanks told off to assist the attack were found stuck in the mud at the first objective, but this had not prevented the Canadians from securing both their objectives, and the battalion reached its appointed position of deployment along the Lille road practically without loss. A short halt here allowed the ground ahead to be reconnoitred, and at 9.30 the battalion advanced, passing through the Canadians who were consolidating their second objective. So effective was the barrage that Thelus Trench was reached and rushed with great ease; little effective opposition was offered, though some 30 prisoners were secured. C and D Companies (Captains Bellman and Wilberforce), who were leading, promptly pushed parties up the communi-

April 9th 1917

1st Battalion See Sketch 27

THE VIMY RIDGE.

April 9th
1917
1st Battalion

cation trench leading to Telegraphen Weg and into the shattered remains of Count's Wood, while No. 14 Platoon, led by Lieut. Hyde and 2nd Lieut. Lewis Barned, secured a cross-roads on the right, despite fire over open sights from some German guns in the Bois du Goulot, which were silenced by the accurate shooting of a covering party. Then, while C and D consolidated Thelus Trench, having established touch with the First Canadian Division on the right and the K.O.S.B.'s on the left, A and B took up the advance.

B, well led by 2nd Lieut. Jenkinson, worked forward round the Northern edge of Count's Wood and, entering the Bois du Goulot from the North, pushed through it, meeting rather more opposition which, however, was speedily overcome, the Germans affording good targets to our Lewis gunners as they made off to the N.E. By 11 a.m. the "Blue Line" had been secured and then A (2nd Lieut. Press) came up on B's right to complete the clearing of the Bois du Goulot and carry the advance on to the "Brown Line," the final objective on its Eastern edge. It, too, was completely successful; a large party of Germans retired hastily in front of it, nine guns of various calibres were captured and many casualties inflicted on the retiring enemy, again mainly by the Lewis gunners, among whom L/Cpls. Bott and Dimmock, Corpl. Ackland and Ptes. Gould and Peachey were conspicuous. By noon the battalion had secured the final objective and had started consolidating it, Lieut. Monypenny and his platoon pushing forward 350 yards ahead of the outpost line and forming an advanced post under heavy fire from machine-guns.

From the Bois de Goulot a magnificent view could be obtained over the country at the foot of the ridge—on fine days the colour of Douai Cathedral could even be made out—and with this advantage in observation it was easy to detect and report to the artillery any German movement in the plain below. The success of the

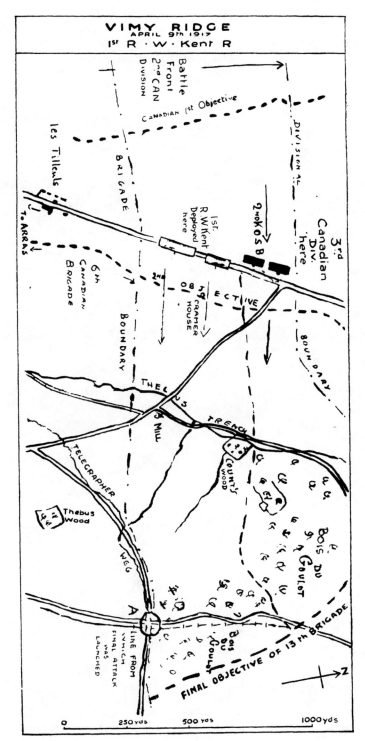

ARRAS.

attack had apparently altogether upset the arrangements of the Germans, for nothing like the vigorous counter-attacks of Loos and the Somme was attempted. A and B reported one or two advances to the artillery and assisted to break them up with long-range rifle and Lewis-gun fire, but all that day and the next consolidation proceeded almost unimpeded by the enemy's shell-fire, though rather more effectively hampered by the difficulty of getting up stores and rations over the desolation between the advanced positions and the old British front line, a task in which Lieut. Thorne, the Quarter Master, displayed quite exceptional zeal and ability. On one occasion, moreover, a convoy of pack animals bringing up rations to the front line came under shell-fire and was thrown into confusion, several horses being hit, but Corpl. Cutter and Pte. Miles did splendid work and brought the rations through nevertheless. On the evening of the 10th a Canadian battalion arrived to relieve the battalion, which went back to Gouy Servins, not so much to rest as to find some of the large working parties required for the bringing forward of the communications and rearward establishments to meet the new situation. As the weather was peculiarly bad—a series of blizzards following in quick succession—and the troops were for the moment on reduced rations, this work proved particularly trying; but the battalion had good reason to congratulate itself, not only on a very fine achievement, but on the lightness of its casualty list. Twenty officers and 655 other ranks had gone into action;[1] only 138 figured in the list, Lieut. Hyde and 13 men being killed, 12 men missing, 2nd Lieut. Lewis Barned and the remaining 111 men wounded.[2]

_{April 9th}
₁₉₁₇
_{1st Battalion}

_{April 10th}

While the 1st Battalion had been achieving notable success at this very low cost the 6th, though encounter-

_{April, 9th}
_{6th Battalion}

---

[1] The "battle surplus," on which the battalion might be reconstructed in case of heavy losses, had included 12 officers with N.C.O.'s and specialists.

[2] Captains Wilberforce and Bellman received the M.C.

OBSERVATION RIDGE.

April 9th, 1917
6th Battalion

See Sketch 28

ing more serious opposition, had been equally successful and scarcely less fortunate as regards losses. The Twelfth Division was in the right centre of the battle front, starting from the suburb of St. Sauveur and advancing between the Arras-Cambria road and the Arras-Douai railway. Its immediate objective was the high ground known as Observation Ridge which runs Northward from Tilloy-lez-Mofflaines towards the Scarpe. The 37th Brigade took the right of the line with the 6th Queen's on the right and 7th East Surreys on the left, the battalion following the East Surreys. On their left came the 36th Brigade, which, with the 37th, was to carry the attack as far as the Division's second objective—the "Blue Line"—after which the 35th was to come through and attack yet a third objective, the "Brown Line."

Here also the artillery had done its work with extraordinary effectiveness, and The Queen's and East Surreys secured the "Black Line" in very quick time, while the supporting battalions got forward almost without any casualties. They had had the great advantage of starting the attack unusually fit and fresh owing to the splendid accommodation afforded close up to the front line by the extensive caves and cellars with which Arras abounded, and bad as the going was in the sleet and snow, the troops advanced confidently. The main obstacle before the battalion was Hangest Trench, which was situated on the Western slopes of Observation Ridge and was flanked on the North by Holt and Heron Works, the latter being on the front of the 36th Brigade; while two main communication trenches running back from the front system to the second, Henley Lane on the North and Havant Lane on the South, had to be cleared to prevent the enemy using them for flanking fire. Considerable opposition was offered, the position was strong and bristled with machine-guns, the tanks which should have co-operated never arrived, and the battalion had to fight hard. It passed through the

OBSERVATION RIDGE.

East Surreys at 7.30 a.m., and by 8.50 reports reached the Brigade that our troops were in Hangest Trench. A little later, however, another message described them as held up in front of that trench, and it soon became clear that as the state of the ground had prevented the troops from keeping quite close up to the barrage some parties of the enemy had managed to put up an effective opposition and had held the attack up in places. The 6th, indeed, had outstripped the troops on their flanks, and at 10.50 a message came back from Colonel Dawson that he had two companies in Henley Lane and Hamel Work,[1] somewhat to the left of and outside his objective, that another company was held up in front of Hangest Trench and that the remaining one had got into Hotte Work on his right.

April 9th, 1917 6th Battalion

These lodgements on the flanks proved most useful in overcoming the resistance in the centre. Lieut. Thomas distinguished himself by pushing on ahead with a small party, and by forcing his way into the enemy's trench he helped greatly to let the rest of his company, B, get forward, and gradually ground was gained. The detachments which had got in on the left worked down from Henley Lane against Holt Work and Hangest Trench, overcoming a stubborn opposition, while that in Hotte Work also made ground inwards, simultaneously getting touch with the Buffs in Houlette Work further to the right. Under this pressure from the flanks the defence of Hangest Trench and Holt Work collapsed, many Germans put up their hands and a substantial haul of prisoners was collected while the battalion pushed forward and secured its final objective without much further trouble. Here, about 1 p.m., the 35th Brigade passed through it on its way to the "Brown Line," on which the battalion set to work to consolidate the position gained; at 3 p.m. it was reported as occupying Hotte Work and part of Holt

---

[1] It seems possible that it was not Hamel Work, but Heron Work, which the left companies had taken.

ARRAS.

April, 1917
6th Battalion

as its main line, with advanced posts on the higher ground in front.

Despite its hard fighting the 6th had got off relatively lightly. Only 30 men had fallen with one officer, 2nd Lieut. Proctor; Captain L. C. R. Smith, 2nd Lieuts. Waterhouse, Duffield, Fuller, Apperley and Kneafsey were wounded with 124 men, another 10 men were missing, a total of 172 out of the 20 officers and 655 other ranks in action.[1] This loss could not be reckoned severe in comparison with the exceptionally heavy casualties inflicted on the enemy and the importance of the gains secured; indeed, the Division's 1,200 prisoners came to more than half its 2,000 casualties, and the day was certainly the most successful that the Twelfth had yet known. Included in the 6th's captures on this day were one gun, which Colonel Dawson endeavoured to secure as a trophy for The Queen's Own, though he was not successful in rescuing it from the clutches of the Division, and a box containing half-a-dozen Iron Crosses which had obviously been sent up with the rations for distribution. These were eagerly annexed by their finders, and it was with some difficulty and for a large price that one corporal was induced to part with his trophy in order that it might be presented to the Brigadier, General Cator, when he next reviewed the battalion.

Meanwhile the 35th Brigade had secured the " Brown Line " after heavy fighting, and in the course of April 10th and 11th the Thirty-Seventh Division, which had come up from behind and passed through, carried the advance further and reached Monchy le Preux. This village stood on higher ground than the country round it and was in consequence a tactical position of some importance, so its retention was a matter of urgency. But the Thirty-Seventh Division had lost heavily and was so exhausted that on April 11th the

[1] The battalion's " effective strength " on April 1st had been 32 officers and 833 other ranks.

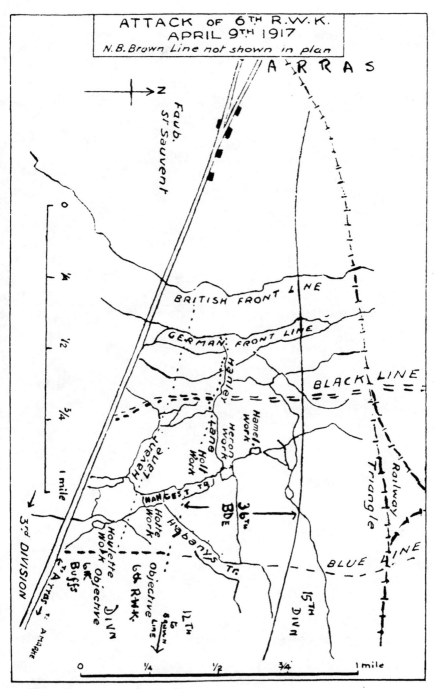

MONCHY LE PREUX.

April, 1917
6th Battalion

37th Brigade had to relieve it. The Brigade had had a hard time since the 9th. It had been unable to shelter in the German dug-outs as many of them had proved to be fitted with delayed-action mines and had blown up with many casualties to their occupants, and the men were exhausted by the work of consolidating trenches in the extremely wintry weather which had set in with the attack and had continued ever since. But they rose to this new demand, and on the evening of April 11th took over the line East of Monchy, the 6th Battalion being on the left.

It was an extremely awkward position; the line here formed a pronounced salient as neither of the Divisions on the flanks had yet got up level. The troops on the left of the battalion were hard to locate, no satisfactory defensive line had as yet been taken up and the position was under heavy and steady shell-fire and intermittent sniping. Moreover, the conditions in the village were indescribably ghastly. One officer writes that the streets were literally " flowing with the blood of horses and men." A brigade of cavalry had been caught in Monchy by German machine-guns, and the place was strewn with dead and dying horses. It was remnants of this brigade whom the 6th had to relieve among others, and the general confusion added greatly to the difficulties of the relief. For tired men it was a severe trial, but Colonel Dawson set his battalion a splendid example of energy and devotion to duty. He was indefatigable, putting the position into a satisfactory state, re-adjusting the line and re-organizing the defence generally; all this, too, was done under heavy shelling with characteristic coolness and disregard for danger. He inspired confidence everywhere and in everybody, and the men responded splendidly to his calls upon them. Finally, after an arduous and exhausting time, the 1st Essex, of the Twenty-Ninth Division,[1] arrived to take over, and the battalion could

[1] This was the same battalion which had relieved the 6th at Gueudecourt in October, 1916 (*cf.* p. 220).

ARRAS.

withdraw to Arras and thence to Montenescourt for a week's well-deserved rest.

April, 1917
8th Battalion

See Sketch 52

April 13th

April 14th

Meanwhile the extension of the battle-zone Northward had brought the Twenty-Fourth Division into the fighting, and on April 12th it co-operated with the Fourth Canadians in a successful advance astride the Souchez River. The 8th R.W.K., being at the opposite end of the Division's line, was not engaged in this, but next day there were indications that the enemy were beginning to withdraw from the trenches opposite and the battalion promptly pushed forward strong patrols. These, led by 2nd Lieuts. Hayward and Tanner, penetrated over half-a-mile into the German positions, driving back the parties left to cover the withdrawal and taking some prisoners. Next day the 8th Queen's pushed on ahead, the battalion consolidating a line through Cité St. Pierre, one of the suburbs of Lens. On the 15th it again took up the advance, but this time encountered much more opposition; and though it made good Cowden Trench just beyond Cité St. Pierre, could progress no further without more artillery support than was available. It had therefore merely to consolidate the ground gained, but while doing this had three officers (2nd Lieuts. Vaughan, Johnson and Woolley) and one warrant officer (C.S.M. Verrall) killed and two more officers wounded by one unlucky shell, a bad blow to the battalion, which had altogether nine officers and 60 men hit in these operations, losing in five days more than twice as many as the previous five weeks in the Calonne sector had cost it.

Between April 12th and the end of the month the fighting on the Arras front continued almost without intermission, though without the brilliant success which had attended the first attack. This was largely because the continuation of the British attack did not form part of Sir Douglas Haig's original scheme. By April 15th he had achieved his purpose. All the tactical features he had desired to secure were in his hands, heavy losses

ARRAS.

had been inflicted on the enemy, many prisoners and guns had been taken, reserves had been attracted to the Arras front, and the British plans would not be served by pressing further at this point, particularly as the advance had already largely out-run the artillery support immediately available, so that each step further would only increase the difficulties of getting guns forward to assist it and of keeping the advanced troops supplied. But it was necessary to go on attacking at Arras to divert the German attention from the great French effort on the Aisne from which so much was hoped; and after the virtual failure of General Nivelle's short cut to victory had thrown the whole Allied plan of campaign utterly out of gear, the British had at all costs to keep the Germans fully occupied lest they should profit by their opportunity and fall in force upon the French when they were suffering from the inevitable reaction consequent on their bitter disillusionment.

In the renewed British attack of April 23rd-24th, when Guemappe and Gavrelle and some other positions were secured, The Queen's Own was not represented; the 1st Battalion, who had moved up to the front again on the 22nd, was held in reserve and spent April 23rd in readiness to move forward, receiving various contradictory orders and reports. The Fifth Division's attack against the Vimy-Lens line between the Vimy-Avion railway and the Souchez River, though gallantly pressed, led to no substantial gains, and when the battalion moved up in the evening to take over the front trenches from the shattered Norfolks it was only an old British line that they occupied. But the enemy attempted no counter-attack, contenting himself with barraging the front line heavily, and the battalion got off without any losses. This was largely because Colonel Dunlop had dug in a little in advance of the old British line, which came in for a very severe but to the battalion quite innocuous shelling. Next night it was relieved by Canadians and was not

ARRAS.

April, 1917
1st Battalion
again actively employed for another ten days, in which interval various small reinforcements arrived which did not quite balance its losses of April 9th, but enabled it to take over 600 men into action when on May 2nd it moved up to Roclincourt for the Fifth Division's next attack.

6th Battalion
Before that the 6th had also returned to the battle-zone, for the Twelfth Division had gone into line between Monchy and the Scarpe on April 25th. The

See Sketch 29
tactical position just N.E. of Monchy was complicated and unsatisfactory. The British front line at this point ran from Rifle Farm, a point due N.E. of Monchy, N.W. along Rifle Trench, but the Northern end of the trench was held by the Germans to its junction with Bayonet Trench. This last trench, part of which also was in German hands, ran North and South parallel with the Western end of Monchy. From April 25th to the end of the month there was sharp fighting for the German portions of Rifle and Bayonet Trenches. Some ground was gained on April 28th by the 35th Brigade, the 6th Battalion being in reserve and employed mainly as carrying parties. Bayonet Trench was then secured and during the next two days all but a small fragment of Rifle Trench was taken. But this left Monchy still in a distinct salient, liable to enfilade fire from the North and North-East, and this very much complicated the task of the Twelfth Division in the big attack arranged for May 3rd.

May 3rd.
This attack was the biggest effort which the British Armies had made since the opening of the Arras offensive. The front extended from Fresnoy to Fontaine lez Croisilles, while further South the Fifth Army attacked the Hindenburg Line near Bullecourt. Of The Queen's Own only the 6th and 7th Battalions were actively engaged; for the 1st, though in readiness to advance, had the attacks of the Seventeenth Corps met with substantial success, was not called upon to do so.

DEVIL'S TRENCH.

To the 6th and 7th, however, May 3rd brought desperate fighting and heavy losses. The Twelfth Division's task was to swing up its left flank level with its right, so as to reduce the salient at Monchy. It put two brigades into its attack, the 37th being on the right with the Buffs and E. Surreys in front, the R.W.K. in support, and The Queen's in reserve. The leading battalions had first to capture the line formed by Scabbard Trench on their left and Devil's Trench on their right, and then to push on to Gun Trench. This was the "Brown Line," beyond it Cartridge and Grenade Trenches formed the "Yellow Line," where the 6th were to pass through and go on to the "Red Dotted Line," half a mile further East. The ground to be crossed was a maze of trenches old and new. But even more troublesome obstacles were presented by sunken roads and shell-holes, organized for defence and far more difficult for the artillery to locate and to register than definite trench-lines. Somewhat similar conditions prevailed at the point where the Eighteenth Division was to attack. This was some way further to the right, the actual first objective of the 55th Brigade being the village of Cherisy on the left bank of the Sensée, which river had to be crossed and a "Red Line" consolidated on the slopes beyond. The 7th, like the 6th, were in support, the Buffs and East Surreys being the attacking battalions.

Both the Twelfth and Eighteenth Divisions began by securing considerable gains. Scabbard Trench and Devil's Trench were crossed and the leading battalions of the Twelfth reached Gun Trench and even penetrated some way further. But at "zero" (3.45 a.m.) it was still dark and it seems that the parties detailed to "mop up" the enemy's front line were not completely successful, for when daylight came parts of Scabbard and Devil's Trenches were still in German hands and machine-gun fire from these points swept No Man's Land and effectually severed communication between

May 3rd, 1917 6th Battalion

DEVIL'S TRENCH.

May 3rd, 1917
6th Battalion

the supports and the advanced troops. The Third Division, too, on the right of the Twelfth had been unsuccessful against the Southern end of Devil's Trench, and all through the morning the Germans were pushing reinforcements into Devil's Trench from which they extended Northwards. When these came forward in strength they were caught by the British guns and pretty severely punished, but they dribbled enough men forward to re-occupy their old front line nearly as far as Harness Lane. Further to the left the 36th Brigade not only secured their portion of Scabbard Trench but reached the "Brown Line," here a continuation of Gun Trench. But on the 37th Brigade's front, the situation remained very obscure. The great difficulty about ordering a fresh bombardment was that it was uncertain whether the troops who had reached the "Brown Line" were holding out or not, and without a fresh bombardment it would have been madness to send the 6th over the top in the face of the German machine-guns.[1]

As the day wore on the German artillery fire increased in volume; it was, however, decided to make a fresh attempt on Devil's Trench under cover of darkness, and after over an hour's artillery preparation, the 6th assaulted about 10.30 p.m., A and B Companies in front line.[2] Intense machine-gun fire swept through them from both flanks: some of the front wave won through to the German trenches, the majority were shot down and the survivors crept back as best they could. Of those who actually reached the German trenches, about 60, headed by 2nd Lieut. Pyrke, pushed on to Gun Trench and established themselves there. Unluckily Colonel Dawson had been hit just before the

---

[1] Later on some few of the Buffs and East Surreys did make their way back, working round to their left towards the frontage of the 36th Brigade, whose advanced troops had finally to fall back to and consolidate Scabbard Trench.

[2] What made Devil's Trench specially hard to capture was that being on the back slope of a ridge it was hard to shell accurately, while the defenders got good targets when the attacking troops came over the crest.

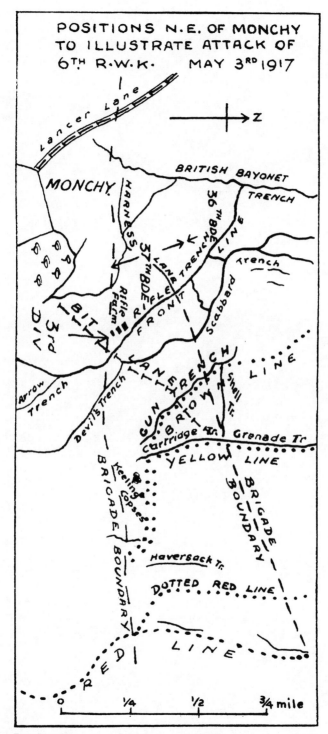

SKETCH 29.

DEVIL'S TRENCH.

attack started and was not available to organize an effort to get through to the help of this detachment. It shows what confidence the battalion had in its young commander that everybody was convinced that had he been present he would have found some way of reaching the little party who were making so fine a stand. Though cut off from help and surrounded by the Germans, they maintained themselves stubbornly for 48 hours, beating off all attacks, till eventually sheer lack of food and water compelled them to surrender. Less fortunate than the 7th in Trones Wood, they had put up a fight which deserved a better fate. But the attack, though gallantly pushed, had failed completely and had cost the 6th over 250 rank and file and eleven officers. Of these Captain E. T. Williams and 2nd Lieut. M. J. Walker were killed, the wounded included, besides Colonel Dawson, Captain Friend, Lieut. G. W. Hill, and 2nd Lieut. Thurburn, while 2nd Lieuts. Antill, Allen, Browning, Ely, Hibbett and Pyrke were taken prisoners. The loss of Captain Williams was much felt; he had served with the battalion since the end of 1914, and had impressed his personality on his brother officers and men as a real leader. The sadly reduced battalion was relieved before dawn by The Queen's, and after a day in support retired to the reserve line to re-organize, Major Alderman, who had been left behind with various details at Arras, and had been kept out of the fight, succeeding to the command in Colonel Dawson's absence.

May 3rd, 1917
6th Battalion

May 3rd had been a disastrous day for the 6th Battalion; it had gone no better with the 7th. The 55th Brigade started well; Cherisy was rushed and cleared and its leading battalions reached the first objective, the "Blue Line," well up to time, though the right flank had to be flung back as touch with the 54th Brigade could not be secured; that brigade had come up against broad belts of uncut wire, sited on a reverse slope where the British guns had been unable to reach them, and had

7th Battalion
See Sketch 30

CHERISY.

May 3rd, 1917
7th Battalion in consequence been held up and had suffered terrible losses. D Company of the battalion, under Captain Latter, had been detailed as " moppers up," and, moving forward behind the leaders, reached the " Blue Line " about 6.15 and began to consolidate a position on the left flank on the road leading North-East from Cherisy to Vis en Artois.[1] Here also the 55th Brigade's flank was " in the air," the Fourteenth Division having apparently failed to get as far forward. The company did not, however, remain here long, being ordered across to the right in order to establish touch between the Buffs and the 54th Brigade. This move Captain Latter carried out with much skill and gallantry, though he was wounded in doing so, but no touch could be obtained, and this flank was quite " in the air." Meanwhile some of the leading battalions had forged ahead and gained a precarious foothold on the final objective, but the insecurity of the left flank caused the East Surreys to ask for reinforcements, upon which 2nd Lieut. F. H. F. Smith went up about 7.30 with half A Company and took post on the left of the " Blue Line," while the rest of A and half B moved across to Cable Trench, the German front line West of Cherisy; the rest of B had now (8.30 a.m.) come up to the old British front line and C was acting as a carrying party.

By this time the enemy were bombarding Cherisy and the British trenches freely, and were attacking the exposed right of the 55th Brigade in force, giving Captain Latter and his men good targets in plenty. The troops who had reached the " Red Line " were soon driven back, and by 11 a.m. the Germans were also pressing hard on the East Surreys in front and from the left flank. Before long the " Blue Line " also became untenable, but the troops put up a fine fight and for some time held the enemy at bay. 2nd Lieut. Smith and his platoons of A made a determined stand in a

---

[1] Approximately at the point marked A on the plan.

CHERISY.

sunken road North-West of the village; D, splendidly led by Captain Latter, who was last seen setting a fine example of gallantry and devotion, offered a stout resistance until overwhelmed by numbers, while the detachments of A and B in Cable Trench, though at one time the retreating British masked their fire, held on for some time and inflicted many casualties on the enemy, until at last sheer weight of numbers forced them back to the British line which C was now manning. Captain Warren did splendid work in covering this retirement; he maintained his position most tenaciously, kept the enemy at bay and was only dislodged from Cable Trench by their getting round both his flanks. *May 3rd, 1917 7th Battalion*

It looked as if the Germans might push on further, but they failed to do so, and upon C the retreating troops rallied and were re-organized. Lieut. Woodhouse was conspicuous in this work, exposing himself fearlessly and setting a fine example. Later on the 7th Queen's were brought up for a fresh attempt on Cherisy, during which the line was held by B and C with A and the 15 survivors who alone remained of D in support. But The Queen's could achieve nothing in face of the machine-guns without much more artillery support than was available, and they lost heavily to no result. All through the next day the 7th continued to hold the line; the Germans kept up a steady shelling but attempted nothing more, and next night the battalion was relieved by the 6th Royal Berkshires and taken back to Beaurains. Its casualties came to 173, Captain Latter and 2nd Lieut. Grist and 22 men were killed, 50 men missing, Colonel Hickson, Captain Warren, six subalterns and 91 men wounded. But the battalion had started the attack much below strength and the losses represented a substantial portion of its effectives. *May 4th-5th*

But the Regiment was not yet clear of the Arras offensive. The ill-success of May 3rd notwithstand-

ARRAS.

May, 1917
6th Battalion

ing, it was still necessary to maintain the pressure to distract the German attention from the French front. The main interest of the next few days centred at Bullecourt, away to the right on the Fifth Army's front, and upon Fresnoy and Oppy on the left, where the Fifth Division was still in action; though round Monchy also activity was desirable, partly in order to improve the local tactical situation. To this end the 6th Battalion, after a short rest, was called back to the front on May 7th and went into line on the extreme left of the Divisional front which now extended to the Scarpe. The battalion was so much reduced that it had to be re-organized in two companies under Captains Thomas and Hodgson-Smith, but even so, these companies were under 150 strong in the trenches, so that the strain on the men was heavy. It was a disturbed corner, the enemy seemed apprehensive of attack and was constantly putting down barrages without any provocation, so the work on the trenches, of which there was much to be done, was carried on under heavy shell-fire. As often happened the company in the front line got off better than the supports, on whom the majority of the German barrages descended. There were no dug-outs, the trenches gave but little protection, and relatively to the numbers available, the casualties, over 40 in all, including 2nd Lieut. Keats killed, were not very light; most of them occurred on the 12th when the enemy retaliated by a severe bombardment of Bayonet and Scabbard Trenches for a renewed attack on Devil's Trench. Another day of heavy shelling was May 16th, when the enemy were making a big but unsuccessful attack on the Fifty-First Division just across the Scarpe, near Roeux, but on this occasion the battalion, though in the front line, escaped without casualties. On the 17th it was relieved after ten very hard days and went back to Montenescourt and then to Ivergny, where it was to get a real spell of rest. Even its "paper strength" was now well below

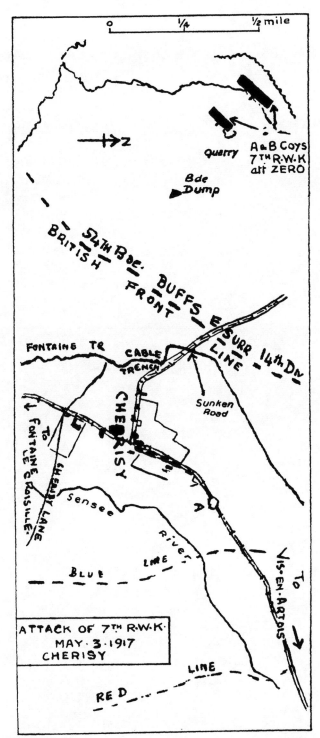

ARRAS.

600, for no drafts had been received to replace the casualties of May 3rd.

While the 6th and 7th Battalions were making their gallant but unsuccessful efforts of May 3rd, the 1st had again come within the area of active operations, but the 13th Brigade was in Corps' reserve on that day, moving up in the evening and taking over trenches North-West of Oppy. Even then the battalion was in Brigade reserve and did not descend the Eastern slopes of the Vimy Ridge, occupying trenches south of Farbus Wood from which a splendid view could be obtained. Here it remained several days, being occasionally shelled and constantly worried by the hostile aircraft, at this time unpleasantly active and successful. After the German counter-attack of May 8th, which recovered Fresnoy, the battalion went up into the front line just West of Oppy, but had no part in the effort of May 9th to recover Fresnoy. This was practically the last important episode in the Arras offensive on that part of the front. Indeed, the policy adopted at this moment indicated the end of the offensive: the Division was to consolidate its position, to do its utmost to harass the enemy and prevent him from strengthening his line, to make all possible use of machine-gun and rifle-fire, to organize its snipers carefully and harass the enemy with its artillery, but no further advance was to be attempted, though further South a more active policy was maintained for some time longer.

Actually the battalion remained in this part of the line till May 23rd, being assiduously shelled, for the enemy, who evidently expected another attack, constantly put down barrages; it was also a good deal bothered by the attentions of the German aeroplanes, who were decidedly in the ascendant at the moment in this quarter, but it escaped with light casualties, having less than 60 for the whole month of May. Early in the month Major Waring had left the battalion to

May, 1917
1st Battalion

ARRAS.

May, 1917
1st Battalion

command a Territorial battalion of the Lincolnshire Regiment, upon which Captain Wilberforce became Adjutant. On May 26th Lieut.-Col. Buchanan-Dunlop had to go sick and return to England; he had commanded the battalion for the better part of two years and had led it through some stern experiences on the Somme and in its day of triumph on the Vimy Ridge, while his careful training and judicious planning had been largely responsible for the conspicuous success of the great Givenchy raid. All were sorry to lose him and, unfortunately for The Queen's Own, on recovering his health he was posted not to one of its battalions, but to one of the Machine-Gun Corps. Major Lynch White had meanwhile taken over command of the 1st Battalion.

CHAPTER XVI

MESSINES.

The heavy casualties incurred in the prolongation of the British offensive at Arras, after all its main objectives had been attained by the brilliant victory of April 9th, had not been the only detrimental results of that excresence on the British Commander-in-Chief's original programme. The urgent need of diverting the attention and resources of the Germans from the Aisne had involved the postponement of his next project until the beginning of June and threw even further back the larger undertaking to which that project was to be the prelude. To free British shipping from the running sore of the use of the chief Belgian ports as German submarine bases was a strong incentive to transferring to Flanders the main British effort. To any offensive in Flanders the recovery of the Messines-Wytschaete Ridge was an indispensable preliminary. Plans for its recapture had been prepared as far back as the autumn of 1916; indeed some of the mines which contributed so much to the success of June 7th had been in readiness for months, and the battalions of The Queen's Own who spent the earlier months of 1917 in the Second Army's country had noted how the enemy's activities increased as the British preparations became increasingly apparent. His guns became more numerous and more active, his aeroplanes more aggressive and inquisitive, and the troops in the line found even " quiet " sectors becoming decidedly " lively " as the spring gave place to summer.

The battalions in question were the 8th, the 10th and the 11th. The 8th had left the Lens front in the middle of April, and had spent three weeks resting and training in pleasant country round Delette. It moved

June, 1917

8th Battalion

MESSINES.

up to Ypres about the middle of May and had a strenuous tour of duty in trenches at the most Easterly point of the Salient, just South of Hooge, coming in for an exceptionally violent bombardment which almost obliterated its trenches, though it very fortunately escaped with no more than 40 casualties. On June 6th it shifted to Dickebusch, its Division being in readiness to extend the area of the attack astride the Ypres-Comines Canal should the success of the main operation warrant it.

<small>June, 1917
10th & 11th
Battalions

See Sketch 31</small>

The 10th and 11th were not very far away, as the Forty-First Division was in the left wing of the main attack. Its objectives were the Dammstrasse, S.E. of St. Eloi, and a line of trenches round Englebrier Farm, N.E. of Oosttaverne. For the attack on the first objective the Division was using the 124th and 123rd Brigades, while the latter employed three battalions; the 10th R.W.K. had come down two days before the attack from a final training in the Reninghelst area and occupied its assembly positions on the night of June 5th-6th, holding the battle front with outposts only. But the enemy were so far from attempting to interfere with the British movements that they had withdrawn from their front line in places, for next night a patrol of A Company found it unoccupied and very badly damaged. Meanwhile the 122nd Brigade, which had been holding the Divisional line since the beginning of the month, was drawn back into support.

<small>June 7th
10th Batt.</small>

Punctually at 3.10 a.m., June 7th, the mines were exploded, the bombardment opened and the infantry pressed forward. The ground over which the 10th was to attack was too rough and boggy for the use of tanks, but even without their help things went well with the Forty-First Division, which met no opposition worth the name till it reached the Dammstrasse, so great had been the effect of the mines and the bombardment. At the Dammstrasse the enemy put up more of a fight, but the 10th was not to be denied.

Lieut.-Colonel A. C. CORFE, D.S.O.
Commanded the 11th Battalion, 1916, 1917, and 1918.
10th Battalion, 1918.

Photo by] [*Death and Dunk, Maidstone.*

Colonel A. WOOD MARTYN, D.S.O., O.B.E.
Commanded 10th Battalion in 1915-1916 and 1917.

MESSINES.

Led by Colonel Wood-Martyn it stormed the position without delay, capturing 40 prisoners and driving the survivors of the defenders in flight before it; then after pushing on a little further it began consolidating a defensive line. It came under more shell-fire while doing this, but the example set by Major Beattie and Lieut. F. W. Roberts, both of whom remained at their posts, although wounded, and continued to direct the work, had much to do with the success with which the line was made good. Lieut. Roberts, too, took command of some men of other regiments who had become disorganized, and got them into order, in which work C.S.M. Cooper also did excellent service. _{June 7th, 1917 10th Batt.}

It was now the 122nd Brigade's turn, and about 5 o'clock it started for an advanced position of assembly behind the Dammstrasse. This was reached without delay and with trifling losses from the rather ineffective reply which the German guns were making to the British bombardment. The 11th was on the left between the 15th Hampshires on its right and a battalion of the Forty-Seventh Division. It had to pass through the 11th Queen's and to capture in succession two lines known respectively as Oblong Trench and Oblong Reserve. _{11th Batt.}

At 6.30 a.m. the 122nd Brigade started its attack. The 11th at once came under enfilade machine-gun fire from the area of the Forty-Seventh Division; then, after a tank had attended to this, it was caught on the other flank by a machine gun in Pheasant Wood, which held up the advance. However, Captain Maltby promptly pushed forward at the head of a small party which included 2nd Lieut. H. J. Greenwood, who, though severely wounded, had continued to lead his company.[1] They soon disposed of this obstacle, capturing the gun and killing or taking its crew, and then the battalion swept on to Oblong Trench, which was

---

[1] Both these officers were awarded the M.C.

MESSINES.

June 7th, 1917
11th Batt.

reached about 7 a.m., and captured after sharp fighting. Oblong Reserve proved a rather more serious matter, but in the end it also was taken, and the 11th set to work to consolidate a defensive line. This had to be sited behind Oblong Reserve as the British barrage was falling a little short and causing some casualties. Despite this, patrols were pushed forward to a track leading N.E. from Englebrier Farm, where they found and cleared several dug-outs and added several prisoners to their bag. There was one attempt at a counter-attack somewhere about mid-day, but the 11th met it with a charge, routed the enemy, captured 25 prisoners, and inflicted heavy casualties. During the afternoon the Twenty-Fourth Division came up and passed through the 122nd Brigade, carrying on the attack to the final objective N.E. of Oosttaverne. Like the 10th Battalion, the 11th had achieved all that was asked of it at a moderate cost, its casualties only slightly exceeding 100.

8th Battalion

In this day's attack the Twenty-Fourth Division were using the 17th and 73rd Brigade, and as they gained all their objectives without having to call on their reserves, the 8th R.W.K. was not engaged in the fighting, but went up into the front line two days later, when its brigade took over from the Twenty-Third Division the ground captured North of the Ypres-Comines railway between Zwarteleen and Klein Zillebeke. While its right company had to hold the Northernmost trenches taken the centre stretched back across what had been No Man's Land to join up with the left in the original British line South of Mount Sorrel. Here the 8th had a strenuous time. The new line needed much work to bring it into a satisfactory state of defence, the enemy were obviously anticipating another attack and put down barrage after barrage so that the battalion had to endure a good deal of shelling and had rather heavy casualties. C.S.M. Greenaway distinguished himself greatly by good

MESSINES.

work in this period, leading his men across the open under intense shelling to occupy a disused trench and averting many casualties by his skilful organizing of the defence.[1] But it was anything but an easy ten days which the 8th spent in these trenches, completing the work done on June 7th. The 10th and 11th had also been kept busy. The former spent the four days following the attack in the positions it had won, extending its line to the right on the 8th and consolidating the position under a shell-fire which increased in intensity as the Germans recovered sufficiently from their surprise and disorganization to bring up more guns. In consequence casualties mounted up considerably and by the time that the 10th returned to Voormezeele on relief they had amounted to 9 officers and 228 rank and file. Of these 5 officers[2] were killed with 30 rank and file. Shortly after this action Colonel Wood-Martyn was compelled to relinquish command owing to ill-health, and returned to England. He had been as successful as a commander in the field as he had in raising and training the battalion, and his departure was much regretted by both officers and men, who were all pleased to hear a little later that he had been awarded the D.S.O.; at the same time Major Beattie, Captain Wallis and Lieut. Roberts received the M.C., and C.S.M. Cooper the D.C.M. for their services on June 7th. June, 1917 8th Batt.

10th Batt.

The 11th had been relieved by a battalion of the Twenty-Fourth Division on the night of June 7th-8th and spent four days in reserve before the 122nd Brigade had to take over the frontage of the Forty-Seventh Division between that of the Forty-First and the Ypres-Comines Canal. The 11th was in the front line in Opal Reserve trench, a continuation N.E. of Oblong Reserve, and had its Battalion Headquarters in the ruins of the White Chateau. It was destined to have an active time as it was desired to push the line

11th Batt.

[1] He was awarded the D.C.M.
[2] 2nd Lieuts. Davies, Dodgson, Mothersell, Foster, and Samuels.

265

OPTIC TRENCH.

June 14th, 1917
11th Batt.

See Sketch 31

forward nearer to Hollebeke, so as to bring it up level on this flank with that already gained by the Forty-First Division. Accordingly at 7.30 p.m. on June 14th three companies of the battalion, with two of the 18th K.R.R.C. on their right, delivered a surprise attack on Optic Trench. The artillery put down a capital barrage and the attack proved speedily successful. On the right B and C Companies captured Optic Trench after a sharp tussle and pushed covering parties of bombers and Lewis gunners forward to Optic Support to protect the consolidation of the captured position. Captain Stallard was conspicuous for his good leading, and 2nd Lieut. Rooney's[1] skill and coolness also contributed appreciably to the success. On the left D captured the junction of Optic Trench and Oblique Row, just East of which it established a block, while bombers working down Oblique Row cleared it as far as the Canal. The operation was a complete success, the whole objective was taken with 15 prisoners while heavy casualties were inflicted on the enemy; but its success was marred by the death of Captain F. G. Frazer, who was killed in going forward under heavy machine-gun fire to bring back some men of D who had overrun their objective. He had distinguished himself repeatedly, had been a most successful company commander and his loss was much felt. Apart from his fall the casualties were light, only just over 30 all told.

June 15th

The 11th did not long enjoy undisturbed occupation of its gains. Next evening, after a heavy bombardment, the enemy advanced in force against Optic Trench from Optic Support and at the same time attacked the barricade on the left flank. The party attacking the barricade made some progress but were driven back by bombers headed by 2nd Lieut. C. P. Webb,[2] who set a splendid example of courage and

[1] Awarded the M.C.
[2] 2nd Lieut. Webb was awarded the M.C.

266

OPTIC TRENCH.

disregard of danger; he was ably seconded by L/Cpl. Chapman, and by their efforts the position at this corner was made secure. Meanwhile the main attack from Optic Support was no less effectively dealt with by rifles and machine guns, 2nd Lieut. Berger[1] showing a fine example of coolness under heavy fire, which greatly encouraged his men; while if the artillery's response to the "S.O.S." signal was a little slow it was most effective when it came. The Germans never reached the British wire, and fell back after suffering heavily. Thus the position was satisfactorily maintained, and when it was handed over two days later to the 12th East Surreys it had not only been well consolidated but a communication trench had been dug back across the 1,000 yards which separated the new line from Opal Reserve. The 11th could certainly look back with considerable satisfaction on the battle of Messines; its casualties had, it is true, amounted to 250, but of these only 40 were killed and missing, amongst them Captain Fraser and 2nd Lieuts. Fenton and Sims, while Captains Stallard and Maltby, Lieut. Gordon-Smith, and 2nd Lieuts. Bernard, Carter, Greenwood and Quartermain were wounded.

It was no more Sir Douglas Haig's intention to continuing pressing on the Messines front after the success of June 7th had given him all he wanted than he had originally meant to prolong the Arras offensive after the middle of April, and for the next few weeks there followed something of a lull on the Flanders front. This was devoted to the necessary preparations for the further offensive, the collection of stores and munitions of every sort, the improvement of communications and of hutting accommodation, and the transfer to the front selected for the new offensive of additional heavy artillery, and of all the Divisions whom the cessation of active operations at other points

---

[1] Lieut. Berger received the M.C. and L/Cpl. Chapman the D.C.M.

HORSESHOE POST.

June, 1917   had rendered available. The Headquarters of the Fifth Army was now moved to the North and took over the Salient from Observatory Ridge Northward on June 10th; and among the Divisions which followed it in the next few weeks was the Eighteenth, so that the arrival at Poperinghe on July 4th of the 7th Battalion brought the battalions of The Queen's Own in the Ypres area up to four.

After its ill-starred venture at Cherisy, the 7th had soon returned to the trenches, having had barely ten days for rest. The sector it took over was not far from the scene of its misfortunes of May 3rd, being between Cherisy and Fontaine les Croisilles. It had an active time, beating off one raid which just reached the trenches and nipping another in the bud by opening fire on the Germans as they were leaving their trenches. On the night of May 31st more serious fighting was started by the capture of a couple of advanced German posts. The attack was made by two parties, that on the right consisting of two platoons of C Company, supported by one of A, the left attack of another platoon of C and a section of D. Both got in successfully, and quickly secured their objectives, driving out the surviving Germans, who bolted, leaving over 20 dead behind. Consolidation was promptly begun, and by next morning the new position, known as Horseshoe Post, had been satisfactorily dug and wired and a communication trench running back from our old line was well advanced.

May, 1917
7th Battalion

June 1st,

June 2nd.   Two nights later, just as the 6th Northamptons were half-way through with the relief of the battalion, the Germans, after some preliminary bombardment, rushed the new post. There was a sharp fight but the Germans were in superior force and drove the survivors of the garrison back to our old lines. Sergt. Woodgate promptly organized a bombing party to counter-attack, but with little success. The situation being

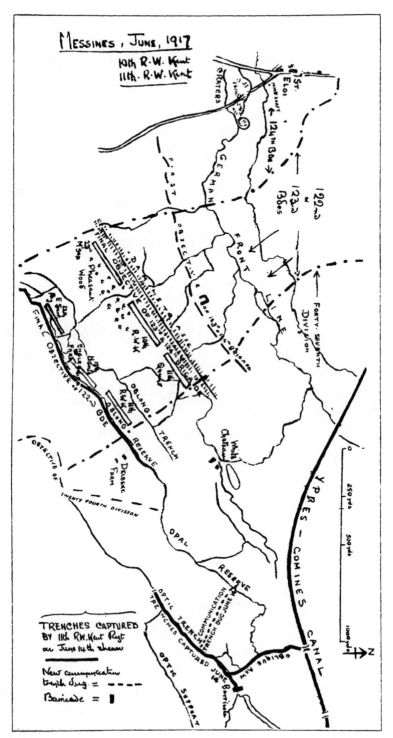

HORSESHOE POST.

very obscure, Colonel Anstruther[1] ordered D Company to attack up the new communication trench on the left, and, well led by Captain Lewin and Sergt. Dungay, they got within a few yards of Horseshoe Post and established a bombing block to secure the communication trench. However, on orders from the Brigade the relief was continued and the Northamptons were left to tackle the recapture of the post. Over 30 casualties had been suffered by the 7th, including 2nd Lieut. Neve wounded. June-July, 1917 7th Battalion

After this the 7th were out of the line for the rest of June, mostly at Coigneux, training; Lieut.-Col. C. H. L. Cinnamond of the Royal Irish Rifles was appointed to the command and took over his duties on June 9th, and then on July 3rd the battalion entrained at Doullens for Flanders. The Division took over the Zillebeke sector from the Thirtieth Division and was at once busily employed upon the preparations for the offensive. This involved an enormous amount of work and many casualties, for the enemy's artillery was exceedingly active, doing its best to hinder the preparations by almost incessant shelling, in which much gas was used, so that the 7th had a bad time, six officers were wounded and four invalided, with proportionate casualties among the rank and file, without the satisfaction of any direct retaliation on the enemy, though the British artillery gave the infantry all the support it could.

During the lull in Flanders a certain activity had been maintained on other parts of the line, mainly to distract the enemy's attention, but partly to improve the local tactical situation at points like Monchy le Preux, where it had been left in an unsatisfactory state at the conclusion of the Arras offensive. Thus the Fifth Division was actively engaged on June 28th when, under cover of an elaborate demonstration along the whole front of the First Army from Hulluch to June-July, 1917 1st Battalion

---

[1] He had been temporarily appointed Lieut.-Col. to command on 19th May.

BEFORE THIRD YPRES.

June-July, 1917 1st Battalion — Gavrelle, real local attacks were made astride the Souchez River and at Oppy. But the Oppy attack was delivered by the 15th Brigade, and once again the 1st Battalion was in reserve and had no more to do than to dig assembly trenches and supply escorts to prisoners, though the next three days found it fully occupied on constructing communication trenches under the most adverse weather conditions. There was constant rain, the men were without shelter, yet the Battalion Diary remarks that " as usual the men became more cheerful as the conditions became more miserable," and the Brigadier of the 15th Brigade was warm in his recognition of its invaluable assistance. The 1st Battalion had returned to the front line about the middle of June, with which began a period of nearly three months' trench duty on the Arleux and Oppy sector, turns in the front line at Arleux alternating with periods in support trenches nearer to Willerval or in reserve at Roclincourt or on the forward slopes of the Vimy Ridge.

Colonel Lynch White had now Major Johnstone as second-in-command; he had been Adjutant of a Territorial battalion of the Royal Warwickshire Regiment in August 1914, which he had accompanied to France early in 1915, he now on June 24th rejoined his own regiment after a long spell of Staff duty. These months were markedly uneventful; the German artillery was not very active, the ascendency which his aircraft had enjoyed in this quarter earlier in the summer had been wrested from him on the arrival of some Sopwith Camels, and though his trench-mortars were troublesome at times their activity usually provoked speedy and effective retaliation. The trenches as usual required any amount of work, in those immediately East of Arleux special arrangements had to be made for the water supply and for enabling the men in the front line to cook hot meals there. This was done by means of "Tommy's cookers," specially constructed in the

BEFORE THIRD YPRES.

regiment by mixing dripping with paraffin and putting it into tins provided with a wick, a plan which worked admirably and made life in the front line much more supportable. Casualties were low, for the enemy were not active and the battalion had much the best of such patrol encounters as took place in No Man's Land. This patrolling was energetically carried on and provided an opportunity to train many of the new hands in this sort of work. The battalion was also able on one of the few occasions when the enemy took the offensive to get effective oblique fire on a party who were trying to rush the right post of the next battalion on the left. But though casualties were few and the sick-rate low, drafts were infrequent and the trench strength remained much under establishment, rarely rising above 500 of all ranks and being more often down to 450. On August 25th Colonel Lynch White left to take an appointment under the First Army and Major Johnstone succeeded to the command. Shortly afterwards the battalion bade farewell to the Vimy area and moved back to billets near Berlencourt in the Canche valley for special training before moving up to Ypres. June-Aug. 1917
1st Battalion

After its heavy fighting on both sides of the Scarpe the 6th Battalion had fairly earned a rest, and from May 19th, when it went back to Montenescourt, near Arras, it was not in action again till the first week of July. This period it spent partly at Ivergny, resting and training, partly at Arras in Divisional Reserve, finding large working parties. It was during this rest period that Colonel Alderman, commanding in Colonel Dawson's absence, received the news that he had been awarded the D.S.O.; he heard it on a lucky day for him; his pony had carried off a prize at the Divisional Horse Show and his long-delayed leave had just come through. Some small drafts arrived during May and June, but the battalion, though up to strength again in officers, had little over 600 rank and file available at the end of its rest. Meanwhile, the Twelfth Division May-July, 1917
6th Battalion

271

BEFORE THIRD YPRES.

June-July, 1917
6th Battalion — had taken over the Monchy sector in the middle of June, just after the Third Division had advanced the British line by capturing some trenches on Infantry Hill. Thus when the 6th returned to the front line its position was a little to the South of the scene of its heavy fighting in May; it was destined to become even more familiar with this section and to see scarcely less severe fighting.

8th Battalion — After its strenuous ten days in the Mount Sorrel sector the 8th Battalion was granted but little rest. By June 26th it was back in front line trenches East of Battle Wood, which, like its last bit of line, were gains made on June 7th. In this sector the front trenches were to be preferred to the support line as they were too near the enemy to be much shelled. However, the Germans were pretty active, and on June 28th tried a raid on a post held by No. 2 Platoon of A Company under 2nd Lieut. Wade. This, however, proved disastrous to them as they found the defenders very much on the alert, and as a result they were beaten off with several casualties. This tour of duty, quite a satisfactory one, was followed by a fortnight near St.

July — Omer, after which a four days' march brought the battalion back to the Klein Zillebeke area, by this time very lively with the preparations for the coming offensive and the German reply. Shelling was heavy on both sides and the mustard gas which the Germans had just introduced was a most unpleasant novelty.

The 8th had several days in the front line N.E. of Klein Zillebeke, marked by a daring attack on Job's Post, a strong point which presented a serious obstacle

July 26th — to a big raid which was in preparation. Accompanied by 8 men Lieut. E. G. Brown worked his way up to the post, surprised it and captured no less than 12 prisoners, a neat piece of work which deservedly earned him a bar to his M.C., won M.M.'s for L/Cpl. Simmons and Pte. Roper and cleared the way for a suc-

July 28th — cessful raid by another battalion. Two days later Pte.

BEFORE THIRD YPRES.

Neal earned a D.C.M. by his devotion and prompti- July, 1917
tude in picking up a bomb which had just been set 8th Battalion
alight by the explosion of a shell and throwing it out
of a dug-out which was full of men, thereby averting a
serious loss of life.

The 10th and 11th Battalions meanwhile were en- 10th & 11th
joying a peaceful July. The Forty-First Division was Battalions
relieved by the Forty-Seventh at the beginning of the
month and had three weeks near Fletre, in which, if
training was by no means neglected, officers and men
were given ample opportunities for rest and recreation.

These were enjoyed to the full, indeed this interval
of rest was quite a halcyon period for the 10th and
11th, and as several drafts were received both battalions
marched back to Ypres in full strength and in excellent
condition and took over the line astride the Canal on
the 24th. This brought them in for a very trying
week before the great attack was launched. The
weather was wet, the trenches had been much knocked
about and were little better than mud-holes, and the
Germans were replying with great vigour to the
British bombardment. Indeed, the week cost the 11th
no less than 80 casualties, many incurred by a fighting
patrol sent out to investigate a report that the enemy
were withdrawing from their front line. This was
found anything but the truth. The Germans were in
force and the patrol suffered heavily in returning to its
own lines. The 10th lost less but had an arduous and
exhausting time in very uncomfortable conditions.

Meanwhile yet another battalion of The Queen's 3/4th Batt.
Own had found its way to France. This was the
3/4th, which, since its reconstitution as an active service unit in July 1915, had been retained at home all
through 1916, constantly expecting orders for France.
The "Second Line T.F." divisions were sent out and
the Sixty-Seventh received orders to prepare for service
overseas, but final orders to embark never came and the
Division was finally broken up in September 1917 and

T 273

BEFORE THIRD YPRES.

June-Aug., 1917
3/4th Batt.

its personnel used for drafts.[1] Three of its battalions, however, had been despatched to France in May. Of these the 3/4th was one, and Colonel Simpson had thus the experience for a second time of taking a T.F. battalion of The Queen's Own on active service.[2]

Landing at Havre on June 1st, the 3/4th proceeded to the neighbourhood of Arras, being attached to the Ninth Division, then holding the sector on the left of the Scarpe near Greenland Hill. On the relief of the Ninth Division in the middle of June by the Seventeenth the battalion was at first attached to the 51st Brigade with which it had some uneventful days in the front line; during the greater part of July it acted as Pioneers and was extremely busy on the construction of communication trenches, and then in August it was definitely posted to the 52nd Brigade in place of the 9th Northumberland Fusiliers, transferred to the Thirty-Fourth Division. This month found it in the front line near the Roeux Chemical Works and was not marked by any great activity. But it gives some clue to the normal wastage of ordinary trench warfare that by the end of August the 3/4th had dwindled from the 1,000 officers and men, who had embarked on May 31st, to little over 850, although it had not taken part in an operation of any note. Among the casualties was Colonel Simpson, who had been invalided in June, being replaced first by Major King of the 10th K.O.Y.L.I., and then by Captain James, from the Lincolnshire Regiment.

[1] The 2/5th R.W.K. was among the battalions broken up, practically all its officers, N.C.O.'s and men were sent out to France as reinforcements; a very large number of them had the good fortune to be sent to the 1st Battalion, to which they proved a very welcome addition.

[2] The officers who went overseas with the 3/4th Battalion were: Colonel A. T. F. Simpson, commanding; Major A. E. Jones, second-in-command; Lieut. W. T. Monckton, Adjutant; Lieut. C. T. Ruse, Quartermaster; Captains B. J. Robinson, T. L. Tanner, J. D. Kennedy, E. W. Stephens, L. R. S. Monckton, E. Watts, F. C. Needham, C. E. Waite, Lieuts. F. S. Fleming, G. Gosselin, S. J. Needham, F. C. Compton, J. A. Beadle, E. S. Nicoll, R. A. E. Starkey, E. C. Vise, V. A. Weeks, F. C. Lovett, H. R. Rainey, H. Ambrose, E. P. Annetts, D. Brook, E. M. Williams, H. Lewis, F. T. Fairhurst, W. C. Clifford, G. G. Richmond, and E. F. Harris.

CHAPTER XVII.
THIRD YPRES.

When at last Sir Douglas Haig launched his long-deferred attempt to force a way over the ridges East of Ypres to the Belgian coast only two battalions of The Queen's Own actually "went over the top" on the opening day. These were the 10th and 11th, to whose Division had been assigned the task of protecting the right flank of the main attack by capturing Hollebeke and clearing the ground across the Canal just East of Battle Wood. Of the two other Divisions then in Flanders in which the Regiment was represented, the Twenty-Fourth was on the left of the Forty-First and made considerable progress East of Klein Zillebeke, forcing its way well into Shrewsbury Forest. But the 8th R.W.K. was in support and merely provided large carrying parties to assist the 1st North Staffords and the 8th Queen's in consolidating Jehovah Trench which they had taken. These parties, however, did splendid work, especially in removing the wounded, a task made all the more difficult by the torrential rain which began to descend almost at the moment the offensive started. {July, 31st, 1917 10th & 11th Battalions} {8th Battalion}

The 7th Battalion also, though within the battle area, was not actively engaged. The Eighteenth Division was in reserve to the Second Corps and only the 53rd Brigade was employed. Its orders were to go through the Thirtieth Division which was attacking through Sanctuary Wood. But here, just astride the Menin Road, the German resistance was most determined and most effective. The Thirtieth Division was checked, and even when the 53rd Brigade was thrown in the advance only reached the line of Dumbarton Lakes and Stirling Castle. {7th Battalion}

THIRD YPRES.

July 31st, 1917
10th & 11th Batts.
See Sketch 32
10th Batt.

But to the 10th and 11th Battalions July 31st was a day of stern and on the whole successful fighting. The Forty-First Division, as has been said, was attacking astride the Canal, the 123rd Brigade being on the Northern side. The 10th[1] was between the 20th Durham L.I., on its left, and the 11th Queen's, on the right, with two companies of the 23rd Middlesex further to the right between the Ypres-Comines railway and the Canal. The battalion hardly started very fresh; it had had six days in the front line under continuous heavy shelling and had suffered a good many casualties. However, exhaustion notwithstanding, there was no faltering. From the first the 123rd Brigade met with stubborn opposition. The 10th Bavarian Division whom they had to face were stout foes and offered a determined resistance,[2] while the barrage which the Germans put down was most effective. Still, all the battalions went forward with determination and mastered the first objective. But in advancing to the second objective they became somewhat disorganized. Casualties had been heavy and the attack lacked weight. Heavy machine-gun fire held it up for a time but about 8 a.m. parties of the 10th and of The Queen's reached the second objective and began to clear it up and consolidate their gains.

A little later some of the supporting companies, B and D, pushed forward along with parties of The Queen's and of the Middlesex who had now come up level nearer the Canal, but their attempt to reach the final objective met with no success and nearly all became casualties. As the men went forward a line of "pillboxes" on the brow of a rise about 100 yards beyond the second objective became unmasked and their fire held up the advance along the front of the 123rd

---

[1] It was now commanded by Colonel Beattie, who had succeeded to the command when Colonel Wood-Martyn was invalided.

[2] One of the Brigadiers of the Division wrote that they were "not the rabbits the special correspondents seem chiefly to hear of."

THIRD YPRES.

Brigade, as the complete lack of cover prevented manœuvre and it was impossible to get the heavy guns on to the obstructing "pill-boxes." At this juncture Captain Holden did splendid work in re-organizing the men who had reached the second objective; he went back more than once to report the situation to Battalion Headquarters, but returned each time to the front line. Good work was also done by 2nd Lieut. Donaldson, who made repeated journeys under heavy fire to maintain touch with the troops on the flanks.[1] It was largely due to the courage and example of these two officers that the second objective was successfully consolidated and maintained in face of heavy fire and despite the retirement of some troops on the left who, after a renewed attempt to advance on the arrival of reinforcements, fell right back to the line of the first objective. Some of these were stopped by Captain Holden and his party and joined in the defence of the second objective. But only about 100 of the battalion could be collected, and it proved necessary to detain some of the ration-carrying parties in order to strengthen the position held by Battalion Headquarters in the first objective. Casualties, indeed, had been heavy, and the list included five officers[2] killed and three[3] wounded, with nearly 230 men, 33 being killed and 56 missing. Moreover, the downpour which set in that evening made the conditions in the front line indescribably uncomfortable and greatly impeded consolidation.

July 31st, 1917 10th Batt.

On the other bank of the Canal the 11th Battalion had fared rather better. No Man's Land had been under very heavy shell-fire while it was forming up for the attack, which rendered all the more difficult Major Beadle's task of superintending the laying of the forming up tapes and the lining up of his battalion along

11th Batt.

---

[1] Both these officers received the M.C.
[2] 2nd Lieuts. Driffield, Dillon, Costin, Woodroffe and Godfrey.
[3] 2nd Lieuts. Green, Grey, and Ledger.

HOLLEBEKE.

July 31st, 1917
11th Batt.

them.[1] Luckily the battalion escaped fairly lightly, and when the British barrage started at 3.50 a.m. it went forward so rapidly that the enemy's counter-barrage came down well behind it and failed to do any damage. Oblique Trench was the objective of the leading companies, A and B, but mist, uncut wire, and the stubborn fight put up by the Bavarians delayed the advance not a little, and only after strenuous fighting was the trench at last cleared, on which A and B began consolidating 150 yards further on. C and D then passed through but found it hard to get on in the face of the machine-gun fire from houses along the Hollebeke road. 2nd Lieut. Preston, however, got well forward and actually worked his way round the village of Hollebeke and established himself with the twelve survivors of his platoon on the final objective.[2] Here he proceeded to bomb dug-outs and capture prisoners, but being quite without support he eventually had to come back to escape being cut off.

In the meantime Colonel Corfe had come up to the front himself and had found that the next battalion to the right had failed to capture the village, and that the advance was held up by machine-gun fire from pill-boxes round Hollebeke Church; accordingly he organized a fresh attack with his characteristic energy and resourcefulness. Already some of A Company had reinforced the exposed right of C, and about 8 a.m. Captain Rooney brought about 40 of B forward to help Captain Lindsay and C carry on the attack into Hollebeke. Despite the heavy fire from rifles and machine-guns these two officers, who led their men with magnificent dash and skill, worked forward into the village, cleared the pill-boxes, mopped up cellars and dug-outs systematically, and successfully established themselves in the ruins. Some 60 prisoners

---

[1] The assembly of the 11th was just to the left of the position captured by it on June 14th.

[2] His position was approximately the point marked A on Sketch 32.

HOLLEBEKE.

were taken and many casualties inflicted on the enemy, who put up a stubborn resistance. By 11.30 a.m. Captain Rooney was able to report that Hollebeke had been cleared. The remainder of the battalion now came forward to assist in consolidating a line East of Hollebeke and only 100 yards short of the final objective, and this did much to help the battalions on the right to get forward also. *July 31st, 1917 11th Batt.*

This day's attack had been carried out under more than ordinary difficulties; the ground, naturally marshy, had been reduced to a frightful condition by the combination of an unusual rainfall and a stupendous bombardment. It had been all but impossible to get forward in the mass of churned-up mud and water. Consolidation in such a state of things was equally difficult. In such conditions as these the example set by a man like L/Cpl. Chapman was of special value. He first went forward alone and captured five Germans in one dug-out and then, when holding an advanced bombing post, though he and his comrades were waist-deep in water, he made light of these hardships and encouraged the others to hold on till relief came. The only compensation was that the ground presented equal obstacles to a counter-attack, which the exhausted survivors of the attack would have been hard pressed to repulse with their rifles and Lewis guns mostly choked with mud. But though the 11th, now under 300 strong, remained in position till the night of August 4th under heavy shell-fire and persistent rain, no counter-attack developed, and at last a battalion of the Thirty-Ninth Division arrived to relieve it. It was all the exhausted men could do to drag themselves back to Lock House, only two miles away; but if the capture of Hollebeke was about the worst experience the battalion ever suffered, it was perhaps its finest exploit, and well deserved Colonel Corfe's bar to the D.S.O., Captain Rooney's bar to the M.C., the M.C.'s granted to Major Beadle, Captain Lindsay and 2nd *Aug., 1917*

THIRD YPRES.

August, 1917
11th Batt.

Lieut. Salmon,[1] the D.C.M.'s which fell to two sergeants named Smith, L/Cpl. Chapman's bar to the D.C.M., and the eleven M.M.'s and bars which were added this day to the eleven won on June 7th and the fifteen of June 14th, a record in the way of distinctions which would be hard to equal. Casualties had been heavy, Captain Squire, 2nd Lieuts. Webb, Westmacott, Ashworth and O. P. Brown were killed or died of wounds with 32 men, 54 men were missing, 7 subalterns and 241 men wounded, while many others went sick with trench feet as the result of the awful weather.

After such an experience the 11th might have looked for a longer rest than merely three days at Reninghelst. But a large draft had just arrived and the battalion had to go back into the line on August 10th, taking over from the 15th Hampshires the position at Hollebeke which it itself had captured on July 31st. The trenches were in an awful state and the enemy plied the position with gas shell, but the battalion escaped with one casualty only, though that was a serious loss, C.S.M. Jennings, a most efficient and gallant warrant officer.

10th Batt.

This tour only lasted three days and then the 11th went right back to the Fletre area to which the 10th had already preceded it. That battalion had remained in the trenches it had captured on July 31st for three most uncomfortable days before being relieved, and then had four days' rest (August 3rd-7th), followed by four in the line, holding the same trenches as it had taken. The chief incident of this tour was a well-conducted raid by a party 15 strong which cleared several of the German " pill-boxes " and machine-gun emplacements which had checked the advance on July 31st; as it yielded 40 prisoners at the cost of only one casualty the raid was in every way a success.

---

[1] This officer had done most daring and useful reconnaissance work and had helped to locate many of the enemy's machine-guns and posts.

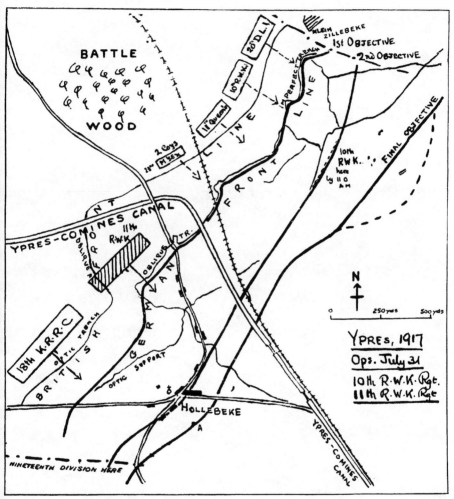

THIRD YPRES.

August, 1917

The persistent rainfall which had made consolidating and holding the captured positions so peculiarly difficult and unpleasant had had other results of graver importance. By transforming the low-lying ground of the Salient into an almost unbroken stretch of bog it effectually prevented any prompt following up of the really substantial success which the centre and left of the attack had achieved on July 31st. It was impossible to move off the roads and tracks, and with movement thus restricted it was easy for the German guns to put down barrages along the few routes open. To relieve the advanced troops, to keep those in front supplied with ammunition and rations, to push forward the stores urgently needed for consolidation, was a sufficient tax on the transport services, and it was out of the question to bring the guns quickly forward to new positions from which they could support effectively an attack on the line to which the Germans had been forced back.

The defenders naturally were not immune from the discomforts and difficulties caused by the rainfall, but delay was all in their favour; they had not so devastated an area to move over, they could use the time to bring up reinforcements of men and artillery and to adapt their defences to their new tactics. These consisted of holding their positions by means of concrete strong points, generally known as "pill-boxes," scattered about irregularly rather than by well defined trench systems. These "pill-boxes" were proof against anything but a direct hit from a fairly heavy gun, shrapnel were impotent against them and it was extremely difficult for the artillery to locate them accurately. Moreover, they were very skilfully sited so as to bring enfilade fire from unexpected directions on points likely to be attacked, and altogether they provided obstacles formidable in themselves and extremely difficult to tackle. Holding their front positions lightly, the Germans kept the bulk of their

THIRD YPRES.

August, 1917 forces further back, so that they could deliver counter-attacks in great strength and with little delay. These methods would in any case have been difficult to overcome, but the persistent bad weather did even more to make the British progress during August so slow, even slower than during the middle period of the Somme in 1916. The troops who attempted to exploit the gains of July 31st had a most difficult task, and it was not because they failed in determination or devotion to duty that progress was so disproportionate to the effort involved and to the losses incurred.

7th Battalion Two battalions only of The Queen's Own saw anything of this disappointing stage of the "Third Ypres." The Eighteenth Division, as has been mentioned, was to have "leap-frogged" the Thirtieth on July 31st had that Division's attack astride the Menin Road been successful. Actually the Thirtieth never reached the point at which the 53rd Brigade should have gone through it, and that brigade's desperate struggle merely secured part of the Thirtieth's first objective near Clapham Junction. Thus when the 54th and 55th Brigades relieved the Thirtieth Division the line they took over was still West of Glencorse Wood and Inverness Copse. The 7th R.W.K., who went into the front trenches on the night of August 3rd/4th found itself just East of Stirling Castle with its left at Clapham Junction. It had a wet and uncomfortable four days in the line. The trenches were in shocking condition, the rain was heavy and continuous and many wounded were lying out in No Man's Land, whom the battalion endeavoured to bring in. But the enemy were inactive, even his guns did little, and though the battalion's patrols were enterprising and had several encounters with the enemy these resulted in few casualties but yielded several prisoners. Relieved on the night of the 7th/8th the battalion was in reserve on August 10th when the Division attacked Glencorse Wood and Inverness Copse and had desperate fighting, losing

THIRD YPRES.

heavily and gaining but little ground. The only men of the battalion to be employed were some "runners" attached to the 55th Brigade Headquarters who did good service, notably L/Cpl. Ursell, whose gallantry and devotion earned him a M.M. On August 11th the 7th went back to Abeele and entrained for Zeggers Cappel, where the Division, which had lost heavily, was to remain for nearly six weeks, training for another effort when its ranks should have been replenished. During this period over 20 officers joined or re-joined the 7th, and in the middle of September a draft of 126 men arrived, though even then the battalion was much under strength. *[August, 1917 — 7th Battalion]*

Meanwhile the 8th Battalion had been kept busy. During August the Twenty-Fourth Division was holding trenches North of the Canal, having one brigade in the line in Shrewsbury Forest, one in support at Dickebusch, and one back in reserve. On this part of the battlefield the fighting had died down, and the 8th's turns of duty in the front line were not very eventful. A big draft which arrived early in August had filled up its ranks and so many new officers had arrived that each company had seven. But at the same time the battalion again lost Colonel Parker's guidance, for another break-down in health compelled him to hand over the command to Major Whitty on September 1st and to go home. As second-in-command to Major Whitty the battalion welcomed back Captain Wenyon, who had been on Staff work since February. *[8th Battalion / Sept., 1917]*

Early in September the Twenty-Fourth Division shifted to the line astride the Menin Road. Here where the ridge reached its highest elevation North of the Canal the advance had met with the most stubborn opposition. Indeed the final objectives of July 31st were not yet in British hands, for the line had only reached the Western portion of Inverness Copse and Glencorse Wood. On September 7th the 8th R.W.K. took over the front line in Inverness Copse from the

INVERNESS COPSE.

September, 1917 8th Battalion 2nd Leinsters. It had D Company North of the road, B and C South of it and A in reserve. The position was not good, communications were difficult to maintain and the fallen trees limited the field of fire and gave cover to the enemy within close range of the line.

Sept. 8th, This was to be turned to account by them next day. Covered by a heavy barrage which completely isolated the front-line posts, they attacked in force, putting in a body of picked "Sturmtruppen" and using flammenwerfer. On the right B Company, under 2nd Lieut. Richardson, and the right of C, under Lieut. H. R. James, met the attack with a most effective fire from rifles and Lewis guns, which brought it to a standstill before it could reach our trenches. But nearer the road the cover of the fallen trees let the enemy get close up and rush C's left post, capturing a "pill-box" and 15 prisoners, the majority of them wounded. 2nd Lieut. Beattie, the platoon commander, set a most gallant example, shooting several of the enemy with his revolver. Then, when forced to withdraw, with the help of Sergt. Purfield, he rallied the survivors of his detachment a little distance in rear and maintained a stubborn resistance with bombs and rifle-fire till help could arrive. In this work 2nd Lieut. Pfeuffar gave great assistance and his bomb-throwing kept the enemy at bay.

Meanwhile Captain Wenyon hurried to the spot, bringing up No. 2 Platoon of the reserve company, A, and promptly organized a counter-attack. This was carried out by men of C Company, in two parties, headed by 2nd Lieuts. Pfeuffar and Beattie, who worked forward till close to the "pill-box," aided by a most effective covering fire from No. 2 Platoon. L/Cpl. Cook did splendid service, getting his Lewis gun into action within short range of the "pill-box" and neutralising the fire of its defenders. This allowed 2nd Lieut. Pfeuffar's party to rush the "pill-box" from the flank. Sergt. Purfield engaged a machine-gun, put

INVERNESS COPSE.

its crew out of action and captured it, and 2nd Lieut. Beattie's party coming up the post was recovered, 15 prisoners were taken and heavy casualties inflicted on the retiring enemy, notably by L/Cpl. Cook, who promptly brought his Lewis gun up to the front line, while D Company got in a most effective flanking fire on them from rifles and Lewis guns. The casualties had been fairly heavy, including 2nd Lieut. Walton and 13 men killed and 2nd Lieut. Hodge wounded; but the battalion earned great credit by its stubborn defence and its prompt and vigorous counter-attack. Captain Wenyon, to whose rapid decision and energy much of the success was due, received the D.S.O., 2nd Lieuts. Pfeuffar and Beattie were awarded the M.C., Sergt. Purfield and L/Cpl. Cook received the D.C.M. Two days later the battalion was relieved and after a short period in reserve moved to Merris on the 16th, and a week later departed with the rest of its Division for quite unfamiliar country, the trenches round Hargicourt facing the Hindenburg Line. It had seen its last of the Ypres Salient. *[Sept. 8th, 1917, 8th Battalion]*

As the 8th Battalion was quitting the Flanders front the 10th and 11th were coming back for another round in the great encounter. They had had over a month out of the line since their last attack, a period spent well back from the front and not very far from Boulogne. As usual recreation and training had been intermingled, the main object of the latter being to replace the numerous casualties among specialists like signallers, Lewis gunners and stretcher-bearers which the attack of July 31st had caused. This was rather more difficult because drafts had been none too numerous and neither battalion was up to strength when they started the forty miles march back to Ypres. By September 18th both were back at Ridge Wood ready for the new attack. *[Sept., 1917, 10th-11th Battalions]*

This time the Forty-First Division was just to the left of its last jumping-off line, being in the centre of

TOWER HAMLETS.

September, 1917 10th & 11th Battalions

See Sketch 33

the Third Corps which was attacking South of the Menin Road. It had the Twenty-Third Division on its left, the Thirty-Ninth on the right and its own objective lay to the South-West of Gheluvelt along the ridge beyond the Basseville Brook to which had been given the name of Tower Hamlets Ridge. The Division attacked with the 122nd Brigade on the left, and the 124th on the right, each on a two-battalion front. In the 122nd Brigade the 15th Hampshires and 18th K.R.R.C. led, the 11th R.W.K. supporting the Hampshires. The 123rd Brigade, including the 10th R.W.K., was kept back in reserve.

11th Batt.

Leaving Ridge Wood camp on the evening of September 18th the 11th moved up to Larch Wood Tunnels. It had a bad time from gas shelling on the way up, found the available shelter already fully occupied and had to spend most of September 19th in trenches outside the shelters under a pretty heavy shell-fire which cost it 40 casualties, including Captain Stone, the commander of C Company and both his subalterns. Lieut. Morley had, therefore, to be sent up from Battalion Headquarters to take command of the company. The actual assembly position in Bodmin Copse was reached after a trying march in pitch darkness along duckboard tracks and under steady shelling, and by 3 a.m. the battalion was in position 200 yards behind the Hampshires. At 5.40 the attack started and the 11th moved forward behind the Hampshires, who at first made rapid progress behind an excellent barrage. But on approaching Java Avenue, a trench running diagonally across the line in front of the first objective, the Hampshires were checked by a strong point which had survived the bombardment. Colonel Corfe with Captains Henderson and Kerr, his acting second-in-command and Adjutant, pushed up to the front to discover what was happening and found the Hampshires hung up along a ditch 40 yards short of the strong point. Nearly all their officers had been hit, so Colonel Corfe

Sept., 20th

TOWER HAMLETS.

at once set to work to re-organize them while waiting for his own leading companies to reinforce. He was badly wounded in the shoulder but carried on nevertheless till B and D Companies came up and carried the whole line forward with a rush, overwhelming the strong point and its defenders and sweeping on to the first objective just short of the Basseville Brook. By 6.15 this had been secured, and an hour later the battalion and the survivors of the Hampshires, who were now mixed up with it, pushed on as arranged across the brook towards the second objective just beyond.

Sept. 20th, 1917 11th Batt.

Captain Henderson, who had taken charge when Colonel Corfe collapsed from loss of blood, led and directed this second stage with ability and coolness. Such opposition as was encountered completely failed to stop the advance. The second objective was taken and handed over to the Hampshires to consolidate; and then about 9.50 Lieut. Morley led the remnants of the battalion, little over 120 with half-a-dozen officers, forward past Tower Hamlets to the ridge beyond. By this time the battalion had altogether outstripped the 18th K.R.R.C. on its right, though on the left the Twenty-Third Division were keeping touch, and most of the casualties in the final stage came from machine-gun fire from the right. Still the objective was reached and Tower Trench taken with nearly 50 prisoners and three machine-guns. But to hold this advanced position without support was difficult. An effort was made by 2nd Lieut. Freeman and a party to throw back a defensive flank on the right, but machine-guns took so heavy a toll of those who tried to dig in here that, after 2nd Lieut. Freeman had been killed and nearly 40 casualties had been suffered, Lieut. Morley decided to fall back to a line 150 yards in front of the second objective, where touch was obtained with the 12th East Surreys who had passed through the 18th K.R.R.C. But the order to withdraw never reached 2nd Lieut.

TOWER HAMLETS.

Sept. 20th, 1917
11th Batt.

Drumgold, who remained in position with about 15 men on the extreme left of the final objective.

The survivors of the attack were not given much time to consolidate their new position before a counter-attack began to develop on the right. But they met and repulsed it by rifle-fire, aided by an effective barrage, and held on unshaken, and by nightfall the line was well dug in and in touch with the Twenty-Third Division. On the right the position was less satisfactory, the 124th Brigade had lost heavily and had failed to reach its final objective; and though the 123rd had been brought up in the afternoon to continue the attack, only the 23rd Middlesex reached to the front in time to go forward with the barrage, and the 10th R.W.K. got only a little beyond the original British front line.

Sept. 21st,
10th Batt.

Next morning, however, a fresh attack was launched by the 20th Durham L.I. on the left of the 123rd Brigade, and as they came up level with the 10th, that battalion joined in. Some progress was made, but machine-gun fire brought the Durhams to a standstill, and the 10th had to halt and dig in just beyond the Basseville Brook. This line, though short of Joist Trench, which had been the objective, was about level with the Tower Hamlets. This line was vigorously counter-attacked in the afternoon and evening—about 4 p.m. the Brigade reported the front line hard pressed and asked for leave to use the 11th Queen's to reinforce the 10th R.W.K.—but the defenders were now well dug in and beat the assailants back. That day

11th Batt.

the 11th also had been severely tried. The enemy started a heavy shell-fire about 4.30 a.m. and kept it up more or less all day while their snipers and machine-gunners were also busy. A small reinforcement was brought up by 2nd Lieut. Thomson, and in the afternoon news was at last received from 2nd Lieut. Drumgold, who was still maintaining his position on the final objective, though casualties had reduced his party by

TOWER HAMLETS.

half. A little later the enemy opened a heavy bombardment and followed it up by a counter-attack. Some troops on the battalion's right began to retire, but they were rallied and brought back to the line by Captain Henderson, who set a splendid example and was ably seconded by Captain Kerr. Thanks largely to these officers and to the steadiness of the remnants of the 11th this counter-stroke was repulsed and the line successfully maintained. When relief came on the following evening, little over 100 of those who had started to the attack remained.[1] Two officers, 2nd Lieuts. Came and Freeman, were killed with 26 men, 53 men were missing, Colonel Corfe and five other officers wounded.[2] The 10th, who were relieved about the same time, had been less punished, Captain Roberts and 2nd Lieuts. Thomas and H. Robinson and 29 men were killed, 24 men missing, Captain Richmond, 2nd Lieuts. Edmett, May and F. B. Brown and about 100 men wounded.

September, 1917 10th & 11th Batts.

Sept. 22nd

This was the end of "Third Ypres" for the Forty-First Division. It had had its full share of fighting and had achieved no small success. Both the battalions of The Queen's Own included in the Division had been well to the fore and the 11th's record was really remarkable. Few units secured so many honours and awards in "Third Ypres"—the battle of September 20th brought a second bar to Colonel Corfe's D.S.O., D.S.O's. to Captain Henderson and Lieut. Drumgold, M.C.'s to Captain Kerr, Lieut. Morley and 2nd Lieuts. Loudoun and Rushton, a D.C.M. to Pte. Smart, two bars to the M.M. and sixteen M.M.'s, making its total of honours since June 7th up to eighty.

The attack of September 20th may be taken as marking the beginning of a second stage in the offensive. There had been some improvement in the weather, enough to allow of the resumption of attacks on a large

---
[1] The battalion had been much below strength to start with.
[2] The total casualties were over 250.

THIRD YPRES.

Sept., 1917   scale and for the next fortnight real progress was made, but for the most part the troops now employed had not been engaged in the earlier fighting. It was at this point that the 1st Battalion renewed its acquaintance with the Salient it had quitted more than two years earlier.

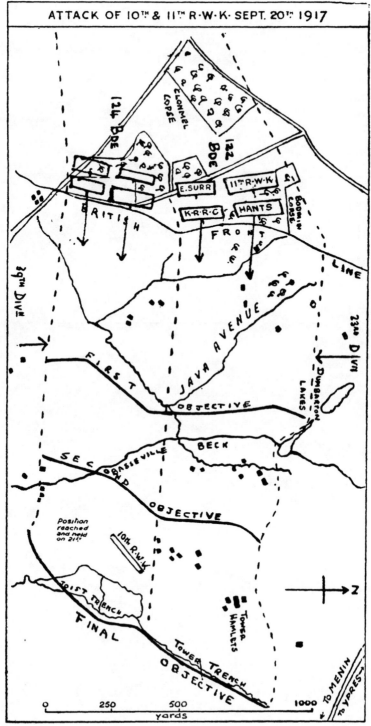

CHAPTER XVIII.

THIRD YPRES.

The heavy fighting which followed the relief of the Forty-First Division was almost the only major operation of 1917 in which The Queen's Own had no share. It was not till the attack of October 4th, officially known as the battle of Broodseinde, that the 1st Battalion first took part in the great contest. By this time the British line had been carried forward through Polygon Wood and into Zonnebeke, while just North of the Menin Road it had got as far as what had once been the hamlet of Veldhoek and was within reach of Polderhoek and Gheluvelt, the latter being the next point of vital tactical importance in this part of the field, though the possession of Polderhoek Chateau would go far to render Gheluvelt untenable even should direct attack fail.

*September-October, 1917
1st Battalion*

The 1st Battalion had had three weeks of rest and training at Berlencourt. A draft of nearly 250 men had brought its depleted numbers up well over 800, several new officers had joined and Colonel Johnstone had now Major Wilberforce as second-in-command, Captain McClenaghan as Adjutant, 2nd Lieut. R. Brown, just promoted from R.S.M., as Assistant Adjutant, and Captains W. R. Cobb, Snelgrove, Bellman and Press as company commanders. It had moved up on September 25th, detraining at Wizernes and marching to a camp in the Brandhoek area. Here the "battle surplus" remained, having been separated from those detailed for the attack. But it was the battle surplus who suffered the first casualties, as on the night of September 27th their camp was bombed by German aeroplanes with disastrous results. Two men were killed and over 20 wounded, along with Captains

THIRD YPRES.

Sept.-Oct., 1917
1st Battalion

Bellman and Nisbet and 2nd Lieuts. Nurse and Stevens. Meanwhile the main body had moved up to "Goldfish Chateau," along with the 2nd K.O.S.B's., as reserves for an attack on the high ground E. of Wieltje Cross Roads. As this attack achieved complete success without the reserves being engaged the battalion returned to Brandhoek, whence it moved to Berthen. Three nights later, just as it was leaving Berthen for Ridge Wood, the battalion in its turn was heavily bombed. However, it got off much better, having only one casualty, though a dozen transport animals were put out of action.

Sept. 30th

From Ridge Wood the battalion moved forward, and on the night of October 2nd/3rd took over the right of the Fifth Division's new frontage, S.E. of Veldhoek. The relief was much delayed by heavy hostile shelling, but was at last accomplished, the battalion's right resting on the Menin Road with the K.O.S.B.'s on its left and the 95th Brigade beyond them astride the head of the Reutel Beek. Hardly had the battalion settled down into its trenches before a heavy bombardment opened all along its line. S.O.S. signals went up from the Thirty-Seventh Division south of the Menin Road, and the enemy debouched from his positions in force. It was misty, and at that early hour, between 5 and 6 a.m., the light was none too good, and the Germans, though received with a hot fire, managed to penetrate to the trenches at several points only to be immediately ejected, leaving dead and prisoners behind. Sergt. Brydon, Corpl. Newman and Pte. Beckett all did fine work in repulsing this attack, and it was largely thanks to the last that the enemy obtained no identifications.

See Sketch 34

October 3rd

Half-an-hour later the Germans returned to the attack, but Lieut. Joel, who was commanding the right company, C, on whom the brunt of the attack had fallen, had taken prompt steps to re-organize and strengthen the defences after the repulse of the first attack.[1]

[1] He was awarded the M.C., while C.S.M. Taylor got the D.C.M.

THIRD YPRES.

C.S.M. Taylor, too, did splendid work, taking command of his platoon when his officer was hit, rallying it and re-establishing the line, while Sergt. Ashby brought up his platoon from support on his own initiative and was most instrumental in beating off the attack. Moreover, the light was now better and this time the Germans were stopped 50 yards short of our wire. Their casualties were heavy and they were increased during the day as survivors who had taken shelter in shell-holes or other cover in No Man's Land offered targets to snipers when trying to regain their own lines. C Company had over 20 casualties, A (Captain Cobb) on the left came off better with only 7, and both could congratulate themselves on a successful morning's work. But as the day wore on the tale of casualties rose as the enemy's artillery activity increased. B Company, in support trenches South of the Menin Road, caught the worst of this shelling and figured largely among the 100 casualties in the day's list.

October 3rd, 1917
1st Battalion

That evening C and A closed to their right and B came up to fill the gap thus created on the left of the line. After midnight company commanders laid tapes on the forming-up positions, and at 5.30 a.m. the three companies were lined up ready for the barrage to begin. The battalion had no very precise objective for the enemy were not holding any well-defined trench line but were relying on "pill-boxes" and shell-holes. On the right C was to advance about 300 yards, on the left B had nearly twice that distance to go to keep touch with the K.O.S.B.'s, who were making for Polderhoek Chateau.

Oct. 4th

At 6 a.m. the barrage came down and the troops went forward. Mud proved the chief obstacle, for the enemy's counter-barrage fell well in rear, and before long prisoners began to arrive at Battalion Headquarters and their escorts reported the objective gained all along the line. More accurate reports, however, indicated that C had come under enfilade machine-gun fire from a

THIRD YPRES.

Oct. 4th, 1917
1st Battalion

"pill-box" south of the Menin Road which the Thirty-Seventh Division had not managed to neutralize, and its losses in consequence were severe. The right had to be thrown back as a defensive flank facing this "pill-box," and before long a platoon of D from reserve, along with a couple of reserve Lewis-gun teams, had to be sent up under 2nd Lieut. Cathcart to reinforce at this point. Elsewhere the objective was taken, Sergt. Hart doing great work by bombing a troublesome machine-gun emplacement and capturing the gun, while considerable losses were inflicted on the enemy, who soon began counter-attacking in some force. By 8.30 a.m. No. 1 Platoon of A was asking for more ammunition, and as the day wore on the counter-attacks continued and the enemy's artillery fire became heavier and more accurate, some guns from the South, near Tenbrielen and Comines, in particular getting in a nasty enfilade fire.

However, shelling and counter-attacks notwithstanding, the battalion held its ground. It was for a time severely pressed, for the Germans were unwilling to let ground of such importance go. 2nd Lieut. Gray, who had taken over command of B on Lieut. Fleming being wounded, re-organized the remains of his company so successfully that despite a loss of two-thirds of its numbers, it beat off several attacks. Corpl. Nicholson, who had done great work in the attack, killing a dozen Germans, now took command of his platoon and then of his company and controlled them with much ability.[1] L/Cpl. Vaughan, too, who had charge of a Lewis-gun team on the open flank, was largely instrumental by his fire in keeping the enemy at bay, while L/Cpl. Smart handled his Lewis gun most effectively though all his team had fallen. L/Cpl. Glen and Ptes. Passy and Broughton in like manner kept their Lewis guns in action single-handed or with but little help, and largely thanks to the skilful way in which the Lewis guns were used the counter-attacks were all repulsed.

[1] Lieut. Gray received the M.C., and Corpl. Nicholson the D.C.M.

294

THIRD YPRES.

By 12.30 p.m. Captain Cobb could report the objective consolidated and the position quite tenable, though reinforcements were needed. The rest of the reserve, two platoons of D, were pushed up accordingly to replace C, now reduced to two officers and twenty men, and later on a company of the 14th R. Warwickshires had to be asked for to bring up ammunition and rifle grenades, which reached the old British front line about 5 p.m. But the position was maintained, splendid work being done by the battalion runners and signallers in maintaining communication and guiding up parties with ammunition and water, while touch was kept with the K.O.S.B.'s, who had finally dug in 200 yards West of Polderhoek Chateau and were holding on there. October 5th saw the survivors of the battalion clinging manfully to their gains. The counter-attacks had ceased but intermittent shelling continued and a steady rain made conditions most uncomfortable. Nevertheless, many wounded were successfully brought in and the position was handed over intact that night to the 15th Brigade. October 4th, 1917 1st Battalion

October 5th & 6th

But it was an attenuated battalion which withdrew to Ridge Camp. Of the 670 who had gone into action, only 7 officers and 283 men were left. 2nd Lieuts. Daniell and Redding had been killed, Captain Cobb, who had been conspicuous both in defence and in attack, died of wounds soon afterwards, Lieuts. Joel, Faunthorpe, Fleming and Gordon and 2nd Lieuts. Brett, Chauncey and Monypenny were wounded, 69 men were killed and 300 wounded. The battalion was therefore in sore need both of rest and of drafts. It had a fortnight out of the line and reinforcements amounting to 12 officers and 400 men,[1] and could take

---

[1] These men came mostly from the 2/5th R.W.K., whose Division, as already mentioned, was being utilized for drafts. This reinforcement was a remarkably fine set. One of the officers of the battalion wrote of them : " They went straight into quite one of the nastiest battles one could have chosen for them and the other men commented on their spirit."

POELCAPELLE.

<small>October, 1917</small>

600 men into action at its next effort. This, however, was not till October 26th, and in the interval considerable progress had been made.

Once the main ridge North of the Menin Road had been secured the chief object of the assailants had been to bring forward the left of the line which ran back North-West from Broodseinde along the Gravenstafel spur and South of Poelcapelle and the Houthulst Forest. Here, however, the ground was lower and the going even worse than on the main ridge. The shelling had so completely broken up the surface that the whole country was a wilderness of shell-holes which the unusual rainfall had converted into a mass of slime and bog. Except on the spurs of rather higher ground the whole country was a mere slough; and only the crucial importance of denying to the enemy that freedom of action which the suspension of the attack would have given him caused the continuation of the offensive despite such persistent bad weather and such fearful difficulties.

<small>7th Battalion</small>

Most unfavourable conditions, therefore, faced the Eighteenth Division when early in October it returned to the Salient to continue the attack, and to add to the handicaps the Brigade was called upon to attack at 24 hours' notice at a point quite different from that which it had expected to assault. The Division had been training to attack the main Passchendaele ridge and had carried out several tactical exercises over a model of the ground till all ranks were familiar with their tasks. Actually it had to attack Poelcapelle and, on the night of October 10th/11th, the 53rd Brigade moved up to the front to relieve the Eleventh Division at that point. That division had attacked Poelcapelle on October 8th, and after losing heavily had captured part of the village, but the Northern end of it along the Staden road had remained in German hands.

<small>Oct. 12th</small>

The relief, which pouring rain, mud that surpassed all previous experience, and intense darkness, rendered

LIEUT.-COLONEL B. JOHNSTONE. D.S.O.
Commanded 1st Battalion. 1917. 1918.

[Photo by] [Lafayette, London.

LIEUT.-COLONEL L. H. HICKSON.
Commanded 7th Battalion in 1917 and 1918.

POELCAPELLE.

exceptionally slow and difficult, had barely been completed before the time fixed for the attack of October 12th. The 7th R.W.K. were on the left of the 55th Brigade, next to the Fourth Division, with the Buffs on their other flank. The plan of attack involved the withdrawal of the companies holding the front line, A and D, to an assembly position some way further back, as the front line ran diagonally to the objectives. Detachments were left along the front line, with orders to rejoin their companies as these came along as the second wave of the attack. But the withdrawal lengthened the distance to be covered, a disadvantage the more serious because of the mud which retarded progress—it was so bad that in places men stuck fast and, being unable to move, were killed where they stood. Even the lightly equipped could hardly move in such a slough; for men encumbered with equipment, weapons and ammunition it was doubly difficult. Thus, though the enemy's barrage was not very effective, the battalion lost quite heavily from rifle and machine-gun fire before it cleared its own front line._October 12th 1917 7th Battalion See Sketch 35_

B Company, on the right, made fair progress at first and accounted for many enemy. Before long, however, they were held up by machine-gun fire from their right flank and from the Brewery, a strong point just East of the Staden road. All the officers became casualties, but Sergt. Tebbitt took command and carried on till, about 6.30 a.m., D reinforced the survivors of B. But even then the opposition was too strong to allow of much progress; casualties were heavy, and 2nd Lieut. Duffield, the only officer left with the two companies, re-organized them in a chain of posts just beyond the original line, and despite heavy fire maintained his ground successfully.[1]

On the other flank C had found the barrage somewhat erratic, indeed several German machine-guns had escaped it and gave a great deal of trouble. The

[1] He was awarded the M.C., while Sergt. Tebbitt received the M.M.

POELCAPELLE.

October 12th 1917
7th Battalion

platoon on the flank, however, got on splendidly. When a machine-gun in a strong point threatened to hold it up, Pte. Ives rushed forward with a Lewis gun, and despite heavy fire knocked the machine-gun out, enabling the platoon to get on. Sergt. Hamblin, who had taken command on the fall of his officer, 2nd Lieut. Michell, led the platoon with so much determination and ability that it reached a strong point[1] only just short of the battalion's objective and well ahead of the rest of the attack. This point it rushed successfully, capturing two officers and 50 men with a couple of machine-guns. From here the party, reduced by casualties to 16 men, became mixed up with the Household Battalion of the Fourth Division with whom they pushed on ahead.

The rest of C were less fortunate. A strong point at the Northern end of the village brought them to a standstill, and though A came up to reinforce it was unable to carry the advance any further, nor could the 8th Suffolks of the 53rd Brigade achieve any more when they, too, pushed forward on the left. Finally, therefore, these two companies dug in a little in front of the line held before the attack. Touch was established with Lieut. Duffield's party and eventually some 120 men were collected and organised, a defensive flank formed on the right and the position consolidated, despite much trouble from snipers. Sergt. Coleman helped greatly in this work, he went up and down the line under heavy fire, encouraging the men and directing their efforts. Sergts. Coombs and Firmer were also well to the fore, but despite the gallantry and determination which the 7th had displayed it had achieved but little to compensate for very heavy losses. The weakness of the barrage[2] and the great difficulties of getting forward over a water-logged stretch of mud there had been no time to reconnoitre were mainly

[1] A on map, B marks limit of platoon's advance.
[2] This was largely due to mud, owing to which many of the guns which should have provided it had stuck fast, and never got into action.

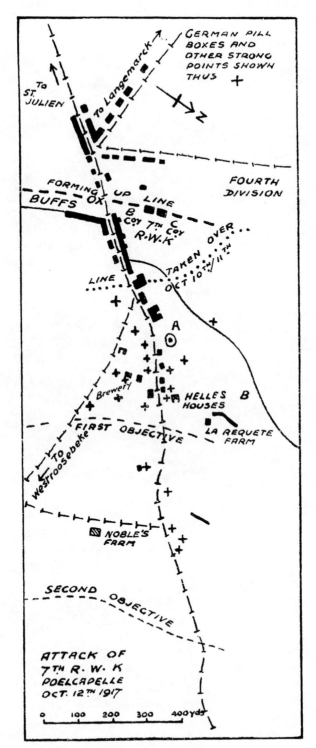

THIRD YPRES.

responsible for the failure to accomplish more, but the battalion hung on all through the next day (October 13th) and maintained its ground until that evening it was relieved by the 8th Suffolks. *October, 1917 7th Battalion*

But its cup was not yet full. When boarding lorries next day to withdraw to the back area, it had the misfortune to be attacked by German aeroplanes, an experience which was becoming unpleasantly frequent, and suffered nearly 40 casualties in addition to those already incurred. These had been serious enough, just half the 600 men who had gone "over the top" were on the casualty list, along with 14 officers, of whom Captain Lewin, Lieut. H. T. Gregory, 2nd Lieuts. Allen, Coles and Michell were killed or died of wounds, Captains Anstruther and F. H. F. Smith being among the wounded.[1] To these the bombing attack added Lieut. Gladwell killed, Captain Heaton, died of wounds, and Captain Hogg and 2nd Lieut. Day wounded. It was a sadly shattered remnant that was left of a battalion which had come up to the front in fine condition and fighting trim.[2] *Oct. 14th*

While the 7th had been finding mud even more formidable than Germans round Poelcapelle, another battalion of the Regiment had been employed in the same quarter of the battlefield, though without being engaged in any real heavy fighting. The 3rd/4th had arrived in the Ypres area on October 4th, and after a week at Proven moved forward when its Division relieved the Twenty-Ninth in the line North-East of Langemarck. But it was only in Divisional reserve, and on October 14th was detailed for work under R.E. supervision in constructing roads between the Pilckem Ridge and Langemarck Church. "Road-making" in *3/4th Batt.*

---

[1] Of the officers who had taken part in the attack, Colonel Cinnamond and Lieut. Duffield were the only two unhurt.

[2] Captain Reynolds, R.A.M.C., the Medical Officer of the Battalion, had done exceptionally fine work during this attack. His name was sent up with a strong recommendation for the D.S.O., but to the disappointment of all ranks he was only awarded the M.C.

GHELUVELT.

Oct.-Nov., 1917
3/4th Batt.

the state to which rain and shell-fire had reduced the ground was arduous and almost unending work, but if uninspiring it was absolutely essential, and, moreover, was not without its dangers, costing the battalion 20 casualties in twelve days. Ten days in back areas followed and then the Seventeenth Division relieved the Fifty-Seventh between Poelcapelle and the Ypres-Staden railway on November 7th. This brought the 3/4th into the front trenches between Requette Farm and the Broombeck two nights later, but by that time active operations on the Poelçapelle front had been suspended, though through shelling and snipers the battalion had over 30 casualties in its four days in the line.

Oct. 24th
1st Battalion

On returning to the fighting line on October 24th the 1st Battalion found itself practically at the point to which it had itself advanced the line on October 4th.

See Sketch 34

B and D Companies occupied the front line North-West of Gheluvelt, A and C being back at Stirling Castle. A day of intermittent shelling intervened between the relief of the 7th K.S.L.I. and the opening of the next attack. This time the battalion's objective was North of Gheluvelt, the village itself being allotted to the Seventh Division, whom it now had on its right astride the Menin Road. The ground was, if possible, more of a bog than it had been three weeks earlier, and merely to move up from support to the assembly trenches was quite exhausting. But somehow the troops got into position in time for "zero," 5.40 a.m.

Oct. 26th

on October 26th, though one platoon of A Company remained behind at Stirling Castle, never having received orders to move. In order to get a satisfactory barrage line it was found necessary to form the attackers up 400 yards in rear of the line gained on October 4th, and the enemy, discovering that this line had been evacuated, promptly re-occupied it, so that when D and B went forward at "zero" they had to fight hard to recover the old front line. They cleared it, however, and moved forward, A thereupon came up in support,

GHELUVELT.

though meeting heavy fire and suffering severely even in reaching the old front.

Oct. 26th.
1917
1st Battalion

Little information came back from the attackers once they cleared the old line, though about 7 a.m. a message was received that Captain Press had been killed, and an hour later an officer of the Machine-Gun Corps came back to report that the troops had gained the first objective and were in touch with the Seventh Division, who had got into Gheluvelt. Shortly afterwards, however, some of the Seventh Division came drifting back upon the old front line of the battalion, having been dislodged by a counter-attack which, it was ascertained later on, led to the survivors of B and D holding the first objective being rolled up from the right flank and rear and killed or taken almost to a man. The attack of the Seventh Division on the South of the road had been held up by Germans in "pill-boxes" on the outskirts of Gheluvelt, which were the key to the situation at this point. By this time Captain Winn had brought C Company up to the front line, and though his attempts to clear these " pill-boxes" proved fruitless, he did great work in organizing a defensive line, rallying men of all units of the 20th Brigade whom the German counter-stoke had forced back, and setting a fine example. Lieut. Lewis Barned, who had been up to the front to collect more accurate information than was available at Battalion Headquarters, came back again to help in securing the right flank and rallying stragglers. He did good service by repairing three Lewis guns which had been put out of action and which he soon rendered serviceable again. Colonel Johnstone, too, was indefatigable in collecting men of all regiments and bringing them up to assist in holding the defensive line. It was largely through the exertions of these three officers[1] that the original line was manned and organized in readiness for the expected counter-attack, which developed early in the evening but withered away

[1] Colonel Johnstone received the D.S.O., and the two others the M.C.

GHELUVELT.

Oct., 1917
1st Battalion

under the fire of the defenders and a most effective artillery barrage. L/Cpl. Sears, who set a fine example and controlled the fire of his men with marked ability, accounted for a large number of the enemy, and thinly though the line was held it was maintained successfully. Shortly afterwards some of the Welsh Fusiliers of the Seventh Division came up on the battalion's right between it and the Menin Road, and a company of the K.O.S.B.'s also arrived to reinforce, while during the night the remnants of the battalion were relieved by the 1st Norfolks.

It was a scanty remnant indeed which reached Ridge Wood Camp. Except for the few who fell wounded near enough to our line to drag themselves back or be fetched in by stretcher-bearers, practically none of B or D Companies ever got back. Those who were wounded at any distance from our line had no chance of extricating themselves from the awful mud which was the dominating feature of the day; it checked the advance of the attack, it impeded and almost prevented communication between front and rear, it choked rifles and Lewis guns so that at critical moments they were out of action. To its all-pervading influence it is chiefly to be ascribed that October 26th 1917 was the worst day in the battalion's experiences in the war. To lose 12 officers[1] and 348 men out of the 16 officers and 581 men who went into action, 225 of the men killed and missing, and to gain not a yard of ground, was a depressing result, even if in the left and centre of the attack ground was won and the line advanced appreciably towards Passchendaele. It was the last major operation in "Third Ypres" in which The Queen's Own was represented. The 1st Battalion was to have another turn in the trenches just North of the Menin Road, but

Nov., 1917

this tour of duty (November 7th/11th) was marked by no serious fighting, though the guns at Comines and

---

[1] Besides Captain Press, 2nd-Lieut. Lovelace was killed, and 2nd-Lieut. Fry was returned as " missing."

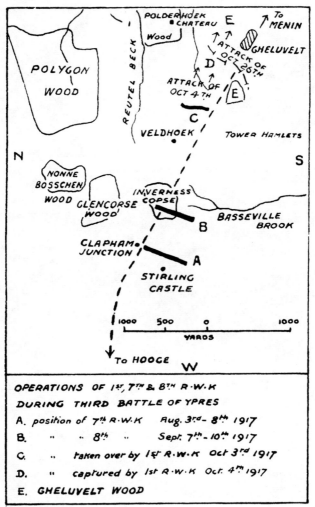

THIRD YPRES.

Tenbrielen still proved very troublesome; actually most of the 25 casualties incurred were caused by one shell which caught the rear platoon of C Company on its way up to the trenches. Conditions were now almost at their worst and imposed inactivity on both sides. After this came relief and a change. November 14th saw the battalion entraining at Ouderdom for Selles, in the Pas de Calais, where it was still resting when ten days later it suddenly received orders to recall all men on leave and detached duties, to dispatch all surplus kit to England, and to hold itself in readiness to entrain for a destination not announced but generally anticipated to be beyond the Alps.

November, 1917
1st Battalion

CHAPTER XIX.

INFANTRY HILL.

June-Oct., 1917
6th Battalion

Of the battalions of The Queen's Own in France one only did not share in the protracted and costly struggle in Flanders. But if the 6th Battalion missed the swamps and mud of " Third Ypres " it was far from inactive, and during the summer and early autumn of 1917 it distinguished itself in no ordinary fashion on several occasions. It is in itself some indication of the vast scale of the war that exploits as gallant and successful as those of the Twelfth Division in this period should not merely have passed unmentioned in the Commander-in-Chief's dispatches but should have received no more than a line or two in the daily communiqués. But to the units involved such actions gave just the same opportunities for the display of courage, resourcefulness, endurance, skill and devotion to duty as did a share in some great battle. Indeed a minor offensive in which some valuable tactical point was captured, or a local counter-attack which won back important trenches naturally meant much to the individual battalion entrusted with the enterprise, and in the story of the 6th R.W.K., the names of Monchy le Preux and Infantry Hill have fully as honourable a place as the Somme or Arras.

When the Twelfth Division went back to the front line in the middle of June some progress had been made both E. and N.E. of Monchy. On the left of its frontage the line had been advanced in front of Scabbard Trench, though the Germans still retained their hold on Devil's Trench. Further to the South much more progress had been made and the advanced position on the slopes of Infantry Hill was well to the East of Monchy. The right sector of the Divisional front

INFANTRY HILL.

ran from the Monchy-Cambrai road to a point N.W. of the Twin Copses which stood half-way between Monchy and the Bois du Sart. The front line here was known as Long Trench; this, however, did not cover the whole frontage and, being held by posts and not continuously, served rather as an outpost line to the line of main resistance in Hook Trench, behind the greater part of which Hill Trench served as a support line. At the Northern end of the line there was a patch of ground in which water was found 18 inches below the surface; here, therefore, digging was impossible, and North of the Green Lane, one of many tracks which led S.E. from Monchy, Hook Trench was a dead end, known as the Hook, only separated by a short space from the Southern part of Devil's Trench. Indeed it was only on June 29th, a few days before the 6th R.W.K. moved up to Monchy, that the 8th Royal Fusiliers had dislodged the Germans from the Hook. *June, 1917 6th Battalion* *See Sketch 36*

The 6th's first turn in the new sector did not bring it actually into the front line; the battalion was in support or Brigade reserve, providing large working parties and having a few casualties. On July 11th, about 5 a.m., the Germans suddenly began bombarding the British positions and then attacked in considerable force over a frontage of nearly half-a-mile, using liquid fire with considerable effect. The garrison of the line attacked put up a stout defence but were overpowered by numbers. Long Trench was lost, and for a time the enemy even got into the Northern end of Hook Trench but were ultimately driven out. On the right a bombing block was established in Long Trench about 80 yards from its junction with Hook Trench; but it was essential to recover the lost ground, and when the 6th took over the front line on July 13th it was with instructions that Long Trench was to be retaken two days later. Actually the weather turned wet and just a quarter-of-an-hour before the time fixed for the assault a message arrived postponing the attack till the *July, 1917* *July 11th*

LONG TRENCH.

July, 1917
6th Battalion

17th; there was only just time to send up the cancelling orders to the front line by a fleet-footed orderly going boldly over the top, but he got through all right, and though the postponement cost the battalion nearly 20 casualties from the shell-fire which the enemy persistently maintained, it permitted careful reconnoitring.

The object of the attack was the consolidation of a line of shell-holes about 100 yards West of Long Trench, which the Germans had been doing their best to convert into a new trench. Long Trench itself was to be occupied and held long enough to cover the consolidation. The 6th were to employ two companies, B on the right, D on the left, one platoon from each company and one of C being detailed to follow the assault and consolidate the new trench. Further to the left, North of Green Lane, the 9th Essex were to co-operate and were to construct a line running back to Hook Trench. On the right a bombing party of the 6th Queen's was to push forward from the block in Long Trench.

July 17th

The attack, which was assisted by a very heavy bombardment by artillery and Stokes mortars, got off well at 4.45 a.m. on the 17th. The leading waves swept over the half-completed new trench with such rapidity that they failed to notice some score of Germans lying prone at the bottom of the trench, and when the consolidating party, following behind with rifles slung, came jumping into the trench on top of them these men showed fight but were promptly and satisfactorily disposed of with picks and shovels. The Queen's bombers, after one check, rushed the block in Long Trench over the top, and then pushed on up that trench killing and taking a good many Germans, while the rest of the trench was captured by B and D after a stiff fight, and several prisoners of the 17th Reserve Division were taken. But to consolidate the captured position was no easy task. The right and centre of Long Trench were under effective enfilade fire from the

LONG TRENCH.

South. On the left the ground was like a basin, the Germans who held the Northern and Eastern edges commanded practically all the posts in the centre and the Essex were before long forced back. The Germans had put down a heavy barrage the moment the attack started and effectually prevented communication between the attacking companies and those in support, and of the fate of B and D no news came back, though the survivors of the pick and shovel men had been forced back to their starting line by German counter-attacks and machine-gun fire.

July 17th, 1917 6th Battalion

Colonel Alderman came up to Hook Trench and pushed out scouts to ascertain the situation, but not till after 2 p.m. did a messenger at last get back. This was Pte. Adams, who had courageously crawled back under an intense fire, creeping from shell-hole to shell-hole, and having to dodge not a few of these which were occupied by Germans. It had taken him nearly five hours to cover the 500 yards he had to cross, but his news was very welcome. It was that Captain Thomas, though wounded, had established himself in Long Trench near the junction with Green Lane, and was hanging on there with a handful of D Company and resisting all efforts to bomb him out. On his way back Pte. Adams had come across another rather larger party under 2nd Lieut. Scott-Marten and Sergt. Glare, who also were clinging to the captured position and had repulsed several German attempts to dislodge them. Immediately this news reached Colonel Alderman he began organizing a fresh attack. The Queen's were asked to make another effort to bomb up Long Trench; the Brigade arranged for artillery co-operation, and thanks to careful preparation and to the dash with which A and C Companies advanced to the help of their comrades, the fresh attack, launched just as it got dark, was a brilliant success. The Germans were taken by surprise and driven completely out of Long Trench, many were taken and more killed, and touch was regained

LONG TRENCH.

July 17th, 1917
6th Battalion

with the tenacious little parties who had held on so long and were still unconquered.

With Captain Thomas were Captain Henderson-Roe (B Company's commander) and 2nd Lieut. Bull. The latter, though wounded, had crawled from shell-hole to shell-hole, collecting water, food and ammunition from casualties and helping wounded, and had done much to keep up the defence. Captain Henderson-Roe, though buried by a shell which burst close to him, had managed to dig himself out, and, in crawling along the lines before he reached Captain Thomas' post, he had collected several wounded, bandaged them and helped them to get into better shelter in shell-holes. Both he and Captain Thomas had richly earned the D.S.O.'s awarded to them, as had 2nd Lieuts. Bull and Scott-Marten their M.C's. and Sergt. Glare and Pte. Adams their D.C.M.'s. Their courage and endurance made the day memorable in the battalion's annals, even apart from the very considerable success with which the operation ended. By next morning the new German trench had been satisfactorily consolidated and wired. Over 150 yards of a communication trench had been dug by the 5th Northamptons, the Divisional Pioneers, to continue Vine Street to the new position, in Long Trench a block had been made at the junction with Green Lane and The Queen's had successfully cleared the Southern end. Corps and Divisional Commanders alike were warm in their appreciation of the battalion's fine work. "It is greatly due to their pluck and tenacity and the splendid defence which Captain Thomas, 2nd Lieut. Scott-Marten and their parties had put up that the ground was secured," was Sir Charles Ferguson's[1] verdict. Naturally in such a fight casualties had been heavy; 2nd Lieuts. Bristow, H. G. C. Mann, Grocott and Rudall and 10 men were killed; 29 men were missing, while in addition to Captains Henderson-

July 18th

---

[1] The old Divisional Commander of the 1st Battalion in August, 1914, was now G.O.C., Seventeenth Corps, in which the 6th were serving.

INFANTRY HILL.

Roe and Thomas and 2nd Lieut. Bull, 2nd Lieut. Thurburn was wounded with 55 men. But the German casualties must have been heavier, over 30 prisoners were taken, many had been killed both in the new trench and in the storming of Long Trench and in the bombing fights, while the artillery had had some fine targets in Germans bolting from Long Trench before the original attack.

July-Aug. 1917 6th Battalion

A fairly quiet fortnight followed, chiefly spent in the reserve lines, finding working parties, and then on August 1st the battalion relieved the 7th East Surreys in Hook Trench. This had again become the front line, as on July 25th a strong German attack on the 36th Brigade had driven out the posts in Long Trench and the trench captured on the 17th and now known as Spoon Trench, though several saps in front of Hook Trench were still in British hands. But the Germans were evidently not yet satisfied with the position, for after a day of desultory shell-fire their artillery and trench-mortars suddenly worked up to a hurricane bombardment about 6 p.m. on August 2nd. This lasted nearly three hours and inflicted great damage on the trenches; but casualties were minimized by the prompt action of the officers in charge, who pushed their men forward to the far end of the saps whereby they not only avoided the shells but were well posted to break up the infantry attacks when, about 9 p.m., these developed.

See Sketch 36

August 2nd

This they did in strength, not only against the 6th, but against The Queen's on their left in Twin Trench and the 7th Norfolks on the other flank. Three times the Germans emerged in force from their trenches, but each time the parapet was manned the moment the German barrage lifted and the attackers were met by a steady fire from rifles and Lewis guns, under which their lines melted away. Their last effort was rather more successful, they reached and entered the Norfolks' trenches and got into several saps on the

THE HOOK.

Aug. 2nd, 1917
6th Battalion

left of the battalion's front and into "the Hook." From another post they were only beaten off by the courage and devotion of Sergt. Lambeth who, though three times buried by explosions, kept his Lewis gun in action and opened a heavy fire as the attackers came on. It was essential to expel the enemy from the ground they had gained, for the line behind was only held by a series of posts, and if the Germans retained their gains they would endanger the whole line. 2nd Lieut. Bankes, whose steadiness and coolness had done much to keep the defence going, despite the heaviness of the shelling, promptly took measures to recapture the lost ground, and counter-attacks soon ejected the enemy from all but the two saps on the left, a machine-gun and several prisoners being taken.

Aug. 3rd,

To these two saps the Germans clung desperately, and at daybreak were still holding the Hook and one sap, a length of perhaps fifty yards. Further attacks were postponed till evening when the sap was quickly retaken, but the night was so bright that an attempt to rush the Hook over the open failed in face of heavy machine-gun fire. Colonel Alderman then organized a barrage of rifle-grenades to assist the bombers and at last, after a strenuous bombing fight lasting an hour-and-a-half, in which 2nd Lieut. Godly led his bombers with great determination and skill, he was able to report to the Brigade the complete recapture of the position. As the survivors of the 40 or 50 Germans who had been contesting possession of the Hook bolted for their own lines they were caught by Lewis guns, which had been waiting this opportunity, and many of them fell. It had been a costly venture for them, their losses had been extremely heavy,[1] while those of the British were very light considering the weight of the bombardment and the vigour and strength of the infantry attack. The 6th had 14 men killed and missing and 2nd Lieut. Godly and about 30 men wounded,

[1] They were estimated at least 200.

INFANTRY HILL.

though as the battalion was very much below strength these losses were proportionately higher than might be thought. It was the more satisfactory to have recovered the Hook because the Germans had evidently attached considerable value to its possession, had intended to incorporate it in their own lines and had actually dug communication trenches leading back to Long Trench. These were promptly blocked, and when the battalion was relieved by the 9th Royal Fusiliers on the 6th Colonel Alderman had the satisfaction of handing over the position intact.

<small>Aug.-Sept., 1917 6th Battalion</small>

After this success, which won the battalion high praise from Divisional, Corps and Army Commanders and brought M.C.'s to 2nd Lieuts. Bankes and Godly, and a D.C.M. to Sergt. Lambeth, the next two months were much quieter; turns in the front line, usually four days at a time, alternated with periods in support or reserve, but in none of its front line tours did the battalion have to carry out an attack, and none of them happened to coincide with German counter-strokes to the raids which the Division continued to make with much success. On August 24th Colonel Dawson returned and resumed command, Captain L. C. R. Smith also rejoined and a dozen new subalterns made their appearance. Drafts, however, were scarcer, and though casualties were few the battalion's trench strength continued very low; of those on its rolls a large number were absent for various reasons. Thus at the end of July there were two officers acting as Town Majors, one each at Brigade Headquarters, a Training Camp and the Divisional Depôt, and two sick in the country, while of the men 11 were at Brigade Headquarters, 19 in different employments under the Division, 7 attached to the R.E., 26 with the Brigade Machine-Gun Company or acting as Brigade snipers; classes and schools, the Divisional Rest Camp and miscellaneous employments accounted for another 23, and with 13 sick and 8 on leave a total of 107 is reached, as com-

311

INFANTRY HILL.

Aug.-Oct., 1917
6th Battalion

pared with just over 500 actually with the battalion. And this, it may be noted, was distinctly below the normal number of absentees; at the end of August there were 148 away to 450 present, so that the strain of holding and repairing the trenches normally allotted to a battalion fell extremely heavily on the small number actually present, especially when deductions have been made for the transport detachment and men regimentally employed. A draft of 103 men, which arrived on September 22nd, did something to improve matters, but when at the end of October the battalion at last left Monchy and the Seventeenth Corps[1] it had only just over 500 rank and file actually present.

Just before this it had achieved about the most successful of its exploits. Raids had been undertaken by most battalions of the Division and it was decided to make just one more on an unusually large scale before the Division quitted the area. At the beginning of October a specially-selected party of one officer and 50 men from each company, the whole commanded by Captain L. C. R. Smith, was detailed to proceed to Beaurains for special training, along with a similar detachment from the 6th Queen's and another of 350 from the 7th Norfolks. The line to be raided lay rather to the South of the quarter where the 6th had so far had their hardest fighting, the objective being

See Sketch 36

the German trenches known as Strap Trench and Buckle Trench, not far North of the Arras-Cambrai

Oct. 14th

road. The 6th attacked from Tool Trench just East of Tite's Copse, having The Queen's on its right and the Norfolks on its left. The German trenches had

---

[1] It was about this time that the 6th lost the services of the Medical Officer, who for two years had bandaged its wounds and dealt with its ailments, major and minor. Captain Carson, R.A.M.C., was a man of character and competence, highly efficient, acute to detect and to discourage in effective fashion any tendency to report sick without just cause, helpful and sympathetic; he had done much for the efficiency of the battalion in more ways than one, and his departure was universally deplored. His M.C. may not figure in the honours won by the battalion, but it was none the less a source of great satisfaction to the 6th's officers and men alike.

BUCKLE TRENCH.

October 14th, 1917
6th Battalion

been systematically bombarded for days before the raid and the actual attack was preceded by an eight hours' bombardment in which one 15-inch howitzer, three 12-inch, twenty 9.2-inch, over sixty 6-inch, twenty-eight 4.5-inch and seventeen 60-pounders took part, to say nothing of seventy-four 18-pounders and twenty trench mortars. The First Army would have been glad of such a weight of metal, with practically unlimited ammunition, behind its attacks in the spring of 1915. During the period of preparations for this raid Colonel Dawson was for the time in command of the Brigade, General Cator had left to take command of the Fifty-Eighth Division, the new Brigadier, Brig.-General Incledon-Webber, of the Irish Fusiliers, had not yet arrived and the senior battalion commander was away sick.

The raid proved a conspicuous success. So good were the communication trenches in this quarter that the stormers reached their assembly positions without a casualty, and advancing behind a most accurate barrage and under cover of smoke they reached Strap Trench with little loss, for the German barrage came down well behind them. The right party of the battalion, under 2nd Lieut. Slade, met a little resistance from a machine-gun and some bombers, but rushed them and swept on in close pursuit of 40 or 50 Germans, whom they chased to Buckle Trench, accounting for the majority. 2nd Lieut. Davy's party, the next to the left, drove a party of Germans from the front line into the British barrage, and then, pressing on to Buckle Trench, took some 20 prisoners and blew up a dug-out full of Germans who refused to surrender. The next party, 2nd Lieut. Parmenter's, had hardly any fighting till it reached Buckle Trench, where about 20 Germans put up a stout resistance with a machine-gun. 2nd Lieut. Parmenter, however, promptly moved to a flank with some bombers while other men covered his movements with rifle-fire; and then attacking from the flank he

BUCKLE TRENCH.

Oct. 14th, 1917
6th Battalion

routed the enemy, taking six and killing the rest. Only the left party, 2nd Lieut. Elliott's, met any real resistance in Strap Trench, for the wire on their front was less well cut and part of the trench was but little damaged; but by taking the defenders of this section in flank they soon dislodged them, shooting them down as they fled.

Seven minutes after " zero " all the objectives had been taken and the raiders were blowing up dugouts and strong points, rounding up prisoners and pushing patrols out beyond Buckle Trench. Everywhere tremendous damage had been done by the bombardment and it was obvious that it had inflicted heavy casualties, quite apart from the large number killed by the raiders. There was plenty of time to complete all that it was intended to do, the Germans had been hit too hard to counter-attack and their artillery fire was ineffectual. Half-an-hour after " zero " the withdrawal began and was concluded in excellent order; the patrols went first, then the men from Buckle Trench, lastly Strap Trench was evacuated under cover of parties lying out in shell-holes in No Man's Land. Casualties had been light. The 6th had only 3 men killed and 12 missing with 2nd Lieuts. Davy and Parmenter[1] and 31 men wounded; The Queen's had about as many and the Norfolks about 70, while those of the enemy could at a quite conservative estimate be put at 400. The prisoners alone taken by the 6th equalled its total casualties, and the killed on the frontage it attacked came to at least 100, while the other two battalions had done equally well. Moreover, when the Germans re-occu-

Oct. 15th

pied their damaged trenches next day, their efforts to repair them added considerably to their casualty list, for they had to expose themselves freely to the snipers and Lewis gunners who were kept busily employed. Altogether the raid was a most conspicuous success and a

[1] He received the M.C., as did also Captain Smith, to whose careful training and skilful leadership much of the success of the raid was due.

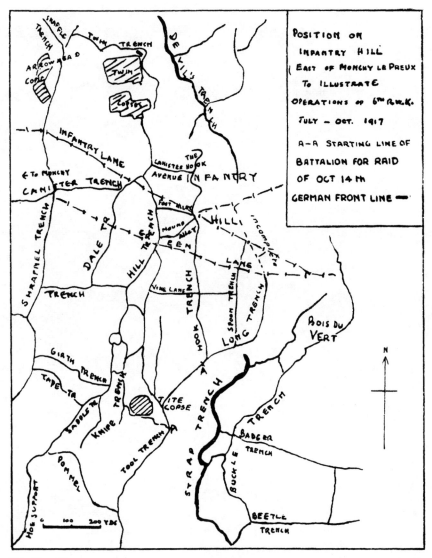

INFANTRY HILL.

triumphal finale to the four months the Division had spent in this quarter. The Army Commander, Sir Julian Byng, spoke warmly of the " complete mastery over the enemy " which it had shown, and of the " dash and determination " which the raiders had displayed. The Corps Commander was not exaggerating when he took leave of the Twelfth Division on its departure from the Seventeenth Corps; " Whether in attack or defence," he wrote, " the Division has done uniformly well and has shown qualities of tenacity and determination which have been an example to all. It has gained a great reputation." To the 6th these words most certainly applied; its stay in the Monchy area had added notable laurels to the regimental record, and though in itself it is no infallible guide to what a battalion had deserved, to have obtained so many honours in what was from the broader point of view only a " side show " is some indication of the way in which those in authority regarded its performances.

October, 1917 6th Battalion

CHAPTER XX

CAMBRAI.

Oct.-Nov., 1917
6th Battalion

The 6th R.W.K. had already found 1917 a most strenuous year before it withdrew from the Monchy sector. But the year had still hard fighting in store for it, one of its biggest successes to be followed by practical annihilation. For some time past a new offensive had been in contemplation in a part of the line which offered better opportunities for the employment of tanks on a large scale than the shell-hole pitted morasses of the Ypres Salient could afford. Since the arrival of the British opposite the Hindenburg Line at the end of March no serious attempt had been made to force its formidable defences. But just for this reason, because there had been no heavy bombardment to break up the surface and create impediments to the progress of the attack there was the more chance that a tank attack on a big scale might prove successful. Preparations for such a stroke were therefore put in hand by the Third Army before the end of October.

The Twelfth Division was among those selected for employment in this new attack. It had spent nearly a month out of the line, part of it devoted to rehearsing an attack in co-operation with tanks, and on November 15th it started its move to the new front, Major Alderman being in temporary command, as Colonel Dawson was in hospital. Every effort was being made to conceal the intended attack from the Germans, there had been no preliminary bombardment, not even any special registration, so that the attack might enjoy the all-important advantage of surprise. The battalion had, therefore, to lie very low, showing no lights at night and keeping movements by day down to the minimum, till shortly before midnight on November 19th it moved out to an assembly position S.W. of

CAMBRAI.

Gonnelieu and formed up with A Company on the right, C on the left, B behind A, and D behind C. The Twelfth Division was on the right of the attack and had orders to form a defensive flank as its attack progressed. In the initial stages the 35th Brigade was on the right and the 36th on the left; the 37th, which was in support, was not to come into action till the leading brigades had taken the first and second objectives, the "Black and Blue lines," when it was to pass through them. Its leading battalions, the East Surreys and the Buffs, were to swing right-handed as they advanced and to continue the defensive flank which the 35th Brigade was to form on the slope overlooking the Scheldt Canal, carrying it along the Bonavis Ridge as far as Lateau Wood. The 6th R.W.K. had to push straight forward till past the flank of the Buffs and then to swing to its right through the Northern end of Lateau Wood. On the way it was to "mop up" the lines which had been stormed by the leading battalions, to capture two fortified positions known as Pam Pam and Le Quennet Farms and to clear its portion of the third objective or "Brown Line." To assist in this, twenty-four tanks were to join the battalion on the "Blue Line." It was a complicated programme, calling for skilful leading and direction-keeping on the part of platoon and company commanders; but the battalion was to prove fully equal to its task, as indeed did the whole Division.

November, 1917
6th Battalion
See Sketch 37

The attack started at 6.20 a.m., and it soon became clear that the careful concealment had been successful and that a complete surprise had been secured. The tanks were most effective in dealing with the wire, strong though it was, and in demolishing the strong points. The infantry following in their wake made rapid progress; little serious resistance was offered by the unprepared Germans, and many prisoners were taken. Thus when the battalion came forward it had little to do till Pam Pam Farm was reached. Here the Germans put up a stout fight, but the tanks helped to

Nov. 20th.

CAMBRAI.

Nov. 20th, 1917
6th Battalion

overcome them and the battalion pushed on to Lateau Wood and Le Quennet, which were reached about 10 a.m. On the left C Company got held up for a time in front of Le Quennet Farm, but Major Alderman, who was well up with the leading line, signalled to a tank and with its aid the point was cleared and occupied. Then, while some of the battalion plunged into Lateau Wood and began clearing it, Major Alderman began organizing an attack on some guns North of Lateau Wood, which he was anxious to secure. He went forward himself with Lieuts. Carré, Bourchier, Newsholme and Stiebel and a small party of men, worked along the edge of the wood and came on a large party of Germans round the guns. But these, instead of standing their ground, bolted at once, under fire from the little detachment which secured the guns and then pressed forward in pursuit only to suffer severely from fire from the Wood. Major Alderman himself fell, mortally wounded, as did Lieut. Carré also; Lieut. Bourchier was killed outright and Lieut. Stiebel badly wounded.

Meanwhile the clearing of Lateau Wood proved difficult — tanks were less useful there — and the battalion had outstripped the Buffs who had had stiff fighting at Bonavis. But gradually progress was made and before long The Queen's came up on the left and joined in the fight; by mid-day their leading company was prolonging the defensive flank beyond Lateau Wood, which had been cleared after a hard fight. 2nd Lieut. Abel, who took command of his company on the fall of its commander, did splendid service at a critical moment, silencing a troublesome strong point by skilfully concentrated rifle-fire which allowed the advance to go forward, while 2nd Lieut. Carey also led, first his platoon and then his company, with skill and initiative, storming the final objective and showing great organizing power in superintending the consolidation. Early in the afternoon the battalion reported

Photo by] [C. Aldridge, Hythe, Kent.

CAPTAIN (A LIEUT.-COLONEL) W. J. ALDERMAN, D.S.O.
Killed in action 20th November, 1917, while temporarily in command of the 6th Battalion.

Face Page 318.

CAMBRAI.

to Brigade Headquarters that it was consolidating a line running North from the N.E. edge of Lateau Wood, in touch on its left with The Queen's, and had sent out patrols to the right to get touch with the Buffs. But though all objectives had been successfully secured the line was weakly held and a grievous loss had been suffered in the death of Major Alderman. Fortunately Colonel Dawson was available, having just returned from hospital, and he at once went forward to superintend the consolidation.

Considering the importance of the success achieved—many prisoners, several machine-guns and the whole battery of 5.9-inch howitzers had been taken near Lateau Wood—the battalion had escaped lightly with under 70 casualties, though with the battalion already weak they were more serious than might appear, while the proportion of officers was high. Besides those already mentioned, Lieut. Sykes and 2nd Lieut. C. W. Clarke had been killed, and Captain Hodgson and 2nd Lieut. Thurlow wounded. In particular Major Alderman's death was much felt throughout the battalion which owed so much to him. In the course of the war the non-commissioned ranks of its Regular battalions provided The Queen's Own with many splendid officers, but if there is one who stands out among them it is Major Alderman. Before the war he had commanded the affection and respect of officers and men : in the war he had given even greater proof of his quality. Promoted to commissioned rank at the very beginning of the war, he had been one of the first officers of the 6th Battalion, had done great service in building it up on sound lines and with high traditions, had accompanied it to France and served with it in the field for two-and-a-half years, as platoon commander, as Transport Officer, as Adjutant, as second-in-command, and as Commanding Officer. He had been in command when the 6th distinguished itself so much at Long Trench on July 17th and in

CAMBRAI.

November, 1917
6th Battalion

repulsing the German attack of August 2nd; both occasions he had played no small part in its success, and no D.S.O. won during the war had been better deserved than his. It was characteristic of his modesty and loyalty that while in command he insisted that the battalion was really Dawson's battalion, that he was only carrying on till Dawson could return, he would only do those things which he was sure Dawson would have wished to do. When in billets he would insist on having Dawson's horse brought round every morning, so that he might satisfy himself that it was being kept fit for him. He has left a noble memory behind him.

November, 20th - 29th

The days following this success saw much hard fighting, but mainly on the left and centre of the battle-front round Moeuvres and Bourlon Wood and Fontaine l'Eveque. On the right there was comparative quiet; no endeavour was made to extend the British gains in this direction and the enemy were also inactive; still there was little rest or relief for the battalions engaged on the 20th. Though much below strength—the 6th had started out barely 600 strong, even including both "battle surplus" and transport, and the rest of the Brigade was in like case—they had to remain in the line, busily employed on consolidation, though in comparison with its scanty "trench strength" the 6th had a terribly long stretch of line to look after. Patrols were pushed out at night to reconnoitre the bridges over the Scheldt Canal, which were found held, while the enemy maintained a steady shell-fire which had inflicted another 30 casualties before November 30th.

On the night of November 24th/25th the Twentieth Division extended to its right, on which the battalion side-stepped to the right and relieved the Buffs in trenches due East of Lateau Wood with its right resting on the road leading down to Vaucelles Bridge. Here again it had a frontage disproportionately large for its numbers, two battalions at strength

THE COUNTER ATTACK.

would not have been too many to hold it; it was obvious to anyone in the trenches that the local situation was none too secure, especially as orders had been issued that the bridges over the canal were not to be demolished. For this there were no doubt good reasons, their destruction would have impeded any effort to widen in a Southerly direction the lodgement which had been made in the German position, but while they remained intact their existence undoubtedly facilitated counter-attacks. The line here consisted of a series of isolated posts, many of which having been part of the Hindenburg Line faced the wrong way and required much work to adapt them to their new purpose, and the whole situation was unsatisfactory. *November, 1917 6th Battalion*

The 6th was still holding these trenches, having been ten days on end in the line, when about 7 a.m. on November 30th a tremendous bombardment was suddenly opened along the whole British front line. It developed rapidly in intensity and within a short time all communications with the front line were severed. The Battalion Headquarters of the 6th R.W.K. were on the reverse slope of a hill behind the Northern end of Lateau Wood. Directly the shelling started Captain Hodgson-Smith, who was now second-in-command, took the whole headquarters party and posted them in a sunken road just in front, ready to form a rallying point should the men in front get pushed in. Before long stragglers were coming back from the N.E. towards the 37th Brigade Headquarters at the Western end of Bonavis Ridge, with Germans behind them. This advance was checked by the Brigade signallers and other details, and in the same way Captain Hodgson-Smith's party began to get targets in Germans advancing on their left, while directly afterwards the Buffs, who were in Brigade support, counter-attacked and recovered Pam Pam Farm, to which the enemy had already penetrated. This counter-stoke, delivered about 8.15 a.m., held the enemy up for a time and *Nov. 30th See Sketch 37*

THE COUNTER ATTACK.

Nov. 30th, 1917
6th Battalion

allowed of the extrication of some of the East Surreys from the front line South of Bonavis Farm. For a time, apparently, the Buffs got touch with the 6th R.W.K. also, for at 10.20 they reported them as holding on.

However, the enemy continued to press hard, especially against the left of the Buffs, and about 10.30 forced them back. As they fought their way to the Hindenburg Support Line the few survivors of the 6th Battalion Headquarters, under Captain Dove, the Adjutant, joined in with them. These had put up a good fight against overwhelming numbers who had at first advanced against them in front and on the left, where, as one survivor writes, "the Germans came pouring on in masses like a Bank Holiday crowd." Those in front the Headquarters' party had promptly shot down, but almost immediately grey figures began emerging from Lateau Wood more to the right, and the post was before long practically surrounded and its garrison overpowered. Captain Hodgson-Smith was twice wounded, the second time very badly, and taken, and only a few got away. Colonel Dawson had been wounded rather before this, exposing himself as usual in the endeavour to discover for himself what was happening, but he had been safely got away. N.E. of La Vacquerie, however, a successful stand was made by about 250 men, mainly Buffs, but including about 60 East Surreys and nearly 20 R.W.K's. Touch was obtained with the 36th Brigade on the right and with the Twentieth Division on the left, and the position was maintained, so that at last the enemy's advance was checked.

Before this, however, the gallant resistance of the companies in the front line had been overpowered. Strung out over a long front—C Company for example had only 4 officers and 42 men to hold a front of 400 yards—they had been subjected to the bombardment followed by attacks in force on both

THE COUNTER ATTACK.

Nov. 30th, 1917
6th Battalion

flanks. The main attack on the Twelfth Division seems to have come against its right from Bantouzelle with a subordinate attack from Voleurs Bridge which made less progress, while the advance which had threatened the 37th Brigade's Headquarters at 8 a.m. and the main pressure on the Buffs after their counter-attack developed more from the North-East, where another weakened and exhausted Division was trying to hold a line too long for its numbers. Apparently the first breach was effected through the very thinly-held front of the Fifty-Fifth Division on the right, for the reports of the survivors of the front-line companies describe the enemy as first assailing them from the right flank. The men, tired as they were and hopelessly outnumbered by fresh troops, put up a fine fight, though the denseness of Lateau Wood and the incomplete state of the defences were all against them, while the fact that the Canal bridges had been left intact, despite all Colonel Dawson's urgent representations to be allowed to demolish them, did prove exceedingly useful, but unfortunately useful to the enemy. Thus, C Company, after a stubborn struggle against heavy attacks in flank and rear, were forced back to a strong point 100 yards East of Le Quennet Farm where the survivors kept the enemy at bay for another two hours, inflicting many casualties on them. At last, however, when every cartridge had been expended, the enemy penetrated into the strong point and compelled the dozen men who were left to lay down their arms. A Company in like manner had first found targets in enemy advancing to their right and had then been attacked in front and flank by large forces advancing on their left more from the direction of Masnières. These, too, they engaged, but to escape being surrounded they had to fall back to some gun-pits a little way in rear. Here, too, they made a stand, but with the Germans already in their rear and on both flanks, ammunition running short and no help forthcoming, surrender could not be long

THE COUNTER ATTACK.

Nov. 30th, 1917
6th Battalion

delayed. The fate of the other companies was much the same. Hardly a man got away; the only men who reached Battalion Headquarters before it was overwhelmed were runners bringing back messages, and the fight which was put up is a page in the history of the battalion of which it has every reason to feel proud. Outnumbered and exhausted, the men did all that was humanly possible and their resistance went far to take the sting out of the German attack and to leave them unable to extend their success or maintain all their gains.

December 1917

During the night a few men managed to rejoin Captain Dove's party which, by the time that the remnants of the 37th Brigade were relieved, had grown to 52 men. Captain Dove, however, was among the few casualties of December 1st, on which day the position remained unaltered, for though the enemy kept up a fairly steady shell-fire he attempted no attack. Early on the 2nd a battalion of the Sixty-First Division took over the line and the 37th Brigade went back to Heudecourt. It was a sad termination to an operation which had opened so brilliantly, but that the Twelfth Division had fought on November 30th under the greatest disadvantages is clear, and though overpowered it had put up a stubborn fight and taken a heavy toll of the enemy. None of the officers in the front line of the 6th R.W.K. escaped. Captain Martyn, 2nd Lieuts. Carey, Sanders and Hodge proved to have been killed, Captain Hodgson-Smith, Lieut. S. G. Wright and half-a-dozen 2nd Lieuts. were taken and nearly 250 other ranks were killed or missing. Colonel Dawson and Captain Thomas, who had also been hit quite early on the 30th, had been safely evacuated.

To the scanty remnant who had reached Heudecourt on the 2nd of December had to be added Captain Hughes and his transport men, the band, who had been acting as ration parties, and a few other details, while on the 4th four more officers and 85 men turned up.

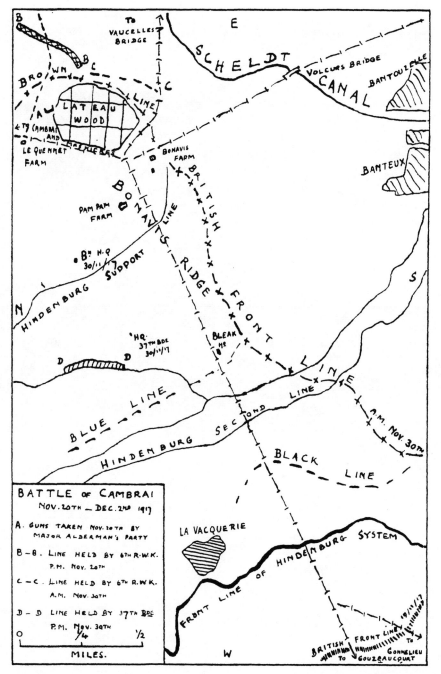

CAMBRAI.

This party, some of the "battle surplus" with 50 of a newly-arrived draft, had been thrown into the line near Chapel Hill as part of a Twelfth Division Composite Battalion early on the 30th, and had held their ground without much loss till the night of December 3rd/4th, playing a useful part in checking the German advance. Altogether, when it left Heudecourt on the 6th, the battalion's numbers had risen to six officers and 225 men. Still even so, the 6th which had fought so well at Arras and on Infantry Hill had been practically wiped out and needed complete reconstruction. It had lost heavily enough more than once before this but had never been quite so near complete destruction.

December, 1917
6th Battalion

From Heudecourt the next move was to Thiennes, where the rest of December was spent in re-organizing. Major Whetham, of the Manchesters, had taken command on December 3rd, and he had Captain Hughes as Adjutant in place of Captain Dove. Small drafts came in at intervals, amounting in all to 160, the return of a few men from leave or hospital or various employments added a few more, and the arrival of Lieuts. Willoughby and Scott and six 2nd Lieuts., with the return of Lieut. Bull, provided enough officers to re-form the companies and to train the new drafts, so that before the end of the year some progress had been made towards reconstructing the battalion.

CHAPTER XXI

PALESTINE.

1917
2nd & 2/4th
Battalions

Nineteen hundred and seventeen had ended less happily on the Western front than it had at one time promised to do, to which disappointment the change of the plan for following up the Somme, the Russian revolution, the scanty success of General Nivelle's much-vaunted short cut to victory, the bad weather of the autumn, the Caporetto collapse and the failure to develop to the full the initial success of Cambrai, had all in varying measure contributed. In the East, however, the year which had opened with one dramatic triumph, General Maude's skilfully accomplished recapture of Kut followed by his brilliantly successful advance on Baghdad, ended with the scarcely less striking and welcome overthrow of the Turkish defences between Beersheba and Gaza and the consequent delivery of Jerusalem.

If the 2nd Battalion in Mesopotamia did not have the good fortune to share in the year's dramatic triumphs, the representatives of The Queen's Own in Palestine had plenty of hard fighting and opportunities of earning distinction. The 2/4th had been heavily engaged, too, earlier in the year. Indeed it was in 1917 that it saw most of its fighting. January found it on the lines of communication in Sinai, but in February it moved up to El Arish, advancing at the end of the month to Sheikh Zowaad, where it had the satisfaction of quitting the sand which it had been eating, drinking and breathing for months past and finding firm ground under its feet again. Here it was in reserve to the outposts which were covering the advance of the railway, and was mainly employed in finding working parties. In March it advanced to Rafa, where it was employed in the outpost line. Towards the end of the month it

2/4th Batt.

Jan.-Feb.

March

PALESTINE.

crossed the old Turco-Egyptian frontier to take its part in the first of Sir Archibald Murray's attempts upon Gaza. *March, 1917 2/4th Batt.*

This effort was really a *coup de main* rather than a deliberate formal attack. It was a repetition on a more ambitious scale of the sudden strokes which had succeeded so well at Maghdaba and Rafa, for while the infantry attacked from the South most of the mounted troops were employed in a wide sweep round the landward side of the town so as to attack it from the East and North-East and cut off the retreat of the garrison. The 2/4th had the distinction of being chosen for a special mission, being detailed along with the Gloucestershire Hussars and a section of 60-pounders, the whole under Colonel Money, to make a demonstration along the sea-coast on the extreme left of the attack to distract the Turks' attention from the other flank.

On March 24th, therefore, the battalion moved up to just beyond Khan Yunus, bivouacked in groves in which it lay hid all next day, and then after sunset advanced to Deir el Belah. About 1 a.m. on the 26th it was on the move again, crossed the Wadi Ghuzze near its mouth, not without some difficulty in finding the passage through the quicksands, and took post at Tel el Ajjul to cover the crossing. At dawn it should have advanced, but a dense sea-fog rolling inland from the coast forbade any movement, and not till 10 a.m. did it lift sufficiently to allow of an advance. Then the battalion deployed, two companies in front line, and pushed forward across the sand-hills. There was but little opposition and casualties were light, about a dozen in all. The advance was continued for about a mile when, as there was no intention of pressing the attack home on this flank, no further progress was attempted, the battalion remaining in the position reached till nightfall, when it fell back a little and formed square round the guns. It was a troubled night, for the Turks opposite kept on firing away and *See Sketch 38 March 26th*

GAZA.

March, 1917
2/4th Batt.

were constantly sending up Very lights; however, they never attempted any counter-attack and with daylight the battalion moved forward again to continue its demonstration. But on the other flank things had gone amiss. After complete success had seemed within the grasp of the attack the arrival of strong Turkish reinforcements developed a very dangerous pressure on the covering screen of mounted troops and the time lost through the sea-fog in the morning proved an important factor in preventing the main infantry attack from achieving its objects. Nightfall came just too soon and the net result was that the troops had to withdraw behind the Wadi-Ghuzze. Substantial captures had been made and heavy losses inflicted on the Turks, but the main object of the attack had not been secured.

During the afternoon of the 27th a hostile column was reported as advancing down the coast from Gaza and some reinforcements of Yeomanry arrived to assist Colonel Money's column. However, the reported advance never developed, and in the evening the column re-crossed the Wadi-Ghuzze and the battalion took up an outpost line on the high ground overlooking the Wadi from the West.

April, 1917

In this line the next fortnight was spent, mainly in improving defences, a task in which the Turks also were busily engaged—and to only too good effect as appeared when, in the middle of April, the second attempt on Gaza was launched. This time the battalion's part was a definite attack, not a mere demonstration, though the ground to be crossed was nearly identical with that traversed on March 26th. The Fifty-Third Division was to push forward with its left on the coast, covering the left flank of the main attack against the Ali el Muntar defences South of Gaza. Its first task was to secure a jumping-off line beyond the Wadi-Ghuzze. This was achieved with little trouble on the evening of April 16th, the battalion being in reserve, and then on April 18th the real attempt began. The

GAZA.

first objective of the 160th Brigade was a hill S.W. of Gaza known as Samson Ridge, after which, if the main attack had got on equally well, the advance was to be continued against a set of trenches just East of the village of Sheik Ajlin. The 2/4th formed the left of the brigade with the 159th Brigade beyond it and the 2/10th Middlesex on the right. April 18th, 1917 2/4th Batt.

At 8 a.m. the advance began, C and D Companies, under Captain Dowling and Major Downes, leading. Almost at once they came under sharp fire, especially from the left, which flank was " in the air," as the 159th Brigade had been held up, and casualties soon began to mount up. Colonel Money[1] was among those hit, on which Captain R. S. Cobb assumed command until in the evening Major Hohler, of the Middlesex Regiment, was sent up. By 11 a.m. A and B, under Captain Hodgson and Lieut. Wood, had had to reinforce the leading waves, and by mid-day the attack seemed about to be completely checked, mainly owing to the heavy casualties among the officers and the enfilade fire from both flanks. The tank attached to the battalion had broken down early in the day, the Division on the right was making very little progress, the Turkish fire was heavy and accurate. Captain H. de B. Wilson, the Adjutant, was killed about this time and the situation seemed critical. However, supports were forthcoming in the shape of the 4th Royal Sussex, and with their assistance the 2/4th got on the move again. Captain Cobb's skilful handling of his Lewis gun did good service in helping the troops to gain ground, and after a hard fight Samson Ridge was reached and stormed. Lieut. Gregson was killed leading the final rush, while Major Downes, by whose determination and good leading the advance had been inspired, fell badly wounded at the foot of the ridge. By this time the tank had been sufficiently repaired to get forward,

[1] Fortunately his wound was not severe and he was able to resume command on May 1st.

329

GAZA.

April 18th, 1917
2/4th Batt.

and it advanced against the El Arish Redoubt opposite Samson Ridge and did considerable execution, until nearly all its crew were hit by armour-piercing bullets. Indeed it would probably have been taken had not Lieut. Dunkerly pushed forward, ascertained how the tank's gun should be worked, kept up a fire which held the enemy at bay, and then, walking in front of the tank under the very heavy fire, got it moving again so that it was successfully guided back to our lines.

With the tank practically *hors de combat*, the troops exhausted by the hard going and the harder fighting, and the Division on the right held up some way from its objective, the task of re-organizing and consolidating was quite enough, and after about 3 p.m. no further advance was attempted. A certain number of men got beyond Samson Ridge and ably led by Captain Hodgson checked the development of a counter-attack, but at dusk they were drawn back to that position, tools were brought up and under Captain Hodgson's guidance and inspiration a tremendous amount of work was put into the digging of trenches.

April 20th

When the 158th Brigade arrived in the small hours of April 20th the position was quite defensible. But the battalion's casualties had been heavy, Lieut. Evans died of wounds that night, making in all three officers killed, of whom Captain Wilson, one of the original officers of the battalion and a most competent and popular Adjutant, was very specially regretted. Nine officers were wounded, 38 men killed, 145 wounded. But while the Fifty-Third Division had not managed to do more than take its first objective, elsewhere much less had been achieved, indeed, the operations as a whole had been a failure. Still, if the whole operation had failed, the 2/4th had acquitted themselves most creditably as was in some measure recognised by the grant of the M.C. to Major Downes, Captains Hodgson and Cobb, and Lieut. Dunkerley.[1]

[1] Colonel Money received a bar to his D.S.O.

PALESTINE.

After this undisguisable check a stalemate followed in the Palestine theatre of war. It was six months before, under a new commander, a much augmented Force renewed the attack. For the 2/4th this was a period of constant hard work on the trenches, varied by occasional " rests " when training took the place of trench construction. This routine was disastrously interrupted one evening in May when, as the battalion was wending its way down a defile to a reserve area behind the Sheikh Abbas Ridge a German aeroplane dropped a bomb with deadly effect right into the middle of D Company, inflicting over 70 casualties. Captain Dillon and 2nd Lieut. Fricker were wounded, of the men 40 were killed on the spot or died of wounds soon after. It was a terrible and distressing moment, and though there was an ambulance with the column and help was prompt in coming to the wounded D was naturally much disorganized by its crippling losses. Apart from this disaster casualties were low, and though the battalion suffered severely from sandfly fever it was well up to strength both in officers and men when active operations were resumed. *April-Oct., 1917 2/4th Batt.*

The considerable increase in the strength of the E.E.F. since the April failure at Gaza, and still more the vast improvements in its mobility and administrative arrangements, made a far less restricted operation possible. There was no need to hurl the whole force against the formidable defences of Gaza, advantage could be taken of the undue extent of the Turkish line in proportion to their strength to threaten it in several places and so compel them to disperse their troops. The Fifty-Third Division was one of those detailed to operate against Beersheba, being charged with covering the left flank of the troops engaged in the capture of the town. Then when the fall of Beersheba allowed General Allenby to develop the second part of his plan and attack the Turkish defences round Tel el Sharia from the high ground N. and N.W. of Beersheba, the *See Sketch 38*

BEERSHEBA.

October, 1917
2/4th Batt.

Division had again to cover a flank. This time it was the right which it had to protect by an advance against the formidable position about Ain Kohleh and Tel Khuweilfeh, to which the Turkish left had retired.

The 2/4th was thus employed rather in covering movements and diversions than in the main decisive stroke, but it had sufficiently severe fighting even so. Moving out from Deir el Balah to Shellal on October 24th, it held the Shellal defences for three days, pushed forward on the 27th to a position between Beit abu Taha and Beersheba, and then on the 30th advanced across the Wadi Hanafish to a new outpost position overlooking the Turkish railway running N.W. from Beersheba. Colonel Money had left to command the 159th Brigade, so Major Jude commanded the battalion.

Oct. 31st

October 31st, the day of the capture of Beersheba, brought the battalion no actual fighting, for no Turkish counter-attack developed from Sharia to disturb the skilfully planned and well-executed stroke at Beersheba.

Nov. 1st

Nor did the next day, when the Division advanced through Beersheba to the hills North of the town, involve more than a hot march and hard work consolidating the new position about El Muwheile.

Nov. 2nd

Next evening, however, the Seventy-Fourth Division took over the line and the Fifty-Third moved into position for the attack it was to make on the following day.

Nov. 3rd

This was to be delivered against the hills about Ain Kohleh and El Khuweilfeh, the 160th Brigade's immediate objective being a ridge known as 1250, North of Ain Kohleh. The 2/4th, with the 2/4th Queen's on the right, carried out the attack, advancing about 1.30 p.m. from the line which the Imperial Camel Corps was holding. Almost immediately they came under heavy fire, mostly from machine-guns, which, in that rugged and difficult country it was extremely hard to locate and no easier to silence when located, as it was

BEERSHEBA.

almost impossible to get artillery forward along the goat tracks which were the only paths. Moreover the bracken which covered the hills gave splendid cover to snipers and made it hard to see where the enemy's line was. However, the troops got on well, Lieut. Nicoll, who was commanding A Company, being conspicuous for his gallantry and good leading, and by 6 p.m. a line of heights North of the track leading to Ain Kohleh had been reached. Here a halt was made for the night in readiness to advance against Hill 1250 at dawn. 2nd Lieut. Cambridge had been killed and Captain Cobb and Lieut. Baker wounded, but the total casualties were under 40.

Nov. 3rd, 1917 2/4th Batt.

At 4 a.m. on November 4th the battalion stood to, and about an hour later such guns as had been got forward opened a brief bombardment while the machine-guns were taken up on to the hills to give covering fire. At 5.20 the attack started. A Company, on the right, got on well and gained its objective, but as the companies on the left were enfiladed by cleverly placed machine-guns and made little progress, it was quite isolated and dangerously exposed, and Lieut. Nicoll, finding it impossible to maintain his advanced position without support, had finally to fall back, but extricated his men with skill and success. Casualties this day had been more serious, Captain Dutton, Lieut. Edmonds and 2nd Lieut. Darlington had been killed with 40 men, 14 more were missing, and 52 wounded, together with 2nd Lieut. Naughton. But if Hill 1250 had not been carried the Turks had been forced to throw so many men into the fight in this quarter of the field that General Allenby could deliver his decisive stroke against their centre without any fear of a counter-attack by the defenders' reserves. Indeed the Turks delivered more than one counter-attack on the Fifty-Third Division in the course of November 4th and 5th, though none of them achieved any success and all came in for sharp punishment, and

Nov. 4th

BEERSHEBA.

<small>November, 1917
2/4th Batt.</small> the Division and the mounted troops co-operating with it had engaged a disproportionately large part of the Turkish army.

<small>Nov. 5th-8th</small> For the 2/4th R.W.K. November 5th was a day without fighting, but it had proved very difficult to get rations or water up to the troops and the men suffered considerable privations. On the 6th the exhausted battalion was called upon for yet another attempt on Hill 1250, which, like its predecessors, was held up by enfilade machine-gun fire from the left flank. However, other troops captured Tel Khuweilfeh and an adjacent hill, and a Turkish effort to recover this last feature was decisively repulsed, with the result that about 5 p.m. on November 7th the outposts of the 2/4th, facing Hill 1250, saw the Turks opposite them beginning to go. Fire was opened on them, but it was not till next day that the battalion's patrols reported the hill all clear and that parties could be sent out to search for any surviving wounded and to bury the dead; it was then they had reason to realize that the casualties had not been all on the attacking side.

<small>Nov. 8th</small>

On November 9th the battalion moved East towards the Hebron road to support the Camel Corps who were being hotly pressed, but before it got up the Turks had retreated. With this, active operations on this side ceased for nearly a month. The main interest of the campaign now centred in the vigorous pursuit of the Turkish main body Northwards. Not till the British main body had turned Eastward and was working its way forward into the difficult hill country leading up to Jerusalem did the Fifty-Third Division advance again.

<small>Nov.-Dec., 1917</small>

This month was spent by the 2/4th mostly in the outpost line near Ras el Nukb. It was a quiet period, mainly spent in re-organizing the battalion, for the enemy was quite inactive. Its total casualties had been 7 officers and 163 men, and in addition 3 officers and 129 men were sent to Hospital during November,

GAZA & BEERSHEBA
TO ILLUSTRATE OPERATIONS OF 2/4 R·W·K· 1917
1 = SAMPSON RIDGE. 2 = EL ARISH REDOUBT.

Face Page 334.   SKETCH 38.

PALESTINE.

quite apart from a lot of men who, from fighting over rocky ground, had got cuts and abrasions which turned septic. By the end of the month the battalion was fully 25 per cent. below its November 1st strength. Colonel Beswick, of the R.W.F., arrived on November 20th to take command, upon which Major Jude reverted to second-in-command, the company commanders being now Captain Hodgson, Major Downes, Lieut. Willows and Lieut. Nicoll. This last officer received the M.C. for his gallantry and good leading on November 3rd and 4th, and the same distinction was conferred on the battalion's Chaplain, the Reverend W. H. Aglionby, who had done magnificent work in going out under the heaviest fire to search for the wounded.   *Nov.-Dec., 1917 2/4th Batt.*

On December 4th the Fifty-Third Division began its advance through Hebron on Jerusalem, the 159th Brigade leading. Hebron was reached and occupied without much opposition, and on the 6th the march North was resumed. On the evening of the 8th the battalion was on the ridge just South of Bethlehem, which was entered by patrols next day and found to be clear. On the 10th it moved forward again, and had the extraordinary experience of marching into Jerusalem with its band playing, and of billeting in the Holy City itself. The advance from Beersheba had been carried out in bad weather; and with only one road for troops, guns and all transport it was really remarkable how well the battalion had fared for rations, while it had entirely escaped casualties, for the Turks, engrossed in opposing the advance of the main body from the Westward, offered hardly any opposition to this advance against their flank, although it was bound to render their position untenable if it succeeded. Several days of hard work on the main Jerusalem-Jaffa road followed, and then on December 15th the battalion moved to the Mount of Olives in preparation for an   *Dec. 4th*   *Dec. 9th*   *See Sketch 59*

PALESTINE.

December, 1917
2/4th Batt.

Dec. 17th

attack on the El Aziziye ridge a little way East of Jerusalem.

This ridge was a strong position, but the attack, carried out at dawn on December 17th by the battalion and the 4th Royal Sussex, was a complete success. B Company, led by Major Downes and well supported by the artillery, cleared the first objective at the point of the bayonet with great celerity, and then A and C, passing through, carried on the attack to the second objective and promptly proceeded to consolidate it. Over 100 prisoners were taken at a total cost of less than 20 casualties, and though the Turks made some attempts to counter-attack these were met by heavy fire and broken up before they could really get going. The importance of this well executed little stroke was that it pushed the Turks further away from Jerusalem and gave more room for developing other attacks to the Northward which were undertaken in the next few days. Thanks largely to the fact that these minor operations had allowed the British to take up a really satisfactory line North and East of Jerusalem, the great Turkish attempt to recover the city which was delivered on the 27th was completely repulsed. But it was a time of such real tension that the battalion had to remain in the line on its captured positions from December 17th to 29th. The weather was wet and stormy, and the troops, who were finding outposts nearly all the time, had much discomfort to undergo. They were not sorry when, after a shift of position on December 29th had merely allowed a company and half to be drawn back into reserve, the battalion was really

Jan. 1st 1918

relieved on January 1st, and taken back to billets in Bireh. After the disappointments in which the 2/4th had shared in the spring it was something to have taken so creditable a part in achievements of such considerable military importance, which had perhaps even more value for political and propaganda purposes.

MESOPOTAMIA.

Further afield the 1/4th and 1/5th Battalions had carried on with their duties, which differed but little from the ordinary routine of a British infantry battalion at an Indian station. The ever-increasing demands for officers for the Indian Army, now under the able administration of Sir Charles Monro in process of rapid expansion, meant that the Territorial units in India were largely drawn upon to provide them. The men who had joined the Territorials before the war or had filled them up at its outbreak provided much excellent material for officers, and many N.C.O.'s and men left both battalions to take commissions. Otherwise the year passed uneventfully for them both till in the autumn the increase of the Indian Army made it possible to mobilize two more Divisions for Mesopotamia, and after nearly three years of garrison duty in India the 1/5th R.W.K. found themselves warned for active service. It was on October 20th that these orders arrived; six weeks later the battalion, which had been brought up to its war establishment by drafts of 100 each from the 4th Buffs and the Kent Cyclists, left Jubbulpore for Bombay. On December 5th it embarked, and after a six days' voyage landed at Basra on the 11th. Five days later it started for Baghdad, where the end of the year found it concentrated in Hinaidi Camp as a unit of the 54th Brigade of the Eighteenth Indian Division. It is some indication of the changes which the composition of the battalion had undergone since the outbreak of war that Colonel Frazer had with him only five other "pre-war" officers of the battalion, Majors Clark, Hills and Neame and Captains Richardson and Hay.[1]

1917
1/4th - 1/5th Battalions

Oct.-Dec., 1917
1/5th Batt.

Dec. 16th

---

[1] The other officers who proceeded to Mesopotamia with the 1/5th were: Captains C. B. Pirie, J. M. Prichard, T. L. Engledow (Adjt.), J. P. Carvoso, E. W. Carvoso, Lieuts. E. M. Neame, T. A. Stokes, J. H. Biggs, and H. F. Hawes, 2nd-Lieuts. C. E. Staddon, V. H. Russell, H. P. Taylor, J. A. Mollen, R. H. Proctor, H. E. Crippen, A. R. Key, A. N. W. Clark, W. T. K. Ware, and W. C. Lane, Lieut.- and Quartermaster H. Cooke.

MESOPOTAMIA.

1917
2nd Battalion

Some time before the 1/5th arrived at Baghdad the 2nd Battalion had at last quitted the Euphrates for the Tigris. That battalion had moved back from Khamisiya to Nasiriya early in January, remaining there employed in the usual routine duties till early in June. The Euphrates line was quieter than ever after General Maude's triumphs at Kut and Baghdad, and the only notable event was the arrival in May of a draft of three officers and 398 men. With the complete reversal of the situation in Mesopotamia the maintenance of so large a force on the lower Euphrates was no longer necessary, and in March orders were issued for the transfer of the Fifteenth Division to the Tigris line. This was gradually effected; Divisional Headquarters moved in April, but the 2nd R.W.K. were left at Nasiriya until troops had been collected from the lines of communication to relieve them. Eventually the battalion quitted Nasiriya on June 7th, reaching Baghdad after a fortnight's journey. The change of station was not, however, accompanied by any immediate activity. The great heat precluded active operations in the summer, and by the time that the weather allowed the Fifteenth Division to deal its highly successful blow at the Turkish forces at Ramadi (September 27th) the 34th Brigade had been shifted to the newly-formed Seventeenth Indian Division under Major-Gen. Leslie, once again parting company with General Brooking to the regret both of that officer and of the battalion. This new formation began concentrating round Baghdad in August, and among its brigadiers was an officer of The Queen's Own in Brig.-Gen. R. J. T. Hildyard, who had originally come to Mesopotamia as G.S.O.I. of General Maude's Thirteenth Division. With the Seventeenth Division the 2nd R.W.K. moved up the Tigris in October as far as Sadiyah, covering 47 miles in 31 hours. This move was in connection with General Cobbe's operations which resulted in the capture of Tekrit; it did not,

See Map B

MESOPOTAMIA.

however, involve the battalion in any fighting nor did active contact with the enemy follow when, early in December, the 34th Brigade began relieving the Meerut Division in the advanced positions about Samara on the latter Division being put under orders for Palestine. This move brought the 2nd R.W.K. to Akab, where it took over a section of the outpost line on the left bank of the Tigris and just West of the Shatt el Adhaim. But even here matters were extremely quiet —a few Turkish deserters came in and their mounted patrols were occasionally seen, but nothing disturbed the ordinary routine, and 1917 ended for the 2nd R.W.K. as uneventfully as it had begun.

Dec., 1917
2nd Battalion

CHAPTER XXII

ITALY.

<small>Nov.-Dec., 1917</small>

Among the reasons for the failure of the Cambrai venture to fulfil the high hopes which its earlier stages had raised must be included one which had special importance for The Queen's Own. Had larger reserves been available the advantages gained on the opening day might have been pressed home and relief afforded to the tired and weakened units which were still holding on November 30th the positions they had taken ten days earlier. Had that been possible the results finally achieved might not have fallen so short of the break through which had at first seemed on the point of being attained. Certainly it was by Divisions which were not exhausted and reduced by the earlier fighting that the great German attack on the Bourlon Wood front was held and so terribly punished. But the collapse of the Italians at Caporetto had introduced a most disquieting element into the strategical situation. It became necessary hastily to detach to Italy British and French divisions which might have accomplished great things had they been available to reinforce the Third Army on the 21st of November. Even before the great tank attack was delivered two Divisions were well on the way to Italy, and two others were starting, while a fifth was waiting entraining orders when the Germans made their counter-attack.

<small>Oct.-Nov., 1917
10th & 11th, Battalions</small>

Among these Divisions were the Fifth and Forty-First, so that in all three battalions represented The Queen's Own in a country which neither the 1st nor the 2nd had ever visited in all their wanderings before 1914. The Forty-First were the first of the two to depart for Italy. Since the attack on the Tower Hamlets Ridge it had had an almost enjoyable

ITALY.

time in a quite unfamiliar part of the line, the coastal sector East of Dunkirk. The 11th reckoned their fortnight in Divisional reserve at La Panne the best time they had had in France. Sea-bathing, football, more leave than had yet been possible, mingled with a little training, formed indeed a pleasant change from the horrors and hardships of the Salient; and except for the unpleasant frequency of night-bombing by German aeroplanes and occasional shelling by high velocity guns the sector was distinctly peaceful.

Oct.-Nov., 1917 10th & 11th Battalions

The 10th Battalion had arrived at Bray Dunes over 850 strong, and during its stay there substantial drafts had brought it well up to strength. Colonel Beattie was now in command with Captain Waydelin as Adjutant. Its stay in the coastal sector was quite without incident, and early in November it moved to Teteghem, where it was training for open warfare when orders to entrain for Italy reached it. The 11th had come out of the Salient very much depleted. In Colonel Corfe's absence Major Beadle was commanding, Captain Jiminez second-in-command and Captain R. Kerr Adjutant, while with Captains Lindsay, Rooney, Preston and H. G. Rogers as company commanders, competent and experienced officers were available to superintend the reconstruction of the battalion and the training of drafts. These last were none too plentiful, and the battalion was still 200 under strength when it entrained for Italy on 13th November. It had been about to take over the front line when the orders were received to be ready to proceed to another front; the wildest rumours were immediately current, Mesopotamia, India, Ireland and Egypt, all figured in turn as the undoubted destination of the battalion, though cynics were confident that the next place in which the 11th would find itself would be the familiar but little desired Ypres Salient.

The journey to Italy was most interesting, novelty compensating for its duration and the impossibility of

ITALY.

**Nov., 1917
10th & 11th
Battalions**

leaving the train for long. Halts were frequent but uncertain in duration—as often as not between instead of at stations—and the four days and a half spent on the train would have been irksome but for the enthusiastic welcome which the troops received all along the Riviera, the inhabitants turning out with presents of fruit, tobacco, flowers and food. The concentration area allotted to the Division was around Mantua, the 10th detraining at Isola della Scala, the 11th at Asola; but directly detrainment had been completed the Division had to start forthwith for the Piave, on which river the defeated Italians were rallying. The plan was to move first to the line Montegaldella-Vicenza, which was to be the line of deployment from which a further advance might be made. It was an open question whether the Italians would maintain the Piave line, and such French and British troops as had reached Italy had to hasten to the critical point. Thus the 10th and 11th had to start on their 100 miles' march practically straight from a five days' train journey—no good preparation for strenuous marching. But the men answered well to the calls upon them, and the 11th distinguished themselves by having fewer men falling out than any other battalion in the Division. The difference of the scenery, with the mountains getting nearer and nearer, and vineyards and maize fields instead of the uninteresting lands of Northern France and Belgium, helped to get the men along; and if maps proved inaccurate and billets often uncomfortable, the plentifulness and cheapness of the wine and fruit were sufficient compensation, and it was great to have exchanged the damp and mud and fogs of Flanders for the sun and brightness of Italy.

November 22nd saw the Adige crossed at Oppano by the 10th, at Albaredo by the 11th, and three days later the Brenta also was passed. Two days' rest followed and then another three days' marching took the Division across the 40 miles between Brenta and Piave

ITALY.

and to the foot of the Montello, a ridge which rose somewhat abruptly out of the low ground and was of the greatest tactical importance in the Piave line. This position was to be taken over on the following day from the Italians. _{*(Feb., 1918, 10th & 11th Battalions)*}

This march across Lombardy had been a memorable experience for the 10th and 11th, as well as no small test of march discipline and endurance. The men were extremely heavily laden, carrying 80 or 90 lb. apiece, and to have accomplished it with but few stragglers or sick was a creditable performance. It had also considerable military value; for though even before the arrival of the British and French contingents the Austro-German advance had been stopped, the knowledge that these reinforcements were hurrying forward unquestionably contributed to encourage the Italians to stand on the Piave. Had they abandoned that line it would have been hard to keep the Austrians out of Venice, and the loss of that city must have reacted most unfavourably on the political situation in Italy and might have had far-reaching consequences. The British Divisions who made that march may therefore claim to have rendered thereby an effective service to the Allied cause, even if after arriving at the Piave they were to see scarcely any fighting worth the name. The Australians had the advantage of position and better facilities for observation, so that movement in the front line had to be avoided; but they were unenterprising, and the Piave complicated patrolling and reduced the opportunities of snipers and machine-gunners. Neither the 10th or 11th attempted any serious raid or had to repel a hostile attack. A patrol across the Piave on February 19th led to a brush with the enemy in which Captain Hindle, of the 10th, distinguished himself, extricating his party from a nasty position by his coolness and determination, and bringing back across the river 2nd Lieut. Nisbitt who had been badly wounded. Ptes. Waite and Stone helped greatly in this and

ITALY.

**Feb., 1918
10th Batt.**

received the M.M. A day later 2nd Lieuts. Weston and Anderson led another patrol across, but had to retire on encountering the enemy in force, effecting their withdrawal without casualties.

**Dec., 1917-
Jan., 1918
1st Battalion**

The 1st Battalion did not leave for Italy till nearly a month after the 10th and 11th. It was kept waiting a fortnight for its entraining orders and did not get away till December 12th, when a six days' train journey through Mâcon, Marseilles and Nice brought it to its detraining station at Fontivilla on the 17th. Then it marched to Bolzenella where it remained until the middle of January. The rest and the change of scenery and climate were very welcome to the battalion, and though it did not receive as large drafts as were needed, over a dozen officers joined or rejoined, among them Lieut. H. S. Doe, who had come out with the battalion as R.S.M. in 1914, and Captain Sutherland, who was awarded the M.C. in the New Year's Honours' Lists, as was also 2nd Lieut. Monypenny.

On January 22nd the battalion's rest came to an end, and it set out for the Piave by march-route. Three days' marching brought it to Arcade, not far from the left bank of that river, and on the 29th it went into the front line again. This consisted of trenches running down to the river bank where they expanded into T-shaped posts, communication being maintained by a good lateral trench some way back. The trenches required a great deal to make them habitable, more particularly in the matter of sanitation, but from the defensive point of view the line was satisfactory enough. The Piave bed was wide, consisting of a number of small channels separated by little islands, the streams being as a rule shallow but rapid, and having the inconvenient habit of changing their channels almost nightly as the melting snow from the mountains swelled the river. The enemy's lines were three quarters of a mile distant, and during the 1st Battalion's stay on the Piave his infantry were extraordinarily inactive; they never

ITALY.

ventured into No Man's Land and all the efforts of the battalion's patrols to secure a prisoner proved unavailing. Patrolling was energetically carried on, the difficulty of fording the streams having been surmounted by the construction of light bridges, for the most part consisting of iron, stakes and wire. This and the activity of the enemy's aircraft were the chief features of this time, nearly two months in all. About the middle of March the Division was relieved by Italians and withdrew to billets at Visnadello, whence it moved back by Fassalta to Villafranca, preparatory to returning to the French front. Two large drafts had joined during March as well as a smaller one in February, and as casualties had been extremely low, under 20 for the whole period, it was quite a strong battalion which at last entrained on April 1st for its return " to the war."

<small>Jan.-April, 1918
1st Battalion</small>

The Forty-First Division had preceded the Fifth back to France as on the outward journey. It had been withdrawn from the front before the end of February, had a three days' march to its entraining area and then began its long train journey in the first week of March. By March 7th it was detraining round Doullens. Both 10th and 11th were fairly up to strength; their battle casualties had been insignificant,[1] though the wastage from sickness had been rather higher. Colonel Corfe had rejoined the 11th on February 11th and resumed command, while the New Year's Honours' List had brought M.C.'s to Major Jiminez and 2nd Lieut. R. O. Russell.

<small>10th-11th Battalions</small>

---

[1] The 11th had only 3 killed and 10 wounded.

CHAPTER XXIII

THE LAST WINTER.

Dec., 1917-March, 1918

The battalions of The Queen's Own which had not been selected for transfer to the comparative rest of the Italian front had found the winter of 1917-1918 in France a trying and strenuous time. The shortage of British man-power had already made itself felt by the man in the trenches through the infrequency and inadequacy of the drafts which had arrived to replace the gaps left by the heavy fighting of the autumn. This was to be further accentuated during the winter months, and in consequence the work thrown upon the small number of available rifles was greatly increased. With fewer men to hold the line either it had to be held in insufficient force or each man's turn of trench duty became longer and more frequent. The strain was consequently much greater; and at the same time no one could fail to realise that the war had taken a very unsatisfactory turn for the Allies. The complete collapse in which the Russian Revolution had culminated had altered the balance in the West by releasing for use there the great forces which the Central Powers had till now maintained on the Russian front. Caporetto had been the first-fruits of this change, and the overwhelming force in which the Germans had delivered their great counter-attack at Cambrai was a scarcely less ominous sign. To this the capture of Jerusalem and the continued successes of the British in Mesopotamia were but a poor off-set, except as an indication that on those subordinate fronts the Allies had attained security for all vital interests, and that with something to spare. From the Eastern theatres, then, the reinforcements so urgently needed on the Western front might have been drawn at the beginning of 1918

THE LAST WINTER.

—as indeed they were ultimately to be. That some means must be found to provide reinforcements was only too clear. All through January the 6th R.W.K. never had more than 500 men present with the battalion, the 7th at that time could only find 170 rifles for the firing-line and, if less depleted than the other battalions, the 8th also was much below establishment. Moreover, in the drafts which did arrive there was too large a proportion of returned sick and wounded, officers and men who had been hit more than once having to go out again, while it was notorious that in certain occupations there were still many exempted men of military age and sound physique. Dec., 1917-March, 1918

The 6th Battalion was fairly lucky in the locality in which it spent this period. After re-organizing at Thiennes it moved to the Lys in January and went into trenches in front of Fleurbaix on the 14th. This was the point where the British line had altered least since the autumn of 1914; the sector had usually been "quiet" and if wet was in a fairly good state. On February 13th the battalion had the satisfaction of welcoming Colonel Dawson back, and next day Captain Dove also rejoined and resumed his duties as Adjutant. During the two months and more the 6th spent on this front its casualties only came to 80, and most of these were incurred in a very successful raid on March 9th or in repulsing subsequent two German attacks. Most of this time the enemy were inactive, only shelled at intervals and in little volume and hardly ever attempted to dispute No Man's Land with our patrols. Indeed a "silent" raid in February found the enemy's front line unoccupied and failed to obtain the identifications wanted. 6th Battalion

This did not satisfy Colonel Dawson, who was determined that it should never be said that the 6th had failed to identify their opponents even if the German front line were unoccupied, and directly he took over command he set to work to plan and organize a

THE LAST WINTER.

March, 1918
6th Battalion
fresh raid. He was a great believer in daylight raids, which he considered involved less confusion than a night raid, gave more chance of inflicting casualties and obtaining information, and above all were calculated to impress our men with confidence in their power to do what they liked with the enemy. Colonel Dawson's plan met with a most conspicuous success.

March 9th
On March 9th a party of 200 men under Captain Ashton raided the trenches known as Index and Index Support. The trenches were half-full of water, so they formed up in No Man's Land. This was a tricky business in the half-light of the dawn, but it was admirably conducted, and passed undetected, being well covered by patrols, and then pushing forward the raiders carried the trenches with a rush. The Germans were completely surprised, a machine-gun and nine prisoners of the 371st Reserve Regiment were taken and heavy losses inflicted on the enemy at a cost of 25 casualties. These, however, included the raid commander, who was mortally wounded, but on his fall Lieut. Elliott took command and led the attack with great dash and determination, setting a fine example. Lieut. Brook also distinguished himself by his contempt of danger and his good leading; he made his way into a "pill-box" from which the enemy refused to come out and killed all its occupants.[1] There was a most effective artillery barrage; the wire had been excellently cut, and the raid, thanks to careful organization and good leading, went splendidly. Here, too, the German front line was practically undefended and only at their second line did they offer resistance.

March, 11th
It was probably in revenge for this blow that two nights later the Germans raided the battalion's lines in force, attacking two posts known as Patrick and Kiwi. At the latter they were decisively repulsed, leaving prisoners and a machine-gun behind, but at Patrick Post their advance was favoured by the shell-pitted state of

[1] Both these officers subsequently received the M.C.

THE LAST WINTER.

the ground, which gave so much cover that they could get quite close up and rush the post, overpowering the garrison, 7 of the 12 men being missing. They were promptly ejected, however, and when a week later they tried to repeat the experiment one of their parties was effectively met by rifle and Lewis-gun fire and driven back, while another ran into a raiding party of The Queen's in No Man's Land and was dispersed. When the 6th moved back to Pont de Nieppe on March 20th it could feel quite satisfied with the last two months, especially as three substantial drafts which arrived in February, 98, 162 and 48 strong respectively, had brought it nearly up to strength again, and on March 23rd another 124 other ranks arrived, while during the period nearly 20 officers had joined. *March, 1918 6th Battalion*

The 7th Battalion had a worse experience. After Poelcapelle there had been a brief rest and then the Division returned to the Salient to hold almost its most unpleasant and swampy sector. This was in what had once been Houthulst Forest and now consisted of some 600 acres of broken tree stumps in a water-logged morass littered with the wreckage of the forest and calculated to swallow anyone who might happen to stray off the duck-board paths which were the only means of reaching the front line. Of course, in such ground the enemy's activities were necessarily limited, mud smothered his shell-bursts and serious attacks were out of question as long as the wet weather lasted. The front line here represented the point reached in the attack of November 9th by the little groups who had dug themselves in just inside the Southern edge of the wood, and the posts were for the most part neither well-sited nor bullet-proof; they were hard to get at, and when the weather turned cold and the ground froze, quiet movement through the wood was made impossible by breaking branches whose noise drew the enemy's fire. Apart from one German raid on January 8th, which was beaten off after the enemy had rushed one *Nov., 1917- March, 1918 7th Battalion*

THE LAST WINTER.

Nov., 1917-
March, 1918
7th Battalion

post and made three of its garrison prisoners, the battalion had far more fatigues than fighting. It was its numerical weakness which made the work so specially arduous and difficult. Whether employed as carrying parties for the front line or on making a track for a tramway, a difficult task in a sea of mud, the men were constantly under shell-fire and had in addition a long and toilsome march from their camp to the scene of their labours. As already mentioned the battalion was down to 170 available rifles for one of its turns in the line in January, and though several new officers appeared drafts were infrequent and small until, just as the battalion was leaving the Salient in February, one of 89 men arrived, followed shortly afterwards by Captains Watts and F. C. Lovett, of the recently disbanded 3/4th Battalion, with four subalterns and 190 other ranks. This was doubly welcome because it was composed of very fine material which went far to fill the gaps which Poelcapelle had left in the battalion's ranks.

The quarter to which the Eighteenth Division was transferred was one with which the British forces were not as yet familiar. After many conferences and consultations it had been finally decided that the British should relieve the French from North of St. Quentin to Barisis, and it was to this new frontage that the Eighteenth made its way. It was assigned the centre sector of the front held by the Third Corps on the right of the Fifth Army, its own frontage extending from North of Travecy to Alaincourt. This was 9,000 yards in extent, a long line for one Division, but the obstacle of the Oise which covered the front was calculated to assist the defence and the plain through which the river flowed was normally marshy. Much work was needed on this new frontage, and the Fifth Army, to which it had been assigned, was dangerously weak. With only twelve Divisions to hold over forty miles it

THE LAST WINTER.

had nothing like the force needed to construct the rearward system of defences that had been designed. *March, 1918 7th Battalion*

That the Germans would throw their last ounce into a great offensive in the spring was beyond all doubt; it was their only hope of securing a favourable decision before the arrival of the great hosts which the United States were preparing should turn the numerical balance decisively against the Central Powers; but at this critical moment the resources of Great Britain were falling short. Just as the British Army was having to extend its frontage it proved necessary to reduce its Divisions from thirteen battalions to ten. But the mere numerical loss was not the only serious disadvantage involved in this reduction. It was undoubtedly a handicap to tactical efficiency. The four-battalion brigade was in every respect the better, more convenient and sounder unit. Moreover, those who were accustomed to four-battalion brigades found it hard to adjust themselves and their methods to the alterations consequent on the reduction of battalions to only three. Dispositions and distributions of reserves and supports which worked well with four battalions were thrown out of gear when applied to three only. Unquestionably in the spring of 1918 the task before the British forces was not a little complicated by the as yet unfamiliar organization. Moreover, the breaking up of battalions which had done good service and acquired no small credit for their regiments, and the transfer of battalions to different brigades and even sometimes to new Divisions, were certainly not calculated to increase cohesion or efficiency.

The 7th Battalion was affected by the redistribution. It had to leave the 55th Brigade and the battalions with which it was accustomed to co-operate and was transferred to the 53rd. This had lost the 8th Norfolks and 8th Suffolks, both of which had been broken up; while the 6th Royal Berkshires had changed their

THE LAST WINTER.

March, 1918
7th Battalion

number on being drafted to their 8th Battalion brought in from the First Division. The only unit of the Brigade unchanged was the 10th Essex.

The 7th had left Flanders on February 8th, detraining at Noyon next day and marching to billets at Mondescourt where the draft from the 3/4th joined. After ten days in reserve the battalion took over the right half of the Northern sector of the Divisional front on February 26th, and spent a fortnight in the line. The village of Moy was on the left of the sub-sector, which was held by defended localities, so sited as to command the intervening spaces with cross-fire and to afford mutual support. There was no continuous trench line, but the defensive system was based on the principle of defence in depth, with a " Forward Zone," about a mile in front of the " Battle Zone " or main line of resistance. Further back still there should have been yet another system of defence, a " Rear Zone," but over the greater part of the Fifth Army's front this was an aspiration rather than a fact. Much work was required on both " Forward " and " Battle Zones," especially on the line recently taken over, and with so long a front to hold and so few men to hold it little labour was available for the third line of defences, while training also suffered considerably. Indeed the 7th had a hard fortnight improving the defences of the " Forward Zone," and as the continuous fine weather had much dried up the marshes which filled No Man's Land, vigorous patrolling proved necessary, in which 2nd Lieut. Vaughan was conspicuous for his enterprise and initiative. This fortnight was followed by a week in Brigade reserve at Ly Fontaine, working on the " Battle Zone," and then on March 19th the battalion returned to the " Forward Zone," taking over the same sector as before. That same day Colonel J. D. Crosthwaite, of the London Regiment, whom the battalion already knew as Brigade Major of its new Brigade, took over the command from Colonel

March 19th

THE LAST WINTER.

Cinnamond, who had held it for nine months. A most efficient commander, to whom the meaning of "fear" was quite unknown; Colonel Cinnamond had gone through many hard times with the 7th which had realized that when he led it into action or took over a piece of line nothing would be left to chance, as far as was humanly possible. <small>March, 1918 7th Battalion</small>

The 8th Battalion was more fortunate during this period than either the 6th or the 7th inasmuch as it remained in the same sector for over five months, and was able to profit by the great amount of work it had put into the trenches. In November Colonel Parker finally left the battalion, his health making this imperatively necessary. The 8th owed him much: he had had the heavy task of building it up again after Loos, and though hampered by persistent ill-health had worked steadily and effectively. The 8th had done well under Colonel Parker and parted from him with real regret. Colonel Whitty, who succeeded him, was transferred the next month to one of the newly-organized battalions of the Machine-Gun Corps, on which the command passed to Major Wenyon, who had joined after Loos as a platoon commander and had rapidly made his way up. The 8th had been very fortunate in its commanders, Colonel Whitty's energy and resourcefulness had been of great service to it and had fully earned the D.S.O. awarded him early in 1917, and under Colonel Wenyon it was to maintain to the full the standards it had already established and to achieve some of its greatest successes, largely thanks to the ability with which it was commanded. <small>Nov., 1917 March, 1918 8th Battalion</small>

The first feature of the winter months was a great display of activity aimed at distracting German attention from the Cambrai attack; this involved constant patrolling which cost the battalion a most competent and popular Intelligence Officer in Lieut. H. J. Dunn. Then on the night of February 3rd D Company raided a German post known to the battalion as <small>Nov., 1917</small>

AA   353

THE LAST WINTER.

Feb.-Mar., 1918
8th Battalion

"Herbert's Post," "Herbert" being the name given to a succession of German sentries who had fallen victims to our snipers at this point. The raid was carried out in two parties, both of which got in and engaged the enemy, inflicting a good many casualties. The right party were counter-attacked by the enemy who lined the parados of the trench, but 2nd Lieut. Carville, finding this too high to climb, extricated his party skilfully, shooting two men himself. 2nd Lieut. Crighton, commanding the left party, was hit, whereupon Sergt. Vanner took command, kept the enemy back by skilful bombing and withdrew his men with little loss, being greatly helped by the tenacity with which 2nd Lieut. Janaway's connecting party in the centre covered their retreat.[1]

See Sketch 41

At the end of February the 8th were taken out for a rest, but had hardly reached Corbie, picking up a couple of good drafts on the way, when their orders for a rest were cancelled and they were sent back to the front, this time at Vadencourt, being now in the Nineteenth Corps (Lieut.-Gen. Sir H. E. Watts), which was holding the left centre of the Fifth Army's line. Here it had a long line to hold in open and rolling country, the "Battle Zone" being on the ridge on which Vadencourt Chateau stands, with an outpost line on another ridge 600 yards further East, the chief feature of which was a tumulus in its centre. The field of fire was good, No Man's Land being nearly 1,000 yards in width, and the swampy valley of the little Omignon river gave some protection to the right flank, while the Vermand-Estrées road marked the left of the "Forward Zone." But the line was a long one for a single battalion, and with only three battalions in each brigade the supports and reserves available were below the proportion needed to make the line secure.

[1] 2nd Lieuts. Janaway and Carville received the M.C., Sergt. Vanner the D.C.M., and Sergt. Allen, who had tried to carry 2nd Lieut. Crighton back, got the M.M.

THE LAST WINTER.

As has been mentioned incidentally one battalion of the Regiment had fallen a victim to the cutting down of the brigades. The 3/4th had moved down from Flanders to the Third Army early in December, did some turns of duty in the Flesquières Salient till the end of January, and received the orders for its disbanding at Velu on February 1st. Of the 35 officers and 729 men on its strength nearly 200 went to the 7th Battalion, mostly from C and D Companies, Captain Needham with three other officers and most of A went to the 8th, while Captain T. L. Tanner and five subalterns took the bulk of B to the 6th.

Feb.-Mar., 1918 3/4th Batt.

In its eight months of active service the 3/4th had had no very special opportunities of distinction; it had taken part in no big attack; but its Divisional Commander in taking leave of it spoke of the fine spirit shown by the battalion in everything it had been called upon to do, and the casualties it had suffered, nearly 200 in all, were some indication that it had had not a little to endure.

CHAPTER XXIV.

THE GERMAN ATTACK.

March 21st, 1918
7th & 8th Battalions

When, on March 21st, 1918, the long-expected German attack at last developed The Queen's Own had two battalions in the front line, exposed to the full weight of the terrific bombardment which ushered it in. For both the 7th and 8th Battalions March 21st began a time of severe trial; both were to suffer terribly, the 7th indeed was almost wiped out, both were to do splendidly and add greatly to their laurels. Before the fighting on the front of the Third and Fifth Armies died down in the middle of April two more battalions had become involved, the 6th coming down from the Lys Valley to stem the hostile advance across the Ancre, the 10th, newly returned from Italy, being thrown in at an earlier stage.

7th Battalion
See Sketch 39

The 7th, as already mentioned, had returned to the "Forward Zone" in its Divisional sector South of St. Quentin two days before the attack. It had barely settled down before, on the afternoon of the 20th, the warning "Prepare for attack" came round. A raid on the front of the neighbouring Corps had revealed the fact that the enemy were massing near St. Quentin and must be on the point of attacking.

A night of anticipation was followed at 4.30 next morning by the outburst of the heaviest bombardment the 7th had ever experienced. At that hour it was still dark, but as dawn came nearer it became evident that the morning was going to be shrouded in the thickest of mists, under cover of which the enemy would be able to approach undetected to within 30 or 50 yards. The mist was the greater disadvantage because it presented the conditions which the new system of defence was least well adapted to meet. This depended on good

THE GERMAN ATTACK.

visibility. The whole scheme of defended localities sweeping intervening spaces with cross-fire was paralyzed by the all-pervading mist. The German tactics of "infiltration," pushing forward through weak points or gaps in the enemy's line and so outflanking the positions at which their advance was held up, could not have been tried under more favourable circumstances than on March 21st. Instead of the garrisons of the posts in the "Outpost Zone" having a good field of fire and supporting each other with enfilade fire they were practically blinded; and as the situation of most of the chief redoubts and defended localities and even of the supporting artillery was well known to the enemy, the mist was no obstacle to their being shelled by the map. At the Battalion Headquarters of the 7th all the overhead shelters were destroyed almost at once, the officers' mess being the first to take fire, and the accuracy of the bombardment was on a parallel with its intensity.

<small>March 21st, 1918 7th Battalion</small>

Shortly after the bombardment opened all wires were cut[1] and except for a few runners and wounded men hardly any of A and C Companies who were in the 7th's front posts got back even as far as Battalion Headquarters at Durham Post on the road from Moy to Ly-Fontaine. Actually the German infantry attack did not develop till about four hours after the bombardment began, by which time heavy casualties and much damage had been inflicted by it. About 8 a.m. the platoon of C, which was in Moy itself, was ordered back to its Company Headquarters on the Western edge of Moy, but found German infantry swarming up the little valleys on both sides. A stout resistance was offered by the platoon, who found good targets for rifles and Lewis guns and inflicted many casualties on the enemy before it was overwhelmed. One of the few

---

[1] Sergt. Hubble, the Signalling Sergeant, did splendid work, going out repeatedly, despite the intense shell-fire, to re-establish communication with the companies. He was cut off by the enemy and nearly taken, but ultimately got back to the British lines after dark.

THE GERMAN ATTACK.

<small>March 21st, 1918
7th Battalion</small> survivors, L./Cpl. Purdham, emptied twenty drums from his Lewis gun into the Germans during this fight. Captain Watts and the small party at C's Headquarters, finding the Germans working round both flanks, effected a retirement to Durham Post about 11 a.m. C's post at Le Vert Chasseur further to the right, which 2nd Lieut. E. A. Thomas's platoon was holding, was attacked rather later. 2nd Lieut. Thomas was wounded at the outset, but the platoon sergeant took charge and put up a fine fight, holding the enemy at bay for some time; indeed it was only after he had been killed and the Lewis gun disabled that the post was finally rushed, only three survivors getting away. A Company on the left was also attacked in overwhelming force, but held out with magnificent devotion and tenacity, inspired by the fine examples set by Lieut. S. A. French and Sergt. Coleman, both of whom died at their post. It was overpowered in the end, but apparently rather after C, for at 11.15 a message from it reached Battalion Headquarters, timed 10.25 a.m., and reporting that the Germans had penetrated the line to its right.

But even after the advanced companies had been overpowered the 7th continued to resist stubbornly. The support company, D, at Drummond Post, just East of the Vendeuil-St. Quentin Road, was attacked in great force about 11 a.m. The Germans got close up to the post under cover of the mist and poured in heavy machine-gun fire from both flanks at close range. The post had already been much damaged by the bombardment, and though the survivors of the garrison put up a good fight they were soon overwhelmed, a few only escaping.[1] This left B Company and Battalion Headquarters manning Durham Post against which the Germans now pressed on.

---

[1] Lieut. Eason, the Company Commander, was among them, managing to reach Battalion Headquarters.

DURHAM POST.

This was first attacked soon after 10 a.m.,[1] but the enemy advancing across the open were driven off by rifle-fire. *(March 21st, 1918, 7th Battalion)* Renewing the attack they got into the post but were promptly ejected. By 11 o'clock, however, they had surrounded it, and a message reporting that the post was still holding out reached Brigade Headquarters shortly before midday. About 11.30 a large body of Germans massing in a sunken road before attacking were skilfully enfiladed by a section directed by the Adjutant, Lieut. Rapson. He was mortally wounded in doing this, but heavy casualties were inflicted on the enemy and the attack was nipped in the bud. About the same time Lieut. Webb, the signalling officer, was hit, and Captain Vaughan, of B Company, was disabled by a wound received when clearing out some Germans who were creeping under the wire; and then at 12.30 Colonel Crosthwaite sent off his last runner down a sunken road with the message, " Boche all round within 50 yards except rear. Can only see 40 yards, so it is difficult to kill the ' blighters.' "

For some hours longer Durham continued its gallant resistance; repeated efforts by the enemy to get in were repulsed by rifle-fire or by bombers in a trench which Lieut. Eason was defending. Soon after 2 p.m. the Colonel was hit and rendered unconscious, and then when the mist lifted the survivors could see the Germans already a long way in rear and realized that there was no hope that a counter-attack would extricate them. Under such circumstances surrender was inevitable.

So effective, however, had been the fight put up in the " Forward Zone " that at midnight the " Battle Zone " of the Eighteenth Division was still intact. If the 7th had been overwhelmed it had done its work and exacted a high price from the enemy. Losses had been heavy;

[1] It is some indication of the way in which the defensive system was disorganised by the fog that the reserve company should have been attacked before even the outposts had been overcome.

THE RETREAT OF THE SEVENTH.

March 21st, 1918
7th Battalion

of the 7th Captain McDonald, the second-in-command, who had been sent back to Brigade Headquarters about 9 o'clock, could collect less than 20, and the Buffs and Berkshires, if in slightly better case, were the merest fragments. But the Germans had been hard hit, too. Had they fared no better elsewhere than they did against the Eighteenth Division, March 21st would have been a black day indeed for them. It appeared from the accounts of prisoners that they had put four Divisions in against the Eighteenth but not even the whole of the objective assigned to the first of them had been reached. But the Divisions on both flanks of the Eighteenth had not managed to keep their "Battle Zones" intact, indeed on the left the Germans were well behind the line on which the Eighteenth were standing;

See Sketch 40

the 54th Brigade, therefore, instead of being available for a counter-attack, had to form a defensive flank. Accordingly, at 1 a.m. on the 22nd, orders had to be given for the Division to conform to the movements of the Corps on the flanks and to fall back behind the Crozat Canal, where a stand was made from about North of Quessy past Menessis to Jussy.

March 22nd

In the fighting of March 22nd along the Canal the remnant of the 7th R.W.K. played little part; it had been taken back to Frieres-Failloeul, where another officer and 60 men, details who had not been in the line, joined Captain McDonald, whose detachment was now organized as one Company of a composite battalion along with the Brigade Trench Mortar Battery and the survivors of the 8th R. Berkshires. The Germans pressed their attacks with vigour, but a heavy price was exacted for such ground as they gained, and when they did get across prompt counter-attacks thrust them back. The Eighteenth had the satisfaction of maintaining its position throughout March 22nd, but when the enemy renewed his attacks next morning it was found that he had managed to get round both flanks and that a retire-

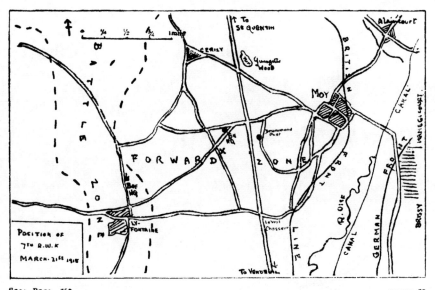

THE RETREAT OF THE SEVENTH.

ment was necessary. In this the 53rd Brigade's composite battalion, till then in reserve, came in for some sharp fighting before retiring to Villequier Aumont, where a stand was so successfully made that when a further retirement to Commenchon proved necessary late at night it was practically unmolested. <small>March, 1918 7th Battalion</small>

Next day saw the survivors of the 7th R.W.K. on the extreme right of the divisional line near Caillouel next the French. There had been time to dig in well and in consequence, despite the heavy shelling to which the line had been subjected, casualties were few and the enemy's advance was well held. But once again the troops on the flank gave, and the Division had to retire during the night through Mondescourt to the Appilly-Grandru road where another stand was made. This was a most successful effort. The high ground overlooking Mondescourt on which the composite battalion and the 8th East Surreys were standing was a good position, and the two battalions, though suffering severely from machine-gun fire, were able to inflict heavy casualties on the enemy and to fight a thoroughly satisfactory rear-guard action. Casualties were heavier this day, the R.W.K. having nearly 40; but the enemy were checked for several hours and the stubborn stand of the 53rd Brigade went far to prevent the Germans from intercepting the Division's retirement over the Oise. This was safely accomplished on the night of March 25th-26th, and the next day saw the little fragment of the 7th in billets at Pontoise. <small>March 24th</small> <small>March 25th</small> <small>March 26th</small>

But it was not to get a rest; although the French, who now interposed between what was left of the Third Corps and the enemy, had checked the German advance at the line of the Oise, the pressure on Amiens was such not even the exhausted and shattered Eighteenth Division could be given rest. It had, therefore, to start at once, and moving by Nampcel and Boves reached Gentelles, just S. of Amiens, on the 28th. Here the composite battalion took up a position

THE RETREAT OF THE SEVENTH.

<small>March, 1918
7th Battalion

See Sketch 45</small> S. and E. of the village but moved forward in the evening to a new position between Hangard and Villers-Bretonneux with the French on the right. This brought it into the front line again and during the next day (March 30th) it was subjected to a heavy bombardment, as the Germans were attacking in force to the South, and it suffered several casualties. That evening it was relieved and taken back to Gentelles, where it was to be reorganized.

On the way round from Pontoise the 7th had picked up its transport at Mantebray and a few officers and men had rejoined from leave or employments, but the battalion as it had existed on the morning of March 21st had been almost obliterated. Sixteen officers, including Colonel Crosthwaite and Captains Watts and Godly, were missing along with the Chaplain (the Rev. G. C. R. Cooke) the M.O. (Captain Moore) and 577 other ranks; two other officers were wounded, and for the reconstruction of the battalion there was only the scantiest nucleus. But no time could be allowed for reconstruction. There was available as reinforcements a body of 20 officers and 500 men, known as the 12th Entrenching Battalion, and this unit was transformed there and then into three companies of the reconstituted 7th R.W.K., Captain McDonald's party, who formed the fourth company, B, serving as a link with the old battalion. Colonel W. Hodson, M.C., of the Cheshires, now took command, and on <small>April, 1st 1918</small> the evening of April 1st this new 7th R.W.K. was thrown into the fight. By this time the character of the battle had greatly changed; the great German offensive was in its last phase; if the Allied line was still to be pushed back in places the long retreat was over.

<small>March 21st
8th Battalion</small> The 8th Battalion's experiences in the great ordeal had been not unlike those of the 7th. March 21st had found it also in the "Forward Zone," it had been subjected to the same tremendous bombardment and had been attacked in great force and under the same

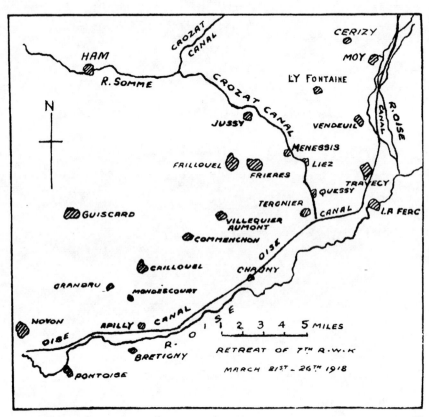

VADENCOURT.

disadvantageous conditions of weather. It added not a little to the strain upon its officers and men that they had just completed a period of ten very hard days and nights in the front line, in which there had been any amount of work and hardly any sleep, 6 officers and over 100 men had been on patrol every night in No Man's Land, which at this point was very extensive, and the whole battalion was very much in need of the relief which was its due.

March 21st, 1918
8th Battalion

Of the two companies in its advanced positions B, on the right, was first attacked by infantry about 5 a.m., when parties of the enemy began attempting to penetrate between the strong points in the "Forward Zone." None of these met with any success, but about 8 a.m. matters became acute, for the next battalion on the right was rushed and overcome, and almost at once the enemy developed an outflanking movement along the Omignon Valley. B were warned just in time to blow up a bridge over the Omignon and to arrange for the defence of the threatened flank. Before long the enemy were pressing hard in front and were well established on the right flank, while simultaneously they began to work down the Bellenglise-Vermand Road and to threaten the company's left also. Nevertheless B put up a splendid fight, beat off all the attacks on its front, and had the satisfaction of punishing the enemy heavily. Not till ammunition failed did B give way, and even then made a desperate effort to cut its way with the bayonet through the Germans who had by this time completely surrounded it. Captain Allworth and most of the survivors were taken, hardly any getting back to the main position.

See Sketch 41

D Company, on the left, had a similar experience. The mist enabled the enemy to penetrate unperceived between its posts, which were overwhelmed one by one, and by 11 o'clock the last of them had gone. But the time which the stubborn defence of the "Outpost Zone" had secured proved invaluable. Had the outposts been

VADENCOURT.

March 21st, 1918
8th Battalion

rushed at once the garrison of the main position at Vadencourt must have been caught like rats in a trap, and had Vadencourt gone the Division would have stood but a poor chance. The delay the outpost companies imposed on the enemy, four hours at the lowest computation, meant that the defenders of the main position were able to deal with the attack in broad daylight and with the mist gone. Some time before 11 a.m. an attack had developed against the main position on the second ridge. It came mainly from the right up the road from Maissemy which had evidently been taken. But the steps which had been promptly taken to destroy the bridge over the Omignon and to form a defensive flank enabled the defence to hold the Germans at bay; the left was secure enough, for the 3rd Rifle Brigade were holding on well, so the enemy had no alternative but to deliver frontal attacks and presented targets of which full advantage was taken, for before mid-day the fog had cleared away. Once a whole battalion came diagonally across the front and was extremely heavily punished, and all the afternoon the 8th maintained its position unshaken, beating off a succession of attacks in force. About 7 p.m. the Germans overcame the resistance of the post at Cooker Quarry on the left, and then began to threaten the 8th from the higher ground on that flank. Nevertheless, until dark the battalion hung on, though both its flanks were now " in the air," keeping the enemy at bay, and then got away covered by a rear-guard under Lieut. Goulden and 2nd Lieuts. Pfeuffar and Tiley. Thanks to this party's determined stand the retirement to the " Battle Zone," the so-called " Brown Line," was carried out unmolested and the new line was satisfactorily taken up and organized, the rear-guard itself managing to get back, to the general satisfaction and surprise. But it was not really very surprising if the Germans should have been incapable of pursuing; the heavy price they had paid for the " Outpost Zone " of

THE RETREAT OF THE EIGHTH.

the Twenty-Fourth Division had clearly taken all the sting out of the attacking Divisions. Sir Douglas Haig's despatch of July 20th 1918 has spoken of the "vigorous resistance of the Twenty-Fourth Division," and the Division had done splendid service by its determined defence of the ridge North of the Omignon. *[March 21st, 1918, 8th Battalion]*

Next morning the German attack was renewed in great force and once again it was favoured by mist. The defence was handicapped by the losses which its artillery had sustained on the previous day, but again the Twenty-Fourth made the Germans fight hard and pay dearly for trifling gains. More than once their attacking waves reached the wire, but none got through in front of the 8th R.W.K., and many who had taken refuge in trenches and shell-holes in No Man's Land were dislodged by rifle-grenades and shot down as they sought to escape. All through the morning the defence held, but bad news came in from the flanks. The enemy was exploiting his advantage at the points where, like Hargicourt and Templeux le Guerard, he had been most successful on the previous day, and by mid-day he was reaching Vermand and Bernes and was round both the Twenty-Fourth's flanks. *[March 22nd]*

Thus about 2 p.m., after what has been described as "a really satisfactory morning," the 8th and two companies of the 13th Middlesex, who had reinforced it, had to go. Their line of retirement lay to the S.W. towards Monchy Lagache, and the move was carried out most successfully, the punishment which the Division had inflicted on its opponents proving once again its surest safeguard. On the rearward way it passed through one of the few Divisions available in reserve, the Fiftieth, deployed on the line Happencourt-Villéveque-Boucly, and under its cover Monchy Lagache was reached and the battalion was gratified to find its transport and a meal. But the enemy's pressure was still so heavy that a further retirement was inevitable; and next day saw the Twenty-Fourth Division on its *[March 23rd]*

THE RETREAT OF THE EIGHTH.

March 23rd, 1918
8th Battalion

way back to cross the Somme at Falvy, covered by the 72nd Brigade and some hastily collected reinforcements. At 10 o'clock the 8th received orders to withdraw and reached the bridges without much difficulty, though the rear party, the 3rd Rifle Brigade and some 9th East Surreys, were more severely pressed. But that day's trial for the 8th came later; after reaching Licourt, four miles West of the river, it was suddenly recalled to the Somme, as the position was reported to be unsatisfactory. It arrived, however, to find it was not required and could go back to Licourt, so the men, already utterly spent with nearly three days of fighting and marching with little rest and scanty rations, had the extra eight miles for no purpose. Still the spirit which the 8th showed was really extraordinary. The battalion kept together in wonderful fashion. Time after time the strength was checked and it was proved that there was not a single man unaccounted for; once three men got cut off, joined another unit, and after wandering all night managed to rejoin their own battalion late next evening. Badly wounded men insisted on keeping with their companies and were with difficulty induced to go to the ambulance, though in the days of ordinary trench warfare they would no doubt have quite welcomed a " blighty " and been off to hospital with promptitude.

March 24th
See Sketch 42

March 24th saw the 8th moving backward again, this time to Chaulnes, only to be ordered off South to Fonches, as the enemy had forced his way over the Somme between the Eighth and Twentieth Divisions and was pressing on. Accordingly, after as speedy a march as was possible, a position was taken up along the Fonchette-Hattencourt road, the 8th now having the remnants of the 1st North Staffords attached to it. Great efforts were made to improve the position, of

March 25th

which work the battalion was to reap the benefit next day, when it was fiercely attacked early in the afternoon. This was one of the hardest fights of the whole

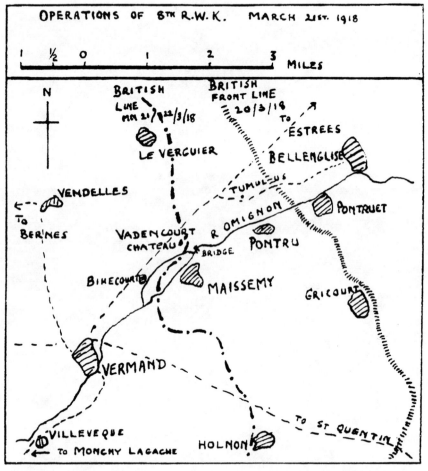

FONCHES CROSS ROADS.

period. The 8th were under heavy fire and the enemy came on in force. The troops on the left were forced to throw their flank back almost at right angles and the position in this quarter was very insecure till the 73rd Brigade managed to push forward to the line of the Fonchette-Omiecourt road. But despite the danger to its flank the 8th stuck resolutely to its trenches and beat off repeated attacks in force, though these were backed up by many machine-guns and by field-guns pushed up to point-blank range. Casualties were heavy. More than one officer fell who had come unscathed through the thick of the earlier fighting. Captain Ewen was killed, 2nd Lieut. Cryer, the acting Adjutant, though badly wounded, remained at duty, setting a fine example and actually assisting in a counter-attack, and the position was held. One wave of the attack left a highwater mark in a party established in old trenches 20 yards from A Company's line, but a prompt and dashing counter-attack led by 2nd Lieut. B. Stephens dislodged them and sent the survivors flying. The 8th had been in many hot places, but undoubtedly Fonches Cross-Roads must rank among the hottest, and the tenacity and determination with which the men fought was infinitely to their credit. It would have been good in fresh troops, after all the 8th had been through it was marvellous. [March 25th, 1918 8th Battalion]

That evening orders were received for yet another retirement, this time to Hallu. To withdraw with the enemy at such close quarters seemed almost impossible, but it was done; and by 3.30 a.m. the battalion was at Hallu, exhausted but refreshed by a meal, and that a hot one which the Transport Section, under the indefatigable Captain Arnaud and his resourceful assistants, Sergt. Shepherd and Corpl. Verrall,[1] managed somehow to produce. But even here there was no long stay. Renewed German attacks once again broke through [March 26th]

[1] The N.C.O.'s subsequently received the M.S.M., a well-merited reward.

THE RETREAT OF THE EIGHTH.

March 26th, 1918
8th Battalion

beyond the right of the 72nd Brigade. Then just as a retirement in echelon from the right was being started the Germans broke through further to the left and threatened envelopment. They were within 200 yards of the 8th but were so hotly received that they could not close, and thanks to a devoted party of the 9th East Surreys, who sacrificed themselves to hold the enemy up, most of the 72nd Brigade got away again.

On reaching Warvillers that evening the 72nd Brigade was re-organized as a composite battalion under Colonel Wenyon, A and C Companies of the 8th still retaining their existence, and this unit took up a position N.E. of Rouvroy, which it maintained for some

March 27th

time next day, despite the loss of Rouvroy. All the German attempts to debouch from the village were stopped, and the ground was held long enough to allow yet a new line covering Vrely and Warvillers to be taken up. Here the composite battalion was on the right in front of Warvillers and gave the

March 28th

enemy a bad time when he attacked next morning. Once again the 8th was tried to the utmost; it was fighting at the tip of a very long and very attenuated salient and the men were utterly spent and exhausted. Still their resistance was as determined as ever. Repeated efforts of the Germans to advance were stopped by rifle-fire, but with ammunition at last beginning to run short—most of the survivors of the 8th had fired thousands of rounds by this time—full advantage could not be taken of targets, so a further retirement was necessary, first to the line Caix-le-Quesnel and then when the right of this was turned to the Bois de Senecat N.W. of Moreuil.

March-April, 8th Battalion

Amiens was now unpleasantly near and must have gone had the retirement had to continue, but the determined resistance of the troops had done its work. The last retirement had brought the Twenty-Fourth Division back through the so-called "Amiens Defence line," and it was now in second line behind the

LIEUT.-COLONEL H. J. WENYON. D.S.O.
Commanded 8th Battalion. 1917. 1918.

BREVET MAJOR T. LIEUT.-COLONEL N. L. WHITTY. D.S.O
Commanded 8th Battalion. 1916-1917.

THE RETREAT OF THE EIGHTH.

Twentieth Division, holding from Thezy on the Moreuil-Amiens railway to the Domart-Amiens road. Here it remained until April 4th when it side-stepped, still in second line, to the left to Bois l'Abbe behind Villers-Bretonneux. *March-April, 1918 8th Battalion See Sketch 45*

During these days the enemy's attacks South of the Somme still continued, but without the overwhelming numbers and vigour which had marked his earlier strokes. The line fluctuated, but if ground was lost in places as a whole the German progress was stayed. The remnants of the 8th, now only five officers and little over 100 other ranks, did not have to go into the front line during this week, and though occasionally shelled, so that they had a few casualties, they got some chances of rest and clean clothes. At last, on April 5th, they were relieved and taken right back to St. Blimont, near St. Valery, to be brought up to strength again. It had been a strenuous and terrible fortnight, of heavy casualties and heavy fighting, of tremendous exertions with hardly any rest; but the battalion had never lost its fighting spirit. Indeed the 8th had surpassed itself. What it had been through before, even in Delville Wood, was insignificant in comparison with what it had gone through in this time. In the words of one of its officers " every man was putting out the greatest he had in him to do," and the battalion's record in these days is beyond praise. It had turned repeatedly to smite the enemy hard every time. If it had given ground it had exacted a full price and overflowing for every yard it yielded. What it owed to Colonel Wenyon's leadership during this time of trial every survivor will emphatically acknowledge, and the bar to the D.S.O. which he received, was richly earned, as were the bar to R.S.M. Rankin's D.C.M., the M.C.'s awarded to Captains S. G. Thompson and Arnaud, Lieuts. Bowen and Goulden and 2nd Lieuts. Cryer, Tyler and Stephens, and the D.C.M.'s bestowed on Corpl. Cherriman and Pte. A. E. Smith.

CHAPTER XXV

THE ELEVENTH DISBANDED.

March, 1918
10th & 11th
Battalions

Long before the 7th and 8th Battalion had succeeded in bringing their pursuers to a stand two other battalions of The Queen's Own had been involved in the great struggle. Of these the 10th was the first to become engaged. Returning from Italy it had detrained in the neighbourhood of Doullens in the first week of March and had since then been quartered at Beaudricourt. The battalion had returned somewhat below establishment, but on March 16th it was brought well up to strength by a draft of five officers and 250 men. But this reinforcement was only available because a most regrettable measure had had to be adopted. On the Forty-First Division's return to France the order had gone out that it, too, was to be cut down to ten battalions, and as one of the junior units of the Division the 11th was among the three to be reduced.

11th Batt.

It may safely be asserted that on no other grounds would the 11th have been selected for reduction. The reputation it had so soon established as a fighting unit, which it had maintained and enhanced in action after action, the remarkable number of honours won by its officers and men, the fact that it was nearly always selected for any particularly difficult task, all marked it out as one of the battalions that the Division could least afford to lose. Brig.-Gen. Towsey, under whom it had served so long, had always sworn by the 11th, whom he was wont to call "Corfe's Irregulars," and both he and the Divisional Commander, Major-Gen. Lawford, were emphatic in their regret at having to part from such a battalion, and in their recognition of the merit of its achievements. The junior Service battalion had certainly added pages to the annals of The

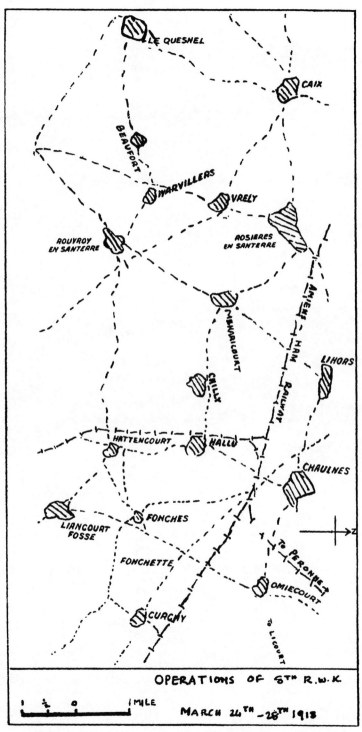

THE GERMAN ATTACK.

Queen's Own by which even its records are notably enriched; it had from the first set itself the ideal of reaching the standards of discipline, determination, tenacity and enterprise, which membership of the Regiment involved. It had attained that aim in no meagre measure. While the bulk of the 11th went off to Reinforcement or Entrenching battalions the draft which joined the 10th included Colonel Corfe himself, whose splendid example and leadership had been so important a factor in the great successes of the 11th. With him came Major Jiminez, Captains R. Kerr and C. F. Hall and Lieut. Hale, Colonel Corfe taking over command of the battalion from Major Wallis, who had been commanding since March 1st when Colonel Beattie had left on a month's special leave. March 1918, 10th & 11th Battalions

When the bombardment which crashed down on the British lines on the morning of March 21st proclaimed in unmistakable fashion the beginning of the German attack, there was little delay about getting the Forty-First Division to the front. It was actually on its way to Albert when the battle opened, but its destination was altered and the trains diverted, and before midnight the 10th R.W.K. had detrained at Achiet le Grand. Next afternoon it pushed forward to Fremicourt on the Bapaume road, and at 5 o'clock orders were received to prepare a position South of Beugnatre which was to join up with the 122nd Brigade on the Beugnatre-Bapaume road. The work had barely been started before the order was cancelled, and the 10th was ordered forward to Beugny to relieve the troops who were holding a line N. and N.E. of that village. These troops belonged for the most part to the Sixth Division, which had been in front line near Lagnicourt when the attack started and had been forced back after two days of heavy fighting and stubborn resistance to a line four miles in rear. March 21st, 10th Batt.

March 22nd
See Sketch 43

By 3 a.m. on March 23rd the 10th was in position, and before daybreak new trenches had been dug, and all March 23rd

371

VAULX VRAUCOURT.

March 23rd, 1918
10th Batt.

four companies were in line, A B C and D from right to left, facing about North just West of Morchies. On its left, though not actually in touch with it, for there proved to be a gap on this flank of nearly 1,000 yards, was the 124th Brigade opposite Vaulx-Vraucourt, on its right the 11th Queen's with the Nineteenth Division beyond them and nearer Beugny. The position was not a good one, the line ran through a valley and observation of what was happening on the flanks was difficult. During the early morning, however, the enemy made little serious attempt to press, though he started shelling about 8 a.m. and machine-guns caused some casualties. One of these was successfully rushed by a patrol ably led by Sergt. White, the crew being killed or taken, but at first the battalion had had few good targets. About 10 a.m. the enemy began to show in strength, delivering an attack in mass which was beaten back, while a whole battalion advanced over the ridge on the 10th's left flank, giving its Lewis-gunners a chance of which they took full advantage. From this time the shelling got heavier, and the enemy attacked repeatedly.

Against the 10th they made no progress, but between 10 and 11 the enemy pushed forward through the gap on the left of the 10th, and about the same time the troops on the right of the 11th Queen's retired. Soon after midday the Germans reached Lebucquière, South of the Bapaume road. On this the Forty-First Division issued orders for its advanced line to retire in conformity with the Nineteenth Division, who were falling back on Beugny. These orders apparently reached The Queen's, some of whom, though not their battalion headquarters, withdrew about 2.30 p.m. as ordered, but they never got to the 10th R.W.K., who continued to maintain their position long after their flanks had been uncovered by the retirement and though the enemy were some distance in rear. Indeed it was 6 p.m. before the Germans finally managed to overcome

372

VAULX VRAUCOURT.

their resistance. About 1 p.m. a runner who had been sent with a message to Brigade Headquarters had returned reporting that the enemy were between the battalion and its brigade and that it was impossible to get through, and shortly afterwards the enemy had begun to threaten from the flanks the trench and sunken road in which the headquarters of the two battalions[1] were defending themselves. For some time these were kept at bay, but converging attacks in increasing strength at last compelled the survivors to surrender to save the numerous wounded who had been brought in to this post. Colonel Corfe himself was among the wounded and the position was perfectly hopeless. The front line companies held out as long, they beat off all attacks and inflicted heavy losses on the enemy, until all ammunition was expended. Casualties had been heavy and the position had long been hopeless. But their long stand had been of great value in keeping the Germans back and enabling the main position of the Division to be maintained intact.

March 23rd, 1918 10th Batt.

To this line but few of the 10th ever got back. Captain Holden displayed great resource in extricating a substantial part of A Company, fighting his way back to the new defensive line in front of Beugnatre through the enemy who threatened to envelope him; here he collected his men with a few survivors of the other companies, but they were a scanty remnant, well under 100 in all. In this work he received great assistance from 2nd Lieut. Cheel and C.S.M. Cooper, both of whom distinguished themselves greatly. Colonel Corfe himself, Major Jiminez, Captains Waydelin and Hall, ten subalterns and over 400 men were returned as "missing." Two officers, 2nd Lieuts. Percy and Cooper, were wounded and the men known to be either killed or wounded came to nearly 50. Those who had reached Beugnatre were promptly reinforced with all the details, some 70 or so, whom Major Wallis

[1] The 11th Queen's had their headquarters in touch with the 10th.

THE GERMAN ATTACK.

March, 1918
10th Batt.

could collect from the transport lines, but they saw no more fighting in this battle, being placed in reserve positions near Bihucourt, when next evening they fell back to Gommecourt. Here a defensive flank was taken up reaching back to Fonquevillers, but on the evening of the 25th the whole 123rd Brigade, now a mere fragment, was withdrawn to Bienvillers to be hastily reorganized before being put into line again near Ablainzeville on the 27th, by which time the 10th's "fighting strength" had been brought up to 18 officers and 204 men, with Major Wallis in command. The 10th's share in the great battle had been briefer than that of either the 7th or 8th, and it had not been fortunate. The miscarriage of the orders which should have reached it turned its own tenacity into a misfortune. It was hard in particular on Colonel Corfe, whose fine record as the commander of a hard-fighting battalion was likely to have brought him before long to the command of a brigade, that his first action at the head of the 10th should have ended in his falling into the enemy's hands. But the fight which the 10th had put up did not go unrecognized; Captain Holden received the D.S.O., 2nd Lieut. Cheel the M.C., C.S.M. Cooper a bar to the D.C.M., Sergt. White the D.C.M., and L/Cpl. Laing and Ptes. Russell and Taylor the M.M.

6th Battalion

Two days after misfortune had overtaken the 10th Battalion the 6th took up the effort to stem the German advance. This battalion had been pushed off in haste from Pont de Nieppe on the 23rd, and after a long and tiring journey in motor-buses had arrived at Bouzincourt just North of Albert early on March 25th. After some hours of waiting the 37th Brigade at last received orders to cross the Ancre and take up the line Montauban-Bazentin le Grand, but as it moved forward these orders were cancelled and Contalmaison substituted as its goal. However, as its leading battalion, The Queen's, reached Ovillers, the Forty-Seventh Division demanded the assistance of the brigade in a counter-

March 25th
See Sketch 44

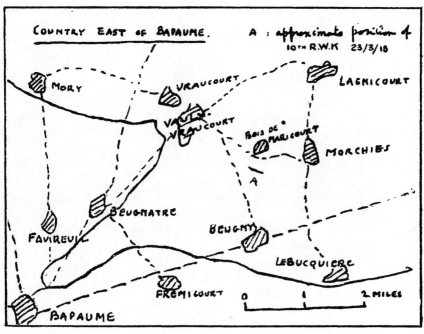

THE STAND ON THE ANCRE.

attack on Pozières on which place the Germans were reported to be advancing. The Queen's and the battalion were detailed for this but before the attack could be launched it also was cancelled and orders were issued to take up an outpost line outside the Bapaume-Albert road near Ovillers, the battalion being on the right of the brigade with the Forty-Seventh Division beyond it. In this position the night was spent. Patrols found Pozières unoccupied, so a screen was formed to cover the destruction of a vast dump at that village which was finally fired about 9.45 p.m. But a position East of the Ancre could no longer be maintained and during the night the Forty-Seventh Division and the fragments which had rallied on it fell back to the right bank, the 37th Brigade following suit as soon as the Forty-Seventh were across. March 25th, 1918
6th Battalion

Crossing the Ancre at Aveluy Bridge the 36th Brigade were found taking up the position just West of the river, so the 37th moved upstream to continue the line to the North. Brigade Headquarters were established at Martinsart and the battalion took up its position in front of Aveluy Wood from opposite Authuille to a point due East of Mesnil, thence the 6th Queen's continued the line Northward to Hamel. Beyond The Queen's were portions of the Sixty-Third Division whom the Twelfth were relieving. The position was not bad as the ground rose fairly steeply from the Ancre, which at this point was quite a considerable obstacle, but there were scarcely any prepared defences. However, by this time the force and pace of the German advance had both abated. They had won much ground but they had paid dearly for their gains, and the difficulties of keeping their advanced troops supplied were already proving a serious handicap, and though they made many attacks these lacked the weight and power of their earlier efforts. That evening some few Germans got into Aveluy Wood, having apparently got through the line of A Company, but they were effec- March 26th

THE STAND ON THE ANCRE.

March 26th, 1918
6th Battalion

tively counter-attacked by Colonel Dawson with the personnel of his battalion headquarters and some Buffs, and driven back with heavy losses, two of their machine-guns being taken, while further to the right B beat off some assailants. A more serious attack on The Queen's was also repulsed and some prisoners taken and the brigade's line was successfully maintained, as was also the case all through the morning and

March 27th
afternoon of the 27th, though shelling increased. That evening, about 6 p.m., the Germans renewed their attack; they had already forced back the troops further to the left, and The Queen's had therefore to evacuate Hamel and throw back their flank. The pressure on the battalion was severe; one attack all along the line was beaten off, but a little later the enemy forced B Company back. Some Germans also got through a gap on the left, but 2nd Lieut. Guess organized a counter-attack which drove them out and re-established the line, and B managed to make a stand along the line of the railway.

March 28th
But the Germans were not done with. The next morning saw the battalion subjected to an intense bombardment and the enemy, who had made some progress further to the right in the direction of Bouzincourt, were able by means of enfilade machine-gun fire to make the railway cutting untenable. B Company fell back, therefore, about 11 a.m., but Colonel Dawson managed to form a defensive flank and to prevent the Germans advancing any further. A company of the 24th Royal Fusiliers, of the Second Division, was placed at his disposal and at 1.45, after half-an-hour's bombardment, he launched a counter-attack, using this company and all the reserves of the battalion. The stroke was delivered with great spirit and success, 2nd Lieut. Slade, who had already headed two counter-attacks, being well to the fore; the enemy was dislodged and thrust down the slopes into the valley, suffering heavily, and at 3 p.m. Colonel Dawson could report that the line had

THE STAND ON THE ANCRE.

been fully re-established. The determination, promptness and energy which he had displayed and which had inspired the battalion to put up so stout a fight were deservedly rewarded by yet another bar to his D.S.O., 2nd Lieuts. Guess and Slade receiving the M.C. *March 28th, 1918 6th Battalion*

Next morning a battalion of the Second Division took over the line, but this did not mean a relief for the 37th Brigade, which merely side-stepped to the right and relieved the 5th Royal Berkshires due East of Bouzincourt. Here the battalion was again attacked that evening, but there was not much vigour in the attempt which was easily repulsed, and the incident was mainly notable because Colonel Dawson sustained yet another wound which incapacitated him for a couple of months, Major Cook[1] replacing him in command. That night, however, the Division was drawn back into Corps Reserve, and the battalion marched back to Warloy-Baillon for a four days' rest. Its casualties on the Ancre had not been heavy, 36 men had been killed or were missing, and in addition to Colonel Dawson, Lieut. Brook and 74 men had been wounded, losses which just about balanced the draft of 124 rank and file which had joined just as the battalion left the Lys front. *March 29th* *March 29th - 30th,*

If by the time the 6th faced the German attacks these had lost some of the intensity which had made the onslaught of March 21st so formidable, it had had to withstand the advance in a hastily adopted and practically unprepared position, and its part in bringing the Germans to a standstill had been most creditable. The Twelfth Division had had to face no less than six German Divisions, and its achievement in standing up successfully against such odds was one of real importance. At the point where the Twelfth had planted itself across the Germans' path the line remained practically un-

---

[1] Major Cook had been transferred to the 6th Queen's from the 7th East Surreys, when that battalion was disbanded in February, 1918.

THE DEFENCE OF AMIENS.

April, 1918
6th Battalion
changed until August saw it begin to move back Eastward.

Actually it was not till the German offensive on the Lys opened that the Allied line from the Somme Northward towards Arras finally became "quiet." When the Twelfth Division went back to the line, on April 2nd/3rd, relieving the Seventeenth opposite Albert, the Germans were still keeping up their bombardments and making minor thrusts to gain local advantages, but they attempted no serious attack. This tour of duty lasted about ten days; the 6th R.W.K. spent the earlier part of it in Divisional reserve at Henencourt, which was very heavily shelled on April 3rd and again on the 5th, on which day the Division had to bring back its right a little to conform to the retirement of the Australians further South. From April 6th to 10th it was in the same trenches East of Bouzincourt as it had held on March 29th. Here it suffered severely from a very heavy bombardment, but no infantry attack followed the shelling. With its relief on the night of April 9th the 6th's part in the defence of Amiens came to an end. Its second tour of duty had cost it 10 killed and over 40 wounded, Captains Tuff and Green and 2nd Lieuts. Stow and G. E. Harris being among the latter.

If the final efforts of the Germans to force their way through to Amiens had not involved the 6th R.W.K. in
7th Battalion any very heavy fighting this was not so with the 7th. Hastily replenished by the incorporation into it of the 12th Entrenching Battalion the re-constituted 7th had been thrust into the line on the evening of April 1st without any time to find itself or get together. It speaks volumes for the straits to which the British Command found itself reduced that after all the Eighteenth Division had gone through it should have been thrust back into the fighting, practically without rest and certainly without any real opportunity for reorganization. But the fragments of four British divisions who were holding the right of the British front S.E. of Amiens

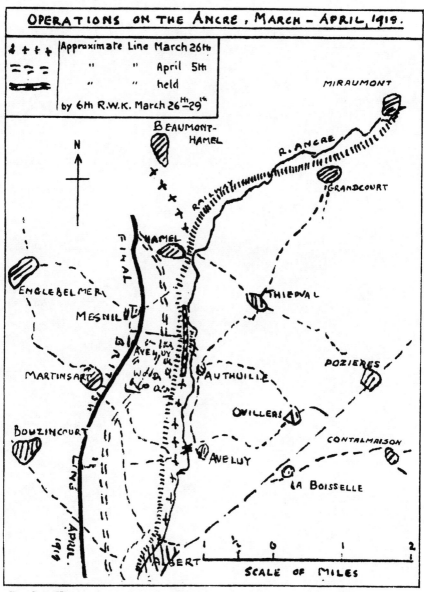

THE DEFENCE OF AMIENS.

were in even worse plight, and on the night of March 29th/30th the Eighteenth, a battered but unbeaten remnant, took over the line from the river Luce to the Marcelcave-Cachy road. On its left was the Villers-Bretonneux plateau, possession of which gave observation over the Somme valley and Amiens itself and was therefore essential to our retention of Amiens. But the Cachy-Gentelles plateau, which the Eighteenth was covering, was scarcely less essential: it gave observation over the valley of the Ancre and Amiens, and its capture would have rendered Villers-Bretonneux untenable. March, 1918 7th Battalion See Sketch 45

At this moment the German advance south of the Somme had been checked on the approximate line Demuin-Aubercourt-Marcelcave-Sailly Laurette. But they were far from having shot their bolt, and were preparing for yet one more attack in force, which was delivered after daybreak on April 4th. But before this the 7th had been sharply engaged. The battalion had taken up its position East of Hangard Wood on the night of April 1st/2nd, having the 8th East Surreys on its left, and the 7th Bedfords on its right, between it and Hangard. In front of the Bedfords on a spur overlooking Aubercourt was a small copse, the capture of which would greatly improve the British line, and the battalion received orders to co-operate with the Bedfords in attacking it, partly by covering their advance with rifle and Lewis-gun fire, partly by pushing forward another company to link up with the new position which the Bedfords were to reach. April, 1918

At 7 p.m. on the 2nd the Bedfords launched their attack, covered by the fire of the 7th. The enemy had apparently seen the troops forming up and opened a heavy fire which brought the attack to a standstill. But the look-out man of the 7th mistook some German lights for the signal on which the assaulting company of the battalion was to go over and it accordingly dashed forward. It was met by heavy machine-gun fire, but April 2nd

THE DEFENCE OF AMIENS.

April 1918, 7th Battalion

persevered in face of it, reached a copse and succeeded in securing it and digging in: a defensive flank was formed to link up with the battalion's line, and this was occupied by Captain MacDonald's company, which was brought up that evening. It proved in the end that this copse was not the real objective, but was one not marked on the map, but, although the flinty character of the ground made the work specially difficult to men as wearied by constant marching and fighting and lack of sleep and rest as were the 7th, the new position was satisfactorily consolidated and was strengthened

April 3rd.

next day: it proved a useful acquisition because it gave command over the enemy's lines so that a German working party which was directed in the open at dawn could be fired upon and dispersed with loss. Two officers, Lieut. A. F. I. Jones and 2nd Lieut. Robinson,[1] were wounded in this operation, but the casualties were not very heavy.

That day (April 3rd) passed off quite uneventfully, but a German prisoner captured near the copse warned his captors that an attack in force would be made on the next morning, and his information

April 4th

proved correct, for April 4th brought the battalion a most strenuous time. At 5 a.m. the enemy's barrage opened and soon developed into a really heavy bombardment. An hour-and-a-half later his infantry swarmed forward. The 7th had two companies in its front line and met the attackers with a steady fire, in face of which and of the excellent barrage which the British artillery promptly put down, the Germans could not advance nearer than 300 yards from the British line. But further to the left the force of the attack broke through the Australians and flung them back almost to the outskirts of Villers-Bretonneux. The 7th Buffs on the left of the Eighteenth Division had to fall back and form a defensive flank.

[1] Cheshire Regiment, attached 7th R.W.K.

THE DEFENCE OF AMIENS.

A second advance against the R.W.K. early in the afternoon was no more successful than its predecessor, but a little later the attack was renewed in force. This time the Germans left the 7th out of the attack, pressing hard against the French at Hangard and on the 6th Northamptons, who had replaced the Bedfords. The French were ousted from Hangard, and to escape being rolled up the Northamptons had to go back, while simultaneously on the battalion's left the Germans broke through the Buffs and East Surreys, whom events further North had compromised. About 5 p.m., therefore, the 7th found the enemy coming through the wood East of the Demuin-Villers-Bretonneux road behind their left, while the retreat of the Northamptons had uncovered their right. But the company in reserve was brought up to form a flank facing North from Hangard Wood Eastward, and as long as their ammunition lasted those in front held on. Then with their retreat in grave danger—for the reserve company was hard put to it to hold its ground—the 7th fell back towards Hangard Wood, losing heavily from the German machine-guns. Here a stand was made, but the battalion had been forced back more than half way through the wood when relief came. The 8th Royal Berks, with the 7th Queen's beyond them, delivered a vigorous counter-attack which checked and thrust back the Germans on the left, beyond them two Australian battalions were even more successful, and to the right the Bedfords came up to help the Northamptons; and, thus covered, the French regained much of the lost ground. The evening closed with the Allied line thrust back but unbroken, and with the two all-important plateaux denied to the Germans. It had been a hard day for the 7th; four officers (Captain Dewdney,[1] 2nd Lieuts. Dainton,[1] Walker[1] and F. G. Norris[1]) had fallen, one (2nd Lieut. Bentley[1]) was taken, two (Cap-

April 4th, 1918, 5th Battalion

---
[1] These officers all belonged to other regiments, but had been attached when the 7th incorporated the Entrenching Battalion.

THE DEFENCE OF AMIENS.

April 1918
7th Battalion

tain McDonald and 2nd Lieut. Ablett) were wounded, and the casualties among the rank and file had been heavy. But its tenacious resistance had been of the greatest service, and was all the more creditable since the battalion was little more than a scratch collection of officers and men largely strangers to each other.

That night saw the battalion relieved and drawn back to Gentelles, where it remained for nearly a week. It was placed at the disposal of the Australians (who had relieved the 53rd Brigade) for counter-attack purposes, but was not employed until, on the morning of the

April 12th

12th, a fresh German attack once more drove the French out of Hangard village and Copse. The situation was critical: the Australians' right was uncovered and the recapture of the position was essential. Accordingly the 7th was sent up to retake the Copse.

The advance was made in the face of a heavy barrage, but nevertheless B Company[1] reached the copse and took several prisoners, though its casualties from shells and machine-gun fire did not allow it to do more than consolidate a line 40 yards from the Western edge of the copse. Still this was enough to achieve the immediate object, and at this critical juncture it was of the greatest value. Other companies prolonged the line to the right, linking up with the French in the valley West of Hangard, while on the left touch was obtained with the Australians, so that an unbroken line was once more established and the Germans prevented from pushing on. This position the 7th maintained till the evening when the 10th Essex came up and, attacking through the battalion's line, retook both the copse and village. Thereupon the 7th were relieved by the Australians and went back West of the Avre to Boves, where and at St. Fuscien, a little further West, it obtained ten days of rest and reorganization.

[1] This was the company formed from the survivors of the 7th; it owed much to C.S.M. Roffey, who was largely instrumental in maintaining the traditions of The Queen's Own in this company and keeping its fighting efficiency up to a very high level.

THE DEFENCE OF AMIENS.

It needed both. The first fortnight of April had cost it 13 officers and 320 men, 2nd Lieuts. Marsh and Blew having been killed on the 12th, when Captain Edwards[1] and 2nd Lieut. Skotowe were mortally wounded. Already nearly half the officers who had joined from the Entrenching Battalion had become casualties, and the battalion was sorely in want of the two drafts who joined it, one of 160 men on the 14th, another of 86 a week later. These were composed of good material, being mainly from the Kent Cyclists and from the 3rd line Yeomanry units hitherto employed in guarding the coasts, and were very welcome. At the same time it had the satisfaction of getting back Colonel Hickson, who had now recovered from the wounds he had received at Cherisy, and was also joined by over a dozen officers. With some of them, notably Lieuts. Smythe and Sutherst, it was a case of rejoining rather than joining, and the others included Lieut. Morley, who had distinguished himself with the 11th Battalion at Ypres in 1917, and Lieut. H. J. M. Harris, who had won the M.C. with the 6th on the Somme in 1916. It was well that it should have been thus reinforced, for it had still a trial to endure in the region between the Somme and Avre.

April 1918
7th Battalion

Repulses notwithstanding, the Germans had not abandoned hope of mastering the Villers-Bretonneux plateau, and their attack in the early hours of April 24th began with a complete success. Partly by using tanks, partly by an overpowering bombardment, they managed to overwhelm the garrison and for the time being the all-important position passed into their keeping. Preparations for a counter-attack in force were immediately set on foot, and the 7th were among the troops ordered up, being lent to the 54th Brigade, which was placed under the orders of the Fifty-Eighth Division to counter-attack between Villers-Bretonneux and Han-

April 24th

---

[1] A.S.C. attached.

VILLERS-BRETONNEUX.

April 24th 1918
7th Battalion
See Sketch 45

gard, the recovery of the actual village being entrusted to the Australians and some of the Eighth Division.

The 7th started off from St. Fuscien at 6 a.m., and after some delays reached an assembly position East of the Cachy-Domart road. Here it deployed with the 7th Bedfords on the left and the 9th Londons (Queen Victoria's Rifles) on the right. At 10 p.m. the advance began, but as touch could not be obtained with the 9th Londons before the attack started D Company was kept back to guard the right flank. The other companies pushed forward steadily, though machine-guns took a heavy toll of them. In this advance Captain Lovett's good leadership was conspicuous, and it was largely through his example and his hold on his men that the objective, the new German positions North of Hangard Wood, was reached and taken. However, the battalion was not in touch with the units on its flanks, and after a gallant effort to retain its gains it recoiled to a position N.W. of the wood, and almost along the Villers-Bretonneux road. Here it dug in, though Colonel Hickson found he had under 200 rifles to hold a front of 800 yards: all the same he managed before long to get touch with the Victoria's, who were found to have reached Hangard Wood, but on the left, where B Company had lost very heavily, there remained a gap.

April 25th

This proved very troublesome next morning, for German snipers and machine-gunners crept forward and established themselves in the gap. However, despite this the battalion held on, 2nd Lieut. Goddard, who had led his company in the attack with conspicuous gallantry, doing good work in keeping his men in hand under heavy fire. Indeed the 7th not only consolidated its position but beat off all the enemy's efforts to oust it from the ground it had won, ground whose retention was essential to the safety of Villers-Bretonneux, which had also been won back. Its part in the action, if not the most conspicuous, had been of the greatest value, and had only been accomplished at a heavy cost, for

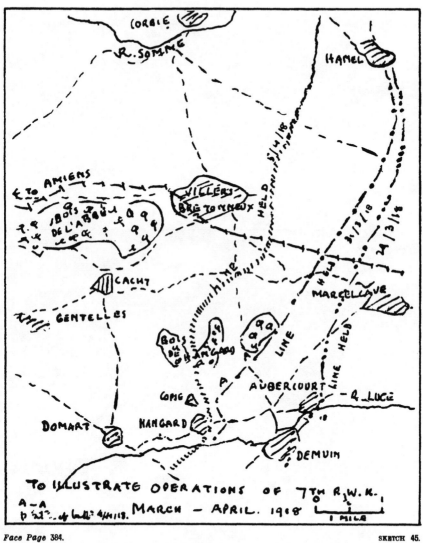

THE DEFENCE OF AMIENS.

the Germans had put up a good fight and gave way most reluctantly. Two officers (Lieut. Farley and 2nd Lieut. Moody) were missing, four (Captain Lovett and 2nd Lieuts. Salt, Singleton-Gates and Chandley) were wounded; and of 481 men who had gone into action 228 were killed, wounded or missing, bringing the battalion's total losses for April nearly up to 600. It had certainly deserved the relief which arrived for it on the night of April 25th/26th in the shape of a Moroccan division. Then at last it was taken right back out of the battle-area to Metigny.

_{April 25th 1918 7th Battalion}

As in the Somme offensive of 1916 the 7th had had a larger share of fighting than any other battalion of the Regiment, so also in the Somme defensive of 1918 it had been in at the beginning and had also shared in the final episode. To have lost forty officers and over a thousand men within three weeks and yet be required to return to the fighting line after less than a fortnight's rest shows what the demands were to which the British infantry of 1918 proved themselves equal. That battalions so constantly shattered, so constantly reconstituted and almost re-created, could possess a full measure of cohesion, training and skill was not to be expected, but it was extraordinary how quickly the new drafts assimilated the old traditions and how they emulated the standards of courage, devotion and endurance which their predecessors had established. It is hard to do justice to the men of the 7th Battalion who went through the long strain of these days, in which they were constantly fighting rear-guard actions against heavy odds under trying and disadvantageous conditions. They were short of sleep—for a fortnight from March 21st they never got a real night's rest; after the first week the supply of rations was erratic and intermittent, when they were not fighting they were usually digging new positions which they often had to evacuate without a fight because things had gone wrong elsewhere. It is rather invidious to single out names

THE DEFENCE OF AMIENS.

<small>April, 1918
7th Battalion</small> for special mention, but there are a few which stand out. Mention has already been made of C.S.M. Roffey and Sergt. Hubble, but Sergt. Smith, the Pioneer Sergeant, who, although 55 years old, proved a marvel of courage and endurance, Pte. Breeds who commanded a platoon with real gallantry and skill, and the resourceful and daring runners, Ptes. Rough, Stacey and Simpkins, should also be remembered as conspicuous for their devotion to duty in a time of special trial.

CHAPTER XXVI

THE CHANNEL PORTS IN DANGER.

While the 6th Battalion was struggling hard to keep the Germans back along the Ancre and the hastily-replenished 7th was going back into the fighting line South of the Somme, the 1st R.W.K. was on its way "back to the war." Its time of quiet on the Italian front had ended on April 1st and on the 6th it was detraining in the Doullens area. Hence it moved to Barly, the Fifth Division being now in reserve under the Tenth Corps. It was thus available for immediate employment when, on April 9th, the second of the great German offensives of the year broke through the Portuguese near Neuve Chapelle. The rapid exploitation of the German success produced an almost more dangerous situation than their success in breaking through the Fifth Army. A comparatively short advance on their part either due West past Merville or North-West past Bailleul would have enabled them to intercept the main lateral communications of the Allied front in Flanders and have placed the all-important Channel Ports in the gravest peril. Reinforcements had to be hurried to the new danger-point. Divisions destined for the Amiens battlefield were hastily diverted Northward, among them the Fifth, which was placed under orders on April 10th to proceed to Thiennes, where it arrived during the night of April 11th/12th. At that moment the acutest danger spot was Merville, into which the Germans had forced their way late on the 11th, for the line just West of the little town was thinly held by an exhausted remnant and only the magnificent resistance of the 4th Guards' Brigade of the Thirty-First Division checked further advance into Nieppe Forest on the critical day of the 12th and

April, 1918
1st Battalion

NIEPPE FOREST.

April, 1918
1st Battalion

gave the Fifth Division time to get into line at that point.

The 1st Battalion did not have a particularly prominent part in stopping the German attack. It was in Brigade reserve on the 13th and though next day it gradually was put in, first one company and then another, to support the 14th R. Warwickshires, by the time that it took over the front line from that unit, on the evening of the 14th, the German attacks had died away. The fresh troops of the Fifth Division had held their own with complete success, an Australian division, also fresh, had come into line on their left and the thrust at Hazebrouck had been definitely checked, henceforward the German efforts were directed further to the North towards the Wytschaete Ridge and Kemmel. Thus, though the battalion had an arduous and exhausting week strengthening the front line of the 13th Brigade, it was not called upon to beat off any attacks. Hostile artillery and aircraft were active, but its losses were slight and it was able to transform the defences into a really formidable line.

April-Aug.,
1918

The Forest of Nieppe was to become very familiar to the 1st R.W.K. From the middle of April to the beginning of August the Fifth Division held this important sector. It was a time of constant activity. The Germans were constantly shelling the front line and subjecting the support and reserve positions to gas shelling, their aircraft concentrated their efforts on night bombing, and their machine-guns were extremely active. But they got as good as they gave. The British guns plied them assiduously with retaliatory fire and the battalion's patrols obtained the upper hand in No Man's Land and brought in much useful information. May saw the battalion visited by the influenza epidemic which was raging on the Western Front; an enormous number of men went sick and one officer, Lieut. R. H. Clarke, who had only just come out, succumbed to it. But against this casualties were low, only

THE PLATE BECQUE.

5 men killed and 3 officers[1] and 30 men wounded for May, and 2 men killed and 19 wounded for the first ten days of June. A good many officers had joined in the meantime, including Captain Kay, one of the subalterns of the 2nd Battalion in August, 1914, and Lieut. Monypenny and Captain Winn, who rejoined after recovery from wounds. Drafts amounting to over 60 were also received. April-Aug., 1918
1st Battalion

June was marked by a singularly successful operation in which the battalion distinguished itself greatly. After a week in front line from the 4th to the 11th, in the course of which a hostile raid was successfully beaten off, the battalion had another week in reserve and a similar period of special training near Steenbecque. By this time the dangerous German offensive against the British and French along the Chemin des Dames had been stopped, and at more than one point local attacks had won back some of the ground lost in March and April. Such a local attack had been planned in the Nieppe Forest sector and was to be carried out by the Fifth and Thirty-First Divisions, the former putting two brigades into the attack, the 13th on the right, the 95th on the left, with the Thirty-First Division beyond the 95th Brigade. The 13th Brigade had the 15th R. Warwickshires on the right, the R.W.K. in the centre and the K.O.S.B.'s on the left. The frontage assigned to the brigade was nearly three-quarters of a mile, and the objective was a line on the top of the slope leading down to the little Plate Becque. June, 1918

See Sketch 46

For the attack the battalion employed two companies, C (2nd Lieut. Monypenny) and B (Captain Scott), as first wave, with A (Lieut. Lewis-Barned) as second wave, and D (Captain Dodson) as reserve. Major Kay was in command as Colonel Johnstone was on duty at Divisional Headquarters. June 28th

An important feature of the scheme was that in order to ensure surprise there was to be no preliminary bom-

---

[1] 2nd-Lieuts. Ouzman, Harrison and Harding.

THE PLATE BECQUE.

June 28th
1918
1st Battalion

bardment. The wire in front of the British trenches had to be cut to facilitate the advance, but the enemy detected nothing and did not appear to be expecting an attack when, at 6 a.m. on June 28th, a heavy barrage was suddenly put down under cover of which the British infantry came dashing forward.

C Company on the right was rapidly and extremely successful. It met scarcely any opposition at the front trenches and went on to the support line almost at once. Here there was more fighting; a machine-gun on the right flank gave much trouble, and the Germans offered a stout resistance. This was, however, overcome after several minutes' sharp fighting hand-to-hand, a special feature of which was the extent and effect with which the bayonet was used, one platoon accounting for no less than 36 of the enemy with that weapon in one farmhouse alone. With such vigour was the attack pressed that the German resistance collapsed completely and the company pushed on, driving the enemy before it and inflicting heavy casualties on them. At the final objective it halted and brought effective rifle and Lewis gun fire to bear on the Germans, now retiring hastily down the slope to the Plate Becque. Patrols were pushed forward to the stream and Sergt. Hirschfield, after posting his section so as to give covering fire, went forward under heavy fire, accompanied by a sapper, to demolish the bridges, and succeeded in destroying three of them; one of them, a stone bridge, being only blown up after two abortive attempts. The company's casualties had been light, not much over a seventh of its strength, but included Lieut. Blott and 2nd Lieut. Aylett: the latter, though hit early in the advance, remained with his men till the final objective was reached and did good service in consolidating it.

The left company, B, had had equal success. At first the men kept so close to the barrage that they sustained several casualties from their own guns, while machine-guns to the left caused much trouble. The

THE PLATE BECQUE.

company commander, Captain Scott, and his second-in-command, Lieut. Smyth, were both killed and nearly 60 men were hit, but despite this the final objective was reached and taken to time, and touch with the K.O.S.B.'s was maintained. 2nd Lieut. Burden adroitly pushed his support platoon into a gap which had opened between B and C, thereby playing an important part in the capture of the final objective. He then took over command and organized the defence of the captured position with marked ability. Here, too, heavy casualties were inflicted on the Germans as they fled down to the Plate Becque; but all attempts to destroy the bridges were prevented by the enemy's machine-guns which put down a most effective barrage. Lieut. Ouzman did splendidly in organizing the consolidation and set a fine example of coolness and courage.

A Company, following as the second wave, reached the German support line to find a party of Germans, wearing Red Cross brassards, throwing bombs at the backs of the wave which had gone on ahead. These men were given short shrift and the support line was occupied; Bonar Farm and other houses near were cleared and several more Germans disposed of in the process. There was some sharp fighting in this "mopping up," for the Germans fought hard, but A soon overcame all resistance. The company then pushed forward reinforcements to help the much depleted B, and all then settled down to consolidate. In this work most valuable assistance was given by two carrying parties of D, which 2nd Lieuts. Garbutt and Whitfield brought up through heavy shell-fire with ammunition and entrenching tools. They were up at the final objective within a few minutes of its capture; and both officers finding the companies in front very short of officers remained in the line, superintending its consolidation. 2nd Lieut. Garbutt was conspicuous for his disregard of danger and 2nd Lieut. Whitfield

THE PLATE BECQUE.

June 28th, 1918
1st Battalion
went across under heavy fire to take command of B Company.

The enemy had been taken by surprise, but he soon recovered enough to develop a very heavy bombardment, which interfered greatly with the consolidation. However, Major Kay hearing of the heavy losses in officers, came up to the front and by his coolness and cheerful example did much to inspire the men with his own resolution. Pte. Hewitt distinguished himself by going forward into the long grass in front and shot down a number of snipers, who were interfering with the consolidation, and Sergt. Norman, who cleared several dug-outs in which German machine-gunners were sheltering, did most useful service. Thus the consolidation was pushed on steadily, though during the

June 28th-30th
next two days the battalion had the misfortune to have Lieut. Monypenny killed, 2nd Lieut. Garbutt wounded, and several casualties among the rank and file, bringing its total losses up to over 120, about a third being killed or missing. But the position was maintained, despite shelling, machine-gunning and the persistent attentions of hostile aircraft, and on the evening of June 30th the battalion was relieved by the 15th R. Warwickshires and marched back through the forest.

The attack at the Plate Becque was a really effective blow, one of the first successful counter-strokes of the summer, an earnest of the reversal of the rôles of attacker and defender which the next few months were to see. The Germans had suffered heavily, over 500 prisoners were taken and 30 machine-guns, and the capture of 6,000 yards of their line not only effected a marked improvement in the local tactical situation, but was a great encouragement to the troops concerned. A minor operation in such a war, Plate Becque is a noteworthy episode in the story of the troops who shared in it. The 1st R.W.K. had carried out to the letter its share of the scheme. Major Kay, who had shown marked skill and ability in his handling of the battalion,

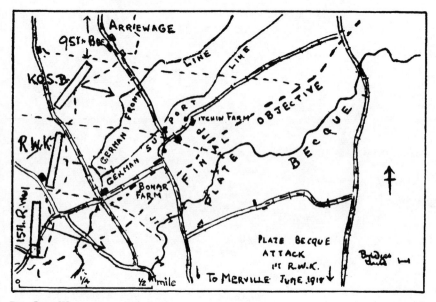

THE LAST SUMMER.

received the D.S.O. and 2nd Lieuts. Burden, Garbutt, Ouzman and Whitfield were awarded the M.C., while Sergt. Hirschfield got the D.C.M., and M.M.'s were given to Sergt. Norman, L-Sgt. Carter, Corpls. Collett and Flint, L/Cpl. Taylor, and Ptes. Saunders, Webster, Lidbury, Bailey, Healing, Brooks, Field and Bunker. June-July, 1918 1st Battalion

After this exploit the battalion had only a short spell of rest: by July 4th it was back in the line. July proved a lively month: the German aircraft were active and troublesome and their guns devoted themselves to maintaining a harassing fire, to which the British guns replied vigorously. A good deal of work was required to make the new line secure, but the battalion was lucky in escaping casualties, and the arrival of three drafts, one of 73 men and two smaller, and half-a-dozen officers, filled the gaps in the ranks which June 28th had made. At the end of July the battalion came out of the line, going back to a rest area behind Hazebrouck till the middle of August.

To the 6th Battalion the summer of 1918 brought a long spell of trench warfare in the line just North of Albert, varied by periods of rest in villages behind the front line like Acheux, Puchevillers and Herissart. These, though beyond the normal attentions of the enemy's artillery, were well within the zone which his air-craft worried with night-bombing, but only one of the periods in the line was marked by any outstanding incident, and though the influenza epidemic did not spare the battalion, casualties in action during May and June did not total more than 40. Against that drafts amounting to some 280 joined with a dozen officers, among them Captain A. E. W. Thomas, who had been wounded at Cambrai, and several officers attached from the A.S.C. In June Colonel Dawson rejoined, though as usual barely recovered from his wounds, and took over command from Major Peploe, who had succeeded to it on Colonel Cook going sick in May. But though by the end of June the numbers " on the strength " of May-June, 1918 6th Battalion

BOUZINCOURT.

May-June, 1918
6th Battalion

the battalion had reached very respectable figures, so many were detached on various duties, courses and employments that the "trench strength" was low, especially when the usual "battle surplus" of officers and specialists had been left out: thus on June 21st those present with the battalion only mustered 23 officers and 582 men, no less than 12 officers and 225 other ranks being also "on the strength" but away from the battalion. The more recent drafts had included a large proportion of very young soldiers of little training, and the task of keeping battalions up to their old level taxed the energies and devotion of the officers and of such experienced N.C.O.'s as were available.

But though at less critical times a battalion which had suffered as much as had the 6th might have expected time to train and assimilate its drafts, the summer of 1918 allowed few chances for rest or quiet. Opposite the British lines in the Bouzincourt sector there was *See Sketch 47* some high ground astride the Bouzincourt-Aveluy road, the capture of which would greatly improve the tactical situation. An attack on this ridge was therefore resolved upon and the 6th was selected for the attempt. It had the left of the line with the 6th Queen's on its right and a battalion of the Eighteenth Division further to the right again. The plan was that the leading waves, A and D Companies, were to push forward beyond the line selected for consolidation and while A raided three areas on the left flank D, with the assistance of a platoon each of B and C, was to hold a forward position well in advance of the line it was hoped to secure. This was to be consolidated by B and C, the advanced troops having orders to maintain their forward position until the line of main resistance had been rendered defensible.

June 30th, 1918

The evening of June 30th had been selected for the enterprise and at 9.35 p.m. the battalion went over the top behind a heavy barrage of artillery, trench-mortars and machine-guns. The front line was rushed without

BOUZINCOURT.

much difficulty, but as the attackers pressed on towards their further objectives more resistance was offered and there was sharp fighting. But the 6th was not to be denied: the men pushed on to the road which had been chosen as the forward position and after some sharp fighting could report that all the objectives had been gained. The three raiding parties carried out their tasks successfully, though a machine-gun among some old Nissen huts on the left somehow escaped detection and the party detailed to reach a sunken road to the East of the huts had to fight really hard. But heavy casualties were inflicted on the enemy, three machine-guns were taken and over 20 prisoners; and The Queen's proved equally successful, though their right flank was exposed by the failure of the battalion of the Eighteenth Division to secure the whole of its objective. By midnight consolidation was well advanced, and about 2.30 a.m. the covering parties fell back as ordered to the main line: they had just previously beaten off a somewhat feeble attempt at a counter-attack.

[margin: June 30th, 1918, 6th Battalion]

July 1st proved a fairly quiet day: there was intermittent shelling by the Germans, and casualties, which in the earlier stages had not been heavy, began to mount up. Much trouble was caused by the overlooked machine-gun among the huts, and a German post in front of the centre proved such a hindrance to the wiring and consolidating parties that an attempt was made to rush it, though without success. Better fortune attended an effort to capture the machine-gun among the Nissen huts, and a strong German counter-attack was decisively repulsed. But though at midnight the 6th R.W.K. still held their line intact, The Queen's had been even harder put to it: they had been attacked several times and the gap on their right proved a source of weakness and they lost a certain amount of ground. During the night the Buffs relieved them.

[margin: July 1st]

BOUZINCOURT.

July, 1918
6th Battalion

July 2nd saw the same sort of thing, intermittent shelling all day followed by attacks at night. At 6.30 p.m. 2nd Lieut. Walthew and 20 men of C Company made a gallant attempt to rush the troublesome post in the centre. 2nd Lieut. Walthew, who had distinguished himself in the original attack by himself killing three Germans who were holding up one of his sections, again displayed great courage and leadership and his men followed him well, but the post was too much for them: all but 6 of the party were hit and the effort failed. Then at 9.30 p.m. there came down a heavy barrage, followed this time by a counter-attack pressed with real determination and force. The battalion put up a stout resistance, but was forced back to the old British line, and the Buffs had also to come back. Early on the 3rd the Buffs took over the whole front line and the 6th were withdrawn into support, retiring that evening to a camp West of Senlis. The casualties had been heavy, eleven officers and 230 rank and file. Captain Catmur[1] and Lieuts. Hart,[1] Hartmann, Stilwell and Elliott were killed, Captain G. W. Hill, 2nd Lieuts. Guess, Standring, Billingham, Walthew and Death wounded.

These losses, however, were soon made good: a draft of 43 men joined on the 3rd, another of two officers and 218 men arrived before the battalion moved on the 10th to Rubempré, where it rested till the 14th, receiving another reinforcement of three officers and 50 men before it moved away to an area S.W. of Amiens, where it remained till the end of the month, training and resting. During this period nine more officers appeared with 86 men, among the officers being Captain Henderson-Roe and Lieut. Scott-Marten, both of whom had so distinguished themselves at Infantry Hill. Thus, when on July 30th the battalion moved back to the fighting line, it mustered over 850 officers

[1] Attached from the A.S.C.

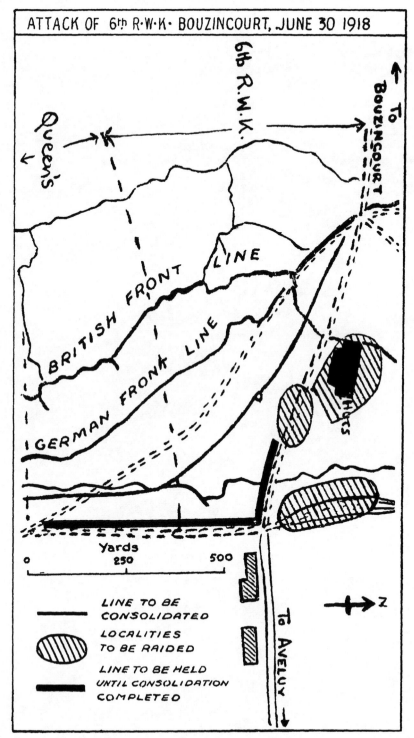

THE LAST SUMMER.

and men "present," though it had fallen well below 500 after the June 30th—July 2nd fight. It was now in the Third Corps which formed the left of the Fourth Army and lay just North of the Somme and S.W. of Albert. <small>July, 1918 6th Battalion</small>

The fortunes of war had brought the 6th Battalion once again, as in May 1917, into the same area as the 7th. The latter had not, since its hard fighting in April, taken part in any operation comparable to the attacks delivered by the 1st and 6th. It had been in and out of the line opposite Albert all through May, June and the beginning of July. This had given time to weld the battalion together, and under Colonel Hickson's influence it had again become a homogeneous unit ready for hard fighting. None of its tours in the line produced either striking incidents or heavy casualties, and some substantial drafts had arrived, including quite a strong leaven of old hands who had already seen much service with the 7th. A good many officers also joined, among them Captain Maltby, formerly of the 11th Battalion, and Captain McDonald, who had made a quick recovery from his Hangard Wood wound. The last three weeks of July the battalion spent training at St. Pierre à Gouy, the Eighteenth Division being then in G.H.Q. Reserve, and finally on July 31st it arrived at La Houssoye North by West of Corbie, where its brigade was in Divisional reserve. <small>May-July, 1918 7th Battalion</small>

The 8th, on the other hand, during this period of strategical inactivity on the British front came in for a good deal of local activity. It had a short rest at the seaside near St. Valerie after leaving the Amiens front and then at the beginning of May went back to its old familiar haunts near Lens. Here the line had altered little since the Twenty-Fourth Division had left the sector. No Man's Land in the St. Emilie sector just North of Lens, which the Twenty-Fourth Division took over from the Canadians, was a mass of tangled ruins on the right, rather more open on the left. A <small>April-July 8th Battalion See Sketch 52</small>

397

THE LAST SUMMER.

May, 1918
8th Battalion

big draft had joined the 8th along with 160 men who had been on leave in England on March 21st and the battalion was well over 800 strong again, while Captain H. S. Brown came back after six months' duty in England to become Major and second-in-command. The battalion at once started patrolling vigorously and before long could report as the result of several brushes with the enemy's patrols that it had established a mastery over No Man's Land, besides repulsing three or four minor attacks.

It, on its part, carried out more than one raid. In May an attack was planned against the enemy's trenches near Conductor Sap, to be carried out in conjunction with a projector attack, a combination which had not been tried before. Actually the gas cylinders fell short; their fumes incapacitated several of the raiders and caused so much confusion that they returned to their trenches. Major Brown then took control, restored order and confidence, and himself laid a tape across No Man's Land which guided the raiders when he launched them to a second attack. This time things went much better: the two parties, led respectively by 2nd Lieuts. Piggott and G. A. E. Wallis, got well into the enemy's trenches and pushed right and left, bombing dug-outs, securing some prisoners and inflicting many casualties. Major Brown meanwhile, having taken up a position on the German parapet near the point of entry, conducted his operations very skilfully and the two subalterns seconded him well, extricating their parties in safety and with few losses. The raid brought well-deserved M.C.'s to all these three officers, and the M.M. to Ptes. Warford, Baker and Bowes, while the prisoners taken proved most valuable for identification purposes. Shortly after this the battalion had the misfortune to lose R.S.M. Rankin, killed by the Germans bombing a football match when the battalion was in reserve. He had been an invaluable

THE LAST SUMMER.

asset to the battalion, notably in the March retreat, and his place was very hard to fill. *May, 1918 7th Battalion*

To the 10th Battalion the summer months had not brought any very conspicuous or important experiences. After being withdrawn from the front between Arras and Amiens it had been transferred to Flanders, but to a part North of that included in the fighting which began on April 9th. Actually the battalion had to take part in the withdrawal on April 16th from the advanced positions round Broodseinde and Passchendaele to a shorter line some distance in rear. The withdrawal was unmolested by the enemy and the rear parties whom the 10th had left to cover the retirement came back in safety. A serious explosion of an ammunition dump at the camp where its details had been left cost the 10th nearly 50 casualties, including Lieut. Anderson and 17 other ranks killed, and destroyed nearly all the battalion records, but it gave 2nd Lieut. Shrimpton a chance of distinction. Though badly shaken he at once organized rescue parties, got soldiers and civilians out of burning buildings, saved a large number of valuable horses, and all this under heavy shelling; for this work he was subsequently awarded the M.C., while C.S.M. Byrne, who had also been most assiduous and resourceful, received the D.C.M. Next to the explosion of this dump the chief feature of the Ypres Salient at this time was the constant gas shelling: the battalion had over 200 casualties from gas in May alone, but despite this and the influenza epidemic from which it, like other units, suffered severely, its numbers were well maintained. In the influenza conspicuous service was done by the M.O., Captain Montgomery, R.A.M.C., whose promptness and resource not only prevented the epidemic spreading, but kept down the numbers evacuated to hospital and consequently lost to the battalion. *April-August 1918 16th Batt.*

Among the officers there were many changes. During this period some old members of the 10th and 11th Battalions reappeared, like Captain Rooney,

THE LAST SUMMER.

April-August 1918
10th Batt.

Major Stallard and Lieut. Lindsay, but Captain Kerr was transferred to the Staff and was succeeded as Adjutant by Captain Holden, who later on gave place to Lieut. Tatham on being shifted to a battalion of The Queen's as Major. The command which had been held by Major Wallis since March 23rd was given in May to Colonel Thesiger, of the Surrey Yeomanry, Major Wallis becoming second-in-command. At the beginning of July the Division, which had been out of the line for three weeks' training near Hazebrouck, relieved the French near La Clytte and remained in that region nearly all August, the chief incident being the attachment to the battalion first of American officers and then of two companies of the 106th American Regiment for instruction and training. September saw the 10th back in the line near Dickebusch, waiting for the extension to its front of that forward movement which had begun on the Amiens front on August 8th.

CHAPTER XXVII

TURNING THE TABLES.

In the whole war no other day saw as dramatic and startling a change as that which the Fourth Army achieved astride the Somme on August 8th, 1918. The whole aspect of affairs was altered. The British Armies which in March had been swept back from the outskirts of St. Quentin to those of Amiens, which in April had been fighting with their backs to the wall and had only just managed to deny to the Germans the vital positions of Amiens, Hazebrouck and the Scherpenberg hills, which during the summer months had asked no more than to maintain the new positions to which the great German onslaughts had thrust them back and to achieve occasional minor successes, local improvements which left the general position unchanged, now suddenly took the offensive on a considerable scale and with results surpassing the utmost the most sanguine had dared to hope for. By Ludendorff's own admission August 8th was "the black day of the war for the German armies," and in that day's victory The Queen's Own were well represented. Included in the Third Corps which formed the left of the attack were the Twelfth and Eighteenth Divisions and in consequence its 6th and 7th Battalions.

The Third Corps' contribution to General Rawlinson's victory has perhaps hardly received adequate recognition. Its attack did not finally secure more than its first objective, and on the evening of August 8th its line was well in rear of that reached by the Australians and Canadians South of the Somme, but its task of forming a defensive flank as the advance progressed was one of particular difficulty, a good deal more formidable in many ways than that of the troops

August. 1918 6th & 7th Battalions

TURNING THE TABLES.

<small>August, 1918
6th & 7th Battalion

Aug. 6th</small>

on its right. The country North of the Somme was cut up by deep ravines which greatly hampered the tanks which were so conspicuously effective South of the river. Further, two days before the day fixed for the offensive a sudden attack delivered by a fresh division of Würtembergers on the 54th Brigade astride the Bray-Corbie road had led to heavy fighting and some

<small>Aug. 7th</small>

loss of ground : this had been partly recovered next day, but fighting was still going on at this point and consequently the plan of the attack was somewhat upset, while the uncertainty as to the exact position prevented the artillery from lending its usual effective support to the infantry who had to rely solely on their own rifles and bayonets.

Moreover, in justice to the Third Corps it must be remembered that while the Australian and Canadian divisions had been spared the brunt of the attacks of March and April, they had the great advantage of having been allowed to retain four battalions in their brigades and were in consequence considerably stronger than divisions from the Mother Country. Indeed one officer writes that he never saw the defects of the three-battalion brigade so apparent as in this battle. The achievement of the Third Corps was by no means the least creditable or substantial part of the battle of Amiens and both battalions of The Queen's Own took their full share in the fighting.

<small>Aug. 8th</small>

On August 8th actually only the 7th was actively engaged. The plan was that the Fifty-Eighth and Eighteenth Divisions should attack from the Somme

<small>See Sketch 49</small>

Northward to just South of Morlancourt; opposite that village a gap of over 400 yards was left, beyond which the Twelfth Division was to engage one brigade, the 35th, in a subsidiary operation designed to encircle Morlancourt and compel its evacuation. The 37th Brigade was in Divisional reserve so the 6th R.W.K. spent the day in readiness at Fravillers, and it was evening before it moved up to Marett Wood West of

402

TURNING THE TABLES.

Morlancourt with orders to continue the attack next morning. *August 8th, 1918*
7th Battalion
See Sketch 48

Far otherwise was it with the 7th, who had a day of desperate fighting. The 53rd Brigade was designed to pass through the troops detailed to capture the first objective of the Eighteenth Division, roughly the line from Malard Wood to Morlancourt, and to push on to Gressaire Wood, a mile-and-a-half further East. From that point a defensive flank was to be formed facing North and connecting up with the left of the Eighteenth Division's original line. The formation of this defensive flank was the special task of the 7th R.W.K., who had the 10th Essex on their right and on their left the 7th Queen's. Special efforts had been made to maintain secrecy: roads had been strewn with straw to muffle the noise of the transport and tanks, though it was hard to conceal the movement of these last, which made a roar which from the interior of a dug-out sounded like the incessant roll and rumble of a heavy barrage.

The 7th was in its assembly position at 2 a.m. and at " zero," 4.30 a.m., moved forward in artillery formation astride the Bray-Corbie road. There was a thick mist which obscured all movement outside a fifty yards' radius, though it was no small compensation that it greatly handicapped the German machine-gunners, the ground was broken and much cut-up with trenches, and connection between the advanced companies and their supports was soon lost. However, direction was successfully maintained and Burke Trench, supposed to be the British front line, was reached up to time. Then, however, difficulties began. The Germans proved to be in great force, for the fog and the broken ground had hampered the tanks very much and The Queen's had had to fight hard even to clear what should have been their " jumping-off line." C Company therefore soon became involved in heavy fighting for Croydon and Cloncurry Trenches which had been lost on

TURNING THE TABLES.

August 8th, 1918
7th Battalion

August 6th, and though they got on they were unable to keep up with the barrage. A, crossing to the South of the Bray-Corbie road, had hard fighting round a chimney called the Brick Beacon and were held up there for some time. By 7 a.m., however, they overcame this resistance and then pushed forward towards some aeroplane hangars about 1,000 yards further on. These they reached after further fighting and then started to dig themselves in. Ultimately about 200 of the battalion established themselves here, mixed up with portions of the 8th Royal Berkshires and in touch with the 10th Essex South of the Bray-Corbie road, while a little later a communication trench on the left was successfully cleared of Germans by Lieut. H. J. M. Harris and touch was obtained with the troops further to the left.

While the rest of the battalion was thus establishing a good defensive flank on the left, B Company, skilfully led by Captain A. V. McDonald, had worked its way forward most successfully. Keeping close to the Bray-Corbie road the company actually caught up the barrage and, pushing on in a gap between A and C, kept with it as far as the final objective, suffering some casualties from machine-guns which, however, were speedily accounted for. On approaching the Brickworks N.W. of Gressaire Wood B swung South of the road, driving back a strong body of Germans just South of the Brickworks, who fell back into Gressaire Wood. The Brickworks proved to be held in force and a first effort to rush them was checked by machine-guns, but at that moment two tanks came lumbering up through the mist, and with their help the Brickworks were stormed and many prisoners taken. It was now about 7.15 a.m., and as the mist began clearing away it became evident that B Company's success in reaching the Brickworks had brought it far beyond the rest of its battalion.

TURNING THE TABLES.

However, though fully 4,000 yards from the starting point and with both his flanks open,[1] Captain McDonald dug in at once and for some time he maintained his ground despite increasing pressure. Further to the right, however, touch was obtained with a company of the 10th Essex due South of the Brickworks which had reached Gressaire Wood, the final objective, but had had to fall back. But the Germans were in force all round and counter-attacks from Gressaire Wood threatened to outflank and cut off the Essex, while they were also advancing against B Company and their enfilade fire was making communication with the troops in rear almost impossible. Accordingly, about 10 a.m. the Colonel of the Essex ordered a withdrawal to the position which the main body of the 7th were consolidating, the so-called " Green Line." This withdrawal was adroitly conducted by Captain McDonald, though the enemy were pressing hard and the task was one of considerable difficulty owing to a German barrage which reinforced their machine-gun fire. Indeed, encouraged by their success in driving back the advanced troops of the Eighteenth Division, the Germans counter-attacked vigorously the line to which these had fallen back. By this time, however, it had been made fairly secure, touch had been established with The Queen's on the left and, well supported by the artillery, the 7th dealt faithfully with these attempts and held tenaciously to their gains.[2]

If the Eighteenth and Fifty-Eighth Divisions had not secured their final objective, they had attained substantial success, while the Twelfth Division's subsidiary attack had established itself successfully on

August 8th, 1918
7th Battalion

---

[1] Sergt. Daniels, who carried out a reconnaissance to the left, went over a mile without finding any other troops.

[2] This action brought a bar to their M.C. to both Captain McDonald and Lieut. Harris Pte. Stacey, a battallion runner, who had done conspicuous work in the March retreat, was again greatly to the fore and obtained a second bar to his M.M., and Sergt. Daniels, the Lewis gun N.C.O. of B Company was another who distinguished himself greatly.

TURNING THE TABLES.

<small>August 1918
6th Battalion

Aug. 9th

See Sketch 48</small>

a line threatening Morlancourt from the North-West. Moreover, the casualties inflicted on the Germans had been very heavy: the Third Corps had taken over 2,000 prisoners, and next day a renewed attack resulted in the capture of the whole of the previous day's second objective. In this attack the 37th Brigade took part and the 6th R.W.K. got its chance.

The line reached on the 8th ran North-East of Ville sur Ancre and was close up to the edge of Morlancourt: the battalion was on the left of the attack with The Queen's and Buffs beyond it, and assembled along the Morlancourt-Ville sur Ancre road. At 5.30 p.m. the attack was launched under a barrage and the battalion pushed forward, meeting most determined opposition. The hostile machine-guns were mostly concealed in the standing crops and in shell-holes, and for a moment the attack seemed bound to be held up. That this did not happen was due to the gallantry and devotion of Sergt. T. J. Harris, who rushed one of these guns at the head of his section and captured it. Twice again as the advance proceeded the same thing happened; each time Sergt. Harris dashed forward against the obstructing machine-gun. In the first instance he was again successful, killing the whole team singlehanded: the second time he was himself shot, but his example had inspired all those round him and the advance swept on. A posthumous V.C. fittingly recognized his splendid achievement. A conspicuous feature of the day was Colonel Dawson's leadership: he went into battle on horseback, exposing himself fearlessly and setting an example of calmness and courage which was most inspiring to his men. 2nd Lieut. H. J. Turner was also prominent in this advance. Machine-guns concealed in the low-lying ground near the river were inflicting casualties on his company, but he skilfully manœuvred his men into a position from which they could take the enemy in flank and rear and so cleared them out of the

Snapshot]

No. 358. Sergt. T. J. HARRIS. V.C., M.M.
6th Battalion.
Killed in action, 9th August, 1918.

way. 2nd Lieut. Upfold also twice successfully disposed of machine-guns which were holding up his platoon, by engaging them in front and thereby diverting the attention from parties who rushed them from the flank. Thus the battalion achieved an advance of over 2,000 yards, captured or destroyed over 20 machine-guns and four trench-mortars, made a substantial haul of prisoners and consolidated its final objective, which ran South-East from the Ancre just East of Dernancourt. In this Captain Henderson-Roe set a splendid example: his left arm was badly shattered early on, but he continued nevertheless to lead his company forward with marked skill and leadership and insisted on remaining at the front until the position had been consolidated. The battalion had somewhat outstripped those on its right, but next day the advance was resumed and a further substantial gain of ground secured, the line getting within a short distance of Meaulté. The attack had cost the 37th Brigade between 500 and 600 casualties, of which the battalion had suffered nearly 200; 2nd Lieuts. A. H. Brown and Walsh were killed with 24 men, 2 men were missing and 157 wounded, together with Captains Henderson-Roe and Tharp, Lieuts. Westendarp and Sweeny and 2nd Lieut. Bensley.[1]

August 9th, 1918
6th Battalion

August 10th

The 6th held the position it had captured until August 12th, when a relief allowed it to be drawn back into reserve. The next few days saw a temporary pause in the operations. By the evening of August 11th General Rawlinson's advance had been pushed to the limits of profitable exploitation: the enemy's resistance had stiffened, he had brought up reinforcements and was holding a strong line and all advantage of surprise was over. But Sir Douglas Haig's plans were largely based on utilizing this factor to the full and surprise could best be achieved by a sudden shift in the

[1] Captain Henderson-Roe and 2nd Lieuts. Upfold and Turner received the M.C.

TURNING THE TABLES.

August, 1918
7th Battalion

point of attack directly the enemy's reserves had been drawn to the breach already effected. All was now in train for the Third Army to take up the attack and in the meantime the Fourth was to consolidate its gains, to press the enemy enough to fix his attention and to take advantage of local opportunities. To the Twelfth and Eighteenth Divisions, therefore, the middle of August was a time of suspended activity, though the latter division remained in front line, having relieved the Forty-Seventh opposite Albert, the 7th R.W.K. going into the support line on the new front on the night of August 10th. Its casualties on August 8th had not been heavy considering the character of the fighting: Lieut. Hackforth-Jones (attached from the Gloucesters) and 2nd Lieut. H. J. Chapman had been killed with 13 men, 43 men were missing, Lieuts. A. V. D. Morley, Bergl and Bell, 2nd Lieuts. W. F. Chapman and Addison and 137 men wounded. These losses in officers were more than made good by new arrivals, though the gaps in the ranks had not been filled before the battalion went over the top again.

1st Battalion

See Sketch 50

It was the Third Army who on August 21st started the second of Sir Douglas Haig's series of blows at the German line. The front to be attacked ran from the Ancre near Miraumont to Moyenneville, a length of nine miles, and the day's operations aimed at gaining the line of the Arras-Albert railway. This was to be a preliminary to a simultaneous attack by the Third and Fourth Armies two days later, with a North and South line through Bapaume as immediate objective and turning the line of the Somme above Peronne as ultimate object.

The Fifth Division was by this time included in the Third Army. The 1st R.W.K. had had nearly three weeks out of the line when on August 20th it moved up to Gommecourt for the new attack. On the 21st it never reached the front line, for though its Division went through the Thirty-Seventh on the left of the

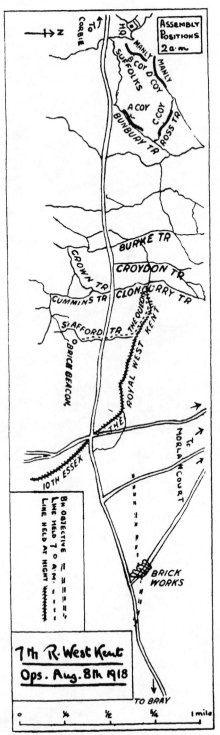

Face Page 408. SKETCH 49.

THE ADVANCE ON BAPAUME.

Fourth Corps and captured Achiet le Petit, establishing a line just short of the railway, it did this with the 15th and 95th Brigades only and retained the 13th in reserve. The next day was spent in reorganizing and then on August 23rd the Third Army struck again with force and effect. This time the Fifth Division led the attack, but once again the 13th Brigade was in reserve and only when the right of the attack was held up in front of Irles did the battalion get its chance. During the day it had moved up from Bucquoy towards Achiet le Petit in the wake of the 15th R. Warwickshires, and it was already 5 p.m. when it received orders to deploy South of Achiet le Petit. It was necessary to attack without a barrage on Irles itself as it was uncertain whether British troops were not actually holding part of the village and the battalion, keeping close to the barrage as its orders prescribed, for the most part missed the village, but by capturing the high ground just South it was largely instrumental in enabling the 12th Gloucesters to make a second and successful attack on Irles.

<small>August 21st, 1918
1st Battalion</small>

<small>August 23rd</small>

The advance was stoutly opposed: German machine-guns inflicted many casualties, and at one time large gaps had been made in the attacking line. Seeing these Lieut. Darlow, who was commanding the company in support, promptly pushed up reinforcements. Splendid service was done by Sergt. Gilbert, who changed his platoon's direction to clear a trench and dispose of a machine-gun which was enfilading the advance, by Corpl. Harris, who put a troublesome machine-gun out of action by rushing it from a flank, and by Pte. Biffen, who brought forward some men who had lost direction and filled a gap in the line with them: 2nd Lieut. Sansom, whose platoon was on the right flank, was also conspicuous; assisted by his runner he rushed and took a couple of machine-guns and his platoon cleared several sunken roads, capturing many prisoners and helping to secure the flank. Thus the

THE ADVANCE ON BAPAUME.

August 23rd 1918
1st Battalion

objective was secured at the moderate cost of only 100 casualties, including Lieut. Steele killed and Captain Winn and 2nd Lieuts. Quigley, Collins, Glass and Cottrell wounded. The prisoners taken about equalled the casualties and the battalion, by digging itself in very effectively, though with only entrenching implements available, formed a strong defensive flank facing Miraumont, which was still in German hands. In organizing this flank Lieut. Milford did conspicuous service; his excellent handling of D Company during the attack had been largely responsible for the lightness of its casualty list, and his example and resolution inspired his men, exhausted by the long advance, to stick to the work of consolidation. While this work was in progress Pte. Larking did good work by going out single-handed and disposing of three troublesome snipers who were interfering with the work, besides surprising and killing the crew of a machinegun, which he took. Moreover, the ground thus secured was of considerable tactical value, dominating Miraumont and the German positions to the East and South and affording an excellent "jumping off" ground for the next stage of the advance.

August 24th

Next morning the New Zealanders passed through the 13th Brigade to continue the advance on Bapaume and the Forty-Second Division resumed the attack on Miraumont. In this the battalion co-operated, bringing Lewis-gun fire on the defenders of Miraumont and reporting to the artillery movements noticed about the place. Patrols were active in clearing up the ground crossed in the previous day's advance in which several prisoners were collected, especially when the Forty-Second Division's progress against Miraumont caught many Germans between it and the battalion. On this Lieut. Darlow took out a patrol and cleared up a gulley where there was a machine-gun which would have held up the advance. Another patrol under 2nd Lieut. Sansom made a notable haul, securing a 5.9-inch howitzer

THE ADVANCE ON BAPAUME.

and four machine-guns, while Colonel Johnstone and his Intelligence Officer, 2nd Lieut. Marke, pushed out to the right and superintended the establishing of touch with the Forty-Second Division. A few more casualties were suffered during the day, mainly from machine-gun fire from Loupart Wood, which was not cleared by the New Zealanders till fairly late in the day, Lieut. Milford and 2nd Lieut. Thorning both being wounded. August 24th
1918
1st Battalion

August 25th saw the Fifth Division shifted to the left to relieve the Thirty-Seventh at Favreuil; the 13th Brigade moving into position East of that village and spending a night of pouring rain in the open ready to continue the advance. This resulted next day in the capture of Beugnatre by the K.O.S.B.'s and 14th R. Warwickshires, who consolidated a position North-East of that village which the battalion took over on the night of August 27th/28th. It had had about twenty casualties in the meantime, partly from shell-fire, partly from German "booby traps" which had taken in some of the more unwary. See Sketch 43

August 26th

By this time the German resistance had somewhat diminished in resolution and on the 28th the battalion was but little troubled by the enemy who merely indulged in some fairly inocuous shelling. Actually he was about to evacuate Bapaume, which the New Zealanders occupied early next day. To cover their left the battalion pushed forward patrols which had some sharp fighting, and then in the afternoon it received orders to assist in securing some high ground to the South-East which overlooked the railway and would afford a capital "jumping-off" ground for the next general advance. August 29th

Considerable opposition was offered; as usual machine-guns gave great trouble, and B and C Companies who were leading had many losses. Lieut. Darlow, who was directing the advance most skilfully, was killed, and 2nd Lieut. King was also hit, command of B Company thus devolving on Sergt. E. J. Smith,

THE ADVANCE ON BAPAUME.

Aug., 1918
1st Battalion

who rose to the occasion splendidly, re-organizing his men, leading them forward under heavy shell-fire and selecting the line to be consolidated. His courage and leadership were thus largely responsible for the success of the attack.[1] Captain Fulcher, too, seeing the attack wavering, pushed up a platoon of his company, which was in support, in the nick of time to carry the advance successfully forward to the objective, while Pte. Cowell, a platoon runner, took command of his platoon on the fall of its sergeant, led it forward with great coolness and skill, using the one Lewis gun most successfully, established it on its proper objective, superintended consolidation, and got touch with the next battalion. 2nd Lieut. Purchase also displayed marked skill and leadership, capturing his objective with 30 prisoners and a couple of machine-guns with insignificant losses and accounting for many of the enemy. These results were achieved at a cost of only 40 casualties, and the operation constituted a most satisfactory finale to the battalion's share in the battle of Bapaume; that night the 95th Brigade relieved the 13th, which remained in reserve while the Division continued its advance beyond Beugny, the enemy now retreating rapidly.

6th & 7th Battalions

For the failure of the German resistance to stiffen as the Third Army's attack was pressed home the cooperation of the Fourth had been partly responsible. General Rawlinson's advance astride the Somme was a threat to the flank of the troops which they could not ignore, but it was only achieved after severe fighting, and both 6th and 7th R.W.K. encountered really stiff opposition. The Twelfth Division was now on the right of the Eighteenth, having come back to the line on August 12th and taken over the central section of the Third Corps front. Before the main attack of the Fourth Army could be delivered it was essential to clear Albert and accordingly on August 22nd, the day after General Byng's advance began, the Third Corps carried

[1] He subsequently received the D.C.M., as did Pte. Cowell also.

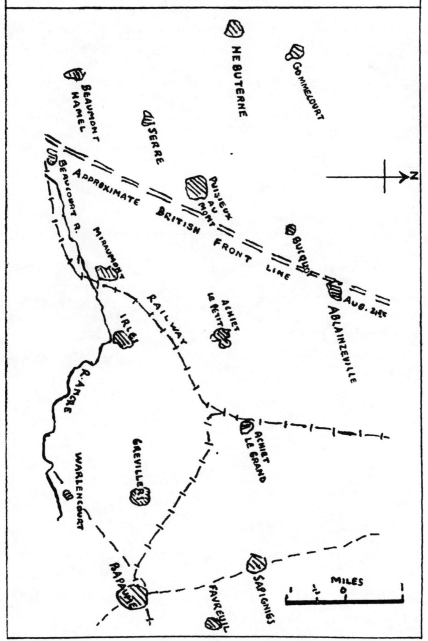

THE ADVANCE FROM THE ANCRE.

out a skilfully-planned enveloping movement which secured Albert and advanced the Fourth Army's left between the Somme and the Ancre well East of the Bray-Corbie road. In this the 53rd Brigade was held in Divisional reserve, so the 7th Battalion took no active part. The 6th also was not actively employed, the attack of the Twelfth Division being delivered by the 35th and 36th Brigades which after heavy fighting reached a position on the Bray-Albert road with the left in Meaulté and the 35th Brigade on the right, half-way to Bray. Cavalry attempted to exploit the success but were held up, and on the 23rd little progress was made. That evening the 37th Brigade was ordered forward to pass through the 35th Brigade shortly after midnight and continue the attack. August 22nd 1918 6th & 7th Battalions

August 23rd

But before this the 7th Battalion had come into action again. Though the Germans had been ousted from Albert they still held Tara and Usna Hills, East of that town, and it was essential to dislodge them. The task was allotted to the 53rd Brigade, reinforced by the 7th Queen's and assisted on its left by the 113th Brigade of the Thirty-Eighth Division which had passed through Albert behind the Eighteenth. "Zero" was fixed for 4.45 a.m. on the 23rd, and punctually to the minute the battalion pushed forward behind the barrage along the light railway which runs up the Tara Valley. The attack was an immediate success. The German resistance was promptly and effectively overcome, a gun and 350 prisoners were taken by the 53rd Brigade and by 6 a.m. the high ground overlooking Bécourt Wood had been secured. Captain Maltby distinguished himself greatly; he took command of the attackers, supervised the consolidation and himself reconnoitred the whole of the new front. 7th Battalion

August 23rd

The capture of Tara and Usna Hills rendered an advance on La Boisselle possible, and early next morning the 8th R. Berkshires attacked this position, C and D Companies of the battalion advancing on their right August 24th

THE ADVANCE FROM THE ANCRE.

<small>August 24th 1918
7th Battalion</small> to cover their flank. By using some old communication trenches these companies reached their objective with little loss, established a line of posts North and West of Bécourt Wood and followed this up later on by pushing a strong fighting patrol through the wood, clearing it up and linking up the 10th Essex on the right with the 8th R. Berkshires at La Boisselle. The Berkshires had been stoutly opposed but eventually cleared the great crater which had been blown in on July 1st 1916 and had been the key of the enemy's resistance. In reducing it they were greatly assisted by Captain Sutherst, who brought up his Trench Mortar Battery to the crater and handled it with conspicuous skill and success. That evening the 55th Brigade took over the line and the 7th went back to Albert for a brief rest. It had had three officers killed (Lieut. J. C. Cobb, and 2nd Lieuts. Watts and Desprez), five wounded (2nd Lieuts. Montague, Hodgkinson, Pigou, Fell and Claridge) and 142 other casualties, but its gains had been important enough to make this seem but a light price.

<small>6th Battalion</small> The 6th had been no less hotly engaged on August 24th. Attacking at 1 a.m. in conjunction with the 36th Brigade on its left it had encountered determined opposition. The ground was so broken as to give splendid cover to the machine-guns which soon brought the attack to a standstill short of its objective, though the left company of the battalion got as far forward as the road running South from Bécordel-Bécourt. A renewed attempt made about 1 p.m. with the aid of three " Whippet " tanks was no more successful, the tanks failing completely. However, the battalion hung on tenaciously to the advanced line reached till in the evening its endurance was rewarded by discovering that its opponents, shaken by the advance of the 36th Brigade to the North and of the Forty-Seventh Division nearer the Somme, had evacuated their position.

THE ADVANCE FROM THE ANCRE.

The next two days saw a steady advance towards and past Fricourt and Mametz, somewhat delayed by fog. There was some hard fighting, though not for the 6th, which was only in support, but on August 27th it took the lead again, passing through the 36th Brigade and pushing forward from the Carnoy-Montauban road with the line Briqueterie-Maricourt as its objective. There was considerable resistance but the 37th Brigade fought its way forward steadily. At one moment the advance was held up by a machine-gun, but Lieut. Willoughby attacked it from the flank and bombed the crew, and, this obstacle disposed of, the advance went on, secured the Briqueterie with a couple of field guns after hard fighting, and even gained ground beyond it, the final line running North-East from Maricourt Wood to Favières Wood and thence North to join up with the Eighteenth Division. August 25th & 26th 1918 6th Battalion See Sketch 48

The last four days had brought that Division on to ground which will always be connected with its memory, even if the Eighteenth of August, 1918, contained but few survivors of its great fight for Trones Wood of July 1916. After only two days' rest the 53rd Brigade had moved on the evening of August 26th to a quarry in the dip between Montauban and the Bazentin ridge with orders to attack and clear Trones Wood. Longueval and Delville Wood were believed to be already in British hands and it was under this impression that the Brigade went forward about 5 a.m. next day, pushing East past the Northern apex of Bernafay Wood, then swinging round to its right to attack Trones and Bernafay Woods from the North.[1] The 7th put in A Company to clear Bernafay Wood while D advanced in the gap between that wood and Trones, which last the 8th R. Berkshires had to tackle. B had orders to establish itself on the 7th Battalion August 25th-26th See Sketch 22 August 27th

---

[1] This attack was to coincide with the Twelfth Division's advance to the line Briqueterie-Maricourt.

415

TRONES WOOD AGAIN.

August 27th 1918 7th Battalion Longueval road a few hundred yards North of the N.W. corner of Bernafay Wood.

It was about 6 a.m. when the Southward move began. A Company had a sharp fight but, well led by Lieut. H. J. M. Harris, in the end cleared Bernafay Wood and regained touch with D, whose advance had been more rapid; these two then started consolidating a line 300 yards South of the wood, though D's left was insecure as the Berkshires, delayed in their advance by machine-guns in Longueval and Delville Wood, which after all had not been taken, had not yet cleared Trones Wood. B Company also were held up by machine-gun fire from nests which the Berkshires had missed and suffered also from enfilade fire from the open left flank in the Longueval direction. They had to be held in support to the Berkshires, whose losses had been very heavy. Then at 8 a.m. came a vigorous counter-attack by a fresh battalion of the Prussian Guard. A Company held on most tenaciously, inspired by the splendid example set by Lieut. Harris. D, taken in flank from Trones Wood, gave ground but made a stand just West of the Wood. 2nd Lieut. Cullerne, who had already distinguished himself by following the barrage so closely that the enemy had no chance to reorganize as it lifted, was prominent in re-establishing the line, and 2nd Lieut. R. B. L. Hill rallied his platoon under heavy fire with much gallantry and determination and helped to beat back the attackers. It was some time before a counter-stroke could be organized, for units had become mixed up and losses had been heavy, but at 8 p.m. D and B Companies took part in a well-planned attack under the Colonel of the Berkshires, which swept the Germans back and succeeded in making good all the objectives of the morning. Many Germans were killed, over 40 machine-guns and 80 prisoners of the Francis Joseph Regiment of the Guard were taken, and Trones Wood, valuable for the excellent observation it gave

THE ADVANCE FROM THE ANCRE.

over the country to the Eastward, was firmly secured. Once again the 7th had cause to be proud of the name of Trones Wood. August, 1918
6th & 7th
Battalions

Thus it was that when on August 28th the Twelfth Division advanced past Maricourt towards Hardecourt it was with A Company of the 7th, who had pushed forward posts towards Maltzhorn Farm, that they established touch. That night the 53rd Brigade were relieved by the 54th. The 7th's losses, 90 in all, including 2nd Lieut. Humpage wounded, had been remarkably light, but it was in sore need of drafts. A day later the 6th also went back to rest. It had been in the advance again but had had little fighting, a few prisoners were secured, but the line Maurepas-Savernake Wood (just South of Combles) was reached almost unopposed. That night the Forty-Seventh Division relieved the Twelfth. In the last five days the 6th R.W.K. had lost nearly another 200[1], but it had taken two field-guns, thirteen trench-mortars, five grenade-throwers and thirty-nine machine-guns in the month, and had in all advanced eleven miles, assaulting no less than seven times. It was a splendid record, the result of good leadership and dogged endurance. See Sketch 48

August 29th

The 7th were not to rest just yet. They had three days in reserve while the 54th Brigade pushed on to Combles and cleared it (August 31st) and the 55th made a most successful advance on the morning of September 1st over the high ground between Combles and St. Pierre Vaast Wood, and the Thirty-Eighth Division cleared Morval only to be checked before Sailly-Saillisel. That afternoon the battalion was lent to the 55th Brigade to capture Saillisel in order to assist the Thirty-Eighth Division, who were renewing their attack. In moving up in daylight from near Guillemont to Priez Farm the battalion ran big risks, for the Sept. 1st

---

[1] 2nd Lieut. Snelgrove and 28 men killed, Lieuts. H. D. P. Hall and Thurlow, 2nd Lieuts. Bassett, Cleverly, Gibson, Jenkins, Miller and Thompson wounded with 153 men, 12 men missing.

THE ADVANCE FROM THE ANCRE.

Sept. 1st, 1918
7th Battalion

enemy had excellent observation facilities, but it reached its assembly position North-East of Frégicourt with surprisingly little loss, though at 6.30 p.m., the hour originally chosen as " zero," only B Company was in place and the attack had to be postponed till 7 p.m. Even then only D had got up to join B, but rather than lose the barrage these two companies attacked without waiting for the others.

It encountered a good deal of opposition from machine-gunners and snipers but the attack went very well, a platoon of Welsh Fusiliers of the Thirty-Eighth Division joined in on the left, and Captain McDonald handled his men most skilfully, while the G.S.O.2 of the Division, Major Hopwood, conspicuous in his " red tabs," joined in the advance with great coolness and daring. By 10 p.m. Saillisel had been cleared, over 30 prisoners had been taken and a good line established East of the village, though it was some time before the battalion could get touch with the Buffs nearer St. Pierre Vaast Wood, so that for a time the battalion was at the point of a salient, being well ahead of the Division on its left. This line was

Sept. 2nd

subjected to incessant shelling next day and German snipers were extremely active. The ground here had been reduced to a wilderness of devastation and shell-holes in the fighting of 1916, and the long grass which covered the waste gave cover to snipers, while the enemy had machine-gun posts on both flanks which proved very troublesome. However, the only counter-attack they tried—in the early morning just after " stand to "—was easily beaten off, the artillery co-operating most effectually, and after dark Captain McDonald pushed out patrols who discovered that the Germans were retiring. Profiting by the excellence of his reports the Brigadier took prompt advantage of the move and pushed troops forward in pursuit, the 7th remaining

Sept. 3rd

in support. Next evening the 55th Brigade—to which the 7th had been attached—was relieved by the Twelfth

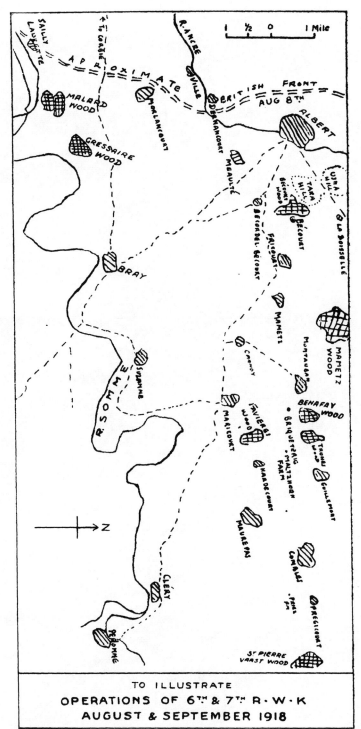

TO ILLUSTRATE
OPERATIONS OF 6TH & 7TH R·W·K
AUGUST & SEPTEMBER 1918

THE ADVANCE FROM THE ANCRE.

Division and went back to Montauban to have more of a real rest than it had enjoyed for weeks. It had earned it; for nearly a month it had been fighting almost remittingly and its victorious advance from the Ancre to the Tortille had covered nearly fifteen miles.   *Sept., 1918 6th & 7th Battalions*

By this time the battle which had started on August 23rd was reaching its close. The Third Corps' capture of the high ground between Bouchavesnes and Morval, coupled with the success of the Australians at Mont St. Quentin and of the Third Army's advance past Bapaume, clinched the fate of Peronne and of the line of the Somme. More than that, there was nothing left for the Germans but to fall back to the Hindenburg Line, and as they withdrew, offering a stubborn rear-guard resistance, the First Army chimed in with its famous piercing of the formidable Drocourt-Quéant Line, one of the few major achievements of the year in which The Queen's Own did not figure. By September 4th the Germans were retiring all along the front, and during the next few days they were thrust back behind the shelter of the outposts of the Hindenburg Line.

Opposite the Third Corps these ran approximately along a line from West of Templeux le Guérard, between Ste. Emilie and Ronssoy and just West of Epéhy and Peizières. In the pursuit to this line and in the various minor operations undertaken to secure a satisfactory starting-off line for the main attack on it, the 7th R.W.K. had no part; the 6th, however, came in for a share. The Twelfth Division had come back into the line on September 4th, relieving the Eighteenth along the Tortille. On the 5th and 6th Nurlu was taken after heavy fighting by the 35th and 36th Brigades, who advanced to the line Lieramont-Sorel le Grand, the 37th Brigade moving forward behind them in reserve. On the morning of the 7th it passed through the outpost line to attack the spur running East of North from Guyencourt towards Heude-   *6th Battalion*   *Sept., 7th*

THE ADVANCE FROM THE ANCRE.

Sept., 1918
6th Battalion

Sept. 8th

court Station, the 6th R.W.K. being on the left. Sharp opposition was encountered and machine-gun fire held the advance up for a time. But this opposition was overcome and the battalion pushed on very rapidly, forcing the Germans to evacuate several positions. Finally all objectives were gained and touch was obtained with the Twenty-First Division on the left, the advance having covered more than two miles. Later on patrols secured Jacquenne Copse and ascertained that Peizières and Epéhy were strongly held. Next morning the Fifty-Eighth Division relieved the Twelfth and the 6th, who had lost four officers (Captain Clifford, Lieut. Willoughby and 2nd Lieuts. Bryan and Daniel) wounded with 68 men, besides another 24 men killed or missing, went back to Vaux Wood, the Division being now in Corps Reserve. Since August 8th the battalion's casualties had come to nearly 500, but in the last few days of August drafts amounting to 8 officers and 340 men had arrived so that its strength had been fairly well maintained. It had been a hard time but one of great success and distinction, and the troops had been mightily encouraged at driving the Germans before them until they were back almost to their starting-line of March 21st of bitter memory.

CHAPTER XXVIII

THE LENS FRONT.

While the 1st, 6th and 7th had been contributing notably to the great victories of August 1918, the other two battalions of The Queen's Own in France had been less actively engaged. As yet the Germans had not had to give ground seriously either round Lens or on the front S.E. of Ypres, and neither to the 8th nor to the 10th R.W.K. were July and August specially noteworthy. The 8th found it busy enough, however, for the hostile aircraft displayed the greatest activity, though after several unsuccessful encounters with the 8th the German patrols completely abandoned all effort to contest No Man's Land. At the beginning of September the first indications were noticed of a German retirement on this front; on the evening of September 1st a platoon under 2nd Lieut. Killick pushed forward into Lens and established a post in what recently had been German territory, under cover of which working parties started clearing the two main roads leading into Lens and set to work establishing a new forward line. By September 12th, when the battalion was taken out for a rest, a good line had been constructed.   *Aug.-Sept., 1918 8th Battalion*   *See Sketch 52*

Returning a week later the 8th soon became involved in a series of sharp actions memorable in the battalion's story, for the Germans were anxious to delay the Allied advance at this point. The first episode was the recapture of a post at the junction of Claud and Canary Trenches which had changed hands several times already. Then on the night of September 23rd/24th the Germans attempted to retake it but were promptly counter-attacked and driven off by Lieut. Trenchard Davis, who led two sections across the open, covered by a rifle-grenade barrage. Next evening half   *Sept. 19th*   *Sept. 23rd-24th.*

DEAN'S POST.

Sept., 24th 1918
8th Battalion

No. 16 Platoon of D Company under 2nd Lieut. D. J. Dean, formerly of the 11th Battalion, took over the advanced post in Canary Trench. Hardly was the relief complete before the enemy attacked from the N.E., but were beaten off. 2nd Lieut Dean promptly repaired and improved his defences and though attacked

Sept. 25th

again held his own. Then about 6 a.m. a heavy barrage was put down, completely isolating the post. But its defenders, though heavily trench-mortared, never wavered, and when the enemy simultaneously attacked down the continuation of Canary Trench and across the open they were again repulsed. After that the day passed quietly, though the garrison was far from idle, any amount of work being done to strengthen the post; and that night the rest of No. 16 relieved the garrison, though 2nd Lieut. Dean insisted upon remaining in charge.

Sept., 26th

Early next morning came another attack, rather half-hearted, which the defenders' rifle-fire stopped easily enough, but it was followed by an intense bombardment which forced the remnants of the garrison back some fifty yards and then at last the Germans could rush the post. Their triumph was not for long; 2nd Lieut. Dean rallied his men and headed a counter-attack across the open; and at the same time 2nd Lieut. Cambrook, whose platoon was in Cinnabar Trench on the right of "Dean's Post," displayed marked promptness and initiative, and by a dashing attack across the open threatened to take the Germans in flank and cut them off. Sergt. Alderman gave him splendid help and the stroke proved most effective. The double attack dislodged the enemy, who bolted, many being shot as they fled.[1] The Germans did not try another attack; they had been too heavily punished, and the equipment which they left about the post would have fitted out a platoon. 2nd Lieut. Dean, who had set a splendid

---

[1] 2nd Lieut. Cambrook, who was badly wounded, subsequently died of his wounds, but had been awarded the M.C.

Lieut. D. J. DEAN, V.C., 8th Battalion.

Face Page 422.

DEAN'S POST.

example of courage and leadership and had handled his command with remarkable skill and judgment, inspiring his men with his own daring and contempt for danger, was fittingly rewarded by the much coveted Victoria Cross, Sergt Skinner, his Platoon Sergeant, who had backed him up splendidly, received the D.C.M., and M.M.'s were given to Sergt. Alderman, Corpls. Eversfield and Goodwin and Pte. Yates. Sept. 26th 1918 8th Battalion

The defence of " Dean's Post " was a notable feather in the 8th Battalion's cap. It was curious that it should have coincided with the third anniversary of the original 8th's tragic baptism of fire. The same devotion which had inspired Colonel Vansittart's men in their attempt to achieve the impossible at Loos had been displayed under more fortunate circumstances and with happier results. But the defence of " Dean's Post " did not stand alone. That afternoon 2nd Lieuts. Trenchard Davis and Killick successfully raided the enemy's post at the junction of Cloud and Cinnabar Trenches; 2nd Lieut. Killick knocked out a machine-gun just as it was opening fire on the raiders, while a dug-out was bombed, other damage done and many casualties inflicted. Next night a German raid was beaten off mainly by the tactical skill of 2nd Lieut. Manley, who kept his men sheltered in a dug-out while the bombardment lasted, brought them out the moment it lifted, placed them so as to get their fire to bear on both of the parties which were advancing and drove the enemy back with heavy losses. 2nd Lieut. Manley was badly wounded and died of wounds later on, but his promptness and insight were suitably rewarded by the M.C. Sept. 27th

The commanding officer of the 8th had ample justification, therefore, for the issue of his congratulatory Special Battalion Order of September 27th. The battalion's conduct had indeed reflected credit on all concerned and promised that when its turn came to pass to the offensive it would fully sustain the records of the

THE HINDENBURG LINE.

<small>September, 1918
8th Battalion</small>

1st, 6th and 7th. That turn was now at hand. On September 29th the battalion was relieved and went back to a camp near Doullens where its Division was concentrated for a short period of training.

<small>Aug.-Sept.
10th Batt.</small>

The 10th Battalion had had a quieter time. It had continued with the usual routine of trench duty varied by periods in reserve; several officers had joined, casualties had been fairly low, the enemy opposite being inactive while the Second Army was still holding its hand till the time to strike was ripe. By the beginning of September the Germans had evacuated practically the whole of the Lys salient created by their success of April and the British line on the right of the Forty-First Division's front had come forward again practically to the front held from the end of 1914 to the battle of Messines. When the 10th left the line on September 18th for a week's rest it had done its last turn of trench duty.

But before either the 8th or 10th took part in the great offensive the 1st, 6th and 7th had all been heavily engaged again. Sir Douglas Haig was now convinced that the breaking of the Hindenburg Line was practicable and that success in this operation would go far to clinch the victories of August and might even bring the war to an end in 1918. Before, however, any attack on the main Hindenburg Line could possibly succeed, the zone of its outer defences must be cleared; and accordingly orders were issued to the Fourth Army to attack on a front of fourteen miles from Holnon to Peizières with the object of establishing itself in striking distance of the main line. As before the Third Corps was on the left of the attack from the Cologne river Northward, having a frontage of 7,000 yards, and, as it had brought up both the Twelfth and the Eighteenth Divisions from reserve, The Queen's Own had once again its 6th and 7th Battalions engaged in the same major operation.

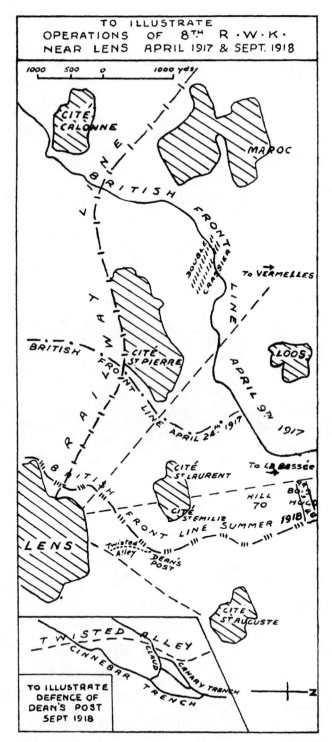

Face Page 424.

SKETCH 52.

EPÉHY.

The Eighteenth Division had the right centre of the Corps line from S.E. of Ste. Emilie to midway between that village and Epéhy, the Twelfth continuing the line North to N.W. of Peizières. In the Eighteenth Division the 54th Brigade reinforced by the 7th R.W.K. had Ronssoy and Basse Boulogne as its first objectives, in the Twelfth the 37th Brigade was held in reserve N. of Guyencourt, ready to go through the other brigades and attack the second objective. Beyond the line Basse Boulogne-Peizières a large number of spurs run in an Easterly or N.E. direction towards the St. Quentin Canal, and the second objective of the day's attack corresponded roughly to the old British outpost line along the top of these spurs. On the Twelfth Division's front the 37th Brigade had a line overlooking Vendhuille as its goal. *Sept., 1918 6th & 7th Battalions. See Sketch 51*

But some days were to elapse before the British line reached its objectives of September 18th. From the start the Third Corps met with most determined opposition and had to fight hard to make any progress. The ground was intersected with trenches, part of the old British defences, and largely owing to this, though partly to the misty weather, the fighting developed into a series of separate struggles for small tactical points in which units got very much split up. The fog made maintenance of direction very difficult, and the 7th, starting from just East of Ste. Emilié, failed to keep up with the barrage. However, by 7 a.m. the leading companies, A and D, had reached Ronssoy Wood and pushed on into the village, establishing a line to the Eastward of it while C mopped up the Wood. Soon after 9 a.m. Ronssoy had been secured, and the 54th Brigade "leap-frogged" the battalion and went on to complete the capture of the first objective. The 7th had done its work most effectively and with but few casualties. Later in the day it withdrew to Ste. Emilie and reverted to its own Brigade. *Sept. 18th 1918. 7th Battalion*

425

EPÉHY.

Sept. 18th 1918
6th Battalion

On the left the Twelfth Division had found stubborn opponents in the Alpine Corps, troops of high reputation and resolution, and the capture of Epéhy and Peizières was as much as could be accomplished. There was no question of the 37th Brigade going through to the second objective; indeed, though Colonel Dawson at first tried to work round North of the village, the 6th itself became involved in clearing Peizières which it reached about 8.30 a.m., nor were the remaining German posts and machine-guns in the village reduced till mid-day. The battalion was then able to push on N.E. towards Limerick Post to assist the Fifty-Eighth Division on the extreme left of the Corps. Working forward on the left by Beech Trench to Fir Support and Plane Trench two companies managed to establish some posts close to Poplar Trench, but could get no further in face of heavy machine-gun fire from that trench and from Lark Spur behind it. Further to the right little progress could be made, and the railway line just East of Epéhy represented the limit of the battalion's advance. Confused fighting continued most of the night on the Twelfth Division's front; further attempts by the 6th R.W.K. against Poplar Trench were unavailing,

Sept. 19th

and early next morning the battalion was relieved by the Fifty-Eighth Division and drawn back behind Epéhy. Its casualties had been light, not much over 40, including three officers[1] wounded. It was to have two days' rest before it was in action again, but for the 7th these were by no means days of rest.

7th Battalion

While only the right of the Third Corps had secured its second objective, over the greater part of the Fourth Army's front that line had been reached, and Sir Henry Rawlinson issued orders for the flanks of the attack to continue their efforts on the 19th. The Eighteenth Division therefore renewed its attack, advancing from Basse-Boulogne against Lempire. This village was flanked to the South by fortified copses known as X, Y

[1] Captain Parmenter, and 2nd Lieuts. Hunt and Woodcock.

EPÉHY.

and Z, and on the North by a trench, St. Patrick's Avenue, parallel to the road to Little Priel Farm, behind which were two fortified posts, Yak and Zebra, with Braeton and Heythorp Posts a little behind them, all on the spur running North from Lempire to the Catelet Valley. These posts were strongly held, for a fresh Division had just been rushed up to this front, and its arrival had been responsible for the stubborn opposition experienced by the Eighteenth Division both on September 18th and on the following day. Sept. 19th 1918 7th Battalion
See Sketch 51

The 7th had a hard time on the 19th. Assembling behind Ronssoy its orders were to follow the 8th Royal Berkshires through Lempire, to clear St. Patrick's Avenue with C Company, secure Zebra Post with B and then push on A to Braeton. This programme could not be carried out. Machine-gun fire from the right disorganized the advance, and the Berkshires had great difficulty in gaining ground and in clearing the way for the 7th to pass through them. By 12.10 p.m., however, they reported their right on its objective, and that one company of the R.W.K. had gone through them, but at 1 p.m. they had still not taken Yak Post, and till that was secured it was useless to advance against Zebra or Braeton. However, C Company bombed its way successfully along St. Patrick's Avenue and by 6 p.m. had secured it almost to its junction with Bird Trench. But it was slightly ahead of the Twelfth Division on its left, who had again met such stubborn resistance that they did not get beyond a line running diagonally N.W. to S.E. from Poplar Trench to the middle of St. Patrick's Avenue. Next day the fighting continued. It was of a desultory order; there was no attack on a large scale, but ground was gained by local struggles in which the 7th pushed patrols forward to Bird Trench and Zebra Post. That evening the Twelfth Division began relieving the left brigade of the Eighteenth and the 7th was accordingly withdrawn to Lempire to cooperate in an effort to secure the defences along the Sept. 20th

EPÉHY.

Sept. 21st 1918
7th Battalion

Hargicourt-Vendhuille road, D Company being put in early on the 21st to attack Sart Farm, while the 10th Essex advanced on its left and the 6th Northamptons on its right.

D achieved its objects, Sart Farm was taken with some prisoners; but an attempt on Egg Post was beaten back and neither Essex nor Northamptons could achieve much. The German opposition was still tenacious, and with the tactical situation very obscure artillery support was difficult to arrange. On the 22nd three distinct attempts were made upon Egg Post, but despite Lieut. Neill's determined leadership all were unsuccessful, though posts were established in Pomponious and Fleeceall Lanes. The effort was renewed on the 24th when A Company was beaten back from Egg Post by machine-gun fire, though Lieut. Cullerne, with some of B, established himself in a trench a little way South of the Post, taking three machine-guns and 12 prisoners

Sept. 22nd

and maintaining his ground.[1] That evening the battalion went back to Maurepas. It had had over 200 casualties since the 18th, including seven officers,[2] but it had hit the enemy hard and had wrested from him ground of real tactical importance.

6th Battalion

The exchange of frontage between the Eighteenth and Twelfth Divisions had brought the 6th R.W.K. to the spot where the 7th had been fighting. It took over St. Patrick's Avenue from 50 yards South of Bird Trench to Yak Post on the night of the 20th/21st and

Sept. 21st

at 5.40 a.m. attacked in the direction of Braeton Post and Bird Lane. The attack was met by heavy machine-gun fire, only a few men reached the wire in front of Braeton, and machine-guns in Mule Trench on the left prevented the retention of what ground was gained in that quarter. But the battalion kept up the pressure,

---

[1] He was awarded the M.C.

[2] Captain Tanner, Lieut. Stevens, and 2nd Lieuts. Peter and Larken were killed; Lieut. Gausden and 2nd Lieuts. Clapham and Robertson wounded.

ÉPÉHY.

many Germans who were retiring across the open towards Heythorp Post were effectively dealt with by the artillery, blocks were made in Bird and Heythorp Trenches and gradually the attack progressed. The junction of Bird Trench and St. Patrick's Avenue was finally made good about 10 p.m., and 300 yards were gained by bombing. This pressure was maintained next morning, and at last, about 3 p.m., after several repulses a fresh attack, organised by Colonel Dawson, whose energy and example inspired the exhausted men with fresh determination, carried Braeton Post and the whole trench line running South to Tombois Farm. The enemy bolted, losing heavily; and the battalion retained its gains undisturbed till that evening the 9th Essex relieved it. In the last few days it had had 36 men killed and missing, Captain G. W. Hill, Lieuts. Bayley and Fleming, 2nd Lieuts. Dark, Darcy, Turner, Warr and Vaughan wounded with 152 men, and was so reduced that it had to be reorganized as two companies. Throughout this period Colonel Dawson's leadership and example had been invaluable; he was constantly up in the front line, superintending operations, encouraging the men and inspiring them to new exertions. His part in enabling the 6th, despite heavy losses and the influx of recruits of little training, to continue to achieve success had been no small one.

Substantial success had been achieved on the 21st and 22nd along the whole front of the Third Corps, whose line was now sufficiently far advanced for effective co-operation in the great attack on the Hindenburg Line which was planned for September 29th. But though the Fourth Army had borne the brunt of the recent fighting and was confronted with the most formidable of the German defences it was not the Allied plan to press at one point only. While the 6th and 7th were enjoying their brief rest the French and Americans took up the attack in the Argonne, the Third and First

Sept., 1918
6th Battalion

Sept. 22nd

GOUZEAUCOURT.

September, 1918

British Armies attacked on the 29th South of the Sensée, menacing Cambrai from the North, while the Fourth threatened to turn it to the South, and on September 28th the Second in turn was let loose against the German defences East of Ypres.

1st Battalion

These extensions of the battle-front involved two more battalions of The Queen's Own in active fighting. The Fifth Division had relieved the New Zealanders in front of Gouzeaucourt in the middle of September. The 1st R.W.K. had received some small drafts since the battle of Bapaume, amounting to about 60 men with 12 officers, two of whom had the misfortune to be hit in their first tour of trench duty: this was when the

See Sketch 53

battalion was in the line from the 14th to the 20th N.W. of Gouzeaucourt, coming in for an increasing activity on the part of the enemy's heavy artillery. On the evening of September 25th it went up again in readiness for the general attack. In this it was told off to capture African Trench, N.W. of Gouzeaucourt, which was about the Southern end of the front attacked. It had the 15th and 14th R. Warwickshires on its left, and the 15th Brigade beyond them.

Sept. 27th

The 13th Brigade was not to attack until over two hours after the advance had begun elsewhere, and before the battalion left its trenches it had been under fire for some time and had some casualties. Its objective was just over the crest of the ridge, out of sight from its starting-line; the configuration of the ground enabled the Germans to get in an effective grazing fire and the attack, though gallantly pressed, was soon brought to a standstill. Even when Colonel Johnstone reinforced his attacking companies, A on the right, then B, then C, with three platoons of his reserve company, D, there was not weight enough to drive the attack home through the grazing fire. Some ground was gained; Sergt. E. J. Smith once again distinguished himself by leading his company forward after all its officers had fallen and establishing them close up to the German

GOUZEAUCOURT.

trenches, and at 8.30 a.m. Lieut. Burden, in the centre, reported the attack held up on his right but going better on his left; a little later some 40 of the battalion were digging in not very far from their objective and ultimately some men of C Company crawled back to report that they had got into a trench but had been held up by a block and a "strong point," and had later on been forced back by bombing. Another party under Corpl. Piggott got within 20 yards of the enemy's trenches and bombed the Germans, but seeing that the position was untenable the Corporal skilfully organized a retirement, which he covered by accurate rifle-fire and by bombing, but was himself mortally wounded in withdrawing. Sergt. Gilbert and Ptes. Burton and Colk all made gallant attempts to work forward and use bombs and rifle-grenades, and L/Cpl. Degavino established his Lewis gun within 40 yards of the enemy and put one of the German machine-guns out of action. But the position was too strong to be mastered and all that could be done was to hang on to the line reached.

_{Sept. 27th, 1918}
_{1st Battalion}

Finding that the officers with the attack had nearly all been hit, Lieut. Corke, who was acting as Intelligence Officer, went up to the front and did great work in organizing the consolidation of the line reached. 2nd Lieut. Ticehurst, the Signalling Officer, was assiduous in laying wires to the forward companies and keeping them in repair, though they were repeatedly broken by the shell-fire. On neither flank had much progress been made, but the battalion hung on and was rewarded for its tenacity next morning when patrols discovered African Trench clear, the enemy having evacuated it so hurriedly as to leave behind his own wounded, some British prisoners, ten machine-guns and a great quantity of ammunition. The attack had cost the battalion three officers[1] killed, and six wounded,[2]

Sept. 28th,

[1] Lieuts. Hemmerde and Lewin and 2nd-Lieut. R. M. Stephens.
[2] 2nd Lieuts. Burden, Bernard, Luscombe, Nott, Smith and Thorning.

FLANDERS.

Sept., 1918
1st Battalion

with 62 men killed, 2 missing and 153 wounded. It had in consequence to be reorganised as two companies of two platoons each and one of three, A and C being temporarily united.

10th Batt.
Sept. 28th

The other battalion to share in the offensive was the 10th. On the opening day of the Flanders attack it was not actively engaged; the Forty-First Division was in reserve to the Nineteenth Corps and only the 124th Brigade, which passed through the Thirty-Fifth Division, reached the front line. The 123rd Brigade followed to Ravine Wood, halted there, and then advanced to pass through the 124th at Kortewilde and continue the attack next morning.

Sept. 29th

September 29th opened fine, but with a ground fog, which made direction-keeping difficult but helped to conceal the advance and so contributed to the surprise of the Germans. So complete was this that the crews of a 4.2-inch howitzer battery were at breakfast when the 10th came rushing in on top of them, and in addition three 77-mm. field-guns, five machine-guns and many prisoners were taken with surprisingly low casualties. By 9.15 the battalion was on the railway N.E. of Comines, but the 23rd Middlesex on its right had been kept back by meeting very stubborn opposition on the canal bank and both that unit and the 10th had outrun the troops on their flanks and found themselves in a pronounced salient under a heavy converging fire from artillery and machine-guns. It was necessary to fall back; and under cover of B Company, which was well handled by 2nd Lieut. Weston, a successful withdrawal to a position a little in advance of the Houthem line was made, though casualties were heavier in the withdrawal than they had been in the advance. Splendid work was done by Corpl. Malyon and Sergt. Pilcher. The former, whose Lewis-gun section had done good service in the advance, covered the withdrawal most effectively and in the end got his gun and his whole party back in safety, although himself wounded. The

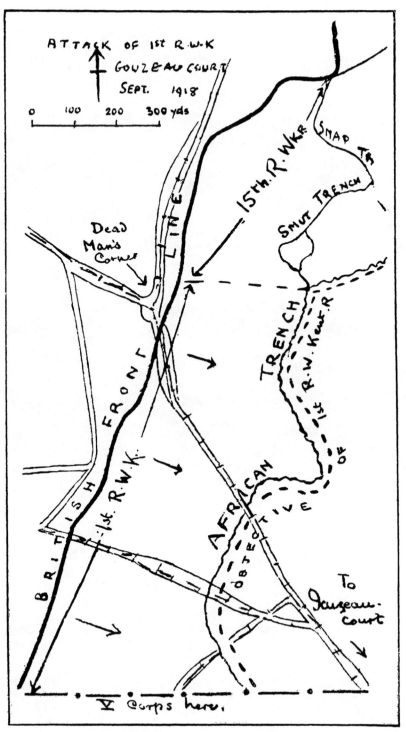

FLANDERS.

Sergeant rallied two platoons which were in disorder because their officers had fallen, and led them forward just in time to repel a counter-attack. The Germans indeed had counter-attacked twice in force hoping to recover their guns; they were met with steady rifle and Lewis-gun fire and by an effective barrage, and lost very heavily without gaining their ends. That night the battalion was relieved by the 10th Queen's. *Sept. 29th, 1918 10th Batt.*

September 29th had been a notable day for the 10th, really its first real experience of open warfare, but it had carried out its unfamiliar task well. Direction and extensions had been well kept, ground had been skilfully used to encircle and outflank the hostile machine-guns; and if losses had been severe—three officers[1] and 35 men killed, 20 men missing and five officers[2] and 90 men wounded—important gains had been made.

The Forty-First Division was now transferred to the left to press the advance on Menin; the move brought it into line just South of the Ypres-Menin road. On October 1st the 123rd Brigade advanced towards Gheluwe, the battalion, which was in reserve, moving through Tenbrielen to the America Cabaret under heavy shelling from Comines. The leading battalions were held up by a trench system called the Gheluwe Switch, which the 10th had to attack next day,[3] when the 122nd Brigade's progress on the left gave the 123rd a better chance to get on. A and B Companies were sent forward about noon and pushed on some way, but a counter-attack on the battalion on their left, which drove that unit back, compelled the two companies to conform, though one platoon of B managed to maintain its ground. Sergt. Pilcher was again to the fore, rallying *October 2nd*

---

[1] Lieut. F. E. Norris and 2nd Lieuts. J. H. Russell and Hickmott.

[2] Captains Hindle and Doubleday, 2nd Lieuts. George, Lawrence and Hudson.

[3] It was on this day that Captain Holden, who had served so long with the 10th Battalion, was killed when in command of the 11th Queen's.

FF

FLANDERS.

Sept.-Oct., 1918
10th Batt.

retiring troops and bringing them into the firing-line in the face of heavy machine-gun fire; and in the end the Germans, who had suffered severely from the rifle and machine-gun fire to which they had exposed themselves, retired in disorder. The Second Army was now practically up to the left bank of the Lys, and for the moment its advance was suspended.

CHAPTER XXIX

THROUGH THE HINDENBURG LINE.

While the Second Army had been carrying the British line in Flanders further in one swoop than all the repeated attacks of 1917 had ever managed to do, an even more decisive success was being secured on the Cambrai-St. Quentin front. In this the Fourth Army attacked on a twelve-mile line from Selency to Vendhuille, with the Third Corps on its left. The special mission of that Corps, which was again employing the Twelfth and Eighteenth Divisions, was to capture the high ground just S.W. of Vendhuille and thereby protect the attack by the Australians and Americans on the tunnel defences round Bellicourt. This brought the 6th R.W.K. into the fight yet once again, but the 7th was in reserve, though its Division came in for heavy fighting. To the North of the Fourth Army the Third co-operated by attacking on the Gouzeaucourt-Marcoing front S.W. of Cambrai, supported by the First Army N.W. of that town. But for the moment the Fifth Division was back in reserve after its sharp fighting of September 27th, and though the Twenty-Fourth was just about to leave the Lens area and to be thrown into the fighting neither the 1st or 8th Battalions took any part in the piercing of the formidable lines which represented the German ne plus ultra, the highest development of the art of constructing field fortifications seen in the four long years of war. _{Sept.-Oct., 1918}

But the 6th, if the only battalion of The Queen's Own engaged in this great battle, played its part well. The 37th Brigade assembled West of the Honnecourt road and North of Catelet Copse and attacked in an Easterly direction with Swallow Trench as its main objective. The 6th was on the left with the Buffs on

6th Battalion
See Sketch 51

THROUGH THE HINDENBURG LINE.

Sept. 29th 1918
6th Battalion

its right. Advancing at 6.30 a.m. the 6th met stubborn opposition, particularly on the left where Dados Lane, a particularly strong position overlooking the valley beyond, defied its efforts. On the right more progress was made; a platoon got into Swallow Trench but it was ahead of the troops on both flanks and after a hard fight it was dislodged. But Catelet Trench was secured, a counter-attack beaten off without much difficulty, and posts pushed forward into Dados Lane and Dados Loop.

Sept. 30th

At dawn next morning the attack was renewed. Once again most stubborn resistance was offered, especially in Dados Loop, but the pressure was maintained and at last Dados Loop was cleared. Once that had happened other gains followed. Stone Trench, Falcon Trench, the Bird Cage and almost all Kildare Trench were taken, and the battalion and the 9th Essex, pressing on, occupied Hawk Trench, with the S.W. part of Ossus Wood. By that evening the Twelfth and Eighteenth Divisions had driven the Germans across the canal and were clearing up Vendhuille. A patrol of the 6th reached the canal bank and found a bridge intact by which infantry could pass over.

But the 37th Brigade was not to exploit its success any further, it was relieved by the Eighteenth Division and retired to Guyencourt, prior to moving away to the quieter portion of the front held by the First Army. After all it had gone through and accomplished in the last two months the Twelfth Division had certainly earned an easier task than to continue to lead the advance of the Fourth Army. In this last fight the 6th had got off lightly, considering the stubbornness of the resistance, but its "strength" was down now below 600. It had captured many machine-guns, trench-mortars and other booty during September, but the continuity and variety of the fighting and the rapidity of the advance had rendered the collection of more than a few of these trophies impossible.

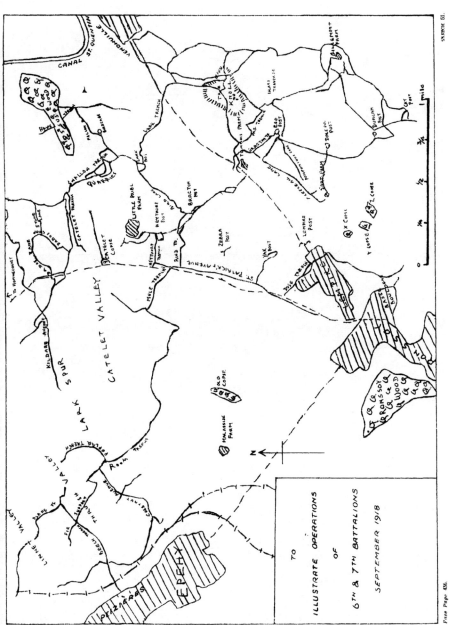

THROUGH THE HINDENBURG LINE.

Once the Hindenburg Line had been broken through the character of the fighting was substantially changed; the Germans had little or nothing in the way of prepared positions in rear of it. What artificial obstacles they were able to oppose to the further advance of the British were improvised. Past were the days of prolonged bombardments, of elaborate and strongly fortified trench systems; for the remainder of the war the fighting was almost entirely in open country for the most part untouched by war. The villages and towns which had yet to be captured were still substantial, not mere names on a map represented on the actual ground only by ruins heaped over an occasional cellar. Conditions were thus much more like those of the opening days of the war, except for the enormous increase in artillery and for all the new weapons and methods of war. _{October, 1918}

The immediate sequel to the breaking of the Hindenburg Line was an attack by the Third and Fourth Armies delivered on October 8th on the front of seventeen miles from Cambrai Southward. In this the 8th Battalion was to get its chance, its Division having been brought up two days earlier to Graincourt, S.W. of Cambrai, where it was in support to the Sixty-Third. This was almost on the extreme left of the attack and had as its objective Niergnies, about three miles from the S.E. suburbs of Cambrai. After hard fighting the Sixty-Third took and held this village, and in the evening the 72nd Brigade came up to pass through and continue the advance by attacking Awoignt. At 5.20 next morning, when it was still dark, the attack started. Opposition was still stubborn, mainly from machine-gun crews. One detachment which was holding up D Company with its machine-guns, thereby covering the destruction of a railway bridge, was successfully rushed by 2nd Lieut. Dean and a party, the guns were taken, the bridge was saved and the advance went on. By 8 a.m. the battalion's objectives had been taken _{Oct. 8th. 8th Battalion See Sketch 54} _{October 9th}

437

THROUGH THE HINDENBURG LINE.

October, 1918
8th Battalion

along with two guns, three tanks and 35 prisoners, its casualties amounting to just 60, including 2nd Lieuts. Winch and Green killed and 2nd Lieut. Taylor wounded. It had been a well-executed movement, and despite the start in the dark direction was well kept.

The 73rd Brigade passing through the 72nd now pushed on at a great pace. Only when, on the evening of October 10th, the leading troops began to approach the river Selle did the resistance stiffen. The 8th, who had followed the advance by Cagnoncles and Rieux to St. Aubert, moved into line West of the river on October 13th, just opposite Haussy. The immediate task was the passage of the river which, if not in itself a major obstacle, certainly needed careful negotiation. All bridges had been destroyed and the Germans kept the high ground above the river under steady shell-fire. On the 14th some patrols of A Company made their way down to Haussy and tried to penetrate into it but were stoutly opposed; at last, however, after heavy fighting two platoons established a lodgment in the West of the village. 2nd Lieut. Piggott and Sergt. Ashdown were both killed and only with much difficulty was the position maintained.

See Sketch 54

October 16th

Two days later came a real attack on Haussy; this was to omit the village itself, but was to secure the high ground lower down the river between it and Montrecourt, and only after that had been successful was Haussy to be attacked. A steady harassing fire, maintained by the artillery on the ground between the river and the railway, had the effect of clearing that area of Germans so that the battalion could assemble beyond the river and be waiting there for the barrage to open at 5.10 a.m. The advance was immediately successful. B Company on the left, though ahead of the battalion on its flank, rushed the railway, taking the enemy by surprise and capturing many prisoners with several machine-guns. D, on the right, was equally successful and by 7 a.m. all objectives had been taken. Splendid

HAUSSY.

service was done by C.S.M. Gutteridge who rallied and reorganized platoons which had come under enfilade fire and had lost their officers, and by pushing forward with a Lewis gun and directing its fire was largely instrumental in breaking up a counter-attack.

October 16th
1918
8th Battalion

The position having thus been secured by the 8th the way was clear for the 9th East Surreys to be put in against Haussy from the North, and they successfully carried the village. But the enemy replied by a furious bombardment of Haussy and followed this up with counter-attacks, ultimately getting into the village from the South where the East Surreys' flank was open and getting behind them. Nearly all Haussy was lost, but Captain Orchardson of D Company promptly organized a defensive flank and prevented the enemy from emerging from the Northern end of Haussy. 2nd Lieut. Cornford, the only other officer left in B and D Companies, also did great work in directing the consolidation and in holding up the German counter-attack, which was brought to a dead stop at a chapel where 2nd Lieut. Cornford held an advanced post all day. Thus the 8th contrived to maintain its ground, although its other flank was also exposed. It was the more creditable that with both flanks " in the air " the 8th guarded them so well that it did not lose a single prisoner. That evening the 7th Northamptons arrived to relieve the battalion, which went back into reserve until October 26th. Its fine achievement had cost it nearly 100 casualties, 2nd Lieuts. Laskey, Bain, Holman and Wallis were killed and Captain Porter wounded, but the action brought M.C.'s to Captains Orchardson, Porter and Selfe, D.C.M.'s to C.S.M. Gutteridge, who died of wounds a little later, Corpl. Stoneman and Pte. Woodmore, and a bar to the M.M. to Pte. Bowes.

By this time the Fifth Division were back at the front again and the Eighteenth were under orders to return. The ten days' rest which the 1st R.W.K. had

THROUGH THE HINDENBURG LINE.

October, 1918
1st Battalion

since the fight for African Trench had been spent in the Ytres area and had brought it a substantial reinforcement in the shape of 162 men from the 12th Gloucesters, for the reduction to a ten-battalion basis which the Fifth Division had so long avoided had at last overtaken it, and the 14th and 15th Royal Warwicks disappeared from the 13th Brigade, being replaced by their 16th Battalion. At the same time half-a-dozen new officers joined with some small drafts and a few men from hospital, while Colonel Johnstone returned to England on three months' leave, leaving Captain R. Brown in command.

October 9th
See Sketch 54

On October 9th the Battalion started for the front, moving by Caudry to Bethencourt and relieving the 63rd Brigade (Thirty-Seventh Division) in the line on the evening of the 12th. The 13th Brigade's frontage ran along the railway East of Briastre, with its right thrown back along the Selle near Neuvilly, the 1st R.W.K. being on the Viesly-Inchy road in support until the 16th, when it took over the front line from the K.O.S.B.'s having two companies in front, each with two platoons on the further side of the Selle. Artillery and aircraft were extremely active on both sides. The Germans made a speciality of firing gas-shell freely at night, but failed to prevent the battalion's patrols from being very enterprising and collecting a great deal of information as to the location of the enemy's wire; this was passed on to the artillery—with highly satisfactory results.

October 16th-19th

The work which the battalion put in during its three days in the line helped to bring about the substantial success achieved by the Fifth Division in the attack of October 20th, but it had no part in the fight, having been relieved on the previous evening and taken back to Caudry; nor was the 13th Brigade employed in the next attack, that of October 23rd, which, delivered on a front from Mazinghein to N.E. of Haussy, brought the British line forward to the Sambre-Oise Canal on the right, to the outskirts of the Forest of

TO ILLUSTRATE OPERATIONS OF 1ST & 8TH R·W·K· OCT. 1918

SKETCH 54.

THROUGH THE HINDENBURG LINE.

Mormal and to the neighbourhood of Valenciennes on the left. In this and the operations of October 26th which exploited and completed its success, the much-enduring 7th R.W.K. were once again to the fore. Not for long could the Eighteenth Division be left out of the fighting.

<small>October, 1918</small>

After relieving the Twelfth Division at Vendhuille on September 30th the Eighteenth had been promptly relieved itself and had gone back to Cardonette near Amiens, where the 7th spent a fortnight in reserve. A dozen new officers arrived, and, though weak in numbers, the battalion was again in condition to give a good account of itself when, on October 17th, it entrained for Roisel. Marching by Villers Faucon and Premont it reached Maurois, S.W. of Le Cateau, on the 19th and went into the line next night, B and D Companies relieving the 9th Manchesters of the Sixty-Sixth Division on the spur just N.E. of the town which had been captured in the attack of October 17th and 18th. Beyond this spur the ground dipped rapidly to the valley of the little Richemont River, rising more steeply on the far side. The 53rd Brigade was on the right of the Division with the 7th R.W.K. on the right and the 10th Essex on the left and the 54th Brigade beyond them. On the right the Twenty-Fifth Division was attacking the Bois l'Evêque, a big wood partially cleared of timber which flanked the line by which the Eighteenth Division would move from its first to its second objective. The enemy seemed to be expecting another big attack and kept on putting down barrages at short intervals, but nevertheless some valuable patrolling work was done, notably by Corpl. Aitchison, whose success in locating German machine-gun positions behind their front line proved of great service when the attack was made.

<small>7th Battalion</small>

<small>See Sketch 55</small>

" Zero " was fixed for 1.20 a.m., instead of dawn, as the moon was full and the attack actually started in bright moonlight. The Germans immediately put

<small>October 23rd</small>

441

ACROSS THE SELLE.

October, 1918
7th Battalion

down a heavy barrage on the forming-up line, but the companies had taken the precaution of moving forward and so escaped it, though some field-guns just behind B's line suffered severely. The battalion made short work of the descent of the slopes leading down to the Richemont; light wooden bridges, specially constructed for the purpose, were laid across; and despite heavy fire, chiefly from trench-mortars, the passage was forced, thanks largely to the very accurate fire of some 4.5-inch howitzers which were supporting the advance. It was not done without loss, however, for 2nd Lieut. Cullerne was killed in leading his men across, and a good many other casualties were suffered. But a dashing attack by B Company took the German post at Garde Mill from the flank and captured it with 70 prisoners; D carried Ervillers Wood Farm at the foot of the rising ground and went on to the hamlet of Corbeau, half-way up the slope, while a detachment of B coming up behind some Germans, who were holding up the advance of the Twenty-Fifth Division, surprised them completely and took another 120 prisoners. A and C then took up the running, clearing the spur N.W. of Pommereuil and reaching the first objective well to time.

Sergt. Gregory was prominent in this advance. He had already done good work on patrol, bringing in valuable information; and he now rushed a machine-gun single-handed, while on reaching the objective he established a couple of posts and " mopped up " a sunken road, capturing several prisoners.[1] Sergt. Sterry, too, pushed out to the front and cleared the ground of snipers with much success. A great haul was made of machine-guns, anti-tank rifles and trench-mortars and nearly 400 prisoners were captured, not far short of the whole strength of the battalion, for the Germans were apparently so completely surprised by the speed of the

---

[1] He received the D.C.M., as did also Corpl. Aitchison and Sergt. Sterry, but the latter, who had already won the M.M. and a bar, was badly wounded and died four days later.

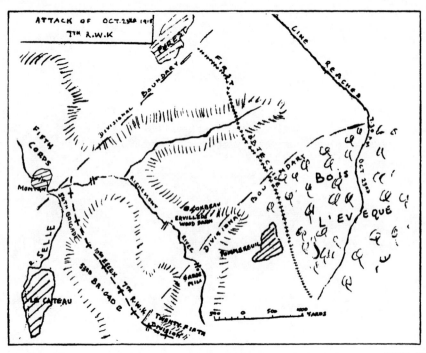

ENGLEFONTAINE.

advance that for once they seemed to lack stomach for a fight, even though the battalion's left was exposed, the Essex having been checked. Indeed, not till some time later did the Berkshires come up and pass through to capture the second objective. Beyond that the attack was carried on by the 55th Brigade, which after hard fighting secured the third objective, just East of Bousies. Next day the 54th and 55th Brigades carried the line forward to just West of the road on the S.W. edge of the Forest of Mormal from Englefontaine to Landrecies. After this brilliant success, in which the Eighteenth Division captured a quite unprecedented number of guns, both field and heavy, there came a week's lull in active operations, to allow of the necessary preparations for the next big stroke, but in this period some successful minor enterprises were carried out, in one of which the 7th was engaged. _{October 23rd 1918 7th Battalion} _{October 24th}

The battalion had concentrated at Corbeau on the evening of October 23rd, moved up to Bousies next day and remained there in support till the evening of the 25th, when it moved forward to co-operate with the 10th Essex and 8th R. Berkshires in an attack on some high ground S. of Englefontaine, known as Mount Carmel. A and C Companies were told off to cover the Berkshires' left by attacking respectively Hecq Church and the cross-roads at the S.E. end of Englefontaine. The country here was very different from the open and rolling downs West of the Selle. It was well wooded, divided into small fields and orchards, enclosed by thick hedges, which, if they provided cover from view and might help to conceal advances, were also serious obstacles to movement. However, at 1 a.m. on the 26th C Company went off with great dash and well led by 2nd Lieut. Oakley,[1] seized their objective and consolidated it, although they were for some time the only British in Englefontaine, as the troops of the Fifth Corps who were co-operating on their left did not

See Sketch 56

October 26th

---
[1] He was awarded the M.C.

THROUGH THE HINDENBURG LINE.

October, 1918
7th Battalion
succeed in clearing the village till much later. A was hardly so successful. Severe machine-gun fire from the outskirts of Hecq stopped them 200 yards short of the church, and as neither Berkshires nor Essex had managed to get beyond the Englefontaine-Robersart road no more progress could be made. A, however, dug in

October 27th
and the two companies held on, while next day the rest of the battalion took over the Berkshires' share of the Brigade frontage. This position it retained till the 29th, and then, after a day's rest at Bousies, re-occupied it again on the 31st. Considering the difficulties of the ground and the advantages it gave to the defence, the battalion's casualties in its last two actions had been low; 2nd Lieut. Cullerne was the only officer killed and only three were wounded, 2nd Lieuts. Hill, Woolley and Lee, while 12 men were killed, 3 missing and 62 wounded.

Meanwhile even the centre of the British line, which had long stood almost stationary, was moving forward

6th Battalion
rapidly and the 6th R.W.K. found that if their transfer to the First Army had brought them to a quarter where there was not the desperate fighting of August and September, there was certainly to be plenty of movement. On joining the Eighth Corps the Twelfth

See Sketch 57
Division found itself in the Avion Sector South of Lens, and here the 6th took over support trenches on October 6th. It had received drafts amounting to over 150 men before the move came, and Major L. C. R. Smith had rejoined and became second-in-command and three other officers had arrived.

Barely had the Division taken over the new front before its patrols discovered that the Germans had began to withdraw, upon which an advance was at once begun. On October 10th the leading troops reached the formidable Drocourt-Quéant line to find it practically undefended, the 6th advancing to and clearing Billy Montigny. The Germans were going back fast enough, but there was a sting in their tails, and

THE ADVANCE FROM LENS.

more than once the British advanced guards had sharp fighting. Thus, when Billy Montigny was cleared, 2nd Lieut. Arnold was mortally wounded and several men were hit, but the battalion's advance forced a strong party of Germans to quit a hamlet known as Jerusalem on the left of its line and heavy losses were inflicted on them as they fled. On the 12th Henin Lietard was occupied, and there the 6th had four days' rest while the 35th Brigade took over the advanced guard duties and pushed on to the passage of the Haute Deule Canal at Auby, North of Douai. On the 18th the 6th was leading again and pushed on to Flines on the Douai-Orchies road, which village it occupied after sharp fighting in which some of the battalion had the rare experience of being actually charged by cavalry, a detachment of which suddenly emerged out of Flines Wood, only to be beaten off with loss. Next day the Buffs went through the battalion, which followed to Beuvry and Mont du Proy between Orchies and St. Amand and came forward again on the 22nd for what was to be its last fight. _{October, 1918 6th Battalion} _{October 19th}

This was for the passage of the little river Decours at Nivelle, N. of St. Amand, which was effected despite some opposition, and then the battalion pushed on to the Scarpe Canal. Here the bridges had been destroyed and the German machine-guns were busy, so the task was attended with considerable difficulties, which were much increased by the flooding of the country on both banks of the canal. But the troops persevered, and on the morning of October 23rd they at last forced their way across, thanks largely to the skill with which Colonel Dawson handled his men, and compelled the enemy to clear away from a bridge they were trying to defend. Thus the passage was secured and the way opened for the Buffs to go through. But before this took place a grave misfortune had befallen the 6th. Colonel Dawson came up from headquarters to visit the front line and inspect the

THROUGH THE HINDENBURG LINE.

October, 1918
6th Battalion

bridge-heads under construction. He completed his inspection and was going back down the road when a stray shell bursting close to him inflicted terrible wounds in the back, chest, left leg and spine. He was quite alone and, though almost unconscious, managed to drag himself into a small empty hut near by. A runner who was passing heard a low whistle and going in found his Colonel. Assistance was promptly forthcoming, but from the first it was realized that his injuries were of the gravest nature. After all he had gone through — it was his seventh appearance in the casualty list—it was the cruellest fate that he should be struck down by almost the last shell fired at the battalion he had commanded so skilfully, which had done such memorable things under him, of which he had been the life and soul, the predominant figure and the chief inspiration, by which he was so valued and loved. A few days later the Twelfth Division was relieved by the Fifty-Second and the 6th, now commanded by Major Smith, went back to Rosult. It had just moved forward again to Lechelle when the

Nov. 11th

news of the armistice reached it. A striking feature of this advance was that in every village the 6th passed through, sometimes on the very heels of the Germans, the inhabitants, old men and women and young children, came out of the houses to gaze in astonishment on troops and uniforms they had never seen before, and then to fall down on their knees at the road-side and thank God for " the Deliverance." It was a wonderful sight which those who saw it will never forget.

10th Batt.

Of all the battalions of The Queen's Own in the Western theatre of war the 10th had the longest spell of fighting in October. After a few days' rest near Kruiseecke it had gone back into the line on the night of the 6th/7th and had a lively time, for German snipers were active and their machine-guns troublesome till a fighting patrol went out on the evening of October 8th and cleared up a particularly obnoxious specimen. Then

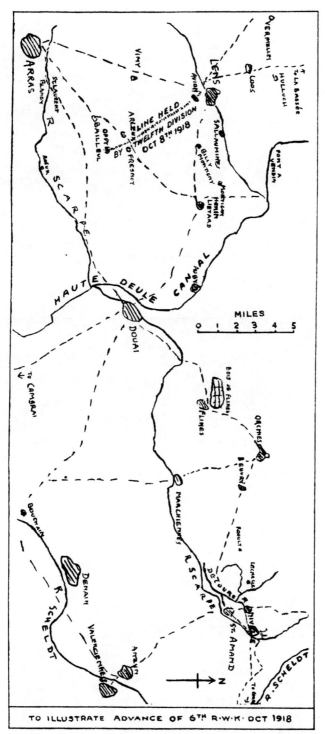

Face Page 446. SKETCH 57.

FROM LYS TO SCHELDT.

after another short rest the battalion took up its position in Divisional reserve for the new attack on the Flanders front. This aimed at effecting the passage of the Lys, after which Lille was to be pinched out by the advance of the Fifth Army from the S.W. in co-operation with that of the Second to the Scheldt. October, 1918 10th Batt.

See Sketch 58

When the attack started, on October 14th, the 123rd Brigade had nothing more to do than to follow up the advance, and as this went well the reserve brigade was not called upon. By evening the Tenth and Nineteenth Corps were established on rising ground overlooking Menin and Wervicq, while on the left the attack made even greater progress, the net result being that on the 19th the crossing of the river was effected by the Division near Courtrai. The 10th was not actively employed in this operation but moved forward into billets in Courtrai next day; its turn was to come. On the evening of the 22nd the 123rd Brigade took over the left of the Divisional front, the 10th Battalion facing S.E. between the villages of Kattestraat and Kwadestraat, with its left on the Kattestraat-Heesteert road. Before the general advance could be resumed it was highly desirable to clear the enemy out of their strong position opposite the 10th in order to straighten the line at this point. On October 23rd therefore the 10th was ordered to make the attempt, though very little artillery support was available. The final objective of the attack was the Avelghem-Waffelstraat road, but before that could be reached high ground 400 yards North of the Hoogmolen-Vierkeerhoek road had to be secured. The battalion attacked with B Company on the right, A and D beyond it and C in reserve. October 20th

October 23rd

The attack came under heavy fire from machine-guns at once, but progress was made nevertheless. However, after some 400 yards had been gained by A and D the fierceness of the machine-gun fire from the chapel E. of Kattestraat pulled them up, and though B reached Hill 66 there was a farm just over the crest from the

FROM LYS TO SCHELDT.

October, 1918
10th Batt.

roof of which several machine-guns fired with most deadly effect. From Hoogmolen Mill, too, other machine-guns swept the front, and as the troops on the flanks had not managed to get as far forward the battalion had finally to fall back at nightfall approximately

October 24th

to its starting-off line. At 2.30 next morning the advance was renewed, this time with C Company in the centre in place of A, but with no more backing from the artillery. Much the same thing happened; ground was gained at first, several German posts were cleared out by D, but machine-gun fire from the left flank held the advance up and D, after holding on to its gains for some time, had to go back for lack of support on its exposed left flank. C also, after actually capturing the farm on the eastern slopes of Hill 66, which had proved such an obstacle on the day before, found it untenable in the face of increasing shelling and a converging machine-gun fire. After maintaining its position for over two hours C withdrew in good order, however, and with surprisingly few casualties.

That night the 11th Queen's relieved the battalion, which was placed in Brigade reserve for the next advance. This was the big attack: ample artillery support was forthcoming and the Germans hastily evacuated the position, offering hardly any resistance. Both

October 25th

the 23rd Middlesex and 11th Queen's made good progress, and D and A Companies—which were attached to these battalions as " moppers-up "—had plenty of work. A had first to clear the houses on the Kattestraat-Heestert road, which involved some sharp fighting but was satisfactorily accomplished; Heestert was reached about 1.30 p.m. and then two platoons were put in to fill a gap between The Queen's and the Middlesex while the other two helped The Queen's to clear up two hamlets, Spichestraat and Raaptorf, 400 yards East of which latter place an outpost line was taken up.

FROM LYS TO SCHELDT.

D Company had had a similar experience. There were houses to be cleared along the Knokke-Hoske road but the German resistance lacked determination and the villages of Hoske and Okkerdriesch were taken without much fighting, after which the company pushed forward to link up with the line already established East of Raaptorf. Meanwhile Battalion Headquarters and B and C had followed in the track of the advance, Headquarters and B ultimately getting to Hoske, C almost to Raaptorf. October 25th 1918 10th Batt.

Next day the advance was continued but without serious opposition and a line was established on the banks of the Scheldt, thus reaching the final objective. Then the Thirty-Fifth Division relieved the Forty-First and the 10th went back to Courtrai to rest. Here a draft of nearly 100 men joined, about replacing the losses in the last advance, which included Captains Harding, Gordon Smith and 2nd Lieuts. Stubbs and Cross killed with 27 men, while 2nd Lieut. S. C. Harris was among the wounded. The battalion was down below 700 strong, its September casualties not having been replaced. October 26th

CHAPTER XXX

THE LAST BATTLE.

October, 1918

By the end of October the victorious progress of the Allied armies had reached a point which brought the end of hostilities almost within sight. Decisive victory in 1918, which had seemed unattainable before August 8th, had been practically achieved. A series of undisguisable defeats had at last demoralized the German armies. Here and there a stubborn opposition was still offered but for the most part the rank and file were more ready to surrender than to resist to the last. Indeed there could be no prospect now of a successful stand by the Germans on any line short of the Rhine, if the Allies could continue the series of hammer-strokes which Marshal Foch and Sir Douglas Haig had been delivering for the past three months. That this might be rendered impossible by the difficulty of keeping the troops at the front supplied with food and ammunition was more to be feared than that the German resistance would stiffen up again to the standard it had reached in August and September. But in the damaged condition of the roads and railways a breakdown in the supply arrangements was highly probable and already the Third and Fourth Armies had had to let nearly a week elapse after the final success on the Selle before

November, 1918

they could repeat their blow. However, by November 4th all was ready for what was to prove the last great battle of the war.

By this time the First Army had come up level with the left of the Third and its capture of Valenciennes had forced the Germans back almost to the junction of the Scheldt with the Condé canal. The frontage to be attacked came to nearly thirty miles, and on it were to be found three Divisions in which battalions of The

THE LAST BATTLE.

Queen's Own were serving. Of these the Twenty-Fourth was almost on the extreme left of the Third Army, being just North of the Rhonelle river opposite the villages of Wargnies le Petit and Wargnies le Grand; the Fifth in the centre of that Army was in support to the Thirty-Seventh Division S.W. of Le Quesnoy, the Eighteenth on the left of the Fourth Army was at Robersart on the Western edge of the Forest of Mormal. Thus the 1st, the 7th and 8th Battalions lined up for the last round in the great encounter. [November, 1918]

Neither the 1st nor 8th, however, were to experience in this last engagement fighting of any severity. When the Twenty-Fourth Division attacked, using the 73rd Brigade as advance-guard, the 17th in support, and the 72nd as reserve, it met surprisingly little opposition. Only at Wargnies le Petit was there real resistance and this was overcome without calling upon the 72nd Brigade. Indeed it was not till November 7th that that brigade passed through the 17th at St. Waast and swept on towards Bavai. Rear-guard parties with machine-guns tried to put up a fight but could not prevent the brigade passing Bavai and getting 2,000 yards beyond it. Here more serious opposition was met. Lieut. H. R. Smith and 2nd Lieut. Everson were killed in trying to push forward in the face of machine-gun fire and the battalion's advance was checked. But next morning the German rearguard had gone and the 8th pushed on with the North Staffords on its right and the 6th Dragoon Guards scouting ahead. There was not much opposition and the day's advance, which covered no less than four miles, was not brought to a stop till Feignies was reached. Here the Germans were standing in a strong position, and with all ranks dead beat from their exertions it was decided not to attack there and then. The soundness of the decision was vindicated next morning when, on the battalion pushing forward, the enemy vacated Feignies with speed; then, the village once cleared, other troops came forward [Nov. 4th 8th Battalion] [Nov. 7th] [Nov. 8th] [Nov. 9th]

THE LAST BATTLE.

<small>November 1918 8th Battalion</small> and passed through the 8th. It had fired its last shot in the war, for before its turn to lead the advance could come round again the Armistice had been declared. Since October 8th, when it had joined in the advance to victory, its casualties had not amounted to 200, mostly incurred in the fights for Awoignt and Haussy (for the last stage had cost it little), and its prisoners alone considerably exceeded its losses. If it had not been engaged in the earlier stages of the advance when the German resistance was at its stiffest, it had had sharp fighting enough, and at Haussy in particular had done splendidly.

<small>1st Battalion</small> Meanwhile the 1st Battalion, which had been in Corps reserve along with its Division at the beginning of the month, had come forward by Beaurain and Louvignies to Jolimetz (November 5th). The 15th and 95th Brigades had been exploiting the success gained by the Thirty-Seventh Division on November 4th and the line had been carried forward East of the <small>Nov. 8th</small> Forest of Mormal. On November 8th the 15th Brigade moved forward, ready to pass through the 95th when the Avesnes-Maubeuge road should be reached. This move involved the passage of the Sambre, negotiated under considerable shell-fire, and by evening the advanced line had been reached and the relief of the 95th Brigade was successfully accomplished despite pitch darkness and heavy rain. Almost the only casualty was Captain McClenaghan, mortally wounded near Pantignies while acting as Brigade Intelligence Officer.

The battalion was now on the left of the Division's line at the S.E. corner of the Bois du Quesnoy with the Forty-Second Division on its left, and the K.O.S.B.'s on the right, the Seventeenth Division being still <small>Nov. 9th</small> further to the right. At 3 a.m. on November 9th the advance was resumed. Hardly any resistance was encountered; by 5 a.m. the Avesnes-Maubeuge road had been reached, and the battalion pushed on beyond to the

THE LAST BATTLE.

Beaufort-Le Pavé road; then, instead of halting there as had been intended, it crossed the Solre river also and gained touch with the enemy near Ferriere La Petite three miles from Maubeuge. Here there was some sharp skirmishing and eventually the battalion took up an outpost line covering Marliere. It was the last stage in its advance. Next morning the Forty-Second Division took over and the battalion fell back to La Puissance Farm, whence it moved back next day, to receive the news of the Armistice on the road between Pont-sur-Sambre and Harpignies, within 20 miles of the spot where it had first faced von Kluck's great host. There was hardly a man and not one officer present on November 11th, 1918, who had heard the first shots fired on August 23rd, 1914. Constantly wiped out, as constantly renewed, the battalion had crowded into those four years and a quarter experiences and losses which put into the shade all that the old Fiftieth had endured in the seven years of the Peninsular, in the Sikh Wars and in the Crimea. But despite all its losses and despite all that it had had to endure throughout the longest four and a quarter years on record it had nobly and fully sustained both the traditions of the old Fiftieth and the high standard which it had itself set up on that memorable August 23rd. *Nov. 9th 1918 1st Battalion* *Nov. 10th* *Nov. 11th*

Unlike the 1st and 8th the 7th Battalion's last encounter with the Germans brought it serious fighting. It had taken over the left portion of its brigade's frontage on the Western edge of the Forest of Mormal on the evening of October 31st and remained there till the attack started on the morning of the 4th. Patrolling was actively carried out, but cost the battalion one officer, 2nd Lieut. Debenham, in an encounter with a German post. 2nd Lieut. Debenham was mortally wounded and the N.C.O. who accompanied him was also hit, but the Germans, after wounding them, surrendered, and the N.C.O. succeeded in escorting his prisoners in, despite his injuries. *7th Battalion* *Nov. 4th*

THE LAST BATTLE.

Nov. 4th, 1918
7th Battalion
See Sketch 56

In the attack of November 4th the battalion had as its first objective the village of Hecq, assigned to C and D companies, after which A and B were to go through to the second objective, a road 500 yards ahead. The attack started in thickish weather at 6.15 a.m., C and D advancing close behind the three tanks detailed to assist them. At a sunken road on the outskirts of the village stubborn resistance was encountered and two platoons of each company had to be left to clear up this area while the rest pressed on into the village. Here also there was hard fighting, particularly for D Company on the right; the tanks were put out of action but the crew of one got out and, pushing forward on the left, did effective service with their machine-guns. In the end C and D made good their line and then A and B, coming forward, carried on the advance at a great rate. Resistance was lessening now, many Germans surrendered, many were shot as they endeavoured to get away through the forest, and the objective was reached and consolidated, the 8th R. Berkshires passing through to continue the advance. For the rest of the day companies remained in the positions reached; the work of consolidating was suddenly interrupted by a party of some 30 Germans who emerged from the wood and attacked A Company in rear with machine-guns and trench-mortars. But A proved equal to the occasion, faced about and shot down the two officers who were leading the party; with their fall their followers' zeal for fighting evaporated, and the rest were easily rounded up, increasing the total of prisoners taken to nearly 200. As against this the battalion had just fifty casualties, including 2nd Lieuts. Pegler, Bolton, and Fuller killed, the last two of whom had only joined in October, while 2nd Lieut. Hewett was wounded. Next day the 7th withdrew to billets in Hecq, moving thence to Le Cateau, where it was still lying when the news of the Armistice reached it.

Nov. 5th

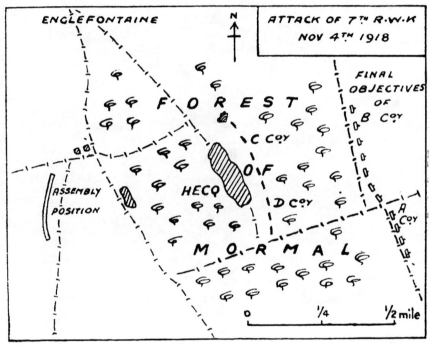

THE LAST BATTLE.

It was the junior Service battalion of The Queen's Own to whom it fell to be the last portion of the Regiment actually in action in the war. The 10th had had nearly a week's rest, mainly at Courtrai, before, on the night of November 4th, its brigade took over the line on the left bank of the Scheldt below Avelghem; the battalion itself not being in front line but at Langestraat. Here it was heavily shelled, the neighbourhood of some 60-pounders being the main reason for the attentions of the German gunners, but it escaped extremely lightly and then on the 9th pushed forward across the Scheldt, the passage of which had been effected on the previous day by the 11th Queen's by means of a small boat, being supported by C Company of the 10th under Captain Waterman, who crossed in the same way. Passing through the line reached by The Queen's the 10th pushed forward steadily all that afternoon, reaching the Nukerke-Renaix road practically without opposition, the only people encountered being Belgian civilians by whom the advancing British were cordially welcomed. Outposts that evening ran along the Renaix-Nukerke road. From this line the advance went forward next day, first to the Renaix-Oudenarde railway, which was reached unopposed. Thence the battalion pushed on, still unopposed, to a line East of Kerkhem; but just as it passed its third objective, Schoorishe, resistance was encountered. But a field-gun had been detailed to accompany the battalion and this, firing over open sights at 800 yards, was mainly instrumental in suppressing the German machine-guns and in letting the battalion reach its final objective near Roovorst just as evening was closing in.

<small>November, 1918 10th Batt.</small>

<small>Nov. 4th</small>

<small>See Sketch 58</small>

<small>Nov. 9th</small>

<small>Nov. 10th</small>

At this point the battalion stood fast next morning and shortly after the 124th Brigade had passed through came the intelligence that the Armistice had been concluded and would come into force at 11 a.m. that day.

<small>Nov. 11th</small>

That the news of the Armistice was received with a kind of bewilderment, almost incredulity, rather than

THE ARMISTICE.

Nov. 11th 1918

with demonstrations of enthusiasm, was perhaps only natural. The diminishing resistance which the Germans had offered in the last few days, their ready abandonment of positions which earlier on would have been stubbornly defended, their readiness to surrender, the unmistakable evidence of the declining efficiency of their administration and the deterioration of their equipment, all these had to some extent prepared officers and men for the approach of the end; but the cessation of hostilities when it came meant so complete a change that it carried with it an air of almost unreality. It was some time before it was possible to realize fully what the conclusion of the Armistice meant, that victory, which in March and April had seemed almost too much to hope for, at any rate infinitely further off than it had been months earlier, had at last been achieved. The abrupt change from being constantly in the presence of danger and sudden death to the practical security of peace conditions had hardly become familiar before a new question began to loom large on the horizon of each individual, the whole collection of problems concentrated in the word "demobilisation."

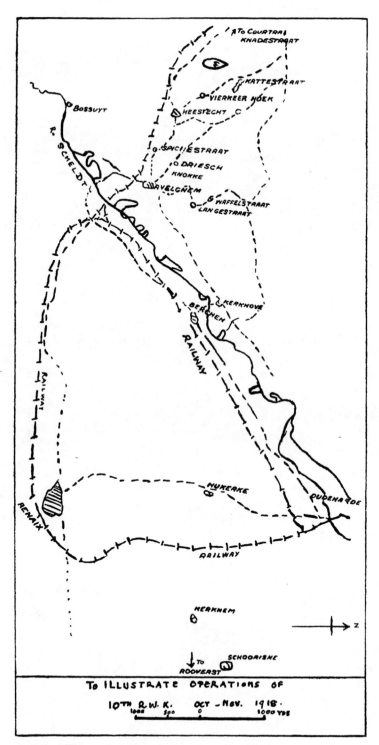

CHAPTER XXXI

EASTERN THEATRES IN 1918.

The heavy fighting which had characterized the year 1918 on the Western Front and had brought to The Queen's Own such heavy losses and so many opportunities of distinction was not experienced in the Eastern theatres. The year ended in Macedonia, in Mesopotamia and in Palestine with striking and dramatic triumphs for the Allies, with the total overthrow of the hostile forces, with the final reaping of the fruits of past exertions. But these triumphs were to some degree the repercussion of the greater and more vital events in the theatre where the fate of the senior partner in the Central Powers' firm was being decided, it was only late in the year that Macedonia and Mesopotamia became the scene of real activity and that the representatives of The Queen's Own in the latter country got a belated chance of striking a blow. In Palestine there had been greater activity, but before the final blow The Queen's Own had ceased to be represented by any unit in that theatre of war.

With the repulse of the Turkish effort to recover Jerusalem the operations in Palestine had entered upon a phase of minor activities. Various small attacks were launched on points of tactical importance with the result that the Turks were gradually thrust back further North towards Nablus and Eastward into the Jordan valley. This was varied by strenuous work on improving roads and by tours of duty in the outpost line. In all these the 2/4th R.W.K. shared. After a spell of road-making in the beginning of January it was employed on January 18th to push forward the Divisional front by the capture of a prominent hill near the Bireh road known as 2984 or Sheikh Abdallah. The assault

1918

2/4th Batt.

January, 1918

See Sketch 59

PALESTINE.

Jan.-July,
1918
2/4th Batt.

which was carried out by C and D Companies under Captains Willows and Cobb was a complete success, the position being captured with little opposition and less loss. But consolidation had not been long in process before the Turks opened a heavy artillery fire which they maintained for some hours, and this and their sniping inflicted a good many casualties, among the killed being Captain Nicoll, who had distinguished himself so much at Hill 1250 in November. However, all their counter-attacks were beaten off and the position was successfully consolidated. Ten days of outpost duty followed, then more road-making; then the battalion returned to the front line in the middle of February to advance again and occupy the village of Beir Dirwan and make several other minor advances, co-operating with the move of the Sixtieth Division against Jericho and with the capture of Rimmon by the 2/10th Middlesex. More road-making while the Division was operating against the commanding height of Tel Asur was

Feb. 15th

followed by a return to Jerusalem on the 15th for a short rest.

From Jerusalem the battalion next proceeded to the warmer if rather depressing climate of the Jordan valley, taking up a position North of Jericho and getting the chance of bathing in the Jordan. It was not actually employed in the operations East of the river but made a demonstration on March 29th to cover the withdrawal of the troops employed on the attack on Amman. April saw it back in the Judæan Hills again

May-July

where it spent the next three months. This was a time of inactivity for the British force in Palestine as a whole, though of plenty of hard work and long spells of duty. The reverses of March and April on the Western Front had exposed the fallacy of the notion that we were "over-insured in the West" and that the road to victory over the German lay in concentrating our efforts on the overthrow of the Turk. All schemes for an offensive in Palestine had to be postponed, two

458

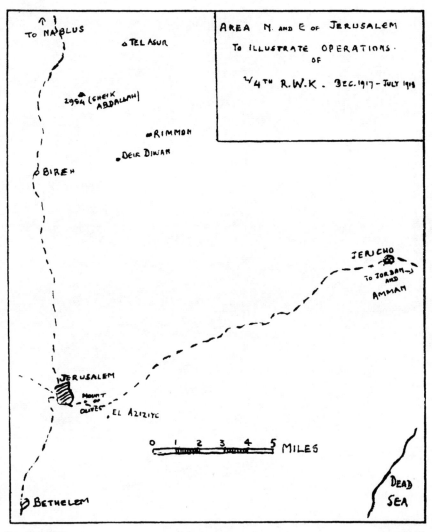

THE 2/4th DISBANDED.

of the British Divisions and many units from the others were hurried to the critical theatre in France and Indian battalions began to appear in increasing numbers to replace them. The Fifty-Third Division was among those to be " Indianized," several of its battalions left for the Western Front, and in June it was announced that as no reinforcements could be sent out from England the 2/4th R.W.K. would have to be broken up to find drafts for the British units retained for service in the "Indianized" Divisions. Actually this fate did not overtake it till the middle of September, and it spent three quarters of June and a week of July undergoing a most unpleasant experience.

It was in line on a ridge overlooking Sinjol on which the enemy concentrated all their available artillery, including a particularly obnoxious 9.4 trench mortar. Every shell fired in the neighbourhood seemed to land on the ridge and the maintenance of the defences in repair meant perpetual hard work, while the activities of the enemy's aircraft were unpleasantly pronounced. A Turkish attack was expected but never came off, and early in July the battalion at last bade farewell to the line and moved into Corps reserve preparatory to being finally broken up. Of the 759 other ranks on its establishment at the end of August nearly half were transferred to the three surviving British battalions of the Sixtieth Division, or to the M.G.C. or other units. Several officers were sent off to various employments, and on September 11th the remainder moved down to Ramleh to entrain next day for Kantara, where they were posted to the Reinforcement Camp. It was hard on the 2/4th that after all its arduous work and many hardships it should have been denied the privilege of adding Allenby's coming triumph of Megiddo to the battle-honours of The Queen's Own, but it had done fine work and had left a most creditable record behind it.

MESOPOTAMIA IN 1918.

1918 2nd and 1/5th Battalions
See Map B

The two battalions of The Queen's Own in Mesopotamia were not destined to see any fighting till 1918 was well advanced. The beginning of the year had found that theatre of war in a somewhat stationary position, and though in March General Marshall set his left wing on the Euphrates in motion, bringing the Turkish force in that quarter to action near Khan Baghdadi and compelling it to surrender, the Seventeenth and Eighteenth Indian Divisions, being on the Tigris, were not employed, nor did they play any very active part in the second of General Marshall's enterprises. This was undertaken in April and May on the other flank against the mountains running Eastward from the left bank of the Tigris some way above Tekrit; it resulted in the capture of Kifri and Tuz Khurmatli and Kirkuk with another substantial haul of prisoners, while the Turks in this quarter retired behind the line of the Lesser Zab.

Jan.-May, 2nd & 5th Battalions

The only direct way in which these operations affected the battalions of The Queen's Own was that there was in consequence much redistribution of the positions of the centre of the force along the Tigris. At the beginning of the year the Seventeenth Division had been established along the river from Sumaikcheh to Samarra, the 2nd R.W.K. being at Akab, while the Eighteenth lay lower downstream, completing its concentration at Baghdad, the 5th R.W.K. being in camp at the Iron Bridge. On the departure of the Lahore Division for Palestine in March the Seventeenth moved upstream to take over the Samarra section which extended nearly to Tekrit. This meant for the 2nd R.W.K. a move forward from Akab to Samarra, begun on March 11th and completed on the 20th, its old position at Akab being taken over by its own 5th Battalion

5th Battalion

which moved upstream for the purpose, covering 72 miles in the course of five days. After spending April at Akab, during which time steady patrolling was carried on without encountering any enemy, the 5th

MESOPOTAMIA IN 1918.

moved out on May 3rd as part of a movable column 1918
which co-operated on the left of the Tigris with the
Third Corps' operations in the Kifri area.

The 5th moved out 19 officers and 727 rank and 5th Battalion
file, a reserve company of all sick and weakly men having been left behind under Major Neame. The
column moved by Samarra to Daur and thence to
Mohammed el Hassan, where it remained over a week,
during which time it was employed on digging a defensive line and then returned to Samarra, to settle
down into occupation of a portion of the bridge-head
defences on the left bank. Here it remained throughout the summer, suffering not a little from the heat by
day, though cool nights did something to mitigate conditions. For Mesopotamia the sick-rate was not high
but a good many officers and men were invalided,
among them Majors Neame and Hills and Colonel
Frazer, in whose absence Colonel Clark was in command
from early in June to September 18th. Captain
Marshall rejoined from the 2nd Battalion and took over
the Adjutancy. A few new officers arrived but no
drafts, and with many men detached on various duties
and occupations the strength of the battalion dwindled
considerably although it had not yet been in action.

Meanwhile the 2nd Battalion was having an equally 2nd Battalion
uneventful time. It remained at Samarra until the beginning of October, finding many guards and men for
various duties so as to relieve other troops for employment on the extension of the railway from Samarra to
Tekrit which was being vigorously pushed on. Early
in July troops had moved forward and occupied Tekrit
to cover the construction of the line which reached that
place in the middle of August. The main object of
this extension was to facilitate the striking of a final
blow at the last important Turkish force in Mesopotamia, the Sixth Turkish Army, which lay entrenched
across the Tigris about 30 miles higher upstream
where the river forces its way through the Jebel

THE ADVANCE ON MOSUL.

October, 1918
2nd Battalion
See Sketch 60

Hamrin range at the celebrated Fattah Gorge. Through this ran the road to Mosul, and though the main object of the operations it was proposed to undertake was the destruction of the Turkish forces, from the political point of view the occupation of Mosul was an objective of importance, if strategically subordinate to the overthrow of the Sixth Army and indeed mainly to be advocated as a means to that end.

2nd & 5th Battalions

These operations were entrusted to General Cobbe's First Indian Corps with two cavalry brigades. Their scope was decidedly ambitious, involving a scheme for driving the Turks back from the Fattah Gorge position to a second line above the confluence of the Lesser Zab and the Tigris, after which the cavalry were to cross the Tigris higher up and plant themselves across the Turkish retreat on Mosul, while the Seventeenth Division on the right bank and the Eighteenth on the left simultaneously pressed forward up the Tigris. In a well-supplied country abounding in good roads the administrative problems involved in this scheme would have been serious; in the Tigris valley above Baghdad they were doubly formidable. On the right of the Tigris a line of steep hills—the Jebel Makhul—runs parallel to the river for many miles upstream from the Fattah position and with the waterless desert beyond these hills effectively protected the Turkish right against an attack in any force, on the left bank the Jebel Hamrin presented a very serious obstacle, while in the valley the so-called roads were hardly practicable for wheeled traffic. The Eighteenth Division were confident their road on the left bank must be the worst in Mesopotamia, but the Seventeenth on the right could not admit the Eighteenth's claim. The troops had therefore to be cut down to the absolute minimum of transport and kit and had no inconsiderable discomforts and hardships to endure in the course of the operations.

For the 2nd R.W.K. the operations began on October 7th when the battalion left Samarra by rail for

THE ADVANCE ON MOSUL.

Tekrit where the Division was concentrating. A fortnight's halt at Tekrit, mainly spent in working on the pushing forward of the railway above Tekrit, was marked by an outbreak of influenza which sent four officers and over 100 men to hospital and sadly reduced the battalion, already none too strong, for no drafts had arrived since the beginning of the year. Then on October 21st the battalion led the advance of the 34th Brigade upstream to Abu Rajash, a 15-mile march. Next day the move was continued to Khan Suraimyah, 27 miles North of Tekrit and 8 miles short of Fattah, and on October 23rd the move against the Fattah position began, the 34th Brigade being in Divisional reserve. By evening the 51st and 52nd Brigades had pressed forward to within four miles of the Turkish lines. Everything seemed to point to a severe fight for the Fattah Gorge next day, but morning showed that the Turks had gone, and General Hildyard's 51st Brigade and the cavalry pushed on after them, leaving the battalion and the rest of the 34th Brigade to assist the artillery to get their guns forward over the apology for a road which ran through the gorge. It was a difficult task and kept the battalion only too well employed till the afternoon of the 26th, when it was ordered up to rejoin its Brigade, the rest of which had already gone forward.

October, 1918
2nd Battalion

October 21st

October 22nd

October 24th

October 26th

Meanwhile the 5th Battalion had come into action. It had moved forward from Samarra on October 8th and halted about ten days at Tekrit. Then on October 19th it advanced thirteen miles, and that night pushed on again to the foothills of the Jebel Hamrin where the 54th Brigade was concentrating, seven miles from the left flank of the Turkish position at the Fattah Gorge. The battalion took up an outpost position and found itself in touch with the enemy. Here its patrols were active and did extremely well in some encounters with the Turkish outposts. On the 23rd the 54th Brigade pushed forward along the crest of the Jebel Hamrin to

5th Battalion
Oct. 8th-18th

THE ADVANCE ON MOSUL.

October, 1918
5th Battalion
attack the left of the Fattah position, on the morning of October 24th in conjunction with the frontal attack by the Seventeenth Division on the right bank of the Tigris. It was a hard and difficult advance over the broken ground along the top of the ridge, ideal country for a delaying action. However, no opposition was encountered and the advance was continued right on into the Turkish position which proved to have been evacuated. Eventually the battalion moved down nearer to the river to support the Seventeenth Division's attack, only to find that it also was going

October 25th forward unopposed. Next day the advance up the left bank continued, the 5th R.W.K. being detailed as escort to the 337th Brigade R.F.A. and coming under a heavy fire in doing so. A and D Companies pushed forward steadily despite the shelling until they had taken up a good position, the 341st Battery coming into action 1,000 yards in rear. This battery, however, suffered severely; the Turkish guns which till then had been shelling the escort without much success managed to get the range of the British guns, bombarded them with 5.9-inch shells, drove the detachments from the guns and inflicted much damage on the material. The escort, however, stuck to their positions until long after the shelling had ceased, and then about 8 p.m. fell back to the river bank on ascertaining that the portions of the battery which remained mobile had also withdrawn. Its casualties, 3 men killed and 2nd Lieut. Gilham and 8 men wounded, were far lower than might have been expected.

The 5th was not again to be actually in action. After re-assembling on the 26th the whole battalion went forward that afternoon to the Lesser Zab, still acting as

October 27th & 28th escort to the guns. For the next two days it remained on the Zab finding outposts, crossed that river on the 29th, and then moved forward to reinforce the 53rd Brigade which had been pushed up to support the cavalry under Generals Cassels and Norton. These

QALAT SHERGAT.

had carried out their programme admirably, fording the Tigris at the Hawaish creek some miles above Shargat and thus interposing between the main body of the Turks and Mosul. Though attacked from the North by reinforcements coming downstream from Mosul the cavalry had hung on in a most exposed and isolated position, had kept back the reinforcements and at the same time barred the retreat of the main body which was retiring upstream under the steady and successful pressure of the Seventeenth Division. <small>October, 1918 / 5th Battalion</small>

In applying this pressure the 2nd Battalion had taken a leading part. When on the evening of October 26th it got up to the front, after an exhausting march of 16 miles, and rejoined its brigade from which it had been for the time detached, it found that the Turks, standing at bay in the naturally strong and skilfully prepared Humr position at the bend in the Tigris just above the confluence with the Lesser Zab, had managed to check the advance of the 51st Brigade, even when it had been reinforced by the 112th Infantry and 114th Mahrattas of the 34th Brigade. The advance, however, had been most gallantly pressed, and before daybreak next day the British patrols reported the enemy to be retiring. The pursuit was as vigorously urged as possible, but the appalling state of the track which did duty for a road prevented its leaders from getting beyond Qalat al Bint and the enemy were able to retire, more or less at leisure, upon an entrenched position three miles south of Shargat. But the day's march was marked by little opposition from the enemy, if by much passive obstruction from the country. <small>October 26th / 2nd Battalion</small> <small>October 27th</small>

October 28th saw the 2nd R.W.K. heading the advance of the 34th Brigade[1] against this new position. <small>October 28th</small>

---

[1] The brigades had been cut down to three battalions apiece a little earlier owing to Indian battalions having been detailed to proceed to Salonica, the 31st Punjabis being selected for transfer from the 34th Brigade. The battalion went into action with 17 officers and 456 men, Captain Aldworth, who had been left in hospital at the Fattah Gorge, appearing just as the orders for the attack were being issued.

QALAT SHERGAT.

October 28th 1918
2nd Battalion

It had the 112th Infantry moving on its right rear echeloned back nearly two miles while the 114th Mahrattas followed in its tracks. The advance was terribly delayed by having to cross the many nalas which intersected its path. More than once all Lewis-gun mules had to be closed to the one point where one of these deep nalas could be crossed. However, after ten miles from its bivouac had been covered the cavalry reported that the enemy had been located, standing in a strong position astride the Mosul Road and about five miles ahead. On this the battalion deployed, B Company on the right, C on the left, D behind C and A, reduced by sickness to four Lewis-gun sections, on D's right rear. Two sections of the Brigade Machine-Gun Company and a company of the 114th Mahrattas were in support.

Under a heavy fire the men pressed steadily forward, keeping direction and intervals admirably, 1,200 yards from the enemy they extended, and though only twelve guns were available to support them, and their fire could not possibly amount to an effective barrage, they swept on against the enemy's front line. All possible use was made of covering fire by the machine-guns, and 200 yards from the enemy's position the company of the 114th came up level with the right. As the advance went forward it came under very effective machine-gun fire, upon which Colonel Woulfe-Flanagan, on his own initiative, ordered the assault, without pausing to wait for the turning movements on his flanks which had been held up by the difficult character of the country.

The assault was immediately successful, largely thanks to L/Cpl. James, who pushed forward to locate a troublesome machine-gun and then rushed it himself, killing the crew, by which act he immediately relieved the situation; 800 yards further on lay the enemy's second line, strengthened at each end by a strong redoubt. Almost without a pause the troops pressed on against this position. On the left

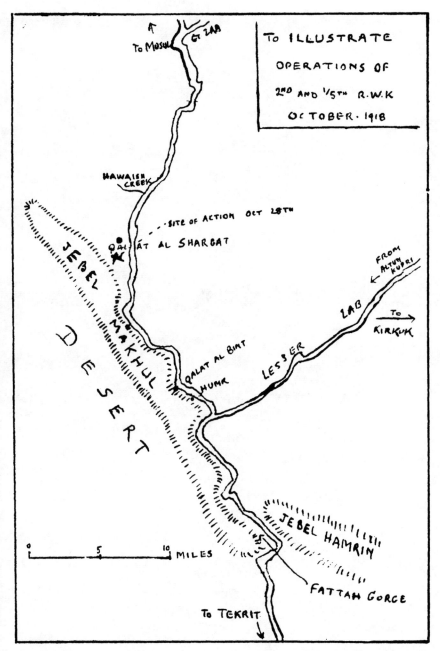

QALAT SHERGAT.

a strong point West of the Mosul road threatened <small>October 28th 1918 2nd Battalion</small> trouble, but Captain Aldworth with a small party promptly advanced against it, working round so as to take it in flank while C.Q.M.S. McCormick with a few men attacked it in front and a section of machine-guns gave effective covering fire, the net result being the capture of the strong point with 100 prisoners and six machine-guns. On the right 2nd Lieut. White and a party of C and D Companies were the first to reach the Turkish line, then 2nd Lieut. Capes arrived on his left with some of B, Captain Piggott and Lieut. Fry prolonged the line to the left, and between them the redoubt on the cliff edge at the end of the line was stormed and the position consolidated, the arrival rather later of the rest of the 114th Mahrattas enabling a gap in the centre to be filled and the position secured. C.Q.M.S. Kemp, on the fall of both officers of C Company, led his men forward with great initiative and ability, while Sergt. Burnham, though himself wounded, continued to lead his platoon, setting a fine example of coolness and perseverance.

The attack had been a brilliant success. The Brigadier, General Wauchope, has written of the "excellent local leadership" displayed. "The West Kent Regiment," he writes,[1] "lost 25 per cent. of their number, but had any mistake been made, had control been lost at any rate over those very widely-extended platoons, had full use not been made of all covering fire available, had the men failed to respond to their leaders, then had their losses been doubled and the issue hung in the balance." The losses had certainly been heavy in proportion to the numbers engaged. Captain Schofield, Lieuts. Northey and Wilson had been killed with 35 men, Captain Pattisson and Lieut. Bennett were wounded and 72 men. But the prisoners taken, 160, alone exceeded the casualties, and the determination

[1] "The Destruction of the Sixth Turkish Army."—*Journal of the R.U.S.I.,* 1919.

THE ADVANCE ON MOSUL.

October 28th 1918 2nd Battalion
with which the battalion had pressed its attack, coupled with a threat to the Turkish flank through the advance of a co-operating column on the left, had sent the Turks back once again. They were effectively cornered now, for all their efforts had failed to dislodge General Cassels and his 11th Cavalry Brigade from their position astride the road to Mosul, and before evening not only had the leading troops of the Eighteenth Division got into touch with him but General Norton's 7th Cavalry Brigade had arrived to reinforce. There was

October 29th
to be one more hard fight when, on October 29th, General Hildyard's 51st Brigade pushing forward against the enemy's main position North of Shargat met severe opposition, culminating in a vigorous counter-attack, only checked with some difficulty by the splendid steadiness and gallantry of the H.L.I. and the 114th Mahrattas whom the 34th Brigade pushed forward as reinforcements. Once again, however, the 2nd R.W.K. was denied the chance of distinction. It was kept back in support and merely dug in in second line, sending forward one small party to assist the 114th Mahrattas.

October 30th
Next morning the battalion stood to arms at 5.30, but as it moved forward for a renewed attack by the 34th and 51st Brigades it was greeted by a bugle-call, reminiscent of manœuvres, which seemed strangely out of place on active service—the "Stand Fast." The whole Turkish force, over 8,000 officers and men, had surrendered unconditionally with thirty guns, eighty machine-guns and all their material. It was a complete and crushing victory, and the share of the 2nd Battalion in bringing it about was singled out for particular praise by the Divisional Commander, who spoke of the "superhuman exertions of all ranks," the initiative of subordinate leaders, the gallantry of the men, the splendid way in which, despite all exertions and exhaustion, they had never failed to respond to the calls made on them. If the 2nd had not been fortu-

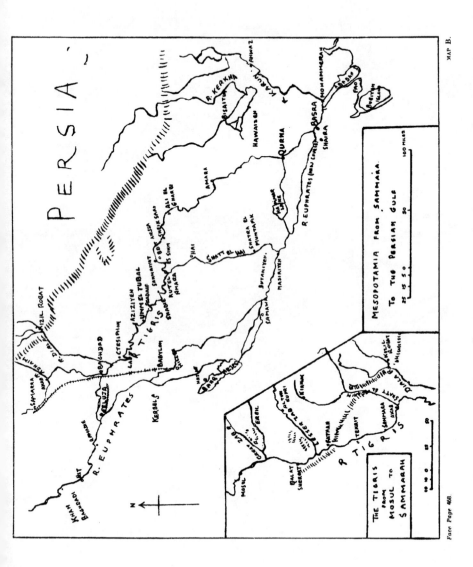

THE ADVANCE ON MOSUL.

nate in getting opportunities of distinction in battle, Nasiriya and Qalat Shergat, its two actions of importance, had shown of what it was capable when given its chance, and the rewards which fell to its lot for its share in the Turkish overthrow speak for themselves. Colonel Woulfe-Flanagan and Captain Aldworth got the D.S.O., Sergt. Burnham, C.Q.M.S. Kemp and L/Cpl. James the D.C.M., C.S.M. Godden, Corpls. Eves and Francis, L/Cpls. Knight and Weston, Ptes. Bromfield, Cheeseman, Locker, Philpott, Rogers and Thompson the M.M.

<small>October, 1918 2nd Battalion</small>

The Turkish surrender had prevented the 5th R.W.K. getting a real chance in action. Any other opportunities it might have hoped for were snatched from it by the news that an Armistice had been concluded with Turkey and that hostilities would cease forthwith (October 31st). On this the Eighteenth Division did actually move forward to Mosul, and the 5th R.W.K., now down to 17 officers and 409 men present, among whom only 5 officers, Colonel Frazer, Major Clark and Captains Hay, Richardson and Marshall had belonged to the pre-war 5th, had the satisfaction of reaching Mosul where the end of the year found it providing guards and picquets for duty in that city, not to mention various fatigues and working parties. For it demobilization was destined to be long deferred. With the 2nd the case was different. On the news of the Armistice it had been sent off at once down to rail-head in charge of 1,000 prisoners. On the way down it picked up both the great-coats and the exiguous 10-lb. kits which it had had to drop by the wayside on the move forward, and on reaching rail-head it was able to hand its charges over to the Lines of Communication staff; after which it was employed on railway construction almost to the end of the month when it moved down to Tekrit, to send off its first batch of 14 men to the United Kingdom for demobilization in the course of December.

<small>5th Battalion

2nd Battalion

November</small>

469

CHAPTER XXXII

DEMOBILIZATION.

Nov.-Dec., 1918

When hostilities were actually suspended on the Western Front it so happened that no single battalion of The Queen's Own was in immediate touch with the retreating enemy; the 1st had withdrawn from the front line the day before the Armistice, the 6th had been back in billets since October 28th, the 7th was at Le Cateau, also in rest, the 8th had been "leap-frogged" on November 9th, while the 10th only missed by a few hours the distinction of being in action up to the last moment. The terms of the Armistice had included the occupation of the German territories West of the Rhine by a mixed Allied force, but to allow of the withdrawal of the Germans behind the Rhine and to facilitate the necessary readjustment of the administrative arrangements, a halt of a week had to be called on the British front, and it was not till November 17th that the advance towards Germany could be resumed, and only on December 1st did British troops cross the German frontier and begin the occupation of the zone assigned to the British forces about Cologne. The opening stages of the advance were carried out by the Second and Fourth Armies, but by the time the frontier came to be crossed the frontage to be occupied did not require more than a single Army command and the final advance was carried out by the Second Army only. This had been very largely reconstructed, and as finally organized did not include any of the Divisions in which The Queen's Own was represented. Later on both the 6th and 10th Battalions were included in the Army of Occupation, but in the period immediately succeeding the Armistice all the five battalions remained at rest, though a certain amount of changes of station took place.

Brevet Major T Lieut.-Colonel W. R. A. DAWSON, D.S.O.
Commanded 6th Battalion, 1916, 1917, and 1918.
Died of wounds, 3rd December, 1918.

COLONEL DAWSON'S DEATH.

For the Regiment the outstanding event for this period was a sad one, the death, on December 3rd, of Colonel Dawson from the wounds he had received at the end of October. From the first their gravity had been clear, but he had struggled long and gallantly for life and it was with the greatest regret that not only his own 6th, but all battalions of The Queen's Own heard the news of his death. His record in the war was truly remarkable: junior subaltern in August 1914, battalion commander in November 1916, a D.S.O. and three bars, a Brevet Major at an age when some subalterns have hardly achieved their second star. Seven times wounded, he had always contrived to get back to his battalion, usually with his wounds barely healed. He had repeatedly refused offers of Staff employment which would have meant leaving the 6th. What he had been to the 6th Battalion only those who served with and under him can say. He had played a large part in building and training it, he had helped to give it high standards and aims. In its first serious engagement at Loos he and his company had been conspicuously successful, in the bitter struggle for the Hohenzollern Craters he had stood out as the life and soul of the defence, and it was under his command that the 6th had achieved the majority of its most striking successes. That after suffering virtual annihilation at Cambrai it had been able in 1918 to accomplish so many brilliant things was largely because it still had Colonel Dawson to lead it and to inspire it afresh with his energy and fighting spirit. But it was not merely for what the 6th had done that Dawson will be remembered, but for his personality, his leadership, his high standards, his devotion to duty, his endurance, his fearlessness and resource in action, above all for the extraordinary confidence he inspired in his officers and men, there was nothing of which the 6th did not believe him capable, nothing which it was not prepared to undertake if he were there to lead it. What made

Nov.-Dec., 1918

DEMOBILIZATION.

Nov.-Dec., 1918 1st Battalion

his influence over his battalion so specially remarkable was his youth.

In the middle of December the 1st Battalion, which had spent the last month in billets at Herbignies near Le Quesnoy, moved forward into Belgium, arriving in new quarters N.W. of Namur on the 22nd, where it was rejoined by a Colour party consisting of Lieut. Lewis Barned, 2nd Lieut. Marke, C.S.M. Hylands and Sergts. Weston and Gilbert, which had been sent off to Maidstone to fetch the Colours from the Depôt. This incident was symbolical of the change from war conditions. Though the agreement signed on November 10th had been called an "armistice" it was in effect nothing short of a surrender on the part of the Germans, and accordingly among the problems which the military authorities had to tackle was that of the reconstruction of the Regular Army on as near an approach to normal lines as the very abnormal conditions then prevailing would admit. The task bristled with difficulties. Four years of war had left but the scantiest remnant of Regulars serving on "pre-war" engagements, and these were scattered about the different battalions, which, whether called Regular or Territorial or Service, were all composed of a mixture of men enlisted on different terms, volunteers "for duration," "Derby" recruits, conscripts, some entitled to a prompt discharge, others liable to be retained with the colours. Thus while those Service and Territorial battalions not required for the various Armies of Occupation in Germany, in Palestine and in other Eastern theatres, had to be disbanded or disembodied as soon as circumstances would allow, the Regular battalions had equally to be reduced to cadres by the demobilization or transfer to other units of all men not available for service with the battalion when reconstructed.

1919

In the same way when the 6th and 10th Battalions were detailed early in 1919 for transfer to the Army of the Rhine they had to be in large measure reconstructed.

DEMOBILIZATION.

The 6th, which had since the beginning of December 1919 been commanded by Captain (Acting Lieut.-Col.) 6th Battalion Peploe, underwent a good many changes, many of its officers and men were demobilized, their places being filled from other battalions of the Regiment or from other regiments. Thus on the final reduction of the 1st Battalion to cadre strength in April Major Kay and over a dozen other officers proceeded to join the 6th. In like manner the 10th received a draft of 200 men from the 1st Battalion, Colonel Hickson from the 7th, half-a-dozen officers, including Captains Penton and Drumgold, from the 8th, and about twice as many from the 2/20th Battalion of the London Regiment. In posting these officers to a battalion of The Queen's Own the authorities were certainly happily inspired, as the 20th London were the old 2nd Volunteer Battalion Royal West Kent and had as their recruiting area Blackheath and Woolwich.

In the middle of March the 1st Battalion moved to 1st Battalion Fleurus, where the reduction to cadre was completed, the last big batch to depart being the 200 men sent to the 10th Battalion. Then on April 17th the cadre, 6 officers and 46 men, started for England, Major R. Brown being in command and having with him Captains Doe, Mattinson and Lewis Barned, Lieut. Marke and 2nd Lieut. Purchase, of whom Captain Doe was an "old original" of August 1914, having gone out as R.S.M., in which post Major Brown had succeeded him in December 1914. There were eight other "old originals" in the cadre who had left Dublin with the battalion in August 1914, Sergts. Keane, Haynes, Cutter and Banfield, Corpl. Weatherall, L/Cpls. Hannant and Wyatt and Pte. Simpson.

Landing at Dover on April 23rd the cadre proceeded direct to Gravesend where they found a reinforcement awaiting them in the shape of a nucleus party under Major Nelson, released from his captivity in Turkey. This party had been formed at Maidstone

DEMOBILIZATION.

1919
1st Battalion and had moved to Gravesend early in April. The two parties between them came to just over 100 officers and men, but to this additions were constantly being made as the battalion was due for service in India, for which country it eventually departed in October, being then fully "up to strength" and having Colonel P. M. Robinson once again in command.

2nd Battalion Meanwhile the other Regular battalion was on its way home from the East. Shortly after the conclusion of the final operations against the Turks the 2nd Royal West Kent had been withdrawn down the Tigris to Tekrit after spending some time on railway construction on the way. Here it received orders in March 1919 that it was to be reduced to a cadre and dispatched to India for embarkation for home. Demobilization had begun some time before this, but the cadre was destined to be a long time on the homeward way. It suffered minor delays both at Baghdad and Basra, and then, on reaching Bombay, found affairs in India in such a disturbed condition and the troubles with Afghanistan so serious that it was dispatched forthwith to Deolali and detained first there and then at Nasik and then at Delhi, so that it did not finally leave India until the end of July. It mustered four officers, Colonel Woulfe-Flanagan, Majors Grey and Hardy, and Captain Bredon, the first two of whom had gone out with it to Egypt in September 1899. Of the forty-six other ranks all but one were wearing the 1914-1915 Star and had had a long dose of service in Mesopotamia. Arriving at Devonport on August 16th the cadre was directed to proceed to Rugeley Camp in Staffordshire. Here were already established the "Home Service Details" destined to form part of the battalion. These had been provided in part from the Depôt, but the majority came from two recruit companies of the 3rd Battalion which had been transferred to the 2nd in June shortly before the disembodying of the 3rd. Thus by September 1919 both 1st and 2nd Battalions were well on the way

DEMOBILIZATION.

towards reconstruction while the 3rd had been disembodied,[1] as had also the Reserve Territorial units.

1919
2nd Battalion

The "first line" Territorials, however, were still abroad; indeed the 1/4th had at last, after over four years of garrison duty, seen something of active service on the Indian Frontier. It had moved up to the Frontier early in 1918, being stationed at Quetta, where it remained until detailed in May 1919 for the operations against the Afghans. The chief action in which it took part was the capture on May 27th 1919 of the Afghan position at Spin Maldak, about the strongest post in Afghanistan, in which the battalion was at last given a chance of distinguishing itself. It took its chance to some purpose, the position being stormed after an action lasting over eight hours in the hottest weather. The Afghan resistance was stubborn, but so well did the 1/4th fight that its Brigadier, B.-Gen. J. L. R. Gordon, presented it with the drums captured from the enemy as a memento. After this action the battalion remained on active service until the conclusion of peace with Afghanistan in September. It then returned to Quetta and was placed under orders for home in October, eventually leaving Karachi on October 30th 1919, just five years since its departure for India. Of the nineteen officers who returned with the battalion only Major A. M. Cohen and Captain R. D. Watney had held commissions in it on the outbreak of war, so greatly had the vicissitudes of the past five years altered the composition even of a battalion which had been debarred from participating in the chief operations of the war. The voyage home was soon accomplished; on November 21st the battalion landed at Plymouth, proceeding to Crowborough, and after a most cordial reception at Tonbridge on November 24th made its way

1/4th Batt.

---

[1] Since August 4th, 1914, no less than 936 officers—almost a full battalion—had done duty with the 3rd Battalion; it had sent 717 officers overseas, 9 of them three times, with 14,527 other ranks, besides sending off to various units at home, exclusive of the Machine-Gun Corps, an additional 4,654.

DEMOBILIZATION.

1919
1/4th Batt. to the Crystal Palace to be finally demobilized. It was two months ahead of its sister unit, the 1/5th.

1/5th Batt. This battalion had been retained to form part of the garrison of Mesopotamia, being quartered in the Mosul district. It had been in large measure reconstructed, being reduced to one company of its own men, another drawn from those men of the 2nd Royal West Kent not eligible for demobilization, and a third of them of the same description from the Highland Light Infantry. It had spent over a year in the Mosul area before it was reduced to cadre and detailed to proceed home. The chief incident of this period was a punitive expedition to Amadia in Central Kurdistan. There had been a good deal of unrest in that district culminating in July in a mutiny among the Gendarmerie and the wiping out of the small post at Amadia. Two columns were despatched to restore order, to one of which, drawn from the 54th Brigade the battalion contributed several officers and men. These operations were brought to a successful conclusion in October and soon after that came orders for home. Leaving Mosul on November 27th, 1919, the cadre negotiated its journey to Basra in three stages, by motor-lorry to rail-head at Shergat, by rail to Baghdad, by river to Basra, where a short delay was caused by the receipt of an order that no fighting troops were to leave the country. By December 27th, however, the embargo had been removed and the cadre reached Bombay five days later, transhipped promptly to a homeward-bound troopship and reached Plymouth on January

Jan., 1920 22nd, 1920. But its home-coming was sadly marred by the death from influenza of its commanding officer, Colonel Clark, who had embarked with it in October 1914, and actually succumbed after the transport

Jan. 23rd reached Plymouth. The next day the cadre disembarked and that following saw it back on Kentish soil at Tonbridge, moving two days later to its own Head-

DEMOBILIZATION.

quarters at Bromley, where disembodiment followed promptly.

Long before the return of the Territorials to England the four Service battalions which had survived till the Armistice had ceased to exist. The 7th and 8th had been the first to go, both being broken up in the early summer of 1919. Before disbandment, however, both battalions had, like other Service battalions, the honour of being presented with a King's Colour. The Eighteenth Division had not been among those selected for the Army of Occupation and therefore remained in the Le Cateau area until the middle of March, mainly occupied in clearing up the battlefields. The 7th had remained at Prémont till the middle of January, then moved to Bertry, where it was reorganized in two companies, one destined for the Army of Occupation, the other for demobilization. At the end of February Y Company departed for the Rhine and from that time demobilization went forward steadily. By March 19th it had proceeded so far that the Division was formally announced to have ceased to exist and its units, which had nearly all been reduced to cadres, were shortly afterwards transferred to England. The cadre of the 7th remained till May at Clary whither it had moved on March 1st, most of its remaining officers left it to join the 6th Battalion on the Rhine, Major Kirk went home to be demobilized in March and was succeeded in command by Major Stewart of the East Surreys, by whom the 7th was brought back to England to be finally mustered out on July 17th.

The 8th Battalion had moved to Tournai towards the end of December, and here its King's Colour was presented to it. The ceremony was performed on February 11th, 1919, by Lieut.-Gen. Sir Arthur Holland, commanding the First Corps. It was the last outstanding incident in the career of the 8th Royal West Kent. Not being required for the Army of the Rhine it was soon drawn upon for drafts for battalions

1919

7th Battalion

8th Battalion

DEMOBILIZATION.

<small>1919
8th Battalion</small>
in that force and the gaps made in its ranks by demobilization were not filled up. On March 5th orders were received for its reduction to cadre strength, and on the 17th a big draft, nearly 150 strong, proceeded to join the 10th Battalion on the Rhine. Other detachments proceeded later to the 10th, to which in all some 250 of the 8th Battalion were transferred, and by the end of April the battalion had been brought down to cadre establishment. It was some time, however, before this cadre was finally broken up. It had left Tournai at the end of March for Lamain, on the road to Lille, where it remained for a couple of months awaiting orders for home. These finally arrived at the end of May, and on June 7th the remnant of the 8th landed at Tilbury, proceeding to Whitchurch in Shropshire, where the last stage in the disbandment of the battalion was carried out.

Thus by the middle of 1919 both the 7th and 8th Battalions had passed out of existence. In their brief but crowded hour both had added many fine pages to the record of The Queen's Own. The 7th will be remembered mostly for its brilliant achievements on the Somme in 1916, for its gallant stand on the fateful March 21st, and for its series of successes in the Hundred Days that closed the war. But perhaps the page in its story to which even greater credit attaches is that which tells how the remnant that was left after March 21st fought on courageously and undismayed, played so great a part in keeping the Germans back from the very gates of Amiens and succeeded in linking up the battalion which was all but wiped out in the defence of Moy with the successors who took full and ample revenge in the Hundred Days. The 8th had the misfortune of starting with losses that might have shaken any battalion; within a month of its landing in France it had to be practically re-created. But the steadiness and tenacity which it showed in its first action, disastrously though that resulted, marked

DEMOBILIZATION.

it all through its career. There are many things in its story on which its survivors may dwell with pride, its stout defence of Delville Wood, the gallantry, enterprise and resource of which it gave such ample proof in the Lens area in 1918. That to one of its members fell one of the two V.C.'s awarded to battalions of The Queen's Own in the war is a notable feature in its record, but if it were the practice of the British Army, as it is of the French, to award distinctions to units as well as its individuals the 8th's surprising gallantry, endurance, discipline and devotion during the "March retreat" could hardly have failed to win reward.

₁₉₁₉
_{7th & 8th Battalions}

The 6th and 10th Battalions remained in existence some months longer. The 6th, after having had the honour of receiving its King's Colour from the Prince of Wales in February, had moved up to Wahn, seven miles from Cologne, and spent a not unpleasant summer in various Rhenish villages, ending up at Lohmar on the Agger, a picturesque spot in forest country, which was a popular holiday resort for the inhabitants of neighbouring industrial towns and villages. Its stay here was uneventful though it had plenty of opportunities of holding its own in friendly competitions with other units, both military and athletic. In August came its orders for home, and on the 18th it started on its last journey, reaching Ripon three days later and at once beginning demobilization. It had been preceded by one day by the 10th Battalion, which had likewise had a quite enjoyable time in the occupied territory and now found itself once more alongside the Senior Service battalion of its Regiment. Here the two battalions remained until November, dwindling gradually as one officer after another departed either to civil life or to some new sphere of military duty, and as batch after batch of men obtained their discharge.

_{6th & 10th Battalions}

In November both were disbanded. Of the 6th it may be said that it will stand out in the annals of The Queen's Own as "Dawson's battalion," and that the 6th

DEMOBILIZATION.

1919
6th Battalion

will be content to be so known. The first formed of the Service battalions, it had been the first to show that it was possible for these new formations on whose successful development such vital issues impended to reach standards of discipline and efficiency that had seemed unattainable when it was ordered to be raised. The way in which the new battalions acquired the spirit and traditions of The Queen's Own is a feature which it is hard to over-emphasize; it was indeed remarkable how the regimental reputation not for gallantry and steadiness in the field only but for discipline and good conduct in camp and billets was maintained by all its battalions. The 6th went through many hard trials but had many triumphs. If on the Somme in 1916 it shared in none of the conspicuous successes that fell to other battalions of The Queen's Own, that was in no sense due to any defect on its part. Its 1917 record with Arras and Infantry Hill and the great success of November 20th may be the more brilliant, but it had really given as good proofs of its quality and spirit at Gun Trench and in the Hohenzollern, at Ovillers, at Pozières and at Le Sars. 1917 brought it also its most crippling disaster, but how the 6th rose superior even to that its brilliant record in 1918 both in defence and attack affords ample proof. The 10th, too, has left a fine record. It was fortunate in being raised by a man of really remarkable ability as a trainer of troops, and though it did not arrive in France until 1916 was well advanced it saw hard fighting enough to satisfy any fire-eater. It belonged to a Division which had a remarkable record of success and in those successes it had a great share, culminating in a prominent part in an episode which has somehow hardly received its due recognition, the great advance through Flanders in the last months of the war.

10th Batt.

In the course of 1919 there had been much discussion of the question of setting up some permanent memorial of the services of the Regiment in the War and

THE UNVEILING OF THE CENOTAPH AT MAIDSTONE, JULY 30th, 1921.

THE WAR MEMORIAL.

commemorating the officers and men, little short of 7,000 in all, who had given their lives during the war. In November a meeting of the Regimental Memorial Fund decided upon setting up at Maidstone a replica of the Cenotaph in Whitehall. Sir Edwin Lutyens, the architect of the Whitehall Cenotaph, agreed to design a replica of rather smaller size, bearing on two sides the inscription: " The glorious dead of The Queen's Own Royal West Kent Regiment," and on the other two the dates MCMXIV and MCMXIX. A site was obtained in Brenchley Gardens and work was pushed steadily on during 1920, having been entrusted to a Maidstone firm, Messrs. Wallis & Sons. It was actually ready for unveiling in the spring of 1921, but owing to the coal strike, the mobilization of the Defence Force and other circumstances, it was not till the end of July that the ceremony of unveiling actually took place. 1919

1920

There was a great concourse of people present to see the unveiling, old members of the Regiment, relatives of the fallen, representatives of local authorities, clergy of all denominations, with a guard of honour of 50 men from the Depôt under Captain Anstruther, and two unarmed parties, one of 100 men from the Depôt, the other of 50 men of the 5th Battalion. The actual unveiling was performed by Major-Gen. Sir Edmund Leach, the Colonel of the Regiment, but as he felt his strength to be unequal to the task of addressing such an assembly, Lieut.-Gen. Sir E. A. H. Alderson undertook this duty; he spoke of the memorial as a tribute to those who had fallen, of the great fame that the war had brought to the Regiment, and of the splendid example The Queen's Own had set, not only in the war, but to generations to come. Then after the Archbishop of Canterbury had blessed and dedicated the memorial came the hymn " O Valiant Hearts, who to your glory come," followed by the Last Post, the hymn " The Strife is o'er," the Reveillé and a blessing July, 1921

THE WAR MEMORIAL.

July, 1921

from the Archbishop. At the close of the service wreaths were laid at the foot of the memorial by Sir Edmund Leach, by Colonels Buchanan Dunlop for the 1st Battalion, Fiennes for the Depôt, and Wood-Martyn for the 10th Battalion, by Captain Mills for the 2nd Battalion and Lieut. Gould for the Old Comrades' Association, with a number in memory of individual officers and men.

This impressive and moving ceremony was followed in the afternoon by the solemn laying up of six King's Colours belonging to Service and Territorial battalions in All Saints' Church, that of the Kent Cyclists who had given so many good drafts to different battalions being deposited along with them. This ceremony began with the parading of the colours at the Barracks from which they were carried through the streets under an escort of 50 men, the colours being carried by officers of the different battalions. Captain Baker carried that of the 2/4th, Lieut. Hill-Reid that of the 3/4th, Captain Hughes that of the 6th, Lieut. Duffield the 7th's, Major H. S. Brown the 8th's and Captain Drayson the 10th's.[1] On reaching the Church the Colours were carried up to the screen while the escort lined the central aisle. A special form of service was conducted by Canon E. H. Hardcastle, in the course of which the Colours were handed over by their bearers to the Vicar and laid upon the altar. After this had been done the Archbishop of Canterbury dedicated a bronze tablet on the North wall of the nave to the memory of all ranks of the Regiment who had fallen in the War. In the address which he delivered the Archbishop spoke of the past history of Maidstone, the Kentish capital, and of its place in English history, and then went on to show that while the Cenotaph, unveiled that morning, the Colours laid upon the altar, and the tablet on the wall commemorated more particularly the part played

---

[1] That of the 11th had already been deposited in the Parish Church at Lewisham.

LAYING UP THE COLOURS.

by West Kent and its Regiment in the great World War, it and all the other local and special memorials should remind people not only of the local effort and the local sacrifice, but of the greater effort and the greater sacrifice of which it had formed a part.

The laying up of the Colours was, as the Archbishop pointed out, as symbolical of the fact that the war was at an end as they themselves had been symbolical of the spirit of devotion, steadfastness and endurance in which the war had been fought. It forms, therefore, a natural termination to the record of The Queen's Own in that great ordeal. Before the outbreak of war The Queen's Own had had a great past and high reputation; the Army and the county of Kent knew its quality and confidently expected that in the time of trial it would acquit itself worthily of that past and would fully sustain the great traditions it had inherited. Of what The Queen's Own accomplished and endured, of the conditions—at times positively appalling—under which its men had to live and fight, of the way in which all its battalions, Regular, Territorial, Service, " Local " and Reserve, not only maintained but enhanced that reputation until the achievements and reputation of the Royal West Kent's became known to the whole British Empire, despite even the cold shadow of the Censorship under which our soldiers had to fight, these pages have given but an inadequate account. Still, even the barest record of achievements so remarkable and varied must in some measure bring out the great strength and power of a great regimental tradition like that of The Queen's Own. The traditions of the Regiment for steadfast courage, for mutual trust, loyalty and discipline among all ranks, contributed much directly and far more indirectly to the great achievements of the years 1914-1918; it was largely because they had so high a standard to aim at and such traditions to maintain that the men who, with little previous military experience,

INVICTA.

July, 1921   replenished all ranks of the old and built up the new battalions succeeded in so greatly enriching the story of the Regiment during the long years of the sternest struggle in history.

APPENDIX I.

A RECORD OF THE WORK AT THE DEPÔT
and of
THE COMFORTS & PRISONERS OF WAR FUNDS.

Compiled from materials
supplied by
COLONEL G. W. MAUNSELL, C.M.G.,
and
LIEUT.-COL. J. P. DALISON.

THE FIRST MONTHS OF THE WAR.

Orders for mobilization reached the Depôt on the 4th August and within a short time nearly all the Regular officers and staff joined their battalions. On the first day of mobilization, 5th August, Colonel G. W. Maunsell took over command from Major P. M. Robinson, C.M.G., and his first duty was to improvise a new staff from retired officers and ex-N.C.O.'s who rejoined on declaration of war.

Major Robinson, however, remained at the Depôt for some days to superintend the mobilization of the Regular units.

After the Reservists had been dealt with, being sent either to the 1st or 3rd Battalion, the mobilization of two Regular medical units was expeditiously carried out.

From this time recruiting became one of the most important works carried on at the Depôt. During the early months of the war, there was first an almost overwhelming rush of recruits, and then a steady flow of men which lasted until the spring of 1915. Recruiting centres were established at Tonbridge, Bromley,

APPENDIX I.

Gravesend, Chatham and Sheerness, where the officers in charge enrolled the men and passed them to the Depôt. These recruiting officers were in close touch with the Kent Territorial Force Association, whose organization greatly assisted in keeping the Centres well supplied with recruits.

At the Depôt the men were provided with accommodation, pay, and as far as possible clothing and equipment—and began their training.

But so great was the rush of men joining that the problem of dealing with them was full of difficulty.

To provide food, the Drill Hall was turned into a mess room, and at one time it was necessary to provide relays of meals lasting nearly all day.

Although strong drafts were sent to the 6th Battalion, which was formed at Colchester on August 14th, the barrack rooms were congested, passages were filled, and men even slept under the trees in the barrack square. At the beginning of September the situation became critical, nearly 3,000 men being in barracks and in requisitioned houses and buildings close by. So on September 4th authority was received for the completion to full strength of the 6th Battalion and for the formation of the 7th Battalion. The men were at once told off into companies, a few ex-Regular N.C.O.'s were allotted to each company, which was then put in charge of some Regular or retired officer.

On the afternoon of the 5th September the two senior Service Battalions of the Regiment were completed, and the drafts were despatched to their training camps. On the 14th September, the 8th Battalion was similarly formed and the 19th October saw the birth of the 9th Battalion.

The reserves of clothing and equipment were soon used up. The 6th and 7th Battalions were fortunate and left Maidstone fairly well equipped, but after their departure no more clothing or equipment was available for some time. So the 8th and 9th Battalions when

APPENDIX I.

they paraded for their departure to their training camps, presented an extraordinary appearance. Very few men possessed any uniform, head gear of every sort was to be seen—straw hats, bowlers, caps, and there were even some top hats amongst them. Many men carried their belongings in suit cases, hand bags, or cricket bags.

For the 8th and 9th Battalions, the provision of officers also became less easy, and any previous experience in military training or in handling men was found to be valuable.

On the departure of the 9th Battalion the barracks became less congested and the Staff were able to give more attention to training, which up to this time had been of a very elementary nature. But recruits still continued to arrive each day in considerable numbers, and many of them were drafted by companies to other regiments. Naturally this was not popular with the men, who were however consoled by the assurance that their companies would be kept intact in their new regiment.

Not the least important work carried out by the Depôt Staff up to the end of 1914 was the selection after interview of candidates for commissions. It is satisfactory to know that the whole of the 200 who were recommended by the Depôt were accepted. In fact the name of the Officer commanding the Depôt became known at the War Office as that of a man whose recommendations could be implicitly trusted, as he put forward only those candidates whom he considered fit to become officers in his own regiment.

On April 10th, 1915, Colonel Maunsell was ordered to take up an appointment in France and handed over command to Lieut.-Col. W. L. Rowe.

RECRUITING.

At about this time it became clear that the enthusiasm which had brought such enormous numbers of men into

APPENDIX I.

the Army during the first months of the War had in some measure abated, and voluntary enlistment was not producing sufficient men to fill the units of the New Armies or even to replace the heavy losses suffered by regiments at the front. Efforts were therefore made to make the voluntary system of enlistment more effective. The Regimental Recruiting Area was divided into five sub-areas, Chatham, Gravesend, Bromley, Tonbridge and Maidstone, working under the Headquarters of Recruiting at Maidstone Barracks. Sheerness was at this time transferred to The Buffs. Later these five sub-areas were reduced to three, but the system remained the same till the end. All recruits raised were sent to the Depôt for first payment, clothing and posting to units.

Area Registration Office.

About August, 1915, the Registration Act was passed, which made it compulsory for every man to register his name, age, occupation and other details with his Local Authority. This information in the case of all men between the ages of 18 and 40 was sent to the Area Office for registration. So on the 8th September the Area Registration Office was opened. To complete and keep up to date the registers, not only was it necessary to increase the existing staff by six female clerks and three or four men returned from the front, but also obtain as much voluntary help as possible. Assistance was given by local ladies and gentlemen, by some of the banks, and on many occasions the staff of the Sessions House assisted by working after hours up to 11 o'clock at night. In spite of all this extra help the Registers were not complete till the middle of October, by which time 50,000 names had been entered. As the scheme developed, this number was largely increased until at the end there were over 82,000 names in the Register.

APPENDIX I.

The principal work in the Area Registration Office was to keep the Register up to date from information supplied from sub-areas of the results of Tribunal cases, medical examinations, enlistments, etc. Work increased rapidly and with it the number of clerks employed, so that the office was transferred to and occupied the whole of the Commanding Officer's house.

The more important increases of work were due to the Derby Group system instituted in December, 1915, which invited men to enlist and be passed at once into the Reserve, to be called up when needed, and to the addition to the Register in 1916 of lads between the ages of 15 and 17.

OCCUPATIONAL INDEX.

Towards the end of 1916 a completely new department had to be established to keep an Occupational Index. Its object was to classify every man on the Register under his occupation so that the number of men in each trade could be readily ascertained. This index contained 36,000 cards: there were 18 main trades with 90 sub-divisions. Early in 1917, the Review of Exceptions Acts was passed. This act authorized the calling up for re-examination of all men rejected for service on medical grounds, after six months from the date of their last examination. As approximately a million men came under the provisions of this Act, the importance of the work it entailed is easily understood, and necessitated a close scrutiny of the Registers. About the middle of 1917, two fresh groups were formed, viz.: for men of 45 to 49 years of age and for men of 50. As each step was taken by Government to meet the demand for men, so the work of registration increased.

Inspection of the Registration Offices were frequent, and the complimentary reports on the accuracy of the work were in great measure the result of the indefatigable work of the Chief Clerk, Q.M.S. R. Giovanni.

APPENDIX I.

Posting of Recruits.

Connected with the work hitherto described was the handling and posting of recruits on their arrival at the Depôt—a difficult task demanding tact and discernment which was most ably and conscientiously carried out for nearly two years by Captain R. H. Eccles, in addition to his other duties.

A recruit on arrival was classified by a medical board according to his fitness for general service, garrison duty, labour, or sedentary work at home or abroad. If unfit, the man was at once discharged. After being classified, he was posted to a suitable unit in accordance with the instructions of the Army Council. To decide how each man could be most usefully employed was no easy matter, and the difficulty was much increased by the large number dealt with, which reached at one time 240 in a day.

Although all possible consideration was shown to the personal wishes of the recruit, it was not infrequent that the necessities of the service demanded that they should be disregarded. And as a rule the older men were sent to fill up the number required as tradesmen, while the younger men were posted to units in the fighting line.

Having been posted, unless he could be dispatched at once to his unit, a recruit was accommodated at the Depôt and received one day's pay each evening. The filling up of the men's documents was a lengthy and tedious business, and kept the Posting Officer and his valuable assistant, Colour-Sergt. Palmer, at work to late hours.

Conscientious Objectors.

Several Conscientious Objectors were dealt with. Those not exempted by the Tribunals were posted to the infantry, and at the Depôt they, like other recruits, were sent to the Quartermaster's Stores to receive their

APPENDIX I.

uniform. This the Conscientious Objector invariably refused to wear, and was at once put in close arrest on the charge of disobedience to orders.

SUBSTITUTION.

About the middle of 1916 another department had to be established to carry out a scheme for substitution, by which Category A men, who were employed in certified trades and could not be spared from such trades, were exchanged with men of lower category obtained from the Army. In each area a Substitution Officer was appointed, and for the West Kent Area, Captain A. H. Pickard. The scheme was explained at public meetings in the chief industrial and farming centres, with the result that many employers sent in lists of men to the Substitution Officer, who obtained substitutes from Headquarters, Eastern Command.

MUNITIONS AREA RECRUITING SCHEME.

In May, 1917, a larger scheme was inaugurated known as the Munitions Area Recruiting Scheme. Captain Pickard became the Munitions Area Recruiting Officer, and working under his jurisdiction were a Dilution Officer, a skilled engineer, from the Ministry of Munitions, an Employment Officer from the Ministry of Labour, and a Substitution Officer from the Ministry of National Service.

The Recruiting and Dilution Officers visited factories and decided what men could be called up for service either without a substitute or on a substitute being found from the Army by the Substitution Officer, or from civil life by the Employment Officer.

The success of the scheme depended in a large measure on cordiality and willing co-operation between the four officers concerned. In the West Kent Area all worked smoothly, so much so that the various M.A.R.O.'s from other areas were sent to Maidstone for instruction, and Captain Pickard was later selected

APPENDIX I.

by the Ministry of National Service to inspect and report on the work of all the officers under their jurisdiction.

Employment Companies.

One other measure was adopted to increase the supply of fit men. All men of high medical category were withdrawn from employment in the spring of 1917, and substitutes for them were found from men in Employment Companies formed of men of low category. The strength of No. 613 Company, formed at Maidstone, was 750. The men were sent to units at home as batmen, storemen, cooks, etc., and their pay was sent to them each week from the Depôt.

Agricultural Companies.

In March, 1917, the Depôt shared in the work of increasing and conserving our supplies of food grown in the country by organising and administering Agricultural Companies. At first one company only was formed under Colonel Lushington with an establishment of 250; the actual strength usually exceeded 400, however. In June three more companies were added, all becoming Agricultural Companies of the Labour Corps. The men of these companies were sent out to work on farms in the district and though a large proportion were unskilled, their services were eagerly sought. The men were paid a minimum wage by their farmer employers on working days and received Army pay on Sundays and when in barracks. At the time of the Armistice the number of men on the rolls of these companies was 3,000.

Sufficient has been said to make clear the enormous volume of work thrown on the Depôt Staff by the various measures taken to raise and maintain a National Army. It may be said that an attempt was made, and was in a large measure successful, to do, during the progress of the war, the work of preparing plans for

APPENDIX I.

mobilizing our man power as a Nation in Arms as well as that of putting those plans into execution. And it was on Depôt Staffs that the work of carrying out the various plans fell.

THE QUARTER-MASTER'S DEPARTMENT.

All the men who passed through the Depôt had to be housed, clothed, equipped and fed. It was fortunate for the successive commanding officers that the Quarter-Master's Department was under the able direction of Major Couch, who had retired on the day before orders for mobilization were received, but at once returned to duty, for on his ability, judgment and integrity implicit confidence could be placed.

The total number of sets of arms and equipment held on charge in mobilization stores was 1,257, all of which were issued to the Army Reservists. Clothing and equipment, etc., was indented for more quickly than it could be supplied, and the reserves held by the Ordnance Department were soon exhausted. Hence arose the remarkable appearance of the 8th and 9th Battalions on their departure from Maidstone. But after their departure all recruits were clothed and equipped by the Depôt.

Commanding Officers were directed to purchase locally. Very little could be obtained as the Territorial Association had already purchased for the units for which they were responsible, but a considerable quantity of such articles as razors, towels, knives, forks, spoons, shirts and socks were procured from the big London stores.

Later the Royal Army Clothing Department issued trade pattern clothing, blue uniform and civilian great coats of various colours, but there was no uniformity for some considerable time. About 1,000 suits of Special Reserve red clothing were sent to the 8th Battalion.

APPENDIX I.

Service Battalions proceeding overseas sent their surplus stores to the Depôt, where the clothing was examined, and serviceable garments were cleaned, repaired and re-issued. When Service dress became available battalions near Maidstone were ordered to hand in their emergency clothing at Maidstone. As this occurred at a time of heavy rain, the clothing got saturated, which was particularly unfortunate for the Quartermaster's staff, while two battalions, whose service dress was delayed and who demanded that only their own clothing should be returned to them, came off badly.

The number of articles issued from the stores is quite impossible to compute, it must have been colossal, and when it is remembered that every article had to be accounted for in his ledger, it is easy to understand why, although the Quarter-Master was seldom seen, there was never any difficulty in finding him.

The number of men for whom rations were drawn was large and often the meals for over 1,000 men were cooked in barracks. At first rations were on a generous scale, but when food became short, rabbits and frozen fish were substituted for meat, and every effort was made to economize. Rabbit skins were carefully preserved and sold, fats of every sort collected for munition factories.

Crops in Barracks.

To increase the supply of food, orders were issued that all Government ground in the vicinity of barracks was to be cultivated. At that time there happened to be plenty of men available in barracks, so soon scores of men were lined out with picks and shovels on the Recreation Ground, the whole of which was dug over in one day. In due course it was planted with cabbages, which brought good profit to the Canteen Fund. The next crop was potatoes, nearly half the seed for which was derived from potatoes voluntarily given by

APPENDIX I.

the men from their rations. But the most lucrative venture was the establishment of piggeries in front of the Mobilization Store, which under the management of R.S.M. Akhurst brought in a profit of £583.

COMMANDING OFFICERS.

In this short record of the Depôt during the war, little mention has been made of the men who carried out their never-ending and ever-increasing work. On May 17th, 1916, Lieut.-Col. W. E. Rowe retired and was succeeded by Lieut.-Col. E. A. Iremonger, formerly a Major in the Durham Light Infantry, and what was thought of the staff of the Depôt by an officer of another regiment may be shown by quoting from a letter he wrote on his departure on April 4th, 1917, when he was succeeded by Lieut.-Col. J. P. Dalison. After stating that he had been privileged to serve in units of three regiments during the War, that in none had the good spirit been surpassed by that of "these most lovable officers and men of The Queen's Own." He concluded, "But for the unswerving loyalty and support you have all accorded me, a total stranger, and regimentally an outsider to you all, life and the performance of one's duty would indeed have been an uphill task." It may be said that the feelings so generously expressed were warmly reciprocated by all ranks. No man could have more jealously guarded the interest and honour of The Queen's Own.

It was perhaps during Lieut.-Col. Dalison's period of command that the stress of work was highest, and he has provided the major part of this short record. His success can perhaps best be judged by quoting from a private letter written by him to the compiler.

"I wanted to say more about the grand way our N.C.O.'s worked all the time and to mention some of them, especially R.S.M. Audsley, who was splendid,

APPENDIX I.

R.S.M. Drew, Q.M.S. Powers, Sergt. Clewes, all wonders in their respective ways.

"But, of course, I think the outstanding figure was dear old Couch. I had said a lot more about him, but lack of space forced me to cross it out."

To appreciate the good work of subordinates is one of the qualities of a successful and efficient Commanding Officer. To say more is unnecessary.

No account of the work at the Depôt during the War would be complete without a description of the funds raised for the welfare of the Regiment.

THE COMFORTS' FUND.

Sir Edward Leach started the Comforts' Fund in September, 1914, by making an appeal for subscriptions to provide comforts for our Battalions at the front. Gifts of money and in kind were quickly received, and by the beginning of October Colonel Maunsell, who was acting as treasurer, had received £290. Mrs. Arundel Martyn received gifts of comforts (shirts, socks, tobacco, etc.) and was sending them out in small parcels to the 1st Battalion once a fortnight. From this comparatively small beginning the Fund developed rapidly, and the 53rd and last list of donations published in the "Queen's Own Gazette" in January, 1919, brought the total receipt of money up to £7,568. Of this sum Lord Harris' County Organization, which included the Society of the Men of Kent and Kentish Men, contributed over £2,400. But the money represents part only of the generosity of the friends of the Regiment—gifts of comforts of all sorts were received in a steady stream. Where many give so generously of their time and money, it is almost invidious to mention names, but perhaps the thanks of the Regiment are especially due to the Roan School for Girls at Greenwich, who not only contributed £600 in cash to the

APPENDIX I.

Fund, but month after month from the very first sent numerous bales of comforts. Equally, too, to Mrs. O. J. Daniell is the Regiment under obligation. For two years she was responsible for the administration of the Fund, superintending the packing and despatching of all parcels of comforts.

GIFTS FROM QUEEN ALEXANDRA.

In April, 1915, Her Majesty Queen Alexandra sent to the 1st Battalion a gift of comforts. The Officer Commanding on returning thanks wrote: " Your Majesty's kindness and thought are a great encouragement to all ranks, and the knowledge that you are following our movements and doings with interest fills us with sentiments of loyalty and devotion to your person."

CHRISTMAS CHEER FUND.

In November, 1915, a special appeal was made by the Officer Commanding the Depôt for money to provide Christmas gifts for our men at the front. The appeal, which was repeated in the three subsequent years, met with a generous response, with the result that £3,169 was handed over to the Comforts' Fund for this purpose. Over half this large sum was collected by a few ladies, and nearly £1,000 was received from the Directors of the *Kent Messenger*, the proceeds of a " Shilling Fund " inaugurated by them.

Thousands of men blessed these friends of the Regiment for their kindly thought and labour.

PRISONERS OF WAR.

For the first three-and-a-half years of the War, our Prisoners of War were looked after by Mr. J. L. Spoor, who was working voluntarily under the Vice-Lieutenant's County Organization. No record is available of the monies expended during this period beyond the fact that several hundred pounds were sent

APPENDIX I.

to Mr. Spoor by the O.C. Depôt at different times and from various sources.

In February, 1918, however, the care of our Prisoners of War was handed over to the Depôt, and a Prisoners of War Care Committee was formed with the O.C. Depôt as Chairman, Captain J. Lees as Hon. Secretary, and Mr. A. P. Margetts as Hon. Treasurer. Mrs. O. J. Daniell undertook charge of stores in addition to her work for the Comforts' Fund, many ladies assisting her.

The total number of Prisoners of War of the Regiment reached 1,863 in Germany and 95 in Turkey during the time of the Committee's management. To our men in Germany 52,203 parcels of food were sent, besides other articles. To arrange for the safe arrival of parcels of food and clothing to our prisoners in Turkey proved a task almost beyond the power of the Committee. But money reached prisoners safely, and the Committee forwarded 846 parcels and expended over £500 in remittances to Turkey.

During the period under review the Committee expended £34,900, of which £33,795 was the cost of the food. This huge sum was received from various sources; grants from the Central Prisoners of War Committee reached £16,300. Subscriptions and donations, which included the money raised by the Local Committee in the county provided £15,700, while the Vice-Lieutenant's (Lord Harris') Organization contributed a further sum of over £2,830, beyond what was given to the Comforts' Fund.

The Regiment therefore received from Lord Harris' Organization the munificent gift of £5,250.

A splendid work was also done by Miss C. K. Macy, of Beckenham, in tracing the whereabouts of soldiers reported missing. By corresponding with prisoners of war and by other means, she was able to bring relief or consolation to the anxious relatives of many of our men.

APPENDIX I.

The "Queen's Own Gazette."

The "Queen's Own Gazette" was one of the very few regimental magazines whose publication was uninterrupted throughout the war. Every month 100 free copies were sent to each battalion and to various hospitals, and the men looked forward to their arrival with great eagerness.

The post of Editor was undertaken by Colonel T. H. Brock early in 1915. Some acknowledgment of the debt owed to him by those responsible for this book is made in the Preface. To the Regiment his work meant that one of the chains which bind its battalions together was never allowed to weaken.

It is impossible to do more than record the activities of the many friends who worked untiringly and gave generously for the welfare and comfort of members of the Regiment. Their work was truly a labour of love, and so to the workers themselves perhaps brought its own reward. It is equally impossible to give expression to the truly heartfelt gratitude of the members of the Regiment, who in all circumstances, however terrible, felt that they were never forgotten, and never neglected by their friends at home.

Photo by] [Chesney, Ltd., London.

LIEUT. C. H. SEWELL, V.C.
3rd Battalion attached Tank Corps.
Killed in action, 29th August, 1918.

APPENDIX II.

ROLL OF HONOUR.

THE SOLDIER.

If I should die, think only this of me:
That there's some corner of a foreign field
That is for ever England. There shall be
In that rich earth a richer dust concealed;
A dust whom England bore, shaped, made aware,
Gave, once, her flowers to love, her ways to roam,
A body of England's, breathing England's air,
Washed by the rivers, blest by suns of home.

And think, this heart, all evil shed away,
A pulse in the eternal mind, no less
Gives somewhere back the thoughts by England
given;
Her sights and sounds; dreams happy as her day;
And laughter, learnt of friends; and gentleness,
In hearts at peace, under an English heaven.

RUPERT BROOKE.

(By kind permission of the Literary Executors of Rupert Brooke and Messrs. Sidgwick & Jackson, Ltd.)

APPENDIX II.

A List in Alphabetical order of Members of
THE QUEEN'S OWN
Who were killed in action, or died of wounds or disease during the Great War, 1914—1919.

Abbey, G.	G/19968	Pte.		Aitkin, D. G.	240826	Pte.
Abbott, A. J.	G/31096	Pte.		Akast, F.	L/10268	Pte.
Abbott, J.	G/9033	Pte.		Akehurst, W.	G/5837	Pte.
Abbott, S. W.	G/4642	L/Sgt.		Akers, H. J.	G/6709	L/Cpl.
Abel, J. E.		2nd Lieut.		Akhurst, A.	S/53	Pte.
Ablett, J.	G/5659	Pte.		Albery, R. E.	G/30203	Pte.
Abnett, A.	L/7748	Pte.		Alcorn, W.	241772	Pte.
Abnett, E.	S/9170	Pte.		Alderman, W. J., D.S.O.		
Abraham, T.	G/3658	L/Cpl.				Lieut.-Col.
Abrey, W.	G/24255	L/Cpl.		Alderton, G.	G/8008	Sgt.
Accleton, E. J.	TF/1957	Pte.		Aldous, G.	G/2093	Pte.
Acott, A.	G/16453	Pte.		Aldous, H. G.	G/30503	Pte.
Acott, B. C.	S/8700	Pte.		Aldous, W.	L/10446	Pte.
Acott, E.	G/2406	Pte.		Aldridge, F. J.	G/24579	Pte.
Acott, F.	L/9540	Pte.		Alexander, G.H.	G/17766	Pte.
Acott, R.	G/13024	L/Cpl.		Alexander, J. L.	240893	Pte.
Acres, A. S.	G/18242	Sgt.		Alexander, S.T.B.	205436	Pte.
Adams, A.	G/1004	Pte.		Aley, A. S.	G/31807	Pte.
Adams, E. W.	L/7645	Pte.		Algate, W.	242111	Pte.
Adams, F.	S/137	Pte.		Allan, W. H.	L/9982	Pte.
Adams, H.	S/9119	Pte.		Allchin, J. H.	G/12586	Pte.
Adams, J.	G/18286	Pte.		Allchin, S. M.		2nd Lieut.
Adams, J. A.	G/8771	Pte.		Allcorn, F. P.	G/12310	Sgt.
Adams, W.	G/26959	Pte.		Allcorn, R.	G/10495	Pte.
Adams, W.	G/15970	Pte.		Allcorn, T. L.	G/5010	Pte.
Adie, C.	G/4177	Pte.		Allen, A.	G/377	Pte.
Adley, S.	G/19391	Pte.		Allen, A.	G/6934	Pte.
Agutter, E. H.	204172	Pte.		Allen, C.	G/24580	Pte.
Ainsworth, G.	203063	Pte.		Allen, C. H.	G/10345	Pte.
Aird, H. W.	G/2574	Pte.		Allen, F. C.	G/3725	Pte.
Airey, R. W.	L/8091	Pte.		Allen, F. J. W.	G/24497	Pte.
Airton, G.	G/8419	Pte.		Allen, G. J.	L/10101	L/Cpl.
Airton, N.	G/19904	Pte.		Allen, G. W.	G/23228	Pte.
Aitken, R. L.	L/7315	L/Cpl.		Allen, H. A.	G/11157	Pte.

APPENDIX II.

Allen, J.	G/25413	Pte.	Andrews, F.	G/24256	Sgt.
Allen, P.	G/20686	Pte.	Andrews, F. C.	G/2270	Cpl.
Allen, S. T.	G/9362	Pte.	Andrews, G. J.	L/7326	Pte.
Allen, T.	S/1095	Pte.	Andrews, J.	L/9940	Pte.
Allen, W. J.	203198	Pte.	Andrews, J.	G/4117	Pte.
Allen, W. K.		2nd Lieut.	Andrews, J. T.	L/8888	Pte.
Allin, W.	241365	Pte.	Andrews, R.	G/4957	Pte.
Allman, G. J.	G/12446	Pte.	Andrews, W. S.	G/11240	Pte.
Allwinkle, C.	G/5975	Pte.	Annakin, I.	G/19406	Pte.
Allworthy, T. E.	241660	Pte.	Anscombe, E.	24498	Pte.
Allum, A. J.	G/18807	Pte.	Anscombe, E. G.	240583	Pte.
Almond, F.	G/12800	Pte.	Ansfield, F.	G/16180	Pte.
Alsop, J.	G/19969	Pte.	Anstead, W.	G/16884	Pte.
Ambrose, J..J	203397	Pte.	Anstiss, H. S.A.	G/10464	Pte.
Ambrose, P. F.	G/18333	Pte.	Ansty, A.	G/25324	Pte.
Ambrose, W. E.	G/18245	Pte.	Anthony, J. W.	L/11430	Pte.
Ames, E. T.	G/18403	Pte.	Apperley, B. L. M.		2nd Lieut.
Ames, H. S.	G/39093	Pte.	Appleby, H. C. S.		
Ames, W.	G/5306	Cpl.		L/10443	L/Cpl.
Ames, W. K.		2nd Lieut.	Appleton, E. J.	L/9396	Pte.
Amess, W.M. F.	L/8985	Pte.	Appleton, W. J.	205434	Pte.
Amis, T.	G/29548	Pte.	Apps, M.	266725	Pte.
Amos, H.	G/24581	Pte.	Apps, T. W.	G/5453	Pte.
Amos, J.	S/8545	L/Cpl.	Arbon, A. H.	G/20928	Pte.
Amos, J. H.	G/858	Pte.	Archer, F.	G/4510	Pte.
Amoss, J.	L/9092	Pte.	Archer, F.	G/17773	Pte.
Anderson, A.	242109	Pte.	Ardley, A. J.	G/6664	Pte.
Anderson, C. K.		Lieut.	Argent, G. W.	G/9660	Pte.
Anderson, D. F.		Lieut.	Argent, J. E.	L/5498	Pte.
Anderson, H.	G/30854	Pte.	Arkle, D.	G/3930	Pte.
Anderson, H.	G/2787	Pte.	Armin, J.	21035	Pte.
Anderson, J.	G/20056	Pte.	Armitage, W. A. J.		
Anderson, J. W.	G/2294	Pte.		G/1304	Pte.
Anderson, R.	200959	Pte.	Armsden, G.	S/8504	Pte.
Anderson, W.	G/8888	Pte.	Armstrong, A.	G/17763	Cpl.
Anderton, H. T.	G/3657	L/Cpl.	Armstrong,W.T.	L/10409	Pte.
Andrew, D.	G/27695	Pte.	Arnell, H. G.	G/18806	Pte.
Andrew, E. L.	G/28897	Pte.	Arnold, C.	S/1118	Pte.
Andrews, A. B.	201187	Pte.	Arnold, F. A.		2nd Lieut.
Andrews, C. J.	201479	L/Cpl.	Arnold, F.	G/4110	L/Sgt.
Andrews, C. J.	205185	Pte.	Arnold, G	G/3349	Pte.
Andrews, D.	G/2376	Pte.	Arnold, G	L/8940	Pte.
Andrews, E. C.		2nd Lieut.	Arnold, J. W.	S/971	Pte.

503

APPENDIX II.

Arnold, P. F.	G/9234	Cpl.	Atkinson, E.	TF/4930	Pte.
Arnold, R.	G/2362	Pte.	Atkinson, G.A.C.	G/3054	Pte.
Arundel, A. H.	G/11229	Cpl.	Atkinson, J.	L/9790	Pte.
Arundell, A.	L/7349	Pte.	Atkinson, T.	G/31911	Pte.
Ash, S. J.	L/7882	Cpl.	Atkinson, T.	G/25976	Pte.
Ashbee, C. J.	G/18334	Pte.	Attenborough, W.		
Ashby, F., *D.C.M.*				G/19407	Pte.
	G/7850	Sgt.	Attwood, A. J.	G/10534	Pte.
Ashby, J. H.	242296	Pte.	Attwood, W. H.	202574	Pte.
Ashby, T. H.	G/20061	Pte.	Atwood, W. C.	L/9427	L/Cpl.
Ashby, W.	G/5238	Pte.	Auckland, G.	G/9096	L/Cpl.
Ashdown, A.	G/378	Sgt.	Austen, A.	G/38822	Pte.
Ashdown, A. C.	L/8230	L/Sgt.	Austen, R. J.	201040	Cpl.
Ashdown, F.	G/2780	Pte.	Austen, W. T.	G/8043	Col-Sgt.
Ashdown, F. J.	G/15514	L/Cpl.	Austin, J.	G/6392	Pte.
Ashdown, H.	G/768	Pte.	Austin, H. F. J.	G/24700	Pte.
Ashdown, P. T.	G/19620	Pte.	Austin, R. A.	G/20203	Pte.
Ashenden, G.	S/9268	Pte.	Austin, T. H.	G/12853	Pte.
Ashenden, H.	S/920	Pte.	Austin, W. F.	G/4766	Pte.
Ashenden, S. R.	G/30568	Pte.	Avard, F. F.	G/24277	Cpl.
Ashford, P. J.	L/10233	Sgt.	Aveling, H.	G/5433	Pte.
Ashley, W.	L/9335	Pte.	Averns, R.	G/17772	Pte.
Ashman, G.	G/11783	Pte.	Avery, E. J.	G/12109	Pte.
Ashman, R. A.	L/10927	Pte.	Avery, G.	G/30502	Pte.
Ashman, W.	G/25944	Pte.	Avery, G.	G/30531	Pte.
Ashton, C. J.		Capt.	Avery, G.	L/9797	Sgt.
Ashton, J. R.	G/27460	Pte.	Avery, H.	G/7724	Pte.
Ashton, S J.	G/2675	Pte.	Avery, H.	G/20058	Pte.
Ashton, W. A.	G/10240	Pte.	Avery, W. S.	G/3688	Pte.
Ashton, W. L.	G/18182	Pte.	Avis, C.	G/11120	Pte.
Ashwell, W. A.	G/10823	Pte.	Avis, W.	G/887	Pte.
Ashworth, B. W.		2nd Lieut.	Axelby, H. K.	G/1547	Pte.
Aslin, P. J.	203315	Pte.	Axell, F.	G/11188	Pte.
Aspell, R.	G/2957	Pte.	Axford, F.	G/23717	Pte.
Astley, E.	G/1555	Pte.	Axtell, G. A.	G/12280	Pte.
Atchison, W. R.	G/3041	Sgt.	Axten, E. G.	L/10820	Pte.
Atherall, G. D.	G/11187	Pte.	Aylward, J.	G/1322	Pte.
Atkin, F. H.	TF/7332	Pte.	Ayres, A. A.	G/6352	Pte.
Atkins, A. D.	203798	Pte.			
Atkins, E. C.	G/17462	Pte.			
Atkins, M. G.	G/12832	Pte.	Bacon, A. C.	G/3199	Pte.
Atkinson, C.	G/2263	Pte.	Bacon, P. R.	G/31446	Pte.
Atkinson, D. P.	G/18152	Pte.	Bacon, W. J.	241691	Pte.

APPENDIX II.

Name	Number	Rank	Name	Number	Rank
Baddeley, F. W.	G/16374	Pte.	Baker, J. E.	L/8183	Pte.
Bagge, W. J.	G/18154	Sgt.	Baker, J. H., *M.M.*		
Bagnall, J. W.	G/21070	Pte.		G/6502	Cpl.
Bagwell, B. J.	G/23373	Pte.	Baker, J. H.	G/1242	Sgt.
Bailey, A.	G/16618	Pte.	Baker, J. W.	G/18694	Pte.
Bailey, A. H.	G/28925	Pte.	Baker, J. W. H.	G/6950	Pte.
Bailey, C.	G/24831	Pte.	Baker, R. J.	G/1711	Pte.
Bailey, C.	G/6650	Pte.	Baker, T.	L/9608	Pte.
Bailey, C. E.	L/5979	Pte.	Baker, T. E.	G/19370	Pte.
Bailey, C. R	G/20943	Pte.	Baker, W.	G/9822	Pte.
Bailey, G.	S/8529	L/Cpl.	Baker, W. E.	G/5450	Pte.
Bailey, G. H.	G/12308	Pte.	Balcombe, W. G.	L/10562	Pte.
Bailey, H. S.	242479	L/Cpl.	Baldock, S. T.	G/5058	Pte.
Bailey, J. C.	S/894	Pte.	Baldwin, A.	L/9672	Sgt.
Bailey, R. J. W.	G/18808	Pte.	Baldwin, A.	G/5294	Pte.
Bailey, W. H.	L/4680	Pte.	Baldwin, J.	G/4643	Pte.
Bain, D. A.	G/11381	Pte.	Baldwin, J. A.	L/10807	Pte.
Bain, J.	L/9480	Pte.	Baldwin, P. F.	G/5914	Pte.
Bain, N.		2nd Lieut.	Baldwin, W.	L/6737	Pte.
Baines, H.	G/2641	Pte.	Balkham, H. G.	G/6632	Pte.
Baird, W.	G/31171	Pte.	Ball, A.	G/11786	Pte.
Baker, A.	G/20941	Pte.	Ball, G.	240973	Pte.
Baker, A. E.	S/806	Pte.	Ball, H. J. C.	G/29979	Pte.
Baker, A. E.	G/3203	Sgt.	Ball, J. J.	G/6584	Pte.
Baker, A. J.	G/18692	Pte.	Ball, J. W.	G/10682	L/Cpl.
Baker, A. P.	G/10573	Pte.	Ball, W.	G/16393	Pte.
Baker, A R.	G/31128	Pte.	Ballard, C. F.	G/18004	Pte.
Baker, B.	G/6905	Pte.	Balls, J.	G/11474	Pte.
Baker, B.	G/18736	Pte.	Bamford, H.	242297	Pte.
Baker, C.	S/696	Pte.	Bampton, H. C.	L/7434	Pte.
Baker, E. G.	205086	Pte.	Bamsey, F. R.	G/6716	Pte.
Baker, F.	L/7229	Pte.	Banagan, F. C.	G/6113	Pte.
Baker, F.	G/23369	L/Cpl.	Bance, T.	201012	Pte.
Baker, F.	G/18055	Pte.	Bandfield, A.	G/132	Pte.
Baker, F. H.	206336	Pte.	Bandy, J. T.	G/6843	C.S.M.
Baker, G.	L/9868	Pte.	Banfield, J. W.	G/19138	Pte.
Baker, H.	241196	Pte.	Banks, D.	L/9853	Pte.
Baker, H.	G/23550	Pte.	Banks, J.	G/15973	Pte.
Baker, H. E. R.	G/4384	L/Cpl.	Banks, P. A., *M.C.*		2nd Lieut.
Baker, J.	201655	Sgt.	Banks, R.	L/6555	Pte.
Baker, J.	G/17602	Pte.	Banks, R.	L/7676	Pte.
Baker, J.	G/18647	Pte.	Banks, W.	S/644	Pte.
Baker, J. A.	G/4994	L/Cpl.	Bannister, G. T.	G/10728	Pte.

505

APPENDIX II.

Name	Number	Rank
Bannister, R.	205442	Pte.
Barber, F. W.	L/10735	Pte.
Barber, H. H.	G/23252	Pte.
Barber, R.	L/8112	L/Cpl.
Barber, S. P.	G/16137	Pte.
Barden, C. E.	L/9603	Sgt.
Barden, G. I.	G/4781	Pte.
Barden, H. A.	L/8358	Pte.
Barden, M.	G/13047	Pte.
Barden, P.	G/2287	L/Cpl.
Barden, Z.	L/8126	Sgt.
Bardoe, S. J.	G/10966	Pte.
Bardsley, P.	G/12768	Pte.
Bareham, A.	G/18810	Pte.
Barfield, G. E.	203302	Sgt.
Barham, A.	S/260	Pte.
Barham, J.	G/16605	Pte.
Barham, J. W.	G/13473	Pte.
Barham, W.	G/3649	Pte.
Baring, C. C.		2nd Lieut.
Barker, A.	G/20294	Pte.
Barker, A. J.	L/8179	Pte.
Barker, A. R.	L/6781	Pte.
Barker, C.	G/18419	Pte.
Barker, C. I.		2nd Lieut.
Barker, C. J.	G/8153	Pte.
Barker, E. J.	S/761	Pte.
Barker, F.	G/14530	Pte.
Barker, H. H.	G/20641	Pte.
Barker, J.	G/14629	Pte.
Barker, J. E.	240788	Cpl.
Barker, P.	G/18289	Pte.
Barker, P. C.	G/29513	Pte.
Barker, S.	L/7849	Pte.
Barker, T.	G/18083	Pte.
Barker, W. C.	G/18949	Pte.
Barksby, W. H.	G/20063	Pte.
Barkwith, F. E.	G/9164	Pte.
Barlow, S.	G/19408	Pte.
Barnard, A. H.	L/8873	Sgt.
Barnard, H. J.	L/8560	Pte.
Barnard, S.	G/10809	Pte.
Barnard, W.	G/12060	Pte.
Barnden, J.	G/10396	Pte.
Barnes, A. C.	G/4397	Pte.
Barnes, A. G.	G/18194	Pte.
Barnes, A. S.	G/8674	Pte.
Barnes, C. J.	G/21050	Cpl.
Barnes, D. S.	L/8182	Pte.
Barnes, E. M.	G/18608	Pte.
Barnes, F.	G/18809	Pte.
Barnes, G.	S/1216	Pte.
Barnes, R.	G/1247	Pte.
Barnes, W.	205415	Pte.
Barnes, W. V.	G/18362	Pte.
Barnet, G. W.	201268	Pte.
Barnett, L. de B.		Capt.
Barnett, N.	G/31651	Pte.
Barnett, W.	L/8146	Pte.
Barnham, J. W. J., M.M.	G/11243	Sgt.
Baron, N.	S/554	Sgt.
Barr, C.	S/8702	Pte.
Barratt, H. C.	G/2714	C.Q.M.S.
Barrett, B.	G/3232	Pte.
Barrett, G.	G/5347	Pte.
Barrett, J.	G/19864	Pte.
Barrett, T. H.	G/646	Pte.
Barrett, T.	L/8168	Pte.
Barrett, T. J.	G/5771	Pte.
Barrie, A. J. M.	240811	Pte.
Barrie, J.	L/10469	Pte.
Barrows, J. E.	G/16039	Pte.
Barrs, N. C.		2nd Lieut.
Barry, J. J.	L/8558	Pte.
Barry, T.	L/8357	L/Cpl.
Bartholomew, H. F.	G/1532	Sgt.
Bartlett, A.	G/2030	Pte.
Bartlett, E. S.	G/902	L/Cpl.
Bartlett, H. J.	G/24572	Cpl.
Bartlett, L. A.		Lieut.
Barton, A. M.	G/24583	Pte.
Barton, F. A.	G/18246	Pte.
Barton, G. H.	G/4164	Pte.

APPENDIX II.

Barton, G. T.	205808	C.Q.M.S.	Batts, C. F.	G/16325	L/Cpl.
			Baulcomb, F.	G/31047	Pte.
Barton, J. H.	G/9693	Pte.	Baulcombe, J. C. S.	G/18288	Pte.
Bartram, A. A.	G/5095	L/Cpl.	Baum, H.	G/20064	Pte.
Bartram, R. J.	L/11558	Pte.	Bax, C.	G/9596	Pte.
Barwell, J. A.	G/20645	Pte.	Baxhill, A. J.	G/31108	Pte.
Bascombe, F.W.	G/10787	Pte.	Baxter, A. C.	G/6795	Pte.
Bashford, W. H.	G/18916	Pte.	Baylis, E. A.	G/3493	Pte.
Baskett, H. G.	205444	Pte.	Baynes, S.	G/8878	Sgt.
Baskett, M. A.	G/7593	Pte.	Beadle, G. J.	G/10324	Pte.
Bass, A E.	G/5282	L/Cpl.	Beagley, F.	S/7889	Cpl.
Bass, J.	G/6453	Pte.	Beake, W. H., M.M.		
Bass, R.	G/30585	Pte.		G/19027	Sgt.
Bass, W. A.	L/9419	L/Cpl.	Beal, R., M.M.	G/18421	Cpl.
Bassett, A.	241183	Pte.	Beale, F. W.	G/4326	Pte.
Bassett, A.	G/1212	Pte.	Beale, J.	G/8262	Sgt.
Bassett, F. E.	G/10038	Pte.	Beale, W.	S/111	Pte.
Bassett, J. B.	G/5497	Pte.	Beames, A.	G/4816	Pte.
Bassett, W.	G/19185	Pte.	Beaney, J.	G/4986	Pte.
Bassett, W. H.	G/6617	Pte.	Beard, J.	G/5753	Pte.
Bassil, J. W.	L/10123	Pte.	Beard, T.	205599	Pte.
Bastecky, V.	G/27834	Pte.	Beasley, W.	G/393	L/Cpl.
Bastin, W. T.	G/9564	Pte.	Beattie, R.	G/8782	Pte.
Batchelor, F. J.	G/1059	Pte.	Beaumont, F.	G/13241	Pte.
Batchelor, T.	L/8156	L/Cpl.	Beavan, R. J.	G/9652	Pte.
Bateman, C. A.	200389	Sgt.	Beckett, A. C.	L/9557	Pte.
Bateman, H. J.	G/458	Pte.	Beckett, C.	G/8579	Pte.
Bateman, W. B. F.			Beckett, F. J.	G/17417	Pte.
	G/31260	Pte.	Beckett, P. A.	2nd Lieut.	
Bater, S.	G/18733	Pte.	Beckham, J.	206377	Pte.
Bates, A. E. H.	G/3991	Pte.	Beckington, W. L.		
Bates, B.	G/11173	Pte.		G/1943	Pte.
Bates, F. G.	G/20623	Pte.	Beckwith, G. W.	S/9092	Pte.
Bates, G.	G/16787	Pte.	Beckwith, W. F.	S/8914	Pte.
Bates, W. G. J.	G/5116	Pte.	Beeching, G. A.	G/28090	Pte.
Bather, R. T.	G/31539	Pte.	Beeley, J. E.	G/10060	Pte.
Bathurst, A.L.L.	G/19023	Pte.	Beeman, A. C.		Capt.
Batsford, A. J.	203566	Pte.	Beer, A.	L/10976	Pte.
Batsford, B.	G/5131	Pte.	Beer, H. J.	G/18248	Pte.
Batten, B.	G/28547	Pte.	Beer, H. O.	2nd Lieut.	
Batten, W. H.	G/470	Cpl.	Beesley, F J.	S/9363	Sgt.
Batterham, A.C.	L/10128	Pte.	Beeson, W.	G/30867	Pte.
Battersby, E. M.		Capt.	Beeston, A.	G/21611	Pte.

507

APPENDIX II.

Beeston, H. L.		Capt.	Benstead, E. V.	G/21071	Pte.
Belcher, A. E.	G/11820	Pte.	Bentley, E.	G/751	Cpl.
Belcher, G.	G/7725	Pte.	Bentley, F.	G/31656	Pte.
Belcher, R.	L/9787	Pte.	Bentley, S. H.	205586	Pte.
Bell, A. J.	L/9937	Pte.	Benton, L. J.	G/2223	Pte.
Bell, H.	G/6131	Cpl.	Beresford, J.	G/5113	Pte.
Bell, J.	G/9143	Pte.	Berriman, E. C.	204473	Pte.
Bell, J.	G/18863	Pte.	Berry, A.	242453	Pte.
Bell, J. A.	G/20454	Pte.	Berry, E. A.	G/7426	Pte.
Bell, J. P.	G/31442	Pte.	Berry, G. E.	G/11908	Pte.
Bell, R. R.	G/31652	Pte.	Berry, W. H.	201388	Pte.
Bell, T.	G/10027	Pte.	Best, T. R.	205033	Pte.
Bellamy, R. A.	G/30534	Pte.	Best, T. W.	G/30875	Pte.
Bellfield, W. H. F.			Beswick, J. J.	G/19972	Pte.
	L/7474	Pte.	Betts, A. H.	G/15508	Pte.
Bendall, F. A.	G/11374	Sgt.	Betts, F.	S/371	Pte.
Bendall, J. M.	G/15121	Pte.	Betts, P. W.	L/9998	Pte.
Benfold, J.	L/10387	Pte.	Bevan, C.	G/5352	Pte.
Benge, F. H.	G/9420	Pte.	Bevan, C. T.	G/24847	Pte.
Benge, G. A.	S/8346	Pte.	Bevan, N. S.	L/11300	Pte.
Benn, A. E.	G/25104	Pte.	Beven, C. H.	G/1175	Pte.
Bennell, A.	G/23756	Pte.	Bevis, A. G.	G/17546	Pte.
Bennett, A.	G/5973	Pte.	Bevis, W.	L/10259	Pte.
Bennett, A. E.	G/11891	Pte.	Bewick, J. J.	G/21371	Sgt.
Bennett, A. E.	G/18418	Pte.	Bewshea, C. A.	G/10069	L/Cpl.
Bennett, C. T.		Capt.	Bickle, F. J.	L/8363	L/Cpl.
Bennett, E. V.	G/8196	Cpl.	Bicknell, H.	G/4262	Pte.
Bennett, F.	G/5642	Pte.	Biggs, W. J.	L/6647	Pte.
Bennett, F. T.	L/10036	Pte.	Bignall, W. R.	G/39460	Pte.
Bennett, H.	G/30844	Pte.	Bignell, J.	L/9726	L/Cpl.
Bennett, H. R.	G/17430	Pte.	Bigsby, E. A.		2nd Lieut.
Bennett, J.	G/17781	Pte.	Billings, P. W.	G/31443	Pte.
Bennett, J.	G/11164	Pte.	Bilner, F.	G/17782	Pte.
Bennett, J. S.	G/38602	Pte.	Bingham, G.	G/25960	Pte.
Bennett, R. W.	G/31000	Cpl.	Birch, C. S.	G/5644	Pte.
Bennett, R. W.	G/6863	Pte.	Birch, F.	G/5191	Pte.
Bennett, T. A.	201842	Pte.	Birch, S. H.	L/10392	L/Cpl.
Bennett, W.	S/9244	Pte.	Birch, W. J.	L/7396	L/Cpl.
Bennett, W.	L/8312	Pte.	Bird, C. W.	G/18336	Pte.
Bennett, W. H.	G/23135	Pte.	Bird, G.	G/1033	Pte.
Bennett, W. J.	G/10582	Cpl.	Bird, G.	G/5664	Pte.
Bennett, W S.	G/10457	Pte.	Bird, G. W. F.	202151	Pte.
Benson, E. E.	242128	Pte.	Bird, W. A. J.	G/18174	Pte.

APPENDIX II.

Name	Number	Rank		Name	Number	Rank
Bird, W. J.	G/7701	Pte.		Blake, H.	G/4074	L/Cpl.
Bird, W. J.	G/18073	Cpl.		Blake, H. V.	G/1842	Pte.
Birkenfeld, W. J. F. G.	G/23636	Cpl.		Blake, J.	G/4845	Pte.
Birks, H.	G/31649	Pte.		Blakeman, A.	G/2138	Cpl.
Birt, J.	L/7786	Pte.		Blakey, C. H.	G/11468	Pte.
Bishenden, H.	G/4873	L/Cpl.		Blandford, W.A.	G/24586	Pte.
Bishop, A.	G/31070	Pte.		Blanks, L.	240295	Pte.
Bishop, A. H.	205051	Pte.		Blannin, G.	G/17308	Pte.
Bishop, A. J.	G/15118	Pte.		Bleach, C. A.	G/19326	Pte.
Bishop, F A.	240454	Pte.		Bleach, F. W.	G/2872	Pte.
Bishop, F. E.	L/4743	L/Cpl.		Blew, P.		2nd Lieut.
Bishop, W. A.	G/11904	Pte.		Blewer, P.	G/25961	Pte.
Bishop, W. G.	205835	Pte.		Bloomfield, A.	G/10564	Pte.
Bishopp, H.	L/8060	Pte.		Bloomfield, L.S.	G/1879	Pte.
Biss, W. J.	G/15474	Pte.		Blow, G. H.	G/19481	Pte.
Bissager, C.	G/21544	Pte.		Blows, H.	G/10000	L/Cpl.
Bitkeathly, A.	G/3705	Pte.		Bloxham, A. J.	TF/1115	Dr.
Bittle, H. T.	L/7637	Pte.		Bloxham, E.	G/17779	Pte.
Black, T. W.	G/39162	Pte.		Bloxham, T. J.	G/19739	Cpl.
Blackburn, B., M.M.	240022	L/Sgt.		Blundell, C. A.	G/2757	Pte.
Blackburn, G.F.	G/4158	L/Cpl.		Blundell, R.	G/3904	Pte.
Blackburn, J.	L/10525	Pte.		Blundell, R. V.	G/5157	Pte.
Blackburn, J.	G/20378	Pte.		Blundell, W. A.	G/3903	Pte.
Blackeby, F.	L/6714	Pte.		Blundell, W. T.	G/4004	Pte.
Blackett, T.	205537	Pte.		Blunden, H. W.	204636	Pte.
Blacklock, A.	G/2510	Pte.		Boakes, A.	G/21043	Sgt.
Blackman, C.	G/4017	L/Cpl.		Boakes, H.	G/1208	Sgt.
Blackman, E. M., M.M.	G/1194	Cpl.		Boakes, H. S.	G/31818	Pte.
Blackman, F.W.	G/31792	Pte.		Boakes, N. W.	G/16965	L/Cpl.
Blackman, H.	L/10429	Pte.		Boaks, G.	240639	Pte.
Blackman, H.	G/12815	Pte.		Boar, A. T.	G/11057	Pte.
Blackmore, F.C.	G/4886	Pte.		Board, F. G.	TF/1846	Pte.
Blackmore, S. S.	G/30876	Pte.		Bobby, H. C.	G/7249	Pte.
Blackstone, H.	G/20653	Pte.		Boden, S.	G/19906	Pte.
Blackstone, O. B.	203530	Pte.		Bodiam, E. P.	G/8394	Pte.
Blackwell, A. R.	G/9285	Pte.		Body, F. W.	L/9525	Sgt.
Blackwell, F. J.	G/12281	Pte.		Boggon, J.	L/10018	L/Cpl.
Blaikie, J.W. D.	L/10161	Pte.		Bolam, P.	L/8622	Pte.
Blain, A. J.	G/15872	Pte.		Bolden, W.	G/18786	Pte.
Blake, G. E.	G/11028	Pte.		Boldron, P. C.	G/8595	Pte.
				Bolton, A. E.	203456	Pte.
				Bolton, B.	G/5382	Pte.
				Bolton, F. J.	L/8581	Pte.

APPENDIX II.

Name	Number	Rank
Bolton, J. C., *M.M.*	G/5441	Cpl.
Bolton, P. J.		2nd Lieut.
Bond, A.	G/11824	Pte.
Bond, D. J.	L/25112	Pte.
Bond, F.	G/5505	Pte.
Bond, H. S. V.	G/818	Pte.
Bond, J. F. W.	G/31658	Pte.
Bond, S. H.	205186	Pte.
Bond, W. E.	G/18077	Pte.
Bonds, J.	L/7534	Pte.
Bone, T.	L/8571	Pte.
Bonfield, E. W.	L/9080	L/Cpl.
Bonham, H.	S/119	Pte.
Bonner, A.	G/3080	Pte.
Bonner, E. V.	G/8002	Cpl.
Bonny, S. G.	G/24418	Pte.
Booker, A. G.	G/26415	Pte.
Booker, E.	G/12728	Pte.
Booker, F.	S/4623	Pte.
Booker, H.	G/962	Pte.
Booker, J.	G/25366	Pte.
Booker, J.	G/9224	Pte.
Booker, J. W.	G/520	Pte.
Boorman, A.	S/133	L/Cpl.
Boorman, F. J.	G/532	Pte.
Boosey, F.	G/5992	Pte.
Boosey, R. H.	L/9394	Pte.
Booth, B. T.	G/28702	Pte.
Booth, E.	L/9568	L/Cpl.
Booth, E.	G/7417	Pte.
Booth, F. G.	L/9131	Pte.
Boothby, W. E.	G/20452	Pte.
Boother, J.	L/7860	Pte.
Boreham, G.	G/9112	Pte.
Borkett, J.	G/7060	Pte.
Borrett, R. W.	205304	Pte.
Borrins, J. V.	G/30683	Pte.
Bostridge, G.	G/5871	Pte.
Bott, R. H.	G/15449	Pte.
Botting, C. V.	G/7277	Pte.
Bottle, R. E.	200262	Pte.
Bottom, G. A., *M.M.*	G/20447	Sgt.
Boucher, W. M.		Lieut.
Boulton, F. J., *M.M.*	G/20748	Pte.
Bourne, D.	L/10174	Pte.
Bourne, F.	242504	Pte.
Bourne, J.	S/8597	Pte.
Bourne, S.	204614	Pte.
Bourne, W. J.	G/10445	Pte.
Bourne, W. T. J.	G/11816	Pte.
Bovis, F.	L/8438	C.S.M.
Bovis, F. T. W.	G/25471	Pte.
Bowater, T. T.	G/21233	Pte.
Bowden, F.	2422115	Pte.
Bowden, R. C.	G/4859	Pte.
Bowden, S. A.	G/18368	Pte.
Bowell, W. R.	G/4118	Pte.
Bowen, F. M. S.		Lieut.
Bowen, W.	L/11172	Pte.
Bowen, W. H.	G/2778	Cpl.
Bower, B. F.	G/6343	Pte.
Bower, E. P.	G/57567	Pte.
Bowes, E.	G/7027	Pte.
Bowles, A. J.	G/17241	Pte.
Bowles, H.H.W.	G/4181	Pte.
Bowles, L.	G/2217	Pte.
Bowles, L. A.	G/11986	Pte.
Bowles, S.	G/4414	Pte.
Bowling, E. R.		2nd Lieut.
Box, C. W.	G/19021	Pte.
Boxall, W.	G/20708	Pte.
Boxall, W. C.	G/9169	Pte.
Boyce, H. T.	G/4679	Pte.
Boyce, W. T.	G/31027	Pte.
Boyes, R. J.	G/16616	L/Cpl.
Boyle, J.	G/2076	Pte.
Boyse, C. F.	G/1344	Pte.
Bracey, A. V.	G/31820	Pte.
Brackley, A. J.	L/9596	Pte.
Bradey, G. A.	G/9614	Pte.
Bradford, C.	L/9766	L/Cpl.

APPENDIX II.

Bradford, C. H.	G/23675	Pte.	Bridgeman, W.B.	G/8925	Cpl.
Bradford, F.	L/8320	Pte.	Bridger, H. M.	G/16171	Pte.
Bradley, J. W.	G/18561	Pte.	Bridges, F. V.	G/23856	Pte.
Bradley, P. W.		Lieut.	Bridgland, V.	202476	Pte.
Bradley, T.	G/3020	Pte.	Brigden, R. W.	G/7598	Pte.
Bradley, W. D.	G/20957	Pte.	Briggs, E. W.	G/21543	Pte.
Bradley, W. H.	L/8123	Pte.	Briggs, T.	G/2897	Pte.
Bradley, W J.	G/21503	L/Cpl.	Bright, H.	G/17599	Pte.
Bragg, C. W.	S/8898	Pte.	Bright, R. J.	G/987	Pte.
Brain, E.	G/24849	Pte.	Brightmore, J.	L/8617	Pte.
Braithwaite, A.	L/8018	Pte.	Brignell, F. T.	G/18379	Pte.
Braithwaite, G.	203992	Pte.	Brill, W.	L/27023	Pte.
Bramble, E. W.	L/9595	Pte.	Brinkley, J.	202919	Pte.
Bramble, H.	G/4705	Pte.	Brinkworth, C.	G/11377	Pte.
Bramble, J. H.	S/8476	Pte.	Brinkworth, L.	G/24589	Pte.
Bramble, S.	G/16298	L/Cpl.	Briselden, C. G. E.		
Brampton, A.	G/18663	Pte.		G/8496	Pte.
Branch, A.	G/11935	Pte.	Brissenden, F.	G/18399	Sgt.
Branch, J. S. P.	L/10223	Pte.	Brister, J. A.	G/16622	Pte.
Brand, S. A.	G/18135	Pte.	Bristow, A.	L/6162	C.S.M.
Brannon, J.	S/962	Pte.	Bristow, C. G.		2nd Lieut.
Braund, G. T	G/19155	Pte.	Bristow, C. R.	G/27303	Pte.
Braund, R.	241387	Pte.	Bristow, E. G.	G/18812	Pte.
Bray, S. G.	G/18054	Pte.	Bristow, L.	S/8933	Pte.
Brazier, H. G.	G/11216	Pte.	Britcher, J. J.	G/19037	Sgt.
Breakspeare, F.	G/5424	Pte.	Britter, H. L.	200093	Pte.
Breeds, W. W.	G/46	Pte.	Britton, F., *M.M.*	240926	Cpl.
Breeze, H. J.	TF/3824	Pte.	Britton, F. T.	G/12133	Pte.
Brennan, J. J.	L/236	Pte.	Briveau, C. H.	G/11249	Pte.
Brenchley, S. A.	G/1587	Pte	Broad, C. N.	G/1601	L/Cpl.
Brett, A.	G/3898	Pte.	Broad, H.	G/3422	Pte.
Brett, F.	241693	Pte.	Broad, T. H.	G/11165	Pte.
Brett, V. A.	G/19936	Pte.	Broadley, W. E.	L/11448	Pte.
Brett, W. H.	G/10535	Pte.	Broadwood, M. F.		2nd Lieut.
Brewer, W. F.	G/16165	Pte.	Brock-Hollinshead, L.		Major.
Brewster, F.	L/5552	Cpl.	Brockwell, C. R.	G/4647	Pte.
Brewster, G. J.	G/19187	Pte.	Brockwell, E. G.	G/11017	Pte
Breze, W.	G/5119	Pte.	Bromfield, T. A.	G/1022	Sgt.
Brickelt, S.	G/10824	Cpl.	Bromley, E. W.	TF/4278	Pte.
Bridge, D.	G/26260	Pte.	Bronwin, H.	G/511	Pte.
Bridge, H.	S/1213	Cpl.	Brook, C.	G/7419	L/Cpl.
Bridge, S.	204371	Pte.	Brook, J.	G/4938	Pte.
Bridgeland, H.	L/10441	Pte.	Brook, W.	G/11619	Pte.

511

APPENDIX II.

Brooke, F. J.	202203	Pte.	Brown, G.	G/3789	Pte.
Brooker, J.	L/8916	Pte.	Brown, G.	G/1990	Pte.
Brooker, J.	S/1106	Pte.	Brown, G.	L/5940	Pte.
Brooker, J. G.	G/798	Pte.	Brown, G.	L/9501	Sgt.
Brooker, W. H.	TF/2683	Pte.	Brown, G. E.	G/4753	Pte.
Brookes, C.	G/18122	Pte.	Brown, G. J.	S/325	Pte.
Brookes, C. E.	G/6276	Cpl.	Brown, G. W.	G/5387	Pte.
Brookes, C. J.	G/23762	Pte.	Brown, H.	G/4087	Pte.
Brooks, G.	L/6289	Pte.	Brown, H.	L/10936	Pte.
Brooks, J.	G/21326	Pte.	Brown, H.	G/4891	Pte.
Brooks, J.	G/3238	Pte.	Brown, H. S.	241011	Sgt.
Brooks, P.	G/75	L/Sgt.	Brown, J.	G/25659	Pte.
Brooks, S. E.	G/20455	Pte.	Brown, J.	G/12863	Pte.
Brooks, W. C.	242274	Pte.	Brown, J.	S/343	Pte.
Brooks, W. T.	L/8330	Pte.	Brown, J. A	G/4173	L/Cpl.
Brooman, A.	G/968	Pte.	Brown, J. E. G.		Capt.
Brooman, H.	G/7418	Pte.	Brown, J. T.	G/18644	Pte.
Broome, H. J.	G/6944	Pte.	Brown, O. P.		2nd Lieut.
Broomfield, E.	G/11616	Pte.	Brown, R. J.	G/320	Pte.
Broomfield, H.	L/10083	Pte.	Brown, T. C.	241880	Pte.
Brotherhood. E.	G/15440	Pte.	Brown, T. W.	G/69	Pte.
Broughton, P. W., *M.M.*	G/3734	L/Cpl.	Brown, T. W. M.	L/10347	Pte.
Broughton, W. L.	S/720	Sgt.	Brown, W.	G/10062	Pte.
Brown, A.	G/1235	Pte.	Brown, W.	TF/1138	Pte.
Brown, A.	L/9802	L/Cpl.	Brown, W., *M.M.*	G/5266	Sgt.
Brown, A. E., *M.M.*	G/18697	Pte.	Brown, W. E.	242405	Pte.
Brown, A. E.	G/9103	Pte.	Brown, W. F.	L/9352	Pte.
Brown, A. H.		2nd Lieut.	Browne, E.	G/568	Cpl.
Brown, C. A.	G/14780	Cpl.	Brouitt, W. R.	G/3896	Pte.
Brown, C. J.	241762	Pte.	Browning, H. N.	G/18420	Pte.
Brown, C. P.	G/9042	Pte.	Brownjohn, W. H. G.	L/10824	Pte.
Brown, E.	G/4244	Pte.	Bruce, J.	G/31306	Pte.
Brown, E. C		Lieut.	Bruce, W. T.	L/9864	Pte.
Brown, E. C.		2nd Lieut.	Brunger, A.	G/3211	Pte.
Brown, E. G.	G/18234	Pte.	Brunger, A. W.	G/4333	Pte.
Brown, E. G.	L/9230	Pte.	Bruton, A.	G/14921	Pte.
Brown, F.	S/7474	Pte.	Bryan, J. W.	G/16739	Pte.
Brown, F. A.	G/11922	Pte.	Bryan, T.	L/8734	Sgt.
Brown, F. E.	L/9923	Pte.	Bryan, W. M.	S/8941	Pte.
Brown, F. P.		2nd Lieut.	Bryant, A.	G/10591	Pte.
Brown, F. R.	G/2600	L/Sgt.	Bryant, C. E.	G/3383	Pte.
			Bryant, C. F.	G/30043	Pte.

APPENDIX II.

Bryant, H.	G/6904	Pte.		Bullock, J.	G/24543	Pte.
Bryant, J. G. G.	G/12009	Pte.		Bulwer, F.	G/26565	Pte.
Bryant, S. S.	G/4676	Pte.		Bunce, W.	G/18794	Cpl.
Bryant, W.	G/4146	Cpl.		Bunce, V.	G/5423	Pte.
Brydon, G., M.M.				Bunting, E. A.	G/832	Cpl.
	G/4746	Sgt.		Bunting, H.	240896	Pte.
Bryett, F. A.	L/9986	Pte.		Burberry, H. A.	G/14720	Pte.
Bryson, R. F.	G/20655	Pte.		Burbury, F. W.		Lieut.-Col.
Bubbers, W. J.	G/27365	Pte.		Burbury, J. F.		2nd Lieut.
Bubear, W.	241313	Pte.		Burchell, A. E.	G/18172	L/Cpl.
Buchanan, J.	G/1621	Pte.		Burchett, G.	G/5031	Pte.
Buchanan, J.	G/16351	Pte.		Burdekin, F.	G/19483	Pte.
Buck, F.	S/300	Pte.		Burden, C. V.	205441	Pte.
Buck, J. G.	G/6638	L/Cpl.		Burden, W.	G/5164	Pte.
Buckby, E. T.	G/30209	Pte.		Burdge, F.	G/3843	Pte.
Buckingham, B.	G/17511	Pte.		Burfoot, W. H.	G/4178	Pte.
Buckingham, P. E.		2nd Lieut.		Burgess, A.	L/10145	Pte.
Buckland, J.	G/6822	Pte.		Burgess, C. W.	242119	Pte.
Buckle, C. C. C.		2nd Lieut.		Burgess, L. H.	G/16997	Pte.
Buckle, H.	G/1227	Pte.		Burgess, W. H.	TF/1511	Pte.
Buckle, M. P., D.S.O.		Major.		Burgin, A.	L/39579	Pte.
Buckley, R. F.	G/23623	Pte.		Burke, C. G.	240932	Pte.
Buckley, W. A.	G/31444	Pte.		Burles, P.	G/12901	Pte.
Buckmaster, E. J.	G/7499	Pte.		Burman, C.	G/8852	Pte.
Bucknole, L. T.	203172	Sgt.		Burnard, H. A.	19133	Pte.
Budd, S. G.	G/1541	Sgt.		Burnell, E. J.	G/11186	Pte.
Buddell, F.	G/8445	C.Q.M.S.		Burningham, E. C.	S/8902	Pte.
Budden, H. G.	G/17590	Pte.		Burningham, O. F.	G/12459	Pte.
Budgen, A.	G/9586	Pte.		Burns, R.	202885	Pte.
Budgen, T.	G/8638	Cpl.		Burr, C. J. F.		Lieut.
Buggey, A. V.	G/8438	Pte.		Burr, R.	G/4927	Pte.
Bull, H.	G/18723	Pte.		Burr, W.	L/8356	Sgt.
Bull, W. A.	L/7629	Pte.		Burrage, V. A.	20945	Pte.
Bull, W. J.	G/4967	Pte.		Burrel, A.	G/20658	Pte.
Bullimore, P. A.	G/31109	Pte.		Burrell, R. F. T.		2nd Lieut.
Bullin, T. J.	L/10072	Pte.		Burrell, W.	G/2735	Pte.
Bullman, H. R. H.		2nd Lieut.		Burren, A.	203340	Pte.
Bullman, W. H.	205888	Pte.		Burrluck, G. E.	L/871	L/Cpl.
Bullock, E. E.	G/29760	Pte.		Burrows, A. F.	L/10489	Pte.
Bullock, E. G.	203014	Pte.		Burrows, J.	L/8119	Sgt.
Bullock, F.	G/242125	Pte.		Burrows, R. H.	G/8521	Pte.
Bullock, H. C.	G/12828	Pte.		Burrows, S. H.	G/23874	Pte.
Bullock, J.	G/30137	Pte.		Burrows, W. J.	G/28713	Pte.

LL 513

APPENDIX II.

Bursell, R. E.	S/31463	Pte.	Butler, W.	L/10423	Pte.
Burstow, A. E.	L/10077	Pte.	Butler, W. W.	G/3807	L/Cpl.
Burt, A. R.	G/9518	Pte.	Butson, H. R.	S/740	Pte.
Burt, C.	G/8379	L/Cpl.	Butterworth, L. C.		
Burt, E.	L/8991	Pte.		G/7100	Pte.
Burt, W.	L/8564	Pte.	Button, A.	L/7635	Pte.
Burt, W.	L/8631	Pte.	Button, F. A.	240416	Pte.
Burtenshaw, W. A.			Button, L.	G/7712	Sgt.
	G/1673	Pte.	Buttwell J., *M.M.*		
Burton, A. J.	G/10593	L/Cpl.		G/1421	Sgt.
Burton, C. W.	G/2753	Pte.	Buxton, F.	G/2090	L/Cpl.
Burton, E. A.	G/20062	L/Cpl.	Buxton, L. A.	G/9444	Pte.
Burton, F. P.	G/2867	Pte.	Byram, H.	G/16533	Pte.
Burton, F. W.	L/8486	Pte.	Byrne, C.	G/10288	L/Cpl.
Burton, F. W	240762	Cpl.	Byrne, H. R.	S/3752	C/Sgt.
Burton, J.,*M.M.*	G/28509	Pte.			
Burton, T.	G/494	Pte.			
Burton, W. E.	G/18139	L/Cpl.	Cable, W.	L/7867	L/Cpl.
Burwell, A. G.	G/10475	Pte.	Cadby, S. A.	L/7463	Pte.
Busby, A. H.	G/622	Pte.	Cade, W. B.	G/4756	Pte.
Busby, G. W.	G/18354	Pte.	Cadell, A. B.	2nd Lieut.	
Bush, A. R.	G/4473	Pte.	Cain, G. H.	G/20983	Pte.
Bush, C. H.	G/28710	Pte.	Cain, H. T.	L/9877	L/Cpl.
Bush, F.	G/23685	Pte.	Callaby, A.	G/7778	Pte.
Bush, R. F. G.	G/2877	Pte.	Caller, C. A.	G/4820	Pte.
Bush, T. H.	241474	Pte.	Caller, E.	G/989	Pte.
Bushell, E. J.	G/15301	Pte.	Calloway, C.	G/4311	Pte.
Bushell, J. W.	G/6271	Pte.	Calnan. G.	10361	Pte.
Bushell, T. V.	G/18428	Pte.	Calnan, J.	L/7255	Pte.
Bushell, W. S.	G/207	Pte.	Calver, R. C.	G/10084	L/Cpl.
Bushnell, S.	203307	Cpl.	Calvert, W. J.	G/6341	L/Cpl.
Buss, R. W.	G/11777	Pte.	Cambridge. T.	2nd Lieut.	
Buss, W. D.	G/9783	L/Cpl.	Came, H. C.	2nd Lieut.	
Butcher, A. E.	204477	Pte.	Camp, G.	203505	Pte.
Butcher, G.	G/8965	Pte.	Camp, W.	G/21235	Pte.
Butcher, G. F.	202478	Pte.	Campbell, E.	G/11275	Pte.
Butler, A. G.	G/10245	Pte.	Campbell, R.	G/18189	Pte.
Butler, A. W.	G/16384	Pte.	Campbell,W.H.	G/5419	Pte.
Butler, F.	G/31	Pte.	Camper, R. S.	L/7806	Cpl.
Butler, H.	L/8866	Pte.	Campin, W. E.	G/25491	Pte.
Butler, J.	L/9648	Pte.	Camplin, E.	2nd Lieut.	
Butler, T. F.	G/5745	Pte.	Camplin, G. A.	G/2718	C.S.M.
Butler, V. T.	G/2861	Pte.	Canbrook, H., *M.C.*	2nd Lieut.	

514

APPENDIX II.

Name	ID	Rank
Candle, G. H.	203995	Pte.
Candler, G. B.	G/2095	Pte.
Cann, W. H.	L/7886	Pte.
Cannings, E. A.	G/8356	Cpl.
Cannon, J.	G/31667	Pte.
Cansdale, A. A.	G/15148	Pte.
Canty, J.	L/6793	L/Cpl.
Capel, T. E.	G/17790	Pte.
Capner, E. C.	G/31131	Pte.
Caraco, R. C.	G/24323	Pte.
Carbett, A. J.	G/17247	Pte.
Card, C W.	G/17961	Pte.
Card, D. R.	G/27411	Pte.
Card, E. F.	G/14706	Pte.
Card, F.	G/3885	L/Cpl.
Card, R.	G/31262	Pte.
Carden, T. A.	S/200	Pte.
Careless, J.	G/5101	Pte.
Carey, M. E.,	M.C.	2nd Lieut.
Carlis, C. F.		Major.
Carlsson, J.	G/24068	Pte.
Carman, R. J.	S/355	Pte.
Carne, F. T.	242034	Pte.
Carnell, H.	G/23720	Pte.
Carpenter, A. D.	G/15716	Pte.
Carpenter, A. G.	L/6594	Cpl.
Carpenter, E. F.	G/8820	Pte.
Carpenter, G.	202480	Cpl.
Carpenter, G. T.	L/7233	Pte.
Carr, A. O.	G/11802	Pte.
Carr, B. R.	G/24433	Pte.
Carr, T. H.	L/9207	Pte.
Carre, G. T.		Lieut.
Carrett, C.	G/4558	Pte.
Carrol, T.	G/11383	Pte.
Carruthers, D. P.	G/8389	Sgt.
Carson, W.	G/5324	L/Cpl.
Carswell, P.	G/10063	Pte.
Carter, C. H.	G/24592	Pte.
Carter, F.	G/13476	Pte.
Carter, G. H.	S/1080	Pte.
Carter. G. L.	L/10001	Pte.
Carter, H.	G/16529	Pte.
Carter, H.	G/6459	Pte.
Carter, H. A.	G/8179	Pte.
Carter, H. C.	G/28723	Pte.
Carter, H. W.	G/30210	Pte.
Carter, J.	G/10565	Pte.
Carter, P. W.	241242	Pte.
Carter. S. C.		2nd Lieut.
Carter, W.	G/603	Pte.
Carter, W. E. J.	G/28725	Pte.
Carter, W. H.	L/7739	Pte.
Carter, W.,	D.C.M.	
	G/767	Sgt.
Cartwright, J.	205075	Pte.
Carver, R.	G/34416	L/Cpl.
Carvey, E.	G/4666	Pte.
Cascarine. L.	201682	Pte.
Casey. J.	G/30951	Pte.
Cassidy, J.	S/9091	Pte.
Cassom, A. E.	G/7216	Pte.
Castle, J. H.	G/10420	Pte.
Catchpole, J.	G/4683	Pte.
Cater, A.	G/24548	Pte.
Cater, J.	G/16763	Pte.
Cathcart, D. A.		2nd Lieut.
Catherwood, C. T.	203656	Cpl.
Catt, A. W.,	M.C.	2nd Lieut.
Catling, W. F.	G/30662	Pte.
Caulder, A.	L/9003	Pte.
Cavanagh, J.	G/3298	L/Cpl.
Cavanagh, W. J.	G/891	Pte.
Cawley, H. F.	G/18355	Pte.
Cawthorne, J.	242143	Pte.
Cecil, T. J.	G/11471	Pte.
Chadney, W. C.	G/7729	Pte.
Chadwick, G. H.	G/38660	Pte.
Chaffer, W. J.	G/25342	Pte.
Chalke, R.	G/18666	L/Sgt.
Chalklin, F. T.	L/9322	Pte.
Challis, W. G.	S/628	Sgt.
Chambers, A.	G/5214	Pte.
Chambers, F.	G/15278	Pte.
Chambers, H. F.,	M.M.	
	G/4928	Cpl.

515

APPENDIX II.

Chambers, W.	G/31626	Pte.
Chambers, W. H.	TF/212	Sgt.
Chamberlain, E.	G/14553	Pte.
Chamberlain, W. C. S/1880		Pte.
Chamberlain, W. J. G/3710		Pte.
Champion, A.	G/15491	Pte.
Champion, C. E.	L/10629	Cpl.
Champion, J.	TF/1330	Pte.
Champion, H.W.	L/8456	L/Sgt.
Champion, T.H.	L/7418	Pte.
Champkin, F.	G/3817	Pte.
Chandler, A. J.	203390	Pte.
Chandler, A. J.	S/8557	Pte.
Chandler, S.	G/840	Pte.
Chandler, W.	G/24682	Pte.
Channon, J. A.	G/2268	Pte.
Chantler, H.	G/18605	Pte.
Chaplin, R. E.	G/4813	L/Cpl.
Chapman, A. E.	L/10789	Pte.
Chapman, C.	G/24500	Pte.
Chapman, C. E.	G/18817	Pte.
Chapman, E. R.	G/18356	Pte.
Chapman, F.	G/17413	Pte.
Chapman, F. W.	S/8635	L/Cpl.
Chapman, G.	G/979	Pte.
Chapman, G. T.	G/14510	Pte.
Chapman, H.	G/623	Pte.
Chapman, H. G.	G/29517	Pte.
Chapman, H. J., *M.C.*		2nd Lieut.
Chapman, J.	G/7730	Pte.
Chapman, J.	L/10365	Pte.
Chapman, J.	L/9857	Pte.
Chapman, J.	G/9135	Pte.
Chapman, L.	G/4104	Pte.
Chapman, L. A.	G/3931	L/Cpl.
Chapman, W.	G/19628	Pte.
Chapman, W. A.	L/10358	Pte.
Chapman, W. J.	242413	Pte.
Chappell, A. T.	G/21642	Pte.
Chappell, C. J.	10537	Pte.
Chappell, G.	G/24245	Pte.
Chappell, H. A.	G/20469	Pte.
Chappell, W. A.	G/19866	Pte.
Chard, J.	G/29492	Pte.
Charles, L.	G/21328	Pte.
Charlesworth, J. J. G/20073		Pte.
Charman, N.	G/25350	Pte.
Charman, W.	L/9450	L/Cpl.
Chatfield, J.	G/2899	Pte.
Chatfield, H.	G/10162	Pte.
Chatfield, H.	L/10102	Pte.
Chatfield, W.	G/17792	Pte.
Cheasman, H.H.	G/9616	Pte.
Checkley, F.	G/10048	Pte.
Chedzoy, A. E.	G/18901	Sgt.
Cheek, G.	240177	L/Cpl.
Cheers, E.	S/8687	Pte.
Cheeseman, A. R.	G/28305	Pte.
Cheeseman, C.	G/24432	Pte.
Cheeseman, E.	G/19333	Pte.
Cheeseman, E.	L/7312	Pte.
Cheeseman, E.	G/2139	Pte.
Cheeseman, H. W. F. G/5162		Pte.
Cheeseman, T.	G/1741	Pte.
Cheeseman, W. A.	G/9311	Pte.
Cheesman, E.	G/19365	Pte.
Chell, A. E.	L/11801	Pte.
Cheshire, F.	G/29362	Pte.
Cheshire, G.	G/929	Cpl.
Chenery, F. H.	G/30880	Pte.
Cheney, W. H.	3643	Pte.
Cheron, H. E.	S/9142	Cpl.
Cherry, R.	G/11061	Pte.
Chesser, A.	G/5639	Pte.
Chessum, A.	G/9551	Pte.
Chessum, A. A.	G/39156	Pte.
Chessum, S.	G/12204	Pte.
Chester, T.	G/7019	Pte.
Chick, E.	G/24685	Pte.
Childerley, F.	G/18129	Pte.
Childs, H.	G/18792	L/Cpl.

516

APPENDIX II.

Childs, J. R.	G/11421	Pte.	Clark, R. A.		205034	Pte.
Childs, W. H.	G/10774	Pte.	Clark, S. G.		G/29763	Pte.
Chiles, H. F.	S/1217	Pte.	Clark, T.		S/8945	Pte.
Chilvers, W. W.	G/1735	Cpl.	Clark, T. H.		L/10092	Pte.
Chinn, C. V.	G/3159	Pte.	Clark, T. H., *M.M.*			
Chittenden, H.	G/2892	L/Cpl.			L/10880	Pte.
Chitty, F. L.	G/20697	Pte.	Clark, T. J.		G/16070	Pte.
Chivers, W. H.	G/10776	Pte.	Clark, W. A.		G/10594	Pte.
Chown, F.	241335	Pte.	Clark, W. F.		G/32245	Pte.
Christian, A. R., *M.M.*			Clark, W. T.		L/10317	Pte.
	G/18364	Pte.	Clarke, A.		G/11033	Pte.
Christmas, F. B.	G/12061	Pte.	Clarke, C.		G/13407	Pte.
Christmas, S. C.	G/7610	Cpl.	Clarke, E.		G/38690	Pte.
Christopher, B. W.	G/25822	Pte.	Clarke, E. A.		L/10459	Pte.
Christopher, T.	G/5830	Pte.	Clarke, F.		L/6518	L/Cpl.
Chudley, F.	G/19977	Pte.	Clarke, F. A.		G/8966	Pte.
Chugg, S. H.	241226	Pte.	Clarke, G.		G/18659	Pte.
Church, F. J.	G/12897	Pte.	Clarke, G.		203445	Pte.
Church, W. H.	G/11230	Pte.	Clarke, G.		S/646	Pte.
Churchill, F. D.	242275	Pte.	Clarke, G.		G/9439	Pte.
Clack, F.	265621	Pte.	Clarke, G. A.		10437	Pte.
Clackett, G. A.	G/4902	Pte.	Clarke, G. E.		G/9310	Pte.
Clackett, W. J.	G/5222	Pte.	Clarke, G. E. C.		G/5605	Pte.
Clamp, L. P.	204077	Cpl.	Clarke, H. W.		G/18134	Pte.
Clapson, G. A.	G/2470	Pte.	Clarke, J. H.		L/11513	Sgt.
Clarey, C.	G/2423	Pte.	Clarke, J. W.		G/5706	Pte.
Clark, A. E.	L/7550	Pte.	Clarke, L. S.	H	204191	Pte.
Clark, A. G.	G/2695	Sgt.	Clarke, R. G.		G/29364	Pte.
Clark, A. J.	L/10675	Pte.	Clarke, R. H.		G/24595	Pte.
Clark, C. H.	204408	Pte.	Clarke, R. H.		2nd Lieut.	
Clark, C. W.	2nd Lieut.		Clarke, W.		S/347	L/Cpl.
Clark, E. W.	G/5910	Pte.	Clarkson, A. M.		G/8082	Pte.
Clark, F. G.	201049	Pte.	Clavey, A.		G/4125	L/Cpl.
Clark, G.	S/8510	Pte.	Claxton, J.		G/17058	Pte.
Clark, G.	201393	Pte.	Clayton, J.		G/17058	Pte.
Clark, G.	205907	L/Cpl.	Clayton, V. A.		G/29622	Pte.
Clark, H.	G/6942	Pte.	Clear, V. R.		G/18053	Pte.
Clark, J.	G/28343	Pte.	Clearey, J. W.		G/5039	Pte.
Clark, J.	G/30888	Pte.	Cleary, T. R.		G/12087	Pte.
Clark, J. A.	G/30890	Pte.	Cleaver, C. L.		G/8089	Pte.
Clark, J. J.	G/30889	Pte.	Clegg, S.		G/11925	Pte.
Clark, J. T.	L/10303	L/Cpl.	Clegg, T.		L/10918	Pte.
Clark, P. J.	G/8004	Sgt.	Cleggett, W. J.		L/9964	Pte.

517

APPENDIX II.

Cleland-Hollamby, D. M.		2nd Lieut.
Clements, C.	L/3976	Pte.
Clements, E.	S/8363	Pte.
Clements, J.	G/13065	Pte.
Cleversley, H.	G/6141	Pte.
Clews, R.	G/25496	L/Cpl.
Clibbon, W. G.	G/6393	Pte.
Clibbon, W. G.	G/4930	Pte.
Clifford, W. J.	G/20213	Pte.
Clift, E. L.	G/1081	Pte.
Clift, H. R., D.C.M.	L/7963	Pte.
Clifton, F.	241609	Pte.
Clifton, G.	G/24688	Pte.
Clifton, G.	G/9216	Pte.
Clifton, J.	G/16555	Pte.
Clifton, W. E.	G/25103	Pte.
Clipsham, A. E.	G/18340	Pte.
Clough, F. T.	G/5869	Pte.
Clough, H. F.		Lieut.
Clough, J.	G/19923	Pte.
Clout, A.	G/18292	Pte.
Clout, G.	L/8423	Pte.
Clover, B. J.	G/29503	Pte.
Clutterbuck, A.	G/7607	Pte.
Clyne, W.	TF/1356	Pte.
Coachworth, E. S.	205679	Pte.
Coates, J. C.		2nd Lieut.
Cobb, J. C.		Lieut.
Cobb, W. R., M.C.		Capt.
Cobby, B.	G/31310	Pte.
Cobley, G. O.	G/6408	Pte.
Cockrane, D.	G/23264	Pte.
Cocks, L. G.	G/30891	Pte.
Coe, C. A.	G/9208	C.Q.M.S.
Coe, G. M.	G/6771	C.S.M.
Coe, W.	G/24944	Pte.
Coffin, S.	240819	Pte.
Cogdell, A.	G/2363	Pte.
Cogger, A. N.	L/6725	Pte.
Cogger, J.	201101	Cpl.
Coggin, S. W. G.		2nd Lieut.
Cohen, A. I.	G/24909	Pte.
Cokeley, J. E.	G/6713	Pte.
Coker, A.	G/40	L/Cpl.
Coldbeck, J.	205446	Pte.
Coldbridge, W.A.	241213	Pte.
Cole, A.	G/9348	Pte.
Cole, A. F.	202086	Pte.
Cole, A. O.	G/20460	Pte.
Cole, A. W.	G/18703	Pte.
Cole, C.	G/78	Pte.
Cole, F.	L/9954	Pte.
Cole, F.	G/10110	Pte.
Cole, G.	L/9384	Pte.
Cole, G. B.	S/8483	Pte.
Cole, H. E.	L/9386	Pte.
Cole, J.	G/7954	Pte.
Cole, J.	205680	Pte.
Cole, J.	G/10246	Pte.
Cole, J. B.	G/15503	Pte.
Cole, J. W.	L/6535	Pte.
Cole, W.	203222	Pte.
Colebrooke, W.	L/8047	Sgt.
Coleman, A.	G/2220	Cpl.
Coleman, A. G.	S/8466	Pte.
Coleman, F.	G/19015	Sgt.
Coleman, G.	G/71	Pte.
Coleman, G. B.	G/10895	Pte.
Coleman, H.	205583	Pte.
Coleman, J.	G/2212	Pte.
Coleman, T. S.	G/2907	Pte.
Coleman, W. F.	G/23692	Pte.
Coleman, W. R.	204625	Pte.
Coles, A. G.	G/2501	Sgt.
Coles, L. H.	G/8951	Cpl.
Coles, R. W.		2nd Lieut.
Colgate, A. P.	G/12132	Pte.
Coling, R.	L/10842	Pte.
Collar, F. A.	G/20215	Pte.
Colleer, H. C.	240828	Pte.
Collett A. E.	G/25936	Pte.
Collier, A. G.	G/18339	Pte.
Collier, G.	S/822	Pte.

APPENDIX II.

Collier, L. E.	G/19191	Pte.	Cook, A. C.	G/1381	Pte.
Collings, H. J.	G/24434	Pte.	Cook C.	G/2554	Pte.
Collins, G. D.	G/2893	Pte.	Cook, C.	G/11749	Pte.
Collins, A. J.	G/31544	Pte.	Cook, C.	S/367	Pte.
Collins, E. H.	G/251	Pte.	Cook, C.	G/6848	L/Cpl.
Collins, F.	G/18102	Pte.	Cook, E.	L/7813	Sgt.
Collins, H.	242147	Pte.	Cook, E. J.	G/14794	Pte.
Collins, J.	TR/10/40332	Pte.	Cook, G.	17787	Pte.
Collins, J.	G/1738	Pte.	Cook, J.	G/5722	Pte.
Collins, J. J.	L/8694	Pte.	Cook, J. H.	G/19751	Cpl.
Collins, R.	G/1640	Pte.	Cook, L.	L/10194	Pte.
Collins, R. S.	G/2389	Pte.	Cook, M.	G/2507	Pte.
Collins, T.	G/3403	Pte.	Cook, P. J.	L/10613	Pte.
Collins, T.	L/8283	Pte.	Cook, R.	L/6534	Pte.
Collins, T.	G/188	Pte.	Cook, S. E.	G/11250	Sgt.
Collins, T. J.	L/10644	Pte.	Cook, W. H.	G/5864	Pte.
Collins, W.	G/674	Pte.	Cooke, A.	L/8143	Pte.
Collis, H.	240293	Pte.	Cooker, F. T., D.C.M.		
Collis, L. B.	242144	Pte.		G/6	Sgt.
Collishaw, F.	205140	Pte.	Cooksey, K. B.		2nd Lieut.
Collison, A.	G/907	Pte.	Coombe, C.	G/15064	Pte.
Collison, J.	266965	Pte.	Coomber, A. J.	S/483	Pte.
Collman, A. G.	G/17144	Pte.	Coomber, C. G.	G/1520	L/Cpl.
Collyer, A. B.	203547	Pte.	Coomber, F.	L/7568	Pte.
Collyer, J.	G/18791	Pte.	Coomber, W. D., M.M.		
Colmar, W. G.	L/9015	Pte.		G/1515	Sgt.
Colston, E. J.	G/18188	Pte.	Coombs, C. S.		2nd Lieut.
Colvin, A.	G/8653	Pte.	Coombs, E. J.	G/19030	Sgt.
Colwell, F.	G/12265	Pte.	Coomes, W.	L/10584	Pte.
Colwell, P.	G/23877	L/Cpl.	Cooney, W. J.	S/842	L/Cpl.
Comer, F. G.	G/29981	Pte.	Cooper, A. G.	G/3042	Cpl.
Comerford, A.	L/6701	Pte.	Cooper, A. H.	240414	Pte.
Comerford, F.	G/11059	Pte.	Cooper, B.	G/31112	Pte.
Commons, F.	G/16336	Sgt.	Cooper, E. G.	G/21462	Pte.
Compson, S. H., M.M.			Cooper, G. S.		Capt.
	G/19059	Pte.	Cooper, H.	G/19490	Pte.
Compton, C. H.		2nd Lieut.	Cooper, H.	G/12020	Pte.
Compton, C. V.	G/24663	Pte.	Cooper, H. H.	G/2394	Pte.
Conlong, T.	G/5524	Pte.	Cooper, J.	L/6654	Pte.
Connolly, J.V.M.	G/14958	Pte.	Cooper, J. A.	G/30066	L/Cpl.
Connolly, W. P.	G/23232	Pte.	Cooper, J. H.	G/4067	L/Cpl.
Conroy, M. J.	205412	Pte.	Cooper, J. W.	G/21074	Pte.
Cook, A. B.	G/21057	Pte.	Cooper, L.	S/62	Pte.

APPENDIX II.

Cooper, P. R.	203828	Pte.	Cosham, W. T.	205331	Pte.
Cooper, P. W.	G/11612	Pte.	Cossey, B. G. J.	G/29987	Pte.
Cooper, R.	G/5683	Pte.	Cosson, J.	G/9639	Pte.
Cooper, R. J.	201834	Pte.	Costin, F.	G/29592	Pte.
Cooper, S.	L/6616	Pte.	Costin, H. W.		2nd Lieut.
Cooper, T. E.	S/495	Cpl.	Cottam, D.	G/6201	Pte.
Cooper, T. H.	G/7285	Pte.	Cottenham, C. A.	G/5043	Pte.
Cooper, T. W.	G/31449	Pte.	Cotterell, C.	G/18075	Pte.
Cooper, W.	232487	Pte.	Cotterell, W.	S/219	L/Cpl.
Cooper, W.	G/2291		Cottis, H. C.	L/9261	Pte.
		R.Q.M.S.	Cottreill, W.	L/9294	Pte.
Cooper, W. S.	203303	Pte.	Cottrell, J. P.		2nd Lieut.
Cooper, W. T.	G/5669	Cpl.	Cottrell, H.	G/8224	Pte.
Coote, B.	G/14600	Pte.	Cottrell, W.	242056	Pte.
Coote, G. B.		Lieut.	Couchman, T. E.	TF/1882	Pte.
Cope, W.	G/1910	Pte.	Couchman, W.	G/12544	Pte.
Copeland, T. W. J.			Coulstock, E.	G/4858	Pte.
	L/5729	Sgt.	Coulstock, J.	S/8620	Pte.
Copeland, W. H.	G/12510	Pte.	Coulter, A. J.	G/1661	Pte.
Copeman, E. H.		2nd Lieut.	Coupe, C. S.	205168	Pte.
Copland, R.	G/21009	Cpl.	Court, E.	G/100	Pte.
Copper, B.	G/110	Pte.	Court, F. J.	203341	Pte.
Copper, S. G.	G/17974	Pte.	Court, W. J.	G/10025	Pte.
Coppin, N.	L/10393	Pte.	Cousens, R. J.	G/18126	Pte.
Coppins, G.	5898	Pte.	Cousens, W.	G/5262	Pte.
Corbett, A. J.	G/17247	Pte.	Cousins, W. W.	L/6563	Sgt.
Corbin, A. (M.M.)	G/17607	Pte.	Coutts, A. E.	G/16630	Pte.
Corbin, W. H.	G/16200	Pte.	Cover, J. A. A.	L/9860	Cpl.
Cork, T., D.C.M.	L/5793	Pte.	Coward, J. H.	G/24680	Pte.
Corkran, W.	S/6998	Pte.	Cowden, A. S.	G/2315	L/Cpl.
Corley, E. C.		2nd Lieut.	Cowlard, C. J.	G/24599	Pte.
Cornbill, B.	205035	Pte.	Cowles, R. E.	G/23011	Pte.
Cornell, A. R. G.	G/1370	L/Cpl.	Cox, A. E.	G/7443	Pte.
Cornford, W. D.		2nd Lieut.	Cox, E.	L/11154	Pte.
Cornish, A. E.	G/31329	Pte.	Cox, E. H.	G/29996	Cpl.
Cornish, A.	G/18056	Sgt.	Cox, H. E.	G/31092	Pte.
Cornwell, A. E.	G/4952	Pte.	Cox, J.	L/7387	Pte.
Corps, G. T.	L/7269	Pte.	Cox, J. W.	G/19489	Pte.
Corte, O. A.	G/11593	Pte.	Cox, R. C.	G/7217	Pte.
Cosgrove, C. S.	205448	Pte.	Cox, S. H.	200206	Sgt.
Cosgrove, J.	G/6580	L/Cpl.	Cox, T.	G/11571	Pte.
Coshall, J. H.	L/10420	Pte.	Cox, W. F.	L/10068	Pte.
Cosham, T.	G/9758	Pte.	Coxhill, A.	G/20217	Pte.

APPENDIX II.

Cozens, E. G.	200621	Pte.	Crook, W. C.	L/9409	Pte.
Crafter, W.	G/1021	Pte.	Cropley, L. A.	G/17532	Pte.
Craig, A. F.		Capt.	Cross, A. J.	L/10355	Pte.
Cramer, L. C.	G/23192	Sgt.	Cross, E. W.	G/12673	Pte.
Cramp, S. W.	G/7860	Pte.	Cross, J. C.	G/10957	Pte.
Crane, W. G.	203796	Pte.	Cross, P. F.		2nd Lieut.
Cranmer, W.	G/9536	Pte.	Cross, S	G/347	Cpl.
Crapper, E.	205608	Pte.	Cross, S. W.		2nd Lieut.
Craston, J.		2nd Lieut.	Crosse, R. G.		Lieut.
Crate, E.	G/17927	Pte.	Crossley, F. J., D.C.M.		
Crawford, R. J.	G/30747	Cpl.		L/5259	C.S.M.
Crawley, L.	G/15526	Pte.	Crouch, A. W.	G/19978	Pte.
Crawley, W. F.	G/11768	Pte.	Crouch, P. J.	L/8284	Pte.
Cray, G.	G/6469	Pte.	Crouch, W.	G/209	Pte.
Craycroft, H. T.	L/7906	Pte.	Croucher, E.	G/6257	Cpl.
Cresswell, E.	G/20078	Pte.	Croucher, F. W.		2nd Lieut.
Crew, F. J.	L/7723	L/Cpl.	Croucher, R.	TF/1976	Pte.
Crick, A.	G/31448	Pte.	Croucher, W. R.	G/23102	Pte.
Crick, H. E.	9258	Pte.	Crout, G. W.	L/9309	Pte.
Crips, F. R.	G/20962	Pte.	Crow, H. S.	G/19272	L/Cpl.
Cripps, E. J.	G/6859	Pte.	Crowe, F J.	G/3072	Pte.
Cripps, W.	L/6252	Pte.	Crowhurst, A.G.	G/4623	Pte.
Crisp, E.	S/956	Pte.	Crowhurst, S.	L/7648	L/Cpl.
Crisp, F.	G/17670	Pte.	Crowhurst, W. J.	G/15327	L/Cpl.
Crisp, G.	G/11384	Pte.	Crowley, R.	G/9394	Pte.
Crisp, H.	G/11385	Pte.	Crown, J.	G/25824	Pte.
Crisp, W.	G/11429	Pte.	Cruckshank, R. J. G.		
Crist, A. C.	G/8574	Pte.		G/711	Pte.
Critchley, J.	G/31664	Pte.	Crust, F.	G/2422	Pte.
Crittle, A. B.	201349	Pte.	Cudby, W.	G/14699	Pte.
Crittle, W.	G/3949	Pte.	Culbert, B. A.	G/4478	Pte.
Croasdell, J. M.	G/19125	L/Cpl.	Cull, A. J.	240963	Pte.
Crocker, E. J.	200957	Cpl.	Cullerne, A. B., M.C.		2nd Lieut.
Crocker, P. J. W.		Lieut.	Culley, G. M. G.		Capt.
Crockford, V.G.	G/9457	Pte.	Cullum, E. J.	G/30882	Pte.
Croft, C. E.	G/5375	Pte.	Cummins, C.	G/146	Pte.
Croft, J. W.	L/10680	Pte.	Cummins, F. C.	G/15315	Pte.
Croft, T. M.	G/21081	Pte.	Cummins, W. J.	G/24501	Pte.
Croft, W.	G/11542	L/Cpl.	Cumnock, A. M.	L/8398	Pte.
Crombie, J. M.		2nd Lieut.	Cunliffe, J. E.	G/4408	Pte.
Crombie, W.	G/8689	Pte.	Cunningham, J. R.	G/6974	Pte.
Crome, G. F.	G/29591	Pte.	Cupit, W. J.	G/10649	Pte.
Crompton, A.	203020	Pte.	Curds, A. E.	G/29624	Pte.

APPENDIX II.

Curling, R.	G/11443	Pte.	Danks, E. W.	G/26352	Pte.
Currie, B. J.	TF/1894	Pte.	Dann, W.	L/8647	Pte.
Currie, P.	G/23434	Pte.	Danzey, H. G.	S/9026	Pte.
Curtis, C.	G/10595	Pte.	Darke, F. F.	S/9229	Pte.
Curtis, E. J.		2nd Lieut.	Darley, G.	G/19278	Pte.
Curtis, H.	240493	Pte.	Darley, R.	L/6078	C.S.M.
Curtis, J.	G/3747	Pte.	Darling, J. G.	205160	Pte.
Curtis, T.	G/31882	Pte.	Darlington, W. C.		2nd Lieut.
Curtis, T. P.	L/10416	Pte.	Darlow, J. W. E., *M.C.*		
Curtis, W.	G/19975	Pte.			2nd Lieut.
Curtis, W. F.	L/10030	Pte.	Darrington, W. J.	201810	Pte.
Cushing, F.	G/2194	Pte.	Dartnell, G.	L/9432	Pte.
Cussell, R.	L/9921	Pte.	Darton, M. J.	G/6742	C.S.M.
Cussins, H.	G/18243	Sgt.	Daubeney, G. R.		2nd Lieut.
Cutbush, H. S.	G/7650	L/Cpl.	Davey, D. G.	G/28730	Pte.
Cuthbert, A. E.	L/10669	Pte.	Davey, E.	G/2345	Pte.
Cuthbert, G.	G/27585	Pte.	Davey, H.	G/24836	Pte.
Cutler, C. H.	L/10574	Pte.	Davey, W. C.	G/13381	Pte.
Cutting, W.	G/18089	Pte.	Davidson, R. T.	G/21429	Pte.
Cutting, W. G.	G/18141	Pte.	Davidson, S. A.	203975	Pte.
			Davies, A. C.	205717	Pte.
			Davies, C. T.		2nd Lieut.
Dabin, R.	G/10421	L/Cpl.	Davies, E.	G/20220	Pte.
Dabner, G. H.	L/8984	Pte.	Davies, F.	G/15527	Pte.
Daborn, F. J.	G/18017	L/Cpl.	Davies, F. W.	L/6335	Sgt.
Dack, S.	G/28937	Pte.	Davies, G.	G/17803	Pte.
Dadson, C.	G/4983	Pte.	Davies, G. E.	L/8711	Pte.
Dale, A. H.	G/30897	L/Cpl.	Davies, J.	G/28349	Pte.
Dale, P. S.	G/19981	Pte.	Davies, N. P.	G/24808	L/Cpl.
Dale, R. J.	G/11858	Pte.	Davies, S. B.	G/5817	Pte.
Dally, G.	G/2448	L/Cpl.	Davies, T.	G/24861	Pte.
Dalton, W. G.	266798	Pte.	Davies, W.	G/21401	Pte.
Daly, R. W.	G/12223	L/Cpl.	Davies, W.	240313	Pte.
Daly, W. G.	S/9116	Pte.	Davies, W. C.	L/5624	Sgt.
Damant, P. A.	G/19157	Pte.	Davies, W.C. F.	G/24469	Pte.
Damary, C. A.	S/669	Cpl.	Davies, W. H.	G/19867	Pte.
Dance, S.	G/11289	Pte.	Davis, A. T.	G/19061	Pte.
Dancey, E. A.	G/7341	Pte.	Davis, E.	G/5655	Cpl.
Dancey, R.	G/18603	Pte.	Davis, F. J.	G/1426	Pte.
Danes, H.	G/5188	Pte.	Davis, F. W.	G/31504	Pte.
Daniel, A. M.		2nd Lieut.	Davis, G	202374	Pte.
Daniels, A. G.	L/10570	Pte.	Davis, G.	G/4977	Pte.
Daniells, R.	G/21408	L/Cpl.	Davis, H. C.		Pte.

APPENDIX II.

Davis, J.	G/1341	Pte.	Debnam, J.	G/18737	Pte.
Davis, S. E.	G/4064	Pte.	Debose, A. H.	L/9680	Pte.
Davis, T.	G/474	Pte.	De Bruin, A. J.	S/425	Pte.
Davis, W. A.	G/12848	Pte.	Deering, W. A.	G/8814	L/Cpl.
Davis, W. H.	G/27400	Pte.	Delderfield, E.	G/18820	Pte.
Davis, W. H.	241757	Pte.	De Leur, H. B. R. A.		
Dawes, A. G.	G/13309	Pte.		G/4661	Pte.
Dawson, C.	G/140	Pte.	Dellar, J. F.	G/30898	Pte.
Dawson, C. H.	204746	Pte.	Deller, T. G.	G/948	Pte.
Dawson, G.	203245	Cpl.	Dellow, H.	L/10297	L/Cpl.
Dawson, H.	G/11191	Pte.	Dempster, E.	G/306	Pte.
Dawson, J.	205155	Pte.	Demsey, J.	G/8536	Pte.
Dawson, R.	G/28552	Pte.	Denby, H.	G/18567	Pte.
Dawson, W. E. G.	241787	Pte.	Dence, L. G.	G/27804	Pte.
Dawson, W. R. A., D.S.O.		Lieut.-Col.	Denne, R. A.	G/20741	Pte.
			Denner, J.	G/469	Cpl.
Dawson, W. H. G., M.M.			Denney, L.	G/1128	Pte.
	202602	Cpl.	Dennis, C. W.	G/4172	Pte.
Dawtry, E.	G/17802	Pte.	Dennis, E.	G/14942	Pte.
Day, A. W.	G/18739	Pte.	Dennis, F.	L/10733	Pte.
Day, B.	L/11628		Dennis, F. T.	L/10734	Pte.
		C.Q.M.S.	Dennis, T. R.	TF/1748	Pte.
Day, C.	G/1769	Pte.	Dennis, W. J.	G/11819	Pte.
Day, E. A.	201337	Pte.	Denny, R.	G/20393	L/Cpl.
Day, J.	L/7612	Pte.	Dent, C. G.	G/5285	Pte.
Day, R.	G/8061	Sgt.	Denton, J.	G/1986	Pte.
Day, R. H.	L/9792	L/Cpl.	Denton, H.	G/8283	Pte.
Day, S.	S/8074	Pte.	Denton, T. J.	S/8699	Pte.
Day, W.	S/9294	Pte.	Denyer, A. E.	G/17610	Pte.
Daynes, F. J.	204010	Pte.	Denyer, F. E.	L/7818	Pte.
Deacon, G. J. O., M.M.			Derrick, J.	G/9021	Sgt.
	G/23458	Pte.	Derry, H.	G/1297	Pte.
Deadman, D.	201943	Pte.	Desprey, W. H.		2nd Lieut.
Deadman, R.	TF/1629	Pte.	Devine, W.	G/16338	L/Cpl.
Dean, A.	G/16212	Pte.	Dew, E.	G/19416	Pte.
Dean, J.	G/12104	Pte.	Dew, W.	G/9697	Pte.
Dean, J. M.	G/23585	Pte.	Dibley, C.	L/10550	Pte.
Dean, L.	G/1953	Pte.	Dickens, H.	G/3696	Pte.
Dean, S.	205681	Pte.	Dickenson, G.	G/1840	Pte.
Dean, W.	L/9393	Pte.	Dickenson, W. D.	205629	Pte.
Dearmer, F.	G/14661	Pte.	Dicker, E. J.	G/31502	Pte.
Death, W. J.	G/26377	Pte.	Dickinson, B. N.		2nd Lieut.
Debenham, H. A.		2nd Lieut.	Dickinson, H. N.		2nd Lieut.

APPENDIX II.

Dickman, W.	265989	Sgt.	Dolley, G. E.	L/8750	Pte.
Dicks, P. R.	G/1860	Pte.	Domeney, S.	G/11124	Pte.
Diggens, A. J.	G/21138	Pte.	Don, V. G.		Lieut.
Dillon, C. E. N.		2nd Lieut.	Donaldson, G.	G/27439	Pte.
Dilloway, C.	G/4063	Pte.	Donoghue, J.	TF/2088	Pte.
Dimmock, E.	S/848	Pte.	Donoghue, J. D.	L/6394	Pte.
Dimon, W.	G/2035	Pte.	Donovan, P., D.C.M.		
Dingle, T.	G/6125	Pte.		L/9831	Pte.
Dinwoody, A.	L/6700	L/Cpl.	Doolan, J.	S/9285	Pte.
Diplock, B.	G/6675	Pte.	Doree, H.	L/5161	Cpl.
Diplock, S.	L/11539	Sgt.	Dorrington, A.	203313	Sgt.
Dipple, J.	G/2366	Pte.	Douch, H.	G/18412	Pte.
Diprose, A. H.	G/4942	Pte.	Douglas, H. G.	G/20624	Pte.
Diprose, H.		Pte.	Dougletty, E. M.	S/8227	Pte.
Divall, F.	G/13396	Pte.	Doust, H.	L/8521	Pte.
Divall, A. E.	L/9089	L/Cpl.	Dove, S. E.		2nd Lieut.
Dive, H. E.	240400	L/Cpl.	Dove, V.	G/6069	Pte.
Diver, F. L.	G/7829	Pte.	Dovey, H.	201385	Pte.
Dix, G.	G/845	L/Cpl.	Dowdall, F. C.	L/10356	Pte.
Dix, H. G., M.C.		2nd Lieut.	Dowdeswell, R.	G/21446	Pte.
Dix, J. R.	G/18014	Pte.	Dowding, W. H.	G/1906	Pte.
Dix, W.	G/16564	Pte.	Dowland, H.	G/997	Pte.
Dixey, A. G. D.	L/9454	Pte.	Down, A. E.	G/9199	Pte.
Dixon, A. E.	L/10847	Pte.	Down, S., M.M.	G/10447	Pte.
Dixon, D.	G/9715	Pte.	Downing, G.	G/8827	L/Cpl.
Dixon, F.	205573	Pte.	Downs, J. E.	G/6609	Pte.
Dixon, G. W.	L/9038	Pte.	Doyle, A. E.	G/7633	Pte.
Dixon, J. R.	G/19914	Pte.	Drake, A. C.	G/6419	Pte.
Dixon, O. G.	204626	Pte.	Drake, H. R.	G/3668	Pte.
Dixon, T.	L/3628		Draper, F.	G/911	Cpl.
		C.Q.M.S.	Drawbridge, T. S.		
Dobbs, R. S.	G/31834	Pte.		G/5363	Pte.
Dobie, W. M.		Lieut.	Dray, A. S.	G/19139	Sgt.
Dobson, J. R.	G/3985	Cpl.	Dray, J. F.	L/9840	Pte.
Dodd, H. N.	G/1223	Cpl.	Drew, C. T.	242152	Pte.
Dodgson, J. H.		2nd Lieut.	Drewell, S. J.	G/31311	Pte.
Dodson, J. E.		2nd Lieut.	Drewett, W. J.	G/9904	Pte.
Dodson, T.	S/1051	Pte.	Driffield, H. G.		2nd Lieut.
Doe, A. A.	G/30895	Pte.	Driscoll, J. E.	G/30900	Pte.
Doe, W.	G/20994	Pte.	Driver, H.	G/13468	Pte.
Doel, P. H.	242155	Pte.	Driver, L.	G/20484	Pte.
Dolden, H. C.	G/8639	Pte.	Driver, R.	242091	Pte.
Dollemore, A. J.	G/2237	Pte.	Driver, T. F.	L/7795	Pte.

APPENDIX II.

Drumm, T.	G/5900	Pte.		Duvall, P.	G/23135	Pte.
Drummond, A. E.	G/21354	Pte.		Dyer, C. H.	L/10316	L/Cpl.
Drury, H. E.	G/12678	Pte.		Dyer, E.	G/4596	Pte.
Dry, S.	G/9277	Pte.		Dyer, E. T.	L/8608	Cpl.
Dryden, E.	G/876	Pte.		Dyer, R. C.	G/30540	Pte.
Dubrey, H.	G/30218	Pte.		Dyke, E.	G/9667	L/Cpl.
Duck, F.	G/20991	Pte.		Dyke, F. H.		2nd Lieut.
Duckett, A.	G/6260	Pte.		Dyke, W.	G/9668	Pte.
Duckworth, H.	G/19417	Pte.		Dykes, A. V.	G/6356	Pte.
Dudman, E., M.M.				Dymond, H.	G/999	Pte.
	G/31017	L/Cpl.		Dymond, R. H. A.	241718	Pte.
Duffield, E. E.	L/10098	Pte.		Dyson, W. C.	G/3645	Pte.
Duffield, T. W.	G/10388	Pte.				
Duffill, G.	G/19495	Pte.		Eacott, S.	G/6200	Pte.
Duffurn, A.	G/9992	Pte.		Eades, J.	G/4312	Pte.
Duffy, F.	L/8633	Cpl.		Eagleton, A. J., M.M.		
Duke, E.	G/18191	Pte.			G/19393	Pte.
Dumville, J. R.	205623	Pte.		Eames, E. G.	S/8392	L/Cpl.
Duncton, H. R.	G/15438	Pte.		Eardley, C. P.	G/30957	Pte.
Dunford, C. E.	205183	Pte.		Earley, G.	S/1164	Pte.
Dungate, T. E.	L/9757	Pte.		Early, C. E.	G/5075	Pte.
Dungworth, E.	205592	Pte.		Easey, E.	G/18099	Pte.
Dunkley, A.	G/4834	Pte.		East, F. W.	G/20083	Pte.
Dunmall, H. J.	G/187	Pte.		East, J. P.	G/20996	Pte.
Dunmore, J. A.	G/11432	Pte.		East, W.	G/24603	Pte.
Dunn, A. E.	G/10876	Pte.		Eastgate, J. S.	G/8339	Pte.
Dunn, C. W.	L/7812	Pte.		Eastland, W.	G/15673	Pte.
Dunn, G.	L/6421	Pte.		Eastman, J.	G/1376	Pte.
Dunn, H. J.		2nd Lieut.		Easton, F.	TF/6058	Pte.
Dunn, J. A.	G/2586	Pte.		Eaton, G. J.	G/1422	Pte.
Durant, R.H.W.	G/3138	Pte.		Ebbs, P. C.	G/31456	Pte.
Durley, G.	G/38741	Pte.		Eckett, E. L.	K/1630	Sgt.
Durrant, G. E.	G/23385	Pte.		Eccles, C. G.		Capt.
Durrant, W.	L/9602	Pte.		Ecclestone, B.A.	G/31132	Pte.
Durrell, C. D.	242089	Pte.		Edbrooke, F. C.	G/31631	Pte.
Dursley, G.	S/8939	Pte.		Eden, T.	G/17036	Pte.
Dutch, W. G.	241637	Pte.		Edey, E.	G/8436	Pte.
Dutnall, B.	L/10616	L/Cpl.		Edmett, A. W.		Lieut.
Dutnall, H.	G/19274	L/Cpl.		Edmonds, L.		2nd Lieut.
Dutton, T. D.		Capt.		Edmunds, F. W.	L/10811	Pte.
Dutton, W.	G/15555	Pte.		Edmunds, H.	G/21186	L/Sgt.
Duvall, H. C.	TF/1961	Pte.		Edney, G.	G/11277	Pte.

525

APPENDIX II.

Edom, E.	G/30807	Pte.	Ellis, J. E.	G/18192	Pte.
Edwards, A. C.		Capt.	Ellis, J. W.	204196	Pte.
Edwards, E.	S/1149	Cpl.	Ellis, J. W.	L/9957	Pte.
Edwards, E.	G/9418	Pte.	Ellis, L. W.	G/81	Pte.
Edwards, E.	G/17331	Pte.	Ellis, S. C.	L/7177	L/Cpl.
Edwards, E. R.	G/29960	Pte.	Ellis, T.	G/3779	Pte.
Edwards, E. W.	201606	Pte.	Ellis, W.	G/2084	Pte.
Edwards, F. W.	G/17354	Pte.	Elsom, E. H.	G/24552	Pte.
Edwards, G. F.	201316	Pte.	Elston, A. E.	G/12155	Pte.
Edwards, H.	G/11887	Pte.	Elton, A. C.		Lieut.
Edwards, J.	G/1376	Pte.	Elve, F. A.	G/4579	Pte.
Edwards, J.	G/4543	Pte.	Elvin, R.	G/10995	Pte.
Edwards, J.	G/4667	Pte.	Elworthy, J.	G/2408	Pte.
Edwards, J. J.	S/8964	Pte.	Ely, J. H.	G/18343	Pte.
Edwards, J. S.	G/8982	Pte.	Ely, R.	G/16706	Pte.
Edwards, R.	G/24823	Pte.	Embley, N.	L/5386	Pte.
Edwards, W. E.	G/8327	Sgt.	Embleton, A.	G/984	Pte.
Edwards, W. F.	G/41	Cpl.	Embury, W. C.	L/5255	Sgt.
Edwards, W. T.	G/1061	Pte.	Emery, G. B.	G/15824	Pte.
Efford, W.	G/7620	Pte.	Emery, J. W.	G/12257	Pte.
Eldridge, P. E.	L/7267	L/Cpl.	Emery, W. G.	L/10569	Pte.
Elgar, W. C.	G/1994	Pte.	England, G. H.	203521	Pte.
Elkins, E.	G/28924	Pte.	England, H.	L/9631	Pte.
Ellen, F. A.	L/9987	Pte.	England, W.	G/11232	Pte.
Ellen, F. G.	G/993	Cpl.	Englefield, H.	G/8084	Pte.
Elkington, P. A.	L/9534 C.Q.M.S.		Errill, G. G.	G/24439	Pte.
Elliott, C. A., M.M.,	G/4974	Pte.	Erskine, D.	L/5837	Sgt.
Elliott, E.	L/10802	Pte.	Escott, H. W.	G/18796	Pte.
Elliott, H.	G/5841	Pte.	Eskdale, R.	G/4709	Pte.
Elliott, R. H.	G/6668	L/Cpl.	Etherton, P.	G/31506	Pte.
Elliott, S. O.	G/31021	Pte.	Evans, A. E.	G/24604	Pte.
Elliott, V. K., M.M.	L/10344	Cpl.	Evans, C. A.	G/18707	Pte.
			Evans, F. V.	204593	Pte.
Elliott, W. L., M.C.	2nd	Lieut.	Evans, G.	G/4583	Pte.
Elliott, W. J.	G/19061	Pte.	Evans, H. W.	G/2211	Pte.
Ellis, C.	G/12518	Pte.	Evans, N. H.		Lieut.
Ellis, C.	G/753	Pte.	Evans, P.	G/160	L/Cpl.
Ellis, E. A.	G/1816	Pte.	Evans, P. G.	L/10226	Pte.
Ellis, E. A.	G/4345	Pte.	Evans, R.	G/1486	Pte.
Ellis, F. B.	205607	Pte.	Evans, S. H.	G/7916	Pte.
Ellis, G. A.	L/7371	L/Cpl.	Evans, W.	G/21493	Pte.
Ellis, G. F.	G/3131	Pte.	Evans, W.	205683	Pte.
			Evans, W. E.	242301	Pte.

APPENDIX II.

Evanson, R. M.	G/16521	Pte.	Farnell, W.J. E.	G/15066	Pte.
Everleigh, F.	G/23528	Pte.	Farr, F.	G/1623	L/Cpl.
Evenden, C. W.	S/779	Pte.	Farr, R.	G/3778	Pte.
Evers, W.	G/26995	Pte.	Farrance, O.	G/11179	Pte.
Everest, A.	L/8833	Pte.	Farrant, W.	G/4706	Cpl.
Everest, A.	L/10093	Pte.	Farrell, W.	G/16412	L/Cpl.
Everett, H. V.	G/59	Pte.	Farrelly, J.	G/1266	L/Cpl.
Everist, J. H., D.C.M.			Farrow, A. E.	266389	Pte.
	G/226	Sgt.	Farrow, H.	G/39144	Pte.
Everitt, H.	G/10973	Pte.	Faulkner, A. J.	G/538	Pte.
Everitt, J. W.	G/5848	Pte.	Faultley, E.	G/14752	Pte.
Everson, H. T.		2nd Lieut.	Fawcett, H.	L/9777	Pte.
Eves, S.	G/1087	Pte.	Fay, B. B.	G/11034	Pte.
Ewen, W. J.		Capt.	Feather, J. H.	G/16525	Cpl.
Exall, A.	L/5473	Pte.	Feather, R. W.	L/8780	Pte.
Excell, L. A.	G/11473	Pte.	Febland, A. J.	G/17225	Pte.
Exell, F., M.M.	G/529	Pte.	Feetham, J.	G/15868	Pte.
Exton, J.	G/18557	L/Cpl.	Felton, F. G.	204164	Pte.
Eyre, B.	G/9932	Pte.	Fenn, P.	G/481	Pte.
			Fennell, G. H.	G/5396	Cpl.
			Fenlon, A. J.	L/10745	Cpl.
Fabian, F. P.	G/10190	Pte.	Fenton, E.	G/21275	Cpl.
Facer, J. R.	G/31173	Pte.	Fenton, A. E.		2nd Lieut.
Facey, W. G.	G/2722	L/Cpl.	Fenwick, J. H.	L/6584	Sgt.
Fagg, A. A.	G/8677	Cpl.	Fermer, A. A.	L/10415	L/Sgt.
Faggminter, J.	G/10783	Pte.	Fermer, J.	G/12471	Pte.
Fairbain, W. F. T.			Ferrier, A. R.	G/14930	Pte.
	G/10539	L/Cpl.	Fever, W. H.	G/4831	Pte.
Faircloth, F.	201449	Pte.	Fewell, G. J.	S/9068	Pte.
Fairhall, E. J.	S/8424	Cpl.	Field, A. H.	G/1844	Cpl.
Fairman, F.	L/9143	Pte.	Field, C. C.		2nd Lieut.
Fairservice, J. A. V.			Field, C. J.	G/12049	Pte.
	S/6350	Sgt.	Field, F. J.	TF/2240	Pte.
Falkner, J.L.H.	L/10230	Pte.	Field, H. F.	L/9000	Pte.
Falkner,R.G.G.	L/10229	Sgt.	Field, W.	G/23279	Pte.
Falp, R.	G/19619	Pte.	Field, W. L.	G/11696	Pte.
Fardon, J.	G/5390	L/Cpl.	Figg, F. P.	G/18196	Pte.
Farey, G. C.	G/12285	Pte.	Figg, R.	G/821	Pte.
Farley, H. W.		Lieut.	Figg, S.	G/5593	Pte.
Farmer, G.	G/12956	Pte.	Filar, H.	202755	Pte.
Farmer, J.	203382	Pte.	File, H. W.		2nd Lieut.
Farmer, J. R.	242325	Pte.	File, W. G.	L/8674	Sgt.
Farnell, W.	G/13340	Pte.	Filmer, C. G.	G/12007	Pte.

527

APPENDIX II.

Filmer, F.	G/4304	Pte.
Filmer, G. T.	G/7531	Pte.
Finch, E. P.	201422	Pte.
Finch, F. J.	L/5521	Pte.
Finch, G. E.	G/19199	Pte.
Finch, J.	S/742	Pte.
Findley, J. B.	G/10182	Pte.
Fish, F.	G/2404	Cpl.
Fish, H. E.	G/30809	Pte.
Fishenden, E. H.	G/24539	Cpl.
Fisher, A. W.	G/2643	L/Cpl.
Fisher, E.	205663	Pte.
Fisher, F.		Capt.
Fisher, F.	G/6273	Pte.
Fisher, F. G.	G/8215	Pte.
Fisher, G. V.	G/2910	Pte.
Fisher, G. W.	205169	Pte.
Fisher, J.	G/2476	Pte.
Fisher, R.	L/7945	Dmr.
Fisher, R. H.	G/7681	Pte.
Fisher, S. C.	G/25126	Pte.
Fisher, W. G., M.M.	L/9041	Sgt.
Fisk, F.	G/6855	Pte.
Fissenden, H.	G/1029	L/Cpl.
Fissenden, R. A.	G/10996	Pte.
Fissenden, S. W.	L/10721	Pte.
Fitch, E. A.	G/31219	Pte.
Fitch, P. E. R.	G/29765	Pte.
Fittal, G. H.	L/7266	Sgt.
Fitton, H.	G/21274	Pte.
Fitton, H. G., C.B., D.S.O., A.D.C.		Brig-Gen.
Fitzgerald, J.	L/7628	Sgt.
Fitzgerald, J.	202970	Pte.
Fitzhugh, A.	G/2257	Pte.
Flack, R.	G/15968	Pte.
Flaye, G.	241735	Pte.
Fleet, W.	G/15142	Pte.
Fleming, J. A.		2nd Lieut.
Fleming, W. J.	G/4011	Pte.
Fletcher, A.	G/982	Pte.
Fletcher, F. W.	240954	Pte.
Fletcher, T.	L/5752	C.S.M.
Fletcher, W. H.	G/31536	Pte.
Flexman, E. L.	205341	Sgt.
Flint, F.	G/20087	Cpl.
Flint, W.	G/19423	Pte.
Flint, W.	G/18822	Pte.
Flood, R. G.	202154	Pte.
Flood, H.	S/737	Pte.
Flowers, H.		2nd Lieut.
Flowers, J.	G/21392	Cpl.
Flowers, T.	G/2629	Pte.
Fogg, E. J.	203943	Pte.
Foley, S.	L/6646	Pte.
Follett, A.	TF/4766	Pte.
Follington, T.	203832	Pte.
Foolkes, A.	G/17137	Pte.
Foord, C.	S/861	Pte.
Foord, E. J.	G/12298	Pte.
Forbes, G.	G/1135	Pte.
Forbes, W.	G/31245	Pte.
Ford, A.	L/10238	Pte.
Ford, C. T.	G/13000	Pte.
Ford, C. W.	L/8693	Pte.
Ford, E.	G/5124	Pte.
Ford, F. H.	G/26417	Pte.
Ford, J.	G/6161	Pte.
Ford, J. B. B.		Capt.
Ford, R.	G/2335	Pte.
Ford, S.	G/4229	Pte.
Ford, S.	G/20224	Pte.
Ford, V. J.	G/11453	Pte.
Fordham, E. G. B.	G/18107	Pte.
Fordham, G.	G/10926	Pte.
Foreman, A. W.	G/23417	L/Cpl.
Foreman, L. S.	G/20339	Pte.
Forsdick, F. W. T.	G/30904	Pte.
Forster, A. T.	S/8259	Pte.
Forster, W.	205908	Pte.
Forsyth, J.		2nd Lieut.
Fostall, L.	240660	Pte.
Foster, A. E.	G/1797	Pte.

APPENDIX II.

Foster, C. A.	G/24967	Pte.	Francis, G.	G/18434	Pte.
Foster, C. R.	G/23833	Pte.	Francis, G.	G/18298	Pte.
Foster, C. W.	G/20295	L/Sgt.	Francis, H.	G/9621	Pte.
Foster, F.	G/11475	Pte.	Francis, P.	G/12809	Pte.
Foster, H. L.		2nd Lieut.	Francis, S.	G/21549	Pte.
Foster, J. T. G.	G/5736	Pte.	Francis, T.	TF/3558	Pte.
Foster, W. C.	G/26263	Pte.	Francis, T.	L/7289	Pte.
Foster, W. J.	G/19587	Pte.	Francis, W. T.	G/355	L/Cpl.
Foster, W. T.	204154	Pte.	Frankis, E.	G/5842	Pte.
Fothergill, H.	G/30675	Pte.	Frankland, V.	G/24441	Pte.
Fothergill, S.	G/8267	Pte.	Frankland, W. J.	G/11725	Pte.
Foulds, J.	L/8696	Pte.	Franklin, F. E.	G/30808	Pte.
Foulger, C. F.	G/8640	Pte.	Franklin, J.	201766	Pte.
Foulger, J. T.	L/10817	L/Cpl.	Franklinde, G. T.		
Fowle, F.	201043	Sgt.		L/8443	Cpl.
Fowle, G.	L/9756	Pte.	Franks, H. C.	G/27311	Pte.
Fowler, A.	G/1446	L/Cpl.	Franks, J. T.	G/4298	Pte.
Fowler, A. J.	S/9197	Pte.	Fraser, F. G., *M.C.*		Capt.
Fowler, D.	G/849	L/Cpl.	Frazer, G. H.	G/21475	Pte.
Fowler, E. J.	G/1432	Pte.	Free, G.	L/9600	Pte.
Fowler, J.	L/6669	Pte.	Free, R. C.	G/18256	Pte.
Fowler, R. G.	L/9760	L/Cpl.	Free, W.	L/9343	Sgt.
Fowler, W.	L/7529	Pte.	Freebourne, E. A.		
Fowler, W. H.	G/5107	Pte.		G/18871	L/Cpl.
Fowles, A.	G/20412	Pte.	Freed, E. V.	S/9260	Cpl.
Fox, A.	G/9218	Pte.	Freeman, C. L.	G/19500	Pte.
Fox, A. W.	G/29669	Pte.	Freeman, C. S.	G/20494	Pte.
Fox, C. J.		2nd Lieut.	Freeman, E.	L/8936	Pte.
Fox, E. J.	242277	Pte.	Freeman, E. A.	G/5976	Pte.
Fox, E. W. E.	G/19966	Pte.	Freeman, F.	L/9266	Pte.
Fox, F. B.	S/63	Pte.	Freeman, F.	G/12495	Pte.
Fox, F. G.	G/24666	Sgt.	Freeman, F. A.	G/29778	Pte.
Fox, F. W.	G/31226	Pte.	Freeman, G.	G/10269	Pte.
Fox, G. E.	G/5373	Pte.	Freeman, H.	S/8217	Pte.
Fox, H.	G/4998	Pte.	Freeman, J. B.		2nd Lieut.
Fox, W. J.	G/8548	Pte.	Freeman, W. D.	L/9383	L/Cpl.
Frampton, N.	206334	Pte.	French, E.	G/1120	Cpl.
Frampton, P. G.	L/9891	Pte.	French, F.	G/14711	Pte.
France, H.	G/18195	Pte.	French, G. A.	G/14675	Pte.
France, H. J. W.	G/31134	Pte.	French, H.	L/7614	Pte.
Francis, A. T.	G/7737	L/Cpl.	French, H. S.	G/18640	Pte.
Francis, E. J.	242278	Pte.	French, S. A.		Lieut.
Francis, G.	S/8714	Pte.	French, T.	G/2589	L/Cpl.

MM   529

APPENDIX II.

French, T. E.	G/11069	Pte.
Freshwater, F. W. C.		
	G/26264	Pte.
Fressingfield, C. W.		
	G/11386	Pte.
Frick, O.	T/2972	L/Cpl.
Fricker, E.		2nd Lieut.
Friday, C. J.	G/23364	Pte.
Friedleben, E.G.	G/6178	Pte.
Friend, D. T.	G/21053	Pte.
Friend, E. P.	G/7738	Pte.
Friend, P. W.	G/11018	Pte.
Froome, S. W.	G/3662	L/Cpl.
Frost, B.	G/9601	Pte.
Frost, C. H.	G/17528	Pte.
Frost, F. W.	G/10135	Pte.
Frost, H. P.	G/24393	Pte.
Frost, J.	L/10324	Pte.
Frost, K.		2nd Lieut.
Frost, L. G.	S/8694	Pte.
Frost, M.	G/18019	Pte.
Frost, M. C.	G/1360	Pte.
Frostick, J. W.	G/11142	Pte.
Froud, F. G.	G/24506	Pte.
Froud, J.	205457	Pte.
Frowen, P.	G/13786	Pte.
Fry, C.	G/5538	Pte.
Fry, E. L.	G/25284	Pte.
Fry, H. C.		2nd Lieut.
Fry, R.	G/28523	Pte.
Fryatt, J.	G/23582	Pte.
Fryer, A.	G/2338	Pte.
Fryer, F.	G/16722	Pte.
Fryer, F.	G/2339	L/Cpl.
Fryer, T.	TF/2271	Pte.
Fuggle, P.	L/11767	Pte.
Fulcher, W.	G/12865	Pte.
Fullagar, P. W.	G/12888	Pte.
Fullager, G. H.	G/8734	Pte.
Fullbrook, E.	G/17612	Pte.
Fuller, B.		2nd Lieut.
Fuller, E.	G/31460	Pte.
Fuller, G.	G/15785	Pte.
Fuller, G. R.	G/4560	Pte.
Fuller, H.	L/9582	Pte.
Fuller, H.	G/7255	Pte.
Fuller, J. D.	G/4100	Pte.
Fuller, M.	G/11089	Pte.
Funnell, A.	G/9953	Pte.
Fyrth, A. J.	G/11923	Pte.
Gabriel, J.	L/5782	Cpl.
Gadd, J.	G/5724	Pte.
Gadd, J.	L/10685	Pte.
Gage, T.	L/11015	Pte.
Gailer, C. R.	G/8483	Pte.
Gale, R.	G/3982	Pte.
Gallant, A. E.	G/21550	Pte.
Gallavan, A.	202121	Pte.
Gallyer, W. R.	L/7273	Pte.
Galpin, F. A.	G/12042	Pte.
Galvin, W.	G/14649	Pte.
Gammon, A.	G/18439	Pte.
Gammon, E.	205073	Pte.
Gammon, G. H. H.		
	G/12187	Pte.
Gander, J.	G/7386	Pte.
Gander, R.	201175	Sgt.
Gane, H.	L/6732	Pte.
Gant, A. J.	G/6583	Pte.
Gapper, G.	241274	Pte.
Gardener, W.	201010	L/Cpl.
Gardiner, T. H.	S/9151	Pte.
Gardner, E.	G/18631	Pte.
Gardner, G.	G/24606	Pte.
Gardner, G. W.	G/11621	Pte.
Gardner, H.	G/4997	Pte.
Gardner, J.	G/24701	Pte.
Gardner, R. W. W.		
	G/19610	Pte.
Garity, J.	G/10890	Pte.
Garland, F. G.	G/3972	Cpl.
Garland, G. J.	G/5812	Pte.
Garland, W.	G/2086	Pte.
Garner, A.	204064	Pte.
Garner, A. E.	G/18257	Pte.

APPENDIX II.

Name	ID	Rank
Garner, H. L.	G/23618	Pte.
Garnett, G.	G/15861	Pte.
Garrett, G.	L/9852	Pte.
Garth, H.	G/18176	L/Cpl.
Garvey, M.	L/7926	Pte.
Gaskins, A. F.	G/19649	Pte.
Gasper, A.	S/9227	Pte.
Gasson, T. W.	G/18635	Pte.
Gaston, J.	G/9425	Pte.
Gate, W.	200005	Pte.
Gates, A.	G/7533	Pte.
Gates, C. G.	G/19291	Cpl.
Gates, S. J.	G/8596	L/Cpl.
Gates, W. T.	G/38739	Pte.
Gatland, S.	G/4978	Pte.
Gaukroger, A.	T/38730	Pte.
Gaulley, A. J.	G/2524	Pte.
Gay, G.	G/2608	Pte.
Gayler, E.	G/11246	Pte.
Gayton, H. B., M.M.	G/6172	Pte.
Gearing, F.	G/9222	Pte.
Gearing, T. H.	G/2244	Pte.
Geddes, A. V.	L/10717	Pte.
Geddes, W. R.	L/11329	L/Cpl.
Gee, G. W.	G/18345	Pte.
Gee, W.	L/5925	Pte.
Gennery, H. A.	G/26248	Pte.
George, E.	241232	Pte.
George, F.	G/8268	Cpl.
George, S.	G/7043	Dmr.
Gerling, A.F. J.	G/31170	Pte.
Gerring, C. P.	204605	Pte.
Gibbins, E., M.M.	G/11077	Pte.
Gibbins, M.	G/24555	Pte.
Gibbon, G. F.	G/18198	Pte.
Gibbons, H. F.	G/10325	Pte.
Gibbons, W. A.	G/2241	Pte.
Gibbs, A.	G/3005	Pte.
Gibbs, A. H.	G/3118	Pte.
Gibbs, A. J.	201473	Pte.
Gibbs, E. B.	G/26644	Pte.
Gibbs, J.	G/1121	Pte.
Gibbs, J. E. W.	G/31050	Pte.
Gibbs, L.		Lieut.
Giblin, E.	L/11107	Pte.
Gibson, F.	G/12209	Pte.
Gibson, H.	L/8206	L/Cpl.
Gibson, J.	L/8007	Pte.
Gibson, P. A.	S/1163	Pte.
Gilbert, A.	L/8541	Pte.
Gilbert, A.	G/15070	Pte.
Gilbert, F. J. C.	G/11702	Pte.
Gilbert, J. T.	G/11454	Pte.
Gilbey, C. J.	L/7540	Sgt.
Gilbey, H.	G/38687	Pte.
Giles, E. V.	L/9107	Pte.
Giles, J. T.	S/1131	Pte.
Gilks, F. E.	G/3210	Pte.
Gill, B.	205591	Pte.
Gill, G.	241360	Pte.
Gill, J. F.	G/2777	Pte.
Gill, W.	G/14667	Pte.
Gill, W.	205654	Pte.
Gillard, A. E.	G/24554	Pte.
Gillard, E. M.	G/566	Pte.
Gillard, L.	G/8507	Pte.
Gillett, A.	G/30596	Pte.
Gillett, F. T.		2nd Lieut.
Gillett, W. C.	L/3732	Pte.
Gillham, W.	203524	Pte.
Gillies, G.	G/12639	Pte.
Gillingham, F.	L/10234	Pte.
Gillis, J. M.	G/3145	Pte.
Gillson, T.	G/18324	Pte.
Gilmore, J.	205520	Pte.
Ginn, G. J. F.	L/9665	Pte.
Gittens, A.	S/4914	Pte.
Gladman, F.	G/5288	Pte.
Gladman, J.	G/28365	Pte.
Gladwell, J. H.		2nd Lieut.
Gladwell, J. J.	G/4794	Cpl.
Glanville, F. C.	L/7850	Pte.
Glasgow, W. H.	G/18824	Pte.
Glass, H.	G/20744	Pte.

APPENDIX II.

Glayzer, S. E.	L/10120	Pte.	Gooderham, F. W.			
Glazebrook, S. W.				G/30576	Pte.	
	L/8020	C.S.M.	Goodhew, W.	G/30911	Pte.	
Glazier, A. E.	G/28749	Pte.	Gooding, H.	L/10850	Pte.	
Gleeson, A.	L/11429	Pte.	Goodlad, J.	S/8846	Pte.	
Glenman, J.	27448	Pte.	Goodman, H.	L/5578	Pte.	
Glossop, F.	G/31688	Pte.	Goodman, W.	G/12831	Pte.	
Glover, B. H.		Capt.	Goodrick, W.	L/7769	Sgt.	
Glover, J.	L/6756	Sgt.	Goodrum, F. S.	205613	Pte.	
Goble, M.	L/10060	Cpl.	Goodsell, H. G.	G/4972	L/Cpl.	
Godden, A. J.	G/2169	Cpl.	Goodsell, H. M.	200833	Pte.	
Godden, G. F.	G/10279	Pte.	Goodwin, A. W.	G/7785	Pte.	
Godden, H.	S/9150	Pte.	Goodwin, E.	G/23156	Pte.	
Godfrey, A. H.	G/6764	Pte.	Goodwin, F. C. R.			
Godfrey, E.		2nd Lieut.		G/18381	Pte.	
Godfrey, G.	L/9429	Pte.	Goodwin, F. J.	S/8309	Pte.	
Godfrey, W.	G/6000	Pte.	Goodwin, L. M.	241594	Pte.	
Godley, G.	G/1875	Pte.	Goodwin, S.	G/18024	Pte.	
Godsell, J. H.	242167	Pte.	Goodwin, W. H.	L/7652	Pte.	
Goff, A. H.	L/10166	Pte.	Goose. G.	G/946	Pte.	
Gold, E. F.	G/20228	Pte.	Gordon, G. T.	203274	L/Cpl.	
Golder, G.	L/7249	L/Cpl.	Gordon, P.	G/4273	Pte.	
Goldfinch, W.	200359	Pte.	Gordon, T. E.	G/8610	Pte.	
Golding, H.	L/9514	Pte.	Gordon-Smith, G.		Capt.	
Golding, J.	L/8698	Sgt.	Gore, G.	G/4129	L/Cpl.	
Golding, P.J. T.	G/8804	Pte.	Gore, S. K.		Lieut.	
Golding, T.	S/79	L/Cpl.	Gore, W. G.	206331	Pte.	
Golding, W. M.	G/30058	Pte.	Gorham, F. J.	G/19203	Cpl.	
Goldsbury, T.	L/11560	Sgt.	Gorman, S. H.	L/7695	L/Cpl.	
Goldsmith, G.	S/9041	Pte.	Gosden, J.	G/4824	Pte.	
Goldsmith, G.F.	G/6698	Pte.	Gosling, E.	TF/2378	Pte.	
Goldsmith, W.C.	L/7284	Pte.	Gosling, R. C.	G/31464	Pte.	
Goldup, T. A.	G/4900	Pte.	Goss, F.	G/18299	Pte.	
Gomm, E. T.	L/9782	L/Cpl.	Gothard, E.	G/19201	L/Cpl.	
Gomm, W.	204482	Pte.	Gott, C.	G/20092	Pte.	
Gonich, L. J.	L/8044	L/Cpl.	Gough, A.	205687	Pte.	
Gooch, C. S.	G/25868	Pte.	Gould, A.	G/12329	Pte.	
Goodacre, J.	G/19927	Pte.	Gould, A. R.	G/19651	Pte.	
Goodall, H.	G/7012	Cpl.	Gould, H. J.	201224	L/Sgt.	
Gooday, W. G.	G/15983	Pte.	Gould, J.	G/3	Pte.	
Goodchild, A.	G/12802	Pte.	Gould, R.	L/7328	L/Cpl.	
Goodchild, E.B.	G/10449	Pte.	Gould, W.	S/2522	Cpl.	
Goodchild,W.E.	L/7768	Pte.	Goulding, R.	G/3681	L/Cpl.	

APPENDIX II.

Gouldsborough, C.	G/6331	Pte.	Green, H. W.	L/9551	Pte.
Gowers, J.	G/6444	L/Cpl.	Green, J.	G/11877	Pte.
Gowland, T.	G/18241	Sgt.	Green, R.	G/4113	Pte.
Graham, E. C.	G/7612	Pte.	Green, S.	G/11912	Pte.
Graham, J.	L/5911	Pte.	Green, T.	G/1765	Pte.
Graham, J. A.	242326	Pte.	Green, W.	G/24328	Pte.
Graham, M. W.		Capt.	Green, W.	L/5937	Sgt.
Graham, W.	G/19504	Pte.	Green, W.	G/31554	Pte.
Grainger, W. E.	L/9415	Pte.	Green W.	G/2700	Cpl.
Gramson, H. J.	G/8176	Pte.	Green, W. E.	G/10951	Pte.
Granger, A. F.	G/19715	Pte.	Green, W. J.	G/18259	Pte.
Granger, G.	G/1054	L/Cpl.	Greenall, J.	G/31553	Pte.
Grant, A. G.	G/7534	Pte.	Greenaway, G.F.	G/1314	Pte.
Grant, J.	G/2622	Pte.	Greenfield, F. S.	G/19724	Pte.
Grant, J. T.		2nd Lieut.	Greenland, G.T.	G/11095	Pte.
Grant, R. W.		Capt.	Greenleaf, C.	G/6523	Pte.
Graves, R.	G/18375	Pte.	Greenslade, A.	G/12895	Pte.
Gravett, A. W.	L/8428	Pte.	Greenslade, A.S.	L/10269	Pte.
Gray, D. G.		2nd Lieut.	Greenslade, V.L.	TF/3085	Pte.
Gray, F. E.	G/2882	L/Cpl.	Greenstreet, R.G.	G/26252	Pte.
Gray, G. M.		2nd Lieut.	Greenwood, C.	G/10729	Pte.
Gray, H.	G/12585	Pte.	Greenwood, E. C., *M.M.*		
Gray, H. A., *M.C.*		Lieut.		G/10527	Pte.
Gray, H. G.	G/18149	Pte.	Greenwood, F. W.		
Gray, J., *D.C.M.*	203072	Sgt.		L/10085	L/Cpl.
Gray, P. H.	G/2521	Pte.	Greenwood, J.	L/10063	Cpl.
Gray, R.	G/30959	L/Cpl.	Greenwood, J. H., *M.C.*		Lieut.
Gray, R.	L/6680	Pte.	Greenwood, S.G.	G/10952	Pte.
Grayland, B.	G/8126	Cpl.	Greenwood, S. W.		
Grayson, J. D.	G/4885	Sgt.		G/23583	Pte.
Grayston, F.C.J.	G/25307	Pte.	Greenwood, W.	G/16527	Pte.
Greagsbey, E.	G/4606	Pte.	Gregan, P.	G/30362	Pte.
Green, A. E.	G/4994	Pte.	Gregory, H. T.		Capt.
Green, A. G.	G/24769	L/Cpl.	Gregory, W.	G/23691	Pte.
Green, A. L.	G/23722	Pte.	Gregory, W. A.	G/635	L/Cpl.
Green, C. E.	G/7477	Cpl.	Gregory, W. J.	203339	Pte.
Green, F.	205786	Pte.	Gregson, A. H.		2nd Lieut.
Green, G.	G/24609	Pte.	Gresty, J. R.	G/27645	Pte.
Green, G. E., *M.M.*			Grey, J. G.	G/6866	Pte.
	G/2049	Sgt.	Grey, W.	G/6535	Sgt.
Green, G. H.	S/610	Pte.	Grief, W. T.	S/832	Pte.
Green, H. A.		2nd Lieut.	Grier, A. J.	242094	Pte.
			Griffin, E.	L/10740	Pte.

APPENDIX II.

Name	Number	Rank
Griffin, E. A.	G/31272	Pte.
Griffin, G. H.	G/6828	Pte.
Griffin, S. G.	G/10431	Pte.
Griffiths, C. J.	G/9013	Pte.
Griffiths, D. W.	L/10656	Pte.
Griffiths, E.	S/837	Pte.
Griffiths, E. T.	G/11646	Cpl.
Griffiths, L.	L/10130	Pte.
Griffiths, V. E.	G/8017	Sgt.
Griffiths, W. H.		2nd Lieut.
Griffiths, W. J.	L/9214	Pte.
Griffiths, W. L.	203023	Pte.
Grigg, E. R.	S/707	Pte.
Griggs, F. W.	G/30729	Pte.
Griggs, H. J.	G/12709	Pte.
Grigsby, C.	S/154	Pte.
Grigsby, H. S.	L/10543	Pte.
Grimes, S.	TF/3433	Pte.
Grimley, W. H.	L/9545	Cpl.
Grimshaw, W.	G/2254	Cpl.
Grimwood, B.	G/30913	Pte.
Grinler, F. C.	G/24699	Pte.
Grinshead, T. C.	G/11572	Pte.
Grist, C. H.		2nd Lieut.
Grist, C. R.	G/2924	Pte.
Gristwood, P. C.	G/7867	Pte.
Grix, C. H.	G/30733	L/Cpl.
Grocott, F. W.		2nd Lieut.
Groom, C. A.	L/8912	Pte.
Groombridge, A.	G/18660	Pte.
Groombridge, H.	L/9967	Pte.
Groombridge, W. E.	G/7242	Pte.
Gross, G. J.		Capt.
Grotier, E.	G/31513	Pte.
Ground, J. K.		2nd Lieut.
Grout, J. G.	240522	Pte.
Grover, C. W. H.	G/9533	L/Sgt.
Grover, G. E.	G/10661	Pte.
Grover, J.	G/6479	Pte.
Groves, H.	L/7478	Cpl.
Groves, W. H.	G/7410	Cpl.
Growns, A.	G/9605	Pte.
Grubb, G.	G/30570	Pte.
Grubb, H. W.	TF/3641	Pte.
Guess, C.	L/8240	L/Cpl.
Guess, E. A.	L/9011	L/Cpl.
Guess, F. J.	L/8545	Cpl.
Guess, S. W.	G/5135	Pte.
Gumb, J.	G/9730	Pte.
Gunn, A.	G/3929	L/Cpl.
Gunn, E. F.	240919	Pte.
Gunn, W. J.	G/23700	Pte.
Gunner, C. W.	L/10673	Pte.
Gurney, E.	G/1754	Pte.
Gurr, G.	G/17326	Pte.
Gurr, J. P.	G/10256	Pte.
Gutherless, H.	205460	Pte.
Gutsell, E.	G/1557	Pte.
Gutteridge, J., D.C.M.	G/1324	C.S.M.
Guyatt, L. A.	G/17338	Pte.
Habgood, C. W.	G/21689	L/Cpl.
Hackett, W. R.		Lieut.
Hackett, W.	G/5667	Cpl.
Hackney, T.	G/24330	Pte.
Hacon, E.	241848	Pte.
Hadaway, W.	L/9374	Pte.
Haddon, F. W.	G/17751	Pte.
Haddow, J.	203487	Pte.
Hadler, G. W.	G/12385	Pte.
Hadley, H.	G/5076	Pte.
Hadrill, W.	L/8955	Pte.
Hadwin, H.	G/19753	Pte.
Haggar, H.	L/10242	Pte.
Hagger, H. C.	G/6763	Pte.
Haggerty, C.	S/8173	Pte.
Hague, H. W.	G/30280	Pte.
Hague, J. W.	G/9071	Pte.
Haigleton, H.	G/2382	Pte.
Haines, P. W.	L/9910	Pte.
Haines, W.	S/773	Cpl.
Haines, W.	200228	Sgt.
Haiselden, F. C.	G/15434	Pte.
Hale, C.	G/30224	Pte.
Hale, C. H.	G/7	Pte.

534

APPENDIX II.

Hale, S. A.	G/26424	Pte.	Hampton, W.	L/8296	Cpl.
Hales, A. L.	G/31470	Pte.	Hamshaw, A.	205446	Pte.
Hall, A.	L/10374	Pte.	Hanch, F.	G/14602	Pte.
Hall, A. F.	G/7605	Pte.	Hancock, W. E.	L/10399	L/Sgt.
Hall, A. K.		Capt.	Handley, F.	G/18946	Pte.
Hall, C.	L/9896	Pte.	Handley, F. G.	G/24450	Pte.
Hall, E.	266001	Pte.	Handscombe, A. E.	L/10007	Pte.
Hall, E.	205874	Cpl.	Hankins, A. J.	G/5383	Pte.
Hall, E.	G/12837	Pte.	Hankins, J. W.	L/10754	Pte.
Hall, E. C.	S/8384	Pte.	Hanmore, F.	L/7403	L/Cpl.
Hall, E. E.	G/17819	Pte.	Hannay, W. A.	G/17554	L/Cpl.
Hall, G. J.	G/31890	L/Cpl.	Hannen, T.	G/20347	Pte.
Hall, H. S. H. H.		Capt.	Harber, G. F.	G/460	Cpl.
Hall, J. H.	G/19992	Pte.	Harboe, A.	L/9161	Pte.
Hall, J. W.	G/3291	L/Cpl.	Harding, A. J.	L/10087	Pte.
Hall, S. A.	G/28378	Pte.	Harding, A. K., M.C.		Capt.
Hall, T. E.	G/5405	Pte.	Harding, C.	10401	Pte.
Hall, W.	G/3920	Cpl.	Harding, F.	G/16729	Pte.
Hall, W.	G/5466	Pte.	Harding, F. O.	G/28376	Pte.
Hall, W.	G/8018	Pte.	Harding, F. W. L.	G/3940	Cpl.
Hall, W. C.	S/2976	Sgt.	Harding, H.	201740	Pte.
Hall, W. E.	G/23197	Pte.	Harding, J. A.	G/20231	Pte.
Halley, W. E.	G/6633	Pte.	Harding, J. M.		2nd Lieut.
Halliday, R. J.	204515	Pte.	Harding, L. J.	G/1377	Pte.
Hallowes, G. B.		2nd Lieut.	Harding, O. C.	240972	Pte.
Halls, S. J.	G/6247	Pte.	Harding, R. D.	G/11893	Pte.
Ham, G.	G/1727	Pte.	Harding, W.	G/38617	Pte.
Hamilton, F. W.		2nd Lieut.	Harding, W.	L/8049	Pte.
Hamilton, H. F.	G/18620	Pte.	Hardwick, W.	G/17620	Pte.
Hamilton, J. A.	G/2031	Pte.	Hardy, C.	G/472	Pte.
Hamilton, W.	G/3024	Pte.	Hardy, G. W.	205641	Pte.
Hammond, A.	G/20229	Pte.	Hardy, H. J.	G/2667	Pte.
Hammond, C.R.	S/8540	Pte.	Hardy, R.	G/5707	Pte.
Hammond, F.G.	G/28525	Pte.	Hardy, W. D.	G/6860	Pte.
Hammond, G.	G/20230	Pte.	Hare, E. W.	G/2809	Pte.
Hammond, H.	G/294	Pte.	Hare, H. B.	G/29370	Pte.
Hammond, H.	G/10567	Pte.	Hare, S.	G/5122	Pte.
Hammond, J.	G/8657	Pte.	Hargreaves, H.	G/1272	Pte.
Hammond, S.C.	G/5001	Pte.	Harland, C. E.	L/8868	L/Cpl.
Hammond, W.	G/31248	Pte.	Harland, H.	205471	Pte.
Hampton, J. P.	G/7388	Pte.	Harland, J.	L/10050	Pte.
Hampton, T.	L/9462	Pte.	Harling, S. G.	G/15423	Pte.
Hampton, T.	G/1198	Pte.	Harman, A.	G/1039	Pte.

APPENDIX II.

Harman, R.	G/11117	Pte.
Harmer, F. H.	S/8164	Pte.
Harmer, W. H.	G/2472	Pte.
Harmes, T. H.	G/9252	Pte.
Harmor, E.	G/15329	Pte.
Harnan, H.	G/5618	Pte.
Harrington, E.	G/31473	Pte.
Harris, A.	G/11395	Pte.
Harris, A. N.		2nd Lieut.
Harris, A. W.	G/360	Pte.
Harris, C. A.	G/4628	Pte.
Harris, D.	G/4227	Pte.
Harris, E. J.	S/8888	Pte.
Harris, G.	G/5111	L/Cpl.
Harris, G. H.	L/9140	L/Cpl.
Harris, H. C.		Capt.
Harris, H. R.	L/8121	Pte.
Harris, J.	G/18827	Pte.
Harris, J.	G/18908	Pte.
Harris, R.	G/2593	Pte.
Harris, R. J.	G/10688	Pte.
Harris, R. J.	G/19141	Cpl.
Harris, T.	L/10132	Pte.
Harris, T. J., V.C., M.M.	G/358	Sgt.
Harris, W. G.	G/11492	Pte.
Harrison, E. D.		2nd Lieut.
Harrison, F. I.		Capt.
Harrison, G. A.	G/5672	Pte.
Harrison, J.	202894	Cpl.
Harrison, J. W.	G/10891	Pte.
Harrison, S.	L/7143	Pte.
Harrison, W.	G/4971	Pte.
Harrison, W.	G/10691	Pte.
Harp, J.	G/5532	Pte.
Harrod, A. G.	241021	Pte.
Harrod, G. J.	240520	Pte.
Hart, A. G.	G/4984	Pte.
Hart, B. B.	TF/6068	Pte.
Hart, E. H.	G/4843	Pte.
Hart, G. F.	L/8895	Pte.
Hart, G. F.	G/5349	Pte.
Hart, H. T.	L/10026	Pte.
Hart, J.	G/10601	Pte.
Hart, L.	241620	Pte.
Hart, W.	G/8644	Pte.
Hartley, W.	G/11662	L/Cpl.
Hartman, G. A.	G/16754	Pte.
Hartman, C. H.		Lieut.
Harvey, A.	G/4076	Pte.
Harvey, A. W.	G/27788	Pte.
Harvey, A. W.	G/9959	L/Cpl.
Harvey, C. T.	L/10879	Pte.
Harvey, E. B. A.		2nd Lieut.
Harvey, E. G.	203509	Pte.
Harvey, T. J.	G/4805	Pte.
Haselden, B.	G/30923	Pte.
Haselden, M.	G/2188	Pte.
Haseldine, G.	G/18347	Pte.
Haslam, J. A.	G/31557	Pte.
Haslam, W. H. W.		Lieut.
Hassall, F.	G/19508	Pte.
Hastings, P.		Major.
Hastings, T.	L/10478	Pte.
Hastings, W. A.	G/12880	Pte.
Hatcher, A. J.	G/5638	Pte.
Hatcher, H.	G/28462	Pte.
Hatcher, T. H.	L/10202	Pte.
Hatto, W. E.	TF/1972	Pte.
Hatton, H. G.	G/30920	Pte.
Hatton, J. F.	G/30921	Pte.
Haundley, H. St. R.	G/166	Sgt.
Hawes, H.	G/1238	Pte.
Hawes, R.	G/12047	Pte.
Hawkes, H. G.	G/20721	Pte.
Hawkins, A.	241642	Pte.
Hawkins, A. F.	L/10928	Pte.
Hawkins, H.	G/11490	Pte.
Hawkins, J.	G/19654	Pte.
Hawkins, J. W.	G/4209	Pte.
Hawkins, L. C.	G/8561	Pte.
Hawkins, R.	G/18618	L/Cpl.
Hawkins, W. J. S.	L/9574	Pte.
Hawksworth, E.	G/15941	Pte.

APPENDIX II.

Hawksworth, G.	L/11443	Sgt.	Head, R.	265006	Sgt.
Hawney, C. F.	G/8358	Pte.	Headford, R.	G/13991	Pte.
Haworth, A.	G/2260	Pte.	Healey, R. E. H.		Lieut.
Haworth, C.	G/2259	Pte.	Healy, E. P.	G/1914	Pte.
Haworth, L. E.	G/21298	Pte.	Heard, A.	G/14785	Pte.
Hay, D. T.		Lieut.	Heard, H. J.	S/71	Pte.
Hayden, G.	G/9094	Pte.	Hearn, H. J.	G/18575	Pte.
Hayes, E J.	G/23229	L/Cpl.	Hearnden, F.	G/6882	Pte.
Hayes, G. E.	G/30619	Pte.	Hearnden, H. C. S.		Lieut.
Hayes, G. S.		2nd Lieut.	Heath, A. G.		Lieut.
Hayes, J.	S/9024	Pte.	Heath, B. A.	G/775	Pte.
Hayes, J.	L/7409	Pte.	Heath, C. W.	G/7742	L/Cpl.
Hayes, J.	G/12545	Pte.	Heath, E. C.	G/2249	Cpl.
Hayes, L.	200922	Pte.	Heath, F.	G/24451	Pte.
Hayes, W.	204439	Pte.	Heath, G.	201345	Pte.
Hayhurst, J.	L/7681	L/Cpl.	Heath, H. F.	G/17825	Pte.
Hayhurst, J.	G/31695	Pte.	Heath, H. T.	G/9212	L/Cpl.
Hayler, A. W. G.	G/2660	Pte.	Heath, J. J.	L/8615	Pte.
Hayler, W. F.	G/18717	Pte.	Heath, J. V.		Lieut.
Hayler, W.	L/7458	Pte.	Heath, W. G.	G/20234	Pte.
Haylock, E. C.	S/9177	Pte.	Heatley, J. F.		2nd Lieut.
Haylor, S. J.	G/5307	Pte.	Heaton, I.		Lieut.
Hayman, H.	202208	Pte.	Heaver, R.	G/8589	Pte.
Haynes, J.	S/9076	Pte.	Hedge, A. C.	L/9448	Cpl.
Haynes, P.	G/3208	Pte.	Hedge, H.	S/92	Pte.
Hayward, A.	G/25940	Pte.	Hedgecock, A. T.	G/5364	Pte.
Hayward, B.	G/24611	Pte.	Hedgcock, J. U.	G/18448	Pte.
Hayward, C. H.	G/24706	Pte.	Hedger, G. J.	G/7596	Pte.
Hayward, E. P.	G/9253	Pte.	Hedges, A. W.	G/31474	Pte.
Hayward, F.	G/8203	Pte.	Hedges, R. T.	G/27309	Pte.
Hayward, G. H.	G/28586	Pte.	Hedges, W. C.	G/16427	Pte.
Hayward, P. E.	G/8455	Pte.	Hedges, W. G.	G/8575	Cpl.
Hayward, S.	202502	L/Cpl.	Heffer, R.	200007	Pte.
Hayward, T. P.	202445	Pte.	Hefford, J. C.	L/10037	Pte.
Hayward, W. G. L.	G/2218	Pte.	Hehir, T. W.	L/9421	Pte.
			Hele, H. L.	242176	Pte.
Haywood, F.	205633	Pte.	Hemsley, A.	G/6272	Pte.
Hazel, A.	G/29931	Pte.	Hemsley, M.	205671	Pte.
Hazel, A. W.	G/31275	Pte.	Hendra, C.	L/7131	Pte.
Hazel, C.	G/26405	Pte.	Henley, C.	G/6180	Pte.
Hazel, J. W.	G/18095	Pte.	Hennis, H.	L/7182	Pte.
Hazelden, J.	G/795	Pte.	Henrick, G.	S/6540	Pte.
Head, C.	G/18977	Pte.	Henry, C.	G/5179	L/Cpl.

APPENDIX II.

Henry, F.	TF/2092	Pte.	Hill, J.		242179	Pte.
Henshall, W. C. E.			Hill, J.		G/30745	Pte.
	G/1759	Pte.	Hill, J. H.		G/18832	Pte.
Hemmerde, C. E., *M.C.*		Lieut.	Hill, J. W.		G/18028	Pte.
Hepburn, A. E.	G/8160	Cpl.	Hiller, F. J.		G/31137	Pte.
Hepworth, C.	205334	Pte.	Hilliard, J. F.		L/9247	Pte.
Herbert, G.	G/1659	L/Cpl.	Hillier, J.		G/940	Pte.
Heron, T.	G/8788	Pte.	Hills, A. E.		G/7259	Pte.
Herridge, R.	241343	Pte.	Hills, B. J.		G/28760	Pte.
Herrington, M.	G/6138	Pte.	Hills, E.		G/6240	L/Cpl.
Herritt, J.	G/19516	Pte.	Hills, J.		S/9014	Pte.
Hewitt, A. G.	G/19837	Pte.	Hills, R. H.		G/8870	Pte.
Hewlett, G. L.	G/10603	Pte.	Hills, T.		G/12814	Pte.
Hews, H.	G/7387	Pte.	Hills, W.		G/4	Pte.
Hibben, A. A.	S/9086	Pte.	Hills, W.		G/18610	Pte.
Hibben, A. V., *M.M.*			Hills, W. J.		G/11850	L/Cpl.
	G/15325	Pte.	Hillsden, B. D.		202923	Pte.
Hibbert, J.	201558	Cpl.	Hinchcliffe, W.		L/7522	Pte.
Hibbett, F.	L/8520	Pte.	Hind, A.		G/31559	Pte.
Hickingbottom, C. G.			Hind, T. L.		G/18168	Pte.
	G/29673	Pte.	Hind, W. G.		G/11234	Pte.
Hickmore, P.	L/7605	Cpl.	Hinge, H.		TF/549	Pte.
Hickmot, S. R.		2nd Lieut.	Hinkley, H.		240100	Pte.
Hicks, T. H.	L/9403	Pte.	Hinks, F.		G/983	L/Cpl.
Hickson, R. H.	205635	Pte.	Hinton, J.		L/10611	Pte.
Hider, F. J.	G/4948	Pte.	Hirchfield, H. J., *D.C.M.*			
Higgins, A. S.	L/10941	Pte.			G/2073	Sgt.
Higgins, G.	G/6658	Pte.	Hiseman, W.		G/24286	L/Cpl.
Higgins, J.	G/20100	Pte.	Hissep, J.,*M.M.*		S/168	Pte.
Higgs, E.	G/23257	Pte.	Hoad, W. A.		201092	Pte.
Higgs, E.	G/2520	Pte.	Hoadley, A. G.		S/665	Sgt.
Higham, T. W.	G/9734	L/Cpl.	Hoadley, H. G.			
Highgate, C. E.	L/8856	Pte.			TR/10/40431	L/Cpl.
Highgate, T. J.	L/10061	Pte.	Hoadley, H. H.		L/8155	Sgt.
Hilder, A. P.	240671	Pte.	Hoadley, J.		G/2286	Pte.
Hilder, M. J.	G/23134	Pte.	Hoadley, R.		G/12080	Pte.
Hill, E. J.	G/17623	Pte.	Hoadley, W.		G/6461	Pte.
Hill, F. E.	L/9169	Pte.	Hobbs, A. B.		G/4159	L/Cpl.
Hill, G.	G/9363	Pte.	Hobbs, A. E.		G/18743	L/Cpl.
Hill, G.	G/1018	Pte.	Hobbs, A. E.		G/27019	Pte.
Hill, G.	205118	Pte.	Hobbs, H. M.		200102	L/Cpl.
Hill, H. B.		Lieut.	Hobday, A. S.		G/8559	Pte.
Hill, H. H.	G/27547	Pte.	Hobden, A.E. J.		G/7303	L/Sgt.

APPENDIX II.

Hobden, C.	G/163	Pte.	Hollman, J. J.	G/21551	Pte.
Hobden, P.	L/7188	Pte.	Hollman, T.	S/622	Pte.
Hobson, F. C.	G/19510	Pte.	Hollman, W.	G/4947	Pte.
Hodge, F. S.	200475	Sgt.	Hollman, W. H.		2nd Lieut.
Hodge, G.	201290	Pte.	Holloway, A.	203474	Pte.
Hodge, L. C.		2nd Lieut.	Holloway, W.	G/1780	Pte.
Hodges, D. A.		2nd Lieut.	Holman,T.P.E.	G/8270	Pte.
Hodges, W. H.	L/8872	Sgt.	Holmans, A. G.	G/4996	Pte.
Hodgkin, F.	L/10555	Pte.	Holmden, T. J.	G/2207	Pte.
Hodgkin, L.	L/9863	L/Cpl.	Holmwood,A.T.	G/1044	Pte.
Hodgkinson, G. A.			Holness, A. T.,	*M.M.*	
	G/6068	L/Cpl.		G/8399	L/Sgt.
Hodgkinson, H.	G/19743	Pte.	Holness, W. P.	G/31471	Pte.
Hodson, W.	G/2284	L/Sgt.	Holt, F. W.	G/1612	Pte.
Hoffman, C. F.	G/11500	Pte.	Holt, W.	G/8315	Pte.
Hogan, D.	L/9439	Pte.	Holyer, F. S.	G/7655	Pte.
Hogben, A. F.	G/18446	Pte.	Homan, J.H.W.	G/19351	Pte.
Hogben, L. S.	G/6707	Pte.	Homes, B.	G/31522	Pte.
Hogdon, W.	S/817	Sgt.	Homes, C.	G/2726	Pte.
Hogg, F.	G/19424	Pte.	Homes, E. C.	G/15298	Pte.
Holden, E.	G/1831	Pte.	Homes, E. H.	G/18624	Pte.
Holden, F.	G/12208	Pte.	Homes, F.	TF/4621	Pte.
Holden, G. E.	G/2101	Pte.	Homes, H. F.	G/1887	Pte.
Holden, V., *D.S.O.*, *M.C.*		Major.	Homes, R. H.	G/28313	Pte.
Holdgate, A. G.	G/20188	Pte.	Homes, W.	G/31696	Pte.
Holdgate, W. J.	G/18833	Pte.	Homes, W.	G/16846	Pte.
Holdin, W.	S/745	L/Cpl.	Homewood, W. L.		
Holdstock, H.	G/506	Pte.		G/8228	Pte.
Hole, E.	G/18652	Pte.	Homewood, W.	G/25367	Pte.
Holkham, C.	G/18609	Pte.	Honess, F.	G/15515	Pte.
Hollamby, B.	G/1027	L/Cpl.	Honeysett, A.	G/4876	Cpl.
Holland, A. J.	G/11183	Pte.	Honeysett, S.	G/4877	Cpl.
Holland, F. J.	G/13125	Pte.	Honeysett,W.H.	G/23627	Pte.
Holland, J. R.	G/18087	L/Sgt.	Hook, A.	G/13394	Pte.
Holland, R.	G/1003	Pte.	Hook, A.	G/1696	Pte.
Holland, R. B.		Capt.	Hook, H.	L/6501	Pte.
Hollands, S. A.	S/9180	Pte.	Hook, T. W.	G/2604	Pte.
Holliday, F. J.	G/10353	L/Cpl.	Hook, W. J.	202111	Pte.
Hollis, A.R.W.	G/10768	Pte.	Hooker, A.	G/8978	Pte.
Hollist, A.	G/19275	Pte.	Hooker, A. W.	G/15401	Pte.
Hollman, F. A.	G/2104	Pte.	Hooker, H. J.	*M.M.*	
Hollman, H.	S/312	Pte.		G/67	Sgt.
Hollman, H. F.	G/51229	Pte.	Hooper, A. L.	G/24487	Sgt.

539

APPENDIX II.

Hooper, F. W.	G/23598	L/Sgt.	Houghton, J. S.			Pte.
Hooper, G. J.	G/10814	Pte.	Hounslow, F.		201735	L/Sgt.
Hooper, W. H.	G/18834	Pte.	House, R. E.		G/16647	L/Sgt.
Hope, A.	G/11209	Pte.	Hovey, H.		L/9090	Pte.
Hope, G. D.	G/11445	Pte.	How, F.		G/18744	Pte.
Hope, P.	L/10752	Pte.	Howard, C. W.		S/1238	Pte.
Hoper, A.	S/317	Sgt.	Howard, E.		S/8737	Pte.
Hopgood, T. W.	G/714	Pte.	Howard, H. J.		G/11405	Cpl.
Hopgood, T. C.	G/6966	Pte.	Howard, H. W.		G/21190	Pte.
Hopkins, C. E.	G/24989	Pte.	Howard, J.		G/5216	Pte.
Hopkins, W.	G/258	Pte.	Howard, J.		202617	Pte.
Hopkins, W. D.	G/30930	Pte.	Howard, L. W., *M.M.*			
Hopper, H.	G/30260	Pte.			G/25982	Sgt.
Hopwood, A. E.	G/20346	Pte.	Howard, P. G.		G/1504	Cpl.
Hopwood, M.	G/16528	Pte.	Howden, E. G.		G/11607	Sgt.
Horlock, A. G.	G/17027	Pte.	Howe, E.		L/9618	Pte.
Horlock, G.	G/8967	Pte.	Howe, L.		G/10828	Pte.
Horn, W. H.	S/1132	Pte.	Howe, T.		G/21324	Pte.
Hornblow, F.	L/7726	Pte.	Howell, E.		G/28635	Pte.
Hornby, S. H.	G/1788	Cpl.	Howell, F.		G/16460	Pte.
Hornby, W.	G/29704	Pte.	Howell, H. S.		L/7939	Pte.
Horne, J. J.	G/4402	Pte.	Howell, N. B.			Lieut.
Horne, W.	G/31564	Pte.	Howell, R. O.		G/28375	Pte.
Horner, A. H.	G/30759	Pte.	Howes, A. E.		G/1783	Cpl.
Hornsby, A.	G/30620	Pte.	Howes, H.		205688	Pte.
Hornsley, A.W.	G/31524	Pte.	Howes, W.		G/3679	Pte.
Horton, A.	202800	Pte.	Howes, W. S.		G/2341	Cpl.
Horton, F.	202624	Cpl.	Howett, C.		200746	Pte.
Horton, J. T.	G/23723	Pte.	Howick, J.		S/8108	Pte.
Horsley, J. E.	G/7021	Pte.	Howlett, A. H.		G/744	Pte.
Horsley, W.	L/7381	Pte.	Howlett, F. C.		G/20510	Pte.
Horswell, C.	G/31801	Pte.	Howlett, R. P.		204012	L/Cpl.
Hoskins, A. J.	G/18127	Pte.	Howlett, S. E.		G/16875	L/Cpl.
Hoskins, H. G.	L/6595	Pte.	Howson, A. E.		L/8463	Cpl.
Hoskins, H. J.	G/1671	L/Cpl.	Howson, J. A.		G/2383	Pte.
Hostettler, A.E.	G/1457	Pte.	Hubble, A. E.		L/10896	Pte.
Hotchkiss, R.H.	G/20185	Pte.	Hucks, C. G.		G/6783	Pte.
Hotham, F. H.		Major.	Hucks, W.		G/8946	Pte.
Hougham, B. W., *M.C.*		Capt.	Hudson, A. E.		G/25867	Pte.
Hougham,W.H.	G/29559	Pte.	Hudson, A. E.		G/9435	Pte.
Houghbow, J.	204209	Pte.	Hudson, G. T.			2nd Lieut.
Houghton, E. T.	G/24828	Pte.	Hudson, W.		242187	Pte.
Houghton, H.	S/224	Pte.	Hughes, E.		G/432	Pte.

APPENDIX II.

Name	Number	Rank
Hughes, E. E. V.	202093	Pte.
Hughes, G.	S/5805	Pte.
Hughes, J.	202257	Pte.
Hughes, J. H.		2nd Lieut.
Hughes, L.	241601	Pte.
Hughes, R.	G/18025	Pte.
Hughes, T.	G/24814	Pte.
Hulbert, G.	S/1142	Pte.
Hulbert, T. G.	L/11740	Pte.
Hull, H. W.	205040	Pte.
Hull, J.	G/3709	Pte.
Hulme, J. W.	G/9587	Pte.
Hulme, W. R.	G/31697	Pte.
Humbersbone, H. S.	L/10058	Pte.
Humble, D.	G/184	Pte.
Hummel, A.	G/7683	Pte.
Humphrey, A. J.	L/10444	Pte.
Humphrey, C.	L/9914	Pte.
Humphrey H.E.	G/7654	Pte.
Humphrey, J.	G/16980	Pte.
Humphrey, T.	G/30929	Pte.
Humphrey, W.A.	G/25227	Pte.
Humphrey, W.J.	240258	Pte.
Humphreys, A.J.	G/31035	Pte.
Humphreys, T. W.	G/17523	Cpl.
Humphries, C. H.	G/11436	Pte.
Humphries, J.	S/8633	Pte.
Humphries, W. H. J.	G/9996	Pte.
Hunt, A. W.	G/1112	Pte.
Hunt, E.	L/7442	L/Sgt.
Hunt, E.	G/9054	Pte.
Hunt, E. H.	205329	Cpl.
Hunt, F.	242422	Pte.
Hunt, F. H.	G/8289	Pte.
Hunt, G.	G/19404	Pte.
Hunt, G.	G/3197	Pte.
Hunt, J.	TF/2020	Pte.
Hunt, J. H.	G/2585	Pte.
Hunt, S.	241241	Pte.
Hunt, W. R.	G/24449	Pte.
Hunt, W. T. O.	G/29735	Pte.
Hunter, A. C.	G/29945	Pte.
Hunter, E. W.	L/10299	L/Cpl.
Hunter, J.	G/1392	Sgt.
Hunter, T. H.	TF/130	Sgt.
Hunter, W.	G/1824	Pte.
Hunter, W. S.		2nd Lieut.
Huntingdon, M. J.	S/8151	Pte.
Hurd, J.	G/5907	Pte.
Hurley, E. F.	L/8524	L/Cpl.
Hurrell, C.	G/10605	L/Cpl.
Hurren, G.	L/6699	Pte.
Hurst, C. W.	G/19517	Pte.
Hurst, E.	241031	Sgt.
Hurst, R. A.	G/11045	Pte.
Hurt, F. E.	G/10819	Pte.
Hurven, J. E.	S/1179	Pte.
Husband, W.	205470	Pte.
Huse, C. F.	G/11835	Pte.
Hussey, E. G.	G/16599	Pte.
Hutchings, S. J.	G/21284	L/Cpl
Hutchings, T.B.	L/7749	Pte.
Hutchinson, A. T.	G/31472	Pte.
Hutchinson, E. W.	G/13311	Pte.
Hutchinson, G.	205624	Pte.
Hutchinson, J.G.	G/2539	Pte.
Hutchinson, W. E.	G/7861	Pte.
Hutley, S.	G/10974	Cpl.
Huxstep, J.	G/12744	Pte.
Hyde, F. C.		Lieut.
Hyde, S. P.	G/5024	Pte.
Hymers, T. H.	L/9156	Sgt.
Hyne, H. C.	G/8931	Cpl.
Igglesden, W.	L/6796	Pte.
Ince, A.	G/24821	Pte.
Indge, A. C.	S/228	Pte.
Indge, F. T.	L/5719	Pte.

APPENDIX II.

Name	Number	Rank
Ingatt, F. C.	G/3729	Pte.
Ingles, F.	241275	Pte.
Ingram, F. E.	G/28771	Pte.
Ingram, G.	S/1205	C.Q.M.S.
Ingram, H.	G/19428	Pte.
Inkpen, W.	G/4809	Pte.
Innes, S.	G/13457	Pte.
Innes, W. J.	G/17519	Pte.
Innocent, E. J.		Lieut.
Inns, J.	G/31138	Pte.
Ironmonger, I.	G/2774	L/Cpl.
Irons, H. H.	G/9809	Pte.
Isaacs, W. J.	242049	Pte.
Isted, A. E.	G/1795	Pte.
Ives, A.	S/9130	Pte.
Izard, W. J.	G/704	Pte.
Izzard, E.	G/11805	Pte.
Izzard, H. H.	200587	Sgt.
Jackman, W. H.	241378	Pte.
Jackson, A.	G/21307	Pte.
Jackson, E.	G/15895	Pte.
Jackson, E. J.	G/17963	Pte.
Jackson, F. H.	203764	Pte.
Jackson, G. B.	L/7747	Cpl.
Jackson, G. E.	G/19429	Pte.
Jackson, H.	G/23008	Pte.
Jackson, J.	G/19430	Pte.
Jackson, J. A.	G/20290	Pte.
Jackson, S.	L/9867	Pte.
Jackson, T.	G/6468	Pte.
Jackson, T.	G/6255	Cpl.
Jackson, W. B.	G/21300	Pte.
Jackson, W. R.	L/10889	Pte.
Jacobs, A. J.	G/7775	Pte.
Jacobs, A. L.	206330	Pte.
Jacobs, B. H.	G/28528	Pte.
Jacobs, G.	G/9618	Pte.
Jacobs, M.	G/23624	Pte.
Jacquet, F. J.	S/174	Pte.
Jakeman, E. C.	G/11185	Pte.
Jakes, F. G.	G/10606	Pte.
Jakings, H.	G/17627	Pte.
James, A.	L/8886	Pte.
James, A. H.	G/24588	Pte.
James, E. A.	203146	C.Q.M.S.
James, E. E.	G/29371	Pte.
James, F. H.	202206	Pte.
James, W. A.	L/9970	Pte.
James, W. J.	241294	Pte.
Jameson, G. A.	L/6543	Pte.
Jameson, S. M.	G/18836	Pte.
Jamieson, J.	G/3264	Pte.
Janes, H., *M.M.*	G/10701	Pte.
Janman, A. G.	G/1522	L/Cpl.
Jaquerey, P.	G/5175	Pte.
Jardine, A.	G/10371	Pte.
Jarrett, R. G.	G/28589	Pte.
Jarvis, C. W. B.		Capt.
Jarvis, D.	205924	Pte.
Jarvis, D.	G/15009	Pte.
Jarvis, J. I.	S/8821	Pte.
Jarvis, T.	G/1598	Pte.
Jay, D. C.	G/18302	Pte.
Jay, F. W.	G/31527	Pte.
Jay, W.	G/38706	Pte.
Jeeves, G.	S/285	Pte.
Jeeves, G. W.	G/1466	Pte.
Jefferies, S. C.	L/9040	Pte.
Jeffery E. T. J.	G/7656	Pte.
Jeffery, P. E.	G/12099	Pte.
Jeffrey, F.	G/12358	Pte.
Jeffrey, J.	S/8374	Pte.
Jeffrey, R.	G/16406	Pte.
Jeffs, G. A.	G/29372	Pte.
Jelf, C.	G/23934	Pte.
Jelley, W. E.	G/25213	Pte.
Jenkins, F.	G/21585	Pte.
Jenkins, H. E.	G/405	Pte.
Jenkins, H. J.	G/11579	Pte.
Jenkins, J. A.	G/2252	Pte.
Jenkins, R. C.	G/5733	Cpl.
Jenkins, T.	L/5621	Pte.
Jenkins, W.	G/30548	Pte.
Jenner, A.	G/534	Cpl.

APPENDIX II.

Jenner, E.	G/8909	Pte.
Jenner, E. J.	240818	Pte.
Jenner, E. J.	G/15627	Pte.
Jenner, H. J.	G/4791	Pte.
Jenner, J. W.	L/8319	Pte.
Jenner, W. C.	L/7541	Pte.
Jennings, C. A.	G/17626	Pte.
Jennings, F.	G/17480	Pte.
Jennings, J. J.	L/9825	Pte.
Jennings, R.	205167	C.S.M.
Jessop, A.	G/119	Pte.
Jessop, C. W. R. A.	G/8119	Pte.
Jewell, J. A.	G/5257	Pte.
Jewhurst, A. W.	L/9705	Pte.
Jewiss, H. C.	G/5128	L/Cpl.
Jiggins, H.	G/18745	Pte.
Job, B. C. K.		2nd Lieut.
Jobbins, J.	G/11196	Pte.
John, G. B.	G/7117	Pte.
Johns, C. F. H.	G/24616	Pte.
Johns, G. H.	G/1411	Pte.
Johnson, A. C.	G/9585	Pte.
Johnson, A. W.	G/18628	Pte.
Johnson, C.	G/8022	Pte.
Johnson, C. J.	L/8597	Pte.
Johnson, E.	G/10169	L/Cpl.
Johnson, E.	G/18303	Pte.
Johnson, E.	G/12148	Pte.
Johnson, E. R.	G/10557	Pte.
Johnson, E. R.	G/3580	Pte.
Johnson, F.	G/19658	Pte.
Johnson, F.	G/18677	Pte.
Johnson, G. W.	G/4787	Pte.
Johnson, H.	L/9202	Pte.
Johnson, H.	205589	Pte.
Johnson, H.	205552	Pte.
Johnson, H.	S/236	Pte.
Johnson, H. W.	TF/2161	Cpl.
Johnson, H. W.	G/26820	Pte.
Johnson, J.	G/21327	Pte.
Johnson, J.	L/10858	Pte.
Johnson, J. L., *M.M.*	G/4078	L/Sgt.
Johnson, J. W.	205472	Pte.
Johnson, N. F.		2nd Lieut.
Johnson, T.	L/7165	Pte.
Johnson, T. P.	L/10062	Pte.
Johnson, W.	205923	Pte.
Johnson, W.	G/1091	Pte.
Johnson, W. G.	240942	L/Cpl.
Johnson, W. T.	G/4204	Pte.
Jones, A.	L/4859	Pte.
Jones, A.	202352	L/Cpl.
Jones, A. S.	G/11790	Pte.
Jones, A. W. G.	L/10439	Pte.
Jones, B. A.	G/6489	Pte.
Jones, C.	G/39512	Pte.
Jones, C.	G/1923	Pte.
Jones, C. S.	G/12873	Pte.
Jones, D.	G/3438	Pte.
Jones, D. C.	G/24809	Pte.
Jones, E.	L/6014	Pte.
Jones, E.	G/27450	Pte.
Jones, E. G.	G/24617	Pte.
Jones, E. J.	L/10279	L/Cpl.
Jones, E. M.	G/353	Pte.
Jones, F.	G/109	Pte.
Jones, F. A.	G/30590	Pte.
Jones, F. C.	G/20296	Pte.
Jones, F. T.	S/479	L/Cpl.
Jones, G.	G/9172	Pte.
Jones, G.	G/10684	Sgt.
Jones, H.	G/3774	Pte.
Jones, H.	G/513	Pte.
Jones, H.	G/13356	Pte.
Jones, H. G.	S/457	Pte.
Jones, I.	L/10542	L/Cpl.
Jones, J. K.	L/5535	Pte.
Jones, M. W. W.	G/29737	Pte.
Jones, P. S.	G/31566	Pte.
Jones, R. A.	G/19561	L/Cpl.
Jones, S.	G/11269	Pte.
Jones, S.	G/18265	Pte.
Jones, S. J.		Lieut.

543

APPENDIX II.

Jones, T.	L/5647	Pte.	Kelcher, J.	202762	Pte.
Jones, W.	G/31703	Pte.	Kelly, J.	G/5332	Pte.
Jones, W.	G/861	Pte.	Kelly, J.	205430	Pte.
Jones, W. A.	G/7501	Pte.	Kelly, J. R.	S/39	Pte.
Jones, W. D.	G/3055	Pte.	Kelly, W.	G/9985	Pte.
Jones, W. D.	L/9830	Pte.	Kelsey, W.	S/9171	Pte.
Jones, W. G.	L/11783	L/Cpl.	Kember, J. H.	G/3934	Pte.
Jordan, G. E.	G/7445	Pte.	Kemery, P.	202412	Pte.
Jordan, H.	G/8750	Pte.	Kemmenoe, G.F.	G/8207	L/Cpl.
Jordan, W. E.	G/19033	Sgt.	Kemp, B.	240407	Pte.
Jordon, G. D.	G/26698	Pte.	Kemp, C. H.	G/10291	Pte.
Josceleyne, C.T.	G/12415	Pte.	Kemp, J. P.	S/8960	L/Sgt.
Josey, B.	G/15384	Pte.	Kemp, S.	G/15245	Pte.
Joslin, F. J.		Major.	Kemp, T.	L/7397	L/Cpl.
Josling, W. E.	S/8590	Cpl.	Kemp, T.	L/4904	Pte.
Joynson, J.	L/11621	Pte.	Kemp, W.	G/12672	Pte.
Judd, F.	242190	Pte.	Kemp, W. E.	G/11268	Pte.
Judd, M. S.		2nd Lieut.	Kemsley, A.	G/18933	Pte.
Judd, W. G.	203250	Pte.	Kenchatt, H.	L/11169	Pte.
Judson, E.	G/21293	Pte.	Kendall, H. A.	L/9905	Pte.
Juniper, A. G.	G/18366	Pte.	Kennard, G.	L/8883	Pte.
Jupp, A. S.	240579	L/Cpl.	Kennedy, W.	G/19115	Sgt.
Jupp, W. T.	G/7446	L/Cpl.	Kensett, H.	G/25364	Pte.
Jury, H. T.	G/99	Pte.	Kent, A.	S/8994	Pte.
Jury, J.	G/23860	Pte.	Kent, E.	G/31357	Cpl.
			Kent, H.	G/25407	Pte.
Kadwill, H. E.	G/9035	Pte.	Kent, P. E.	G/11760	Pte.
Kamester, J.	G/18923	Pte.	Kent, W.	205473	Pte.
Kane, W.	G/3424	Pte.	Kenward, F. S.	G/4738	Pte.
Kay, G.	G/21390	Pte.	Kenward, V. E. T.		
Kay, G. R.	G/39004	Cpl.		G/2754	Pte.
Kealey, A.	G/2127	Cpl.	Kerfoot, S. B.	G/20418	Pte.
Keeble, A. E.	L/9112	L/Cpl.	Kersey, J. E.	L/7619	L/Cpl.
Keeble, F. C.	G/15898	Pte.	Kersey, W. J.	L/9759	Pte.
Keeble, W.	G/27799	Pte.	Kerwood, C.	203481	Pte.
Keefe, F.	G/11517	Pte.	Kettle, P. W.	L/9024	Pte.
Keefe, R.	G/17390	Pte.	Kevan, T. J.	S/1020	Sgt.
Keel, J.	TF/2487	Pte.	Kidd, J. W.	G/8070	Pte.
Keeler, C.	G/2523	Pte.	Kight, A.	L/6719	Pte.
Keeley, G.	S/385	Pte.	Kilburn, F. H.	202008	Pte.
Keenlyside, G. F. H.		Capt.	Kilby, A.	G/16524	Pte.
Kees, G. E.	G/24558	L/Cpl.	Kiley, J. J.	G/10339	Pte.
Keily, H. C.	G/2489	L/Cpl.	Killick, F.	201161	Pte.

APPENDIX II.

Killick, T.	G/24406	Pte.	Kitchener, W.	G/8792	Pte.
Kimber, H. J.	L/9114	Pte.	Kitchingham, S.	G/1934	Pte.
King, A. F.	G/4066	Pte.	Kitsell, W. H.	G/613	Pte.
King, A. H.	G/8023	Pte.	Klein, W.	G/21361	Pte.
King, A. J.	G/31323	Pte.	Kluckner, E.	200101	Pte.
King, A. J.	G/24618	Pte.	Knapp, A. F.	G/15380	Pte.
King, C. A.	L/10051	L/Cpl.	Knapp, G. E.	G/8412	Pte.
King, E.	G/15051	Pte.	Knapp, R. F.	G/18802	L/Cpl.
King, F.	G/18304	Pte.	Kneller, A.A.F.	L/10263	Cpl.
King, F. C.	G/17837	Pte.	Knevett, G. W.	L/8881	Pte.
King, G. W.	G/9984	Pte.	Knight, A. E.	L/9925	Dmr.
King, H. B.	S/9040	Pte.	Knight, C. E.	L/9171	Pte.
King, J.	G/10028	Cpl.	Knight, E. C.	G/7321	Pte.
King, J. R. A.	G/14621	Pte.	Knight, F. E. S.	202138	Pte.
King, P. J.	T/24620	Pte.	Knight, H.	L/7974	Pte.
King, R.	G/2192	Pte.	Knight, H.	G/335	Pte.
King, S. A.	G/31158	Pte.	Knight, H.	G/19432	Pte.
King, S. E.	G/9227	Pte.	Knight, J.	G/18456	Pte.
King, T.	G/24660	Pte.	Knight, J. B.	G/18240	Pte.
King, T. W.	G/2454	L/Cpl.	Knight, J. O.		2nd Lieut.
King, W.	G/25865	Pte.	Knight, S. T.	G/24713	Pte.
King, W.	202632	L/Cpl.	Knight, W.	241618	Pte.
King, W.	202061	Pte.	Knight, W. T.	G/434	Sgt.
King, W.	G/19659	Pte.	Knott, A. J.	G/23406	Pte.
King, W.	G/30936	Pte.	Knott, D. J. V.		2nd Lieut.
King, W.	S/8917	Pte.	Knott, E. A.	G/9863	Pte.
King, W. J.	L/10118	Pte.	Knowler, G. E.	L/10483	Pte.
King, W. T.		2nd Lieut.	Knowles, C.	242195	Pte.
Kingston, H. G.	S/8944	Pte.	Knowles, E.	G/10609	L/Cpl.
Kingswood, A.	S/350	Pte.	Knox, J. R.	G/19997	Pte.
Kinnell, J.	G/23057	Pte.	Kysh, C. J. A.		Lieut.
Kirby, F. A.	G/6452	Pte.			
Kirby, T. W.	G/6164	Pte.	Lacey, L. E.	G/6487	Sgt.
Kirby, W.	G/2863	L/Cpl.	Lacy, C.	205477	Pte.
Kirby, W. H.	G/11890	Pte.	Lacy, H. B.	G/10732	Pte.
Kirby, W. J.	G/13488	Pte.	Lacy, W. E.	203358	Sgt.
Kirkham, G. H.	G/19602	Pte.	Ladbury, W.	S/394	Pte.
Kirkham, W. L.		2nd Lieut.	Lade, T. J., M.M.	G/16162	Sgt.
Kirkpatrick, J., M.M.	G/17838	Pte.	Ladley, G.	G/20110	Pte.
Kirrage, C. I.	L/11752	Pte.	Lagden, P.	G/392	Pte.
Kitchen, C.	G/7485	Pte.	Lake, F.	G/20693	Pte.
Kitchen, L. D.	G/30231	Pte.	Lake, W. O.	L/9016	Pte.
			Laker, A.	G/17994	Pte.

APPENDIX II.

Laker, C.	240378	Pte.	Larking, E. T.	S/652	L/Cpl.
Laker, P. G.	G/18980	Pte.	Laskey, G., *M.M.*		2nd Lieut.
Lakey, M.	205191	Pte.	Latimer, H.		2nd Lieut.
Laking, L.	205896	Pte.	Latter, F. E.	G/4103	Pte.
Lamb, E. E.		2nd Lieut.	Latter, F. R.		Capt.
Lamb, F.	G/20106	Pte.	Latter, G. F.	G/28	Pte.
Lamb, J.	L/5516	Pte.	Latter, T.	G/19166	Pte.
Lamb, W.	G/23842	L/Cpl.	Latter, W. J.	265156	Sgt.
Lamb, W.	G/8620	C.S.M.	Lauchlan, R.	G/25116	Pte.
Lambe, A. W.	G/17840	Pte.	Lauder, W.	G/6613	Pte.
Lambert, E. A.	G/10086	Cpl.	Launchbury, J. F.		
Lambkin, T. O.	G/18459	Pte.		G/24624	Pte.
Lampard, A. C.	G/15569	Pte.	Laundy, J.	G/8187	Pte.
Lancaster, J. E.	G/5623	Pte.	Laurel, I.	L/5159	Pte.
Lane, E. W.	G/1301	Pte.	Laurence, R.	205476	Pte.
Lane, H.	203971	Pte.	Laurence, S.		2nd Lieut.
Lane, H. J. P.	G/79	Pte.	Lavender, C. J.	G/4061	Pte.
Lane, H. S.	L/9239	Pte.	Lavender, D.	G/9548	Pte.
Lane, P.	TF/4790	Pte.	Lavender, H. L.	204165	Pte.
Lane, R. E.	241607	Pte.	Law, C.	202197	Pte.
Lane, W.	L/6766	Pte.	Law, G. W.	G/8171	Pte.
Lane, W.	S/9180	Pte.	Law, R. A.	G/8175	Pte.
Lanfear, A. W.	G/20263	Pte.	Law, T.	G/11122	Pte.
Lang, C. G.	G/6735	Pte.	Law, W.	G/18207	L/Cpl.
Lang, E. A.	G/6736	Pte.	Law, W.	G/18722	Pte.
Lang, G.	S/525	Sgt.	Lawes, F.	L/10157	Pte.
Langdon, A. E.	G/1787	Pte.	Lawford, P. J.	S/8794	Pte.
Langdon, A. J.	G/25005	Pte.	Lawrence, A.	L/9569	L/Cpl.
Langdon, C. W.	G/34940	Pte.	Lawrence, C. C.	G/2273	Pte.
Langford, G.	L/8355	Pte.	Lawrence, C. E.	L/9024	Cpl.
Langham, W. G.	L/7935	Pte.	Lawrence, H.	L/10203	Pte.
Langley, A. E.	G/31481	Pte.	Lawrence, H.	G/38627	Pte.
Langley, E. H. W.			Lawrence, J. A.	G/6424	L/Cpl.
	G/9527	Pte.	Lawrence, J. H.	G/24790	Cpl.
Langley, H. J.	G/11528	Pte.	Lawrence, J. R.	204458	Pte.
Langridge, H.	L/10428	Pte.	Lawrence, J. W.	G/23368	Pte.
Lankester, J.	G/11713	Pte.	Lawrence, W.	G/5861	Pte.
Lannon, O.	204423	Pte.	Lawrence, W.	G/29537	Pte.
Lansdowne, H. J.	G/10980	Pte.	Lawson, C. D. N.		2nd Lieut.
Lapham, H. E.	L/10211	Pte.	Lawson, J.	G/1419	Pte.
Large, C. R.	G/23474	Pte.	Lawson, S.	G/2838	Pte.
Lark, F. W.	G/17839	Cpl.	Layer, E. W.	240710	Pte.
Larkin, P. E.	G/1865	Cpl.	Layton, F.	G/30973	Pte.

APPENDIX II.

Layton, H.	G/3960	Pte.	Lettington, F.	G/6426	Pte.
Leach, B.	G/5025	Pte.	Leverett, H. J.	G/17422	Pte.
Leach, C. E.	G/8752	L/Cpl.	Levett, L. A.	G/3624	Pte.
Leach, G.	203419	Pte.	Levett, R. H.		2nd Lieut.
Leakey, W.	G/1639	Pte.	Levette, C.	G/2356	Pte.
Leaney, G.	L/5232	Cpl.	Levins, W. H.	240620	Sgt.
Leaney, G. W.	G/5102	Pte.	Levison, G.	G/1717	L/Cpl.
Leaney, J.	G/31351	Pte.	Levitt, A.	L/8951	Pte.
Learner, G.	G/3019	Pte.	Levitt, G.	G/8569	C.S.M.
Leatherdale, D. R.		2nd Lieut.	Lewin, E. C.		Lieut.
Le Bean, J.	G/2497	Pte.	Lewin, F. H., $M.C.$		Capt.
Lee, A. H.	242425	Pte.	Lewin, F. H.	G/4001	Pte.
Lee, C.	G/10332	Pte.	Lewington, A.W.	G/1897	Sgt.
Lee, C. A.	G/19400	Pte.	Lewinstein, H.		2nd Lieut.
Lee, F.	TF/3630	Cpl.	Lewis, A.	G/3765	L/Cpl.
Lee, G. H.	G/20529	Pte.	Lewis, C.	G/19947	Pte.
Lee, G. J.	G/25345	Pte.	Lewis, C.	G/30943	Pte.
Lee, H.	L/7443	Pte.	Lewis, C. J.	G/31120	Pte.
Lee, H. T.	G/14505	Pte.	Lewis, D. E.	G/4673	Pte.
Lee, J.	S/1934	Pte.	Lewis, E.	204485	Pte.
Lee, T.	G/2011	Pte.	Lewis, E. G.	G/15012	Pte.
Lee, W. S.	G/15443	Pte.	Lewis, E. J.	G/15956	Pte.
Leece, J.	G/31707	L/Cpl.	Lewis, F.	G/30550	Pte.
Leek, A.	203558	Pte.	Lewis, F. D.	G/24864	Pte.
Leeming, H.	G/31705	Cpl.	Lewis, G.	G/17459	Pte.
Lees, W. T.	202799	Pte.	Lewis, G. R.	G/3342	Cpl.
Leete, P. J.	G/30972	Pte.	Lewis, J.	G/3418	Pte.
Legard, G. B.		Capt.	Lewis, P. H.	G/8538	Pte.
Legge, F.	205854	Pte.	Lewis, R.	G/2021	Pte.
Legge, R.	G/3436	Pte.	Lewis, S.	G/17957	Pte.
Leggett, C. J.	203549	Sgt.	Lewis, T. R.	G/28559	L/Cpl.
Leggett, F.	G/11002	Pte.	Lewis, W. A.	L/7526	Pte.
Leitch, G.	G/19742	L/Cpl.	Lewis, W. A.	G/18116	Cpl.
Lend, J.	L/10860	L/Cpl.	Lewsey, W. A.	G/18571	Pte.
Lengthorn, T.	G/1006	Pte.	Life, S.	G/23561	Pte.
Lennie, W.	G/17374	Pte.	Lilley, A. J.	G/11937	Pte.
Lenning, J.	G/45	Pte.	Lilley, C.	G/11723	Pte.
Lenoir, H. E. T.	G/31045	Pte.	Lilley, H. A.	G/1413	Pte.
Lenton, J. W.	G/18267	Pte.	Lilley, W.	G/21556	L/Cpl.
Leon, F.	202125	Pte.	Limley, J.	242201	Pte.
Leonard, J.R.L.	G/13827	Pte.	Lincoln, T. J.	G/3233	Pte.
Lester, G. L.	G/25980	Pte.	Lind, A. J.	L/9069	Pte.
Lettington, F.	G/4184	Pte.	Lindley, J.	205642	Pte.

APPENDIX II.

Lines, G. J. F.	S/9036	Sgt.	Lomax, C. L.	G/18843	Pte.
Lines, H. C.	G/27812	Pte.	Long, A. R.	L/5842	Pte.
Lines, J. J.	205557	Pte.	Long, C. L.	G/18602	Pte.
Linfield, G. F.	G/4640	Pte.	Long, F. R.	G/21558	Pte.
Linge, J., M.M.	G/518	Pte.	Long, H.	G/12966	Pte.
Linge, L. E.	G/2225	Pte.	Long, H.	G/2096	Pte.
Link, W.	205576	Pte.	Long, T. I.	G/11316	Pte.
Linn, J. T.	205149	Pte.	Long, W.	G/15444	Pte.
Linnell, W.	G/1008	Pte.	Long, W. J.	G/5048	Pte.
Lipscombe, J.	200999	Sgt.	Longbottom, W.	G/30768	Pte.
Lipscombe, J.	G/16851	Pte.	Longhurst, A. R.	G/9059	Pte.
Lipscombe, S.	G/6512	L/Cpl.	Longhurst, J.	G/5268	Pte.
Lister, J.	G/7648	Sgt.	Longhurst, L. N.	G/17633	Pte.
Litten, F. C. P.	G/19281	Pte.	Longley, J.	G/9642	Pte.
Little, C. R.	G/18460	Pte.	Longman, C. F.	G/2902	Pte.
Little, E. F.	G/29538	Pte.	Longuehaye, J. S.		2nd Lieut.
Little, J.	G/16538	Pte.	Lonsdale, J. W.	G/1158	Pte.
Little, J.	204607	Pte.	Loosely, A. G.	G/28966	Pte.
Little, J.	202411	Pte.	Lord, S. G.	L/10551	Pte.
Little, T., M.M.	G/18410	Pte.	Lorimer, W. S.	G/8938	Pte.
Little, W.	G/9577	Pte.	Lott, H.	G/10880	Pte.
Little, W. A.	G/1802	Pte.	Loughery, G.	L/9148	Pte.
Littleboy, F. G.		Lieut.	Loveday, H.	G/18844	Pte.
Livesey, R. W.	G/6277	Pte.	Lovegrove, C.	S/657	Pte.
Livingstone, D. C.	G/24562	Pte.	Lovelace, R. D. W.		2nd Lieut.
Llewellyn, W. E.	S/692	Sgt.	Lovell, A.	G/8206	L/Cpl.
Lloyd, A.	G/1826	Pte.	Lovell, B.	G/21123	Pte.
Lloyd, A. V.	S/264	Pte.	Lovell, F.	G/1915	L/Cpl.
Lloyd, F.	S/9201	Pte.	Lovell, W. S.		2nd Lieut.
Lloyd, J.	G/31154	Pte.	Lowe, A. H. S.	242241	Pte.
Lloyd, J.	205123	Pte.	Lowe, C. J.	G/8645	Pte.
Lloyd, R.	S/9287	Pte.	Lowe, F. W.	G/26378	Pte.
Lloyd, T.	L/10684	Pte.	Lowe, W.	G/2939	Pte.
Loader, H.	G/4588	Pte.	Lower, E. J.	204619	Pte.
Loames, A. J.	G/1082	Pte.	Lownds, J. T.	G/20107	Pte.
Lock, C. R.	G/11676	Pte.	Loyner, H. W.	G/18266	Pte.
Lock, J. J.	L/10830	Pte.	Lucas, A.	L/8370	L/Cpl.
Locke, G. H.	G/18842	Pte.	Lucas, B. H.	G/38	Pte.
Lockett, A. G.	G/30710	Pte.	Luck, A. R.	G/24891	Pte.
Lockley, F. J.	G/20128	Cpl.	Luck, J.	L/8959	Pte.
Loeber, W. E. M.	204225	Cpl.	Luck, N. A.		2nd Lieut.
Loft, A.	G/5718	Pte.	Luckhorst, A.	G/8850	Pte.
Logan, H. H.		Capt.	Luckie, A.	G/339	Pte.

APPENDIX II.

Lucking, H. G.	G/18161	Pte.
Luckman, W.	G/2098	Cpl.
Lucy, T.	S/3328	Pte.
Luddenham, T. G.	L/11143	Pte.
Luesley, E. J.	G/8990	Pte.
Luff, H. T.	G/1337	Pte.
Lumb, J. E.	L/11660	Pte.
Lunn, C. H.	L/8554	L/Cpl.
Lunn, E. J.	205099	Pte.
Lusted, G.	G/24415	Cpl.
Lusted, J. S.	G/5512	Pte.
Lusted, W. J.	G/1354	L/Cpl.
Luxford, C.	G/7349	Pte.
Luxon, J. H.	G/6805	Cpl.
Luxton, M.	241233	Pte.
Lynds, R. W.	G/24508	Pte.
Lynham, A. S.	G/8988	Cpl.
Lyon, A.	G/14624	Pte.
Lyons, H. E.	L/8863	Pte.
Lyons, R. W.	G/6018	Pte.
Macaulay, E.	200425	Pte.
Macdonald, W.	G/2167	Pte.
Mace, H. O.	G/24740	Pte.
Macey, E. W.	G/24775	Pte.
Macintyre, W.D.	G/1762	Pte.
Mackelden, B.A.	G/6667	Pte.
Mackenzie, S.	L/10707	Pte.
Mackenzie, W. J. B.	G/4593	Pte.
Mackey, J.	204436	Cpl.
Mac Nicol, D. O.		Lieut.
Madgwick, G.	G/26423	Pte.
Magrath, S.	G/24402	Pte.
Magson, E.	G/30975	Pte.
Maguire, F. W.	G/8425	Pte.
Maindonald, E. W.	G/21018	Pte.
Mainwaring, J.	203034	Pte.
Makepeace, A.A.	G/15738	Pte.
Malcolm, G. P.	G/20193	Pte.
Malins, E. A.	G/5793	L/Cpl.
Mallyon, L.	G/23588	Pte.
Maloney, J. D.	S/298	Pte.
Malpass, C. E.		Capt.
Mange, E. G.	G/18238	Pte.
Manges, G.	G/15119	Pte.
Mankelow, H. C.	G/18982	Pte.
Manketelow, C. A.	G/15694	L/Cpl.
Mankey, A.	G/2066	Pte.
Mankilow, W., M.M.	G/656	Pte.
Manktelow, B.	G/3892	Pte.
Manktelow, G. T., M.M.	G/2132	Cpl.
Manley, C. P. H., M.C.		2nd Lieut.
Manley, H. D.	G/21428	Pte.
Mann, H.	G/6661	Pte.
Mann, H. G. C., M.C.		2nd Lieut.
Mann, W.	G/23626	Pte.
Mannering, J.	G/11205	Pte.
Manning, A.	G/30236	Pte.
Manning, G.	G/16141	Pte.
Manning, H.	L/7430	Pte.
Manning, J.	L/8831	L/Cpl.
Mansbridge, J.H.	G/25291	Pte.
Mansell, W.	G/1480	Pte.
Mansfield, G. T.		2nd Lieut.
Mansfield, W. J.	G/8130	Sgt.
Mant, T.	G/4027	Pte.
Manuel, W. C.	G/29377	Pte.
Maple, H.	G/1456	Pte.
Mapp, J.	S/8329	Pte.
Marchant, D. T.	L/11440	Pte.
Marchant, F.	201053	Cpl.
Marchant, F. G. W.		2nd Lieut.
Marchant, P.	G/543	Pte.
Marchant, R.F.J.	G/9309	L/Cpl.
Mardell, W. T.	G/25931	Pte.
Mark, M. C.	G/5620	Pte.
Markham, J. T., M.M.	S/424	C.S.M.
Marks, A. W.	L/7234	Cpl.
Marks, H.	G/20538	Pte.

APPENDIX II.

Markwick, H.	200550	Pte.
Markwick, J.	202801	Pte.
Marlow, V. T.	G/8759	Pte.
Marsden, A. M.	G/11909	Pte.
Marriott, J. A.	G/3699	Cpl.
Marsh, A. W.	G/2610	Cpl.
Marsh, C. S.	266283	Pte.
Marsh, E. H.	G/15600	Pte.
Marsh, F. S.	G/21019	Pte.
Marsh, F. W.	G/25224	Pte.
Marsh, J.	G/25358	Pte.
Marsh, J.	G/19213	Pte.
Marsh, M. *M.M.*	G/8641	Pte.
Marsh, R. H.		2nd Lieut.
Marsh, R. W.	G/658	Sgt.
Marsh, S.	G/25320	Pte.
Marsh, W.	G/19334	Pte.
Marsh, W. H.	G/12584	Pte.
Marshall, J.	G/6778	Cpl.
Marsland, C. F.	G/18161	Cpl.
Martin, A.		2nd Lieut.
Martin, A. H.	L/10417	L/Cpl.
Martin, C.	G/18468	Pte.
Martin, C.	G/3838	Pte.
Martin, C. H. H., *M.M.*	G/7570	Pte.
Martin, D.	240812	Sgt.
Martin, D.	G/23123	Pte.
Martin, D.	241249	Pte.
Martin, E.	G/23589	Pte.
Martin, F.	G/7345	Pte.
Martin, F.	G/8661	L/Cpl.
Martin, F.	G/10558	Pte.
Martin, G.	S/946	Pte.
Martin, G.	L/11609	L/Cpl.
Martin, G. H.	L/9119	Pte.
Martin, H.	G/10709	Pte.
Martin, H. A.	G/20537	Pte.
Martin, H. C.	TF/2591	Pte.
Martin, H. J.	G/31347	Cpl.
Martin, H. J.	242077	L/Cpl.
Martin, H. W.	L/8447	L/Cpl.
Martin, J.	L/8878	Pte.
Martin, J.	G/7745	Pte.
Martin, J.	L/7875	Pte.
Martin, J.	G/15985	Pte.
Martin, J. F. A.	G/9754	Pte.
Martin, J. S.	G/8304	Pte.
Martin, J. W.	G/2142	Cpl.
Martin, R.	G/9516	Pte.
Martin, R.	S/981	Pte.
Martin, R. J.	G/20240	Pte.
Martin, T. G.	G/11934	Pte.
Martin, W. A.	G/10041	Pte.
Martin, W. E.	G/16342	Pte.
Martin, W. G.	203792	Pte.
Martin, W. J.	G/6744	L/Cpl.
Martyn, E. S.		Capt.
Masey, A. V.	G/17760	L/Cpl.
Maskell, W. J.	L/9686	L/Cpl.
Maslin, H.	L/4158	Sgt.
Mason, C.		2nd Lieut.
Mason, F. C.	202264	Cpl.
Mason, G.	S/9135	Pte.
Mason, H. W. K.	G/24570	Pte.
Mason, J.	G/2758	Pte.
Mason, T.	G/10133	Pte.
Mason, W.	G/4049	Pte.
Massey, W. L. S.	205330	Cpl.
Masters, A.	G/1554	Pte.
Masters, W. J.	G/10432	Pte.
Mather, A. G.	G/5207	Pte.
Mather, G.	203116	L/Cpl.
Matheson, R. K.		2nd Lieut.
Matthews, A. F.	G/30772	Pte.
Matthews, C. J.	G/7637	Pte.
Matthews, E.	G/1739	Pte.
Matthews, E.	G/5211	Pte.
Matthews, F.	G/2896	Pte.
Matthews, F.	L/10245	Pte.
Matthews, H.	202727	Pte.
Matthews, H. L.	G/17634	Pte.
Matthews, J. B.		Capt.
Matthews, J. C.	G/17498	Pte.
Matthews, M. L. W.		Capt.
Matthews, O.	G/5563	Pte.

APPENDIX II.

Maundrell, S.A.	G/9137	Pte.	McGarry, B.	S/220	Pte.
Maunton, A.	G/934	Cpl.	McGrath, J.	G/1123	Pte.
Maunton, W. C.	G/4805	Pte.	McGregor, R.H.	G/5557	Pte.
Maxwell, G. F.	G/9989	Cpl.	McIntyre, W.W.	G/17855	Pte.
May, C. W.	TR/10/40094	Sgt.	McKay, R. C.	G/7265	Pte.
May, F.	G/7815	Pte.	McLeod, J.	G/11438	Pte.
May, G.	G/5658	Pte.	McLinden, E.	242215	Pte.
May, R. J.	241342	Pte.	McNeil, W. J.	L/9927	Pte.
Mayatt, H. W.	G/903	Pte.	McPherson, T.	L/9255	Pte.
Mayatt, L.	G/361	Cpl.	McQueen, A. A.	G/7634	Pte.
Mayes, G. H.	204152	Pte.	McVicar, M.	G/5333	Pte.
Mayger, R. J.	G/4740	Pte.	Meacock, A.	G/5218	Pte.
Mayhew, F. L.	G/28487	Pte.	Mead, O.	G/39069	Pte.
Maynard, G. W.	G/3133	Pte.	Mead, P.	G/19277	Pte.
Maynard, H.	G/17467	Pte.	Mead, W.	G/15376	Pte.
Maynard, H. L.	G/10299	Pte.	Meaden, A.	G/19356	Pte.
Maynard, S.	G/8244	L/Cpl.	Meader, A.	G/27131	Pte.
Maynard, T.	G/1134	Pte.	Meades, S.	G/2950	Pte.
Mayne, W. H.	L/10198	Pte.	Meadows, E. H.	G/24721	L/Cpl.
Mayne, W. W.	G/5249	Pte.	Meadows, G.W.	G/20116	Pte.
Mayor, A.	G/3056	Pte.	Meakins, R. W. S.		2nd Lieut.
Mays, F.	G/15925	Pte.	Mears, F.	201409	Pte.
McCall, A. J.	G/3107	Pte.	Meayers, R. C.	202937	Pte.
McCallum, J., M.M.	G/1616	Cpl.	Medcalf, D.	G/15239	Pte.
			Meddings, C. J.	G/18846	Pte.
McCarthy, F.	G/27655	Pte.	Medhurst, A.	G/332	Pte.
McCarthy, F. M.	S/14	Pte.	Medhurst, F. A.	G/2164	Pte.
McCarthy, J.	L/8350	Pte.	Medhurst, J.	G/8625	L/Cpl.
McCarthy, J.	G/8879	Pte.	Medhurst, S.	G/4168	Pte.
McCarthy, P.	G/11592	Pte.	Medhurst, W.	S/980	Pte.
McClenaghan, G. M.		Capt.	Medhurst, W. T. S.	G/20694	Pte.
McConnachie, J.	G/16391	Pte.	Meehan, J.	G/5884	Pte.
McConnell, E.A.F.	241372	Pte.	Meeks, J.	S/8728	Pte.
McCormack, J.	G/9139	Pte.	Meggs, A. W.	G/1147	Cpl.
McCullock, H.	G/31249	Pte.	Melbourne, E. H.	L/9599	Pte
McDonald, A.	G/11392	Pte.	Meldrum, H.	241020	Pte.
McDonald, P.	G/5331	L/Cpl.	Melloy, P.	G/18558	Pte.
McDougall, A. E.	L/10770	Boy.	Mepham, P. W.	G/1283	Pte.
McEvoy, P. J.	G/16994	Pte.	Mepham, W. A.	L/9500	Pte.
McFarlane, D.	L/6339	Sgt.	Mercer, A. R.	G/7747	L/Cpl.
McFarlane, J.M.	G/29	L/Cpl.	Mercer, A. R.	201291	Pte
McFerran, W.	G/12231	Pte.	Mercer, H.	200373	Pte.
			Mercer, H. F.	G/5939	Pte.

551

APPENDIX II.

Mercer, J.	G/4855	Pte.	Miller, J. J.	G/3153	Pte.
Mercer, T.	S/726	Pte.	Miller, R. H.	G/97	Sgt.
Mercer, W. F.	L/9836	Pte.	Miller, W.	G/24863	Pte.
Merrett, H.	G/9361	Pte.	Milligan, W.J.H.	L/8784	L/Cpl.
Merrin, F.	G/5522	Pte.	Millington, C. G.	205658	Pte.
Merritt, H. J.	G/23149	Pte.	Millington, F. W.		
Merritt, H. R.	G/17850	Pte.		G/298	Cpl.
Merritt, P. J.	G/4065	Pte.	Mills, A.	G/31418	Pte.
Merritt, W.	S/4956	Pte.	Mills, A. A. A.	205690	Pte.
Merton, P. O.	G/1774	Pte.	Mills, C. T.	G/5856	Pte.
Message, F. C.	G/12309	Pte.	Mills, D.	G/1874	Pte.
Mewes, S. C.	G/2448	Sgt.	Mills, E. T.	G/11156	Sgt.
Mewett, F. C.	G/18918	Cpl.	Mills, F.	G/15593	Pte.
Michell, A.	2nd Lieut.		Mills, G. D.	G/15451	L/Cpl.
Middlemiss, A.	G/19612	Pte.	Mills, H.	G/2920	Pte.
Middleton, A.	G/17851	Pte.	Mills, H. J.	G/11053	Pte.
Middleton, D.J.	G/8468	Sgt.	Mills, J. C.	203458	Pte.
Middleton, E.	G/20115	Pte.	Mills, L. W. H.	204232	Pte.
Middleton, F. G.	203965	Pte.	Mills, P. H.	G/7365	Pte.
Middleton, L.	G/7046	Pte.	Mills, P. T.		Capt.
Middleton, S.A.	G/11251	Cpl.	Mills, R.	S/2449	Sgt.
Milborn, A.	G/21195	Pte.	Millyard, G. T.	G/20117	Pte.
Miles, A.	L/10027	Pte.	Milne, S. J.	205404	Pte.
Miles, A. J.	G/10716	Pte.	Milne, W.	G/31018	Pte.
Miles, C.	G/31852	Pte.	Milner, A.W.A.	G/4334	Pte.
Miles, F. A.	G/7473	Pte.	Milner, P.	205639	Pte.
Miles, F. J.	G/4773	L/Cpl.	Milton, J.	240984	Pte.
Miles, G.	G/15929	Pte.	Mindenhall, C. H.	203500	Pte.
Miles, G.	G/15388	Pte.	Minnett, H.	G/27348	Pte.
Miles, G. H.	2nd Lieut.		Minter, S.	205853	Pte.
Miles, H.	G/23569	L/Sgt.	Mires, A, H., *D.C.M.*		
Miles, H. R.	G/19593	L/Cpl.		L/94517	Pte.
Miles, J.	G/12546	Pte.	Mires, B.	S/7501	Cpl.
Milledge, J. F.	G/3678	Pte.	Mitchell, A.	S/106	Sgt.
Milledge, T. A.	G/13033	L/Cpl.	Mitchell, A. H.	G/417	Pte.
Millen, W. G.	G/26	Cpl.	Mitchell, C.	G/2208	Pte.
Miller, B.	L/7367	Sgt.	Mitchell, D.	S/9400	L/Cpl.
Miller, C. H.	G/7862	L/Cpl.	Mitchell, H.	L/9045	Pte.
Miller, D.	TF/4938	Pte.	Mitchell, H. A.	200834	Sgt.
Miller, F.	G/14927	Pte.	Mitchell, H. J.	G/6841	Sgt.
Miller, F. A.	G/3946	Pte.	Mitchell, H. S.		Lieut.
Miller, G.	G/5414	Pte.	Mitchell, R. H.	G/31364	Pte.
Miller, J.	G/11951	Pte.	Mitchell, W.	G/16991	Pte.

APPENDIX II.

Mitchell, W.	G/20195	Pte.
Mitchell, W. J.	242207	Pte.
Mitchell, W. J.	G/17847	Pte.
Mizon, G. W.	G/18044	Pte.
Moat, C. O.	G/15302	Pte.
Moat, W. A.	G/15582	Pte.
Mockridge, E. J.	242204	Pte.
Molyneaux, E.	G/7082	Pte.
Monckton, A.	L/7158	Pte.
Monckton, O.	G/1681	L/Cpl.
Monckton, P. S.	G/31282	Pte.
Mond, B. A.	G/18331	L/Cpl.
Monday, C. S.	S/8670	Pte.
Money, G. J.	G/8837	Pte.
Monk, L. J.	G/41113	Pte.
Monk, W. G. E.	G/10955	Pte.
Monkton, A. E.	G/17134	Pte.
Montague, G.	241193	Pte.
Monypenny, P. B. S. G.		Lieut.
Moody, A.	G/12159	Pte.
Moody, A. E.	L/8037	Cpl.
Moody, F.	L/6506	Pte
Moody, T. A.	L/7141	Pte.
Moon, C., M.M.	G/653	Pte.
Moon, H. W.	G/241	Sgt.
Moon, J.	G/1420	Sgt.
Moon, S.	G/63	Pte.
Moore, A.	G/6758	Pte.
Moore, C.	G/8145	Pte.
Moore, H. E.	G/118	Pte.
Moore, J.	L/5267	Pte.
Moore, W.	G/838	L/Cpl.
Moore, W. J.	G/27540	Pte.
Moores, A. E.	G/12051	Pte.
Moores, J. T.	G/5343	Pte.
Moorhouse, W.		Lieut.
Moreton, H.	S/8578	Pte.
Moreton, R.	L/7474	Pte.
Morford, E. J. W.	G/19169	Pte.
Morgan, A. E.	G/8114	Pte.
Morgan, A. J.	G/11003	Pte.
Morgan, A. T.	G/4055	Pte.
Morgan, C. E.	L/8567	Pte.
Morgan, E.	G/10466	Pte.
Morgan, H. A.	242097	Pte.
Morgan, R.	G/3785	Pte.
Morgan, T	G/8518	Pte.
Morley, A. L.	G/12407	Pte.
Morley, J. T.	G/19434	Pte.
Morley, J. W.E.	G/26425	L/Cpl.
Morphett, W.	G/5006	Cpl.
Morris, A.	L/9057	Pte.
Morris, A. C.	G/13346	Pte.
Morris, C. E.	L/8567	Pte.
Morris, E.	G/16813	Pte.
Morris, E. J.	G/9322	L/Cpl.
Morris, G.	G/1237	Pte.
Morris, G.	G/23365	Pte.
Morris, G.	G/21331	Pte.
Morris, J. B.	G/28561	Pte.
Morris, J. W.	203441	Pte.
Morris, J. W.	241695	Pte.
Morris, T. A.	G/31359	Pte.
Morris, W J. S.	200356	Pte.
Morrish, W. E.	L/7999	C.Q.M.S.
Morrison, G. A.	G/5866	Pte.
Morrison, G. E.	G/23138	Pte.
Morrison, H. F.	G/10833	Pte.
Morrison, J. F.	L/8827	Sgt.
Morrow. A., M.M.	G/11101	Cpl.
Morshead, J.	G/5293	Pte.
Mortby, A. H.	L/9329	Pte.
Morten, E. T.	G/19440	Pte.
Mortimer. H.	G/1424	Pte.
Mortlock, A. G.	G/939	Pte
Morton, A.	205634	Pte.
Morton, J. H.	G/18847	Pte.
Morton, J. W.	G/27470	Pte.
Mose, W. H.	205666	Pte.
Moseley, F. J., M.M.	G/28350	Cpl.
Moseley, R. G.	S/437	Pte.
Moses, N.	G/18395	Sgt.
Moss, G. H.	G/17846	Pte.
Moss, J.	L/6625	Pte.

553

APPENDIX II.

Mothersill, J. N.	2nd Lieut.	
Mott, W. J.	L/8408	Pte.
Moulding, E. J.	241347	Pte.
Moulton, E.	G/14697	Cpl.
Moulton, R. H.	G/2559	Pte.
Mount, E. W.	204584	Pte.
Mowson, G. H.	G/13231	Pte.
Moxey, S. C.	G/1819	Pte.
Moyce, H.	L/10816	Pte.
Moyce, J.	241760	Pte.
Mudge, A. E.	G/24627	Pte.
Muggeridge, J.	S/203	Pte.
Muggleton F. R.	G/6556	Pte.
Muggridge, E. F.	L/9712	Sgt.
Muggridge, H. G. C.	G/24488	Cpl.
Muggridge, H. O.	G/5314	Pte.
Mullarkey, J. J.	L/11592	Sgt.
Mullen, J.	G/4381	L/Cpl.
Mullin, J.	G/18724	L/Cpl.
Mummery, W.	L/8437	Pte.
Muncaster, F.	G/18211	Pte.
Muncey, H. H.	G/823	Cpl.
Muncey, H. J.	TF/2122	Pte.
Munday, J.	G/4255	Pte.
Munday, G.	G/2426	Pte.
Munday, W. H.	G/26259	Pte.
Mundy, W. J.	G/9171	Pte.
Munn, W.	G/5079	Pte.
Munroe, E.	L/10863	Pte.
Murkett, F. W.	G/31805	Pte.
Murking, R. T.	G/5354	Pte.
Murphy, F. H.	G/25977	Cpl.
Murphy, J. C.	L/9980	Pte.
Murrant, W. H. E.	L/8388	L/Cpl.
Murrell, W. J.	L/9087	Pte.
Mussell, E. S.	L/7471	Sgt.
Mussell, J.	L/9245	Cpl.
Myers, F.	G/19999	Pte.
Myers, F.	G/18208	Pte.
Myers, J.	S/271	Pte.
Myers, S. G.	G/10460	Pte.
Myner, T. A.	L/5570	Sgt.
Myson, H.	G/4147	Pte.
Nall, M.	G/19717	Pte.
Napper, J.	G/31283	Pte.
Nash, A. J.	204486	Pte.
Nash, C. W.	G/11892	Pte.
Nash, H.	G/11306	Pte.
Nash, H.	G/20664	Pte.
Nash, R. J.	G/4771	Pte.
Nash, W. G.	204429	L/Cpl.
Nash, W. J. S.	242286	Pte.
Neal, A.	G/19152	L/Cpl.
Neal, F.	G/8773	Pte.
Neal, G. A.	G/13471	Pte.
Neal, P. V.	G/8663	Pte.
Neat, R. H.	G/25282	Pte.
Neck, A. J.	S/896	Pte.
Neenan, J. J.	G/1733	Pte.
Negus, W. J.	G/18091	Pte.
Neil, W. G.	G/3037	Cpl.
Neill, W.	G/8640	Pte.
Nevard, P.	G/24723	Pte.
Neville, N.A.O.	G/20546	Pte.
Newbold, P.		2nd Lieut.
Newbrook, E. J., D.C.M.	L/5706	C.S.M.
Newell, H.	S/9053	Pte.
Newell, H. W.	L/10370	Pte.
Newell, P. W.	L/9948	Pte.
Newell, W. G.	L/9093	Pte.
Newick, F.	G/31368	Pte.
Newland, E.	G/17393	Pte.
Newling, W. L.	G/11704	Pte.
Newman, A. C.	L/9928	Pte.
Newman, F.	G/8473	Sgt.
Newman, J.	G/3130	Pte.
Newman, L.	G/2216	Sgt.
Newport, E. J.	G/17862	Pte.
Newport, W. H.	G/18212	Pte.
Newstead, T.	G/10785	Pte.

APPENDIX II.

Newton, S. H.	G/31308	Cpl.
Newton, W.		Capt.
Nichol, A.	203124	Pte.
Nicholas, O. R.		Lieut.
Nicholas, S. N.	G/18213	Pte.
Nicholas, W.	G/24629	Pte.
Nicholls, C.	G/11145	Pte.
Nicholls, C. J.	L/8814	Cpl.
Nicholls, G.	S/8677	Pte.
Nicholls, H.	G/2004	Pte.
Nicholls, H.	G/1449	Pte.
Nicholls, H.A.E.	L/9197	L/Cpl.
Nicholls, T. L.	L/8988	Pte.
Nicholls, W.	TF/2496	Pte.
Nichols, E. N.	G/16198	Pte.
Nichols, J. H.	204510	Pte.
Nicholson, J.	L/6582	Pte.
Nicoll, E. S., *M.C.*		Capt.
Nightingale, W. A.	G/6803	Cpl.
Nind, A. L.	L/9604	Pte.
Nixon, J.	L/8202	Pte.
Nixon, J.	G/4383	Pte.
Noakes, F.	L/9778	Sgt.
Nobbs, W. E.	L/10716	Pte.
Noble, A.	G/5410	Pte.
Noble, C.	L/8176	Pte.
Noble, C. H. T.	240873	Cpl.
Noble, G.	L/8125	Dmr.
Noble, G.	L/6507	Pte.
Noble, H.	L/8032	Pte.
Nokes, C. E.	G/2591	Pte.
Norburn, W., *M.M.*	G/770	Cpl.
Norbury, A.	204374	Pte.
Norfolk, G. E.	G/17203	Pte.
Norman, C.	G/24872	Pte.
Norman, E.	G/23272	Pte.
Norman, E. J.	G/30999	Sgt.
Norman, G. H.	G/18120	Pte.
Norman, H. E.	L/9979	Pte.
Norman, M.	G/23617	Pte.
Norman, T. S.	G/30572	Pte.
Norman, W.	G/5942	Pte.
Norman, W. H.	G/1763	Pte.
Norman, W. H. G.	G/5940	Pte.
Norris, A.	G/27402	Pte.
Norris, C. R.	G/9495	Pte.
Norris, F. C.	201015	Pte.
Norris, F. E. E.		Lieut.
Norris, K. A. A.		2nd Lieut.
Norris, T. C. J.	G/10778	Pte.
Norris, W. J.	G/20548	L/Cpl.
Norris, W. W.	G/497	Pte.
North, A.	240747	Cpl.
North, J. L.	G/20549	Pte.
Northey, M. A.		Lieut.
Norton, H. J.	G/18472	Pte.
Nottingham, T.	G/18683	Pte.
Nowell, F. H.	G/5472	Pte.
Nudds, A. V.	S/8991	L/Cpl.
Nunn, E. A.	G/24368	Pte.
Nunn, H.	241038	Pte.
Nurden, H.	L/7357	Sgt.
Nute, C.	203001	Pte.
Nuttall, N.	L/10749	Pte.
Nye, A.	G/7659	Pte.
Nye, H. S.	G/18475	Pte.
Nye, J. B.	G/7834	Pte.
Nye, S. J.	G/700	Sgt.
Oakes, T. A. V.	S/8889	Pte.
Oakley, H. J.	G/11123	Pte.
Oakley, S. B.	G/17395	Pte.
Oaten, J.	G/2328	Pte.
Oates, N.	241278	Pte.
Oates, T. V.	G/19090	L/Cpl.
Obbard, J.	G/26221	Pte.
Obee, W. T.	L/8216	Pte.
Oborn, W. H.	G/24232	Pte.
O'Callaghan, J.	L/10353	Pte.
O'Connell, D. J.	202777	Pte.
O'Connor, B. J.	293367	Pte.
Oddy, S.	G/19876	Pte.
O'Donohoe, M. G.	L/8592	Sgt.
Ogan, G. J.	G/20550	Pte.
Ogden, W. G.	L/10041	L/Cpl.
O'Grady, A. W.	G/4933	Pte.

555

APPENDIX II.

O'Grady, J.	G/9915	Pte.	Packer, W. J.	S/786	Pte.
Older, O.	G/1288	Pte.	Packham, A. S.	G/1977	Pte.
Oldham, R.	G/5345	Pte.	Packham, E. W.	G/19095	Pte.
O'Leary, L. R.	203571	Sgt.	Packham, J.	L/8353	Pte.
Oliver, G.	G/1622	Pte.	Packman, B.	G/2736	Pte.
Oliver, G. R.	G/20153	Pte.	Padbury, H. J.	G/31854	Pte.
Oliver, H. W.	G/20154	Pte.	Padgham, L.	G/21119	Pte.
Oliver, H. W.	G/6902	Pte.	Page, A. H.	G/18383	Pte.
Olney, E.	G/24630	Pte.	Page, A. W.	G/8513	Pte.
Onions, W.	G/4315	Pte.	Page, E.	G/18486	Pte.
Oram, W. E.	G/573	Pte.	Page, E. W.	G/9109	Pte.
Orchard, W. S.	G/15484	Pte.	Page, F.	G/15848	Pte.
Orme, W.	G/2725	Pte.	Page, G.	G/5016	Pte.
Osborne, B.	205305	Sgt.	Page, H.	G/14791	Pte.
Osborne, C. R.	G/908	Pte.	Page, H. F.	L/8565	Pte.
Osborne, H. C.	S/1109	Pte.	Page, J.	L/8807	Pte.
O'Shea, J.	L/6259	Pte.	Page, J.	G/31053	Pte.
Osmotherly, A.	G/6015	Pte.	Page, J. O.	G/17875	Pte.
Ottley, F. W.	L/9984	Pte.	Page, L. J.	G/747	Pte.
Outred, H.	G/2296	Pte.	Page, W.	L/7342	Pte.
Outred, L.	G/12227	Pte.	Page, W.	G/18069	Pte.
Ovenden, N.	G/696	Cpl.	Page, W.	G/11152	Pte.
Ovendon, T.	G/28247	Pte.	Pain, A. G.	G/31726	L/Cpl.
Overbury, E. H.	204406	Pte.	Paine, C.	L/9646	Pte.
Oversly, J. O.	G/31721	Pte.	Paine, C. W.	L/11195	Pte.
Overy, R. W.	G/233	Pte.	Paine, F. G.	G/30516	Pte.
Owen, C.	L/668	L/Cpl.	Paine, F. P.	G/19297	Pte.
Owen, C. F.	G/550	Pte.	Paine, W. W.	M.M.	
Owen, D.	S/9061	Pte.		G/7395	Pte.
Owen, G. P.	S/9004	Pte.	Painter, P. W.	G/185	Cpl.
Owen, J. H.	G/13357	Pte.	Palfrey, F. G.	G/17642	Pte.
Owen, W. J.	204459	Pte.	Pallot, A.	S/9212	Pte.
Owers, W. T.	G/7456	L/Cpl.	Palmer, A. V.	201106	Pte.
Oxborrow, W.E.	G/39152	Pte.	Palmer, A W.	200090	C.S.M.
Oxbrow, J.	G/5987	Pte.	Palmer, E. G.	G/30504	Pte.
Oxenbridge, G. H.	TF/3644	Pte.	Palmer, F.	241326	Pte.
Oxlade, A.	G/24631	Pte.	Palmer, F. C. Q.	G/18051	Pte.
Oxley, C.	G/7660	Pte.	Palmer, G.	G/8165	Pte.
			Palmer, G. J.	L/10389	Pte.
Pace, G., M.M.	S/156	Sgt.	Palmer, J.	G/24731	Pte.
Packard, C R. J.	G/4340	L/Cpl.	Palmer, O.	203264	C.S.M.
Pack-Beresford, C. G.		Major.	Palmer, T.	G/28502	Pte.
Packer, F. G.	L/7715	Pte.	Palmer, V. J.	G/6641	Cpl.

APPENDIX II.

Palmer, W.	G/18358	Pte.
Palmer, W. E.	G/21203	Pte.
Pankhurst, F.	G/10943	L/Cpl.
Pankhurst, W.	L/10765	Pte.
Pannett, T., M.M.	L/10385	Cpl.
Panting, A.	G/8097	Cpl.
Panton, F.	205618	Pte.
Panton, F. J.	G/28254	Pte.
Paradine, G. H.	G/16048	Pte.
Parfett, S.	G/11348	Pte.
Parish, J. H.	G/15020	Pte.
Parke, A., M.M.	206342	Pte.
Parker, A. E. L.	G/18153	Sgt.
Parker, A. W.	G/28112	Pte.
Parker, E.	G/18606	Pte.
Parker, H.	G/23711	Pte.
Parker, P. H.	G/4077	Pte.
Parker, R. H.	G/9942	Sgt.
Parker, R. J.	S/252	Pte.
Parker, S.	241344	L/Cpl.
Parker, W. C.	G/11688	Pte.
Parker, W. J.	G/7347	Pte.
Parkes, A.	G/3806	Pte.
Parkes, W. U.	G/8113	Pte.
Parkin, A. H.	205698	Pte.
Parkinson, L.	G/19124	Cpl.
Parkinson, W.	G/17510	Pte.
Parks, G.	G/493	Pte.
Parks, E. W.	G/24912	Pte.
Parks, H.	200413	Pte.
Parmenter, A.	G/16319	Pte.
Parmenter, P.	S/8634	Pte.
Parnall, W. L.	203005	Pte.
Parncutt, J. G.	TF/5432	Pte.
Parnell, A. W.	G/38702	Pte.
Parr, E.	G/18308	Pte.
Parramore, C.	G/11965	Pte.
Parrin, A.	TF/2316	Pte.
Parris, F.	201427	Pte.
Parrott, F.	L/9091	Pte.
Parrott, F.	240435	Pte.
Parry, C. J.	G/20555	Pte.
Parry, H.	G/24566	Pte.
Parsons, A.	G/5495	Pte.
Parsons, A. S.	202234	Pte.
Parsons, C. R.	G/19792	Pte.
Parsons, E. L.	G/2665	Pte.
Parsons, H.	G/38683	Pte.
Parsons, J.	G/28137	Pte.
Parsons, R. E.	L/5973	Pte.
Partlett, F. A.	G/956	Pte.
Pascoe, C. T.	G/10602	Cpl.
Pashby, T. G.	L/9611	Pte.
Pashley, W. S.	G/9127	Cpl.
Patching, A.	G/31141	Pte.
Paterson, G.	G/6964	Pte.
Patey, G.	G/24728	Pte.
Patmore, H.	240901	Pte.
Patmore, R.	G/3083	Pte.
Patston, W.	L/6451	Pte.
Pattenden, A.	L/8477	Pte.
Pattenden, A.	G/12969	Pte.
Pattenden, C.	G/8741	Pte.
Pattenden, T. E.	200558	Sgt.
Pattenden, W. E.	201253	Pte.
Paul, A. E.	G/3118	Pte.
Paveley, H. G.	G/2854	Pte.
Paveley, H. M.	G/31778	Pte.
Pavey, A. S.	205165	Pte.
Pavier, W. J.	G/945	Pte.
Paxton, F. F.	G/6362	Pte.
Paxton, W. E.	204609	Pte.
Pay, A. J.	G/29681	Pte.
Pay, T.	L/8476	Pte.
Payliss, F. W., M.M.	G/1962	Pte.
Payne, A.	G/4700	Pte.
Payne, C. B.	G/21753	Pte.
Payne, C. H.	G/18889	Cpl.
Payne, C. W. T.	203539	Pte.
Payne, E.	L/5980	Pte.
Payne, E.	G/196	Cpl.
Payne, E. T.	I./7948	L/Cpl.
Payne, T. E.	L/9693	Pte.
Payne, T. R.	G/708	Pte.
Payne, W.	G/2276	Pte.

APPENDIX II.

Payne, W. H.	S/1012	Pte.
Payton, C. M.		Lieut.
Peachey, H. J.	G/8748	Pte.
Peacock, F.	266945	Pte.
Peacock, J.	G/25500	Pte.
Peacock, J. T.	L/9278	Sgt.
Peacock, W.J. C.	G/24727	Pte.
Pearce, A. E.	G/21204	Pte.
Pearce, C. A.	G/23873	Pte.
Pearce, G. H.	G/12118	Pte.
Pearce, L. A.	L/10338	Pte.
Pearce, P. V.	204666	Pte.
Pearce, R.	G/19535	Pte.
Pearce, T. W.	240908	Pte.
Pearce, W. J.	G/9406	Pte.
Pearman, G. A.	L/9542	Pte.
Pearn, A. S.	242052	Pte.
Pearse, A.	205697	Pte.
Pearson, A.	G/12817	Pte.
Pearson, A. E.	G/7813	Pte.
Pearson, A. I.	205653	Pte.
Pearson, A. J.	G/26556	Pte.
Pearson, E. J.	G/5073	Cpl.
Pearson, F. C.	G/19829	Pte.
Pearson, G., D.C.M.	S/1086	C.S.M.
Pearson, G.	G/2966	Pte.
Pearson, H. G.	204004	Pte.
Pearson, J.	G/4013	Pte.
Pearson, J.	G/17985	Pte.
Pearson, W.	G/16617	L/Cpl.
Pearson, W.	G/14511	Pte.
Peat, W. G.	G/438	Pte.
Peck, C.	G/6652	Pte.
Peck, E.	G/5388	Pte.
Peddlesden, W., M.M.	G/1441	Pte.
Peerless, R.		Pte.
Peet, A.	G/19534	Pte.
Peglar, H. S.		2nd Lieut.
Pegrum, H. R.	G/29647	Pte.
Peirce, R.	L/7989	Pte.
Pell, F. G.	202650	Pte.
Pelling, E. J.	G/18615	Pte.
Pelling, F.	G/23912	Cpl.
Pembroke, J. F.	L/1189	Pte.
Pembroke, J.	S/8763	Pte.
Pendlebury, V.W.	G/17868	Pte.
Penfold, J. E.	G/6361	Pte.
Penfold, J. J.	L/10690	Pte.
Penfold, L. E.	G/12000	Pte.
Penfold, P. E.	G/6338	L/Cpl.
Penfold, W. R.	G/3828	Pte.
Penhale, H. W.	G/9368	Cpl.
Penn, C. J.	L/6695	Pte.
Penn, G.	G/30780	Pte.
Penn, L.	266157	Pte.
Pennett, A. E.	G/2522	Pte.
Penney, F. W.	G/10665	Pte.
Penney, W. H.	L/4558	C.S.M.
Penny, H.	L/7528	Pte.
Pentecost, A.	G/1257	Pte.
Pentecost, L. D.	203344	Pte.
Penwill, J. E.	G/28078	Pte
Pepper, B. L.	G/7224	Pte
Pepper, C. G.	L/9369	Pte.
Pepper, W. G.	242524	L/Cpl.
Perchard, C.	G/23193	Sgt.
Percival, F.	L/7594	Pte.
Percival, R.	G/5286	Pte.
Percival, W. T.	G/19744	Pte.
Perfect, G.	G/23154	Pte.
Perfitt, F. H.	L/10190	Pte.
Perkins, A.	S/8824	Pte.
Perkins, C.	S/9333	Pte.
Perkins, E. V.	241350	Pte.
Perkins, H.	S/1079	Pte.
Perkins, J. H.	G/25917	L/Cpl.
Perks, A.	G/19538	Pte.
Perrin, A.	G/869	Pte.
Perrin, H. J.	G/4759	Pte.
Perrin, W.	G/310	Pte.
Perry, A.	L/6698	Pte.
Perry, J., M.M.	G/25615	Pte.
Perry, L.	G/18774	Sgt.
Peskett, T.	L/10382	Pte.

APPENDIX II.

Peters, F.	G/10644	Pte.
Peters, J.	L/7630	Pte.
Peters, W. M.	S/146	Pte.
Peterson, F.	G/8628	Pte.
Pethers, W.	G/9429	Pte.
Pett, A.	G/21135	Pte.
Pettifer, H.	G/20123	Pte.
Pettifer, T.	G/13418	Pte.
Pettitt, A. H.	G/1069	Pte.
Pettitt, F. B.	G/10553	Pte.
Pettitt, J.	G/11984	Pte.
Phelps, W.	S/9188	Pte.
Phelps, W.J. H.	G/763	Pte.
Phillips, A. E., *M.M.*	G/21522	L/Cpl.
Phillips, C.	G/31155	L/Cpl.
Phillips, C. W.	241714	Pte.
Phillips, E. W.	L/6172	Pte.
Phillips, G. W.	L/9182	L/Cpl.
Phillips, J.	G/17865	Pte.
Phillips, M.	G/3440	Pte.
Phillips, W. A.	G/9588	Pte.
Phillips, W. C. O.		Capt.
Phillips, W. H.	241314	Pte.
Philpott, A J.	L/9935	L/Cpl.
Philpott, F. T.	G/39448	L/Cpl.
Philpott, H.	G/18481	Pte.
Philpott, T.	G/4795	Pte.
Philpott, W.	G/7371	Pte.
Philpott, W.	G/25322	Pte.
Philpott, W. J.	213346	Pte.
Phipps, G. E.	L/8555	Pte.
Phyall, S. E., *M.M.*	G/386	Pte.
Pickard, A. H.	206366	Pte.
Pickard, W. V.	S/8576	Pte.
Pickering, H.	L/6486	Sgt.
Pickering, J. S.	G/5927	Pte.
Picket, W. C. S.	205722	L/Cpl.
Pickett, J.	G/7226	Pte.
Pickles, A.	G/21329	Pte.
Pidoux, G.	G/6496	Pte.
Pierce, G.	204621	Pte.
Pierce, H., *M.M.*	G/1957	L/Cpl.
Pierce, P. T.	G/4812	Pte.
Piercy, C. F.	241064	Pte.
Piercy, F. H.	202272	Pte.
Piggott, A.E. G.	L/9858	Pte.
Piggott, D. T., *M.C.*		Lieut.
Piggott, H.	203272	Pte.
Piggott, W., *M.M.*	G/23271	Cpl.
Pigott, F., *M.M. & Bar*	202235	Pte.
Pigott, R. B.	G/18482	Pte.
Pike, T. H.	202065	Pte.
Pike, J. H. C.	G/9366	Pte.
Pilcher, L. G.	G/7639	Pte.
Pilcher, H. J.	G/18396	Sgt.
Pillman, R. L.		Capt.
Pinchback, F.	G/2091	Pte.
Pinder, S. G.	G/2076	L/Cpl.
Pinion, F.	G/1353	Pte.
Pink, G. W.	L/9051	Pte.
Pink, D. S.	G/7000	Cpl.
Pinks, J. T.	L/10271	Pte.
Pinson, R.	G/134	Cpl.
Piper, C.	G/18771	Sgt.
Piper, F.	G/24298	Pte.
Piper, H.	L/9411	Pte.
Piper, J.	G/2298	Pte.
Piper, J.	G/2106	Pte.
Piper, J. J.	G/11322	Pte.
Piper, P.	G/8979	Pte.
Piper, S. J.	266206	Pte.
Pitter, J.	G/667	Pte.
Place, J.	L/10693	Pte.
Planner, W. C.	S/795	Cpl.
Plant, P. W.		2nd Lieut.
Plastow, A. G.	24701	Pte.
Pledge, H. A.	G/29512	Pte.
Pluckrose, E.	L/10137	Pte.
Plumb, M. B.	G/13474	Pte.
Plumbe, E.	21357	L/Sgt.
Plumbridge, A.	G/852	Pte.

APPENDIX II.

Pocock, H. C.	G/5417	Pte.		Potts, A.	206424	Pte.
Pocock, W. A.	L/10897	Pte.		Potts, F.	G/9161	Pte.
Poet, J. H.	G/1517	Pte.		Potts, J.	G/15976	Pte.
Poile, G. R.	G/13474	Pte.		Povey, W. F.	G/20662	Pte.
Poland, H. A.		2nd Lieut.		Powditch, C.	G/3136	Pte.
Pollard, H. L.	G/17396	Pte.		Powell, E. N.	G/8055	Pte.
Pollard, R. B.	203171	Sgt.		Powell, F. A.	G/1641	Pte.
Pollard, T.	G/21314	Pte.		Powell F. W.	L/11198	Pte.
Pollard, W. W.	G/9293	Pte.		Powell, H.	G/1010	Pte.
Polley, A. P.	G/14774	Pte.		Powell, J. W.	L/8328	Sgt.
Polley, H. J.	G/18048	L/Cpl.		Powell, P. H.	205347	Pte.
Polley, R. A.	G/7638	Cpl.		Powell, R. C.	G/6404	Sgt.
Pollitt, W.	G/10017	Pte.		Powell, T. A.	G/24807	Pte.
Pont, F.	G/7434	Pte.		Powell, W.	G/28403	Pte.
Ponting, E. A.	201079	Cpl.		Powell, W. H.	203251	Sgt.
Pook, J. H.	G/1517	Pte.		Power, E.	G/1850	Pte.
Poole, C.	241154	Pte.		Powles, C.	G/21117	Pte.
Poole, E.	G/19594	Pte.		Pownall, L. H. Y.		Lieut.
Poole, J.	G/2106	Pte.		Poynter, A.	G/7676	L/Cpl.
Poole, F. H.	L/10188	Pte.		Pracy, H. R.		2nd Lieut.
Poole, R. A.	G/466	Pte.		Pragnall, G. F.		Capt.
Pooley, S. J.	G/9247	Cpl.		Pratt, H.	G/11082	Pte.
Poolton, W.	G/21562	Pte.		Pratt, H.	G/8485	Pte.
Pope, J. J.	G/4784	Pte.		Pratt, J.	G/15859	Pte.
Pope, P.	S/782	Pte.		Pratt, J.	G/9336	Pte.
Pope, W. J.	203003	Pte.		Pratt, P.	G/11782	Pte.
Poore, A. E.	G/12361	Pte.		Pratt, W.	G/5436	Pte.
Port, G.	G/15340	Pte.		Preedy, G.	202720	Pte.
Porter, F.	G/5360	Pte.		Prentice, G.	G/18803	L/Cpl.
Porter, H. T.	18903	Pte.		Prentice, H.	G/3168	Pte.
Portfleet, A. P.	G/31331	Pte.		Press, G. W.		Capt.
Posnett, R.A.H.	G/20557	Pte.		Preston, E. J.	G/20007	Pte.
Postill, E.	G/20121	Pte.		Preston, F.	G/24726	Pte.
Postle, H.	G/7396	Pte.		Preston, L. G., M.C.		Capt.
Pott, G. W.	TF/2288	Pte.		Preston, W. S.	G/18728	Pte.
Potter, B.	205200	Pte.		Prett, M. T.	G/18484	Pte.
Potter, F. C.	G/6025	Pte.		Prettyjohn, G.	G/20656	Pte.
Potter, G. M.	G/2954	Pte.		Prevett, A. E.	G/7295	Pte.
Potter, J. A.	G/19536	Pte.		Prewer, W. J.	242219	Pte.
Potter, J. E.	G/4614	Sgt.		Price, A. E., M.M.		
Potter, S.	203485	Pte.			G/23464	Pte.
Potter, S .	G/8144	Pte.		Price, J.	G/123	Pte.
Potter, W. C.	G/6218	Pte.		Price, W.	G/3433	Pte.
Potter, W. G.	L/7914	Pte.		Prichard, A. A.	203465	Pte.

APPENDIX II.

Name	Number	Rank
Pride, W.	G/3870	Pte.
Prime, W.	G/10117	Pte.
Prior, A. G.	G/11362	Cpl.
Prior, F.	G/11368	Pte.
Prior, H.	G/16213	Pte.
Prior, H. G. R.		Lieut.
Prior, H. W.	G/29714	Pte.
Prior, R. E.	G/16243	Pte.
Prior, W.	G/18272	Pte.
Pritchard, J.	205711	L/Sgt.
Proctor, W.	L/6734	L/Cpl.
Proctor, W. H.		2nd Lieut.
Prosser, F. J.	G/3173	Pte.
Prosser, W.	G/5044	Pte.
Prout, B.	G/28019	L/Cpl.
Pryer, F. A.	G/12039	L/Cpl.
Pryke, G.	G/18949	Pte.
Pryor, H. W.	G/12373	Pte.
Pullen, A.	G/20361	Pte.
Pullen,, W.	G/20120	Pte.
Pulley, A. G.	G/1307	Pte.
Pullin, H. V.	204630	Pte.
Pulling, W.	242333	Pte.
Pulman, T.	G/2876	Pte.
Puplett, W. F.	L/9253	Pte.
Purcell, C. A.	L/10323	Pte.
Purcell, C. P.	L/9063	Pte.
Purcell, F. C.	G/3454	Pte.
Purcell, M. J.	G/5172	Pte.
Purdy, T. C.	G/9196	Pte.
Purser, J.	G/17146	Pte.
Pursey, J.	G/14569	Pte.
Purver, B. A.		Capt.
Purvis, R.	S/575	Sgt.
Puttock, A. G.	L/10096	Pte.
Pycroft, H.	G/14732	Pte.
Pye, W. H.	G/475	Pte.
Pye, W. W.		2nd Lieut.
Pyke, A. E.	L/10216	Pte.
Pyke, F. S.	241336	Pte.
Pyman, A. J. K.	240991	Pte.
Pynn, J. H.	G/3927	Pte.
Quaife, H. S.	G/9680	Pte.
Quibell, L. S.	G/9768	Pte.
Quick, J. H.	TF/4651	Pte.
Quinnell, G. H.	G/12475	Pte.
Quinnell, H.	G/4557	Pte.
Rabbeth, W. G.	G/9082	L/Cpl.
Rabey, W. T.	G/8591	Pte.
Radford, A. S.	G/15141	Pte.
Ralph, J. D.	L/10395	Pte.
Ralph, W. J.	G/12834	Pte.
Ramm, H.	G/18313	Pte.
Ramsden, J.	205490	Pte.
Randall, A.	G/2387	Pte.
Randall, C. E.	241163	L/Cpl.
Randall, G.	205180	Pte.
Randall, S. H.	L/8418	Pte.
Randall, T. A.	G/2773	L/Cpl.
Rankin, H. B.	G/3142	Pte.
Rankin, R..	D.C.M. G/1219	R.S.M.
Ransley, E.	G/18495	Sgt.
Ransom, C. J.	L/8395	Pte.
Ransom, H.	G/18489	Pte.
Ransome, E. G.	L/4921	C.S.M.
Ransome, W. F.	G/18490	L/Cpl.
Rapson, H. T.		Capt.
Rasey, T. P.	204923	Pte.
Rash, C. W.	G/17470	Pte.
Ratcliffe, P. W.	G/11807	Pte.
Ratcliffe, R. H.	G/10300	Pte.
Raven, H. G.	L/7894	Pte.
Ravenscroft, E.	G/20756	Pte.
Ray, J. W.	G/2528	Pte.
Raymond, F.	G/314	Pte.
Rayner, G. W.	S/939	Sgt.
Rayner, O. W.	G/15152	Pte.
Rayner, W. T.	G/10142	Pte.
Raynes, F.	L/9890	Pte.
Raynes, J. R.	G/4674	Pte.
Raynor, T.	G/3887	Pte.
Read, B.	G/2058	Pte.
Read, B. C.	G/5056	L/Cpl.
Read, G.	L/10578	Pte.

APPENDIX II.

Read, G.	G/17336	Pte.	Reynolds, G.	G/11779	Pte.
Read, H.	G/8649	Pte.	Reynolds, G.	203252	Pte.
Read, J. G.	242450	Pte.	Reynolds, W. T.	24227	Pte.
Read, T. W.	G/20568	Pte.	Rhind, W.	S/517	Pte.
Read, W. T.	G/12355	Pte.	Rhodes, F. C.	G/9848	Pte.
Reay, I.	G/19726	Pte.	Rice, I. S.	L/9198	Pte.
Record, V. R.	200298	L/Sgt.	Rice, W. J.	G/17653	Pte.
Redding, E. J.		2nd Lieut.	Rich, H.	G/17349	Pte.
Redford, A.	G/5173	Pte.	Rich, H.	205527	Pte.
Redford, T.	G/5528	Pte.	Richards, A.	TF/1416	Pte.
Redgrave, J. E. B.	G/17502	Pte.	Richards, A.	G/1330	Pte.
Redler, H. T.	G/10524	Pte.	Richards, D. T.	203133	Pte.
Reed, A. E.	L/9527	Pte.	Richards, G.	L/5794	Pte.
Reed, A. G.	G/21100	Pte.	Richards, G.	G/2386	Pte.
Reed, E., M.M.	G/6785	Sgt.	Richards, G. F.	G/5461	Pte.
Reed, H.	L/6002	Pte.	Richards, H. E.	G/28806	Pte.
Reed, H. G.	G/391	Pte.	Richards, L. F.	G/27370	Cpl.
Reed, W.	G/21563	Pte.	Richardson, A.	S/427	Pte.
Reeder, J. S.	201210	Pte.	Richardson, A. B.		2nd Lieut.
Rees, D.	G/31594	Pte.	Richardson, C. J.	G/7306	L/Cpl.
Reeve, C. E.	G/20172	Pte.	Richardson, E.	G/5377	L/Cpl.
Reeves, A. H.	G/11715	Pte.	Richardson E. J.	L/9473	Pte.
Reeves, F.	G/17878	Pte.	Richardson, G.	L/8302	Pte.
Reeves, H. J.	L/7767	L/Cpl.	Richardson, G.W.	205723	Pte.
Reeves, J.	S/9238	Pte.	Richardson, H. G.		
Reeves, J.	204461	Cpl.		G/18661	Pte.
Reeves, W.	L/8322	Pte.	Richardson, J.S.	G/13434	Pte.
Reffell, G. S.	G/23879	L/Cpl.	Richardson, N.	205431	Pte.
Regis, C.	S/915	Sgt.	Richardson, R.	G/6256	Pte.
Reid, D.	G/10418	Cpl.	Richardson, T. A., M.M.		
Reid, H. P.	G/10837	Pte.		G/17458	Pte.
Reilly, F.	S/1073	L/Cpl.	Richardson, W.	L/7319	Pte.
Reilly, W., M.M.	G/218	Pte.	Richardson, W. A. I.		2nd Lieut.
Relf, E. F.	G/1205	Pte.	Riches, G.	G/13278	Pte.
Relf, H. A.	G/1310	Cpl.	Riches, W. E.	G/20016	Pte.
Rennie, J.	242233	Pte.	Richmond, A.P.	G/409	Pte.
Restell, P. J. D.	L/10078	Pte.	Rickard, A.	L/6592	Pte.
Revelle, R. C.		2nd Lieut.	Rickard, J. N.	G/30981	Pte.
Rey, E. C.	204241	Pte.	Rickards, J.	G/10743	Pte.
Reynolds, B.	G/13344	Pte.	Ricketts, C.	G/28407	Pte.
Reynolds, C.	G/4141	Pte.	Ricketts, J. M.W.	203423	Pte.
Reynolds, F.	G/24263	Pte.	Ricketts, G. E.	G/5690	Pte.
Reynolds, F. J.	G/28805	Pte.	Ricks, A.	G/18494	Pte.

APPENDIX II.

Riddall, F.	G/9951	Pte.	Roberts, R. G.	G/29383	L/Cpl.	
Riddle, E.	G/19321	Pte.	Roberts, T. W.		2nd Lieut.	
Riddles, F. H.	G/8415	Pte.	Robertshaw,P.T.	G/20023	Pte.	
Ride, A.	G/24639	Pte.	Robertshaw, W.	G/20022	Pte.	
Ridge, A.	G/6438	Pte.	Robertson, G.	L/6558	Pte.	
Ridgers, J.	L/6621	L/Cpl.	Robertson, H.L.	G/18642	L/Cpl.	
Ridges, W. H.	203249	Pte.	Robertson, J.	G/18906	Pte.	
Ridgley, H. T.	G/24384	L/Cpl.	Robertson, W.	G/16389	L/Cpl.	
Ridgway, L.	240739	Cpl.	Robertson-Ross, P. M.		Capt.	
Ridley, F. W.	G/20565	Pte.	Robinson, A. A.	G/2063	Pte.	
Ridley, H.	G/4008	Pte.	Robinson, A. G.	L/9697	Cpl.	
Riess, T. G.	G/145	Sgt.	Robinson, A. H.	L/9906	Pte.	
Rigden, G. E.	G/20019	Pte.	Robinson, G.	L/9791	Cpl.	
Riggs, A. C., M.M.			Robinson, G.	L/11682	Pte.	
	L/10520	Pte.	Robinson, H.	TF/3678	Pte.	
Riggs, C. E.	G/31426	Pte.	Robinson, H.	G/192	Pte.	
Riggulsford, H. T.	L/10023	Pte.	Robinson, H.	G/18651	Pte.	
Riley, S. J.	G/18219	L/Cpl.	Robinson, H.	G/1576	Pte.	
Riley, G.	L/10701	Pte.	Robinson, H.	G/17650	Pte.	
Ringe, G.	G/2337	L/Cpl.	Robinson, H.		2nd Lieut.	
Ringland, J.	G/423	Pte.	Robinson, H. E.	G/11707	L/Cpl.	
Rippon, B. A.	205648	Pte.	Robinson, L.W.	G/177	Pte.	
Risley, E. C.	G/18732	Pte.	Robinson, W.	205644	Pte.	
Rivers, F. C.	202756	Pte.	Robinson, W. G.	G/4826	Pte.	
Rivett, E.	G/16118	Pte.	Robinson, W. J.	241811	Pte.	
Rivett, F.	202983	Pte.	Robson, A.	L/10604	L/Cpl.	
Rix, W.	G/13448	Pte.	Roche, R. J.	Major and Q.M.		
Rix, W.	G/2635	L/Cpl.	Rochester, C. W.	G/27787	Pte.	
Robbins, A. H.	G/20180	Pte.	Rodda, R.	204631	Pte.	
Robbins, H.	G/21532	L/Cpl.	Roddam, J.	G/18170	Pte.	
Robbins, W. G.	G/19737	Sgt.	Rodney, B. W.		2nd Lieut.	
Roberson, F.	L/9362	Pte.	Rodwell, R.	G/15342	Pte.	
Roberts, A.	S/9271	Pte.	Rodwell, W.	G/10275	Pte.	
Roberts, D. L.	L/10573	Pte.	Roff, G.	200603	Pte.	
Roberts, E.	G/6838	Pte.	Roffey, H.	G/17325	Pte.	
Roberts, E. J.	L/6320	Pte.	Rogers, A.	L/7281	Cpl.	
Roberts, F.	S/235	Pte.	Rogers, A.	L/6258	Sgt.	
Roberts, F. W., M.C.		Capt.	Rogers, B.	L/8373	Pte.	
Roberts, G.	G/5303	Pte.	Rogers, E. J.	G/1313	Pte.	
Roberts, H.	G/9304	Pte.	Rogers, F.	G/2869	Pte.	
Roberts, H. J.	G/10434	Pte.	Rogers, H.	L/9510	Pte.	
Roberts, J.	G/13312	Pte.	Rogers, H.	G/1245	Pte.	
Roberts, J. E.	G/24835	Pte.	Rogers, H. G.	G/24641	Pte.	

APPENDIX II.

Rogers, J. A.	G/17487	Pte.		Rowell, W.	G/13190	Pte.
Rogers, M.	G/9384	Pte.		Rowing, W. S.	S/9057	Pte.
Rogers, O. J.	L/7375	Cpl.		Rowlands, H.M.	G/7442	Pte.
Rogers, T.	G/3441	L/Cpl.		Rowlands, W.	G/20013	Pte.
Rogers, T.	G/8896	Pte.		Rowles, A. E.	G/3007	Cpl.
Rolfe, F. G.	G/4962	Pte.		Rowlston, R.	G/4758	Pte.
Rolfe, F. W.	202659	Pte.		Royal, A.	G/28940	Pte.
Rolfe, P.	G/15095	Pte.		Royle, A. W.	L/7831	Pte.
Rolfe, S.	L/6721	Pte.		Royle, J.	G/31598	Pte.
Rollins, J.	G/5146	Pte.		Royle, J. A.	G/18157	Cpl.
Rollins, J.	G/223	Pte.		Roythorne, R.	L/8154	C.S.M.
Rollins, W.	G/7268	Pte.		Ruby, J.	TF/2477	Pte.
Rollinson, A.	G/29527	Pte.		Ruck, E. W.	G/24733	Cpl.
Rolph, E. H.	G/2532	Sgt.		Ruck, W. J.	G/17545	Pte.
Romerill, A.J.H.	G/10282	Pte.		Rudall, B. A.		2nd Lieut.
Rook, S.	G/25480	Pte.		Rudd, B.	G/28852	L/Cpl.
Rookley, J.	G/17651	Pte.		Rudd, E.	203131	Pte.
Root, A.	G/18327	Pte.		Rudge, G. J. W.	G/20563	L/Cpl.
Roots, W.	S/856	Sgt.		Rudge, T. W.	S/6582	Pte.
Roper, G.	G/27006	Pte.		Ruewell, J.	G/1873	L/Cpl.
Roper, W. J.	G/3184	Pte.		Ruffie, H.	G/17648	Pte.
Roscoe, A., M.C.		2nd Lieut.		Rule, A.	TF/1976	Pte.
Roscoe, D. J.	242313	Pte.		Rumens, W. E.	G/9786	Pte.
Rose, G.	L/9356	Cpl.		Rumley, E.	G/12391	Pte.
Rose, R. R.	G/12307	Pte.		Rundle, G.	G/227	Pte.
Rose, S., M.M.	G/12053	Pte.		Russell, A. E.	G/15275	Pte.
Rose S.	G/10999	Pte.		Russell, A. N.	G/12103	Pte.
Rose S. J.	L/9331	Pte.		Russell, A. S.	203352	Pte.
Rose, W.	L/9878	Pte.		Russell, B.	L/10867	Pte.
Rose, W. H.	G/31055	Pte.		Russell, D.	L/7226	L/Cpl.
Rosendale, W.A.	L/9773	Pte.		Russell, E.	L/9385	Pte.
Rosendale, S.	L/10380	Pte.		Russell, F.	L/10664	Pte.
Ross, R. C.	G/4233	L/Cpl.		Russell, J.	205730	Pte.
Ross, W. V.		Capt.		Russell, J.	G/8031	Pte.
Rossiter, B.	G/8287	Pte.		Russell, J.	S/395	Pte.
Routledge, W.	L/7753	Pte.		Russell, J. A.	242438	Pte.
Row, N. D.	G/31785	Pte.		Russell, J. E.	206364	L/Cpl.
Rowcliffe, A.	S/8825	L/Cpl.		Russell, J. G. H. S.		2nd Lieut.
Rowden, W. H.	G/10187	Pte.		Russell, J. W.	G/6614	Pte.
Rowe, C.	G/18942	Pte.		Russell, O.	203781	Pte.
Rowe, W.	G/4903	Pte.		Russell, S. H.	G/2113	Pte.
Rowe, W. E.	G/25863	Pte.		Russell, T.	G/18500	Pte.
Rowe, W. J.	G/18499	Pte.		Russell, W.	G/6547	Pte.

APPENDIX II.

Rust, E. W.	G/321	Pte.
Ruth, W.	G/4047	L/Sgt.
Rutherford, T. T.	G/11299	Pte.
Rutley, H. W.	L/10067	L/Cpl.
Rutt, J.	G/3664	Pte.
Rutt, O.	G/28853	Pte.
Ryall, A. E.	G/24567	Pte.
Ryan, D.	G/17412	Pte.
Ryan, E. P.	L/7667	Pte.
Ryan, F. G.	S/1167	Pte.
Ryan, G.	L/10670	Pte.
Ryan, J. P.	L/8142	L/Cpl.
Ryan, M.	G/18274	Pte.
Rye, E.	G/31979	Pte.
Rye, H. J.	G/11413	Pte.
Sacker, A. A. J.	S/9110	Pte.
Sackett, R.	242237	Pte.
Saddington, G. H.	G/1435	Sgt.
Saddleton, G. F.	G/18509	Pte.
Sadler, A. J.	G/15431	Pte.
Sage, A.	L/8200	Pte.
Sage, F.	206372	Pte.
Sage, J. S.	L/10571	Pte.
Saint, R.	S/8956	Pte.
Sale, W. H.	201178	Cpl.
Sallis, A. F.	G/24743	Pte.
Salter, A. E.	G/18150	Pte.
Salter, J. W.	G/16112	Pte.
Sampson, A.	G/1942	Cpl.
Sampson, C.	G/11554	Pte.
Sampson, R.	G/1539	Pte.
Sams, A.	241677	Pte.
Sams, C.		2nd Lieut.
Samuel, G. G.		Lieut.
Samuel, W. B.	203183	Pte.
Samways, S. G.	S/674	Pte.
Sandell, L. W.	G/20767	L/Cpl.
Sanders, C. A.	G/11238	Pte.
Sanders, F.	G/28411	L/Cpl.
Sanders, F. J.	L/8203	Pte.
Sanders, S. E.		2nd Lieut.
Sandford, J.	L/8737	Pte.
Sands, E.	G/1408	Pte.
Sands, F.	G/16539	Pte.
Sands, W.	S/1150	Pte.
Sandwell, W.	G/17569	Pte.
Sansom, J. H.	G/1107	L/Cpl.
Sansom, C. J.	240920	L/Cpl.
Sansome F. S.	241703	Pte.
Santes, J.	G/2738	Pte.
Santon, J. W.	205934	Pte.
Sapey, A. C.	G/18316	Pte.
Sargeant, A. H.	G/15901	Pte.
Sargeant, J. E.	G/9681	Pte.
Sargent, S. A.	G/7646	Pte.
Sargent, W.	G/23129	Pte.
Saunders, A. J.	G/8234	Pte.
Saunders, A. V.	L/10181	Pte.
Saunders, D.	G/57	Cpl.
Saunders, E.	G/11866	Pte.
Saunders, E.	G/19098	Pte.
Saunders, F. H.	G/12322	Pte.
Saunders, J. H.	G/11614	L/Sgt.
Saunders, T. W.	G/1257	Sgt.
Saunders, W. B.	L/4607	C.S.M.
Saunders, W. H.	G/7592	Pte.
Saunderson, J.	L/10106	Pte.
Savage, J. E.	G/15269	Pte.
Saveall, G.		2nd Lieut.
Saville, A. E.	G/28914	Pte.
Saville, B.	205496	Pte.
Saward, B. L.	G/9069	Pte.
Saward, J. C.	L/7632	Sgt.
Sawford, W.	G/4987	Pte.
Sawkins, E. A.	G/5155	Pte.
Sawyer, A. B.	G/27802	Pte.
Sawyer, F. G.	G/510	Pte.
Saxby, E. J.	240823	Pte.
Sayer, H.	205088	Pte.
Sayers, J.	TF/7318	Pte.
Sayers, K. R.		Lieut.
Scading, W. J.	G/131	Cpl.
Scanlon, W.	L/10966	Pte.
Scarratt, R. L.	G/13301	Pte.

APPENDIX II.

Schofield, A.	21337	Pte.	Sears, S. J.	G/4960	Cpl.
Schofield, E. W. N.	G/2168	Pte.	Seates, J.	G/17655	
			Seddon, J. T.	G/26249	Pte.
Scholeberg, H.	G/31224	Pte.	Sedge, F. C.	G/24296	Pte.
Scholey, S.	G/597	Pte.	Seeds, W.	L/8514	Pte.
Scoffield, C. D.,	242440	L/Cpl.	Seeney, G.	G/2967	Pte.
Scotchmur, W. T.	201313	Pte.	Selby, H. J.	G/1925	Pte.
Scott, A. E. M. M.	G/23885	Pte.	Self, A. E.	G/18061	Pte.
Scott, A. T.	L/9221	Pte.	Sellen, C.	G/21130	Pte.
Scott, E. C.	205625	Pte.	Sellens, J. W.	L/6596	Pte.
Scott, G. W. H.	G/30556	L/Cpl.	Selley, J.	241230	Pte.
Scott, H.	G/13484	Pte.	Selves, J.	S/159	Pte.
Scott, J. J., M.C.		Capt.	Semark, F.	TF/2590	Pte.
Scott, J. M.	L/6613	Pte.	Sendles, W.	L/11185	Pte.
Scott, T.	G/5341	Pte.	Sessions, H. G.	G/11640	Pte.
Scott, W.	205418	Pte.	Sewell, A. G.	L/10797	L/Cpl.
Scott, W.	242315	Pte.	Sewell, C. H., V.C.		Lieut.
Scotting, R.	G/13234	Pte.	Sewell, D. C. C.		Lieut.
Scotton, E. R.	G/29386	Pte.	Sewell, H.	G/18317	Pte.
Scrace, H.	G/12175	L/Cpl.	Sexton, A. E.	G/18221	Pte.
Scriven, F.	L/6676	Pte.	Shand, H. F.	G/24492	Pte.
Scriven, W.	G/5371	Pte.	Shand, J.	L/8968	Pte.
Scudder, W. R.	S/1113	Pte.	Shambrook, J.	G/19677	Pte.
Scully, J.	L/6743	Pte.	Shannon, A.	G/6765	Pte.
Scutt, S. V.	S/897	Pte.	Sharman, E.	G/3674	Pte.
Seabrook, E. F. W.	G/28823	Pte.	Sharp, A.	G/11153	Pte.
Seager, A.	G/750	Pte.	Sharp, C.	G/18518	Sgt.
Seager, C.	L/10937	Pte.	Sharp, E.	L/6581	Pte.
Seal, G.	L/8761	Pte.	Sharp, E. T.	G/19678	Pte.
Seal, H.	G/28541	Pte.	Sharp, F.	L/5411	Pte.
Seal, J.	G/1025	L/Cpl.	Sharp H. H.	G/25947	Pte.
Seal, R. D.	S/1018	Cpl.	Sharp, J.	G/5325	Pte.
Seaman, H. R.	L/8627	Cpl.	Sharp, O. R.	L/8626	Cpl.
Seamark, W.	G/3918	Pte.	Sharp, P.	G/24465	Pte.
Seammence, F. H.	L/10025	Cpl.	Sharpe A.	G/4171	Pte.
			Sharpe, A. E.	L/10449	Pte.
Seanor, T. H.	G/31599	Pte.	Sharpe, J.	G/19551	Pte.
Searle, E.	L/8132	Pte.	Sharpe, R. S.	G/1037	Pte.
Searle, H. S.	241287	Pte.	Sharples, F.	G/4288	Pte.
Searle, W.	201115	Pte.	Sharratt, A. A.	G/7129	Sgt.
Searle, W.	G/17890	Pte.	Shattock, H. E.		Lieut.
Sears, A.	G/10508	Pte.	Shaw, A.	S/9084	Pte.
			Shaw, B.	G/23959	L/Cpl.

APPENDIX II.

Shaw, C. A.	202405	Pte.		Shorter, F. S.	G/6250	Pte.
Shaw, C. J.	G/19553	Pte.		Shorter, H. B.	G/8584	Pte.
Shaw, C. R.	G/24646	Pte.		Shorting, G.	G/2547	Pte.
Shaw, F. W.	L/9624	Pte.		Shrubb, A. T.	205062	Pte.
Shaw, F. W.	G/11794	Pte.		Shrubb, J. W.	240166	Pte.
Shaw, G. A.	203295	Pte.		Shrubsole, F.	G/10667	Pte.
Shaw, H.	G/18898	Pte.		Shufflebotham, S. H.		
Shaw, H. J.	G/9633	L/Cpl.			G/28870	Pte.
Shaw, W.	L/8260	Pte.		Shuttlewood, A. E. P.		
Shean, J.	L/7531	Pte.			G/21216	Pte.
Sheen, W.	G/1729	Pte.		Shuttleworth, H.	G/19926	Pte.
Sheldon, J.	G/17493	Pte.		Sibbald, W.	L/7524	Sgt.
Sheldon, T.	G/5490	Pte.		Sibbons, W. A. A.	G/6874	Pte.
Sheldrake, W.	TF/2134	Pte.		Sibley, F.	G/14956	Pte.
Sheldrick, E. W.	G/18348	Pte.		Silcock, J. C.	G/5709	L/Cpl.
Shelton, F.	G/9167	Pte.		Silver, G. M.	G/7067	Pte.
Shepherd, E. G.	L/8964	Pte.		Simcoe, F.	G/28864	Pte.
Shepherd, J.	G/20129	Pte.		Simes, J.	G/12427	Pte.
Shepherd, W.	G/19452	Pte.		Simmonds, F.	G/25363	Pte.
Shepherd, W. D.	242246	Pte.		Simmonds, F. J.	G/11583	Pte.
Shepherd, W. H.	G/10628	Pte.		Simmonds, W. G.	G/5064	Pte.
Sheppard, D. A.	G/19727	Pte.		Simmonds, W. T.	G/9026	Pte.
Sheppard, G. H.	L/11447	Pte.		Simmons, A. L.	G/5686	Cpl.
Sheppard, H.	G/2349	Pte.		Simmons, E. G.	G/4980	Pte.
Sheppard, H. W.	241651	Pte.		Simmons, W. J.	G/18593	Pte.
Sheppard, J. W.	G/8579	Pte.		Simon, E.	G/7466	L/Cpl.
Sheppard, S.	G/18782	L/Cpl.		Simons, H. G.	G/27451	Pte.
Sheppey-Greene, N. G. S.		Lieut.		Simons, W.	G/16305	L/Cpl.
Sheriff, K.		2nd Lieut.		Simons, W. S.	G/8460	Pte.
Sherwood, R. V.	TF/4547	Pte.		Simpkin, G.	G/2332	Pte.
Shields, A.	G/18	Pte.		Simpson, F.	G/25338	Pte.
Shields, H.	G/38650	Pte.		Simpson, J.	G/39046	Pte.
Shilco, E., *M.M.*	204389	Pte.		Simpson, R.	203997	Pte.
Shilling, T. A.	202536	Pte.		Simpson S.	G/3660	Pte.
Shine, A. G.	204805	Pte.		Simpson, T.	G/699	Sgt.
Shinn, L. J. T.	G/19252	Pte.		Simpson, W.	241895	Pte.
Shirley, S.	203297	Pte.		Sims, H. B.	G/8885	Pte.
Shoebridge, J.	G/12315	Pte.		Sims, V. A.	G/7475	Pte.
Shoebridge, S. A.	241587	Pte.		Sims, W. A.	G/542	Pte.
Shoesmith, C. W.	201262	Pte.		Sinclair, E. C.	G/10655	Pte.
Shopland, E. J.	G/13421	Pte.		Sinclair, E. W.	G/6703	Pte.
Short, F. C.	G/7329	Pte.		Sinden, H. A.	G/11744	Pte.
Short, F. L.		Capt.		Singleton J.	S/8364	Pte.

APPENDIX II.

Singyard, E.	G/25294	Dmr.	Smith, A.	G/24377	Pte.
Sivey H.	G/2859	Pte.	Smith, A.	G/38809	Pte.
Siviett A. E.	G/25313	Pte.	Smith, A.	203140	Pte.
Sivyer H. A.	G/11113	Pte.	Smith, A.	G/8691	Pte.
Skeen, T.	G/29388	Pte.	Smith, A.	G/8535	Pte.
Skeggs, J. A.	G/10849	Pte.	Smith, A.	G/18756	Pte.
Skeggs, T.	G/23638	Pte.	Smith, A. C.	G/29568	Pte.
Skelton, C.	G/6003	Pte.	Smith, A. E.	S/8926	Pte.
Skerritt, C. H.	L/5284	Pte.	Smith, A. H.	L/10621	L/Cpl.
Skidmore, H.	202364	Pte.	Smith, A. H.	L/9010	Dmr.
Skiller, J.	S/510	Pte.	Smith, A. J.	G/11104	Pte.
Skilton, A. W.	L/10240	Pte.	Smith, A. L.	G/619	Pte.
Skinner, A. E.	202537	L/Sgt.	Smith, A. T.	L/10556	Pte.
Skinner, D. H.		Capt.	Smith, C.	G/30555	Pte.
Skinner, E.	G/31334	Pte.	Smith, C.	205583	Sgt.
Skinner, F.	G/10243	Pte.	Smith, C. A.	G/9804	L/Cpl.
Skinner, H.	G/3714	Pte.	Smith, C. H.	G/953	L/Cpl.
Skinner, J.	L/7785	Pte.	Smith, C. H.	L/8497	L/Cpl.
Skinner, J.	203241	Cpl.	Smith, C. W.	G/12821	L/Cpl.
Skinner, R.	200974	Sgt.	Smith, D.	G/1619	Pte.
Skinner, R. F.	G/1510	Pte.	Smith, E.		2nd Lieut.
Skipper, T. H., D.C.M.	201103	Sgt.	Smith, E.	241382	Pte.
Skottowe, G.		2nd Lieut.	Smith, E.	G/18319	Pte.
Slack, F.	L/7415	Pte.	Smith, E. A.	G/20572	Pte.
Sladden, E. G.	G/15460	Pte.	Smith, E. C.	G/24649	Pte.
Slade, A.	G/4638	Pte.	Smith, E. E.	S/10111	Pte.
Slade, A. H.	G/12370	Pte.	Smith, E. E.	L/10681	Pte.
Slade, J.	G/524	Pte.	Smith, E. H.	G/4128	Pte.
Slarks, W.	G/19336	Pte.	Smith, E. J.	G/5827	Pte.
Slater, C.	G/31396	Cpl.	Smith, E. J.	G/3471	Pte.
Slater, H.	205529	Pte.	Smith, F.	G/6454	Pte.
Slater, J. N.	G/31872	L/Cpl.	Smith, F.	G/11650	Pte.
Slater, J. W.	L/9243	Pte.	Smith, F.	G/11941	Pte.
Slaymaker, A.G.	G/10203	Pte.	Smith, F.	G/10615	Pte.
Sleath, F. W. G.	240864	Cpl.	Smith, F.	G/8309	Sgt.
Slight, W. A.	G/12604	Pte.	Smith, F., M.M.	G/25919	Sgt.
Sly, P. H. C.	G/16449	Pte.	Smith, F. C.	L/8059	Sgt.
Smale, J. C.	G/2820	Pte.	Smith, F. C.	241254	Pte.
Smele, R. G. E.	G/21790	Cpl.	Smith, F. G.	G/4213	Cpl.
Smith, A.	G/17019	Pte.	Smith, F. S. G.	G/1479	Pte.
Smith, A.	G/13492	Pte.	Smith, F. W.	L/8421	Pte.
Smith, A.	G/20133	Pte.	Smith, G.		2nd Lieut.
Smith, A.	S/8823	Pte.	Smith, G.	G/20028	Pte.
			Smith, G.	S/1243	Pte.

APPENDIX II.

Smith, G. A.	L/7655	Pte.		Smith, S.	G/14582	L/Cpl.
Smith, G. A.	G/8355	L/Cpl.		Smith, S.	G/4154	Pte.
Smith, G. H.	L/8504	Pte.		Smith, S. G.	S/8453	Pte.
Smith, G. W.	G/31160	Pte.		Smith, T.	G/5530	Pte.
Smith, H.	S/747	Pte.		Smith, T. C.	G/1126	Pte.
Smith, H.	G/9877	Pte.		Smith, T. W.	G/12472	Pte.
Smith, H.	G/31387	L/Cpl.		Smith, W.	G/1743	Pte.
Smith, H.	G/94	Cpl.		Smith, W.	G/20179	Pte.
Smith, H.	G/20578	Pte.		Smith, W.	S/5778	Pte.
Smith, H.	G/2384	Pte.		Smith, W.	S/8426	Pte.
Smith, H.	L/1103	Pte.		Smith, W.	G/14578	L/Cpl.
Smith, H.	G/30630	Pte.		Smith, W.	L/10539	Pte.
Smith, H.	L/11554	Pte.		Smith, W.	G/24744	Pte.
Smith, H.	240127	Pte.		Smith, W.	G/8841	Cpl.
Smith, H. A.	G/10616	L/Cpl.		Smith, W.	G/23130	Pte.
Smith, H. E.	G/11000	Pte.		Smith, W. A.	G/25927	L/Cpl.
Smith, H. F.	204597	Pte.		Smith, W. A.	G/24475	Pte.
Smith, H. H.	G/28867	Pte.		Smith, W. A.	G/2358	Pte.
Smith, H. R., M.C.		Lieut.		Smith, W. F.	G/30247	Pte.
Smith, H. U.	G/1871	Pte.		Smith, W. G.	205336	Pte.
Smith, H. W.	G/4991	Pte.		Smith, W. G.	G/9191	Pte.
Smith, H. W.	G/12151	Pte.		Smith, W. H.	G/5018	Pte.
Smith, H. W. J.	G/19617	Pte.		Smith, W. H.	G/17521	Pte.
Smith, J.	G/12148	Pte.		Smith, W. H.	S/379	Pte.
Smith, J.	G/28147	Pte.		Smith, W. H.	204643	Pte.
Smith, J.	G/29718	Pte.		Smith, W. J.	G/943	Pte.
Smith, J. C.	G/19959	Pte.		Smith, W. J.	205336	Pte.
Smith, J. J.	L/9586	Pte.		Smithers, F. G.	L/9269	Pte.
Smith, J. W.	G/15004	Pte.		Smithyes, F. T.	G/20571	Pte.
Smith, L. C. W.	G/1311	Pte.		Smoothy, F. L.	G/3924	Pte.
Smith, L. E.	G/24650	Pte.		Smyth, E. P.		Lieut.
Smith, N.	G/4143	Pte.		Smyth, W. O.	G/7091	Pte.
Smith, P.	G/3500	Pte.		Smythe, C.M.M.	G/816	Cpl.
Smith, P. A.	G/18091	Pte.		Snare, T. D. J.	G/5171	Pte.
Smith, P. E.	L/1052	Pte.		Snelgrove, F. A.		2nd Lieut.
Smith, P. E.	G/10276	Pte.		Snell, H.	G/1503	Pte.
Smith, P. J. H.	G/17966	Pte.		Snelling, L.	G/15554	Pte.
Smith, P. T.		Lieut.		Snook, W. A.	200062	Pte.
Smith, R.	203235	Pte.		Snooks, F. E.	L/9707	Cpl.
Smith, R.	S/275	L/Cpl.		Soane, N.	G/16696	Cpl.
Smith, R.	G/30072	Pte.		Soans, W. H.	S/324	Pte.
Smith, R.	G/19389	Pte.		Somerfield, G.	G/9669	Pte.
Smith, R. H.	G/18130	Pte.		Songhurst, A. J.	G/19296	Cpl.

APPENDIX II.

Sonky, J. E.	G/6355	Pte.
Sontag, H. J.	G/3731	Pte.
Sorrell, J.	L/10545	Pte.
Sorrell, L.	L/8612	Pte.
Sotham, R. C.		Lieut.
Souton, H.	G/18517	Pte.
South, F.	205913	Pte.
South, H.	G/11175	L/Cpl.
South, T. J.	L/8586	Pte.
South, W. E.	S/1065	Sgt.
Southall, F. W.	G/2204	Pte.
Southee, H. J.	S/194	Cpl.
Southgate, H. A.		2nd Lieut.
Southwell, L.	G/31060	Pte.
Spackman, A.	S/1854	L/Cpl.
Spain, L. W.	G/4749	Pte.
Sparks, B.	G/30491	Cpl.
Sparrow, A.	G/14637	Pte.
Sparrowhawk, R.G.	201144	Pte.
Spear, L. J. H.	G/15101	Pte.
Spearing, S. W.	G/1144	L/Cpl.
Spence, B. A.	G/25849	Pte.
Spence, E.	G/30248	Pte.
Spence, J.	205912	Pte.
Spence, S. C.	G/31123	Pte.
Spencer, C.	G/11980	Pte.
Spencer, C. A.	G/8830	Pte.
Spencer, T.	G/28565	Pte.
Spendiff, W. G.	203998	Pte.
Spicer, D.	S/979	Pte.
Spicer, G.	242507	Pte.
Spilett, S. T.	G/4863	Pte.
Spink, W.	L/10426	Pte.
Spinks, A. E.	L/9115	Pte.
Spinks, F. R.	G/28901	Pte.
Spinks, G.	G/2772	Pte.
Spooner, A. C.	L/9380	Pte.
Spooner, W.	G/23571	Pte.
Spoore, S. G.	G/15107	Pte.
Spottiswood, A. B.		
	G/15345	Pte.
Spratt, H. O.W.	204425	Pte.
Spratt, J.	G/8292	Pte.
Spratt, T.	G/19001	Pte.
Sprigge, R. A.	G/8779	Pte.
Springett, A.	G/12830	Pte.
Springett, E.	L/6490	Pte.
Springett, G. T., M.M.		
	G/10838	Sgt.
Springett, L. A.	G/7269	Pte.
Springett, W. T. R.		
	G/4864	Pte.
Spurdon, W.	L/7194	Pte.
Spurling, A. C.	G/13463	Pte.
Spurrell, G. F.	G/7717	Cpl.
Squire, F.		2nd Lieut.
Squires, H. E.	G/20442	Pte.
Squirrell, F.	G/18136	Pte.
Stacey, A. J.	G/30994	Pte.
Stacey, H. A.	G/15945	Pte.
Stackpool, T.	S/397	Pte.
Staff, W. W.	240832	Sgt.
Stafford, W. G.	L/9810	Pte.
Staines, C. W.	G/17471	Pte.
Staines, J. M.	202308	Pte.
Staines, S.	G/25964	Sgt.
Stalker, D.	G/1620	Pte.
Stambridge, T. H.		
	G/2266	Pte.
Stamp, A.	240479	Sgt.
Stanbridge, P.	G/19686	Pte.
Standen, G. W.	G/25215	Pte.
Standen, J. R.	L/8678	Dmr.
Standing, T.	G/23324	Pte.
Standing, T. R.	240026	Sgt.
Standley, H. H.	202715	Pte.
Stanford, W.	L/6807	Pte.
Stanley, C. C.	G/13060	Pte.
Stanley, D.	G/9840	L/Cpl.
Stanley, H. W.	G/20132	Pte.
Stannard, H.	G/2369	Pte.
Stansell, L. B.		2nd Lieut.
Stanton, G.	S/210	Pte.
Stanton, G. M.		2nd Lieut.
Stanyon, A.	G/28857	L/Cpl.
Staples, J.	L/7128	Pte.

APPENDIX II.

Staples, N.	G/7056	Pte.
Staples, S.	G/12263	Pte.
Stapleton, F.	G/17896	Pte.
Stapleton, G. F.	G/9048	Pte.
Stapleton, G. H.	G/9589	Pte.
Stapleton, H. A.	G/15563	Pte.
Stapleton, T. R.	S/108	Pte.
Stapley, E.	S/10	L/Cpl.
Stapley, P. E.	G/31392	Pte.
Starkey, A.	G/484	Sgt.
Starling, W. J.	G/8500	Sgt.
Startup, R. B.	L/8251	Sgt.
Steane, A.	S/967	Pte.
Stears, S.	G/23810	L/Cpl.
Stedman, A.	L/8501	Sgt.
Stedman, G. W.	L/9228	Sgt.
Stedman, S.	G/998	Pte.
Stedman, T. W. F.	L/8015	Pte.
Steed, D.	S/239	Pte.
Steed, J. R.	G/4092	Pte.
Steel, F.	G/21528	Pte.
Steel, J. R.	L/8858	Pte.
Steel, S. J.	L/8766	Pte.
Steel, A. C. J.		2nd Lieut.
Steer, G. H.	G/3303	Pte.
Steer, W.	G/2953	Pte.
Steggall, P. G.	G/8532	Cpl.
Steggles, S. G.	G/18124	Pte.
Stein, J.	G/20161	Pte.
Stemp, J.	S/516	Pte.
Stenning, W. J.	G/17889	Pte.
Stenson, J.	L/11471	Pte.
Stephens, A. E.	G/25955	Pte.
Stephens, R. M.		Lieut.
Stephens, S. T.	G/23867	Pte.
Stephenson, A.	L/9873	Pte.
Stephenson, P.S.	G/14519	Pte.
Stephney, R. A.	G/25943	Pte.
Sterry, M.J., D.C.M.	G/21501	Sgt.
Stevens, A. J.	G/21025	Pte.
Stevens, A. S.	G/3809	Pte.
Stevens, C. E.	G/19177	Pte.
Stevens, C. J.	G/10113	Pte.
Stevens, E.	S/9307	L/Cpl.
Stevens, E.	G/11388	Pte.
Stevens, H. E.	G/13021	Pte.
Stevens, H. F. B.		Lieut.
Stevens, J.	G/30825	Pte.
Stevens, P.		Lieut.
Stevens, P. J.	201373	Pte.
Stevens, R. A.	G/9207	Pte.
Stevens, T.	L/10213	Pte.
Stevens, W. G.	L/8763	Pte.
Stevenson, A.	G/25861	Pte.
Stevenson, F. J.	S/8855	Pte.
Stewart, J. B.	G/16383	Pte.
Stewart, J. R.		2nd Lieut.
Stewart, S. J.	202453	Pte.
Stibbon, T.	205660	Pte.
Stickings, W. T.	L/7521	Sgt.
Stickles, A. J.	G/6673	Pte.
Stigand, C. H., O.B.E.		Major.
Stiles, H. J.	S/7544	Pte.
Still, C.	G/28592	Pte.
Stilwell, M. J.		Lieut.
Stirling, D.	G/31603	Pte.
Stock, A.	L/7694	Cpl.
Stock, P.	G/11569	Pte.
Stock, S.	L/10183	Pte.
Stockbridge, A.	G/18565	Pte.
Stockbridge, T. J.	G/14957	Pte.
Stodart, S. M.	G/23143	Pte.
Stokes, C.	G/15354	Pte.
Stokes, H.	G/30249	Pte.
Stokes, J. H.		Capt.
Stone, A. T.	S/393	Pte.
Stone, C.	G/20577	Pte.
Stone, C. J.	G/3194	Pte.
Stone, D. A.	G/8184	Pte.
Stone, G. H.	G/17970	Pte.
Stone, J.	L/7705	L/Cpl.
Stone, T. W.	G/28498	Pte.
Stone, W.	G/25428	Pte.

APPENDIX II.

Stoneham, H.	G/848	Pte.	Sullivan, J. L.	L/9543	Sgt.
Stoner, E.	G/17968	Pte.	Sullivan, M.	S/8477	Pte.
Stones, T. F.		2nd Lieut.	Sullivan, W.	G/1093	Sgt.
Stonham, F. K.	G/7685	Pte.	Sully, A. J.	206354	Pte.
Stoor, C. R.	G/19227	Pte.	Summers, P. C.	G/7128	L/Cpl.
Stow, E. E.	G/6691	Pte.	Summers, W. G.		Capt.
Strachan, H. A.	G/11146	Pte.	Surkitt, W. A.	G/19894	Pte.
Strand, A. J.	G/18508	Pte.	Suter, G. E.	205646	Pte.
Stratford, H.	G/12440	Pte.	Suter, R.	G/2274	Pte.
Stratton, S. V.	G/29750	Pte.	Sutherland, J. L. C., *M.C.*		Lieut.
Stratton, T. W.	G/15355	Pte.	Sutton, J. E.	G/20033	Pte.
Streatfield, B.R.	G/1558	Pte.	Sutton, R.	G/5471	Pte.
Streatfield, E.H.	G/12173	Pte.	Sutton, V. C. M.		2nd Lieut.
Streatfield, G.	G/9603	Pte.	Sutton, W. G.	G/12349	Pte.
Streatfield, T. B. M.		2nd Lieut.	Swain, A. E.	G/31750	L/Cpl.
Street, E.	G/1718	Pte.	Swain, A. J.	L/8834	Pte.
Streeter, E. L.	G/6280	Pte.	Swaine, F. J.	G/25127	Pte.
Streeter, G.	G/2889	L/Cpl.	Swales, R. J.	G/1665	Cpl.
Stretton, H. G.	G/24742	Pte.	Swan, H.	G/991	Pte.
Stringer, W.	202670	L/Cpl.	Swan, H.	G/11882	Pte.
Stringer, W. J.	202541	L/Cpl.	Swan, J.	G/2541	Pte.
Stroud, F.	G/12306	Pte.	Swan, J. V.	G/25850	Pte.
Stroud, F. R.	G/15463	Pte.	Swansbury, F.	G/18591	Cpl.
Stuart, W. E. M.		2nd Lieut.	Sweeney, J. H.	S/6896	Pte.
Stubbs, A. J.		2nd Lieut.	Sweetman, A.	G/3357	Pte.
Stubbs, H.	L/7195	Pte.	Sweetman, A. E.	G/4155	Pte.
Stubbins, T.	G/5270	Pte.	Sweetman, F.	G/5458	Pte.
Strudwick, D.	G/17654	Pte.	Sweetser, P.	G/12246	Pte.
Strudwick, G.	G/7369	Pte.	Swift, J.	205628	Pte.
Sturge, G. F.	G/2826	Pte.	Swift, W.	G/2040	Pte.
Sturgess, C. J.	G/18650	Pte.	Swindell, F. G.	G/10204	Pte.
Styles, A.	G/53	Pte.	Swindell, F. J. *M.M.*		
Styles, A. G.	G/3801	L/Cpl.		G/3256	Pte.
Styles, C. T.	G/6287	Pte.	Swingwood, R.	G/28566	Pte.
Styles, F.	242443	Pte.	Sydenham, E.G.	G/901	Pte.
Styles, J.	G/4422	Pte.	Sykes, J.	205563	Pte.
Sullivan, B.	242245	Pte.	Sykes, N.	G/20128	Pte.
Sullivan, D.	L/6153	Pte.	Sykes, W. E.		Lieut.
Sullivan, G.	200544	Pte.	Symonds, H. J.	G/7723	Pte.
Sullivan, J.	G/6124	Pte.	Symonds, J. E.	S/1228	Pte.
Sullivan, J.	S/7139	Pte.			
Sullivan, J.	L/10318	Pte.	Taber, J., *M.M.*	G/6130	Cpl.
Sullivan, J.	202944	Pte.	Taberer, A.	G/30700	Pte.

APPENDIX II.

Tabrett E. G.		Pte.	Taylor, H.		G/31761	Pte.
Taft, R.	S/82	Pte.	Taylor, H.		205603	Pte.
Tagg, E. V.	G/284	Pte.	Taylor, H. A.,		M.C.	2nd Lieut.
Talbot, W. R.	G/18090	Pte.	Taylor, H. G.		G/2944	L/Cpl.
Tall, W.	TF/2458	Pte.	Taylor, H. S.		G/8127	Pte.
Talmay, B.	G/23333	Pte.	Taylor, J.		G/31758	Pte.
Talman, F.	G/24230	L/Cpl.	Taylor, J.		S/357	Pte.
Tamsitt, F.	G/2853	Pte.	Taylor, J. H.		G/34	Pte.
Tancock, S. G. A.	206367	Pte.	Taylor, J. R.		G/27475	Pte.
Tanner, T. L.		Capt.	Taylor, M.		G/24915	Pte.
Tanner, W. H.	241356	Pte.	Taylor, P.		G/2051	Pte.
Tapley, T.	G/10163	Pte.	Taylor, P. E.		G/18525	Pte.
Tapp, F.	L/10921	Pte.	Taylor, R.		G/3093	Pte.
Tapp, H. G.	L/6723	Dmr.	Taylor, R.		G/25241	L/Sgt.
Tapsell, F. S.	G/23278	Pte.	Taylor, S.		203159	Pte.
Tarring, L. W.	240734	Cpl.	Taylor, S.		240850	Pte.
Tasker, H.	G/1056	L/Cpl.	Taylor, T. H.		G/18626	Pte.
Tate, A.	L/11035	Pte.	Taylor, T. J.			2nd Lieut.
Tattersall, J.	G/20657	Pte.	Taylor, T. J.		G/10843	Pte.
Taun, W.	205531	Pte.	Tavlor, V.J.W.		G/10584	Pte.
Tavinor, A.H.G.	G/29390	Pte.	Taylor, W. E.		G/12889	Pte.
Tayler, W. N. C.		Lieut.	Taylor, W. T.		G/15479	Pte.
Taylor, A.	G/2027	Sgt.	Teagre, A. V.		G/204	L/Sgt.
Taylor, A. C.	G/2445	Pte.	Teasdale, H.		G/21291	Pte.
Taylor, A. C.	202410	Pte.	Tebboth, H. J.		G/15280	Pte.
Taylor, A. R.	G/18960	L/Cpl.	Tedder, A. W.		L/7570	Sgt.
Taylor, B.	G/4956	Pte.	Tedder, T.		G/17661	Pte.
Taylor, C. E.	G/13436	Pte	Tedham, R. R.		G/27279	Pte.
Taylor, C. G.	G/2828	Pte.	Tennyson-Smith, J. A.			Lieut.
Taylor, C. W.	L/9597	Pte.	Terry, A.		G/19457	Pte.
Taylor, D.	G/654	Pte.	Terry, A. C.		G/60	Pte.
Taylor E.	241818	Pte.	Terry, A. G. C.		G/3860	Pte.
Taylor, E. H.	G/7760	Pte.	Terry, A .J. V.		L/9274	Pte.
Taylor, F.	G/8068	Sgt.	Terry, H.		201344	Pte.
Taylor, F.	G/6759	Pte.	Terry, T. C.		G/2105	Pte.
Taylor, F. C.	G/12356	Pte.	Terry, W. J.		G/5768	Pte.
Taylor, F. M.	242253	Pte.	Teskey, W. C.		241694	Pte.
Taylor, F. T.	G/19566	Pte.	Tester, J.		G/31032	L/Cpl.
Taylor, G.	G/12547	Pte.	Tester, J. A.		G/5290	Pte.
Taylor, G.	G/7786	Pte.	Thacker, A. E.		G/5023	Pte.
Taylor, G.	G/24362	Pte.	Thacker, F.		G/29396	Pte.
Taylor, G. F.	G/9029	Pte.	Theim, E. W.		G/38656	Pte.
Taylor, G. W.	L/6024	Pte.	Thomas, A.		G/6102	Pte.

APPENDIX II.

Thomas, A. E.	224254	Pte.
Thomas, C. E.	G/7274	Pte.
Thomas, D. R.	G/24803	L/Cpl.
Thomas, F.	L/6803	Pte.
Thomas, F.	G/12354	Pte.
Thomas, G.	203973	Pte.
Thomas, G. L.	G/31604	Pte.
Thomas, H. G.	M.M.	
	G/567	Cpl.
Thomas, J.	G/24784	Pte.
Thomas, J.	G/10429	Pte.
Thomas, J. J.	S/9364	Pte.
Thomas, S. J.		2nd Lieut.
Thomas, W. R.	G/3758	Pte.
Thompson, A.	G/25956	Pte.
Thompson, A.	G/20292	Pte.
Thompson, B.	G/16392	Cpl.
Thompson, C.	205497	Sgt.
Thompson, C.F.	G/24908	Pte.
Thompson, E.	G/11206	L/Cpl.
Thompson E.W.	G/6579	Cpl.
Thompson, F.	L/10430	Pte.
Thompson, G. F.	204404	Pte.
Thompson, G.S.	G/18223	Pte.
Thompson, G.W.	G/11488	Pte.
Thompson, H.,	D.C.M.	
	L/10619	Cpl.
Thompson H.	G/19459	Pte.
Thompson, H.G.	G/23580	Cpl.
Thompson, J.	S/7881	Pte.
Thompson, J.	G/2108	Pte.
Thompson, J.	204384	Pte.
Thompson, J. C.	206362	Pte.
Thompson, J.H.	L/7750	Pte.
Thompson J. S.	G/19564	Pte.
Thompson, M. H.		2nd Lieut.
Thompson, R.	205407	Sgt.
Thompson, R.W.	205902	Pte.
Thompson, W.	G/10707	Pte.
Thompson, W.	G/25117	Pte.
Thompson, W. H.		
	TF/2002	Pte.
Thompson, W.J.	S/8932	Pte.
Thompson, W. R. J.,	M.M.	
	G/8900	Pte.
Thompson-Smith, K.		2nd Lieut.
Thomson, F.	203945	L/Cpl.
Thorn, A. G.	203004	Pte.
Thorn, F. W.	G/28833	Pte.
Thorne, C. L.	G/16518	Cpl.
Thorne, J. R.	L/6308	Pte.
Thornton, A. C.	G/5228	Pte.
Thornton, H. T.		2nd Lieut.
Thornton, J. G. H.		
	G/8452	Pte.
Thornton, W.	G/10543	Pte.
Thorogood, A.J.	G/24345	Pte.
Thorogood, F. W.		
	G/10893	Pte.
Thorogood, G.W.	203634	Pte.
Thorogood, J.	G/19693	Pte.
Thorpe, H. C.	G/12182	Pte.
Thorpe, L.	205566	Pte.
Thorpe, W.	G/8453	Pte.
Threadgold, E. C.		
	G/18764	Pte.
Thulborn, E.	G/18123	Pte.
Thunder, G. L.	G/24748	Pte.
Thurling, W.	S/262	Pte.
Thurmer, V. C.	G/19255	Pte.
Thurnall, H.	L/10079	Pte.
Tice, W. H.	L/6206	Pte.
Tick, A. J.	L/8196	Pte.
Tickner, E.	G/494	Pte.
Tickner, G. H.	G/5470	Pte.
Tidd, J.	G/18854	Cpl.
Tierney, A. G.	L/9996	Pte.
Tilbe, E.	G/18522	Pte.
Tilby, H.	L/10566	Pte.
Tiley, B. H.	G/24478	Pte.
Till, J.	G/17363	Pte.
Till, J.	G/4424	Pte.
Tiller, G. A.	L/10035	Cpl.
Tillett, W.	G/6554	Pte.
Tilley, S. J. C.	G/1845	Pte.
Tilley, T. H.	G/23005	Pte.

APPENDIX II.

Tilling, C. T.	G/4343	Pte.	Townsend, T.	S/1193	Pte.
Tillyard, G. S.	TF/4115	Pte.	Townsend, W.	G/9563	Pte.
Timms, W. R.	G/9611	Pte.	Townshend, A. F.		Lieut.-Col.
Timpson, W. H.	L/9445	Pte.	Toyne, M. R.	G/30838	Pte.
Tindall, F.	G/5007	L/Cpl.	Traill, W., *D.C.M.*		
Tingcombe, E. J	G/19047	L/Cpl.		L/8535	C.S.M.
Titchener, G.	G/3296	Pte.	Trainer, H. F. T.	L/10206	Pte.
Titchener, R. J.	G/4393	Pte.	Travers, F. C.	G/28831	Pte.
Tite, H. W.	240807	C.S.M.	Traveller, E. H.	G/8895	Pte.
Titley, T. A.	240859	Pte.	Travis, T.	G/38653	Pte.
Tobechnich, M. W.			Treble, A. W.	G/20252	Pte.
	G/30349	Pte.	Tree, A. G.	G/12082	Pte.
Tobin, B.	G/15202	Sgt.	Treliving, J. W.	L/9200	Pte.
Tobin, J.	G/2331	Pte.	Trewkitt, S.	205539	Pte.
Todd, A. F.	L/6672	Pte.	Trick, W. T. H.	G/20592	Pte.
Todd, G. A.	G/25492	Pte.	Triplow, C.	G/1129	L/Cpl.
Todd, T. J.	G/19102	Pte.	Triplow, W. W.	G/7761	Pte.
Tolhurst, E. G.	G/4897	Pte.	Tripp, W.	G/17492	Pte.
Tolley, A.	G/19390	Pte.	Trodd, F. B.	G/23846	Pte.
Tombs, L. B.	G/29402	Pte.	Trodd, W. P.	G/5514	Pte.
Tomei, C. J.	G/10844	Pte.	Trott, A.	G/25786	L/Cpl.
Tomlin, A.	G/15865	Pte.	Trott, S.	G/17662	Pte.
Tompkins, H. S.	G/3748	Pte.	Trotter, E. B., *M.C., D.C.M.*		
Tompkins, T.	205182	Pte.			Lieut.
Tompsett, W. R.	G/7635	Pte.	Truelove, H. G.	G/26527	Pte.
Tomsett, E. A.	G/24664	L/Cpl.	Trueman, G. W.	L/10152	L/Cpl.
Toombs, J. C.	S/9265	Sgt.	Truman, A. J.	G/20035	Pte.
Toomey, G. D.	G/12952	Pte.	Truman, J. G.	L/10448	Pte.
Topley, W. S.	203316	Pte.	Trundle, J. R.	204257	Pte.
Topliss, A. V.	G/26528	Pte.	Truscott, F C.	G/11957	Pte.
Torrison, R.	L/9284	Pte.	Truscott, F. H.	G/17451	L/Cpl.
Totham, E.	202776	Pte.	Tubey, D. J.	G/21069	Pte.
Tovell, W.	S/8527	Pte.	Tuck, B. C.	G/18072	Pte.
Towler, C. J.		2nd Lieut.	Tucker, A.	G/4530	Cpl.
Town, A.	G/10234	Pte.	Tucker, E.	G/23152	Pte.
Towner, F. J.	G/12040	Pte.	Tucker E.	G/8037	L/Cpl.
Towner, G.	L/9222	Pte.	Tucker, G.	G/4862	Pte.
Towner, G.	201448	Pte.	Tucker, J.		L/Cpl.
Towse, C. H.		Capt.	Tucker, J. J.	G/24470	Cpl.
Townsend, G.	G/6610	Pte.	Tuckerman, A. P.	241203	Pte.
Townsend, G.	G/18584	Pte.	Tuff, C. T.		Capt.
Townsend, H. J.	G/9562	Pte.	Tugwell, A. G.	L/10674	Pte.
Townsend, S.	G/607	Pte.	Tulett, W. A.	G/827	Pte.

575

APPENDIX II.

Tuley, W.	G/10842	Pte.	Underdown, A.	204668	Pte.
Tullett, H. W.	G/11265	Pte.	Underhill, H. J.	G/12005	Pte.
Tully, J.	L/10932	Pte.	Underwood, A. W.		
Tumber, E. D.	S/9071	Sgt.		G/19359	Pte.
Tunaley, H.	G/23484	Pte.	Underwood, F.		2nd Lieut.
Tunley, A.	G/19568	Pte.	Underwood, J.	L/5620	Pte.
Turk, A. H.	L/10173	Pte.	Underwood, J. H.		
Turnbull, M. D.	G/11647	L/Cpl.		G/5477	Pte.
Turner, A.	L/7673	Pte.	Underwood, W.	G/20137	Pte.
Turner, A. B.	G/18278	Pte.	Underwood, W.	G/20039	Pte.
Turner, A. F.	S/8925	Pte.	Ungretta, A.	G/15739	Pte.
Turner, C.	L/9684	L/Sgt.	Unwin, F. W.	G/2914	Pte.
Turner, C.	G/8223	Pte.	Upton, G. H.	L/10324	Pte.
Turner, E.	G/23335	Pte.	Upton, H.		Pte.
Turner, E. F.	G/48	Pte.	Upton, T.	L/7327	L/Sgt.
Turner, E. W.	214270	Pte.	Upton, W. J.	L/7996	Pte.
Turner, F.	L/9353	Pte.	Upward, H.	G/14796	Pte.
Turner, G.	G/17415	Pte.	Usborne, C.	G/12474	Pte.
Turner, G. A.		2nd Lieut.			
Turner, G. F.	G/25872	Pte.	Vale, F.	G/1971	Pte.
Turner, H. A.	G/17899	Pte.	Valentine, V.	G/11803	Cpl.
Turner, H. J.	G/14380	Pte.	Valentine, W. J.	L/8109	L/Cpl.
Turner J. E.	G/19025	Pte.	Vallins, H. W.	240466	Pte.
Turner, J. F.	S/8362	Pte.	Vance, W.	G/31608	Pte.
Turner, J. H., M.C.		2nd Lieut.	Vandell, H. T.		2nd Lieut.
Turner P. G.	G/26257	Pte.	Vant, J. R.	G/183	Sgt.
Turner, R.	G/11331	Pte.	Varney, A.	G/3347	Pte.
Turner, S. R.	G/1073	L/Cpl.	Vass, F.	G/435	Pte.
Turner, W.	L/7484	L/Cpl.	Vater, F. H.	G/4675	Pte.
Turner, W. G.	S/8718	Pte.	Vaughan, A. E.	204645	Pte.
Turner, W. H.	G/2253	Pte.	Vaughan, E. J.	G/4138	Pte.
Turner, W. W.	G/8051	Sgt.	Vaughan, F. S.		Lieut.
Turpin, C.	G/15742	Pte.	Vaughan, H. C.	G/16089	L/Cpl.
Turvill, G.	G/20625	Pte.	Vaughan, R. C.		2nd Lieut.
Tween, F. C.	G/2933	Pte.	Vaughan, T. H., M.M.		
Tween, J.	G/4264	Pte.		G/31563	Pte.
Twelvetrees, B.		2nd Lieut.	Veale, J. R. S.	L/5652	Pte.
Tye, W.	203237	Pte.	Venn, M. J.	G/7461	Pte.
Tyler, L. H.	240071	L/Cpl.	Venner, E. W.		2nd Lieut.
Tyman, M.	G/18520	Pte.	Venner, V.	G/540	Pte.
			Venters, W. S.	L/11181	Pte.
Uden, A. E.	L/7996	Pte.	Vercoe, W. H.	G/20139	Pte.
Uings, L.	L/11186	Pte.	Verrall, G. T.	S/923	C.S.M.

APPENDIX II.

Verrall, R. C.	L/7248	Sgt.	Wale, F.	G/13075	Pte.
Vicat, H. J.		2nd Lieut.	Wales, F. J.	G/9882	Pte.
Vickers, A. T.	G/8406	Sgt.	Walford, C.	G/9233	Pte.
Vickers, W. H.	L/7359	Pte.	Walk, E. J.	G/6747	L/Sgt.
Vidler, T.	L/10286	L/Cpl.	Walker, A. E.	G/29626	Pte.
Vigus, H.	G/19361	Pte.	Walker, C.	L/10565	Pte.
Viles, W. A.	G/8039	Pte.	Walker, C. G.	G/5517	L/Cpl.
Villers, J.	G/1240	Pte.	Walker, E. B.		2nd Lieut.
Vincent, B.	G/5447	Pte.	Walker, F.	S/8185	Sgt.
Vincent, H.	G/18893	Pte.	Walker, F.	G/8280	Pte.
Vine, H.	G/23468	Pte	Walker, G.	L/7828	Pte.
Vines, F.	241244	Pte.	Walker, J.	L/7816	Pte.
Vinicombe, L. F.		2nd Lieut.	Walker, M. J. L.		2nd Lieut.
Virgo, R. C.	G/7354	Pte.	Walker, R. J.	L/10160	Pte.
Vitler, H. J.	G/21137	Pte.	Walker, W J.	G/1719	Pte.
Vivash, J. B.	G/4145	L/Cpl.	Walkling, J.	G/2214	Pte.
Voce, E.	G/20040	Pte.	Wall, E. J.	G/18529	Pte.
Voice, G.	G/7304	Sgt.	Wall, F.	G/5679	Pte.
Vose, A. W.	G/21404	Pte.	Wall, G.	L/8450	Pte.
Vousden, F.	S/917	Pte.	Wallace, C.	L/9636	Pte.
Vousden, G.	G/26838	Pte.	Wallace, W.	G/8362	Pte.
Vousden, R.	L/10654	Pte.	Waller, A.	203952	Pte.
			Waller, A. J.	G/21108	Pte.
Wacher, J. S.		2nd Lieut.	Waller, R.	G/7793	Pte.
Wackett, A. H.	204589	Pte.	Waller, T. E.	G/15446	Pte.
Wade, O. J.		2nd Lieut.	Waller, W. G.	G/8345	Pte.
Wadey, H. E.	G/11256	Pte.	Wallis, A. P.	G/3799	Pte.
Wady, H. H.		Pte.	Wallis, E. G.	204493	Pte.
Waghorn, A. J.	G/18540	Pte.	Wallis, G. A. E., M.C.		2nd Lieut.
Waghorn, C. J.	L/10121	Pte.	Wallis, H.	G/180	Pte.
Waghorn, E., M.M.			Wallis, J. H.	G/459	Pte.
	L/7545	L/Cpl.	Walls, J.	G/9248	Pte.
Waghorn, L. P.		2nd Lieut.	Walmesley, H. H.		
Waghorn, T. H.	S/9139	Sgt.		G/31618	Pte.
Waghorn, W.	L/7854	Pte.	Walmesley, J.H.	G/4290	Pte.
Wainwright, W. G. F.			Walsh, E. G.	G/1652	L/Cpl.
	241820	Pte.	Walsh, R. C.	G/2182	Sgt.
Waite, S. R.	G/19270	Pte.	Walsh, W. L. H.		2nd Lieut.
Wakefield, C.G.	G/9948	Pte.	Walter, G. J.	G/4923	Pte.
Wakeman, P. A.	G/16987	Sgt.	Walter, W. H.	G/2675	Pte.
Wakenell, G. F.	240157	Pte.	Walters, C. W.	G/536	Sgt.
Walden, J.	L/9664	Pte.	Walters, G. E.	G/30849	Pte.
Walders, J.	G/6058	Pte.	Walters, R.	G/31029	Pte.

PP 577

APPENDIX II.

Walters, T.	S/609	Pte.	Warren, T.	G/5523	Pte.
Walton, J. H.	G/10959	Pte.	Wash, W.	L/5934	Pte.
Wandsbury, S.	G/12771	Pte.	Washington, A. E.	G/19720	Pte.
Wannell, W., D.C.M.	L/7361	Sgt.	Washington, W. J.	G/18328	Pte.
Wappett, W.	G/31925	Pte.			
Warbis, H. J.	241873	Pte.	Waterhouse, G. W.		2nd Lieut.
Warburton, S.	204143	Pte.	Waterman, A.	G/2135	Pte.
Ward, A. E.	G/1290	Sgt.	Waterman, E. R.	201034	Pte.
Ward, A. T.	L/9357	Pte.	Waterman, L.	G/9604	Pte.
Ward, B. J.	L/5587	Pte.	Waterman, P	L/10623	Pte.
Ward, C. W. A.	L/10003	Sgt.	Waterman, W.A.	203190	Pte.
Ward, E. H.	G/15366	Pte.	Waterman, W.R.	L/11145	Pte.
Ward, F. G.	G/18109	Pte.	Waters, A.	G/6570	Pte.
Ward, G.	L/7934	Pte.	Waters, A. A.	L/9915	Cpl.
Ward, G.	G/4069	Pte.	Waters, G.	G/12107	Pte.
Ward, G.	205510	Pte.	Waters, H.	200179	L/Cpl.
Ward, G. A.		2nd Lieut.	Waters, H.	L/10671	Pte.
Ward, H.	G/20044	Pte.	Waters, J. W.	G/12890	Pte.
Ward, H.	L/9172	Pte.	Waters, T. J.	G/23096	Pte.
Ward, H.	203912	Pte.	Watkins, F.	G/21033	L/Cpl.
Ward, H.	241216	Pte.	Watkins, G.	202686	Cpl.
Ward, H. E.	L/8710	Pte.	Watkins, G. W.	G/31065	Pte.
Ward, J.	G/871	Pte.	Watkins, H.	G/20606	Pte.
Ward, R. E.	S/9031	Pte.	Watkins, H. C.	G/24531	Pte.
Ward, W. H.	G/20599	Pte.	Watkins, L.	G/20607	Pte.
Ward, W. W.	G/19107	Pte.	Watkins, T.	G/3439	Pte.
Warden, F.	G/3195	Pte.	Watkinson, R.	G/19570	Pte.
Ware, J. A.	G/1358	Pte.	Watson, A.	G/9346	Pte.
Waring, F.	G/3751	Pte.	Watson, A.	S/8515	Pte.
Waring, W.	G/2652	Pte.	Watson, A.	G/3953	L/Cpl.
Warman, W.	240794	Cpl.	Watson, A.	G/19463	Pte.
Warner, A. E.	G/1855	Sgt.	Watson, A. G.	G/17912	Pte.
Warner, E. A.	202985	Pte.	Watson, C. S.	G/28910	Pte.
Warner, G.	L/7495	Pte.	Watson, D. J.	G/24846	Pte.
Warner, J. G.	L/5699	Pte.	Watson, G.	G/18996	Pte.
Warner, J. H.	L/8270	Pte.	Watson, G. F.	G/16045	Pte.
Warner, W. J.	G/10108	L/Cpl.	Watson, H.	G/20046	Pte.
Warnett, W.E.S.	L/9666	L/Sgt.	Watson, H.	G/2627	Pte.
Warrell, A.	TF/1751	Pte.	Watson, H. C.	G/5081	Pte.
Warren, A.	S/9141	Pte.	Watson, L. E.	G/11422	Pte.
Warren, A. F. T.	G/20197	Pte.	Watson, R.		2nd Lieut.
Warren, R.	G/8328	Pte.	Watson, T.	G/10928	Pte.

APPENDIX II.

Watts, C.	L/7149	Dmr.	Weeks, J.	G/8991	Pte.
Watts, D. H.		2nd Lieut.	Wehmer, F. A.	L/9431	Pte.
Watts, E. A.	G/5801	Pte.	Wein, M.	G/30831	Pte.
Watts, G.	L/5750	Pte.	Welch, A.	G/11551	Pte.
Watts, G. J.	S/1117	Pte.	Welch, H. R.	266824	Pte.
Watts, J.	L/6327	Pte.	Welch, J.	S/1148	Pte.
Watts, J.	G/7764	Pte.	Welch, T.	G/1767	Pte.
Watts, P. J.	G/6071	Pte.	Welfare, C.	G/17945	Pte.
Watts, R. K.		2nd Lieut.	Wellard, E.	G/12374	Pte.
Watts, W. A.	L/8405	Cpl.	Weller, A.	L/8874	Sgt.
Wayling, E. T.	G/9136	Pte.	Weller, C. L.	G/2129	Pte.
Weadon, C. W.		2nd Lieut.	Weller, W.	S/266	Cpl.
Weatherhogg, J.	G/30636	L/Cpl.	Weller, W. A.	G/24453	Cpl.
Weatherill, A.F.	G/5451	Pte.	Wellfare, W.	L/8307	Pte.
Weaver, W. J.	G/13455	Pte.	Wellings, B.	G/21224	Pte.
Webb, A. B.	S/75	Pte.	Wellings, T. H.	G/29546	Pte.
Webb, A. T.	G/3094	L/Cpl.	Wellman, J.	TF/2280	Pte.
Webb, C. G.	G/9832	L/Cpl.	Wells, A. C.	G/18560	Pte.
Webb, C. P., M.C.		2nd Lieut.	Wells, C.	G/8429	L/Cpl.
Webb, E. A.	200168	Pte.	Wells, G.	G/12316	Pte.
Webb, F. G.	G/1032	Pte.	Wells, H.	G/571	Pte.
Webb, G.	G/24799	Pte.	Wells, H. C.	G/6751	C.S.M.
Webb, G. E.	G/19464	Pte.	Wells, H. E.	G/30847	Pte.
Webb, H.	G/29723	Pte.	Wells, H. T.	205706	Pte.
Webb, J.	S/4717	Pte.	Wells, H. W.	G/10402	Pte.
Webb, L.	L/9150	Pte.	Wells, J. E.	L/8285	Pte.
Webb, P. B.	G/9291	Sgt.	Wells, T. H.	G/18678	Pte.
Webb, R.	G/24482	Pte.	Wells, W. C.	G/18614	Pte.
Webb, S.	G/5542	Pte.	Wells, W. H.	201401	Pte.
Webb, S. H.		2nd Lieut.	Wenbourne, H. W.		
Webb, T. H.	G/2668	Pte.		G/18531	Pte.
Webley, C. E.	G/18229	Pte.	Wenham, C. A.	G/11094	Pte.
Webster, E. A.	G/19466	Pte.	Wenham, G.	203218	Cpl.
Webster, G.	G/5180	Pte.	Wesson, R. J.	G/20254	Pte.
Webster, G. F.	G/19467	Pte.	West, A.	G/20611	Pte.
Webster, H. J.	G/2527	Pte.	West, A. E. V.	G/15279	Pte.
Webster, J. G.	G/30851	Pte.	West, A. G.	G/12883	Pte.
Webster, P.J.E.	G/2836	Pte.	West, C. R. J.	G/21001	L/Sgt.
Webster, T. G.	G/8922	Pte.	West, F.	G/10561	Pte.
Webster, W. H.	S/403	Pte.	West, G. F.	242482	Pte.
Weedon, A.	G/3859	Pte.	West, H. S.	G/11697	Pte.
Weedon, H. L.	G/2504	Pte.	West, J.	205506	Pte.
Weedon, S. C.	TF/1102	Pte.	West, J. F.	G/3943	Pte.

APPENDIX II.

Name	Number	Rank
West, R. G.	G/24693	Pte.
West, S. J.	203395	Cpl.
West, T.	TF/1913	Pte.
West, W. A.	L/8826	Pte.
West, W. J.	G/4015	Pte.
West, W. J.	L/7467	Pte.
West, W. W.	G/24496	Cpl.
Westborn, J. P., D.C.M.	L/8539	Pte.
Westbury, F.	G/20255	Pte.
Westcott, G.	L/7805	Pte.
Westcott, J.	G/5489	Pte.
Western, J. G.	L/9887	Pte.
Westhueser, O.	200493	Cpl.
Westmacott, F.C.		2nd Lieut.
Weston, E. G.	205508	Pte.
Weston, H. G.	G/9721	C.S.M.
Weston, J.	G/7463	Pte.
Weston, O.	G/10942	Pte.
Weston, R.	G/6710	L/Cpl.
Weston, W. S.	G/11043	Pte.
Whacker, H.	L/8404	Pte.
Whale, W. T.	G/15144	Pte.
Whatford, J.	G/21573	Pte.
Whatling, H.W.	G/11242	Pte.
Whatmough, A. V.	L/16092	Pte.
Wheal, J. H.	G/10658	Pte.
Wheat, D.	G/19469	Pte.
Wheatcroft, T. H.	G/38658	Pte.
Wheatley, G.	G/8	L/Cpl.
Wheatley, J. H.	G/20601	L/Cpl.
Wheatley, P.	G/24612	Pte.
Wheelan, J. M.	G/24401	Pte.
Wheeler, A., M.M.	G/9300	C.S.M.
Wheeler, C. W.	G/25929	Pte.
Wheeler, E.	G/126	Cpl.
Wheeler, G. W.	G/10763	Pte.
Wheeler, J.	G/39329	Pte.
Wheeler, J.	S/5702	Pte.
Wheeler, S.	G/14409	Pte.
Whenday, A. E.	G/19285	Pte.
Whennell, E.	G/7560	Pte.
Whiffen, W.	G/11119	Pte.
Whiffin, W. E.	240213	Pte.
Whiffin, W. G.	TF/4268	Pte.
Whiles, T. P.	G/29544	Pte.
Whitaker, W. G., M.M.	G/11873	L/Cpl.
Whitcombe, S.J.	G/15462	Pte.
White, A.	G/1409	Pte.
White, A. D.	G/113	Pte.
White, A. W.	S/509	Pte.
White, C. A., M.M.	G/19151	Sgt.
White, D. V. A. H. S.	200238	C.S.M.
White, E.	G/19721	Pte.
White, E.	L/7817	Pte.
White, E. E.	203214	Pte.
White, F.	G/141	Pte.
White, F. W.	L/5289	Pte.
White, H.	G/2465	Pte.
White, H. M.	G/326	Pte.
White, I. E.	G/805	Pte.
White, J.	L/6406	Pte.
White J.	S/9235	Pte.
White, J.	S/319	Pte.
White, J.	G/24766	Pte.
White, L. S.		2nd Lieut.
White, P. H.	TF/3582	Pte.
White, R.	L/8063	Pte.
White, S. W.	G/8129	Sgt.
White, T.	G/2042	Pte.
White, T.	G/2785	Pte.
White, T. W., M.M.	L/8740	Pte.
White, W.	G/12526	Pte.
White, W. T.	L/8980	Pte.
Whitehall, J.	G/24654	Pte.
Whitehead, C.D.	G/16025	Pte.
Whitehead, G.	203155	L/Cpl.
Whitehead, T. R.	S/7838	Pte.

APPENDIX II.

Whitehorn, A.S.	L/7193	Pte.	Wilkins, W. T.	G/20167	Pte.
Whitehouse, L.	G/11851	Pte.	Wilkinson, C. J.	G/5412	Pte.
Whitehouse, P. J.		2nd Lieut.	Wilkinson, F.	L/10677	Pte.
Whiteley, W.	203154	Pte.	Wilkinson, J. W.	205432	Pte.
Whiteman, C.W.	G/18543	Pte.	Wilkinson, R. A. W.		
Whitman, B. F.	G/19267	L/Cpl.		L/10294	Pte.
Whittaker, A.	G/442	Pte.	Wilkinson, W.	G/11327	Pte.
Whittaker, T.E.	G/24764	Cpl.	Wilks, S.		Lieut.
Whittaker, W.	L/6519	Sgt.	Willard, J.	G/58	Pte.
Whittle, S.	G/16362	Pte.	Willcocks,	L/9589	L/Cpl.
Whitwood, H.	240569	Pte.	Willden, S.	201076	Pte.
Whyatt, A. H., M.M.			Willett, L.	L/11146	Pte.
	G/3497	Pte.	Williams, A. J.	S/9402	Cpl.
Whybrow, W.R.	G/18781	Pte.	Williams, C.	G/11845	Pte.
Whyman, H.	G/11270	Pte.	Williams, C. J.	G/7583	L/Cpl.
Whyman, L. J.	L/11039	L/Cpl.	Williams, D. G.	G/8664	L/Cpl.
Wickenden, J.E.	L/10151	Pte.	Williams, D.W.	G/24765	Cpl.
Wickens, P.R.S.	G/1066	Pte.	Williams, E. H.	G/11795	Pte.
Wickens, S.	G/3015	Pte.	Williams, E. J.	204407	Pte.
Wickens, S. F.	G/11618	L/Cpl.	Williams, E. J.	G/13353	Pte.
Wicker, F. A.	G/959	Pte.	Williams, E. T.		Capt.
Wickham, F. J.	G/4748	Cpl.	Williams, E. V. G.		
Wicks, G. J.	G/18538	L/Cpl.		G/26525	Pte.
Wide, W. J.	G/17914	Pte.	Williams, F.	G/5682	Pte.
Wiffen, C. F.	G/18858	Pte.	Williams, F. C.	L/9683	L/Cpl.
Wiffen, S.	G/24363	Pte.	Williams, F. E.	203178	L/Cpl.
Wigan, W. L.		Lieut.	Williams, F. G.	L/9841	Sgt.
Wiggin, J.	L/10635	Pte.	Williams, G. F.	G/14521	Pte.
Wiggins, F. B.	206358	Pte.	Williams, H.	S/173	Pte.
Wiggins, S. J.	G/28582	Pte.	Williams, H.	G/4688	Pte.
Wiggins, W.	L/9324	Pte.	Williams, H. A.	L/7314	Pte.
Whightman, A. E.			Williams, H. C.	G/23882	Pte.
	G/12479	L/Cpl.	Williams, I.	242320	Pte.
Wilcox, C.	G/11286	Cpl.	Williams, J.	G/31613	Pte.
Wilder, F.	L/10129	Pte.	Williams, J. A.	G/8147	Pte.
Wildey, H. E.	G/26267	Pte.	Williams, J. T.	G/3459	Pte.
Wiles, A.	TG/1939	Pte.	Williams, L. G.	G/31295	Pte.
Wilkin, G.	G/38685	Pte.	Williams, O.G.J.	S/1237	Pte.
Wilkins, A. J.	G/5800	Cpl.	Williams, P.	G/7355	Pte.
Wilkins, E. J.	G/23139	L/Cpl.	Williams, R. M.	G/29018	L/Cpl.
Wilkins, F.	G/20049	Pte.	Williams, R. W.	G/4135	Pte.
Wilkins, H. G.	L/11638	Pte.	Williams, S.	G/6349	Pte.
Wilkins, T. W.	G/8040	Pte.	Williams, V.	203230	Pte.

581

APPENDIX II.

Williams, W.	G/6075	Pte.
Williams, W. E.	G/19833	Pte.
Williams, W. J.	G/21538	Sgt.
Williamson, F.A.	265364	Pte.
Willimott, W.	240820	Cpl.
Willis, A. E.	G/18869	Pte.
Willis, E. C.	G/10671	Pte.
Willis, J.	S/469	Pte.
Willis, S.	G/17946	Pte.
Willis, S. G.	G/10898	Pte.
Willison, A. G.	G/6935	Pte.
Willott, R. R.	241340	Pte.
Willoughby, D. H.	G/15991	L/Cpl.
Willoughby, F.	L/7884	Pte.
Willoughby, W. A.	G/2562	Pte.
Wills, A.	G/16602	Pte.
Wills, A.	G/24755	Pte.
Wills, H. G.	G/23701	Pte.
Willsher, H. E.	G/15979	Pte.
Wilson, A.	G/18228	Pte.
Wilson, A.	G/2542	L/Cpl.
Wilson, A.D. L.		Lieut.
Wilson, A. K.	205650	Pte.
Wilson, E. C.		Lieut.
Wilson, D.	G/14735	Pte.
Wilson F.	G/10015	L/Cpl.
Wilson, F.	G/19360	Pte.
Wilson, H. G.F.	G/18940	Pte.
Wilson, H. I. De B.		Capt.
Wilson, H. W.	G/3480	L/Cpl.
Wilson, T.	G/19470	Pte.
Wilson, J. A.	G/5875	L/Cpl.
Wilson, J. E.	G/21571	Pte.
Wilson, R.	205534	Pte.
Wilson, R. A.	G/4292	Pte.
Wilson, R. S.W.	G/17477	Sgt.
Wilson, T.	G/20050	Pte.
Wilson, T.	G/4594	Pte.
Wilson, T. A.	L/10836	Pte.
Wilson, T. E.	242257	Pte.
Wilson, W.	S/314	Pte.
Wilson, W.	G/5558	Pte.
Wilson, W.	G/18279	Pte.
Wilson W. E.	G/9874	Pte.
Wilson, W. H.	L/7439	Pte.
Winch, E. N.		2nd Lieut.
Wineyard, C.	G/13308	Pte.
Winfield, P. J.	G/1289	Pte.
Wingate, F. J.	G/23157	Pte.
Wingrove, B. A.	S/9145	Pte.
Wingrove, F. H.	240125	Pte.
Winn, J.	L/9621	Pte.
Winsett, E. A.	G/17987	Pte.
Winter, C.	L/7912	Pte.
Winter, F. A.	L/10168	Pte.
Winter S. J.	L/9173	Pte.
Winterflood, A. E.	G/23854	L/Cpl.
Wisdom, F. G.	G/5012	Pte.
Wise, F. J.	203275	Pte.
Wise J.	G/4617	Pte.
Wise, W.	G/8800	Cpl.
Wiseman, A. S.	G/25406	Pte.
Wiseman, W. J.	G/13074	Pte.
Wiseman, W. O.	204724	Pte.
Wiskin W. J.	L/10894	Pte.
Withall, J.	G/23565	Pte.
Witham, W.	G/7232	Pte.
Withnall, A.	G/31615	Pte.
Wolfe, A. W.	L/10154	Pte.
Wolfe, W.	G/8364	Pte.
Wood, A.	G/5226	Pte.
Wood B. V.		2nd Lieut.
Wood, C.	G/20198	Pte.
Wood, C. A.	L/7569	Pte.
Wood, E.	G/5068	Pte.
Wood, E. E.	L/9949	L/Cpl.
Wood, E. L.	G/19179	Pte.
Wood, F.	G/10546	Pte.
Wood, F.	G/7714	Sgt.
Wood, F. A.	G/439	L/Cpl.
Wood, G. W.	G/20145	Pte.
Wood, H. F. A.	G/6474	Pte.
Wood, H. J.	G/10673	Pte.

APPENDIX II.

Name	Number	Rank
Wood, T. G.	G/695	Pte.
Wood, V.	G/13091	Pte.
Wood, W.		Capt.
Wood, W.	G/23855	Cpl.
Wood, W.	G/15969	Pte.
Wood, W.	G/18226	L/Cpl.
Wood, W. C.	G/12467	Pte.
Wood, W. H.	G/7298	Pte.
Woodall, A.	242446	Pte.
Woodard, R. J.	G/25094	Pte.
Woodbridge, H. R.	202317	Pte.
Woodcock, F.H.	L/10465	Pte.
Woodcock, J.M.	G/7330	Pte.
Wooddeson, H. L.	G/10674	Cpl.
Woodgate, C.	G/5823	Pte.
Woodgate, E.H.	G/6351	Pte.
Woodgate, H.	L/9912	Sgt.
Woodgate, J. A.	G/23616	Pte.
Woodgate, R. A.	G/1852	Pte.
Woodger, A. E.	G/12134	Pte.
Woodhams, H.	L/8561	Pte.
Woodhams, W.	G/4392	Pte.
Woodhead, E.	G/24534	Pte.
Woodhouse, J.A.	G/19468	Pte.
Woodhouse, W.	G/12340	Pte.
Woodley, W.	G/2848	Pte.
Woodman, A.	G/10055	Pte.
Woodman, N. E.	G/28841	Pte.
Woodroffe, A. H.		2nd Lieut.
Woodrow, H.	G/19104	Pte.
Woods, C.	G/25379	Pte.
Woods, D. C.	G/12194	Pte.
Woods, F. C.	G/18057	L/Sgt.
Woods, G.	G/17246	Pte.
Woods, H. C.	G/11389	L/Cpl.
Woods, J.	G/19763	Pte.
Woods, S. F.	G/18082	Pte.
Woodward, C.	G/10390	Pte.
Woodward, G.	G/10333	Pte.
Woodward, W.	L/9416	Dmr.
Wookey, H. C.	G/31083	Cpl.
Woolard, F.	G/13481	Pte.
Woolard, W. J. C.	G/30990	Pte.
Wooley, H. A.	G/11930	Pte.
Woolf, C. H.	241027	L/Cpl.
Woolford, H.	S/9042	Pte.
Woolford, H.	203936	Pte.
Woolford, R.	S/8942	Pte.
Woollard, B.	G/17486	Pte.
Woolley, E.	L/10561	Pte.
Woolley, H. G.		2nd Lieut.
Woolven, J.	G/17399	Pte.
Worby, E. W.	G/28323	Pte.
Wormald, H. B.	G/2170	Sgt.
Worms, A. E.	G/8377	Pte.
Worsfold, W. C.	S/882	Sgt.
Worsford, A. V.	G/11844	Pte.
Worsley, E. J.	G/18535	Cpl.
Worsley, H.	203516	Pte.
Worth, T. H.	G/4250	Pte.
Worthington, H. W.	G/19589	Pte.
Wrack, W. C.	G/8807	L/Cpl.
Wraight, V. T.	G/18547	Pte.
Wren, C.	L/6122	Pte.
Wright, A.	L/7358	Pte.
Wright, A. G.	G/24485	Pte.
Wright, C. E.	G/9704	Pte.
Wright, C. P.		2nd Lieut.
Wright, E. J.	L/6746	Pte.
Wright, F.	G/24659	Pte.
Wright, G.	G/20610	Pte.
Wright, H.	G/24538	Pte.
Wright, J.	G/4403	Pte.
Wright, J. H.	G/1734	Pte.
Wright, J. S.	G/6089	Pte.
Wright, L.	G/19327	Pte.
Wright, L. C.	G/28840	Pte.
Wright, S. G.	G/1764	Pte.
Wright, T.	G/6938	Pte.
Wright T. W.	G/6701	L/Cpl.
Wright, W.	G/20053	Pte.
Wrighton, A. P.	G/14575	Pte.

APPENDIX II.

Wrigley, J. H.	G/22136	Pte.	Yorke, C. H.		2nd Lieut.	
Wyatt, A.	L/5018	Pte.	Youlton, F. J.	G/23120	Pte.	
Wyatt, E. J.	G/3235	Pte.	Young, A.	G/12149	Pte.	
Wyatt, R.	G/322	Pte.	Young, A. G.		2nd Lieut.	
Wyatt, R. J.	G/29407	Pte.	Young, A. J.	G/4804	Pte.	
Wyborn, N.W.A.	265402	Pte.	Young, A. W.	G/20617	Pte.	
Wybourne, A.	S/8656	Pte.	Young, B. A.	S/9144	Pte.	
Wycherley, C.T.	G/4016	Pte.	Young, C. H. A., *M.M.*			
Wycherley, J. L.	G/5463	Pte.		G/502	Sgt.	
Wykes, A.	L/6560	Pte.	Young, D.	20095E	Pte.	
Wylie, L. J.	G/30845	Pte.	Young, E.	G/2277	Pte.	
Wyre, A.	G/24484	Pte.	Young, E. M.	G/24758	Pte.	
			Young, F. J.	G/4071	Pte.	
Yardley, W.	L/10008	Pte.	Young, G. J.	G/21228	Pte.	
Yarnton, J.	G/4562	Pte.	Young, H. A.	G/20055	Pte.	
Yates, J.	G/18934	Pte.	Young, H. J.	G/2173	Pte.	
Yates, J. S.		2nd Lieut.	Young, L.	G/19110	Pte.	
Yates, T.	G/1939	Pte.	Young, T. F.	G/169	L/Cpl.	
Yeldham, E. S.	G/414	L/Cpl.	Young, W.	G/24262	Pte.	
Yell, F. D.	G/15990	Pte.	Young, W. J.	L/9083	Pte.	
Yeo, A. F.	G/31622	Pte.	Youngman, A.O.	G/20257	Pte.	
Yeo, F. G.		2nd Lieut.				
Yeomans, W.	G/737	Pte.				
Yews, W.	G/3780	Pte.	Zillwood, J. F.	G/7042	Pte.	
York, F. E.	200858	L/Cpl.	Zimmern, L.	G/17489	Pte.	
York, W. T.	G/14746	Pte.	Zincraft, V. E.	G/1140	Pte.	

APPENDIX III.

HONOURS, REWARDS AND DECORATIONS AWARDED

to Members Past and Present of
The Queen's Own Royal West Kent Regiment.

(The ranks shown are those held at the time of award).

VICTORIA CROSS.

Lieut. D. J. DEAN.

An account of the exploit for which Lieut. Dean was awarded the V.C. is given in Chapter XXVIII. (Page 422).

Lieut. C. H. SEWELL, 3rd Battalion, attached Tank Corps.

When in command of a section of Whippet Light Tanks in action this officer displayed most conspicuous bravery and initiative in getting out of his own Tank and crossing open ground under heavy shell and machine-gun fire to rescue the crew of another Whippet of his section which had side-slipped into a large shell-hole, overturned and taken fire. The door of the Tank having become jammed against the side of the shell-hole, Lieut. Sewell, by his own unaided efforts, dug away the entrance to the door and released the crew. In doing so he undoubtedly saved the lives of the officer and men inside the Tank, as they could not have got out without his assistance. After having extricated the crew, seeing one of his own crew lying wounded behind his Tank, he again dashed across the open ground to his assistance. He was hit in doing so, but succeeded in reaching the Tank, when a few minutes later he was again hit, fatally, in the act of dressing his wounded driver. During the whole period he was within full view and short range of the enemy machine-guns and rifle - pits, and throughout, by his prompt and heroic action, showed an utter disregard for his own personal safety.

APPENDIX III.

VICTORIA CROSS (continued).

No. 358 Sergt. T. J. HARRIS.

The action which won for Sergt. Harris the V.C. is described in Chapter XXVII. (Page 406).

No. 55295 L/Sergt. G. JARRATT, Royal Fusiliers, formerly 12th Battalion.

For most conspicuous bravery and devotion in deliberately sacrificing his life to save others, near Pelves, France, on 3rd May, 1917. He had, together with some wounded men, been taken prisoner, and placed under guard in a dug-out. The same evening the enemy were driven back by our troops, the leading infantrymen of which commenced to bomb the dug-outs. A grenade fell in the dug-out, and without hesitation Cpl. Jarratt placed both feet on the grenade, the subsequent explosion blowing off both his legs. The wounded were later safely removed to our lines, but Cpl. Jarratt died before he could be removed. By this supreme act of self-sacrifice, the lives of these wounded men were saved.

No. 1987 Corpl. F. G. COPPINS, Manitoba Regiment, served for four years in the 1st Battalion.

For conspicuous bravery and devotion to duty when, during an attack, his platoon came unexpectedly under fire of numerous machine-guns. It was not possible to advance or retire, and no cover was available. It became apparent that the platoon would be annihilated unless the enemy machine-guns were silenced immediately. Cpl. Coppins, without hesitation and on his own initiative, called on four men to follow him, and leapt forward in face of intense machine-gun fire. With his comrades he rushed straight for the machine-guns. The four men with him were killed and Cpl. Coppins wounded. Despite his wounds, he reached the hostile machine-guns alone, killed the operator of the first gun and three of the crew, and made prisoners of four others, who surrendered. Cpl. Coppins, by this act of outstanding valour, was the means of saving many lives of the men of his platoon, and enabled the advance to be continued. Despite his wounds, this gallant N.C.O. continued with his platoon to the final objective, and only left the line when it had been made secure and when ordered to do so.

APPENDIX III.

K.C.B.

Alderson, E. A. H., *C.B.*, Lieut.-General.

K.C.M.G.

Western, W. G. B., *C.B.*, Major-General.

C.B.

Bush, H. S., *C.M.G.*, Bt.-Colonel.
Leslie, W. S., *C.M.G.*, *D.S.O.*, Brig.-General.
Martyn, A., *C.M.G.*, Brig.-General.
Nepean, H. E. C. B., Colonel.
O'Dowda, J. W., *C.M.G.*, Brig.-General.
Pedley, S. H., Colonel.
Robinson, P. M., *C.M.G.*, Lieut.-Colonel.

C.S.I.

Fagan, E. A., *C.M.G.*, *D.S.O.*, Brig.-General.
Isacke, H., *C.M.G.*, Brig.-General.
Nepean, H. E. C. B., *C.M.G.*, Brig.-General.
O'Dowda, J. W., *C.B.*, *C.M.G.*, Brig.-General.

C.M.G.

Annesley, W. H., *D.S.O.*, Bt.-Major.
Bonham-Carter, C., *D.S.O.*, Brig.-General.
Buchanan-Dunlop, H. D., *D.S.O.*, Bt.-Lieut.-Colonel.
Bush, H. S., Bt.-Colonel.
Crosse, C. R., *M.V.O.*, Lieut.-Colonel.
Fagan, E. A., *D.S.O.*, Brig.-General.
Harrison, C. E. C. B., Bt.-Colonel.
Hewett, E. V. O., *D.S.O.*, Major.
Hildyard, R. J. T., *D.S.O.*, Bt.-Lieut.-Colonel.
Isacke, H., Bt.-Colonel.
Martyn, A., Brig.-General.

APPENDIX III.

C.M.G. (continued).

Maunsell, G. W., Bt.-Colonel.
Nepean, H. E. C. B., Lieut.-Colonel.
O'Dowda, J. W., Bt.-Colonel.
Price, T. R. C., *D.S.O.*, Bt.-Lieut.-Colonel.
Snow, H. W., *D.S.O.*, Bt.-Lieut.-Colonel.
Whitehead, J., *D.S.O.*, Bt.-Lieut.-Colonel.
Umfreville, P., Bt.-Lieut.-Colonel.

C.I.E.

Watney, C. N., *T.D.*, Lieut.-Colonel.

C.B.E.

Grove, E. A. W. S., *C.B.*, Brig.-General.
Harrison, C. E. C. B., *C.M.G.*, Bt.-Colonel.
Umfreville, P., *C.M.G.*, Bt.-Lieut.-Colonel.
Wintour, F., *C.B.*, Brig.-General.

THIRD CLASP TO D.S.O.

Dawson, W. R. A., *D.S.O.*, Lieut.-Colonel.

SECOND CLASP TO D.S.O.

Corfe, A. C., *D.S.O.*, Lieut.-Colonel.
Dawson, W. R. A., *D.S.O.*, Lieut.-Colonel.

CLASP TO THE D.S.O.

Corfe, A. C., *D.S.O.*, Lieut.-Colonel.
Dawson, W. R. A., *D.S.O.*, Lieut.-Colonel.
Fagan, E. A., *C.M.G.*, *D.S.O.*, Brig-General.
Wenyon, H. J., *D.S.O.*, Lieut.-Colonel.

APPENDIX III.

D.S.O.

Alderman, W. J., Captain.
Aldworth, T. P., Captain.
Annesley, W. H., Bt.-Major.
Anstruther, P. N., *M.C.*, Captain.

Bazley-White, R. B. L., Captain.
Belgrave, H. D., Bt.-Lieut.-Col.
Bonham-Carter, C., Bt.-Lieut.-Col.
Buchanan-Dunlop, H. D., Major.

Cooke, J. C., *M.C.*, Major.
Corfe, A. C., Lieut.-Col.

Davies, P. M., Lieut.-Col.
Dawson, W. R. A., Captain.
Drumgold, A., 2nd Lieut.

Elgood, G., Major.

Fagan, E. A., Lieut.-Col.
Frazer, F. A., Lieut.-Col.

Grant, A. K., Major.

Hall, P. S., Lieut.
Henderson, G. D., *M.C.*, Captain.
Henderson-Roe, C. G., Captain.
Hewett, E. V. O., *C.M.G.*, Major
Hewitt, A. S., Major.
Hibbert, O. Y., Captain.
Hickson, L. H., Lieut.-Col.
Hildyard, R. J. T., *C.M.G.*, Bt.-Lieut.-Col.
Hitchins, C. F., Lieut.-Gen.
Holden, V., *M.C.*, Captain.

Ingram, C. R., Major.

Johnstone, B., Lieut.-Col.

Kay, J. K., Major.
Kitson, C. E., Bt.-Lieut.-Col.

Leslie, W. S., Bt.-Lieut.-Col.

MacNeece, W. F., Captain.
Martyn, A. Wood, Lieut.-Col.

Nelson, J. W., Major.
Norman, E. H., Major.

Peploe, H., Lieut.-Col.
Phillips, A. E., Major.
Pragnell, G. F., Captain.
Price, T. R. C., Major.
Pullman, A. H., Major.

Russell, J. R., Lieut.

Snow, H. W., Bt.-Major.
Stanhope, Earl J. R., *M.C.*, Major.

Taylor, C. W. H., Bt.-Major.
Thesiger, the Hon. E. R., Major.
Thomas, A. E. W., *M.C.*, 2nd Lieut.
Tillie, W. K., *M.C.*, Lieut.-Col.
Tulloch, R. M. G., Major.
Tronsdell, A. J., *M.C.*, Captain.

Vansittart, E., Colonel.

Waring, H. A., Lieut.-Col.
Wenyon, H. J., Captain.
White, H. B. H., Lieut.
White, R. L., Major.
Whitehead, J., Bt.-Lieut.-Col.
Whitehead, J., Major.
Whitty, N. I., Major.
Wilberforce, W., *M.C.*, Lieut.-Col.
Willis, W. J., Major and Qr.-Mr.
Woulfe-Flanagan, R. J., Bt.-Col.

APPENDIX III.

O.B.E.

Aldworth, T. P., *D.S.O.*, Captain.
Brewis, C. D., Major.
Brock, R. G. C., Major.
Cohen, Sir H.B., *Bart.*, Major.
Dykes, K., *M.C.*, Major.
Hewett, E. V. O., *D.S.O.*, Lieut.-Col.
Hewitt, A. S., *D.S.O.*, Lieut.-Col.
Hudson, E. J., Bt.-Major.
Ingram, C. R., *D.S.O.*, Major.

Martyn, A. Wood, *D.S.O.*, Lieut.-Col.
Norman, E. H., *D.S.O.*, Lieut.-Col.
Phillips, C. E. S., Bt.-Major.
Prescott-Roberts, P. A., Lieut.-Col.
Pritchard, J. M., Captain.
Sheppard, E. W., *M.C.*, Captain.
Smithers, H., Major.
Soames, W. F., Major.
Stigand, C. H., Major.
Watney, R. D., Major.

M.B.E.

Brown, G. W., Captain.
Burrows, J. D., Captain.
Campbell, M., Captain.
Coulter, P. A., Lieut.
Holland, E. S., Captain.
Jones, O., Captain.

May, E., Major.
Nash, W., Captain.
Rogers, H. G., *M.C.*, Captain and Qr.-Mr.
Graham Wigan, A. J., Lieut.

SECOND CLASP TO M.C.

Harris, H. J. M., *M.C.*, Lieut.

McDonald, A. V., *M.C.*, Captain.

CLASP TO M.C.

Brown, E. G., *M.C.*, Lieut.
Brown, R., *M.C.*, Captain.
Doble, G. F., *M.C.*, Lieut.
Dove, W. G., *M.C.*, Captain.
Harris, H. J. M., *M.C.*, Lieut.
Hindle, G. W., *M.C.*, Captain.
McDonald, A. V., *M.C.*, Captain.

Maltby, R., *M.C.*, Captain.
Preston, L. G., *M.C.*, Captain.
Rooney, T., *M.C.*, 2nd Lieut.
Sansome, B., *M.C.*, 2nd Lieut.
Sutherst, D. V., *M.C.*, Captain.
Tanner, D. W. F., *M.C.*, 2nd Lieut.

APPENDIX III.

M.C.

Abel, J. E., 2nd Lieut.
Anstruther, P. N., Captain.
Antill, H. B., Lieut.
Arnaud, J. N., Captain.
Attey, G. A., 2nd Lieut.

Bainton, H. W. E., Lieut.
Baker, G. B., 2nd Lieut.
Baker, R. P., Captain.
Balbernie, A. G., Captain.
Bankes, P. A., 2nd Lieut.
Bartholomew, R., Captain.
Battye, C. F., Captain.
Beattie, H. W., 2nd Lieut.
Bellman, J. F., 2nd Lieut.
Bengough, L., Captain.
Berger, C. C., 2nd Lieut.
Bozman, E. F., Lieut.
Bracken, H., Lieut.
Brett, D. A., 2nd Lieut.
Brook, D. B., Lieut.
Brown, E. G., 2nd Lieut.
Brown, H. S., Major.
Brown, R., 2nd Lieut.
Buckingham, P. E., 2nd Lieut.
Bull, K. R., 2nd Lieut.
Burden, A. E. J., 2nd Lieut.

Cale, R. H., 2nd Lieut.
Cambrook, K. H., 2nd Lieut.
Carey, M. E., 2nd Lieut.
Carville, M. H., 2nd Lieut.
Catt-Carré, A. W., Lieut.
Cheel, E. S., 2nd Lieut.
Clarke, V. S., Captain.
Clifford, W. C., Captain.
Cobb, R. S., Lieut.
Cobb, W. R., Lieut.
Cooke, J. C., Captain.
Cooper, F. T., 2nd Lieut.
Corke, F., Lieut.
Cozens, F., Captain.

Cryer, J. B., 2nd Lieut.
Cullerne, A. B., 2nd Lieut.

Darlow, J. W. E., Lieut.
Densham, J. M., M.M., 2nd Lieut.
Dibben, T. L., 2nd Lieut.
Dix, H. G., 2nd Lieut.
Doble, G. F., 2nd Lieut.
Doe, H. S., Lieut.
Donaldson, A. J., 2nd Lieut.
Dove, W. G., Captain.
Duffield, C. A. W., Lieut.
Dunkerley, C. L., 2nd Lieut.
Dykes, K., Lieut.

Elliott, W. J., 2nd Lieut.
Evans, H. G., Lieut.

Frazer, F. G., Captain.
French, R. S., 2nd Lieut.
Fulcher, E. J., Lieut.

Garbutt, J. R., 2nd Lieut.
Gingell, L. A. H., 2nd Lieut.
Goddard, W. J., 2nd Lieut.
Godly, P. C. T., 2nd Lieut.
Goulden, E. O., Lieut.
Goulds, E. W., Lieut. & Qr.-Mr.
Gray, H. A., 2nd Lieut.
Greenwood, J. H., 2nd Lieut.
Guess, H., 2nd Lieut.
Guest, T. J., Captain.

Hall, W. D. de, Lieut.
Harding, A. K., Captain.
Hardy, A. E., Captain.
Harris, H. J. M., 2nd Lieut.
Hayley, J. D., No. 5614, C.S.M.
Hayward, G. S. L., 2nd Lieut.
Hemmerde, C. E., 2nd Lieut.
Henderson, G. D., Lieut.

APPENDIX III.

M.C. (continued).

Henderson-Roe, C. G., D.S.O., Captain.
Hibbert, O. Y., D.S.O., Major.
Hill, R. B. L., 2nd Lieut.
Hindle, G. W., Captain.
Hinds, G. V., Lieut.
Hodgson, C., 2nd Lieut.
Holden, V., Captain.
Hougham, B. W., Captain.
Hughes, E. G. V., Captain.

Jagger, B. E. G., 2nd Lieut.
Janaway, F. J., 2nd Lieut.
Jenkins, E., 2nd Lieut.
Jimenez, F. J., Captain.
Joel, G. J., Lieut.
Judge, C. F., 10171, C.S.M.

Kent, R. D., 2nd Lieut.
Kerr, R., Lieut.
Killick, R. N., D.C.M., Lieut.
Kirk, F. T., Major.
Knight, C. W. R., Captain.

Lawrence, S. R., 2nd Lieut.
Levelis-Marke, P. H., 2nd Lieut.
Lewin, F. H., 2nd Lieut.
Lewis-Barned, de S. H., Lieut.
Lindsay, J., Captain.
Loudoun, C. W., 2nd Lieut.
Lovett, F. C., Captain.

McDonald, A. V., 2nd Lieut.
Mainwaring, T. L., 2nd Lieut.
Malpass, C. E., Captain.
Maltby, R., Lieut.
Manley, C. P. H., 2nd Lieut.
Mann, H. G. C., 2nd Lieut.
Metford-Lewis, T. A., 2nd Lieut.
Milford, C. S., Lieut.
Monckton, W. T., Captain.
Moneypenny, P. B. S. G., Lieut.

Morley, A. V. D., Lieut.
Moulton-Barrett, E. F., Captain.
Needham, S. J., Lieut.
Nicoll, E. S., Lieut.

Oakley, A. H., Lieut.
Orchardson, J. C., Captain.
Ouzman, W. J. C., 2nd Lieut.

Parmenter, J. H., 2nd Lieut.
Pfeuffar, K., 2nd Lieut.
Phillips, E. O., 2nd Lieut.
Piggott, W. T., 2nd Lieut.
Preston, L. G., 2nd Lieut.
Purchase, A. J., 2nd Lieut.
Puttick, A. J., Captan.

Razell, A. N., 2nd Lieut.
Reynolds, A., 5435, R.S.M.
Roberts, F. W., Lieut.
Rogers, H. G., Lieut. & Qr.-Mr.
Rogers, W. J., Lieut.
Rooney, T., Lieut.
Roscoe, A., 2nd Lieut.
Rowe, J. W. F., 2nd Lieut.
Rushton, F. W., 2nd Lieut.
Russell, R. B., Lieut.

Salmon, E. C. H., Lieut.
Sansom, L. B., 2nd Lieut.
Scott, J. J., Lieut.
Scott-Marten, P., 2nd Lieut.
Sheppard, E. W., 2nd Lieut.
Shrimpton, H. L., 2nd Lieut.
Slade, H. G. B., 2nd Lieut.
Smith, H. R., Lieut.
Smith, L. C. R., Captain.
Smithers, N., Captain.
Squibb, E., 2nd Lieut.
Stallard, C. F., Captain.
Stanhope, J. R., Earl, Major.
Stephens, B., 2nd Lieut.

APPENDIX III.

M.C. (continued).

Stern, C., Captain.
Stevens, H. F., Lieut.
Stokes, J. K., Captain.
Sutherland, J. L. C., Captain.
Sutherst, D. V., 2nd Lieut.

Tanner, D. W. F., 2nd Lieut.
Tapp, A., Lieut. & Qr.-Mr.
Taylor, H. A., 2nd Lieut.
Thomas, A. E. W., Lieut.
Thorne, R., Captain & Qr.-Mr.
Ticehurst, J. V., 2nd Lieut.
Tillie, W. K., Captain.
Tindall, C. G., Lieut.
Trenchard-Davis, C., Lieut.
Trotter, E. C. B., D.C.M., 2nd Lieut.
Turner, R. W., Lieut.
Tyler, P. H., 2nd Lieut.

Upfold, S. J., 2nd Lieut.

Vince, W. R., 2nd Lieut.

Waddington, T. T., Captain.
Waite, C. E., Major.
Wallis, F. A., Captain.
Wallis, G. A. E., 2nd Lieut.
Walthen, R. B., 2nd Lieut.
Warren, H., Captain.
Warren, W. F., 6184, R.S.M.
Waydelin, F. W., Captain.
Webb, C. P., 2nd Lieut.
Weston, E. F., 2nd Lieut.
Whitby, L. E. H., Captain.
Whitfield, W. F., 2nd Lieut.
Wilberforce, W., Captain.
Wilkin, H., Captain.
Willoughby, L., Lieut.
Wilson, A. J., Lieut.
Wilson, P. A., Captain.
Wingfield-Stratford, G. E., Captain.
Winn, H. P., Captain.
Woodcock, H. N. H., 2nd Lieut.
Woodhouse, D. E. M., Lieut.
Woodyear, R. P., 2nd Lieut.
Wright, S. G., 2nd Lieut.
Wright, T. C., 2nd Lieut.

D.F.C.

Dutton, A. C., 2nd Lieut.
Emden, C. S., Captain.

MacNeece, W. F., D.S.O., Lieut.-Col.

CLASP TO D.C.M.

Andrews, C., D.C.M., 2679 Cpl.
Chapman, W. F., D.C.M. 18549 L./Cpl.
Coleman, A., D.C.M. 1201 Sgt.
Cooper, J., D.C.M. 6884 C.S.M.

Rankin, R., D.C.M. 1219 R.S.M.
Smith, E. J., D.C.M. 205707 Sgt.
Taylor, T. R., D.C.M. 7811 C.S.M.

APPENDIX III.

D.C.M.

Adams, T.	9337	Pte.	Donohou, F. G.	23321	Sgt.
Aitcheson, J. D.	205388	Sgt.	Donovan, P.	9381	Pte.
Allison, E. E.	7316	Pte.	Dunk, W.	3818	C.S.M.
Andrews, C.	2679	L/Cpl.	Edwards, J.	6460	L/Sgt.
Ashby, J.	7850	Sgt.	Elliott, A. G.	5619	C.S.M.
Black, W. J.	8509	Pte.	Everist, J.	226	Cpl.
Banfield, C. F.	200965	Cpl.	Foot, W. G.	2240	Sgt.
Bax, T.	8840	Cpl.	Forsdick, P. V.	17810	Pte.
Blunt, W. H.	7895	Cpl.	Gallagher, C.	11263	Cpl.
Bridger, W.	8725	Bdsmn.	Garrod, F. W.	16014	L/Sgt.
Brown, F. J.	289	Pte.	Gilbert, A. T.	10247	Sgt.
Budgeon, W.	7709	Cpl.	Glare, J. R.	6085	Sgt.
Bunsell, E.	8438	Pte.	Goldsmith, P. H.	7504	L/Cpl.
Burnham, W.	5776	Sgt.	Gray, J.	203270	Cpl.
Bye, E. T.	9311	Bdsmn.	Greenaway, F.	2539	C.S.M.
Byrne, W. J.	205807	CSM	Gregory, V. A.	976	L/Sgt.
Carter, W.	767	Sgt.	Gutteridge, F.	1324	C.S.M.
Chambers, C.	203531	Sgt.	Hamblin, C.	3489	Sgt.
Chapman, W.	G/1927	Cpl.	Hammond, A. B.	6348	Sgt.
Chapman, W. F.	18549	L/Cpl.	Hanscombe, R. A.	G/4263	Pte.
Cherriman, E. H., M.M.	6525	Sgt.	Hatch, G. E.	7725	Cpl.
Clift, H. R.	7963	Pte.	Harris, G.	4041	Cpl.
Coleman, A.	1201	L/Cpl.	Hawkes, J. H.	8130	L/Cpl.
Cook, A.	1269	Cpl.	Haydon, S. M.	11448	CQMS
Cook, A. E.	630	Sgt.	Hayley, J., M.C.	L/5614	R.S.M.
Cook, A. T.	4232	L/Cpl.	Haynes, T.	L/10114	Sgt.
Cooker, F. T.	6	Sgt.	Herbert, W.	8746	Pte.
Coomber, J. W.	280	Sgt.	Hibbet, M. H.	8053	C.S.M.
Cooper, J.	6884	C.S.M.	Hillyard, R. J.	1998	Cpl.
Cork, T.	5793	Pte.	Hirschfield, H. J.	2073	Sgt.
Cowell, J.	5723	Pte.	Hooker, W. H.	9441	Cpl.
Cox, H. W.	11136	Sgt.	Howe, G.	8739	Pte.
Cozens, F.	8181	Sgt.	Halford, H., M.M.	8756	Sgt.
Cresswell, H.	718	Sgt.	Hylands, H. T., M.M.		
Crossley, F. J.	5259	C.S.M.		8168	C.S.M.
Daniels, G. H.	24797	Sgt.	Ives, L.	12076	Pte.
Davis, B., M.M.	8505	Sgt.	James, C.	10857	L/Cpl.
Dennington, E.	7847	Sgt.	Jenner, G.	657	Pte.

APPENDIX III.

D.C.M. (continued).

Name	Number	Rank
Johnson, G. H.	7982	Pte.
Keleher, W.	10471	Pte.
Kemp, L. G. L.	8349	C.S.M.
Killick, R. N.	178	Cpl.
Kingston, J.	15455	Pte.
Laffling, A. F.	5084	L/Sgt.
Lambeth, F. G.	362	Sgt.
Levey, R.	1535	Sgt.
Liddamore, F.	1036	L/Cpl.
Logan, R. J.	24785	Pte.
Malyon, J.	18681	L/Cpl.
Markham, W.	7544	Sgt.
Marsh, H. G.	4911	Sgt.
Mills, W. H.	932	C.S.M.
Mires, A. H.	94517	Pte.
Mitchell, W.	1374	C.S.M.
Moore, M.	88	Pte.
Moore, E. G.	7825	Sgt.
Murphy, C.	243	Sgt.
Neal, G.	21132	Pte.
Newbrooke, E. J.	5706	C.S.M.
Nicholson, W. D.	7032	Cpl.
Norrington, V.	4202	L/Cpl.
Nurse, W.	8308	Sgt.
Ogilvie, G. T.	5915	L/Cpl.
Pannett, R. J. G.	9103	Pte.
Pearson, C.	1086	C.S.M.
Penny, W. H.	4558	C.S.M.
Pitcher, A. E.	265396	Sgt.
Playford, A. E.	8413	Pte.
Portwain, H. J.	8595	Pte.
Purfield, A. J.	2640	Sgt.
Rankin, R.	1219	C.S.M.
Rawlings, R. T.	23640	L/Cpl.
Redmond, J. V.	4289	C.S.M.
Robinson, A. J.	8759	Sgt.
Roffey, A. T.	1575	C.S.M.
Rutherford, G. A.	9218	Pte.
Scammell, G.	11699	L/Cpl.
Seale, A.	2200	L/Cpl.
Skeer, W. T.	6530	R.S.M.
Skipper, T. H.	210103	Sgt.
Smart, E. J.	2432	Pte.
Smith, A. E.	2506	Pte.
Smith, E. J.	205707	Sgt.
Smith, H. W.	18511	Sgt.
Sterry, M. J., M.M.	21501	Sgt.
Stoneham, H.	G/28898	Cpl.
Stroud, M. P.	6694	Sgt.
Sutton, J.	4266	Sgt.
Taylor, T. R.	7811	C.S.M.
Terry, H. W.	2206	Sgt.
Thompson, H.	10619	Pte.
Tomkins, C.	470	Sgt.
Traill, W.	8538	Sgt.
Turnball, J.	8192	Pte.
Vanner, E. C.	19191	Sgt.
Vickers, G.	8896	Pte.
Wade, J. F.	G/21109	Sgt.
Wannell, W.	7361	Sgt.
Warner, W. F.	8499	L/Sgt.
Wesborn, J. P.	8539	Pte.
White, J.	19762	L/Sgt.
Wicken, J.	2340	C.S.M.
Woolmore, A. J.	G/29694	L/Cpl.
Wright, D.	7261	Sgt.
Young, J.	241	L/Sgt.

SECOND CLASP TO M.M.

Name	Number	Rank
Stacey, F., M.M.	1042	Pte.
Whaites, F., M.M.	205401	Pte.

APPENDIX III.

CLASP TO M.M.

Barnham, J. W. J.,	11243	Sgt.	McAllum, J. H.	1616	L/Cpl.
Bennett, D.	579	Sgt.	Marshall, A.	10137	Sgt.
Bowes, E.	11894	Pte.	Norris, C. C.	11679	Pte.
Britton, D.	G/246	Pte.			
Cherriman, E. H.	6425	Cpl.	Phillips, A. E.	G/21522	L/Cpl.
Cook, A. E.	G/873	Pte.	Piggott, F.	202235	Pte.
Correll, J. S.	G/19856	C.S.M.	Povey, A. T.	G/11071	Sgt.
Douglas, P. J.	9871	Cpl.	Rough, J. T.	16535	Pte.
Draper, S. J.	18411	Pte.	Rumbold, W. T.	26710	Sgt.
Fairbrother, E.	6552	Pte.	Smith, T. C.	7718	Sgt.
Feast, W.	7564	Cpl.	Stacey, F.	10421	Pte.
			Stacey, M. J.	21501	Sgt.
Gardner, C.	10600	Sgt.	Toomer, W. E.	21002	Sgt.
Green, L.	19122	Sgt.	Tweed, J. B.	17481	Cpl.
Greenwood, E.	10527	Pte.			
Haydon, G. W.	12393	Sgt.	Vaughan, C.	8832	Pte.
Hollands, F.	G/18441	Sgt.	Waller, W. J.	G/10846	Pte.
Hooker, W. H.	9441	Cpl.	West, G. W.	35	Pte.
Hubble, F.	1562	Pte.	Whaites, F.	205401	Pte.
			White, T. W.	8740	Pte.
Jackson, A.	21063	Sgt.	Wiles, A. L.	18532	Cpl.
Jennings, L. H.	165	Cpl.	Worsley, E.	G/18181	Cpl.
Laing, F.	6942	L/Cpl.	Yates, A.	15263	Pte.

M.M.

Abbott, W. E.	24577	Pte.	Anderson, H. G.	G/31909	Pte.
Acott, W.	G/640	Pte.	Apps, F. A.	10622	L/Cpl.
Adkin, S. L. V.	5210	Cpl.	Arnold, J. T.	1148	L/Cpl.
Agar, H. N.	206340	Cpl.	Arundell, A. H.	11129	Pte.
Akehurst, A. H.	19049	Pte.	Ash, S. J.	7882	Cpl.
Alderman, R.	12712	Sgt.	Attenborough, F. K.		
Aldred, A. B.	G/21513	L/Cpl.		G/30032	Sgt.
Aldridge, A. J.	11584	Sgt.	Attwood, A. B.	465	Cpl.
Allchin, J. H.	12586	Pte.	Austin, S.	7482	Pte.
Allen, H. C.	7416	Sgt.			

APPENDIX III.

M.M. (continued).

Name	Number	Rank	Name	Number	Rank
Bailey, A. W.	17539	Pte.	Blackman, W. J.	10172	L/Cpl.
Baker, J.	4646	Pte.	Blake, H.	G/19027	Sgt.
Baldwin, C.	G/9676	L/Cpl.	Blandford, G. A.	4108	Pte.
Baldwin, C. F.	2158	Sgt.	Bodie, J. A.	484	Pte.
Balls, W.	1808	L/Sgt.	Bolton, J. C.	5441	L/Cpl.
Bamblett, C. E.	8588	Pte.	Bond, H. E.	G/8201	Cpl.
Barber, G. S.	2414	L/Cpl.	Bond, J.	G/30606	Pte.
Barden, G.	756	Pte.	Bonner, E. C.	9090	Pte.
Barden, A.	1544	Pte.	Boorman, A. G.	25888	Pte.
Barnham, J. W. J.	11243	Cpl.	Booth, W. A.	9992	L/Cpl.
Barrow, A. E.	8264	Pte.	Botting, G.	9917	Sgt.
Bartholomew, C.	L/7916	L/Cpl.	Bottom, G. A.	20447	Cpl.
Barton, G. E.	10576	Pte.	Boulton, J.	20748	Pte.
Bartrick, E. F.	G/28709	Pte.	Bowes, E.	11894	Pte.
Batchelor, E.	25939	Pte.	Boylar, G. S. B.	10535	L/Cpl.
Batchelor, E. J.	29963	Pte.	Bradley, J. E.	12153	Pte.
Bates, A. J.	2717	Cpl.	Bradman, E.	7292	C.S.M.
Batten, A. E.	1624	Pte.	Braggs, A. B.	19814	Pte.
Baughan, J.	12	Sgt.	Branch, G.	8687	Pte.
Beat, R.	8421	Pte.	Branegan, A. G.	26954	Pte.
Beale, J.	6684	L/Cpl.	Brazier, C. R.	2102	L/Cpl.
Bealtie, T.	G/16402	Sgt.	Breed, S.	1632	Pte.
Beckett, R. W.	17746	Pte.	Breeds, H.	204659	Pte.
Bellamy, J. J.	204472	Cpl.	Bridges, H.	15513	Cpl.
Belts, J. O.	G/10588	Pte.	Bridges, H.	17171	Pte.
Bench, F. G.	G/17394	Cpl.	Bridle, J.	9320	Pte.
Bennett, D.	579	Sgt.	Brittain, D.	246	Pte.
Bennett, P.	4245	Pte.	Britton, F.	240926	Cpl.
Bensted, H.	202587	Pte.	Broad, W. G.	2246	Pte.
Biffin, E.	241961	Pte.	Brooker, C. W.	26953	Sgt.
Bilby, H.	8298	Sgt.	Brooker, M. R.	66799	Pte.
Billings, C. G.	G/2411	Pte.	Brookman, W. H.	8488	Sgt.
Binks, H.	18187	L/Cpl.	Brooks, J. A.	20207	Pte.
Bird, R.	18427	Cpl.	Broomfield, E.	11616	Pte.
Bishop, A. F.	9132	Pte.	Broomfield, G.	G/23087	Pte.
Bishop, S. G.	8234	Sgt.	Broughton, P. W.	3734	L/Cpl.
Blacker, G.	240420	L/Cl.	Brown, A. E.	G/18697	Pte.
Blackford, J.	G/10975	Sgt.	Brown, A. S.	8238	Cpl.
Blackhorn, V.	240922	Sgt.	Brown, C. R.	20593	L/Cpl.
Blackman, E.	1104	Pte.	Brown, F. J.	289	Pte.

APPENDIX III.

M.M. (continued).

Brown, H. J.	202592	Pte.	Cogdell, A.	2363	Pte.
Brown, K. G.	204178	Pte.	Colbran, G. T.	G/18790	Pte.
Brown, J. W.	G/28718	Pte.	Cole, J.	G/38703	Pte.
Brown, W. H.	5266	Cpl.	Cole, W. S.	18105	Pte.
Browne, S.	9142	L/Cpl.	Coleman, A.	1201	Sgt.
Boyden, G.	4746	Sgt.	Coles, E.	5799	Pte.
Buck, G.	3713	Sgt.	Colk, C. J.	29663	Pte.
Bunker, H. G.	28333	Pte.	Collett, H. E.	10024	Cpl.
Burbridge, G. W.	18968	L/Cpl.	Collins, L. R.	10538	Pte.
Burley, F.	242121	Pte.	Colman, T. W.	19922	Sgt.
Burton, J.	28509	Pte.	Compson, S. H.	19059	Pte.
Bush, W. J.	5603	Pte.	Cook, A. E.	G/18697	Pte.
Butcher, H. H.	8010	Sgt.	Cook, W. W.	24283	Cpl.
Butwell, J.	1421	L/Cpl.	Coomber, H. T.	200163	Sgt.
Bygrave, A.	18251	Pte.	Coomber, W. D.	1515	Sgt.
			Cooper, F. W. H.	8072	L/Sgt.
Cahill, E.	5017	Pte.	Coppard, R.	2971	Pte.
Callaghan, J. P.	10335	Pte.	Corbin, A.	17607	Pte.
Calow, J. W.	7076	Pte.	Cordingley, T.	10741	Pte.
Camplin, P.	3485	Cpl.	Correll, J. S.	19856	Sgt.
Cannon, F. A.	4256	Pte.	Cottenden, G.	203212	Cpl.
Carlton, S. F.	5678	Pte.	Court, H. J.	15424	Pte.
Carnell, H.	367	Sgt.	Coward, A. J.	6330	L/Cpl.
Carter, W.	240737	Sgt.	Cox, A.	17797	Pte.
Cater, H. H.	265215	Sgt.	Cozens, F.	8181	Cpl.
Cave, W. T.	7691	Pte.	Cronk, S.	8129	C.Q.M.S.
Chambers, H. F.	4928	L/Cpl.	Cross, F. A.	204745	Pte.
Chandler, L. W.	292	Sgt.	Crowhurst, L.	205833	Pte.
Cheeseman, C. N.	1550	Pte.	Cutter, C. J.	9780	Cpl.
Cheeseman, H.	L/9713	Pte.			
Cherriman, E. H.	6525	Pte.	Dade, A. E.	L/8132	L/Cpl.
Cherrison, G. A.	202599	Sgt.	Dadson, R. C.	10708	Pte.
Chesson, C. W.	655	Sgt.	Dann, F. L.	265674	Sgt.
Christian, A.	18364	Pte.	Darley, R.	—	Sgt.
Christopher, H.	202768	Pte.	Davidson, D. J.	333	C.S.M.
Clark, H.	G/19234	L/Cpl.	Davis, B.	8505	L/Sgt.
Clark, T. H.	10880	Pte.	Dawson, W. H. G.	202602	Cpl.
Clarke, G. W.	G/18409	Sgt.	Deacon, D. J.	23458	Pte.
Clifton, A.	9178	Pte.	Dean, J.	18016	Pte.
Clifton, G.	24688	Pte.	Dean, F. S.	6980	Pte.

APPENDIX III.

M.M. (continued).

Degavine, E.	7734	L/Cpl.	Farmer, E. E.	2396	Pte.
Delaney, R. W.	10881	Sgt.	Farrow, A.	586	Pte.
Dent, A.	8517	L/Cpl.	Faulkner, W.	7838	Sgt.
Dewing, W.	4683	Sgt.	Feast, W.	7564	Cpl.
Dibbs, W. H. R.	G/29951	Cpl.	Fenlon, A. J.	10745	Pte.
Dickson, E.	7167	Pte.	Fever, F.	21077	Pte.
Dilley, E.	203948	L/Cl.	Field, A.	G/24322	Pte.
Dimmick, A. G.	7585	L/Cpl.	Field, A. E.	5217	Pte.
Doe, G. E.	21076	Pte.	Field, H. S.	31115	Pte.
Donovan, M.	1130	Cpl.	Field, J. T.	31151	Pte.
Doole, R. E.	19578	Pte.	Fishenden, G. L.	9373	Pte.
Douglas, P. J.	9871	Pte.	Fisher, W. G.	9041	Sgt.
Down, F.	10447	Pte.	Fittall, G. H. B.	2438	Pte.
Downs, J.	G/21380	Sgt.	Flack, W. W.	15120	L/Cpl.
Dowsing, E.	645	Pte.	Flight, P. T.	5575	Pte.
Drake, J. R.	1319	Pte.	Flint, F.	20087	Cpl.
Draper, S. J.	18411	Pte.	Foran, T.	10350	Cpl.
Durden, H. G. C.	274	L/Cpl.	Foster, G. A.	11154	L/Cpl.
Dyer, C. R.	19112	C/Sgt.	Francis, A.	10694	Pte.
			Francis, E. T.	G/11308	L/Sgt.
Eagleton, A. J.	19393	Pte.	Francis, G.	18434	Pte.
East, J.	1384	L/Cpl.	Franklin, G.	7456	C.S.M.
Eckett, G.	560	Pte.	French, A.	3494	Cpl.
Edgar, D. R.	460	Pte.	Frewer, H. A.	2696	Pte.
Edwards, C.	23721	L/Cpl.	Frith, J. W.	11223	L/Cpl.
Elliott, C. A.	4974	Pte.	Frost, G. H.	10552	Sgt.
Elliott, V. K.	10344	Pte.	Fryer, J. T.	5161	Pte.
Ellis, H. B.	18431	Pte.	Fuller, W.	537	Pte.
Ellis, P.	499	Pte.			
Erskine, J.	G/21521	L/Cpl.	Gard, F. A.	30961	Pte.
Etheridge, A.	10050	Pte.	Gardiner, C.	10600	Sgt.
Etherington, J.	18885	L/Cpl.	Gayton, H. B.	6172	Pte.
Evans, A. R.	21064	Pte.	Gearing, A. J.	265663	Sgt.
Everist, A. J.	201075	Pte.	Gibbins, E.	11077	Pte.
Eversfield, J.	201117	Cpl.	Gilbert, J.	9879	Sgt.
Eves, R.	L/6569	Sgt.	Glen, J.	957	Cpl.
Excell, F.	529	Pte.	Goble, G. W.	202921	Pte.
			Goddard, F. J.	31135	Pte.
Fairbrother, E.	6552	Pte.	Godden, J. S.	10642	Pte.
Farino, T.	G/24097	Pte.	Goff, H.	205342	Sgt.

APPENDIX III.

M.M. (continued).

Goldberg, S.	G/21511	Pte.	Hicks, R. E.	18300	L/Cpl.
Goldie, W.	18380	L/Cpl.	Hickton, J. T.	10011	Pte.
Goodall, R. J.	G/12142	Pte.	Hissey, J.	168	Pte.
Gooden, F. W.	L/7407	C.S.M.	Hodinott, A. V.	21531	L/Cpl.
Goodison, J. H.	9851	Pte.	Holford, F.	7454	L/Cpl.
Goodwin, W. G.	240904	Pte.	Hollands, E. H.	18445	Sgt.
Gould, G.	23253	Sgt.	Hollands, F.	18441	Cpl.
Gray, G. R.	8924	L/Cpl.	Hollick, L. H.	6559	Cpl.
Gray, J.	10004	Pte.	Holness, A. T.	G/8399	L/Sgt.
Gray, S. D.	9894	Cpl.	Holway, W.	8393	C.Q.M.S.
Green, G. E.	2049	Sgt.	Homewood, E.	12292	Pte.
Green, L.	19122	Sgt.	Hood, E. T.	L/10362	Pte.
Greenpass, D.	1286	L/Cpl.	Hooker, H. J.	67	Sgt.
Greenwood, E.	10527	Pte.	Hooker, W. H.	9441	Pte.
Grover, C. W. H.	9333	L/Cpl.	Hopwood, F. W.	6750	Sgt.
			Horan, W.	31164	Pte.
Haines, W.	200228	Sgt.	Hounslow, L.	17765	Pte.
Hale, E. T.	9277	Cpl.	Howard, L. W.	25982	L/Cpl.
Hall, A. J.	17168	Pte.	Howe, W. B.	7318	Pte.
Hall, F.	18026	Pte.	Howes, H. E.	7802	Cpl.
Hall, H.	9615	Pte.	Hoyle, E. W.	5410	L/Cpl.
Hall, H.	21045	Pte.	Hubble, F.	1562	Pte.
Hammond, F. W.	2239	Pte.	Hughes, J. J.	21034	L/Cpl.
Hannant, E. F.	9263	Pte.	Hulford, H.	G/8576	Sgt.
Hannis, J.	24710	Pte.	Hunt, A. G.	201386	Pte.
Harrington, W.	10447	Pte.	Hunt, J. A.	G/9344	Cpl.
Harris, C.	10337	Cpl.	Hunter, G. M.	9927	Pte.
Harris, G. E.	5824	Pte.	Hylands, H. T., *D.C.M.*		
Harris, J. J.	8092	L/Cpl.		8162	C.S.M.
Harris, T. J.	358	Cpl.	Ingles, A. E.	15079	L/Cpl.
Harris, T. P.	18829	L/Cpl.	Ives, C. R.	210357	Pte.
Hart, F. J.	10352	Sgt.			
Hatchley, G.	6605	Sgt.	Jackson, A.	21003	Cpl.
Hawkes, F. H.	4684	Cpl.	James, H.	10701	Pte.
Hawkins, A. J.	19579	Pte.	Jarman, A. J.	18752	Pte.
Hayden, G. W.	12393	L/Cpl.	Jarrett, T. F.	5003	Pte.
Haynes, R. H.	G/9798	Cpl.	Jasper, W.	3661	Cpl.
Herbert, H.	7435	Pte.	Jeffery, H. J.	7782	Sgt.
Hester, R.	9270	Pte.	Jeffery, W.	8111	Sgt.
Hibbin, A. V.	15325	Pte.	Jeffs, C. J.	9924	Pte.

APPENDIX III.

M.M. (continued).

Jeffs, S.	17832	Pte.	Levitt, G.	8569	Sgt.
Jenner, G.	657	Cpl.	Lewin, E. G.	164	Pte.
Jennings, L. H.	165	L/Cpl.	Lewis, E. A.	10719	Pte.
Jones, C.	62369	L/Cpl.	Lewry, A.	16717	Cpl.
Johnson, F.	9108	Cpl.	Lidbury, J. H.	4978	Pte.
Johnson, J. L.	4078	Sgt.	Life, W. E.	8133	L/Cpl.
Johnson, T. E.	11459	L/Cpl.	Little, T.	18140	Pte.
Joyce, W. P.	1415	Sgt.	Lindsay, A. J.	398	L/Cpl.
Judd, E. J.	3192	Pte.	Linge, J.	518	Pte.
Judge, W. J.	18385	Pte.	Lock, F.	202711	Pte.
Jupp, F.	9995	L/Sgt.	Loft, N. E.	6042	Sgt.
			Long, J.	7804	Pte.
Kamester, J.	18923	Pte.	Longman, F. S.	G/3401	L/Cpl.
Kelly, M. L.	21536	Pte.	Lonsdale, J.	5226	Pte.
Kelway, C.	19210	L/Cpl.	Looker, F. G.	G/10227	Pte.
Kemp, D. A.	10268	Pte.	Loudwell, S. W.	G/2305	Pte.
Kevern, W. H.	18679	Pte.	Lovell, E. W.	6671	L/Cpl.
King, A.	201622	Pte.	Lucas, F. J.	G/21481	Pte.
King, A. G.	7801	Pte.	Lucas, J. W.	2209	Pte.
King, E. S. G.	18924	L/Cpl.	Luckett, E. G.	2099	Pte.
Kirby, E. G.	2578	Sgt.	Luff, E. H.	9019	Pte.
Kirkbride, J.	7320	Pte.			
Kirkpatrick, J.	17838	Pte.	McAllister, J.	201964	Pte.
Kirrage, F. G.	11279	Pte.	McCallum, J.	1616	L/Cpl.
Kisby, W.	18036	Pte.	McCormick, D. H.	20184	L/Cpl.
Knell, A. T.	24311	Pte.	McDonald, A.	3380	L/Cpl.
Knevett, A.	7519	Cpl.	Mackenzie, P.	5071	Sgt.
Knight, B.	G/23668	Cpl.	Major, W. E.	15377	Pte.
			Manktelow, G. T.	2132	Cpl.
Lade, T. J.	16162	Sgt.	Manktelow, W.	656	Pte.
Laing, F.	6942	L/Cpl.	Mann, F. W.	8339	Sgt.
Lang, H. H.	202577	Pte.	Manning, E. O.	3219	Pte.
Langley, G. H.	9528	Pte.	Markham, J. T.	424	Sgt.
Larkin, R. P.	10567	Pte.	Marsh, M.	8641	Pte.
Laskey, G.	7713	Sgt.	Marshall, A.	10137	C.S.M
Lawrence, F. G.	25107	Cpl.	Marshall, C. A.	G/18463	Sgt.
Leach, S. J.	25204	Pte.	Marslin, W.	9401	C.Q.M.S.
Leary, J.	6142	Pte.	Martin, C. H.	7570	Pte.
Leigh, F.	G/10515	L/Cpl.	Martin, R. L.	G/18470	Cpl.
Le Petit, W.	31255	Pte.	Mason, F. W.	201074	Pte.

APPENDIX III.

M.M. (continued).

Masters, T.	24335	Pte.	Offen, G.	G/15480	Sgt.
May, V.	24337	Pte.	Oliver, H. G.	15391	Pte.
Mead, G.	50974	Pte.	Orbell, J.	G/18601	L/Cpl.
Meads, C.	13303	Pte.	Osborne, G. A.	2232	Cpl.
Mealing, H.	5142	Pte.	Otway, J. W.	17949	L/Cpl.
Medhurst, F.	200867	Sgt.	Owen, S. C.	11218	Sgt.
Meen, A.	2672	Pte.			
Merritt, H.	8413	L/Cpl.	Pace, G.	156	Sgt.
Miles, A.	7898	L/Cpl.	Packman, H.	18478	Pte.
Miles, A.	150	L/Cpl.	Page, E. C.	485	Sgt.
Miles, P. J.	1325	Pte.	Paine, W.	7395	Pte.
Miles, W. J.	L/6684	Pte.	Pankhurst, P.	735	Pte.
Miller, A. W.	2662	Pte.	Pannett, T.	10385	Cpl.
Milliner, F.	638	Pte.	Park, J. T.	21377	Pte.
Mills, H. V.	11236	Cpl.	Parren, C. G.	18487	Pte.
Mitchell, A.	8105	Sgt.	Parrott, A. G.	16003	Pte.
Mitchell, S. C.	17635	Pte.	Parsons, A. E.	8842	Pte.
Mitchell, W., D.C.M.	1374	Sgt.	Parsons, H.	242062	Pte.
Moffatt, G.	883	Pte.	Passey, F. L.	L/10199	Pte.
Moodnick, B.	242046	Pte.	Paylis, F. W.	1962	Pte.
Moody, F.	23850	L/Cpl.	Payne, A. C. J.	8159	Sgt.
Moon, C.	653	Pte.	Payne, C. P.	11324	L/Sgt.
Morris, R.	240384	Pte.	Peddlesden, W.	1441	Pte.
Morrow, A.	11101	Cpl.	Peerless, G. E. T.	2203	Pte.
Moring, A.	241799	Pte.	Penfold, F.	G/30627	Pte.
Mortimore, A.	G/23712	L/Cpl.	Pennell, J. H.	9798	C.S.M.
Moseley, J.	23850	L/Cpl.	Perrin, A.	869	Pte.
Moss, L.	17845	Pte.	Perry, J.	25615	Pte.
Munro, F.	8075	Cpl.	Peskett, G.	8323	L/Cpl.
Munro, W. J.	1511	Sgt.	Phillips, A. E.	G/21522	L/Cpl.
Neaves, H. G.	39445	Pte.	Phillips, S. A.	205877	Pte.
Newman, C. P.	498	L/Cpl.	Philpott, W. J. F.	G/4743	Pte.
Norburn, W.	770	Cpl.	Phyall, E. C.	521	Pte.
Norman, F. W.	G/26254	Pte.	Phyall, S. E.	386	Pte.
Norman, G.	23127	Sgt.	Pierce, F. A.	4014	Pte.
Norris, C. C.	11679	Pte.	Piggott, F.	202235	Pte.
Norton, H. J.	18472	Pte.	Piller, W.	4451	Pte.
Nye, J.	697	Pte.	Pink, H. P.	2437	Cpl.
			Ploughman, F. A.	28794	L/Cpl.
Oaten, E. E.	4733	Sgt.	Pope, H. F.	L/5698	Pte.

APPENDIX III.

M.M. (continued).

Poet, A.	G/23697	L/Cpl.	Scott, A.	3866	Sgt.
Potter, G. A.	G/30781	Pte.	Scott, A. E.	23885	Pte.
Pountain, A. L.	20118	Pte.	Scott, J.	4934	Sgt.
Povey, A. T.	G/11071	Sgt.	Scrace, H.	12175	Pte.
Price, A. E.	23464	Pte.	Scripps, J. J. H.	570	Pte.
			Scrivener, F.	10105	Pte.
Rabbitt, J.	8226	Sgt.	Scroby, A.	18049	Pte.
Raines, E. A.	18754	Pte.	Sears, S. J.	4960	L/Cpl.
Rapley, E. G.	25941	Pte.	Senebiratne, D. B.	G/30032	Cpl.
Reader, W.	5640	Pte.	Senior, C.	205189	L/C.
Redley, J. R.	31147	L/Cpl.	Sharratt, A. A.	7129	Sgt.
Reed, E.	6785	Pte.	Shewry, T. G.	2909	L/Cpl.
Reilly, W.	218	Pte.	Shilco, E.	204389	Pte.
Richardson, T.	17458	Pte.	Shillery, J.	242131	Pte.
Rickwood, A.	18491	Pte.	Sidgwick, J.	7081	L/Sgt.
Riggs, A. C.	10520	Pte.	Simmonds, G. W.	38	Cpl.
Roberts, C. A.	19244	Sgt.	Simmons, F.	203958	Cpl.
Roberts, H. G. W.	9705	Pte.	Simmons, R. G.	7435	Pte.
Roberts, W. R.	8636	L/Cpl.	Simpkins, J.	2174	Pte.
Robertson, W.	16389	Pte.	Singer, H. M.	20688	Sgt.
Robinson, A. F.	8759	Sgt.	Skelton, T. A.	G/21362	Cpl.
Rogers, W.	L/9849	Pte.	Skelton, W. C.	5949	Pte.
Roper, R. T.	7590	Pte.	Skerry, P.	3852	Pte.
Rose, S.	12053	Pte.	Skidmore, P.	24745	Pte.
Rough, J. T.	16535	Pte.	Skinner, G. A.	8530	Sgt.
Rowswell, T.	6862	Pte.	Slade, L. C.	9442	L/Cpl.
Rudd, H. S.	204460	Sgt.	Smart, E.	2432	Pte.
Rumbold, W. T.	26710	Sgt.	Smartt, R. D.	11308	L/Sgt.
Rumens, H.	572	Pte.	Smith, C.	5520	Sgt.
Russell, G. W. C.	L/11325	Pte.	Smith, C. E.	1893	L/Cpl.
Russell, H.	8565	Pte.	Smith, C. S.	21445	Cpl.
			Smith, F.	25919	Sgt.
Saddington, G. H.	1435	Sgt.	Smith, F. W.	L/11590	Pte.
Sadler, F.	10382	Sgt.	Smith, R. E.	910	Pte.
Saunders, A.	179	Pte.	Smith, T.	31753	Pte.
Saunders, T. H.	11014	L/Cpl.	Smith, T. C.	7718	Sgt.
Savage, A.	18617	Pte.	Smith, W.	7640	L/Cpl.
Savage, R. W.	23099	Pte.	Smythe, C.	816	Pte.
Saxby, H.	11467	Pte.	Soame, N.	16696	L/Cpl.
Scarborough, W.	5618	Pte.	Sorenson, H.	20011	Pte.

APPENDIX III.

M.M. (continued).

Springbett, G. T.	10838	Sgt.	Tolhurst, J. S.	21105	L/Cpl.
Stacey, F.	10421	Pte.	Toomer, W. E.	21002	Sgt.
Stanley, C.	G/19766	Sgt.	Tovey, E. L.	G/3025	C.S.M.
Stansell, L. B.	19045	L/Cpl.	Tark, R.	5676	Pte.
Stares, J.	5938	L/Cpl.	Turk, T. A.	G/30839	Pte.
Stears, H. G.	10422	Pte.	Turner, A.	2723	L/Cpl.
Sterry, M. J.	21501	Pte.	Turner, E.	985	Sgt.
Stockley, H.	G/29387	Pte.	Turner, S.	8860	Sgt.
Stone, W. A. V.	19795	Pte.	Tutton, C. F. J.	8675	L/Cpl.
Streatfield, H. E.	354	Pte.	Tweed, G. W.	7355	L/Sgt.
Stroad, W.	13022	Pte.	Tyler, H.	6969	Pte.
Studd, F. R.	13254	Pte.	Tyrell, A. H.	1498	Pte.
Sutton, J., D.C.M.	G/4266	C.S.M.	Tyrell, H. T.	18148	Pte.
Swift, E.	5250	Pte.	Unsworth, J.	G/21286	Pte.
Swift, H. B.	3217	Pte.	Ursell, S. W.	G/10178	L/Cpl.
Swindell, F. J.	3256	L/Cpl.	Vaughan, G.	8832	Cpl.
Swinyard, W. E.	8609	Sgt.	Vicars, W. J.	24257	Sgt.
Swyer, C. W.	1538	Pte.	Vick, A. J.	16035	Pte.
Taber, J.	6130	Pte.	Vigor, J. A.	G/25981	Sgt.
Taber, J. E.	894	L/Cpl.			
Taggart, T.	G/21127	Pte.	Waghorn, C. L.	G/1989	Sgt.
Talbot, W. H.	7756	Pte.	Waghorn, E.	7545	Pte.
Tarry, F. T.	4299	Cpl.	Waite, H.	21222	Pte.
Tasker, T. W.	14527	Pte.	Wakefield, A. W.	29991	Pte.
Taylor, C. A.	15156	Sgt.	Wallen, J.	10544	Pte.
Taylor, H.	20134	L/Cpl.	Waller, W. J.	10846	Pte.
Taylor, R.	7622	L/Sgt.	Wallis, P.	10148	Cpl.
Taylor, W.	18526	Pte.	Wallond, A.	11137	Pte.
Taylor, W. A.	11647	Pte.	Wareham, A. W.	242103	Pte.
Tebbitt, F. J.	9334	Sgt.	Warford, H. G.	10702	Cpl.
Thomas, H. G.	567	Cpl.	Warne, W. T.	241324	Pte.
Thompson, W. R. J.	G/8900	Pte.	Warren, F. J.	G/38659	Pte.
			Warren, H. W.	9869	Pte.
Thomson, C. E.	G/31756	Sgt.	Waterhouse, E.	G/79026	L/Cpl.
Tidd, C.	1484	Pte.	Watkins, W.	24776	Pte.
Tilling, F. J.	31294	Pte.	Watson, A. W.	3187	Pte.
Tipler, H.	28321	Pte.	Watson, D. S.	200879	Pte.
Todd, D.	203546	Pte.	Watts, W. P.	31416	Sgt.

APPENDIX III.

M.M. (continued).

Webb, A.	8321	Pte.	Wiles, A. L.	18532	Pte.	
Webb, A.	9909	Pte.	Will, J.	6610	C.S.M.	
Webb, A.	10021	Pte.	Williams, C. D.	9279	Sgt.	
Webberley, F.	14614	Pte.	Williams, F. F.	10094	Pte.	
Webster, J.	20052	Pte.	Willison, W.	G/3683	Pte.	
Weldrake, G.	20293	Pte.	Wilson, F.	5245	Pte.	
Weller, P.	2131	Sgt.	Wilson, G.	6639	Pte.	
Weller, W.	G/12011	Pte.	Winder, J.	9302	Pte.	
Wells, C.	8429	L/Cpl.	Witherden, C. J.	416	L/Cpl.	
Wells, E. H.	2074	Cpl.	Withers, C. T.	240676	CQMS	
Wells, G.	4547	Pte.	Witt, S.	539	Pte.	
Wells, S. G.	7597	Pte.	Wood, H. W.	5825	Pte.	
Wesley, B. A.	2144	Pte.	Woodcock, R. E.	L/7992	Pte.	
West, G. W.	33	Cpl.	Woodcock, W. J.	24849	Pte.	
Westbury, A. W.	3819	Sgt.	Woodrow, C. W.	18994	Cpl.	
Weston, E. F.	8927	Sgt.	Woods, J.	8430	Pte.	
Weston, H.	L/9507	L/Cpl.	Wookey, G.	10575	Cpl.	
Whaites, F.	205401	Pte.	Woodgar, G.	25355	Pte.	
Wheeler, A.	9300	Sgt.	Wooltonton, F.	G/18955	Pte.	
Wheeler, A. J.	17909	Pte.	Worsley, E.	18181	L/Cpl.	
Wheeler, J. H.	1317	Pte.	Wright, H. J.	18534	Pte.	
White, C. A.	19151	Sgt.	Wright, W.	17162	Pte.	
White, T. W.	8740	Pte.				
Whittaker, W. G.	11873	Pte.	Yates, A.	15263	Pte.	
Whyatt, A. H.	3497	Pte.	Yeoman, C. F.	24793	Cpl.	
Whyman, A.	10292	Pte.	Young, C.	502	Sgt.	
Wickham, H.	428	Cpl.	Young, C.	203689	Pte.	
Wilby, F.	10155	L/Cpl.	Young, J. G.	20439	Pte.	

M.S.M.

Aiano, R.	265541	Sgt.	Carrington, W.	5186	R.Q.M.S.
Austin, C.	2839	Sgt.	Childs, H.	6334131	RSM
Bailey, E.	G/6541	Sgt.	Clarke, H. S.	24078	Cpl.
Basham, W. A.	15978	Pte.	Cronk, S., *M.M.*	8129	R.Q.M.S.
Bevan, H.	914	Pte.	Crook, E.	L/10799	Cpl.
Bilby, H.	8298	Sgt.	Eley, C. E.	6292	Pte.
Brooks, J.	120	Cpl.	Farmer, A.	6958	Pte.
Bushell, W. K.	265018	Sgt.	Fraiser, W. H.	8015	Sgt.
Carr, W. C.	1886	Sgt.	Gale, G.	8549	Pte.

APPENDIX III.

M.S.M. (continued).

Gale, M.	200272 C.Q.M.S.	Page, P.	G/634	Cpl.
Gibson, A. B.	11523 L/Sgt.	Pallett, W. F.	L/9761	L/Sgt.
Gilham, W.	200173 C.S.M.	Pinnigar, W. G.	G/8169	Sgt.
Gillespie, W. J.	45476 C.S.M.	Powers, E. J.	1089	Q.M.S.
Green, A. C.	205320 Sgt.	Pragnell, F. T.	8074	Sgt.
Green, H. A.	L/9178 Sgt.	Pronger, E.	GSSR/101	Sgt.
Green, L. J.	7254 St.-Sgt. Cook	Pollard, W.	6334101	R.S.M
Hardwick, H.	G/828 C.S.M.	Pullen, H. C.	359	Pte.
Hare, F. E.	5997 C.S.M.	Quinlan, J. T.	L/8442	C.Q.M.S.
Harise, E. P.	7946 Sgt.	Reynolds, A., M.C.	5347	R.S.M.
Harrigan, W.	L/8972 Cpl.	Rogers, W. E.	G/2269	C.Q.M.S.
Hill, A. E.	G/376 Pte.	Roots, E. N.	9264	Sgt.
Holland, F.	GSSR/808 C.Q.M.S.	Rowland, W. A.	L/7790	C.S.M.
Hyde, J. T.	920 R.S.M.	Shappard, G. G.	1369	Sgt.
Ifould, F. A.	1347 R.Q.M.S.	Shaw, B.	23959	L/Cpl.
Jenner, G.	280 C.S.M.	Simmonds, A. E.	11981	C.S.M.
Johnson, W. L.	5971 R.Q.M.S.	Smith, A.	8742	Sgt.
Keattch, A.	10559 Cpl.	Smith, G.	4466	Sgt.
Kemp, L. G. L., D.C.M.	L/8349 C.S.M.	Smith, P. S.	19176	Sgt.
King, S. F.	L/5905 R.Q.M.S.	Steed, L. W.	240468	Cpl.
Latter, W. A.	8416 Pte.	Stubbings, H. E.	816	Sgt.
Lewis, L. H.	6530 Sgt.	Swain, H. R.	G/2888	Sgt.
Lidbury, J. H.	4978 Pte.	Swan, C.	L/7719	C.S.M.
Loft, W. H.	L/9152 Sgt.	Tench, F.	558	R.S.M.
Longden, J.	11624 Sgt.	Thomas, A. M.	928	R.Q.M.S.
Lowry, A. J.	L/8656 C.Q.M.S.	Thomas, G.	G/11608	Sgt.
Lynch, T. G.	881 Sgt.	Trufitt, J.	5449	Sgt.
Manger, H. E.	S/1000 R.Q.M.S.	Turner, H.	240018	R.S.M.
Mannerings, A. T.	8583 Sgt.	Verrall, H. R.	2779	Cpl.
Maynard, C.	C.S.M.	Ward, E.	222815	L/Cpl.
Miles, J.	L/5309 C.S.M.	Ward, W. A.	200457	Sgt.
Mitchell, J.	9225 Pte.	Watts, G.	G/17911	Cpl.
Morgan, J.	240069 C.S.M.	Webster, J. W.	G/25084	Sgt.
Mynheer, A. V.	6334195 Sgt.	Wells, A.	1506	Q.M.S.
Newton, E. J.	L/8782 Sgt.	Whitburn, A. K.	200648	Sgt.
		Wood, W.	725	Sgt.

APPENDIX III.

FOREIGN DECORATIONS.

BELGIUM.

Ordre de Leopold

Officier.

Martyn, A. Wood, *D.S.O.* Lieut.-Col.

Chevalier.

Coke, J. R., Captain

Ordre de la Couronne.

Commandeur.

Martyn, A., *C.B.*, *C.M.G.* Brig.-Gen.

Officier.

Prescott-Roberts, P. A., Lieut.-Col.
Wenyon, H. J., *D.S.O.*, Lieut.-Col.

Croix de Guerre.

Andrews, C., *D.C.M.* 2679 L/Cpl.
Chapman, W. F., *D.C.M.* 18549 L/Sgt.
Coke, J. R. Captain
Cooper, C. 5820 Pte.
Davis, W. G. 11695 Sgt.
Harris, H. 389 R.S.M.
Hooker, W. H., *D.C.M.*, *M.M.* 9441 Cpl.
Knox, A. D'E. Major
Lang, F. 6397 Pte.

Martin, F. 6216 R.S.M.
Martyn, A. Wood, *D.S.O.* Lt.-Col.
Naylor, J. 24796 C.S.M.
Patchin, R. C. 28382 Cpl.
Prescott-Roberts, P. A. Lt.-Col.
Scott, A. 3866 Sgt.
Selby, C. W. P. Lieut.
Sharrad, W. 9220 Pte.
Tucker, J. 24770 Cpl.
Turner, J. E. 8300 Cpl.
Wenyon, H. J., *D.S.O.* Lt.-Col.

Decoration Militaire.

French, A., 3494 Cpl.

APPENDIX III.

EGYPT.

ORDER OF THE NILE.

2nd Class.
   Leslie, W. S., *C.M.G.*, *D.S.O.*, Brig.-General.
   Western, Sir W. G. B., *K.C.M.G.*, *C.B.*, Major-General.

3rd Class.
   Stigand, C. H., Major.

4th Class.
   Bazley-White, R. B. L., *D.S.O.*, Captain.
   Brock, R. G. C., Major.

MILITARY STAR.
   Brock, R. G. C., Major.

FRANCE.

LEGION D'HONNEUR.

Commandeur.
   Alderson, Sir E. A. H., *K.C.B.*, Lieut.-General.

Officier.
   Bonham-Carter, C., *D.S.O.*, Bt-Lieut.-Colonel.
   Snow, H. W., *D.S.O.*, Bt.-Major.
   Whitehead, J., *D.S.O.*, Bt.-Lieut.-Colonel.

Chevalier.
   Ingram, C. R., *D.S.O.*, Major.
   Price, T. R. C., *D.S.O.*, Major.
   Prescott-Roberts, P. A., Major.
   Stanhope, Earl J. R., *D.S.O.*, *M.C.*, Major.

CROIX DE GUERRE AVEC PALMES.
   Western, W. G. B., *C.B.*, Major-General.
   Wilson, A. J., Lieut.

APPENDIX III.

CROIX DE GUERRE.

Allen, W. V., 30655, Pte.
Cannon, A. F., 4256, Pte.
Corfe, A. C., *D.S.O.*, Lieut.-Colonel.
Crabb, J., 29553, Pte.
Dobson, C., 16395, L/Cpl.
Engledow, F. L., Captain.
Hewitt, A. S., *D.S.O.*, Major.
Mellors, P. W., 30944, Pte.
Morris, F., 30774, Pte.
Osmotherly, W., G/9475, Pte.
Pickett, W. E., 19093, Pte.
Smith, A., 8742, Sgt.
Smith, G. W., G/530, L/Cpl.
Stroud, M. P., I./6694, R.S.M.
Thomas, A. E. W., *D.S.O.*, *M.C.*, Lieut.
Vaughan, T. H., 31563, L/Cpl.
Wingfield-Stratford, G. E., *M.C.*, Captain.
Woodyear, R. P., *M.C.*, 2nd Lieut.

MEDAILLE MILITAIRE.

Bennett, D., *M.M.*, G/579, R.S.M.
Cork, T., 5793, Pte.
Cozens, L., 1050, C.S.M.
Doe, H. S., R.S.M.
Hatch, G., 7725, Cpl.
Jackson, W. G., 9366, Sgt.
Kelway, C., 19210, L/Cpl.
Selves, W., 8566, C.S.M.

MEDAILLE D'HONNEUR.

Butler, J., G/973, R.Q.M.S.
Verrall, H. R., G/2779, Cpl.

APPENDIX III.

GREECE.

Order of the Redeemer.

Commander.
Taylor, C. W. H., Bt.-Major.

Order of King George I.

Disney-Roebuck, C. D., Lieut.-Colonel.

ITALY.

Order of the Crown of Italy.

Commander.
Western, W. G. B., *C.B.*, Major-General.

Cavalier.
Watts, A. A., Lieut.

Bronze Medal for Valour.

Beattie, T., 16402, R.S.M.
Hayden, G. W., *M.M.*, 12393, Sgt.

PORTUGAL.

Military Order of Aviz.

Chevalier.
da Silva, C., Lieut.

ROUMANIA.

Star of Roumania.

Chevalier.
May, E., Major.
Watts, A. A., Lieut.

Medaille Barbatie Si Credinta.

Carrington, W., 13156, C.S.M.
Kingston, J., 15455, Pte.
Walker, P. W., 4840, R.S.M.

APPENDIX III.

RUSSIA.

Order of St. Anne.

3rd Class.
Woulfe-Flanagan, R. J., Lieut.-Colonel.

Order of St. Vladimir.

2nd Class.
Le Cocq, F. B., Captain.

Order of St. Stanilas.

2nd Class.
Daniell, O. J., Major.

Medal of St. George.

Bridger, W., 8723, Bandsman.
Bye, E. T., 9511, Bandsman.
Edwards, J., 6460, Cpl.
Floyd, F. G., 6025, Pte.
Howe, G., 8734, Pte.
Portwain, H. J., 8595, Pte.
Turnbull, J., 8192, Pte.
Young, J., 241, L/Sgt.

SERBIA.

Order of the White Eagle.

Adams, C. F., Major.
Hildyard, R. J. T., *C.M.G.*, *D.S.O.*,
                    Bt.-Lieut.-Colonel.
O'Dowda, J. W., *C.M.G.*, Bt.-Colonel.
Taylor, C. W. H., Bt.-Major.

APPENDIX III.

CROSS OF KARA GEORGE.

Gold Medal.
McKelvey, J., 9702, Pte.
Medhurst, A. H., 9907, Pte.
Salisbury, H., 9575, Bandsman.

Silver Medal.
Golding, G. E. M., 9020, L/Cpl.
Heritage, R., 8042, Pte.
Hooker, E. F., 203327, Dr.
Locke, W., 8768, Cpl.
Martin, J., 9502, Pte.
Pangbourne, C., 8550, Pte.
Quittenden, N. A., 9902, Pte.
Shand, J., 8968, Pte.

2nd Class with Swords.
Twort, R. T., 202544, Pte.

UNITED STATES.

DISTINGUISHED SERVICE MEDAL.

Bonham-Carter, C., *C.M.G.*, *D.S.O.*, Brig.-General.

PROMOTIONS.

The following officers were granted promotion in rank as a reward for services during the war :—

To Major-General.
Colonel W. G. B. Western, *C.B.*

To Hon. Major-General.
Colonel F. F. Johnson, *C.B.*

APPENDIX III.

To Brevet-Colonel.

Bt.-Colonel C. Bonham-Carter, *D.S.O.*
Lieut.-Colonel H. S. Bush, *C.M.G.*
Lieut.-Colonel E. D. Caird.
Lieut.-Colonel E. A. Fagan, *C.M.G.*, *D.S.O.*
Bt.-Lieut.-Col. R. J. T. Hildyard, *C.M.G.*, **D.S.O.**
Bt.-Lieut.-Colonel H. Isacke, *C.M.G.*
Bt.-Lieut.-Colonel W. S. Leslie, *D.S.O.*
Lieut.-Colonel A. Martyn.
Lieut.-Colonel J. W. O'Dowda, *C.M.G.*
Lieut.-Colonel R. J. Woulfe-Flanagan.

To Brevet-Lieut.-Colonel.

Major H. D. Belgrave.
Major C. Bonham-Carter.
Major H. D., Buchanan-Dunlop, *D.S.O.*
Major A. K. Grant, *D.S.O.*
Major R. J. T. Hildyard, *C.M.G.*, *D.S.O.*
Major C. F. Hitchins, *D.S.O.*
Major B. Johnstone, *D.S.O.*
Major C. E. Kitson, *D.S.O.*
Major W. S. Leslie.
Major T. H. C. Nunn, *D.S.O.*
Major T. R. C. Price, *D.S.O.*
Major P. M. Robinson, *C.M.G.*
Major H. W. Snow, *D.S.O.*
Major R. M. G. Tulloch, *D.S.O.*
Major J. T. Twisleton-Wykeham-Fiennes.
Major P. Umfreville, *C.M.G.*
Major H. A. Waring, *D.S.O.*
Major J. Whitehead, *D.S.O.*

APPENDIX III.

To be Brevet-Major.

    Captain W. H. Annesley.
    Captain L. Bengough, *M.C.*
    Captain W. R. A. Dawson, *D.S.O.*
    Captain A. E. Hardy, *M.C.*
    Captain E. J. Hudson.
    Lieut. J. Le Fleming (on promotion to Captain).
    Captain E. F. Moulton-Barrett, *M.C.*
    Captain C. E. S. Phillips.
    Captain H. W. Snow.
    Captain C. W. H. Taylor.
    Captain N. I. Whitty, *D.S.O.*
    Captain G. E. Wingfield-Stratford, *M.C.*

To be Major.

    Captain and Qr.-Mr. F. Grey, *D.C.M.*

To be Captain.

    Lieut. and Qr.-Mr. G. A. Barnes.

Granted a Higher Rate of Pay.

    Lieut. and Qr.-Mr. E. Mills.
    Lieut. and Qr.-Mr. H. G. Rogers, *M.C.*

APPENDIX IV.

MENTIONED IN DISPATCHES.

(The rank shown is as stated in the *Gazette*, in the case of more than one mention the highest rank is given. Only honours granted before the war are mentioned).

SEVEN TIMES.

Buchanan-Dunlop, H. D., Lieut.-Colonel.

O'Dowda, J. W., Brig.-General.

SIX TIMES.

Bush, H. S., Colonel.
Hildyard, R. J. T., Brig.-General

Martyn, A. Wood, Lieut.-Colonel.
Tillie, W. K., Lieut.-Colonel.

FIVE TIMES.

Belgrave, H. D., Lieut.-Colonel.
Bonham-Carter, C., Brig.-General
Dawson, W. R. A., Lieut.-Colonel
Elgood, G., Major.
Fagan, E. A., Brig.-General.
Grant, A. K., Lieut.-Colonel.
Ingram, C. R., Major.

Martyn, A., Brig.-General.
Norman, E. H., Lieut.-Colonel.
Robinson, P. M., Brig.-General.
Snow, H. W., Lieut.-Colonel.
Umfreville, P., Brig.-General.
Western, W. G. B., *C.B.*, Major-General.

FOUR TIMES.

Annesley, W. H., Lieut.-Colonel.
Brock, R. G. C., Major.
Hewitt, A. S., Lieut.-Colonel.
Isacke, H., Brig.-General.
Lepper, J. G., Captain.
Leslie, W. S., Brig.-General.
May, E., Captain.

Maunsell, G. W., Colonel.
Peploe, H., Lieut.-Colonel.
Price, T. R. C., Brig.-General.
Rogers, E. S., 15319, L/Cpl.
Taylor, C. W. H., Major.
Walker, P. W., 4840, R.S.M.
Whitehead, J., Lieut.-Colonel.
Wilberforce, W., Lieut.-Colonel.

APPENDIX IV.

THREE TIMES.

Alderman, W. J., Captain.
Aldworth, T. P., Captain.
Balbernie, A. G., Captain.
Davies, P. M., Brig.-General.
Harrison, C. E. C. B., Colonel.
Johnstone, B., Lieut.-Colonel.
Kitson, C. E., Lieut.-Colonel.
Lambert, C. F., G/15927, Sgt.

Loft, W. A., 9152, Sgt.
Moulton-Barrett, E. F., Major.
Nepean, H. E. C. B., Brig.-Gen.
Smithers, H., Major.
Tulloch, R. M. G., Major.
Wenyon, H. J., Lieut.-Colonel.
Whitty, N. I., Lieut.-Colonel.

TWICE.

Adams, C. F., Major.
Alderson, E. A. H., *C.B.*, Lieut.-General.
Allen, G., Lieut. and Qr.-Mr.
Bradshaw, C. R., Lieut.-Colonel.
Bredon, A. S., Captain.
Brewis, R. D., Major.
Buckle, M. P., *D.S.O.*, Major.
Cooke, J. C., Major.
Corfe, A. C., Lieut.-Colonel.
Crook, E., L/10799, Cpl.
Crosse, C. R., Lieut.-Colonel.
Dinwiddy, M. J., Captain.
Doe, H. S., Lieut.
Frazer, F. A., Lieut.-Colonel.
Griffith-Boscawen, Sir A. T., Lieut.-Colonel.
Grey, F., *D.C.M.*, Captain and Qr.-Mr.
Hardy, A. E., Major.
Harman, A. S., 15543, Sgt.
Hart, A. C., Captain.
Hewett, E. V. O., Lieut.-Colonel.
Hibbert, O. Y., Captain.

Hitchins, C. F., Lieut.-Colonel.
Hudson, E. J., Captain.
Hughes, E. G. V., Captain.
Legard, G. B., Captain.
Lewis, S. H., Captain.
McKenzie, B., Lieut.
MacNeece, W. F., Captain.
Middleton, C de C., Captain.
Nelson, J. W., Major.
Nunn, T. H. C., *D.S.O.*, Lieut.-Colonel.
Pallett, W. F., 9767, Sgt.
Palmer, G. H., Captain.
Pedley, S. H., Colonel.
Phillips, A. E., Major.
Rogers, H. G., Lieut. and Qr.-Mr.
Scott, A., 3866, Sgt.
Stanhope, J. R., Earl, Major.
Simpson, A. T. F., *V.D.*, Colonel
Stigand, C. H., Major.
Wilberforce-Bell, P. F., Captain.
Wingfield-Stratford, G. E., Major
Waring, H. A., Lieut.-Colonel.
Woulfe-Flanagan, R. J., Lieut.-Colonel.

APPENDIX IV.

ONCE.

Alexander, A.	18058 Sgt.		Bough, E.	7909 C.Q.M.S.
Allan, G. H.	6299 Q.M.S.		Bowman, J.	14385 S.Q.M.S.
Allen, H.	8729 Pte.		Bozman, E. F.	Lieut.
Andrews, G. J.	7326 Pte.		Bridger, W.	8725 Bdsmn
Anstruther, P. N.	Captain		Brockies, F.	191 L/Cpl.
Arnaud, J. N.	Captain		Brooks, S. E.	9584 Sgt.
Atwood, A. A.	1655 Sgt.		Brotherhood, A. A.	200169 Sgt.
Austin, W.	203254 R.S.M.		Brown, A.	9802 L/Cpl.
Ayers, H. V.	2nd Lieut.		Brown, R.	2nd Lieut.
Bailey, C. E. W.	202468 Sgt.		Brown, W. C.	L/9772 C.S.M.
Baker, A.	265960 R.Q.M.S.		Burbage, A. E.	41370 C.Q.M.S.
Baker, E.	492 L/Cpl.		Burbridge, H.	551 Pte.
Baker, G. J.	311 Cpl.		Burloch, J.	9871 L/Cpl.
Baker, J. E.	6306 Q.M.S.		Burdett, G. P.	Lieut.
Ballard, W.	8 Pte.		Burnett, C.	2152 C.Q.M.S.
Banfield, C. F.	200965 Cpl.		Burrows, J. D.	Captain
Banister, A. E. H.	Captain		Butler, J.	973 R.Q.M.S.
Banning, W. S.	6295 Q.M.S.		Butters, G. H.	G/41398 Cpl.
Barden, H. A.	8358 Pte.		Bye, S. T.	9511 Bdsmn.
Barr, C.	8702 Pte.			
Barrett, F. L.	Captain		Calow, J. W.	7076 Pte.
Batchelor, T. W.	8055 Sgt.		Canning, A. T.	9088 Pte.
Battams, J. N. S.	Lieut.		Carre, M. H.	2nd Lieut.
Bax, T.	8840 Cpl.		Carrington, W.	5168 R.Q.M.S.
Bazley-White, R. B. L.	Captain		Carter, H. S.	Lieut.
Beaumont, H. W.	7555 Pte.		Cartwright, A. C.	20325 Pte.
Beech, W. H.	L/8810 Sgt.		Cathcart, A. J.	Lieut.
Beeching, H. C. W.	Major		Catt, A. W.	2nd Lieut.
Beezer, W. J.	225 Pte.		Chambers, F.	6266 Pte.
Bellman, J. F.	2nd Lieut.		Chandler, A. J.	1557 Pte.
Bengough, L.	Captain		Chivers, W. P.	8232 Sgt.
Bennett, C. T.	Lieut.		Christmas, S. W.	9304 Sgt.
Bennett, H. B.	Lieut.		Clark, A. N. W.	Lieut.
Bergl, B.	21005 L/Cpl.		Clark, C. D.	Major
Biggs, G.	864 Pte.		Clark, H. S.	240728 Cpl.
Bishop, S. G.	8234 Sgt.		Clarke-Richardson, T.	Captain
Blazey, C. G.	240506 C.S.M.		Clear, A.	7680 Sgt.
Bolter, E. A.	G/3962 S.M.		Clibbens, T. A.	23629 C.Q.M.S.
Bond, C. W.	9203 Pte.		Clift, J. R.	18291 L/Cpl.
Borrett, G. W.	9861 Pte.		Cohen, Sir H. B., Bart.	Major

APPENDIX IV.

Once (continued).

Coke, J. R.	Captain	Edwards, J.	6460	L/Sgt.
Coles, W. E.	240318 CQMS	Edwards, L. C.	23721	L/Cpl.
Collins, F.	8199 Cpl.	Eldridge, P. E.	7267	L/Cpl.
Cook, A.	241936 Sgt.	Eley, C. E.	6292	Pte.
Cooke, J. H.	Captain & Q.M.	Elliott, A. G.	5619	C.S.M.
Coomber, H. J.	200163 Sgt.	Engledow, F. L.	Lieut. Col.	
Coomber, W. D.	1515 Sgt.	Evans, D. E.	200351	Pte.
Cooper, A. H.	1893 Pte.	Evans, H.	Lieut. & Q.M.	
Corham, H.	Lieut.	Evans, L. R.	203325	CQMS
Corke, J. F.	Captain	Eversden, A. J.	19066	Pte.
Couch, J.	Major & Q.M.	Evens, W. E.	240033	Sgt.
Coulter, P. A.	Lieut.			
Cozens, F.	Captain	File, W. G.	8674	Sgt.
Crisford, M. C.	6259 C.S.M.	Fisher, A. E.	9360	Pte.
Crisp, S. J.	203242 L/Cpl.	Fisk, H.	21078	Pte.
Cronk, L.	8129 R.Q.M.S.	Floyd, F. G.	6025	Pte.
Croucher, W.	8096 Pte.	Francis, A. B. C.	Captain	
		Francis, C. M.	Lieut.	
Dalison, J. P.	Lieut.-Col.	Frazer, F. G.	Captain	
Dando, G. W.	2nd Lieut.	Fuller, W.	587	Pte.
Daniell, O. J.	Major	Funnell, H. J.	10163	Sgt.
Darley, R.	6078 C.S.M.			
Davies, W. M.	17635 Sgt.	Gammon, F. T.	200032	Sgt.
Davis, A. C.	2nd Lieut.	Gilbert, J.	9829	L/Cpl.
Dillon, E. W.	2nd Lieut.	Glazebrook, J. W. S.	8020	C.S.M.
Disney-Roebuck, C. D.	Major	Golding, H.	9514	Bdsmn.
Dix, W.	2nd Lieut.	Gould, S. E.	51381	Sgt.
Dix, W.	508 L/Cpl.	Goulds, E.	4596	R.S.M.
Dixon, T.	3628 Sgt.	Goulds, E. W.	Lieut. & Q.M.	
Dolley, E. D.	8749 Sgt.	Govey, H.	Lieut.	
Don, V. G.	2nd Lieut.	Graham, M. W.	Captain	
Dowsett, A. W. E.	200161 Sgt.	Gray, J.	203270	Sgt.
Dowker, L. A.	6594 S/QMS	Green, L.	7254	S/Sgt.
Dowling, G.	Captain	Greenhalf, F.	2808	Pte.
Druce, C.	Captain	Greenway, F.	2530	C.S.M.
Drumgold, A.	2nd Lieut.	Griffe, G.	200225	Cpl.
Dykes, K.	Major	Grove, E. A. W. S., C.B.		
			Brigadier-Gen.	
Eccles, R. H.	Captain	Guest, T. J.	Captain	
Edkins, W. A. J.	19810 Sgt.	Gutteridge, J.	1324	C.S.M.

APPENDIX IV.

ONCE (*continued*).

Haines, C. W.	200228 Sgt.	Jeffreys, A. G.		Colonel
Haizelden, W.	5754 C.S.M.	Jenkins, C.	18451	Pte.
Hall, P. S.	Lieut.	Jimenez, A. J.		Major
Hall, W. D. de P.	Lieut.	Johnson, F. F., *C.B.*		
Hammond, R. P.	18742 Sgt.		Hon. Major-Gen.	
Hardwick, H.	828 Sgt.	Johnson, F. P.		Captain
Harnett, F. F. E.	Captain	Johnson, G. P. S.		Captain
Harper, G.	1952 Cpl.	Johnson, W. L.	5971	R.Q.M.S.
Harris, C.	10337 Cpl.	Jones, A.	6671	L/Cpl.
Harris, H. C.	Captain	Jones, W.	5705	Sgt.
Hawkes, J. H.	8130 Sgt.	Jones, W. H. W.	6298	Q.M.S.
Haworth, A. G.	2nd Lieut.	Jordan, J.	5133	Cpl.
Hay, J. H.	Captain			
Heath, A.	7919 L/Cpl.	Kay, J. K.		Major
Heaton, I.	Captain	Keattch, A.	10559	Cpl.
Hemmerde, E. C.	2nd Lieut.	Keeble, W. H.	7138	
Henderson, G. D.	Captain		C.S.M. Instr.	
Henderson-Roe, C. G.	Captain	Kelsey, W. E. D.		2nd Lieut.
Hickson, L. H.	Lieut.-Colonel	Kemp, H.	L/9135	Pte.
Hind, G. V.	Lieut.	Kennard, G.	8883	Pte.
Hines, J. C.	7665 Cpl.	Kennedy, J. H.		Captain
Hissey, J.	168 Pte.	Kingham, J. W.	4010	R.Q.M.S
Hobbs, W.	202130 Sgt.	Knell, G.	3881	Cpl.
Holden, V.	Major	Knight, J.	6369	L/Cpl.
Holroyd, V. H.	Captain	Knowles, E.	10609	Pte.
Holway, W.	8393 C.Q.M.S.			
Horton, E.	41389 Sgt.	Lakey, J. G.	8744	L/Cpl.
Howe, G.	8739 Pte.	Lallery, J.	6294	
Howell, N. B.	Lieut.		Supt. Clerk (W.O.)	
Hulford, H.	8576 Sgt.	Lambert, A.	G/24717	Pte.
Humphreys, T.	9699 Pte.	Lambourne, C.	27717	L/Cpl.
Hunt, R.	4471 Sgt.	Langton, H. A. H.	9735	Pte.
Huxter, R. J.	10183 Pte.	Laurie, J. D., *V.D.*		Lieut.-Col.
		Lawrie, A. J.	202636	Sgt.
Jackson, R. D.	Captain	Layton, E. C.		Lieut.
Jackson, W. G.	9366 Sgt.	Lees, J.		Captain
Jarrett, D. G.	108 C.S.M.	Le Fleming, M. R.		Lieut.
Jarrett, E. H.	Lieut. & Q.M.	Levey, G. T.	6864	Cpl.
Jarrett, T. F.	5003 Pte.	Lewin, F. H.		Captain
Jeeps, P. C.	30763 Pte.	Lewis, L. H.	6630	L/Sgt.

APPENDIX IV.

ONCE (*continued*).

Liebenrood, E. C.	Major	Nash, N.		Captain
Lines, G. F.	9036 Sgt.	Newbrook, E. J.	5706	C.S.M.
Linge, J.	518 Pte.	Newell, H.	10370	Pte.
Loft, J.	2310 R.Q.M.S.	Newton, W.		Captain
Longden, J.	11624 Cpl.	Nisbet, D. J.		2nd Lieut.
Lucas, F. L.	Lieut.	Norburn, W. E.	770	L/Cpl.
		Norris, F. G.		2nd Lieut.
MacAllister, J.	201964 Pte.			
McCarthy, J.	8350 Pte.	Obee, G. H.	9066	Pte.
McKelvey, J.	9372 Pte.	Oliver, S.	15257	Pte.
Mackey, P.	202637 L/Cl.	Ogle, W. M.		Captain
McLeland, N. P. K. J. O'N. Capt.		Owen, G.	9745	Pte.
Macmarquis, F. S. G/14688 Sgt.				
McVicar, W.	3869 R.S.M.	Packman, J.	8353	Pte.
Madgett, C.	Captain	Page, A.	8174	Sgt.
Mannerings, T. A.	8583 Sgt.	Page, H. F.	8568	Pte.
Marslin, W.	9401 Sgt.	Palmer, H. A.	6031	Sgt.
Marshall, T. D.	Captain	Palmer, W. V.		Captain
Martin, H.	265919 Sgt.	Pannett, R. H. J.	9103	Pte.
Masters, T. W.	9342 Sgt.	Parker, W. H.	41388	Sgt.
Matthews, M. L. W.	Captain	Payton, C. M.		Lieut.
Mattison, W. H.	Captain	Pearce, F. W.	2460	Sgt.
May, H. G.	24237 C.Q.M.S.	Penny, W.	4558	C.S.M.
Meadowcroft, G. D.	Captain	Percy, P. A.		2nd Lieut.
Medhurst, A. H.	9007 Pte.	Perrin, A.	869	Pte.
Michie, H. G.	2nd Lieut.	Perrin, H. T.	201085	Sgt.
Mills, E.	Lieut. & Q.M.	Pickford, G. F.	27692	Sgt.
Mires, C.	9459 Pte.	Peterkin, C. S.	10123	CQMS
Mitchell, A.	8105 Sgt.	Phillips, C. E. S.		Bt. Major
Mitchell, J.	9225 Pte.	Picton, H. W.	9102	Cpl.
Molony, C. V.	Major	Piggott, W.	23271	Cpl.
Monckton, W. T.	Captain	Pinneger, W. G.	8169	Sgt.
Morgan, A.	41402 L/Sgt.	Playford, A. E.	8413	Pte.
Morgan, J.	2075 Sgt.	Pointer, W.	41368	CQMS
Morrish, J. H.	2nd Lieut.	Potts, T. H.	21394	Sgt.
Mortley, C. V. S.	240297 Cpl.	Powell, J.	8329	Sgt.
Morton, J. H.	L/11983 Sgt.	Prescott-Roberts, P. A. Lieut-Col.		
Moss, J. S.	9263 L/Sgt.	Presnall, J.		Captain
Murphy, W. F.	Lieut. & Q.M.	Prior, A. W.		Bt.-Colonel
Muspratt, V. E.	Major	Prior, W.	240348	Sgt.

APPENDIX IV.

Once (continued).

Pronger, E.	101	Sgt.	Simmons, A. E.	11981	C.S.M.
Pullman, A. H.		Major	Simpson, D.		Lieut.
			Skeer, W. T.	6530	R.S.M.
Quilter, H.	240610	Sgt.	Smellie, C. A.,		Lieut.
Quirk, J. M.	202016	Sgt.	Smith, G. C.	G/41363	R.S.M.
			Smith, S. B.		Captain
Rawlings, C.	G/41371	Sgt.	Smith, S. C. E.	8268	C.S.M.
Reeves, A.		Captain	Soames, W. F.		Major
Reynolds, A.	5435	R.Q.M.S.	Stanley, C. T.	240705	L/Cpl.
Robinson, H. J.		Captain	Steane, A.	967	L/Cpl.
Robinson, W.	6590	Sgt.	Stearn, J.	9109	Pte.
Rogers, C.	14769	Pte.	Stenson, J.	203537	Sgt.
Rogers, E. S.	15319	L/Cpl.	Stevenson, G. E. de St. C.		Major
Rogers, R. G.		Captain	Stigand, A. G.		Captain
Rolls, F.	9960	Pte.	Stokes, J. H.		Captain
Rose, V. C.	554	Sgt.	Stroud, M. P.	6694	Sgt.
Rowe, J. W. F.		Captain	Stubbings, H. E.	813	Sgt.
Rowe, R. P. P.		Captain	Style, R. C.		Brig.-Gen.
Roythorne, R.	8154	C.S.M.	Swan, C.	7719	C.S.M.
Russell, F.		Captain	Syme, J. R.	9001	Q.M.S.
Russell, J. R.		Lieut.			
Rutherford, G. A.	8439	Pte.	Tarry, F. T.	4299	Cpl.
Ryan, J.	3142	L/Cpl.	Tatham, T. E.		Captain
			Taylor, L.		Captain
Salisbury, H.	9575	Pte.	Taylor, T. R.	7811	C.Q.M.S.
Satterthwaite, R. E.		Captain	Thomas, A. E. W.		Captain
Saunders, H.	240590	L/Cl.	Thorne, A. G.	203204	Pte.
Saward, J.	7562	Sgt.	Thorpe, C.	11147	Pte.
Scarratt, A.	2871	Pte.	Toombs, J. C.	9265	Sgt.
Schooling, L. F.		Lieut.	Townshend, A. F.		Lt.-Col.
Sear, W.	6297	Q.M.S.	Trapps, W. A.	18580	Pte.
Searight, A. F.		Captain	Trousdell, A. J.		Captain
Seccombe, G.		Captain	Trufitt, J.	5449	Sgt.
Selby, C. W. P.		Lieut.	Tuly, W. A.	9401	Sgt.
Selves, W.	8566	C.S.M.	Tutt, G.	318	Cpl.
Semark, J.	6422	C.Q.M.S.	Twisleton-Wykeham-Fiennes,		
Shand, J.	8968	Pte.	J. T.		Major
Shaw, B.	23959	L/Cpl.			
Shrimpton, H. L.	2nd	Lieut.	Vansittart, E.		Brev.-Col.
Sibbald, W.	7524	Sgt.	Vaughan, F. S.		Lieut.

621

APPENDIX IV.

ONCE (*continued*).

Venables, E. F.	Lt. Col.	White, H. B. H.		Captain
Vigers, A. A.	Captain	White, R. Lynch		Major
		White, W. F.		2nd Lieut.
Waddington, T. T.	Captain	Whitehouse, A. J.	8110	L/Cpl.
Wade, J. F.	21109 Sgt.	Wiffen, W. E.	1515	Pte.
Wade, R.	Lieut.	Wild, C. H.		2nd Lieut.
Walker, E. V.	2nd Lieut.	Wildsmith, B.	18563	Cpl.
Wallace, C. L. W.	Lt.-Col.	Wilks, J. H.	7613	Pte.
Wannell, H.	7631 Sgt.	Willis, W. J.	Major & Qr. Mr.	
Ward, G.	7934 Pte.	Wintour, F., *C.B.*		Colonel
Ward, J. D.	2nd Lieut.	Wood, J. R.	Lieut. & Qr. Mr.	
Waring, W. A.	Lieut.	Woodhead, J.	24534	Pte.
Warren, W. F.	6184 R.S.M.	Woodman, L. A.	201545	Sgt.
Watkins, A. H.	8005 C.S.M.	Woollett, E. B.		Captain
Watson, A. W.	3187 Pte.	Workman, C.	9837	Cpl.
Webster, W.	25084 Sgt.	Wright, F.	200034	R.Q.M.S.
Wells, E. H.	2074 Cpl.	Wright, J. D.	6296	Q.M.S.
Westborn, J. B.	8539 Pte.	Wright, T. K.		Major
Weston, E. F.	2nd Lieut.			
Whiston, H. C.	1414 L/Cpl.	Young, H.	8583	Q.M.S.

APPENDIX V.

UNITS OF THE QUEEN'S OWN AND THEIR COMMANDING OFFICERS.

August 4th, 1914, to November 11th, 1918.

(NOTE.—Officers on the Active List of the Regular Army, Special Reserve and Territorial Army are given their permanent rank held on the date of assuming command : Officers of the Retired List and of the New Armies their temporary rank. Acting rank is not shown. Only honours earned before the war are mentioned. The date given is that on which command was assumed, where it has been impossible to discover the exact date, the month only is mentioned. The names of officers who acted in command for short intervals between the departure of a commander and the arrival of his successor are omitted).

THE DEPÔT.—Mobilized, August 4th, 1914.

In Command.

Major P. M. Robinson, C.M.G.	August 4th, 1914.
Colonel G. W. Maunsell	August 5th, 1914.
Lieut.-Col. W. E. Rowe	April 10th, 1915.
Lieut.-Col. E. A. Iremonger	May 20th, 1916.
Lieut.-Col. J. P. Dalison	April 5th, 1917.
Major G. D. Lister	October 2nd, 1918.

1ST BATTALION. — Mobilized, August 4th, 1914. Embarked, August 13th, 1914. Served in France and Flanders to December 11th, 1917. In Italy to March 31st, 1918. In France and Flanders to April 23rd, 1919. Reformed at Gravesend.

In Command.

Lieut.-Col. A. Martyn	August 4th, 1914.
Major M. P. Buckle	October 13th, 1914.
Capt. H. D. Buchanan-Dunlop	November 3rd, 1914.
Major P. M. Robinson, C.M.G.	November 19th, 1914.
Major H. D. Buchanan-Dunlop	September 13th, 1915.
Major R. Lynch White	September 12th, 1916.

APPENDIX V.

Major H. D. Buchanan-Dunlop   November 15th, 1916.
Major R. Lynch White   May 26th, 1917.
Major B. Johnstone   August 25th, 1917.
Major J. K. Kay   October, 1918.
(Lieut.-Col. Martyn returned to the Battalion from 1st to 3rd. Nov.)

2ND BATTALION.—On August 4th, 1914, was stationed at Multan. Mobilized, January 17th, 1915. Embarked, January 30th, 1915. Served in Mesopotamia; embarked for home as a cadre, July 26th, 1919. Reformed at Rugeley.

In Command.
Lieut.-Col. S. H. Pedley   August 4th, 1914.
Major R. J. Woulfe-Flanagan   January 14th, 1916.

3RD BATTALION.—Mobilized, August 4th, 1914. Disembodied, July 29th, 1919.

In Command.
Lieut.-Col. Sir A. Griffith-   August 4th, 1914.
          Boscawen
Major C. D. Barrow   April 22nd, 1916.
Lieut.-Col. E. V. O. Hewett   March 3rd, 1918.

1/4TH BATTALION.—Mobilized, August 4th, 1914. Embarked, October 29th, 1914. Served in India, taking part in the Afghanistan Expedition with the Baluchistan Force, May 6th to September 11th, 1919. Embarked, October 30th, 1919. Disembodied, November 24th, 1919.

In Command.
Lieut.-Col. C. N. Watney   August 4th, 1914.

Major C. B. Robb took over command on October 8th, 1918, and was in command during the Afghanistan Expedition.

2/4TH BATTALION. — Formed, April 25th, 1915, as a Kent Composite Battalion, and was renamed on June 14th, 1915. Embarked, July 18th, 1915. Served in Gallipoli, Egypt and Palestine. Disbanded, September 13th, 1918.

In Command.
Colonel A. T. F. Simpson   Appointed on formation.
Major H. Smithers   August 15th, 1915.
Major E. J. F. Vaughan   October 20th, 1915.
    (Devon Regiment)

624

APPENDIX V.

Colonel A. T. F. Simpson	December 22nd, 1915.
Lieut.-Col. A. E. Norton (W.I.R.)	March 3rd, 1916.
Captain E. W. Dillon	June 26th, 1916.
Lieut.-Col. N. Money (Shropshire Yeomanry)	July 27th, 1916.
Major P. Jude (The Buffs)	October 28th, 1917.
Lieut.-Col. W. Beswick (R.W.F.)	November 20th, 1917.

3/4TH BATTALION. — The home service portion of the 1/4th Battalion was formed in September, 1914, and known as the 4th (H.S.) Battalion until October 22nd, 1914, as the 4th (Reserve) Battalion till February 9th, 1915, and as the 2/4th till it became the 3/4th on June 14th, 1915. Embarked, May 31st, 1917. Served in France and Flanders. Disbanded, March 27th, 1918

In Command.

Colonel A. T. F. Simpson	Appointed on formation.
Lieut.-Col. J. D. Laurie	April 25th, 1915.
Colonel A. T. F. Simpson	June, 1916.
Captain E. James (Lincoln Regiment)	August 10th, 1917.

4/4TH BATTALION. — Formed July 14th, 1915. Became 4th (Reserve) Battalion on June 16th, 1916. Combined with 3/5th Battalion September 1st, 1916. Disbanded in May, 1919.

In Command.

Lieut.-Col C. Disney-Roebuck	Appointed on formation.
Major R. McKergow (Sussex Yeomanry)	January 1st, 1917.

1/5TH BATTALION.—Mobilized, August 4th, 1914. Embarked, October 29th, 1914. Served in India. Embarked for Mesopotamia, December 5th, 1917. Embarked for home, December 27th, 1919. Disembodied, January 28th, 1920.

In Command.

Lieut.-Cól. F. A. Frazer	August 4th, 1914.
Major C. D. Clark	June 10th, 1918.
Lieut.-Col. F. A. Frazer	September 18th, 1918.

s s

APPENDIX V.

2/5TH BATTALION. — Formed, October, 1914. Disbanded, November 14th, 1917. Reserve Battalion.

In Command.

Major E. B. Willis	Appointed on formation.
Major E. B. Savage	September 7th, 1916.
Major C. L. Willoughby-Wallace	November 21st, 1916.

3/5TH BATTALION.—Formed, July 12th, 1915. Amalgamated with 4/4th to form 4th (Reserve) Battalion, September 1st, 1916.

Major E. S. Jenyns   Appointed on formation.

6TH BATTALION. — Formed, August 14th, 1914. Embarked, June 1st, 1915. Served in France, Flanders and Germany. Disbanded, November, 1919.

In Command.

Major P. M. Robinson, *C.M.G.*	Appointed on formation.
Colonel G. E. Even, *C.B.*	November 14th, 1914.
Lieut.-Col. E. F. Venables	January 3rd, 1915.
Major C. S. Owen (R.W.F.)	November 29th, 1915.
Lieut. W. R. A. Dawson	November 16th, 1916.
Captain W. J. Alderman	May 3rd, 1917.

(Was temporarily in command when killed in action on November 20th, 1917).

Captain W. R. A. Dawson	August 27th, 1917.
Major P. Whetham (Manchester Regiment)	December 1st, 1917.
Captain W. R. A. Dawson	February 18th, 1918.
Lieut. W. C. Cook (E. Surrey Regiment)	March 29th, 1918.
Captain H. Peploe	May 14th, 1918.
Major W. R. A. Dawson	June 6th, 1918.
Major L. C. R. Smith	October 23rd, 1918.

APPENDIX V.

7TH BATTALION.—Formed, September 5th, 1914. Embarked, July 26th, 1915. Served in France and Flanders. Disbanded, July 16th, 1919.

In Command.

Colonel A. W. Prior	Appointed on formation.
Major J. T. Twisleton-Wykeham-Fiennes	October, 1915.
Major A. E. Phillips	November 28th, 1916.
Major E. M. Liddell (D.W.R.)	January, 1917.
Major A. E. Phillips	February, 1917.
Major L. H. Hickson	April, 1917.
Captain P. N. Anstruther	May 3rd, 1917.
Major C. H. L. Cinnamond (R.I. Rifles)	June 9th, 1917.
Captain J. D. Crosthwaite (1st Batt., London Regt.)	March 18th, 1918.
Major A. E. Phillips	April 2nd, 1918.
Major L. H. Hickson	April 15th, 1918.
Major A. E. Phillips	July, 1918.
Major L. H. Hickson	August 23rd, 1918.

8TH BATTALION.—Formed, September 12th, 1914. Embarked, August 30th, 1915. Served in France and Flanders. Disbanded, June 14th, 1919.

In Command.

Colonel E. Vansittart	Appointed on formation.
Major J. C. Parker	October 6th, 1915.
Major N. I. Whitty	August 30th, 1916.
Major J. C. Parker	January 20th, 1917.
Major N. I. Whitty	November 3rd, 1917.
Lieut.-Col. H. J. Wenyon	December 26th, 1917.

9TH BATTALION.—Formed, October 24th, 1914. Became 22nd Training Reserve Battalion, September 1st, 1916.

Lieut.-Col. O. J. Daniell	Appointed on formation.

APPENDIX V.

10TH BATTALION.—Formed, May 12th, 1915. Embarked, May 4th, 1916. Served in France and Flanders till November 9th, 1917; in Italy till March 2nd, 1918; then in France, Flanders and Germany. Disbanded on January 3rd, 1920.

	In Command.
Lieut.-Col. A. Wood Martyn	Appointed on formation.
Major W. F. Soames	September 15th, 1916.
Lieut.-Col. A. Wood Martyn	February 10th, 1917.
Captain S. H. Beattie (Northampton Regiment)	June 10th, 1917.
Major F. A. Wallis	March 1st, 1918.
Lieut.-Col. A. C. Corfe	March 15th, 1918.
Major F. A. Wallis	March 23rd, 1918.
Major the Hon. E. R. Thesiger (Surrey Yeomanry)	May 7th, 1918.

11TH BATTALION.—Formed, May 12th, 1915. Embarked, May 3rd, 1916. Served in France and Flanders till November 9th, 1917; in Italy till it returned to France and was disbanded on March 16th, 1918.

	In Command.
Lieut.-Col. H. L. Searle	Appointed on formation.
Lieut.-Col. A. F. Townshend	February, 1916.
Lieut.-Col. A. C. Corfe	September 15th, 1916.
Lieut. J. C. Beadle (R.E., Kent Yeomanry)	September 20th, 1917.
Major A. J. Jimenez	January 8th, 1918.
Lieut.-Col. A. C. Corfe	February 21st, 1918.

12TH BATTALION.—Formed, February 5th, 1916. Became 99th Training Reserve Battalion, September 1st, 1916.

Colonel A. G. Jeffrey	Appointed on formation.

1ST HOME SERVICE BATTALION. — Formed, April 1st, 1916. Became a Battalion of the Royal Defence Corps, April 15th, 1918.

Lieut.-Col. C. W. Warden	Appointed on formation.

APPENDIX V.

THE VOLUNTEERS.—The Volunteer Regiment of The Queen's Own was formed in 1917 by the amalgamation into four Battalions of nine Battalions previously allotted to the West Kent and Mid Kent Groups of the County Volunteers.

Regimental Commandant.—Colonel C. E. Warde, M.P.

1ST VOLUNTEER BATTALION.—Colonel J. Rowlandson.

2ND VOLUNTEER BATTALION.—Lieut.-Colonel A. C. Borton.

3RD VOLUNTEER BATTALION.—Major Sir Philip Dawson, Kt.

4TH VOLUNTEER BATTALION.—Major C. H. Gray.

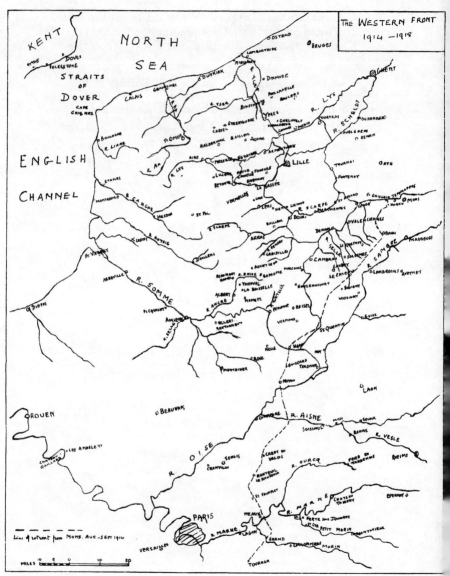

MAP A.